7,20

D1329370

RC

A HISTORY OF

Music in England

A HISTORY OF
Music in England

BY

ERNEST WALKER

———————

THIRD EDITION
REVISED AND ENLARGED BY

J. A. WESTRUP

OXFORD
AT THE CLARENDON PRESS
1952

Oxford University Press, Amen House, London E.C.4

GLASGOW NEW YORK TORONTO MELBOURNE WELLINGTON
BOMBAY CALCUTTA MADRAS CAPE TOWN

Geoffrey Cumberlege, Publisher to the University

First Edition 1907
Second Edition 1924
Reprinted 1931, 1939, 1940

PRINTED IN GREAT BRITAIN
AT THE UNIVERSITY PRESS, OXFORD
BY CHARLES BATEY, PRINTER TO THE UNIVERSITY

PREFACE TO THE THIRD EDITION

THE purpose of this edition is to incorporate the results of recent research and to bring the story of English music nearer to the present day. This has involved not only a large number of small emendations and alterations, but also a substantial amount of new material. Much of this additional matter is so closely interwoven with the original text that it would not have been practicable to indicate its authorship. I must therefore assume complete responsibility for the book in its present form.

J. A. W.

OXFORD, 1951

PREFACE TO THE FIRST EDITION

THE purpose of this book is to sketch the main features of English music from its earliest artistic manifestations to the close of the nineteenth century. I use the term 'English' in default of any other that is more exactly comprehensive; but the chapter on folk music will be found to contain references to the melodies of Scotland, Ireland, and Wales, as well as to those of England itself. And, further, I have taken 'English music' to include 'music made in England', not solely 'music composed by Englishmen'; to adopt the latter signification alone would, I thought, in dealing with a country where foreign influences have played a large part, have unduly limited the scope of the book, and I have in fact, for practical purposes, considered as Englishmen those composers who, though of foreign blood, have made England their home and have produced for an English public all the works by which their name survives. Of these the greatest is of course Handel, who, as a naturalized Englishman who spent over forty-five years of his life in this country, has justly won a place in the *Dictionary of National Biography*; I have disregarded the few works he wrote for Italian and German audiences, but it seemed impossible to avoid treatment of the others, especially as their influence here has been so colossal.

I have thought it best to concern myself primarily with the actual music, and only secondarily with biographical minutiae and general antiquarian research, which, in a work of larger dimensions, would naturally have received closer attention than they do here; it seemed to me that a book of this size demanded a sort of treatment which left little room for details more suited to a biographical dictionary, a history of social customs, or the publications of an archaeological society. It is true that at present considerable research among manuscripts and rare printed books is still indispensable for the proper understanding of the artistic position of some of our greatest men (and, after all, scoring from part-books is a very fascinating if somewhat tedious occupation); but my primary object throughout has been to offer aids towards the elucidation of all the music that is of real self-sufficing importance, and to refrain from obscuring this end by the prosecution, to more than a slight extent, of side issues, however interesting. In a word, the book has been designed from

the standpoint of a musician rather than from that of an antiquarian; and even then more for the general music-lover than for
the technically erudite.

To conclude any history that reaches to our own day is far from
easy; fresh vistas seem continually to arise and to demand treatment
in footnotes and appendixes. After considerable hesitation, I have
thought it best to refrain from mentioning by name any living English composer who was born later than 1860. This date has been
chosen so as to include all those whom it was impossible not to
specify, and at the same time to avoid any sitting in judgement
upon younger men; entitled though we may be to criticize here and
now the individual productions of the latter, yet their total output
can hardly yet be able to challenge opinion on their work as a whole.
Of course serious qualifications are anyhow necessary in criticizing
the work of any living composer; but, as Rückert says in the poem
so perfectly set by Brahms,

> Mit vierzig Jahren ist der Berg erstiegen,
> Wir stehen still und schau'n zurück,

and a judgement of some kind becomes for the first time possible
(though, even among these older men, I have purposely refrained
from mentioning more than five—the surviving four of the five
'Leaders of the Renaissance', as they are called in Mr. Fuller Maitland's *History of English Music in the Nineteenth Century*, and the
one other whose star is of later ascendence). Nevertheless, I thought
it necessary, for the due completion of my scheme, to give a brief
general sketch, without mentioning names, of the course of the most
recent music in England and of the trend, as it appears to me, of the
work of the younger generation.

As to the plan of the book, I have hesitated somewhat. I wished,
so far as I could, to give a consecutive picture of the course of English music while avoiding the disadvantages which a merely piecemeal chronological system entails. I therefore thought it best to
refrain from breaking up the subject except where a fairly tangible
line could be drawn, though the result is that the chapters are few
in number, and somewhat disproportionate in length—and especially disproportionate considering the fact that in English music
twenty years at one time are far more important than a hundred at
another; and with a similar motive I have further, within these comparatively self-contained sections, separated the biographical and

historical details from the critical examination of the actual music. I am fully sensible that this method has the disadvantage of dividing, sometimes by a considerable number of pages, the facts of a composer's life from the features of his works; but on the whole it seemed to me that this might be regarded as being balanced by the rather more compact treatment of purely artistic questions which it renders possible. The concluding chapter on 'General Characteristics' will be found to deal with various miscellaneous matters not specifically connected with any one period, and consequently difficult to include in the earlier portion of the book.

I should have been glad, had it been feasible, to print many more and also longer musical examples; but I have tried to select some which may fairly serve as illustrations of the various points of interest, without of course in any way claiming to be exhaustive specimens of their composers' methods. My urgent desire is to stimulate the reader to acquire for himself as much first-hand knowledge of the music as possible; in an examiner-ridden age we are far too much inclined to attach an altogether ridiculous and harmful importance to parrot-like memorizing of mere dates and facts, that can never be more than the dry bones of a living art.

Apart from the standard older general musical histories, and such authorities as the *Dictionary of National Biography*, Grove's *Dictionary of Music and Musicians*, Eitner's *Quellen-Lexicon*, the prefaces to modern scholars' reprints of old music, and the musical press (including articles in the publications of the 'Internationale Musik-Gesellschaft'), I would express special indebtedness to Dr. Wilibald Nagel's *Geschichte der Musik in England* (which ends, unfortunately, at the death of Purcell), Mr. Henry Davey's *History of English Music* (dealing with the complete subject, but from a standpoint somewhat different from that adopted in the present work), Mr. J. A. Fuller Maitland's *History of English Music in the Nineteenth Century*, and the volumes of the *Oxford History of Music* by Sir Hubert Parry, Prof. H. E. Wooldridge, and Mr. Fuller Maitland. But my main authority throughout has been the music itself, printed and manuscript. For loan of music and assistance in various libraries my cordial thanks are due to Dr. H. P. Allen, Mr. J. M. Duncan, Miss A. Ruth Fry, Mr. J. A. Fuller Maitland, Mr. W. H. Hadow, Dr. B. Harwood, Mr. A. Hughes-Hughes, Mr. M. J. Nash, Mrs. Reginald Poole, Miss Gertrude Sichel, Mr. W. R. Sims, Mr. W. Barclay Squire, and the Very Rev. T. B. Strong, as also to

Mr. F. Jekyll for the Scottish folk-tune 'O cuckoo of the grove', taken down by him from the lips of Mr. J. Robertson, a fisherman of Mull.

ERNEST WALKER

Balliol College, Oxford
July, 1907

CONTENTS

I. THE BEGINNINGS OF ENGLISH MUSIC	1
II. MUSIC IN THE FIFTEENTH AND EARLY SIXTEENTH CENTURIES	18
III. MUSIC OF THE MID-SIXTEENTH CENTURY	48
IV. THE MADRIGALIAN ERA	72
V. MUSIC UNDER CHARLES I AND THE COMMONWEALTH	150
VI. PURCELL AND HIS CONTEMPORARIES	172
VII. HANDEL IN ENGLAND	217
VIII. HANDEL'S CONTEMPORARIES	243
IX. MUSIC UNDER THE LATER GEORGES	265
X. EARLY VICTORIAN MUSIC	291
XI. THE ENGLISH RENAISSANCE	316
XII. MUSIC IN THE TWENTIETH CENTURY	344
XIII. FOLK MUSIC	361
XIV. GENERAL CHARACTERISTICS	386
BIBLIOGRAPHY	403
INDEX TO MUSICAL EXAMPLES	415
GENERAL INDEX	425

ERRATA

On p. 41, two lines from bottom, and p. 44, bottom line,
for *Coronea* read *Corona*

I

THE BEGINNINGS OF ENGLISH MUSIC

THE early history of English music, as of European music in general, is concerned almost entirely with works which form no part of our normal experience of the art. If we take familiarity as a criterion we may easily accept the view that such music is primitive and crude. Modern scholarship, by insisting more and more on performance, has shown that this view is false, that medieval music is not inaccessible because it is remote, and that canons of beauty are not the discovery of a later age. The amount of early music that has survived is inconsiderable, if we compare it with the huge legacies of the eighteenth and nineteenth centuries; we may, in consequence, be led to generalize on insufficient evidence. But the gaps in our material do not absolve us from the necessity of exercising our imagination. Music, of whatever period, does not consist of symbols on paper; it is designed to be sung and played, and to give pleasure.

Fixing our eyes chiefly, as in this book we shall always do, on the actual music that has come down to us, we shall not occupy much space in describing the earliest musical activities, the nature of which we know only at second hand. The Teutonic, Scandinavian, and Celtic races all held in high esteem the bards who, whether itinerant or dwelling in a fixed locality, filled an important place in the social economy of the times by their narrative singing of the deeds of heroes past and present; and though in England the spread of Christianity and, as a secondary result, of the ritual music of the Church, weakened their position, yet the harpers, or minstrels (as, after the Norman invasion, they were also styled), long continued to be held in an honour which the more severe moralists of later days, such as John of Salisbury, were inclined to condemn. We know nothing whatever of the music the harpers played and sang,[1] but, on the other hand, we know from the writings of Giraldus Cambrensis (Gerald Barry), Archdeacon of St. David's in Wales, who flourished in the latter part of the twelfth century (a little later than John of Salisbury), some facts about the contemporary music of the people themselves, at any rate in some parts of these islands.

[1] Cf. p. 374.

In his *Topographia Hibernica* he refers in enthusiastic terms to the excellence of instrumental playing in Ireland, which, to judge from his description, must have been of an unusually advanced kind; he adds that Scotland and Wales were gradually rivalling Ireland in this matter, and that in Scotland, in particular, playing was of a high order of merit.[1] In a later work, *Descriptio Cambriae*, he remarks that the Welsh do not sing their tunes in unison, as is the custom elsewhere, but with as many parts as there are singers, 'all finally uniting in consonance and organic melody under the sweetness of B♭'.[2] And further, he goes on to say that the inhabitants of the northern part of Britain (that is, beyond the Humber) make use of a similar kind of harmony in singing, but only in two parts; and that they do this not so much by art as by a habit which long practice has rendered natural. He adds, indeed, that the children, as soon as they begin to sing, insensibly drop into the same custom of never singing any melody except in parts, and conjectures that the practice was handed down by the Danish and Norwegian invaders.[3] This conjecture finds some support in the thirteenth-century hymn in honour of St. Magnus from the Orkneys (then part of the Norwegian kingdom), which consists mainly of parallel thirds.[4]

Many and elaborate deductions have been drawn from these words of Giraldus, but the information that they give us is really very slight. His remark on the Welsh part-singing that 'it is their custom to sing in a body, and you can hear as many different songs as you see persons',[5] certainly does not, on the face of it, suggest anything except extemporization by a dozen or more singers at once. Yet Giraldus can hardly have meant to describe what, if these words are taken literally, would be mere confused noise. Both his insistence on the 'B♭' (whatever it may mean), and the reference

[1] Works, ed. J. S. Brewer and J. F. Dimock, vol. v (1867), pp. 153–5.

[2] 'In unam denique sub B mollis dulcedine blanda consonantiam et organicam convenientia melodiam.' This obscure remark has been interpreted in various ways; most probably it means (and indeed this explanation is borne out by the fragments of early English music that are in existence) that the music either was or could have been generally written with a B♭ in the signature. 'Semper tamen ab B molli incipiunt,' an expression in Giraldus's account of Irish music, perhaps means the same thing; but the matter is far from clear.

[3] Ibid., vol. vi (1868), pp. 189–90.

[4] Printed in G. Adler, *Handbuch der Musikgeschichte* (2nd ed., 1930), p. 167.

[5] 'Ut in turba canentium, sicut huic genti mos est, quot videas capita tot audias carmina discriminaque vocum varia.'

to the Northumbrian two-part singing as 'similis symphonica harmonia' imply that there was some sort of method in the Welsh choruses; it is conceivable that he is referring to some kind of round. It is surprising that, if we accept Giraldus's word for it (and he was a widely travelled and cultured man) no other people except the Welsh and Northumbrians had adopted this practice. But we know absolutely nothing of the real nature of this popular part-singing what intervals were used or anything else; and in default of all evidence we have no right to devise (as has not infrequently been done) fantastic accounts of the invention of modern harmony by the British laity.

A few fragments of information about early medieval church music as practised in England have come down to us. In the main, of course, ritual music followed the same general lines in all countries under the ecclesiastical guidance of Rome: we learn from Bede that in 680 Benedict Biscop brought to Wearmouth a skilled singer from Rome, 'that he might teach in his monastery the system of singing throughout the year as it was practised at St. Peter's in Rome';[1] and the Council of Clovesho in 747 decreed that chanting should be 'in accordance with the sample that we have received in writing from the Roman Church'.[2] We also have some information about methods of performance in the twelfth and thirteenth centuries. The *Speculum Charitatis* of Aelred, Abbot of Rievaulx in Yorkshire in the middle of the twelfth century, contains a long passage of objurgation of the elaborate church music, with its complicated singing and its powerful accompaniments, including various other instruments besides the organ; independence of voice-parts, with interspersing of rests (known as 'hocket'), and the knowledge of time-divisions are clearly indicated.[3] John of Salisbury, about the same date, inveighs against the excessive devotion to advanced church music in much the same fashion as he inveighs, as we have already seen, against minstrels; but his language gives us no exact information, except that he particularly disliked the Phrygian

[1] Works, ed. J. A. Giles (1843–4), vol. iii, p. 80; ed. C. Plummer (1896), vol. i, p. 241.
[2] J. D. Mansi, *Sacrorum Conciliorum Collectio*, vol. xii (1766), col. 399; A. W. Haddan & W. Stubbs, *Councils and Ecclesiastical Documents*, vol. iii (1871), p. 367.
[3] J. P. Migne, *Patrologia*, Latin series, vol. cxcv (1855), cols. 571–2. The seventeenth-century translation by William Prynne is quoted in P. A. Scholes, *The Puritans and Music* (1934), p. 215.

mode.[1] A treatise of the following century, from the Abbey of Bury St. Edmunds but now in the British Museum (Royal 12 C, vi, fol. 59), gives us more details; as its authorship is unknown, the writer is usually referred to as the 'Anonymus of the British Museum' or Anonymus IV (from his position in the first volume of Coussemaker's *Scriptores*). Here we learn that the interval of the third was favoured by English musicians 'in patria quae dicitur Westcuntre'.[2]

Apart from this passage the early English theorists tell us nothing of the individual music of their native country; their writings concern the general musical practice of their day throughout western Europe, without any avowed reference to different local customs, did such exist. The chief, and indeed only noteworthy, among those who wrote before the fifteenth century are Joannes Cotto, Jean de Garlande, the 'Anonymus of the British Museum', Walter Odington, and Simon Tunsted—to whom reference is here made by their best known names, though the first has been sometimes anglicized into John Cotton, and the second anglicized or latinized into John Garland or Joannes Garlandius. Cotto has generally been regarded as an Englishman, though this is by no means certain; his treatise[3] was written about 1100, before the period of measured music. It is chiefly concerned with monophonic music, and treats at length questions of notation and also the proper forms of the plainsong melodies; only one chapter is devoted to diaphony or *organum,* where Cotto expounds the new system under which contrary movement was taking the place of the old parallel or oblique methods, and the former note-against-note motion was being varied occasionally by slight ornamentation. The musical treatises of the next three writers probably all belong to the century between 1220 and 1320, though the dates of the first two are doubtful. Jean de Garlande seems to have been an Englishman, born at Oxford about 1180 or 1190, who when a comparatively young man settled in France, and remained in that country for the rest of his life; if the identification of him with the author of *De musica mensurabili positio*[4] is correct, he was a versatile writer on many of the other

---

[1] *Policraticus*, ed. C. C. J. Webb (1909), vol. i, pp. 39–44. Extracts are quoted in *The Oxford History of Music*, vol. i (2nd ed., 1929), p. 290.

[2] C. E. H. de Coussemaker, *Scriptorum de musica medii aevi nova series* (1864–76, facsimile ed. 1931), vol. i, p. 358.

[3] J. Smits van Waesberghe, *Johannis Affligemensis De Musica cum Tonario* (1950). The problem of the author's name and origin is discussed by the editor on pp. 22–33. Cf. L. Ellinwood in *Notes*, Sept. 1951, pp. 650–9.

[4] Coussemaker, op. cit., vol. i, pp. 175–82.

liberal arts as well as music, and acquired great celebrity in Paris as poet and scholar. The *De mensuris et discantu*[1] of the 'Anonymus' (of whose English nationality there seems little doubt) dates from the latter part of the thirteenth century; it contains, indeed, a reference to 'the late King Henry'; which would seem to require 1273 as the earliest year. Walter Odington, whose *De speculatione musicae*[2] may with confidence be dated somewhere about the beginning of the fourteenth century, was a monk at Evesham Abbey, and is mentioned in a document of 1316 as among the mathematicians of Oxford; his treatise deals with acoustics, prosody, plainsong, and composition, and is one of the fullest and most instructive authorities on the whole subject of descant. To Simon Tunsted (d. 1369), head of the English branch of the Minorite Franciscans, is commonly attributed the treatise *De quatuor principalibus*,[3] which deals with mensurable music in rather more advanced form; Ravenscroft, in his *Briefe Discourse* (1614), frequently refers to it, though he ascribes it to Dunstable.

We have now to consider such actual music as we possess, written by Englishmen before the time of Dunstable. Before the thirteenth century we have very little that can be quoted; the *organa* in one of the Winchester Tropers of the eleventh century[4] are not musically decipherable with any confidence, and we are largely thrown back on the examples contained in the theoretical treatises. One interesting fragment is a two-part setting of part of a hymn to St. Stephen apparently deriving from St. Augustine's, Canterbury, and dating from the twelfth century:[5] this piece, written in alphabetical notation, is a harmonization of a plainsong melody (in the lower part) on the methods of what Wooldridge calls 'irregular *organum*'—parallel, contrary, and oblique motion being all employed. Attention has been drawn to the pentatonic flavour of the upper part. It begins:

Ex.1

Ut tu - o⸺⸺⸺ pro - pi - ti - a - - - - tus

[1] Ibid., pp. 327–65.   [2] Ibid., pp. 182–251.
[3] Ibid., vol. iv, pp. 200–98.
[4] Cambridge, Corpus Christi College, 473; edited, with some facsimiles, by W. H. Frere (1894).
[5] Oxford, Bodleian, Bodley 572, fol. 49ᵛ; facsimile in H. E. Wooldridge, *Early English Harmony*, vol. i (1897), pl. 1.

Examples in contemporary continental manuscripts prove, however, that this sort of work was in no way peculiar to England. To the same century, though rather later, belongs the *conductus* 'Redit aetas aurea',[1] which celebrates the accession of Richard I (1189).

Medieval English monody is poorly represented. As part of the Angevin Empire in the second half of the twelfth century England had close contacts with the troubadours and trouvères, more particularly since Eleanor of Aquitaine, who was a patron of their art, was the wife of Henry II. But Norman French remained the literary language until the thirteenth century, and even then the examples of English songs with music which have survived are very few and hardly enable us to say to what extent musicians were indebted to French models. The songs of St. Godric,[2] as we might expect from their subject, seem to be derived from plainsong. As an example of the few purely secular songs of the thirteenth century we may quote one of the two versions of 'Worldes blis ne last no throwe',[3] which in its sombre pessimism represents one aspect of the English temperament:

Ex. 2

---

[1] The first section is printed in A. Einstein, *A Short History of Music* (5th ed., 1948), p. 206.

[2] Facsimile in George Saintsbury, *History of English Prosody* (1906), vol. i. See also J. B. Trend, 'The First English Songs', in *Music and Letters*, Apr. 1928, pp. 111–28.

[3] Oxford, Bodleian, Rawl. G. 18, fol. 105ᵛ; facsimile in Wooldridge, op. cit., pl. 23. The notation of the original, as of the majority of troubadour and trouvère songs, is non-mensural. The song is here transcribed in the second (iambic) rhythmic mode.

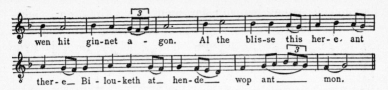

wen hit gin-net a - gon. Al the blis-se this her-e, ant

ther-e— Bi - lou-keth at hen-de— wop ant—— mon.

(The world's joy lasts no time at all, it departs and fades away at once. The longer I know it, the less value I find in it. For it is all mixed with troubles, with sorrow and misfortune, and at the last, when it begins to pass away, it leaves a man poor and naked. All the joy, both here and there, is finally encompassed by weeping and lamentation.)

The other aspect—a joyous acceptance of life—finds expression in the famous *rota* 'Sumer is icumen in', a four-part canon in the unison on the following melody, the other three voices entering successively at intervals of two bars:

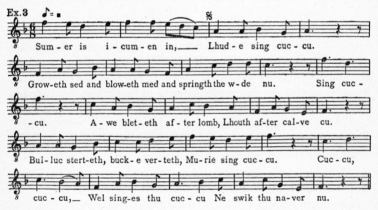

Ex.3

Sum - er is i - cum - en in,—— Lhud - e sing cuc - cu.

Grow-eth sed and blow-eth med and springth the w-de nu. Sing cuc -

- cu. A - we blet-eth af - ter lomb, Lhouth af-ter cal-ve cu.

Bul - luc stert-eth, buck- e ver-teth, Mu-rié sing cuc - cu. Cuc - cu,

cuc - cu,— Wel sing-es thu cuc - cu Ne swik thu na-ver nu.

(Summer has come, loudly sing cuckoo. Now is the seed growing and the meadow flowering and the forest springing to life. Sing cuckoo. The ewe bleats after the lamb, the cow lows after the calf, the bullock leaps, the buck breaks wind. Merrily sing cuckoo. Cuckoo, cuckoo, well dost thou sing cuckoo. Never cease now.)

combined with a *pes* in two lower parts, consisting of a persistent repetition of the following:

Ex.4

Sing cuc - cu nu,—— sing cuc - cu

Sing cuc - cu, sing cuc - cu nu——

7

thus making six-part harmony, beginning:

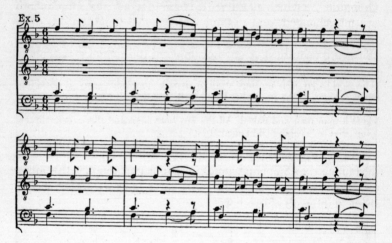

The piece occurs in a manuscript written at Reading Abbey and now in the British Museum (Harl. 978);[1] it is dated, on palaeographical and other evidence, about 1240,[2] and the words have been identified by linguistic experts as Berkshire or Wiltshire thirteenth-century dialect. Not a particle of evidence exists for describing it, as some older writers have done, as a Northumbrian round; nor, indeed, have we any adequate grounds for dogmatizing at all about the authorship of either words or music. It is interesting, however, to notice that religious words in Latin have been added beneath the English text, and that the original form of the melody,[3] still decipherable in spite of the erasures, was different in several respects.

This extraordinary production, which combines beauty of sound and ingenuity of workmanship, has no exact parallel in early music; its form is unlike that of any other early work we possess—though

[1] Facsimile in Grove's *Dictionary* (4th ed.), vol. v, frontispiece.

[2] See B. Schofield, 'The Provenance and Date of "Sumer is icumen in"', in *The Music Review*, May 1948, pp. 81–6. Schofield rejects, on palaeographical grounds, the arguments for assigning the *rota* to the early fourteenth century advanced by Manfred F. Bukofzer in *University of California Publications in Music*, vol. ii, No. 2, pp. 79–114.

[3] Printed in A. T. Davison and W. Apel, *Historical Anthology of Music* (1946), No. 42. Cf. *The Oxford History of Music*, vol. i (2nd ed., 1929), pp. 181–2.

the two-part *pes* follows the method of the rondel as described by Odington,[1] in which all the parts begin together and subsequently are interchanged; and examples of canonic imitation are to be found in works of the Notre Dame school (late twelfth and early thirteenth centuries). A good example of the rondel is the following,[2] of which the opening section may be quoted:

Among the other thirteenth-century pieces are several written in a popular style, for instance, a setting of 'Salve virgo virginum'[3] which begins:

The phrase is repeated to different words, with a couple of added passing-notes in the middle voice; its first half is then repeated a

[1] Coussemaker, op. cit., vol. i, p. 247.
[2] Oxford, Corpus Christi College, 489, No. 9.
[3] Brit. Mus. Arundel 248, fol. 155 (where the same music is also used for a French text); facsimile in Wooldridge, op. cit., pl. 36. The above transcription adopts a modal interpretation of the notation. For an alternative version see *Music and Letters*, Apr. 1935, p. 81.

third time (with a slight modification of the second half), and the little composition ends with a coda:

'Jesu Christes milde moder',[1] dating from about the same time, is also noteworthy as exemplifying what—if we may judge from contemporary continental work—was a specifically English smoothness of movement. This smoothness shows itself particularly in a fondness for parallel thirds, together with crossing of parts. Two-part writing of this kind was known as 'gymel'—an English version of the Latin *cantus gemellus* (twin song)—though the term does not actually occur in manuscripts before the fifteenth century. Interchange of thirds is found already in the *conductus* mentioned on p. 6, but the systematic use of this type of harmony seems to date from the thirteenth century. The two lower parts of Exs. 7 and 8 are an example of gymel, to which a third part has been added. Another example, without the addition of an extra part, is the following English hymn to the Virgin:[2]

[1] Wooldridge, op. cit., pl. 35. Transcription in G. Reese, *Music in the Middle Ages* (1940), p. 389.
[2] Oxford, Corpus Christi College, 59, fol. 113ᵛ; facsimile in R. Morris, *Old English Homilies* (Early English Text Society, O.S., vol. liii).

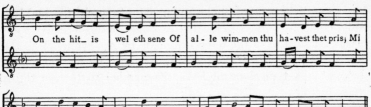

On the hit_ is wel eth sene Of al - le wim-men thu ha-vest thet pris; Mi

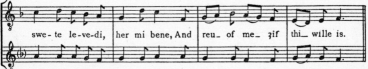

swe- te le-ve-di, her mi bene, And reu_ of me_ ʒif thi_ wille is.

(Blessed be thou, queen of heaven, comfort of men and joy of angels, spotless mother and pure maiden—there is none other such in the world. It is easy to see that of all women thou hast pre-eminence. My sweet lady, hear my prayer and pity me if it is thy will.)

This practice illustrates the reference made by Anonymus IV to the use of the third by English composers (see p. 4). Before long it developed into a form of three-part writing in which parallel sixths also were employed, the three parts together offering successions of $\frac{6}{3}$ chords. This new development, to which the name 'English descant' has been given,[1] later spread to the Continent, where it appears in the early part of the fifteenth century under the name *fauxbourdon*. There was one important difference: in 'English descant' the tune was in the lowest part, in *fauxbourdon* in the upper part. *Fauxbourdon* itself, which is in essence a form of improvised part-singing, was in turn imitated by English composers, and instructions for singing it appear in English treatises of the fifteenth and early sixteenth centuries, including one in Scots which has a section beginning: 'Quhat is Faburdoun?'[2]

The earliest example of 'English descant' appears to be at the end of a late thirteenth-century Te Deum,[3] beginning (the plain-song is in the lowest part):

Ex.10

In te, Do - mi - ne, spe - ra - - - vi

[1] See M. F. Bukofzer, *Geschichte des englischen Diskants und des Faux-bourdons nach den theoretischen Quellen* (1936).
[2] Brit. Mus. Add. 4911; printed in Bukofzer, op. cit., pp. 158–60.
[3] Cambridge, Gonville and Caius College, 334, fol. 2; printed in Bukofzer, op. cit., No. 18.

The same style is found in several of the pieces written by Worcester composers about 1300.[1] The existence of this school of composers reminds us of the reference made by Anonymus IV to the practice of music in the 'Westcuntre'. The following wordless introduction[2] is a typical example of the parallel sixths and thirds characteristic of 'English descant':

We find also in the works of these anonymous musicians vivid evidence of that close association between church music and secular melody which occurs also on the Continent at the same period. There are obvious affinities between 'Sumer is icumen in' and the troped Sanctus[3] beginning:

Particularly attractive is the three-part motet 'Puellare gremium',[4]

---

[1] Printed in *Worcester Mediaeval Harmony*, ed. Dom Anselm Hughes, (1928).　　　　　　　　　　[2] Ibid., p. 125 (facsimile on p. 124).

[3] Ibid., p. 50.

[4] Ibid., p. 100 (with some errors in the transcription of both words and music).

built on an instrumental ostinato which bears the marks of a popular origin:

In the three-part setting, which begins as follows, the phrases of the ostinato are separated by rests:

13

The technique of 'English descant' was applied also to pieces in which the tune was no longer in the lowest part, e.g. this fourteenth-century setting of 'Angelus ad virginem'[1]—a hymn referred to by Chaucer[2]—where the melody, which is considerably older, is in the middle part:

Ex. 15

---

[1] Cambridge, Univ. Lib. Add. 710, fol. 130; facsimile in Wooldridge, op. cit., pls. 46–7. The G in the last bar is written A in the manuscript. The words in square brackets are supplied from Brit. Mus. Arundel 248, fol. 154 (Wooldridge, op. cit., pl. 34), where there is also an English version, beginning 'Gabriel fram evene King'.   [2] *The Miller's Tale*, 3216.

The same technique was incorporated in compositions for four voices, a form of writing which English composers seem to have favoured more than their contemporaries on the Continent. Examples from the early fourteenth century are the motets 'Ave miles coelestis curiae[1] (on a hymn in honour of St. Edmund the martyr) and 'Petrum Cephas ecclesiae'.[2]

Among the earliest specimens of purely instrumental music are three dance tunes in two-part harmony, contained in the same manuscript as 'Sumer is icumen in'.[3] In accordance with the normal practice of the thirteenth and fourteenth centuries they consist of a series of short sections (known as *puncti*) which afford opportunity for contrast and repetition. The two instrumental parts, marked *cantus superior* and *cantus inferior*, appear to be of equal importance. In No. 3 the tune is in the lower part for sections 1 and 2 and is then played a fifth higher by the upper part in sections 3 and 4, and in a slightly ornamented form in section 5:[4]

Ex. 16

[1] Printed in M. F. Bukofzer, *Studies in Medieval and Renaissance Music* (1950), p. 30.
[2] Printed in J. Stainer, *Early Bodleian Music* (1901), vol. ii, p. 24 (facsimile in vol. i, pls. 10–11).
[3] Brit. Mus. 978, fol. 8ᵛ–9; facsimiles in Wooldridge, op. cit., pls. 18–19. Transcriptions of Nos. 1 and 2 in Davison and Apel, op. cit., No. 41.
[4] The clash in the third bar of section 3*a* is inevitable if the two parts are to retain their independence.

This piece also exhibits another common characteristic of medieval dances—the use of varied endings, known in French as *ouvert* and *clos*: the first half of each section ends with a half close, the second half with a full close. To the thirteenth century also belongs a dance tune which is purely monophonic, apart from a section in three parts at the end.[1] This very lively piece, which seems to be in duple time, is markedly instrumental in character; passages like the following:

Ex. 17

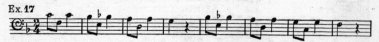

must have been part of the stock-in-trade of minstrelsy.[2] Particularly interesting are two keyboard dances (the earliest known in Europe), which are preserved, together with some motet transcriptions in an early fourteenth-century manuscript formerly at Robertsbridge Abbey in Sussex (Brit. Mus. Add. 28,550, fol. 43–3ᵛ);[3] they are written in a form of tablature familiar later in

[1] Oxford, Bodleian, Douce 139, fol. 5ᵛ; facsimiles in Stainer, op. cit., vol. i, pl. 7, and Wooldridge, op. cit., pl. 24. Transcription in Davison and Apel, op. cit., No. 40c.

[2] If this is string music, the convenience of the player would be a strong argument for the suggested E♭.

[3] Facsimiles in Wooldridge, op. cit., pls. 42–3. Transcriptions in J. Handschin, 'Über Estampie und Sequenz', in *Zeitschrift für Musikwissenschaft*, 1929–30, pp. 14–18. Parts of the second piece are printed in Davison and Apel, op. cit., No. 58.

16

fifteenth-century German organ music, the upper part being in staff notation and the lower represented by letters.[1] Here, too, we have a series of *puncti*, with the 'open' and 'closed' endings. It is by no means certain, however, that the pieces are of English origin.

[1] See W. Apel, *The Notation of Polyphonic Music* (1942), pp. 37–40.

II

MUSIC IN THE FIFTEENTH AND EARLY SIXTEENTH CENTURIES

WITH the beginning of the fifteenth century we are able for the first time to observe something in the nature of a national school of music. In the previous chapter, indeed, we have noticed a few points which, even in the scantiness of our records, still serve to separate the work of England from that of other countries. But now styles begin to diverge in a manner that attracts more attention; and by the end of the period dealt with in this chapter we can recognize in the musical world definitely competing methods of expression. A substantial amount of fifteenth-century music has survived. Two manuscript volumes, respectively in the Bodleian Library at Oxford (Selden B 26)[1] and in the library of St. Edmund's College at Old Hall in Hertfordshire,[2] supply between them about two hundred pieces covering the first half of the century. A third, now in the British Museum (Egerton 3307),[3] includes nearly sixty works. Many others exist on the Continent in the so-called Trent Codices[4] and in manuscripts at Bologna, Modena, and Aosta,[5] and still others, of less importance, in different parts of England. Some of the most noteworthy pieces exist in different versions; and altogether we cannot complain of paucity of material.

The most important of these composers is certainly John Dunstable, about whom has gathered a curious mass of legend and untrustworthy rhapsody. There is no reason to connect him with the town of Dunstable in Bedfordshire, and of biographical details we have virtually none. The date of his death was 1453, according to an epitaph copied by the seventeenth-century antiquary John Stow from his tomb in St. Stephen's, Walbrook, London; in another

[1] See J. Stainer, *Early Bodleian Music*, 3 vols. (1901).
[2] See *The Old Hall Manuscript*, ed. A. Ramsbotham, H. B. Collins, and Dom Anselm Hughes, 3 vols. (1933–8).
[3] See B. Schofield, 'A Newly Discovered 15th-Century Manuscript of the English Chapel Royal', in *The Musical Quarterly*, Oct. 1946, pp. 509–36, and M. F. Bukofzer, ibid., Jan. 1947, pp. 38–51.
[4] Printed in *Denkmäler der Tonkunst in Österreich*, years vii, xi (1), xix (1), xxvii (1), xxxi, xl.
[5] See G. de Van, 'A Recently Discovered Source of Early 15th-Century Polyphonic Music', in *Musica Disciplina*, vol. ii (1948), pp. 5–74.

epitaph preserved in John Weever's *Ancient Funerall Monuments* (1631) he is described as 'an astrologian, a mathematician, a musitian, and what not'.[1] Some astronomical treatises under his name exist in the Bodleian and at St. John's College, Cambridge; and in the latter of these he is described as musician to the Duke of Bedford, who became regent of France in 1422 and died at Rouen in 1435. The fact that the bulk of his music is to be found only in foreign manuscripts also suggests that he spent much of his life abroad; and, indeed, his fame seems to have been at its highest outside his own native country. The poem *Le Champion des Dames*, written by Martin le Franc about 1440, explains the superiority of the heads of the contemporary French school, Dufay and Binchois, as compared with their predecessors, by their adoption of the methods of the English school, and especially of Dunstable; and Tinctoris, the celebrated Flemish theoretician, who flourished in the latter half of the century, names Dunstable as the leader of the English school that was the 'fount and origin' of what virtually seemed a new art, so wonderfully did it surpass all previous music.[2]

Tinctoris is inclined to ascribe the great advance in music during the century very largely to the institution of royal and princely 'chapels', in imitation of the Papal choir at Rome, which were now being gradually created in most parts of Western Europe; they afforded musicians both a more dignified position and also greater artistic opportunities than could be secured by the ordinary church appointments, and consequently attracted the best performers of the time, and incited them towards advanced composition. Henry V possessed a 'complete chapel full of singers',[3] which followed him to France; and we know that the Old Hall manuscript, containing compositions from the pen of the king himself,[4] along with many others, is a collection of the music sung in St. George's Chapel, Windsor. But of the lives of all these composers we know practically nothing. Leonel Power (d. 1445), who seems to have been the most famous after Dunstable, wrote a treatise (forming part of a volume,

---

[1] Both epitaphs are printed in Grove's *Dictionary* (4th ed.), vol. ii, p. 112.

[2] 'Quo fit ut hac tempestate facultas nostrae musicae tam mirabile susceperit incrementum quod ars nova esse videatur, cuius, ut ita dicam, novae artis fons et origo apud Anglicos, quorum caput Dunstaple exstitit, fuisse perhibetur' (Coussemaker, op. cit., vol. iv, p. 154).

[3] C. A. Cole, *Memorials of Henry V, King of England* (1858), p. 68.

[4] See M. F. Bukofzer, 'The Music of the Old Hall Manuscript', in *Studies in Medieval and Renaissance Music* (1950), pp. 78–9.

the preservation of which is due to Tallis, who acquired it at the dissolution of the monastery of Waltham Holy Cross),[1] in which he prohibits consecutive unisons, fifths, and octaves. Aleyn, a composer of less note, has been identified, with some probability, with a Johannes Alanus, author of a motet of which the *triplum*, beginning 'Sub Arturo plebs vallata', refers to several English musicians.[2] Of the other composers whose names have come down to us with their compositions— Jervays, Forest, Benet, Bedingham, Standley, Stove, Markham, Cooke, Sturgeon, Damett, Burell, Byttering, Tyes, Excetre, Pycard, Rowlard, Queldryk, Fonteyns, Oliver, Chyrbury, Typp, Swynford, Pennard, Lambe, Mayshuet, and one or two more whose names are illegible—we know nothing certain, except that some of them were members of Henry V's Chapel Royal;[3] and many pieces are anonymous. We have more information about a later fifteenth-century composer, John Hothby, whom we now know solely by his theoretical treatises; he settled in Italy about the middle of the century, first in Florence, secondly in Ferrara, and afterwards in Lucca, where he remained for nearly twenty years, dying, however, in England in 1487, when on leave of absence. We also have traces of his having visited Spain, France, and Germany; he was a member of the Carmelite Order, and a prominent theologian. He was held in the highest estimation abroad, and a contemporary poem asserts that no one equal to Ottobi (as his name was written) could be found 'between the Ganges and Cadiz'.[4]

Tinctoris, in a continuation of the passage from which quotation has already been made, remarks that at the time he wrote (about 1475) the English composers, after having led, had now come to learn from the Flemish; the latter, he says, 'are from day to day discovering novel methods', but the former 'are always continuing in the old paths'.[5] Indeed, it is abundantly true that England, after having had in Dunstable a musician without foreign rival, could not, fifty years later, produce any one comparable with Josquin des Près. The shifting of the balance had as a matter of fact begun almost immediately; Dunstable's younger contemporaries, Dufay

---

[1] Brit. Mus. Lansdowne 763 (No. 15). Printed in M. F. Bukofzer, *Geschichte des englischen Diskants und des Fauxbourdons* (1936), pp. 132–6.

[2] Printed in *Denkmäler der Tonkunst in Österreich*, year xl, pp. 9–11.

[3] Bukofzer, *Studies in Medieval and Renaissance Music*, loc. cit.

[4] Coussemaker, op. cit., vol. iii, p. xxxi.

[5] Ibid., vol. iv, p. 154.

and Okeghem, and Obrecht still more, had advanced quickly on the new road, and the methods of the succeeding Flemish composers ruled the musical world unchallenged. Later on, England learnt all the secrets of the new art of its former pupils, and it is to Flemish influence that we owe so much of the music of the sixteenth century in England and elsewhere.

With the cessation of the Wars of the Roses (1455–85) music in England took a new lease of life; humanism obtained a firm position, and there was a general revival of interest in art and learning. But, many as were the literary foreigners who journeyed across the channel, it is more than doubtful if any of the prominent Flemish musicians, scattered all over western and central Europe though they were, came among them; and, indeed, it is not till about the second decade of the sixteenth century that we can see in any English work any really definite signs of Flemish influence, transmitted, no doubt, by travelled English musicians, as well as by the foreign performers settled at the court of Henry VIII, and also by circulation of manuscripts and printed books. We have the names and specimens of the music of a considerable number of composers during the fifty years after the death of Richard III (1483–5); but of their lives we know but little, and, in the case of many, nothing. Robert Fayrfax, who in his time was 'in great renowne and accounted the prime Musitian of the Nation',[1] was organist of St. Alban's Abbey, one of the chief gentlemen of the Chapel Royal in London, and Doctor of Music at both Cambridge and Oxford Universities; he died in 1521, but the exact year of his birth is unknown. Other distinguished composers were William Cornyshe, master of the children of the Chapel Royal from 1509 to his death about 1523; Richard Sampson (d. 1554), dean of the Chapel Royal, who became Bishop of Chichester and later of Lichfield and Coventry; Richard Davy, who was organist of Magdalen College, Oxford, in 1490; Hugh Aston, who was a music student at Oxford in 1510;[2] and John Taverner (d. 1545), who was master of the choristers at Cardinal's College (later Christ Church), Oxford, from 1526 to 1530. Others who deserve mention are Gilbert Banaster (d. 1487), William Newark (d. 1509), Robert Cooper, Richard Bramston, Nicholas Ludford, William Pashe, Thomas Lovell, John Dygon, and Henry

---

[1] Anthony Wood (Oxford, Bodleian, Wood D 19 (4), fol. 50).
[2] For a discussion of his supposed identification with an archdeacon of York who died in 1522 see *Tudor Church Music*, vol. x, pp. xiii–xvii.

VIII himself; but the various manuscripts scattered about English libraries contain in all several hundreds of works of the period—all, with but a small handful of exceptions, vocal, and chiefly designed for ecclesiastical use.

Though a few of the fifteenth-century composers, especially Power, are represented both in the English and in the continental manuscripts, yet on the whole those whose names appear in the former are not in the latter, and vice versa; but the large quantity of anonymous music of the time prevents us from drawing any very definite conclusions. This anonymous music—chiefly, so far as can be judged, earlier than 1450—is of very miscellaneous nature; the custom of allowing each voice to sing different words is still in vogue, and we find examples, to English words, of the ballade form popular in France with Machault and his school, or again specimens of fifteenth-century gymel (or two-part *fauxbourdon*), where the composer's frank delight in consecutive sixths becomes very wearying, or again little things like the two-part song 'Alas, departynge is ground of woo',[1] which in their way aim, and far from unsuccessfully, at real, genuine beauty of sound and emotional expression. But all this work, though sometimes, as in 'Alas, departynge', of very high merit, is very simple in design; and the time was now coming when composers sought after more advanced things. Stainer's *Early Bodleian Music* contains some notable three-part songs of the period, such as the beautiful 'Go hert hurt with adversite' and 'Nesciens mater virgo', the bright and rhythmically spirited 'Tappster, drynker', and the elaborate and skilful 'Tota pulchra es',[2] and a large number of anonymous carols of the period, many of which have been printed in various collections, remain in different manuscripts. A roll of thirteen from the library of Trinity College, Cambridge, has been published in convenient form,[3] and gives a good notion of the rather more ambitious music of the earlier part of the century. They are written sometimes for two, sometimes for three voices; and the three-part work, though containing no imitation, is considerably more elaborate than the attempts of nearly all previous musicians in England. The best

[1] J. Stainer, *Early Bodleian Music* (1901), vol. ii, p. 72.
[2] Ibid., pp. 68, 137, 168, 177.
[3] *English Carols of the Fifteenth Century*, ed. J. A. Fuller Maitland (n.d.). W. S. Rockstro's additional parts, though carefully done, are entirely unnecessary anachronisms; but as they are typographically distinguished, no confusion need arise.

known of the set is No. 7,[1] a song of thanksgiving after the battle
of Agincourt—a famous piece which has often been reprinted in
different shapes. It is a two-part song (though beginning, as was not
uncommon, with a powerful unison phrase) followed by a three-
part chorus; the central portion, to English words, is based on a
very fine tune that may well be of popular origin:

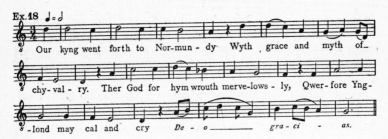

The concluding chorus is as follows:

* ♩ in the M S.

A slightly different version is in the manuscript in the Bodleian
Library at Oxford (Selden B 26) mentioned on p. 18.[2] In general
the carols of this period may be regarded as examples of popular
polyphony. For the most part they are straightforward harmonizations of simple tunes, the words being written in the lowest part.
One example—'Glad and blithe mote ȝe be'[3]—is not only a translation of the Christmas sequence 'Laetabundus' but uses an ornamental version of the plainsong melody in the upper of the two

[1] Facsimile in *English Carols of the Fifteenth Century*, frontispiece.
[2] Printed in J. Stainer, *Early Bodleian Music*, vol. ii, p. 128 (facsimile in
vol. i, pl. 66).
[3] Stainer, op. cit., p. 134.

parts. Elsewhere we may very well suspect the influence of folk-song, as in 'Deo gracias'. The frank and direct style of these pieces, which has obvious affinities with the part-writing described in chapter I, may be illustrated by the three-part refrain of 'Now wel may we merthis make':[1]

A good deal of the church music preserved in the Old Hall manuscript is also very simple in style, consisting of little more than harmonizations of plainsong melodies. Much of it is conventional, even naïve; but simplicity does not necessarily exclude artistry. The following opening of a Gloria by Thomas Damett[2] shows not only technical skill (note the fragment of imitation in the third and fourth bars) but also a genuine feeling for musical expression:

---

[1] Stainer, op. cit., p. 109 (facsimile, pl. 51).
[2] *The Old Hall Manuscript*, ed. A. Ramsbotham, H. B. Collins, and Dom Anselm Hughes, vol. i, p. 144.

There are, however, a number of pieces which show definite signs of continental influence in the use of close imitation (sometimes even of canon) and what has been termed 'isorhythmic' technique—that is to say, the unifying of a composition by the repetition of extended rhythmical patterns. The beginning of a Gloria by Pycard[1] may be quoted as an example of both methods. The last four bars of the quotation show the beginning of a second section which repeats the rhythmical pattern of the first (bars 1–24). Such a device is obviously artificial, but not more so than other structural conventions which have been employed by composers at other periods. The sustained accompaniment provides a simple harmonic background to the upper parts. The plainsong melody on which the composition is based (part of a sequence) is in the tenor. It will be noticed that the contratenor and tenor do not create independent harmony: the composition is virtually in four parts, and in fact the original manuscript provides an alternative *solus tenor* (omitted in this quotation) which combines the contratenor and tenor into a continuous whole:

Ex. 22

---

[1] Ibid., p. 92. See also vol. iii, pp. xxiv–v, and M. F. Bukofzer, 'The Music of the Old Hall Manuscript', in *Studies in Medieval and Renaissance Music*, pp. 60–2.

Passages of this kind—and many others—show how clear at this time was the conception of harmony as a sequence of chords, not merely as the result of combining independent parts. Such a conception was natural in composers who had behind them the traditions of 'English descant' described in the last chapter. It also made it possible for them to place the plainsong *canto fermo* in the treble or a middle part, or even to let it migrate from one voice to another, instead of confining it to the tenor. Nor did the old traditions prevent the more adventurous men from writing progressions which went beyond the established conventions. Sometimes the accidentals marked in the manuscript indicate harmonies which would have been unlikely to result from editorial conjecture—for example, the chromatic opening of an Agnus by Chyrbury,[1] or this passage from a setting of the Creed by Leonel Power:[2]

[1] *The Old Hall Manuscript*, vol. iii, p. 116.
[2] Ibid., vol. ii, p. 194.

Ex. 23

The simple harmonic structure of so many of the pieces in the Old Hall manuscript may be paralleled by the contemporary Passion according to St. Luke—the earliest known Passion setting—which is preserved in the British Museum (Egerton 3307). The style of this is very largely syllabic, with frequent use of repeated notes. As was customary in the later Passions, the setting, which is in three parts, does not include the Evangelist's narrative or the words of Christ but is reserved for those portions of the text which were spoken by individuals or groups of people in the story. The following extract[1] includes the last two sections—the prayer of the penitent thief and the words of the centurion:[2]

Ex. 24

[1] The complete Passion is printed by M. F. Bukofzer, 'A Newly Discovered 15th-Century Manuscript', in *The Musical Quarterly*, Jan. 1947, pp. 43–51. The manuscript also contains an incomplete Passion according to St. Matthew.
[2] Luke xxiii, 42 and 47.

The bulk of the Old Hall manuscript was evidently completed before Dunstable acquired his reputation. Only one complete composition by him[1]—a setting of the hymn 'Veni, sancte spiritus'—is included, as a later addition, and even then without any indication of the author's name. Quite apart from this, very little of Dunstable's work is found in English sources. The continental manuscripts, on the other hand, present us with a considerable amount of material. Some sixty pieces by him, or attributed to him, survive,[2] and a sufficient number of these have been printed to make it possible to form an estimate of his work. In the case of the beautiful setting of Giustiniani's 'O rosa bella',[3] of which there are a large number of copies, the attribution to Dunstable is so weak that there is no sufficient justification for assigning it to him. The problem of works which are attributed to him in one manuscript and to Power in another is more difficult; but it is not solved by the convenient expedient of assuming that Power and Dunstable were the same person.

Dunstable was clearly more susceptible than his English contemporaries to continental influences; but he remained none the less an English composer, with that fondness for smooth harmonic progressions and for melodies suggested by the harmony which is one of the characteristics of English music at this time. His three-part motet 'Quam pulcra es',[4] of which the end may be quoted, is a delicate example of that English suavity which seems to have made such an impression on continental musicians:

---

[1] The incomplete 'Ascendit Christus' (fol. 57ᵛ), said to be by Forest, is attributed to Dunstable in the Modena manuscript (printed in *Denkmäler der Tonkunst in Österreich*, year xl, p. 53). See Ex. 29.

[2] For a list see C. Stainer in *Sammelbände der internationalen Musikgesellschaft*, 1900–1, pp. 8–13, supplemented by M. F. Bukofzer in *Acta Musicologica*, 1936, pp. 111–18 and G. de Van in *Musica Disciplina*, 1948, pp. 22–54.

[3] Printed in Davison and Apel, *Historical Anthology of Music*, No. 61 (after *D.T.Ö.*, year vii, pp. 229–32, including the reproduction of a transcriber's or printer's error in bar 39: the upper part should be a third lower, as a comparison with the facsimile in *D.T.Ö.* will show).

[4] Bologna, Liceo Musicale 37, fol. 284ᵛ–5 (facsimile in Wooldridge, *Early English Harmony*, pl. 59–60). Another version from the Trent manuscripts is printed in *D.T.Ö.* year vii, pp. 190–1. The version in Grove's *Dictionary* (4th ed.), vol. ii, pp. 112–13, which purports to be a transcription of the Bologna manuscript, is actually a conflation of the Bologna and Trent versions, with unspecified emendations. The words are a compilation from the Song of Solomon, vii, 4–7, 11–12.

* Semibreve B in the original

English origin is also very apparent in the nobly expressive 'Crux fidelis',[1] beginning:

[1] *D.T.Ö.*, year vii, p. 183.

Here the plainsong melody is in the middle part (the contratenor);[1] the tenor supplies a simple accompaniment in the style of English gymel, while an independent and decorated part is written above for the treble voice. The opening of this motet is one of the most astonishingly distinguished passages of simple music of any age. Simplicity, as we have seen, was not peculiar to Dunstable; but he excelled in using it to achieve eloquence. The ebb and flow of this section of a 'Kyrie eleison'[2] is beautifully contrived:

The other sections use the same thematic material with variation and elaboration.

These examples represent only one side of Dunstable's art. There is also a love of complexity, evident particularly in his isorhythmic motets, which include the setting of 'Veni, sancte spiritus' found in the Old Hall manuscript. In these works a highly organized rhythmical pattern is used as a framework on which are interwoven contrasted melodic lines. The upper parts, so far from suggesting artificial restrictions, have rather the character of free arabesques. The opening of the isorhythmic motet 'Praeco praeeminentiae'[3]

---

[1] See M. F. Bukofzer, 'John Dunstable and the Music of his Time', in *Proceedings of the Musical Association*, 1938–9, pp. 25 and 29.

[2] *D.T.Ö.*, year xxxi, p. 106.

[3] *D.T.Ö.*, year xl, p. 46.

(for St. John the Baptist's day) will serve as an illustration. The *canto fermo* is in the tenor; the contratenor is without words:

Ex. 28

The style of this owes much to tradition; in addition to the iso-rhythmic structure (which cannot be demonstrated in a short example) we may note also the use of different texts—a survival of thirteenth-century practice—and the long-sustained *canto fermo* in the tenor. Very different in character is the motet 'Ascendit Christus'.[1] The first and third sections are in two parts, the second and fourth in three parts. In the three-part sections the melody of the antiphon 'Alma redemptoris' is introduced in the tenor; but instead of being announced in long notes it is treated with the

---

[1] Ibid., p. 53. Cf. *supra*, p. 28, n. 1.

same rhythmical freedom as the upper parts. It is no longer a mere foundation: the three voices participate on equal terms, and all sing the same words. Our example shows the second section, where the plainsong melody appears for the first time:

We find also motets in which there is no *canto fermo* in a lower part; instead the plainsong appears, in a highly ornamented form, in the treble, as in the motet 'Regina coeli',[1] while the lower parts provide an accompaniment which may be simple or as elaborate as the melody. Others again, like 'Quam pulcra es', quoted above, appear to be entirely original, without any dependence on a plainsong theme. There is thus a considerable variety in Dunstable's work, in spite of a general similarity of idiom; and if there are times when he seems more resourceful than inspired, there is nothing to cause us to question the high regard in which he was held by his contemporaries.

More than thirty years separate the death of Dunstable from the accession of Henry VII (1485–1509). It is hardly surprising that changes of style should be apparent in the work of composers active during that reign. In many respects there is a strong adherence to tradition: we find the same love of smoothness in melody and harmony. But there is also a more intimate relationship between the individual melodic lines and a new sense of direction in the harmony. Several of the motets in the Eton College manuscript appear to be designed on entirely original material. Such independence of a *canto fermo* is not new; but its adoption as a normal method of composition results in a greater freedom in the lower parts. There is also a new awareness of the sonority to be achieved by writing in five or six parts, and this fullness of sound is skilfully used as a contrast to sections of two-part or three-part writing. The opening of a 'Salve regina' by Browne[2] is an excellent example of such sonority, and also of the new feeling for harmonic progression. The music unfolds like a flower responding to the sun:

Ex. 30

---

[1] *D.T.Ö* year xl, p. 49.   [2] Eton College, MS. 178, fol. g 8.

The fine quality of Browne's work makes it surprising that we know virtually nothing about him. We should have expected that a composer who could produce such intimate and finely drawn music as this section of a 'Stabat mater'[1] would have enjoyed a considerable reputation:

This example will also illustrate the unification achieved by an intimate relationship between the parts. Sometimes this relationship is more precise, for instance in this extract from a 'Salve regina' by Cornyshe:[2]

---

[1] Eton College, MS. 178, fol. c 2.   [2] Ibid., fol. g 7.

Ex. 32

But more often it is the result rather of a unity of feeling than of exact imitation. The opening of this same 'Salve regina'[1] is an admirable example of a unified polyphony created by the combination of individual melodic lines:

Ex. 33

[1] Ibid., fol. g 6.

Where the melodic lines have a less marked individuality the result may be to emphasize more strongly the sequence of harmonies. There is very little elaboration in this setting of the centurion's words from Davy's *St. Matthew Passion*,[1] but the resulting simplicity is all the more moving:

The reputation which Fayrfax enjoyed in his lifetime is not entirely borne out by his work. Too often he seems to pursue smoothness to the point of dullness. It may well be that his contemporaries took a particular delight in this continuous euphony; but the modern listener is conscious rather of a lack of personality. The following extract from his *Regali* Mass,[2] which includes some

[1] Eton College, MS. 178, fol. ee 9.
[2] Oxford, Bodleian, Mus. Sch. e. 376–81.

neatly contrived imitation, may serve as a specimen of his work. The whole passage is a setting of the single word 'Benedictus':

Like his contemporaries he also delighted in the effective contrast provided by the massive sonority of several parts. A passage like the following—from the Gloria of the *Albanus* Mass[1]—is little more than an elaboration of a simple sequence of common chords, with little individuality in the part-writing; but here the restricted range of the harmony finds compensation in the richness of the sound:

[1] Ibid.

Ex. 36

It has been suggested that Fayrfax was the composer of the anonymous *O quam suavis* Mass,[1] which is certainly contemporary, but there is no positive evidence in support of this suggestion. The familiar features of early Tudor music appear in this

[1] Edited by H. B. Collins (Plainsong and Medieval Music Society).

38

work—the smoothness of harmony, the frequent use of appoggiaturas, and the long, serpentine phrases for single syllables. More
significant is the considerable use made of imitation—the result, no
doubt, of Flemish influence; an extract from the Creed will give a
fair idea of the style:

With this we may compare the corresponding section of Aston's
Te Deum Mass: [1]

[1] *Tudor Church Music*, vol. x, p. 15.

Here the imitation, though less consistent, is equally effective. Imitation, as well as florid elaboration, plays an important part in Aston's work. His two Masses, based, like those of his contemporaries, on plainsong themes, are imposing structures, designed to exploit the skill of trained singers as well as the familiar contrasts in sonority.

Imitation was not confined to church music. Several of the concerted songs reproduced in the volumes of the Plainsong and Medieval Music Society[1] also show a considerable amount of imitative writing (though of a fairly simple kind) and also some sense of structural design: Cornyshe's vigorous and effective

[1] *Songs and Madrigals by English Composers of the Close of the Fifteenth Century* (1891) and *Madrigals by English Composers of the Close of the Fifteenth Century* (1893).

'Hoyda, hoyda, joly rutterkyn' and Browne's 'Margarit meke' are
in a regular rondo form. The fine three-part 'A, my dere son',[1]
concerning the authorship of which the manuscript (Brit. Mus.
Add. 5465) is silent, contains canonic writing which, very plain
though it is, is more akin to contemporary Flemish methods than
to those of Fayrfax, and also approximates to the foreign style in
its remarkable expressiveness and attention to the sentiment of the
words. There are also definite signs of Flemish influence in a small
manuscript collection dating from the year 1516 (Brit. Mus. Royal
11 E, xi); the motet 'Quam pulcra es' by Sampson which is found
in it[2] shows considerable maturity of manner.

The same influence can be observed in the work of Taverner,[3]
the most important composer of Henry VIII's reign, though he is
also faithful to the English tradition. There is in his music both
suavity and vigour. The former may be illustrated by the opening of
the motet 'Quemadmodum', which is without words in our sources:

Ex. 39 ♩=○

Vigour is to be found in the splendid setting of the words 'Deum
de Deo' from the Creed of his masterpiece, the Mass *Coronea
Spinea* (the plainsong is in the second tenor):

[1] Unfortunately the reprint in the Plainsong and Medieval Music Society's
volume is disfigured by the addition of an organ part and by a transcriber's
error on the sixth page.

[2] The first part was printed by Wooldridge in *The Oxford History of Music*,
vol. ii (1st ed.), pp. 323–4.

[3] His church music is in *Tudor Church Music*, vols. i and iii.

Both appear in this three-part extract from the Gloria of the same work:

Taverner has his mannerisms, among them a fondness for scale passages. The device is very effectively used in the Sanctus of the Mass *The Western Wynde*—a work which is in effect a set of variations on a secular melody, here heard in the soprano:

He is also capable of stiffness, for instance, in the Mass *O Michael*, where the 'Crucifixus' of the Creed includes a too persistent sequence. But there are many places where sequence is handled with brilliant effect, notably in the Agnus of the Mass *Gloria tibi Trinitas*;[1] and in general he threads the mazes of polyphony with extraordinary ease and assurance, sometimes resorting to a simple antiphony between upper and lower voices (as in the Masses *Small Devotion* and *Mater Christi*[2] and some of the motets), at other times developing his melodic lines with a freedom and exuberance that recall the work of his immediate predecessors. There are passages where florid melody in a vivacious rhythm takes complete command, for instance the very striking opening of the Sanctus of the Mass *Coronea Spinea*:

[1] Quoted in *The Oxford History of Music*, vol. ii (2nd ed.), pp. 167–71.
[2] In both these Masses the tenor part is missing. Fellowes (*English Cathedral Music*, p. 42) suggests that the title *Small Devotion* is a copyist's error for *In all Devotion*.

Above all there is in his music a spaciousness and a feeling for growth that make it one of the most impressive monuments of early sixteenth-century polyphony.

Of the compositions of Henry VIII himself,[1] though he wrote a considerable number of them, very little need be said; he was an eclectic of the feeblest kind, producing sometimes, as in the three-part motet 'Quam pulcra es', dull exercise-work, sometimes, as in 'In tyme of youthe', an amateurish and equally dull mixture of incongruous methods, and sometimes, as in the song 'Pastyme with good companye', harmonizing a plain tune, which though bright has very little quality, in a fairly pleasing but decidedly elementary manner. The beautiful anthem 'O Lord, the maker of all thing', which for a long time was attributed to him, is palpably of later date (see p. 63). It is, however, conceivable that an earlier setting of these words in the 'Wanley' manuscript (Oxford, Bodleian, Mus. Sch. e. 420–2) is by the king.[2]

In addition to the ecclesiastical music in which the highest endeavours of these composers are shown there remains a considerable quantity of other music, both vocal and instrumental, of the period centring round the year 1500; and one of the first examples of music-printing in England—Wynkyn de Worde's song book of 1530 (of which only the bass part survives in the British Museum) —is almost exclusively secular. There seems to have been a particular vogue for three-part songs of a simple popular character, known as 'freemen's songs' (a corruption of 'three men's songs'). In some cases the tunes, which are generally in the tenor, may very well be traditional, but it is impossible to be certain. It is interesting to note that composers like Cornyshe, who was active in the composition of elaborate church music, were not averse to writing simple pieces of this kind. Since Henry VIII himself tried his hand at this form of music, we may suppose that they were popular at court and in high society generally—an example of sophistication

[1] Edited by Lady Mary Trefusis for the Roxburghe Club (1912).
[2] See E. H. Fellowes, *English Cathedral Music* (2nd ed., 1943), pp. 41–2.

for which there are plenty of parallels in other countries and other periods. A feature common to many of the songs of this time is that they are written in the Mixolydian mode.

All through this period, and indeed both earlier and later, the concerted vocal music would seem to have been, as a rule, supported by instruments doubling the voices. Not indeed that we have much ground for dogmatizing about details; we cannot tell with any certainty whether portions that lack words were vocalized, or sung to the same words as are fitted to simultaneous vocal parts (where such exist, and where the words can be so fitted, as is not always the case) or merely played. But we know that motets and chansons were sometimes, like madrigals in later times, performed instrumentally without any voices at all; and it seems most probable that the numerous initial, central, and final *ritornelli* which often occur in the music of these centuries were purely instrumental —where they are found, without any hint of words, at the very beginning of the composition, there can indeed be but little doubt. Sometimes they are of some elaboration, as in the two-part song 'Now wolde I fayne sum merthis mak', where the final symphony opens with a point of imitation and is of some length, or in the quaintly beautiful three-part 'Abyde y hope hit be the beste': the central *ritornelli* are particularly noticeable in the two-part 'I have set my hert so hye' (*c.* 1425).[1] Later on we often see instances of similar character (Sheryngham's two-part song 'My wofull hart', printed by Burney,[2] is an excellent specimen) and there are also in existence numerous lengthy pieces with titles suggesting vocal music, but entirely devoid of words, which probably were meant, at any rate primarily, for instrumental performance; and all through we notice evidence, greater or less in degree, that purely unaccompanied vocal music of an artistic kind was, if known at all, distinctly rare. Down to 1600, or later, music was often published with mere casual indications of a few words here and there; perhaps the singers knew the rest of the words by heart and fitted them in as they thought best, or perhaps they simply vocalized—a habit which indeed was not infrequently, so we gather from Morley's *Plaine and Easie Introduction* (1597)[3] and other sources, employed by indolent singers even when the words were written in full.

[1] Stainer, op. cit., vol. ii, pp. 51, 66, 161.
[2] *A General History of Music* (1776–89), vol. ii, p. 544. The original is in Brit. Mus. Add. 5465, fol. 7ᵛ.   [3] p. 179.

In the first years of the sixteenth century we also find some interesting specimens of instrumental composition, unaffected by any vocal considerations. These occur in a manuscript at the British Museum (Royal App. 58) and include an anonymous 'My Lady Carey's Dompe'[1] and a 'Hornpipe'[2] by Hugh Aston, both attempts at the variation form and showing very clear feeling for keyboard style in their scale passages, combinations of different rhythms, and contrasted colour effects. 'My Lady Carey's Dompe', though shorter and less elaborate than the 'Hornpipe', is much more musical and expressive, and is, in its slight way, a really charming little piece.

[1] Printed in A. T. Davison and W. Apel, *Historical Anthology of Music* (1946), No. 103.
[2] Printed in J. Wolf, *Music of Earlier Times*, No. 24.

III

MUSIC OF THE MID-SIXTEENTH CENTURY

WE need not linger much over the biographical details of the lives of the mid-sixteenth-century composers; indeed, the information we possess is but scanty, and dates have often to be supplied approximately, if at all.

Christopher Tye was born about 1500; he was a singer at King's College, Cambridge as a boy and in early manhood, and from 1541 to 1561 was master of the choristers at Ely Cathedral. In later life he took orders in the reformed Church, and seems largely to have abandoned composition. He died in 1573. He wrote much music for the ecclesiastical service, both in the older and the newer forms; during the reign of Edward VI, whose musical tutor he was, he produced a setting of the first fourteen chapters of the *Acts of the Apostles*, to a metrical translation of his own.

Robert White (b. *c.* 1530) was Tye's son-in-law, and seems to have succeeded him as master of the choristers at Ely. He left Ely in 1566 and later became master of the choristers at Westminster Abbey. He died in 1574. The majority of his compositions are to Latin words; only four English anthems can certainly be attributed to him. He also left a small quantity of instrumental music.

Thomas Tallis was born probably about 1505; he was organist of Waltham Abbey for some years before its dissolution in 1540, and subsequently a gentleman of the Chapel Royal, a post that he retained through all the changes of state religion till his death in 1585. His compositions include specimens of all the forms practised in his day; but the great majority are vocal and ecclesiastical in character. In 1575 he and William Byrd (see p. 72) were granted a monopoly, of twenty-one years' duration, of the right of printing music and music-paper—the first known issue of Letters Patent of such a kind.[1] The first work the joint grantees issued was their own *Cantiones Sacrae* (1575), seventeen of the thirty-four being by Tallis.

Of the lives of the other contemporary composers we know still less than we do of those of Tye, White, and Tallis; we have little

---

[1] E. H. Fellowes, *William Byrd* (2nd ed., 1948), pp. 7–8.

more than their names and their works. John Shepherd was as a boy a chorister of St. Paul's Cathedral, and was subsequently— from 1542 to 1551, with a couple of intervals—connected with Magdalen College, Oxford, as organist and Fellow. John Redford, organist of St. Paul's Cathedral (d. 1547); Robert Parsons, a gentleman of the Chapel Royal at the beginning of the reign of Elizabeth (d. 1570); John Thorne (d. at York, 1573); Robert Johnson, a Scottish priest who fled to England (to be distinguished from his namesake, the song-writer, for whom see p. 74); Osbert Parsley (1511–85), for fifty years a lay clerk at Norwich—all these flourished about the same time and devoted themselves exclusively, or nearly so, to ecclesiastical work, to both English and Latin words. Of John Marbeck, lay clerk and one of the organists of St. George's Chapel at Windsor, we know a little more; he was arrested as a Protestant heretic towards the end of the reign of Henry VIII, and narrowly escaped burning—in 1550 he issued his well-known *Booke of Common Praier noted*,[1] and, having escaped persecution under Mary, produced in the following reign several vigorously Protestant theological books. He died about 1585, a little before William Mundy, a gentleman of the Chapel Royal for nearly thirty years under Elizabeth, who seems nevertheless to have been a secret adherent of the older faith: Richard Farrant was also attached (with intervals of a few years) to the Chapel Royal from some time in the reign of Edward VI till his death in 1581. Some secular music by these last two composers is in existence; but the bulk of their work was, like that of most of their contemporaries, written for church use. William Blitheman (d. 1591), though also connected with the Chapel Royal, and master of the choristers of Christ Church, Oxford, was, on the other hand, chiefly an instrumental composer; he was the master of Bull, the great musician of similar tastes in the next generation. Richard Edwards, of somewhat earlier date (d. 1566) was, like Blitheman, connected both with Christ Church and with the Chapel Royal; he was chiefly a lyric poet and dramatist, and it is not certain that the music of the well-known composition attributed to him (see p. 66) is really, as the words undoubtedly are, from his pen.

It does not lie within the province of this history to deal with the ecclesiastical changes that took place at the Reformation save in so far as they affected the music sung in the churches; but, with the

---

[1] Facsimile edition with commentary by J. Eric Hunt (1939).

exception—which is one of the greatest magnitude—that an enormous mass of music was destroyed in the process of suppressing the monasteries, and also under the Protestant régime of Edward VI, the actual artistic upheaval was far less considerable than we might have imagined. Ecclesiastical polyphony had begun as an elaboration of Gregorian chant; but in the course of time it grew away from this strict dependence. The plainsong itself gradually began to be modified and to disappear; in many compositions, from Dunstable downwards, it survives only in the opening intonation and perhaps a few places in the later course of the piece, and ecclesiastical music was increasingly written on themes merely suggested by the plainsong, on themes of a secular character (though this happened less frequently in England than elsewhere, the three Masses on the folksong 'Western wynde' by Tye, Shepherd, and Taverner, being the only notable instances), or finally on entirely original material.

The pre-Reformation Mass music had grown so elaborate that it sometimes omitted words altogether[1] or caused different sentences to be sung simultaneously, and the canticles had similarly tended to become unintelligible; the Reformers wished to allow the words to be heard by the congregation, but this was the whole sum of the change in method. The complaint was directed towards the over-complexity of the setting, not towards the plainsong itself; the Gregorian tones were taken over *en bloc*, and the subsequent Anglican chants were gradually evolved out of them by processes of harmonizing and rhythmicizing and gradual shedding of plainsong material—parallel with a similar development in general ecclesiastical music, in which fragments of plainsong survived here and there for some considerable time. And so we find purely syllabic unharmonized adaptation and imitation of the plainsong, as in Marbeck's historically famous Prayer-Book, or purely syllabic harmony, entirely rhythmless apart from the words, as in an extremely dull service by Heath printed in John Day's *Certaine notes set forthe in foure and three partes* (1560),[2] or the kind of work exemplified in services of Thomas Causton[3] and others, which, while not obscuring the words at all, use contrapuntal devices to a certain extent. There exist also early and rather awkward adaptations to

[1] See Dom Anselm Hughes, 'The Text-omissions in the Creed', in *Missa O quam suavis*, ed. H. B. Collins (Plainsong and Medieval Music Society).

[2] Day omits the Benedictus and Agnus Dei. The complete service is in the 'Wanley' manuscript, *c.* 1546–7 (Bodleian, Mus. Sch. e. 420–2).

[3] See *Tudor Church Music*, 8vo ed., Nos. 94 and 95.

English words of two of Taverner's Masses.[1] The modern anthem, which first came into being at this time, is a product partly of the Latin motet and partly of the elaborate psalm-settings, half-way between chants and anthems, which we find in the works of Byrd and Gibbons and other post-Reformation composers.

The ideal of the extremists in England and at the Council of Trent was identical—the total abolition of all polyphonic church music; this ruinous artistic calamity being averted, nothing very much happened—nothing, at least, of a kind really to affect the work of the great composers. Tye and Tallis were no more hampered by having to write the only very sparingly polyphonic *Acts of the Apostles* settings, or the plain 'Dorian' service, than any modern composer is by occasionally producing solid and earnest official work outside the lines of his normal development. It is true that a considerable number of composers of slenderer artistic powers seem to have found the temporary difficulties of the situation insoluble; but the leaders of music were implicated neither in the inartistic extremes which caused the reaction nor in those which resulted from it. No doubt, during the full flush of the re-forming movement, the great works of Tye and White and Tallis remained unheard except in private; but their composition went on all the same. Organs were temporarily silenced (this indeed was the first step for the reformers to take, as there seems no doubt that the complaints of over-elaboration were directed at least as much at the excessive floridity of the organists' accompaniments to the plainsong as at anything done by the singers); but the musical establishment of the Chapel Royal remained virtually unaltered through all the ecclesiastical upheavals, and the only fresh form of composition that resulted was the psalm tune, a purely Protestant invention. Towards the end of Henry VIII's reign Miles Coverdale had published a collection of Lutheran tunes under the title of *Goostly Psalmes and Spirituall Songes* (which was soon suppressed), and under Edward VI we find examples of psalters with psalm tunes, sometimes plain and sometimes slightly polyphonic in harmony: several more musically important collections published by John Day appeared early in Elizabethan times, and subsequent issues of various kinds are numerous (see p. 397).[2]

---

[1] *Tudor Church Music*, vol. iii, pp. 143–98 (cf. E. H. Fellowes, *English Cathedral Music*, p. 42).

[2] For the whole subject see the very detailed and admirable article 'Psalter' by H. E. Wooldridge in Grove's *Dictionary* (4th ed.), vol. iv, pp. 267–81.

In Scotland the results of Knox's reforming eloquence were far more drastic than anything that happened in England. There seems to have been a considerable school of Scottish composers, if we may judge from the manuscript St. Andrews Psalter,[1] which, though written in 1566, contains Latin motets of no doubt earlier date by several named native musicians, together with instrumental pieces, and harmonized psalm tunes and canticles: Thomas Wode, the transcriber, is a strong opponent of the new inartistic régime. Of the early sixteenth-century Scottish composers Robert Carver (b. 1491) deserves particular mention. He composed a number of elaborate pieces of church music including a Mass on 'L'homme armé' and a motet, 'O bone Jesu', for nineteen voices.[2] To the same period belongs a theoretical treatise in Scottish dialect (Brit. Mus. Add. 4911)[3] containing many extracts from anonymous masses and motets. But when the Genevan order of things was established all ecclesiastical music except psalm-singing was forbidden, and from that day to this Scottish church music has, apart from the psalm tunes, been an absolute desert.

The church music of this period, as also that of Byrd in slightly later times, offers one special difficulty to the historian. We have abundant ocular evidence of the adaptation of an English version to music originally written for Latin words; but in very many cases we cannot be sure whether the work is originally English or not, as the Latin form may easily have been lost. This uncertainty entirely debars us from attempting to draw universally applicable deductions from supposed differences of style between the musical settings of the two languages; all we can do is to take each individual work on its own merits, and refer to it by its most familiar title.

The three great names of this period are Tye, White, and Tallis; and of these Tye, the earliest in date of birth, shows the greatest affinity with the methods of the previous time. Most of the older angularities and harshnesses which still survived in the work of many of his contemporaries have indeed disappeared in his own; but there is still, in much that he wrote, a good deal of stiffness of style that we very rarely find in White or Tallis. The six-part *Euge*

---

[1] The *cantus*, *tenor*, and *bassus* are in Edinburgh University Library, the *contratenor* in the British Museum (Add. 33933). A supplement is at Trinity College, Dublin.

[2] Edited by J. A. Fuller Maitland (Year Book Press).

[3] Part of this is printed in M. F. Bukofzer, *Geschichte des englischen Diskants und des Fauxbourdons* (1936), pp. 158–60.

bone[1] Mass, though very grandiose and finely built throughout, and generally accepted as the most complete specimen of Tye's mature powers, is not—at any rate except to those endowed with special appreciation of the type—altogether free from the charge of dryness. But it is perhaps doubtful if this Mass, though certainly one of Tye's very largest works, quite deserves the pre-eminence that has usually been accorded to it. More striking is the Mass *The Western Wynde*,[2] founded on the melody previously used by Taverner, which makes considerable use of the melismatic style characteristic of the earlier sixteenth-century composers. The opening of the Agnus may be quoted (the melody is in the alto):

---

[1] *Old English Edition*, vol. x. The title is Tye's own, but there seems to be no 'Euge, bone' nor 'Euge, serve bone' antiphon that shows anything like the musical phrase which is the basis of this Mass.

[2] Brit. Mus. Add. 17802–5.

Among the other works written for the Roman service we may specially notice a five-part 'Miserere mei, Deus',[1] with its sombre three-part opening and its fine brightening at the words of confidence:

[1] Brit. Mus. Add. 5059, fol. 38.

or the five-part 'Omnes gentes plaudite manibus', with its ringing jubilant trumpet-calls:[1]

[1] Edited by H. B. Collins (Chester).

both of which, in their very different ways, represent the highest level of Tye's pre-Reformation music. We cannot of course be quite certain as to chronology, but at any rate there is a considerable probability that the works with Latin words are earlier than those with English. His work to English words strikes out a fresh vein; in contrapuntal dignity and massiveness it is, indeed, intimately connected with the earlier style, but the simplified methods which, as we have seen, the exigencies of the situation obliged Tye to adopt in the bulk of his *Acts of the Apostles* settings, show their traces in a certain melodious and bright directness of utterance, lacking, it may be, something of the grandeur of the former work, but showing more close regard to smoothness and beauty of sound, and also sometimes curiously akin in turn of phrase to the style of the contemporary folk-songs, one of which, as we have already noticed, he had, in his younger days, utilized as the theme of a Mass. Anthems like 'I will exalt thee'[1] or the splendid 'Praise ye the Lord, ye children'[2] show something quite new in English music; and the smaller works, in their slighter style, show also the same vigorous, straightforward expression, in which we see very definitely the beginnings of modern rhythm, fused without any rude break into the older interweaving and unaccentuated counterpoint. Tye does not, it is true, show much of the kind of imaginative subtlety that we find so preeminently in the best work of Tallis and, indeed, in smaller men like Mundy; he works on broad lines, and does not dwell with special fondness on any details. Indeed—though the adjective is perhaps an anachronism—we may say that he, more than any other of his contemporaries, sought to produce music that would be popular; but popularity with him was never inconsistent with musicianship of a kind that is among the permanent glories of the English school.

Tye's son-in-law, White, is a great composer whose fame is of comparatively recent date. He does not altogether show his master's versatility; practically all his works are of the solidly contrapuntal order, and melody of the kind that is common in Tye's later style is very rare. But still his music is definitely of the newer school; the old angularity of phrase is much less frequent than in the earlier work of Tye, and the material is thoroughly mastered. A sort of delicate grave charm hangs round his compositions; take for example the splendid setting of 'Peccatum peccavit' from the five-part 'Lamentations':[3]

Ex. 47 ♩ = ♩

[1] *Tudor Church Music*, 8vo ed., No. 59.
[2] Ibid., No. 58.
[3] *Tudor Church Music*, vol. v, p. 14.

or the anthems 'The Lord bless us' or 'O how glorious art thou' or 'O praise God in his holiness',[1] the last of which, with its magnificent setting of 'Praise him in the cymbals and dances', shows more vigour and movement than his quietly dignified genius ordinarily attained. Though in essential grandeur of phrase his style is not inferior to those of Tye and Tallis at their best, it is as a rule, so to speak, more feminine than theirs; it is easy to see its close connexion with Tye's in technique, but, speaking generally, there is less directness and more subtlety. The individuality of utterance is very remarkable; in a very few years English music had travelled miles beyond the older purely impersonal attitude of the mere handmaid to the Church. Tye, White, and Tallis are the three men to whom this advance is primarily due; and White, though far the least known of the three, is fairly to be reckoned—even remembering that Palestrina and Lassus were contemporaries—as among the very greatest European composers of his time.

But great geniuses as were Tye and White, Tallis was a greater

---

[1] There are two versions, one in four parts, the other in eight. For a discussion of the problems which they present see *Tudor Church Music*, vol. v, pp. xxvi–vii.

still; he had more versatility of style than either, and his general handling of his material was more consistently easy and certain.[1] Not, indeed, that we need give many words to what is to most Englishmen his best known work—his harmonization of the Prayers, Responses, and Litany, and his Morning, Communion, and Evening Service in the Dorian mode; beautifully pure and severe all through, it is the merest note-against-note harmony, with hardly a vestige of the imitative contrapuntal methods which were, throughout Europe, the glory of the century. It is in contrapuntal work that the real Tallis is alone displayed; take for example this truly noble opening of a 'Lamentation' that is far too little known:

Ex.48

[1] His Latin church music is printed in *Tudor Church Music*, vol. vi.

or such massive utterances as the five-part 'Absterge Domine' (*Cantiones Sacrae*, No. 2) or the first 'Salvator mundi' (ibid., No. 1) or 'Derelinquat impius' (ibid., No. 13) or the most familiar of his great masterpieces, 'O sacrum convivium' (ibid., No. 9), the English version of which, 'I call and cry', was later published by Barnard (1641).[1] The majestic, architectural splendour of works like these and many others may quite fitly claim for them a place by the side of the best contemporary Italian music; in comparison with them the 'Dorian' service drops at once into its proper merely parochial position. In massive music like this we see Tallis at his grandest; there are none of the angularities of phrasing that, as we have just seen, sometimes slightly, for a present-day hearer, mar the effect of occasional works by Tye, even if we feel, retrospectively, that there is still something lacking which Byrd was soon to supply. But Tallis also could, when he so pleased, employ with equal success a tenderer and more expressively graceful style, as in the exquisite little anthem 'O Lord, give thy holy spirit';[2] here he comes very near to what, as we shall shortly see, were the favourite methods of Redford or Mundy but are but slightly exemplified in Tye or White. In sheer technical facility the famous forty-part motet 'Spem in alium non habui'—written for eight choirs of five parts each—is equal to anything that the great music of any century or country can show. But the really most astonishing thing about it is that it is a splendid work of art also. It is true that, by the very nature of the case, it cannot show the same qualities of clearness and flexibility that we see in such works as those previously named: but, following the bad example of early historians, most writers have confined themselves far too

---

[1] *Tudor Church Music*, 8vo ed., No. 74.
[2] Ibid., No. 68.

exclusively to its purely ingenious qualities, which, very remarkable as they are, have always been well within the reach of the highly skilled mathematical musician, whether a genius like Tallis or a mere trifler. Of course, the more the purely technical difficulty presses, the greater is the chance that the artistic element will drop aside; and it is really extraordinary that in spite of the superlative risk of his endeavour Tallis should have produced in this motet a work so finely organized in form, so large and striking in thematic material and, on the whole, so varied in harmony and expression. But, nevertheless, though the great composer, like the great performer, has the power for artistic *tours de force* when he chooses to exercise it, yet neither the one nor the other is seen at his very greatest in such efforts; at a certain point, however perfectly the thing is done, we cannot help becoming unduly conscious of the cleverness of it. And so, far from representing 'Spem in alium non habui' or a thing like the astonishing seven-part canon, 'Miserere nostri' (*Cantiones Sacrae*, No. 34) as Tallis's supreme masterpiece, we turn back to works like the five-part motets in the *Cantiones Sacrae*, with their continually varied but always majestic choral colour, their massively sweeping and vitalized phrases, and their superbly confident manliness of style.

Tye, White, and Tallis were certainly considerably the three greatest English composers of the mid-sixteenth century; but there are several others who, though producing work less in quantity and, as a rule, slighter in texture, have also a high place in the roll of true musicians. The anthem 'Rejoice in the Lord always',[1] the manuscript of which is anonymous, was attributed by Hawkins[2] to Redford. The ascription has been generally accepted, but without good reason, since the music appears to be designed for the words of the *First Prayer Book* of 1549 and Redford died in 1547.[3] Causton was suggested by Davey;[4] but his work seems to me on the whole[5] so much more stiff, though it is of good quality, as to mili-

---

[1] Ibid., No. 55. In the original, which is an organ transcription (Brit. Mus. Add. 30513, fol. 69v), only the first five words are given; the remainder have been added from the Authorized Version by a later hand, without any precise indication of how they are to fit the music.

[2] *A General History of the Science and Practice of Music* (1875 ed.), p. 929.   [3] A. W. Reed, *Early Tudor Drama* (1926), p. 55.

[4] *History of English Music* (2nd ed., 1921), p. 119.

[5] See especially the separate Te Deum and Benedictus in Brit. Mus. Add. 31226, fol. 70v, and 'O most high and eternal King', in Day's *The whole psalmes in foure partes* (1563).

tate against the probability of his having had a special inspiration for a polished masterpiece like this. On the other hand the style is so similar to that of William Mundy's 'O Lord, the world's saviour' (see p. 63) that I feel strongly inclined to ascribe 'Rejoice in the Lord always' to him. Anyhow, the anthem could worthily be signed by the greatest composer of the time; it is of singular purity and clearness, not quite so mature as the finest work of a man like Tallis, but full of a sort of youthful gravity of a most fascinating type, with a rare spiritual fragrance in its exquisitely tender closing bars:

Ex. 49

Farrant, who is one of the later composers, dying about the same time as Tallis, has left a service in A minor[1] (printed in G minor by Boyce) which is one of the most gracefully dignified of all services, reminding us in general style of Tallis's 'Dorian' service, but less austere and massive. Farrant's music has, indeed, a certain femininity about it, using the word in its very best sense; anthems like 'Hide not thou thy face',[2] with its antiquely tender, almost childlike, close:

Ex. 50

and still more 'Call to remembrance',[3] a tiny gem of perfect lustre, show qualities that the men of stronger and wider vision were sometimes inclined to overlook. The still better known 'Lord, for thy tender mercies' sake',[4] usually ascribed to Farrant or to the elder John Hilton, is probably either by Tye or by someone very

[1] Te Deum and Benedictus: *Tudor Church Music*, 8vo ed., No. 62. Magnificat and Nunc Dimittis: ibid., No. 33.
[2] Ibid., No. 60.   [3] Ibid.
[4] *Church Music Society*, No. 26.

much under his influence. There is only late and untrustworthy evidence as to its authorship, and the music itself is very characteristic of Tye's style.[1]

Farrant is a most attractive composer, and his best works have always had an honoured place in English cathedrals; but a strange neglect has fallen over most of the music of his greater contemporary, William Mundy, who was probably the strongest genius of his day after the three leaders, while his one fairly familiar work —the very sincere and expressive 'O Lord, the maker of all thing'[2] —has been ascribed, in defiance of all evidence, to Henry VIII. The contrapuntal service printed in Barnard's part-books is one of the very finest of all written for the English ritual; it is free from the sort of harmonic squareness of those of Tallis and Farrant, and forecasts rather the methods of Gibbons, though Mundy cannot equal his successor's majesty. The anthems 'O Lord, the world's saviour' and 'O Lord, I bow the knees'[3]—from which we may quote the close of the former[4] and the opening of the latter:

Ex. 51

Ex. 52

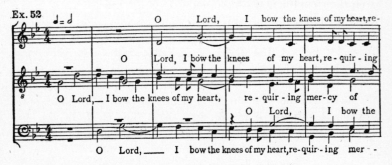

[1] See G. E. P. Arkwright in *S.I.M.G.*, 1905–6, pp. 563–80.
[2] *Tudor Church Music*, 8vo ed., No. 38. Cf. G. E. P. Arkwright in *The Musical Antiquary*, Jan. 1911, p. 123.   [3] Both printed by Barnard.
[4] The remarkable but very beautiful C in the alto part of the second bar is in both the *decani* and the *cantoris* part-books.

are both, in their different ways, strikingly beautiful works, rather less childlike and more elaborate than those of Farrant, but not at all inferior in tenderness. Occasionally, as in the verse anthem 'Ah, helpless wretch' he fails to achieve more than rather stiff though refined work of a simple, hymn-like character, and he never, even at his best, reaches the heights of the greatest things of Tye or White or Tallis; yet he is certainly one of the outstanding men of his time, and deserves to be far more widely known.

Indeed, the level of ordinary English ecclesiastical music at this time was on the whole distinctly high. The numerous part-books (Brit. Mus. Add. 17802–5, containing nearly ninety works, many of them by the greatest men of the time, is an inexhaustible treasure-house) contain a mass of motets and anthems and services, nearly all of which are thoroughly solid musicianly work, not, it is true, showing much variety of style, but at the same time plainly the production of a school of composers differing in various features from their continental contemporaries. No doubt the work of the lesser men may not infrequently incline towards a certain stiffness and pedantry; but under all the circumstances there is singularly little. Not, indeed, that all this music demands any detailed notice; it is little more than a reflex—more or less bright, according to the composer's talent—of the work of the men already mentioned. Shepherd, Thorne, Johnson, and Parsons are perhaps the most note-worthy; 'Esurientes implevit' (part of a Magnificat) by the first named, which Burney printed,[1] is a good specimen of his solid, straightforward, if rather dull, music, Thorne's 'Stella caeli', printed by Hawkins,[2] has excellent qualities, and Johnson's finely austere

---

[1] *A General History of Music* (1776–89), vol. ii, p. 587. The original is in Brit. Mus. Add. 17802–5.
[2] *A General History of the Science and Practice of Music* (1875 ed.), p. 360. The original is in the Royal Music Library, Brit. Mus. RM. 24, d 2, fol. 161ᵛ.

style is well represented by the very long[1] motet 'Ave, Dei patris
filia' or the shorter 'Dum transisset Sabbatum',[2] with its beautifully
expressive treatment of the final 'Alleluia'. Shepherd's 'French
Mass'[3] is a good example of the reaction against the older style
of polyphony based on a *canto fermo*. The title implies an imitation
of continental methods, a conscious adoption of a closely knit style
which avoids the older elaboration. Each section begins with the
same melodic fragment, treated in close imitation, and homophony
is used for the sake of contrast, for instance at the end of the Gloria:

But perhaps Parsons is the best of these lesser men; his elaborate
service (there is some seven-part writing in it) that is printed in
Barnard's collection, is finely contrapuntal—the harmonic method
of Tallis's 'Dorian' service is only slightly employed—and the six-
part canonic 'Deliver me from mine enemies, O God' is notably
solid and smooth. But there are composers of whom we know far
less than we do of these, who were capable of producing work quite
on the same level—for example, the very expressive 'O God, for thy
name's sake' of the obscure John Franctynge, that we meet with in

---

[1] The score in Brit. Mus. Add. 5059 occupies thirty-two pages.
[2] Edited by H. B. Collins (Chester).
[3] Ibid.

the middle of much that is uninteresting in Brit. Mus. Add. 31226, or this picturesque example of word-setting from Parsley's 'Lamentations' (the psalm-tone is in the upper part): [1]

Ex. 54

The religious struggles of the times naturally engrossed men's thoughts, and consequently composers' energies also, with the result that secular vocal music during this period occupied an altogether subordinate position; some half-dozen works, and those quite slight and unimportant, are all that Tye, Tallis, and White seem to have produced between them. Farrant, Parsons, Johnson, and others of less general fame are represented by works which are virtually early madrigals; but nearly all of them (both Burney and Hawkins printed specimens) fall far below the best contemporary sacred music in artistic interest. The numerous anonymous pieces of the kind include the only one that is now remembered, 'In going to my naked bed';[2] the words are known to be by Richard Edwards,

[1] *Tudor Church Music*, vol. x, p. 250.
[2] *English Madrigal School*, vol. xxxvi (at the end).

and Hawkins's conjecture that the music is also by him has been generally accepted and is perhaps likely enough, in default of any evidence to the contrary. This charming little piece is still a great favourite with madrigal societies; and it certainly shows an expressiveness of style which is curiously absent from contemporary secular music as a whole.

The manuscript Mulliner Book (Brit. Mus. Add. 30513),[1] from which it is taken, is of much value as containing, along with a considerable number of transcriptions of vocal music (including 'Rejoice in the Lord always'), a mass of keyboard pieces which afford a clear indication of the development of instrumental music during the mid-sixteenth century; other manuscripts contain many more, and the 'Fitzwilliam Virginal Book', which will be described in the following chapter, has some of this earlier date, but all the best seem to be contained in Thomas Mulliner's collection. Historically they are of great interest as showing the development of keyboard technique. Some of the pieces are written in an imitative style similar to that of vocal polyphony; but there are a large number which are purely instrumental in conception, and though the style is sometimes monotonous, with the same contrapuntal 'species' persisting for long stretches at a time, or indeed throughout the whole piece, there is also evidence of ingenuity and imagination. The following—the concluding verse of a Te Deum setting by William Blitheman[2]—is a fairly simple example of the florid treatment of a *canto fermo* (the plainsong is in the middle part):

Ex.55

---

[1] *Musica Britannica*, vol. i.
[2] Brit. Mus. Add. 30513, fol. 76.

Such verses were designed to alternate with the verses sung to the plainsong melody by the choir. Among the transcriptions of vocal polyphony in this manuscript is part of the Benedictus of Taverner's Mass *Gloria tibi Trinitas*, beginning at the words 'in nomine'.[1] The use of initial words as titles was normal in such transcriptions, as in organ verses; there is in the same manuscript an 'In nomine' by Richard Alwood[2] on a different plainsong. The antiphon 'Gloria tibi Trinitas', however, seems to have had a particular attraction for composers. For well over a century it was used as the *canto fermo* of instrumental pieces in the polyphonic style, whether for viols or for keyboard; and it became traditional to acknowledge Taverner's example by calling such pieces 'In nomine', though the title no longer had any significance.

It will be most convenient to defer to the next chapter a detailed description of sixteenth-century instrumental music; in the stage represented by the Mulliner book the ecclesiastical influence, as shown in the great preponderance of elaborations of plainsong melodies (whether intended for liturgical use or as voluntaries), is still very marked—the two by Tallis on 'Felix namque' in the Fitzwilliam book[3] are typical—and the secular element appears only fitfully. The pieces by Redford are among the most enterprising in the Mulliner collection; the following setting of the plainsong

[1] Brit. Mus. Add. 30513, fol. 41v. The original Benedictus is in *Tudor Church Music*, vol. i, p. 148; an adaptation of the 'in nomine' section to the English words 'In trouble and adversity', originally published in Day's *Certaine notes* (1560), is in vol. ii, p. 199.

[2] Ibid., fol. 27v.

[3] Edited by J. A. Fuller Maitland and W. Barclay Squire (2 vols., 1899), Nos. 109 and 110.

'Eterne rex altissime'[1] shows a very happy treatment of an ostinato figure suggesting the chiming of bells:

Those by Blitheman, himself a great executant, show forecasts of the virtuoso fireworks of his pupil Bull, some of whose rhythmical devices are also foreshadowed in such things as a short 'Miserere' fantasia by William Shelby,[2] which combines three different measures unintermittently from start to finish—an example of mathematical calculation of a kind which seems to have had considerable attraction for contemporary composers.

These relics of the old 'proportional' system find their parallels

[1] Brit. Mus. Add. 30513, fol. 30v.
[2] Ibid., fol. 47v.

in other survivals of past methods with which we meet occasionally, even in the works of the greatest composers of the period. Half a century later, Morley refers to a motet of Dunstable, in which the syllables of a word are separated one from another by lengthy rests, as a specimen of remote antiquarian barbarism;[1] but we find exactly the same thing at the end of the first 'Osanna' of Tye's *Euge bone* Mass,[2] where the movement of the lowest part is quite astonishingly clumsy:

The great composers of the mid-sixteenth century are among the chief glories of English art, and yet, in a short work like the present, it is necessary to pass them over comparatively quickly; their music includes very many compositions of noble quality, where descriptions and quotations would be of much artistic interest, but it is all on the same general lines. It was not till the later Elizabethan times that composers acquired real versatility of style, on more than the slenderest of scales; and, unless it were possible to treat the earlier composers with the fullness required by monographs, the individual works of Tallis and the rest must needs seem very much alike, even while we remember what has been already said about their occasional differences of method. Byrd himself, who possessed far the most intense and concentrated vision among musicians of his time, touches many more springs; and the great madrigalians, even if men of one general mind, seem to manage somehow to present it more or less in instalments. But Tye, White, and Tallis—even when we allow for the two periods of the first-named and the power of working on different lines which the last displayed—seem to give out the whole

---

[1] *A Plaine and Easie Introduction* (1597), p. 178.
[2] *Old English Edition*, vol. x, p. 42.

of themselves in every single work in which they give anything at all of their best; practically any of their notable pages will serve to illustrate their genius. A very lamentable amount of noble music still remains inaccessible save to the special student; but when it is brought to light, we must not expect to be able to say anything new about the men who wrote it. All their genius was turned into a narrow groove—narrower indeed, relatively, than that followed by their immediate predecessors, who had lived in less spiritually serious times; but it afforded splendid opportunities, and they were splendidly met.

IV

THE MADRIGALIAN ERA

THE long-lived William Byrd (1543–1623) is the typical figure of the music of this period, in every form of which—instrumental, secular, vocal, and ecclesiastical—he left numerous works. He is said (though the statement does not rest on contemporary evidence) to have been a pupil of Tallis, and was appointed organist of Lincoln Cathedral (of which town he was probably a native) when about twenty years of age; he subsequently joined the Chapel Royal, and remained in the service of the court throughout his life, though an avowed Romanist and suffering some inconvenience in consequence. Mention has been made in the previous chapter of the monopoly in music-printing (for a term of years) granted to Tallis and Byrd in 1575 (see p. 48), which on the death of the former in 1585 became Byrd's sole property. The works published during his lifetime include two sets of *Cantiones Sacrae* (1589 and 1591), and another set the joint composition of himself and Tallis (1575), two books of *Gradualia* (1605 and 1607), *Psalmes, Sonets, and Songs of Sadnes and Pietie* (1588), *Songs of Sundrie Natures* (1589), and *Psalmes, Songs, and Sonnets* (1611), besides some detached vocal and instrumental pieces; three Masses, the numerous pieces in the 'Fitzwilliam Virginal Book', a number of motets, and various other works have survived in manuscript.[1]

Byrd's juniors, Thomas Morley and Orlando Gibbons, were musicians of very nearly equal fame and versatility. Morley was born in 1557 and died in 1602, or perhaps a little later; he was a pupil of Byrd, and was a gentleman of the Chapel Royal from 1592 to his death, having previously held the office of organist at St. Paul's Cathedral. His compositions include several books of canzonets, madrigals, balletts, and songs with accompaniment, together with anthems and services for church use, and instrumental music of all kinds; he edited various collections of vocal and instrumental music, the most notable being the set of madrigals known as *The Triumphes of Oriana* (1601), and also published in 1597 one of the first regular theoretical treatises to be issued in England,

---

[1] A performing edition of Byrd's complete vocal and instrumental works has been published by E. H. Fellowes (Stainer & Bell).

under the title of *A Plaine and Easie Introduction to Practicall Musicke*. In 1598 he obtained a fresh patent for the exclusive printing of music books, that granted to Tallis and Byrd having lapsed.

Orlando Gibbons (1583–1625) was the son of one of the Waits or town musicians of Oxford,[1] and was the younger brother of two other musicians, Edward Gibbons being successively master of the choristers of King's College, Cambridge, and a priest-vicar (though a layman) of Exeter Cathedral, and Ellis Gibbons contributing two madrigals to the *Oriana* collection. Orlando was a pupil of his eldest brother at Cambridge, and was subsequently organist of the Chapel Royal and of Westminster Abbey; he died suddenly at Canterbury, whither he had travelled in connexion with the festivities for the reception of the Queen of Charles I, and was buried in the cathedral. Gibbons was a less prolific composer than Byrd or Morley, and very little of his work remains now in manuscript; his music includes services, anthems and hymn tunes, a collection of madrigals and motets, fantasies for strings, and dances and other pieces for the virginals.

Many of the other notable composers of the time were less versatile, and devoted their energies more exclusively to one or two departments. As a rule we have but scanty details of their biographies. We know little of the personality of John Wilbye (1574–1638), one of the greatest, except that he was for many years in the service of the Kytson family at Hengrave Hall; of John Bennet, as of John Ward, we know virtually nothing except the music. Thomas Bateson (d. 1630) was successively cathedral organist at Chester and Dublin, and seems to have been the first musical graduate of Trinity College, Dublin; Thomas Weelkes (d. 1623) was organist of Winchester College and Chichester Cathedral. John Farmer seems to have been a predecessor of Bateson in the Dublin organistship; George Kirbye (d. 1634) lived in Suffolk; John Mundy (d. 1630), son of the William Mundy mentioned in the preceding chapter, was organist of Eton College and afterwards Marbeck's successor at St. George's Chapel, Windsor; John Hilton the elder (d. 1608), lay-clerk at Lincoln Cathedral, was afterwards organist of Trinity College, Cambridge; Michael East (d. 1648), perhaps the son of Thomas East (by whom, as assignee first of Byrd and afterwards of Morley, much of the most important music of the time was published), was organist of Lichfield Cathedral; Richard Carlton was a minor canon

[1] Grove's *Dictionary* (4th ed.), supplementary volume, p. 237.

of Norwich Cathedral; Thomas Tomkins (1572–1656) was a pupil of Byrd, and organist of Worcester Cathedral and the Chapel Royal— meagre details like these represent the sum of our knowledge of the lives of men among the most distinguished musicians of the time. Many of them seem to have written principally madrigals, though a considerable quantity of ecclesiastical music from the pens of Weelkes, Ward, Tomkins, and one or two more, is in existence, and there is also instrumental music by several of them; others, while also confining themselves principally to secular vocal music, turned their attention rather to accompanied songs, and were, as a general rule, lutenists. The chief of these was John Dowland (1563–1626), who started life in the service of the English Ambassador at Paris, and subsequently travelled extensively in Germany and Italy. From 1598 to 1607 he was lutenist to the King of Denmark; and in 1612, after some years of obscurity in England, he was appointed one of the 'musicians for the lutes' at the court of James I. Other composers of more or less the same tendencies were Thomas Ford (*c.* 1580–1648), whose only published work, *Musicke of sundrie kindes*, appeared in 1607; Francis Pilkington (d. 1638), a minor canon of Chester Cathedral, who produced two sets of *Madrigals and Pastorals* in addition to the 'ayres' by which he is now more widely known; Robert Johnson, one of the court lutenists to both James I and Charles I, who set two songs from *The Tempest*; John Cooper (d. 1627), who, after a temporary residence in Italy, altered his name to Coprario and was the master of William Lawes; William Corkine, John Danyel, Thomas Greaves, Robert Jones, Philip Rosseter (d. 1623), and Thomas Campian (1567–1620), a physician by profession and a poet of very high distinction, who published several books of vocal music with lute accompaniment (one in conjunction with Rosseter), as well as songs for masques and a treatise on counterpoint.

Others again there were who, though occasionally diverging into other fields, devoted themselves mainly to ecclesiastical work. Among them were John Milton (d. 1647), whose musical abilities were celebrated by his great son in a Latin poem; he was a contributor to the *Oriana* collection, but chiefly set religious words. Adrian Batten (d. 1637), connected successively, as boy and man, with Winchester Cathedral, Westminster Abbey, and St. Paul's Cathedral; Nathaniel Patrick (d. 1595), organist of Worcester Cathedral; Edmund Hooper (d. 1621), organist of Westminster

Abbey; Elway Bevin, a pupil of Tallis, and organist of Bristol Cathedral and gentleman of the Chapel Royal; Richard Dering (d. 1630), many of whose works were published abroad; William Daman, who was born at Liége and became one of the court musicians to Queen Elizabeth; and Thomas Ravenscroft, a graduate of Cambridge—all wrote chiefly services, motets, or anthems, though Bevin and Ravenscroft were also theoretical writers, and the latter was further known as editor of both secular and ecclesiastical collections.

John Bull (c. 1562–1628), on the other hand, was, first and above all, an instrumental composer, his vocal writings (all ecclesiastical in character) being apparently very few in number; he held organist's posts at Hereford Cathedral and the Chapel Royal, but was chiefly famous as a writer for the virginals, on which he was a performer of astonishing virtuosity. In 1613 he quitted England for the Netherlands and in 1617 was appointed organist of Antwerp Cathedral, a post that he retained till his death. Giles Farnaby seems also to have been most distinguished as a composer of music for the virginals, though he wrote canzonets and other vocal work besides.

The religious changes of the times caused the emigration of many English Catholics, among whom was Peter Philips, one of the most prominent of Elizabethan composers; he was an ecclesiastic who spent nearly all his life in the Netherlands, publishing a large quantity of madrigals and religious motets. He was generally known either by the Latin or the Italian version of his name, and his music seems to have been but slightly familiar to his contemporaries in England; the 'Fitzwilliam Virginal Book' (which was, as a matter of fact, transcribed by another Catholic refugee) contains a considerable number of instrumental compositions by him. He is said to have died in 1628, in which case his publications dated 1630 and 1633 were posthumous, though not so described.[1] Counterbalancing, however, to some extent the virtual denationalization of Philips, the two Ferraboscos, both called Alfonso, have, to all intents and purposes, to be reckoned as English musicians; the elder was the son of a musician of Bologna, but seems to have come to England at an early age. He remained in the service of Queen Elizabeth (though with occasional periods of residence abroad) till 1578, when he removed, apparently without the Queen's per-

[1] Grove's *Dictionary* (4th ed.), vol. iv, p. 141.

mission, to take a post under the Duke of Savoy at Turin; he died at Bologna in 1588. He was familiarly known in England as 'Master Alfonso', and enjoyed an exceptional reputation; his madrigals, though published in Italy, were reproduced in English collections, and large quantities of his manuscripts exist in English libraries. His son (d. 1628) was exclusively an Englishman, and was one of the chief court musicians under both James I and Charles I; he frequently collaborated with Ben Jonson, whose intimate friend he was, and left behind him a large quantity of instrumental music and songs, as well as a number of motets, often erroneously ascribed to his father. His three sons, the last of whom died as organist of Ely Cathedral in 1682, carried the musical reputation of the family into the fourth generation.

With the defeat of the Armada in 1588 the danger of religious upheaval passed away from England; and musicians turned with a curious suddenness, and with almost complete unanimity, to follow secular ideals. Since 1530 only one collection of non-ecclesiastical music had been printed—a book of songs for three, four, and five voices composed by Thomas Whythorne and issued in 1571:[1] but between 1588 and 1630 well over eighty vocal collections, containing between 1,500 and 2,000 pieces, nearly all secular in character, were published in part-books, and many more still remain in manuscript. Religious music was not indeed neglected, but for the time it was virtually altogether overshadowed; Boccaccio was more generally attractive than the Bible,[2] and the increase in luxury, combined with the flood of new interest in literature and the drama, rapidly brought about a condition of things in which music, even in its noblest aspects, was primarily regarded as an after-dinner recreation for persons of culture. A well-known passage in Morley's *Plaine and Easie Introduction* (1597) implies, if taken literally, that inability to sing at sight from part-books was regarded as a sign of deficient education. Some allowance must be made here for the claims of advertisement: it does not follow that madrigals were performed only by amateurs or that a high standard of accomplishment was universal. Peacham, in his *Compleat Gentleman* (2nd ed., 1634),[3] says:

[1] Eleven have been edited by P. Warlock (Oxford University Press). Cf. P. Warlock, *Thomas Whythorne: an unknown Elizabethan composer* (1927).
[2] W. Nagel, *Geschichte der Musik in England* (1894–7), vol. ii, p. 114.
[3] p. 100.

'I desire no more in you than to sing your part sure, and at the first sight, withall, to play the same upon your Violl, or the exercise of the Lute, privately to your selfe.' There is no doubt, however, that there was a very great general interest in musical matters, and that the capacity for vocal and instrumental performance was widely diffused among the upper classes. To a large extent this enthusiasm owed its germs to foreign influences, and especially to those emanating from Italy, a country that was being more and more brought into close literary and artistic relations with England; and it is to Italy that we primarily owe the development of our madrigals, perhaps on the whole the greatest musical treasure we possess, though its glory lasted only some thirty years.

As we have seen, concerted vocal music was written to secular words by Englishmen of earlier times, but it is not till towards the close of the sixteenth century that the English madrigal proper makes its appearance. It is a combination of two elements—the contrapuntal secular music of the Italians and their resident masters of Netherlandish blood, and the harmonic Italian quasi-popular songs such as the *frottole*, of which numerous examples were published in the earlier part of the century. All the English madrigal-writers show both the contrapuntal and the harmonic elements in their works, and indeed generally combine them in the same composition; there is not that steady and purely unemotional contrapuntal interlacing which robs the older Netherlandish madrigals, exquisitely beautiful though they mostly are, of the necessary secularity of manner, nor is there that rather uninteresting and elementary method of harmonizing chord by chord which soon causes the *frottole* to pall on the reader or listener. Even in the subsidiary form of madrigals known as balletts or *fa las*, where the markedly rhythmical element is especially prominent and the whole tendency is in the direction of plainly melodic swing, there is still an attention to the delicate shades of individual part-writing which, even if there were not (as there usually are) occasional contrapuntal passages, would prevent us from regarding them merely as harmonized tunes. If we like to say so, the English madrigal is an artistic compromise, of astonishing perfection and success.

The first madrigals published in England were those in Byrd's *Psalmes, Sonets, and Songs of Sadnes and Pietie* (1588). They were followed in the same year by a collection due to the enterprise of a music-lover named Nicholas Yonge, who had procured copies from the Continent and had daily performances in his private house; in the autumn of 1588 he brought out fifty-five of the best Italian and Italianized Netherlandish composers, to English translations, with the addition of two by Byrd. Twenty-four more were published by him nine years later, and in the meantime others had been issued under different auspices: but this interest in foreign works was quickly swamped by the flood of native madrigals that began to pour from the press. The most famous of these publications was that known as *The Triumphes of Oriana*, which was edited by Morley and issued in 1601; this is a collection of twenty-five madrigals by nearly all the most distinguished English composers of the time, and was, no doubt, modelled on an earlier Italian collection entitled *Il trionfo di Dori* (1592), to which Palestrina, Marenzio, and others had contributed. The poems, which are of no sort of special literary value, are intended as compliments to Queen Elizabeth (Oriana is the name of the heroine in the romance of Amadis of Gaul). One of them, 'Hard by a crystal fountain' (here set by Morley) had appeared in the second volume of Yonge's *Musica Transalpina* (1597) as the translation of a madrigal by Giovanni Croce originally published in *Il trionfo di Dori*. This may very well have suggested to Michael Cavendish the composition of his 'Come gentle swains'—the first English madrigal with the refrain 'Long live fair Oriana', first published in 1598 and subsequently rewritten for *The Triumphes of Oriana*; and this in turn may have suggested to Morley the compilation of a complete collection of Oriana madrigals.

Many collections of madrigals and similar music have on the title-page the words 'apt for viols and voices', and Byrd tells us quite plainly that his *Psalmes, Sonets, and Songs* (1588) were originally written for solo voice and strings. The same composer's *Psalmes, Songs, and Sonnets* (1611) are described as 'fit for Voyces or Viols', in spite of the fact that the music is said to be 'framed to the life of the words'. There is no doubt whatever that viols were regularly employed in the performance of madrigals, and we may guess that they were often played as purely instrumental pieces. As they were invariably published in separate part-books, there was no sort of practical difficulty about such a proceeding, and indeed in many cases the words are printed in so casual and incomplete a fashion as to suggest that, even when they were sung, the singer was allowed a very free hand. Haphazard methods like these (and, as we shall shortly see, they were not confined to madrigals) may strike us as inartistic: but we must not forget the essentially private character of such music in older days. It was, to a large extent, the recreation of artistically minded friends who were quite willing, if a work could not be performed in one way, to do it in any other rather than go without their pleasure; ideal considerations affected them no more than they affect today any small handful of music-lovers gathered together behind closed doors. Secular choral music was totally unknown in England till the Purcellian epoch; the ecclesiastical compositions themselves were in all probability never performed by more than a very few voices to a part, and post-Reformation works written to Latin words, like Byrd's *Cantiones Sacrae*, were no doubt (except in a private Catholic chapel here and there) sung, just as madrigals were, by a few friends sitting round a table.

The solo song with string accompaniment, so far from being an offshoot of the madrigal, actually preceded it. This is evident not only from what Byrd tells us about the original form of his *Psalmes, Sonets, and Songs* (1588), but also from the existence of other songs which are certainly earlier than the publication of that volume. One of these—Thomas Whythorne's 'Buy new broom'[1]—was printed in 1571; others survive in manuscript. Some of them were written for the plays presented by the companies of choirboy actors,[2] which Shakespeare satirized in *Pyramus and Thisbe*. A more significant development is the publication of lute-songs or 'ayres', which began in 1597 with Dowland's *First Book of Songs or Ayres*. By this time the solo song with lute accompaniment was a commonplace on the Continent: transcriptions for this medium had been published as early as 1509, and original compositions from 1535 onwards. In England, on the other hand, it seems to have been still a novelty, though instruction books in playing the lute appeared in English in the 1560's.[3] The pieces in Dowland's first book are not in fact exclusively solo songs, since parts are provided for three other voices (see p. 80). Apart from the four songs for voice and bandora

[1] Printed in P. Warlock, *The Second Book of Elizabethan Songs* (Oxford University Press), p. 20.

[2] See [G. E. P. Arkwright], 'Early Elizabethan Stage Music', in *The Musical Antiquary*, 1909–10, pp. 30–40, and 1912–13, pp. 112–17.

[3] See R. Newton, 'English Lute Music of the Golden Age', in *Proceedings of the Musical Association*, 1938–9, p. 68.

printed in William Barley's *A new Booke of Tabliture* (1596), one of which at least is a transcription, the first completely independent solo ayres to be published in England are to be found in Cavendish's *14 Ayres in Tabletorie to the Lute* (1598).

The term 'ayre' was mainly reserved for lute-songs. Works like Morley's *Canzonets or Little Short Aers*, Weelkes's *Ayeres or Phantasticke Spirites*, and the younger Hilton's *Ayres or Fa Las*, which belong to the literature of the madrigal, are an exception. Unlike the madrigals, which were issued in separate part-books, the lutenists' ayres were published in single volumes. If they are not exclusively for solo voice, the various parts, vocal and instrumental, face different ways on two adjacent pages, so that the performers may sit round a small table and all be able to read their music more or less conveniently; as a rule, however, the uppermost vocal part is printed with the lute accompaniment annexed, so that these two could be combined by one performer. The madrigals, again, are invariably unbarred; while in the ayres the tune-part and the lute accompaniment are barred more or less regularly, while the other parts, vocal and instrumental, are as a general rule left without bars. Rosseter bars his tune and accompaniment throughout in the strict modern way; the others are more casual as regards the length of the bars, which now, and indeed for long afterwards, were regarded not as a substitute for the time-signature, but merely as a general help to the eye. The accompaniment, however, is the chief difference; and it seems quite certain that to sing 'Awake, sweet love' or 'Since first I saw your face' as unaccompanied part-songs is to do violence to their composers' intentions. Many sets—for example, Jones's second book (1601), Rosseter's book, half of which is by Campian (1601), Ferrabosco's set of 1609, the third and fourth books of Campian (?1617) and others—contain none but solo songs; and where there are four voice parts printed, the composers indicate, most charitably, numerous ways in which the music can be sung, but seem always to omit to say that it can be performed unaccompanied. The title-page of Dowland's *First Booke of Songes or Ayres* (1597) tells us that they are 'so made that all the partes together, or either of them severally, may be song to the Lute, Orpherian, or Viol de gambo'; which, if it were taken literally, would imply the possibility of, say, the alto part being sung by itself with nothing but the bass viol part for accompaniment. Jones's *First Booke of Songes and Ayres* (1600) has an exactly similar title-page, and Campian's *Divine and Morall Songs* and *Light Conceits of Lovers* (?1613) are directed 'to be sung to the Lute and Viols, in two, three, and four parts: or by one Voice to an Instrument'; while in Jones's *Musicall Dreame* 'the First part is for the Lute, two Voyces, and the Viole de Gambo; The Second part is for the Lute, the Viole, and foure Voices to Sing; The Third part is for one Voyce alone, or to the Lute, the Basse Viole, or to both if you please'—where apparently one voice might be allowed to sing entirely unaccompanied. There are cases where the lute accompaniment does not entirely agree with the four-part setting; but the discrepancy is rarely serious.

Sometimes the same publication includes both ayres and madrigals or religious motets, in which case the parts of the latter are printed facing different ways, all unbarred. The chief example of this is the collection issued in 1614 of fifty-three *Teares or Lamentacions of a Sorrowfull Soule* made by Sir William Leighton, one of the court band of Gentlemen Pensioners, during a period of imprisonment for debt; eight were set by himself, and the remaining forty-five by Byrd, Gibbons, Dowland, Milton, Johnson, Ford, Hooper, Kindersley, Gyles, Coprario, Bull, Pilkington, Lupo, Jones, Peerson, Weelkes, Ward, Wilbye, Ferrabosco, and Timolphus Thopul (an anagram for Th. Lupo). There are seventeen 'Consort Songs'—the cantus with a treble viol and tablature for the lute, the altus with a flute and tablature for the cittern, the tenor with tablature for the bandora, and the bassus with a bass viol; the remaining number consist of twelve songs in four parts and twenty-four in five, all being of the nature of madrigals save in so far as the words are of a religious character.

It is also not at all uncommon to find instrumental pieces included in the vocal publications. Many of these are found in the volumes of ayres, and consist of pieces for the lute or 'lyra' viol; Tobias Hume's *Musicall Humors* (1605) contains several curious attempts at realistic programme music for the latter instrument. Byrd's *Psalmes, Songs, and Sonnets* (1611) contain two fantasias for viols, one in four and one in six parts; East's *Third Set of Bookes* (1610) have several more; and other similar collections now and then show isolated specimens.

Even in the purely ecclesiastical music itself the new ideas are very visible in the frequent appearance of 'verse' anthems and services containing portions for solo voices and independent instru-

mental accompaniments for organ or viols—features entirely unknown in previous times. There seems, indeed, no doubt that the
'full' anthems and services which are now sung unaccompanied
were formerly supported all through by the organ, at any rate so
far as the top and bottom parts and the chief 'leads' of the others
were concerned: but towards the end of the century we find evi-
dences of a partiality for more varying colour. The researcher
among contemporary manuscripts will meet not infrequently with
arrangements of the older choral music, such as an adaptation of
Tallis's well-known 'I call and cry' ('O sacrum convivium') 'for two
countertenors, to the organs'; sometimes the verse anthems show
the solo voices entering vaguely every now and then in alternation
with the full portions, sometimes there are definitely contrasted
sections of equal importance, and sometimes (as in Tomkins's
'Through thee will we overthrow our enemies') the work is designed for one solo voice 'to the organs', with a little, and quite
subordinate, chorus work—Morley's 'Out of the deep' is indeed
found in more than one form, and no doubt considerable latitude
was allowed. Anyhow, there was no differentiation of technique,
and the instruments and voices performed exactly the same kind
of music. It seems certain, however, that the solo singers habitually
introduced ornamentation not written by the composer; and this
custom, though kept well within artistic bounds for some time, was
obviously open to grave abuse.

The authorship of the poetry—often of exquisite beauty—which
all these composers set is never directly named; and the absence of
any real evidence forbids us to assert dogmatically, as is often done,
that the same men wrote both words and music. We know, indeed,
from the preface to the Rosseter-Campian book of 1601, that Campian set his own poetry; but there is nothing whatsoever to tell us
the authorship of the songs set by Rosseter. Campian, who published poetry apart from his ayres, seems always to have set his
own verses; but we have no direct evidence about any one else.
The same problem faces us with the madrigals, though, as a rule,
the poetry of these is not of such exceptional merit; and all we can
do is to point, on the one hand, to a case like that of Campian, and
on the other to the occasional instances of the same words being set
by different composers, and the occasional occurrence of poetry
which we know to be by Shakespeare or Spenser or Marlowe or
Jonson or Sidney or Raleigh. No doubt the matter never caused any

trouble to music-lovers then or for long afterwards; and even now how often is the authorship of the words of a song mentioned on a concert programme?

The Elizabethan age saw also the first beginnings of English stage music. We have seen already that music played an important part in the plays acted by choirboys of the Chapel Royal, St. Paul's Cathedral, and elsewhere. Ample provision was also made for it on the professional stage; and the masque, an offshoot from the main dramatic movement, attracted much attention from composers like Campian, Coprario, and the younger Ferrabosco, many of whose most charming songs were written for such works. However, the masques did not reach their full artistic development till the next period, though from the start they foreshadowed the future opera in the important place which they assigned to vocal music.

A considerable number of composers of this period were further distinguished as the writers of theoretical works. Morley's elaborate and still very interesting *Plaine and Easie Introduction to Practicall Musicke*,[1] which first appeared, with a dedication to Byrd, in 1597, is written in the form of a conversation between two pupils and a master; it consists of three parts, dealing respectively with notation and sight-singing, counterpoint, and general composition, and also contains valuable lists of authorities, both theorists and composers. Still more historically important is Campian's *New Way of making fowre parts in Counter-point* (1613);[2] this, though less practical than Morley's, is considerably more modern in tendency, and was in great request during the Restoration period. Ravenscroft's *Briefe Discourse of the true (but neglected) use of Charact'ring the Degrees . . . in Mensurable Music* (1614) and Dowland's translation (1609) of Ornithoparcus's *Micrologus* (one of the most famous of continental treatises, first published in 1517), also deserve mention as showing the interest taken in scientific questions by composers, even when, as in the case of Dowland, their own work was chiefly in the lighter vein. Henry Peacham, a pupil of the celebrated Italian madrigalist Orazio Vecchi, is unknown as a composer save for one work written, in honour of James I, as a supplement to his Βασιλικὸν δῶρον εἰς τὰ ἐμβλήματα Βασιλικά;[3] but his *Compleat*

---

[1] Facsimile edition, with introduction by E. H. Fellowes (Shakespeare Association, 1937).
[2] Reprinted in Percival Vivian's edition of Campian's works (1909).
[3] Brit. Mus. Harl. 6855, art. 13, fol. 37v–38.

Gentleman (1622)[1] contains numerous interesting references to, and criticisms of, contemporary musicians.

Only a comparatively small quantity of instrumental music was published during the madrigalian era; but several of the collections of vocal music include, as we have seen, a few instrumental pieces, and, as has already been noted, the madrigals might be played on viols. The two most important publications were Gibbons's three-part Fantasies for viols (*c.* 1610) and *Parthenia*[2]—the joint work of Byrd, Bull, and Gibbons, and the earliest engraved music for the virginals in England; this was issued in 1611 and was frequently reprinted. Morley's *First Booke of Consort Lessons* (1599),[3] consisting of twenty-three pieces by various composers for 'the Treble Lute, the Pandora, the Citterne, the Base-Violl, the Flute, and the Treble Violl', may be taken as a specimen of the rest of the instrumental music that issued from the press; but our manuscript authorities are, at any rate so far as virginal music is concerned, much more valuable. Various manuscripts in the British Museum (including the Royal Music Library), New York Public Library, Paris Conservatoire, and Christ Church, Oxford, contain large quantities of virginal music by Byrd, Gibbons, and others,[4] and 'My Ladye Nevell's Booke'[5] at Eridge Castle consists of forty-two pieces by Byrd alone; but our chief source is the 'Fitzwilliam Virginal Book'[6] at Cambridge. This collection of 297 pieces was probably made by a member of a Cornish Catholic family of the name of Tregian, which, owing to religious difficulties, emigrated to the Netherlands; the title of 'Queen Elizabeth's Virginal Book' given by Hawkins is without the least warrant, and, indeed, the dates in the manuscript, several of which are later than 1603, are convincing in themselves, apart from external evidence. The composers represented are Blitheman, Bull, Byrd, Giles Farnaby, Richard Farnaby, Gibbons, Hooper, Inglot, Edward Johnson, Robert Johnson, Morley, John Mundy, Oldfield, Parsons, Peerson, Philips, Richardson, Strogers, Tallis, Tisdall, Tomkins, Warrock, and a few foreigners such as Sweelinck.

---

[1] The second edition (1634) has been reprinted with an introduction by G. S. Gordon (1906). [2] Facsimile edition, with notes by Otto Deutsch (1942).
[3] Reprinted by the New York Public Library (1935).
[4] For details see the article 'Virginal Music' in Grove's *Dictionary* (4th ed.), vol. v, p. 545, and supplementary vol., p. 651.
[5] Edited by Hilda Andrews (1926).
[6] Edited by J. A. Fuller Maitland and W. Barclay Squire, 2 vols. (1899).

English instrumentalists and instrumental compositions seem to have been well known abroad, especially in Germany. English dance tunes had been published at Breslau as early as 1555;[1] and about the beginning of the seventeenth century numerous pieces by various Englishmen, attached as violists or lutenists to foreign courts or settled in foreign towns, saw the light at Hamburg, Frankfort, Utrecht, Nuremberg, Lübeck, Berlin, and elsewhere.[2] There seems, indeed, considerable reason for supposing that these composers, artistically unimportant in themselves though they are, did much to influence the composition of instrumental music on the Continent. The Thirty Years War (1618–48) interrupted but did not put a stop to this intercourse; as late as 1653 William Young published at Innsbruck a set of sonatas dedicated to the Archduke Ferdinand.

A few words may be said concerning the instruments for which Elizabethan composers wrote. The virginal or virginals (the plural form was in common use for keyed instruments) was in effect a harpsichord. In the course of the seventeenth century the name came to be applied particularly to instruments of a rectangular shape, of which a number of examples have survived; but in the period which we are discussing the word was used indiscriminately of any keyboard instrument in which the strings were plucked by plectra. The favourite bowed string instrument was the viol (in Italian, *viola da gamba*), which differs from the violin family (*viola da braccio*) not only in the number of strings and their tuning, but also in the use of gut frets on the finger-board and a distinct style of bowing.[3] A chest of viols (so called from the special cupboard in which they were kept) consisted normally of six instruments—two trebles, two tenors, and two basses. The violin family, which includes violas and 'cellos, was already known in England in the late sixteenth century. It was in use at the court of James I, where a composer for the violins was appointed in 1621;[4] and an inventory of instruments at Hengrave Hall[5] (where Wilbye was employed), dated 1602–3,

[1] *Viel feiner lieblicher Stücklein, Spanischer, Welscher, Englischer, Frantzösischer composition und tentz.*

[2] A number of dance movements for instrumental ensemble by William Brade (d. 1630) are printed in B. Engelke, *Musik und Musiker am Gottorfer Hofe*, vol. i (1930).

[3] See in general G. Hayes, *The Viols and Other Bowed Instruments* (1930).

[4] H. C. de Lafontaine, *The King's Musick* (1909), p. 53.

[5] Printed by E. H. Fellowes, *English Madrigal School*, vol. vi, p. x.

includes a chest of six violins—presumably two violins, two violas, and two 'cellos—as well as a chest of viols. It was not, however, until the Commonwealth that the violin began to come into general use, outside a limited aristocratic circle. Most of the string ensemble music of the reigns of Elizabeth and James I seems to have been written for the viols: when the violin is mentioned it is generally as an alternative—for instance, in Anthony Holborne's *Pavans, Galliards, Almains and other short Aeirs . . . for Viols, Violins, or other*[1] *Musicall Winde Instruments* (1599), and Dowland's *Lachrimae . . . for the Lute, Viols, or Violons* (1605).

Instruments of the lute species were in general use. The ordinary lute had six chief strings (the lower five were doubled, making eleven in all), which were normally tuned:

The plucking was done with the fingers of the right hand, those of the left being engaged in stopping the strings on the fretted fingerboard; the tone, though faint, has great purity and charm and considerable capacity for colour. Lute-players did not employ the ordinary musical notation, but had a 'tablature' of their own, of which the following is an example:[2]

d	c	a	a		c	e	a	e	d		a	d	c		e
a		e			c	e	a	e	d		a	d	c		e
			f		d		b	f	f	d	b	a		f	e	f
c							e			a			e		e
		c	a			c	c			e	c				c
a				d	c		a							c	

a	b	d	c	a	d	c	a	c	e	f	e	a
a	b	d	c	a	d	c	a	c	e	f	e	a
a	d	b	a		d	b	a	f	d	c
a	c	a	c			c
c	a	d	c	e		a	c
	d	c	f	a	c	d		a

The letters represent rising semitones on each string, 'a' being the open note; the superimposed signs indicate the time values from a minim (♩) to a quaver (♪), each sign being supposed to remain in

---

[1] i.e. 'alternatively'.
[2] For a translation into staff notation see Ex. 88, p. 134.

force until contradicted. Similar tablature was sometimes used for *viola da gamba* music; this 'lyra' or 'lero way' method is chiefly found in the latter part of the seventeenth century. There were other instruments of the same general character but differing in details; among these were the cittern and its variants, the pandora (or bandora), and the orpheoreon—all of which differed from the lute in the fact that, having no 'chanterelle' or melody string, they were used primarily for accompaniment. There was also the theorbo or double-necked 'archlute', which was in the seventeenth century frequently used, as an alternative to a keyed instrument, in supplying the chords of a figured bass; it remained in artistic use later than any other member of its family, and is found in the score of Handel's *Esther* and other contemporary works.

Wind instruments seem to have been mainly the preserve of professional players. The cornett—generally made of wood, with finger holes and a cup-shaped mouthpiece—was in use at the court, in the theatre, and in cathedrals as a support to the voices. Examples of its use in private music-making would be hard to find. The establishment at Hengrave Hall, which included four cornetts, was clearly exceptional. The same is true of the recorder, or beaked flute, which did not become popular with amateurs until Restoration times. In the well-known scene in *Hamlet* (III, 2)[1] the recorder-players are professionals: there is nothing to show that Hamlet, any more than Guildenstern, could play the instrument. The transverse flute was also used in Elizabethan times. It appears, for instance, in the Hengrave Hall inventory, and is represented playing in consort in the picture of the masque at Sir Henry Unton's wedding (*c.* 1596).[2] Its vogue, however, among amateurs dates from the eighteenth century, when the recorder became obsolete. The sackbut (or trombone) was used, like the cornett, in cathedrals and in court masques. It also appears in the Hengrave Hall inventory—a further indication of the ambitious scale of professional music-making practised there.

We may now enter on an examination of the actual music left us, either in manuscript or in print, by the composers of this period. Turning first of all to the ecclesiastical music, we are immediately met by the towering figure of Byrd, whose religious compositions

[1] Discussed at length in C. Welch, *Six Lectures on the Recorder* (1911), pp. 157–83.
[2] National Portrait Gallery. Reproduction in F. W. Galpin, *Old English Instruments of Music* (3rd ed., 1932), pl. liv (facing p. 278).

include Masses, Latin motets of various shapes and sizes (the *Cantiones Sacrae* and *Gradualia*), and a quantity of work with English words—psalms, anthems, carols, &c.—contained in the three mixed sacred and secular collections of *Psalmes, Sonets, and Songs of Sadnes and Pietie, Songs of Sundrie Natures*, and *Psalmes, Songs, and Sonnets*, as well as a considerable number of pieces preserved in manuscript. The three Masses[1] are respectively in three, four, and five parts; they probably were written at about the same period,[2] and they differ singularly little in quality, the considerable differences that they show being exclusively due to the relatively more or less complex structures. Thus the three-voice Mass is necessarily the simplest in texture and scope; Byrd secures, it is true, a variety of expression and a continually shifting play of vocal colour that are quite astonishing in view of his slender material, but the work aims throughout primarily at grace, not at strength—and indeed nothing could be more tender and serene than the exquisite Agnus Dei, the beginning of which may be quoted as an example of Byrd's mastery both in technique and in feeling:

<hr />

[1] *Tudor Church Music*, vol. ix.
[2] See E. H. Fellowes, *William Byrd* (2nd ed., 1948), p. 52.

The four-voice Mass is designed on more grandiose lines. Not, indeed, that it yields to its slighter companion in delicacy of expression—the wonderfully pathetic setting (in the Gloria) of the words 'Fili unigenite Jesu Christe' or the perfect last page of all, where the music fades away in long-drawn peaceful harmonies, are full evidence of that; but the bulk of the Gloria, and especially the first part of the Sanctus, show a more powerful touch than anything in the three-voice Mass. The extra part of the five-voice Mass gives Byrd still more opportunity for elaboration of method; music like the splendid setting of the Incarnatus or the very noble Sanctus shows him in his largest mood. The three rank together as, beyond all conceivable question, the finest settings of the Mass that exist from an English hand; they are not so suave and broad as the work of Palestrina, but they are somehow more human and personal, and show, like all Byrd's great work, a strangely fascinating mixture of ruggedness and tenderness.

In the nature of the case, however, the words of the Mass do not afford Byrd, intimate though their appeal is to him, the opportunities for the display of his versatile genius so much as his other religious works, which vary considerably in scope and manner. Sometimes, as in the 'Turbarum voces' (printed in the first set of *Gradualia*)[1]—a three-part setting of the crowd choruses in the Passion according to St. John—he attempts definite drama; but in this line, with his essentially reflective genius and his natural fondness for spacious contrapuntal design, he met with no success at all. Not, indeed, that he could not be dramatic when the occasion arose—dramatic, that is to say, after a style that is carefully welded with the character of the work as a whole. One of the very finest passages in one of his greatest masterpieces—the superbly festal and ringing six-part anthem 'Sing joyfully unto God'[2]—paints the trumpet at the words 'Blow the trumpet in the new moon' in a gorgeously up and down surging passage consisting of four and a half $\frac{4}{2}$ bars on the chord of F major, half a bar on that of C major, and three bars on that of G major; and the less-known but nearly equally fine five-part 'Sing we merrily unto God our strength' (*Psalmes, Songs, and Sonnets*, Nos. 20 and 21)[3] has a very similar though less extended effect. But such definite pictorialism, sustained for so long, is rare in Byrd's

[1] *Tudor Church Music*, vol. vii, p. 202.
[2] Ibid., vol. ii, p. 288.
[3] *English Madrigal School*, vol. xvi, p. 106.

works, though it is true that he is fond of momentary word-painting of a quaintly suggestive character; we may notice, for example, how in 'Posuerunt morticinia' (*Cantiones Sacrae*, I,[1] No. 12) the movement becomes more animated at the reference to the 'fowls of the air', or remark in 'Effuderunt sanguinem' (ibid., No. 13) the realistic setting of 'in circuitu Ierusalem', or in 'Vigilate, nescitis enim' (ibid., No. 16) the suddenness and excitement of the treatment of the word 'repente' or the drowsiness of 'dormientes':

Ex. 59

But quaintnesses like these—more common with Latin than with English words—never for a moment mar the dignified flow of these works, the best of which (and their general level is exceptionally high) are among the very finest music of the austerely noble kind that England, or any other country for that matter, has ever produced. It so happens that the English versions (first printed by Barnard) of 'Ne irascaris, Domine', with its second part 'Civitas sancti tui' (*Cantiones Sacrae*, I, Nos. 20 and 21)—'O Lord, turn thy wrath' and 'Bow thine ear'—have made these particular numbers more familiar to cathedral-goers than the rest of the collection from which they come; but exceedingly fine as they are, they are far from standing alone. Byrd has a very remarkable capacity for pathos, as is especially noticeable in such motets as 'Sed tu, Domine, qui non derelinquis' (ibid., No. 7, the second part of 'Tristitia et anxietas'), or 'Vide Domine afflictionem' and its second part 'Sed veni, Domine' (ibid., Nos. 9 and 10), or the extraordinarily impressive three-part 'From depth of sin' in the *Songs of Sundrie Natures* (No. 6);[2] yet

---

[1] *Collected Vocal Works* (ed. Fellowes), vol. ii.
[2] *English Madrigal School*, vol. xv, p. 32.

'O quam gloriosum' (*Cantiones Sacrae*, I, No. 22), in pure and bright major throughout, is equally successful in its realization of the joyful serenity of its words, 'Laetentur coeli' (ibid., No. 28) is overwhelmingly vigorous in emotion, the six-part setting of the versified 121st Psalm in the *Songs of Sundrie Natures* (No. 45)[1] secures, by continual recurrence to the same kinds of chords and phrases, an effect of wonderfully rich and warm placidness, and the motet 'Non vos relinquam orphanos' from the second set of *Gradualia*[2] runs through the whole gamut of happiness up to its soaringly triumphant last page. Indeed, there is perhaps no English music of greater or more lasting attractiveness, and the range of expression is, when the limitations of the medium are remembered, altogether extraordinary. Subtleties of style that we usually associate with far more modern days meet us at every turn; as an example we may quote the beautiful passage in 'Domine, tu iurasti' (*Cantiones Sacrae*, I, No. 15), where the austere, sombre music suddenly softens and sweetens at the idea of the 'land flowing with milk and honey':

---

[1] Ibid., p. 264.
[2] *Tudor Church Music*, vol. vii, p. 318.

The most elaborate of Byrd's settings of English words is the 'Great Service'[1]—a brilliant application of the principle that there should be, so far as possible, one note to each syllable. Such a principle imposes certain limitations of style; but Byrd's setting proves that there is no reason why it should restrict invention. The grouping of the voices takes full advantage of the opportunities offered by a double choir; and throughout, even in the simplest homophonic passages, there is a rhythmical freedom which gives life to the words and to the individual voices. In the long tradition of Anglican church music the 'Great Service' remains unsurpassed. One cannot, however, resist the impression that Byrd was using his technique and imagination to solve a problem which was not of his choosing. We miss the feeling that the music springs, so to speak, instinctively from the words, as it does in the three Masses. Centuries of tradition lay behind Byrd's setting of the Latin liturgy; in his English services he was following a practice which was not only recent but was also contrary to his own inclinations. The wealth of fine polyphony in the 'Great Service' cannot obscure the fact that the English words had not for the composer that 'abstrusa atque recondita vis' (that secret hidden power) to which he refers in the dedication of the first book of *Gradualia* (1605). The two sets of *Gradualia*—perhaps the ripest product of Byrd's genius—illustrate wonderfully well the extent to which Latin texts could fire his imagination. It is not merely that the settings are picturesque: the very essence of the words seems to be translated into sound. One has only to think of

[1] *Tudor Church Music*, vol. ii, p. 123.

the quiet intensity of 'Ave verum corpus'[1] or 'O admirabile commercium',[2] the joyful confidence of 'Alleluia, ascendit Deus',[3] or the
almost voluptuous adoration of 'O quam suavis est':[4]

The same qualities of imagination are to be found in the *Cantiones
Sacrae*—in the massive 'Laudibus in sanctis', the text of which is a
version in elegiacs of Psalm 150, or the jubilant 'Haec dies' (both
from the second set of 1591).[5] The latter work is remarkable not
only for the brilliant syncopation in the middle section:

[1] Ibid., vol. vii, p. 127.
[2] Ibid., p. 223.
[3] Ibid., p. 286.
[4] Ibid., p. 253.
[5] *Collected Vocal Works* (ed. Fellowes), vol. iii.

but also for the fivefold sequence in the bass which runs through the concluding section like a rod of steel. If the earlier *Cantiones Sacrae* published in association with Tallis in 1575 are more experimental in character, there is none the less much in them that foreshadows the mastery of the later years—for example, the profoundly simple 'Emendemus in melius'[1] or 'O lux, beata Trinitas',[2] with its happy antiphonal treatment of a five-beat rhythm:

As a rule Byrd seems to have required for the full flow of his religious inspiration a certain amount of solemnity; it is with some difficulty that he unbends to handle smaller things, the touch is

---

[1] *Tudor Church Music*, vol. ix, p. 61. [2] Ibid., p. 99.

often less sure and the fire burns less clearly. The carols are among
the best; the well-known five-part 'Lullaby'—one of its composer's
loveliest things, and indeed one of the most exquisitely tender and
delicate blossoms in all music—is a recurrent refrain to a Christmas
carol that forms one of the *Songs of Sadnes and Pietie* (No. 32),[1]
and No. 35 of the *Songs of Sundrie Natures*[2] shows another somewhat similar example, with a carol for solo mezzo-soprano, accompanied by four viols, alternating with a very charming choral refrain
(No. 24) for two trebles and two altos. But, on the whole, if we wish
to see Byrd's noble genius at its highest, we must take compositions
where there is ample space for its expression; miniature work was
not, as a rule, congenial to it—nor, as a matter of fact, was contrapuntal ingenuity such as is shown in the technically amazing but
not otherwise interesting eight-part *recte et retro* canon 'Diliges
Dominum Deum' (No. 25 of the Tallis-Byrd *Cantiones Sacrae* of
1575),[3] about which, as about Tallis's not dissimilar works, far too
much has been written.

We may now turn to the church music of Gibbons; his primary
difference from Byrd is that he owes nothing directly to Roman influences but stands before us as virtually the father of pure Anglican
music. Tallis and others had, indeed, sometimes sacrificed artistic
convictions in order to enable the words to be clearly heard by
every listener; but then they fell back on the old traditional Latin
and repaid themselves by purely contrapuntal works. Gibbons was
the first of the really great men to adopt, in musical matters, the
sort of *via media* which the Anglican Church has always so much
favoured; his famous 'Short Service' in F[4] cannot be said to pay
any special attention to requirements of clearness in the words, as
imitation is freely employed, but, on the other hand, he set nothing
but his native language, and his music shows none of that sort of
mystical austerity that has always been typical of composers under
Roman influences, and is plainly notable in Tallis, Tye, White, and
Byrd alike. He was an English artist, and nothing more; and as such
he is one of our glories. Though he never reaches the same depths
of etherealized tenderness and mystic sublimity as Byrd, he has,
perhaps, more variety of style; and his easy mastery over all his
material enabled him to succeed brilliantly in anything he touched.
The service in F just mentioned is, indeed, one of the most 'four-

---

[1] *English Madrigal School*, vol. xiv, p. 172.   [2] Ibid., vol. xv, p. 135.
[3] *Tudor Church Music*, vol. ix, p. 149.   [4] Ibid., vol. iv, p. 30.

square without blame' of all Anglican services; finely massive from
start to finish, melodious and yet perfectly strong, technically
polished and yet never dry, it very worthily holds its eminent place
in the roll of church music. And yet Gibbons—differing sharply in
this matter from Byrd—is hardly completely at home with purely
ritual words like those of a service; his art demands for its full exercise something more individualized, something with a bearing on
human emotion. And so we see him at his greatest in anthems like
'Hosanna to the Son of David',[1] or 'Lift up your heads',[2] or 'O clap
your hands',[3] the words of which forcibly suggest action and movement; and, though in a totally different mood, the whole feeling of
the solemn yet lovely 'Behold, thou hast made my days as it were a
span long' (a verse anthem with viols)[4] is similarly essentially personal and direct. Magnificent works like these take rank side by side
with the masterpieces of the older men; if they lack something of
the high aloofness, they add expressive colour. Taken at its proper
speed 'Hosanna to the Son of David' sounds like a peal of bells:

Ex. 64

---

[1] *Tudor Church Music*, vol. iv, p. 208.
[2] Ibid., p. 220.   [3] Ibid., p. 236.   [4] Ibid., p. 147.

and similarly 'Lift up your heads' and 'O clap your hands' (especially its second part 'God is gone up') are charged through and through with vitality. All the details are flawless, and yet the whole is conceived as a unity from start to finish; and the great massive onset of the music is one of the things most worthy of remembrance in English art.

Anthems like these are Gibbon's typical masterpieces; yet his church music shows unusual versatility. Sometimes, as in the extremely fine short six-part anthem 'O Lord, in thy wrath rebuke me not',[1] from which we may quote a passage of singularly touching beauty:

he approaches very near to the austere tenderness of Byrd—indeed, this anthem is perhaps the oldest in spirit of all Gibbons's great things, and again he can, though only in passing, foreshadow the florid declamation of fifty years later. Thus the verse anthem 'Glorious and powerful God',[2] which contains fine five-part choral

---

Ibid., p. 267.   [2] Ibid., p. 173.

work of the strict type, with a beautiful interweaving 'Amen' to conclude, starts with a bass solo that might be from the pen of Purcell:

and again, in the long and very large and massive 'See, see, the Word is incarnate',[1] we have one solitary piece of 'Restoration style' in the middle of solid modal choral work. However, these forecasts of future methods are rare and tentative; in essentials Gibbons is very emphatically one, though the latest, of the polyphonists. It is, indeed, only occasionally that he writes strictly in the old ecclesiastical modes; and when he does so he is, as a rule, rather stiff and monotonous. But in seriousness of outlook and solidity of workmanship he is one with the older men; and passages such as those just mentioned—almost frivolous though they probably seemed to a purist like Byrd—do not really alter our judgement.

The church music of Weelkes is remarkable for including no fewer than ten services, none of which, however, is complete (though three have been successfully reconstructed, in whole or in part, by Fellowes).[2] Many of his numerous anthems have suffered the same

[1] *Tudor Church Music*, vol. iv, p. 271.
[2] *Tudor Church Music*, 8vo ed., No. 96; 'Evening Service for two trebles' (Stainer & Bell); Short Morning and Evening Service for four voices (Stainer & Bell).

fate. Enough, however, has survived to show that in this field he was a composer of solid musical gifts, even though we miss in his anthems the vivid imagination which is so remarkable in his madrigals. The well-known 'Hosanna to the Son of David'[1] is less jubilant than Gibbons's setting of the same words, but is none the less a dignified and sonorous piece of part-writing. Perhaps he is seen at his best in the seven-part 'O Lord, arise into thy resting place',[2] the opening of which, austere and tinged with a curious regret, may be quoted:

[1] Ibid., No. 9.
[2] Ibid., No. 63.

In the case of Tomkins we are better served by our sources: his church music was published posthumously under the title *Musica Deo sacra* (1668). It includes several services,[1] one of which—the third service—is unusually elaborate in texture. Of his ninety-three anthems nearly half are verse anthems: the large proportion is to be explained by the fact that, though eleven years senior to Gibbons, he survived him by thirty-one years—his long life spanned the reigns of Elizabeth, James I, and Charles I, and he died only four years before the Restoration. He was, however, equally a master of the older polyphonic style. The five-part 'O God, wonderful art thou',[2] with its chains of suspensions, has an emotional fervour and a sense of climax that are very impressive in effect. Again, in 'O praise the Lord, all ye heathen'[3] he handles twelve parts with skill and imagination; the whole piece is rich in contrasts and altogether a splendid example of massive choral writing.

Though Byrd, Gibbons, Weelkes, and Tomkins are the only notably prominent names among the composers of religious music during this period, we must not think that they stood alone. It is true that the current was setting strongly in the direction of secular art, but, nevertheless, the ecclesiastical services claimed the occasional attention of nearly all the best musicians, even though some of the great madrigalists did comparatively little in this field. Wilbye's Latin motets 'Homo natus de muliere'[4] and 'Ne reminiscaris, Domine'[5] are distinctly uninteresting; but at any rate one

[1] *Tudor Church Music*, vol. viii.
[2] *Tudor Church Music*, 8vo ed., No. 99.   [3] Ibid., No. 100.
[4] *Old English Edition*, vol. xxi, p. 24.
[5] Ibid., p. 31

of his two contributions to *The Teares or Lamentacions of a Sorrowfull Soule*—where there is no definite connexion with any church ritual—is far finer, and this song or psalm or whatever we like to call it, 'O God, the rock of my whole strength,'[1] is remarkably expressive and beautiful, and the end is exquisite (notice especially the purposely dead-sounding disposition of parts on the last chords):

It is easy to see here that the style is to all intents and purposes madrigalian, whatever the words may be; Wilbye had, indeed, so far as we can see, no ecclesiastical tinge at all. But this does not apply to Bateson, whose seven-part anthem 'Holy, Lord God Almighty'[2] is noble music, severe but full of beauty. Bennet's 'The almighty Trinity' also deserves notice; and Morley, though perhaps (as we shall shortly see) the most absolutely secular of the madrigalists, produced some of the finest religious work of the time, small in bulk though his contributions are. His Burial Service in G minor—simply harmonic, with a little plain counterpoint (the finest example existent of the style)—is throughout wonderfully serene, tender, and strong, and the expressiveness of the setting of 'Suffer us not at our last hour for any pains of death to fall from thee' has no superior anywhere. This is much his best-known sacred work, but there are some remarkable Latin motets from his pen: the opening of his 'Agnus Dei'[3] (printed at the end of his *Plaine and Easie Introduction*) is not surpassed anywhere in Elizabethan music for purity of utterance and intensity of feeling:

[1] *English Madrigal School*, vol. vi, p. 176.
[2] Edited by J. F. Fitzgerald (Novello).
[3] Edited by R. R. Terry (Novello).

His Dorian mode verse service, again, is at least as fine as that of Tallis, and his evening service in G minor, if not so striking, is still first-rate work; while the verse anthem 'Out of the deep'[1] is very expressive and stately. With the increasing vogue of secular solo songs, verse anthems containing solo and instrumental passages gradually came, as we have already seen, into existence side by side with the older 'full' anthems; but there was as yet no real differentiation of style. The verse anthems of Byrd and Gibbons and all the rest (except perhaps Ward, who, as we shall shortly have occasion to observe, in certain respects stands outside the general tradition) are as untouched by secular rhythm as anything in the strict *a cappella* manner; and the expression is always similarly grave and dignified.

Though some of the best-known madrigalists wrote comparatively few religious compositions, others divided their energies more evenly between the two departments. Philips produced a large mass of work of both kinds; but, as with his model Palestrina,

---

[1] *Tudor Church Music*, 8vo ed., No. 71.

there seems to be but little secularity about his non-religious music. Peacham, in his *Compleat Gentleman*,[1] says of Philips: 'He affecteth altogether the *Italian* veine'; and, indeed, his permanent residence abroad influenced his style very greatly, and in no respect more than in the curious impersonality which it as a whole displays. Just occasionally, as in the very beautiful closing portion of 'Hodie Beata Virgo Maria' (No. 11 of the five-part *Cantiones Sacrae* of 1612 —a collection which may fairly be taken as representing Philips at his best), or in this exquisite passage from the middle of the motet for the feast of St. John the Evangelist (No. 3 of the same set):

we see something very like the delicately austere but yet thoroughly human tenderness of Byrd; and in 'Beata Agnes' (No. 10) we have, indeed, in the very expressive rhythmical antiphony of the words 'quem quaesivi, quem amavi,' something that is almost modern in its emotional manner. But, as a rule, Philips is a very solid and massive, but not at all distinctive composer; his work, both in secular madrigals and in ecclesiastical choral music, is full of very fine,

[1] 2nd ed. (1634), p. 102.

polished workmanship, but the material is, generally speaking, not much more than the residuum of the great Italians, to whose influence is added, in much of the church work, that of Sweelinck. There is the unmistakable 'grand style'; but it is, in Philips's hands, by no means inconsistent with a certain monotony or even dullness. He is not without English traits; he uses entirely unprepared augmented triads in a manner which, fairly common in England, was exceedingly rare abroad, and the lilting 'Noe' refrains with which he ends some of his religious motets are not at all unlike the secular work of some of his countrymen. But, taken as a whole, he certainly stands outside the line of purely English composers—though much more so in his vocal than in his instrumental work, to which we shall return later. His church music is characteristic of the general development on the Continent in its frequent alternation of polyphony in the old manner with richly sonorous homophony—the motet 'O virum mirabilem',[1] for the feast of St. Francis of Assisi, will supply an example:

[1] Edited by H. B. Collins (Chester).

Like his Italian contemporaries he also takes a particular delight in contrasts of block harmony between different sections of the choir, for instance, in the motets 'Gaudent in coelis' and 'Cantantibus organis'.[1]

His contemporary Richard Dering also enjoyed considerable, though less extended, reputation. Both Philips and Dering adhered to the older faith, and published nearly all their works abroad; and both alike had but little influence in England, though Dering's music seems for a time to have had considerable vogue at Cambridge,[2] and his three-part motets (then in manuscript)[3] were great favourites with Cromwell. Some of his motets show real dignity and power, though not of a specially individual kind. He was clearly in sympathy with the modern methods of his time. He published his motets with a *basso continuo* for the organ, which in some works—for example, 'Anima Christi',[4] where the voices are heard individually—is indispensable. He is up to date, too, in his use of appoggiaturas and suspensions: the end of 'Jesu, dulci memoria'[4] is a good example, or the following passage from the six-part 'O vos omnes':[4]

[1] Both edited by R. R. Terry (Novello).
[2] Thomas Mace, *Musick's Monument* (1676), p. 235.
[3] They were eventually published by Playford in *Cantica Sacra*, 1662.
[4] Edited by J. F. Bridge (Bosworth).

Equally neglected, and, though much less technically mature, considerably more original, are the anthems of Ward; the elaborate verse anthem 'Let God arise' is a remarkable work, very vitalized and powerful, and others are but little below it. Ward is one of the most daring and modern ecclesiastical composers of the madrigalian time. He cannot claim anything remotely like the position of a man like Gibbons in sheer musical worth—indeed, his actual thematic material is not, as a rule, specially striking—but he is full of anticipations of much later times, and, indeed, is not infrequently almost Purcellian in spirit; he has real dramatic expressiveness, and, with all the occasional uncertainty of handling which prevents him from being a really great man in the full sense of the word, his anthems—curiously more advanced in tone than his madrigals—deserve much more study than they have hitherto received. An evening service, printed in Barnard's collection, is also noteworthy.

Among the other sacred compositions of the time there may also be mentioned Ravenscroft's quietly expressive verse anthems 'O Jesu meek' and 'Ah, helpless wretch',[1] the pure and stately but not

---

[1] *Church Music Society*, No. 3.

as a rule specially distinguished work of Batten ('Hear my prayer,
O God',[1] with its very beautiful ending to the words 'O that I had
wings like a dove', is the finest); Daman's sincere and expressive
'Miserere';[2] Bull's 'Almighty God, who by the leading of a star',[3]
and 'Deliver me'—not very remarkable, but thoroughly dignified
and free from the exaggerations of his instrumental work; Hooper's
short but noteworthy 'O thou God almighty'; Patrick's fine service
in G minor;[4] Bevin's 'Dorian' service and other works on the Tallis
model, at some distance behind; and Kirbye's fine and solemn 'O
Jesu, look',[5] in which his massive if slightly heavy style is well displayed. A word may also be given to some reprinted anthems of
Milton, Ford, and East, though they are inferior to those already
mentioned; Milton's 'O had I wings'[6] (one of four written for Leighton's *Teares or Lamentacions of a Sorrowfull Soule*) is free from his
usual stiffness of manner; Ford's 'Let God arise'[7] is good strong
music, though without any special features ('My griefs are full', from
the still unpublished 'Songs of verse and chorus in three parts',[8]
is, however, considerably finer); and East's 'Awake and stand up'[9]
and other similar anthems are solid work. But in the music of this
period there is nothing like the same wellnigh universally high level
attained in the sacred as in the secular field; Byrd and Gibbons are
the giants, and others also did some very fine work, but the artistic
heart of the nation had turned away from the Church.

We may now turn to the consideration of the secular vocal
music; and as Wilbye's sixty-five madrigals[10] represent the style
in its greatest glory, we may therefore fitly describe them in some
detail. Each of the two sets contains madrigals in three, four, five,
and six parts; in all there are fourteen three-part, fourteen four-
part, twenty five-part, and sixteen six-part (with one extra, in six
parts, that was contributed to the *Oriana* collection). There is no
real development of style to be noticed in the later collection, except

---

[1] Edited by G. Bantock (Curwen).
[2] *Old English Edition*, vol. xxi, p. 35.
[3] *Tudor Church Music*, 8vo ed., No. 91.
[4] Edited by J. E. West (Novello). Morning and Evening Service, edited by
I. Atkins (Oxford University Press).
[5] *Tudor Church Music*, 8vo ed., No. 18.
[6] *Old English Edition*, vol. xxii, p. 17.
[7] *Musical Antiquarian Society*, vol. xiv, p. 61.
[8] Oxford, Christ Church, 736–8.
[9] *Musical Antiquarian Society*, vol. xiv, p. 129.
[10] *English Madrigal School*, vols. vi and vii.

in regard to the three-part madrigals, which are considerably more advanced in the 1609 set than in that published in 1598, beautiful as at least two of the latter are; and Wilbye seems to be able to deal with equal mastery with words of the most diverse kind. The works by which he is best known—'Flora gave me fairest flowers' (I, 22) and 'Sweet honey-sucking bees' (II, 17)—represent him in his delicately graceful and lighter mood; they are marked by exquisite polish and charm, but are (at any rate the former) less characteristic than some others. To the same general type belong the four-part 'Lady, when I behold' (I, 10), the three-part 'So light is love' and 'As fair as morn' (II, 4 and 5), the six-part 'Stay, Corydon, thou swain' (II, 32); all bright and dainty, full of subtle detail (the lovely interweaving of parts and syncopated complications in 'So light is love' are very notable), and delightful from start to finish. But these represent Wilbye at his slightest; they fulfil their aim quite perfectly, but they do not aim at more than grace. We see him in rather more reflective mood, tender and expressive, with a vein of quiet sadness, in the three-part 'Weep, O mine eyes' (I, 4) and 'Come, shepherd swains' (II, 1), the four-part 'Adieu, sweet Amarillis' (I, 12), and the five-part 'Down in a valley' (II, 21); but these again can be paralleled, though only rarely in such a degree of perfection, in other contemporary madrigal-books.

Wilbye seems, indeed, to have resembled Byrd and Gibbons in so far as his heart was really most in his serious work. He could, it is true, be frankly gay (as they hardly ever succeeded in being), and could produce masterpieces like 'Happy streams whose trembling fall' (II, 10), which combine all the distinctive excellences of the composers who primarily sought only for charm of sound; but he is seen at his greatest when the words give him emotional chances. In the first set there are the three-part 'Ye restless thoughts' (I, 6), with its dreamy unrest, and the four-part, 'Alas, what hope of speeding' (I, 9), with its passionate last cry, and in the second set the very sombre and strong 'I live and yet methinks I do not breathe' (II, 7); and among the six-part madrigals there are 'Long have I made these hills and valleys weary' (II, 34), the powerful, gloomy 'When shall my wretched life' (I, 25), and 'Thou art but young, thou sayest' (I, 29), where underneath all the freshness and beauty we feel a deep emotional undercurrent, which finally rises to the surface in a sort of great sob, on plain massive chords in a different rhythm, to the words, 'Oh me, that I were young again!' But still more remarkable in some ways are the four-part 'Happy, oh happy he' (II, 16) and the five-part 'All pleasure is of this condition' (II, 19), the closing bars of each of which must be quoted. The latter of these two is throughout in a grey mood, with its feeling, so to speak, dulled and resigned; but just at the end, to the words 'with gnawing grief and never-ending smart', the voices, after some most striking anticipatory harmonic progressions, build themselves up in a sort of last cry of despair—superbly managed both technically and emotionally—and then sink slowly back:

Ex. 73

But perhaps even more wonderful is the close of 'Happy, oh happy he'—the words of which form what is practically a religious poem ending:

> Deeming his life a scene, the world a stage,
> Whereon man acts his weary pilgrimage,

on which Wilbye's sombre and restrained music fades slowly into darkness with one poignant utterance of extraordinarily pathetic dignity:

Perhaps, indeed, music could hardly show anything finer than the setting of the word 'weary' here, if the passage is sung—as all madrigals should be sung—with the very utmost sensitiveness of expression as regards both tone and rhythm.

Wilbye had, indeed, a singular gift for setting individual words from an emotional point of view, as, for example, 'in despair' from 'Long have I made these hills and valleys weary' (II, 34) or 'yet thou of sighs' from 'Oft have I vowed how dearly I did love thee' (II, 20), or from the same madrigal the passage where the bass voice steadily falls (chiefly chromatically) from the upper B♭ to the low G to the words 'suff'rest my feeble heart to pine with anguish'; other instances are the opening bars of 'Unkind, O stay thy flying' (I, 20), or the setting of 'what uncouth jar' in 'I live and yet methinks I do not breathe' (II, 7), or that of the word 'sobs', in 'Of joys and pleasing pain' (I, 26), to a clean augmented chord with no note prepared. Wilbye is, indeed, often harmonically very daring, but he nevertheless always shows a rare instinct for sheer beauty of effect; and however closely he may paint the emotion of individual words, he never sacrifices the broad sweep of his massive structures. Indeed, both as a technical musician and as an expressive artist, he is one of

the very greatest figures in English music; his total output, compared
with that of many of his contemporaries, was not large, but its splendid quality places him, along with Purcell, at the head of English
secular composers.

Bennet, Bateson, and Weelkes form a trio of madrigalists whose
work ranks only a little below that of Wilbye; between the three
there is very little to choose, and each is among the great English
composers. Bennet[1] is best known by the very pathetic and beautiful 'Weep, O mine eyes' (No. 13) and the brilliant 'All creatures now
are merry-minded'[2] in the *Oriana* collection; but others that are
much less known are also very fine. The classic tranquil dignity of
'O grief, where shall poor grief?' and 'O sweet grief' (Nos. 15 and 16)
is very striking, and nothing could well be lovelier than the close of
the former:

Apart from half a dozen slight works contributed to Ravenscroft's
Briefe Discourse (No. 1, 'The hunt is up', is very breezy and piquant),

[1] *English Madrigal School*, vol. xxiii.
[2] Ibid., p. 85.

Bennet produced only one book of madrigals, and this is shorter than usual, containing only seventeen works; but considerable variety of style is shown, though there are no examples of the 'ethical madrigal' of Wilbye and Gibbons. Besides those already mentioned, the music-lover's attention may be specially directed to the very graceful 'Come, shepherds, follow me' (No. 5), 'Whenas I glance' (No. 10), with its delightful coquettish ending, the tranquilly beautiful 'O sleep, fond fancy' (No. 12), with its dreamy close on a bare fifth, or the, no doubt intentionally, concluding madrigal 'Rest now, Amphion' (No. 17), containing an ingenious and charming treatment of the words 'Discording concords make the sweetest song'. One madrigal 'Thirsis, sleepest thou?' (No. 8), the words of which mix up Melibeus and London town in a curious way, seems to be intended to be humorous; but Bennet is more successful in his ordinary moods. He shows some tendency—decidedly more than Wilbye or Gibbons—towards distinctively modal harmony, as, for example, in 'Cruel, unkind' (No. 11), but still he is in most respects quite modern in his chord progressions, and his love of delightfully unexpected interrupted cadences is one of his most salient features.

The genius of Bateson[1] seems to have been attracted more towards picturesqueness and a sort of virginal charm than towards pathos or seriousness of emotion; in technical polish he is quite unsurpassed, and his two large Oriana madrigals—'Hark, hear you not?' (I, 22) and 'When Oriana walked to take the air'[2]—rank with the best in Morley's collection, though they were not in fact included in it (see p. 127). But on the whole he shows less variety than Bennet; the dewy freshness of 'Beauty is a lovely sweet' (I, 1), 'The nightingale' (I, 3), 'And must I needs depart then' (I, 14), 'Sweet Gemma' (I, 15), 'Sweet, those trammels of your hair' (II, 6), and many others, is altogether irresistible, but our memory is very liable to become confused among them. As is the ordinary rule in madrigal books (though there are plentiful exceptions) the five- and six-part works are statelier and larger in scope than the others; and at the end of 'Music some think no music is' (I, 28), where the words rise in mood to the idea of 'music sprung of heav'nly race', Bateson very successfully rises with them, while in the five-part 'Strange were the life' (I, 17) and 'Sadness, sit down' (II, 16) and the six-part 'Thirsis, on his fair Phillis' breast reclining' (I, 26), the tone is more

[1] *English Madrigal School*, vols. xxi and xxii.
[2] Ibid., vol. xxi, p. 1.

grave and contained than usual. But on the whole Bateson lives in the history of music (as does Herrick, whose poetry is a curiously close artistic parallel) chiefly by virtue of the exquisite finish of his lighter style. A feature which is almost peculiar to him—though it does not occur in his very best work—is a curious fondness for very careful piecemeal word-painting of an almost exaggerated kind; he is not infrequently inclined to sacrifice perfect continuity of texture for the sake of accurate descriptiveness of the words as they come. 'Come follow me, fair nymphs' (I, 5) is a regular hunting narrative of a quaintly realistic order; 'Dame Venus hence to Paphos go' (I, 8) begins with a sort of march-rhythm depicting the fact that 'Mars is gone to th' field'; and several other madrigals, such as 'Live not, poor bloom' (II, 7) show this same liking for pictorialism and what may be called 'short views'. Not indeed that Bateson's polish of harmonic style ever deserts him even when he inclines to scrappiness; but we miss in these particular madrigals (which, however, as has been said, are not his best) the serenely large sweep of the purest method. As an example of Bateson in his happiest mood we may perhaps quote the beginning of 'Hark, hear you not?' (Oriana's farewell, I, 22):

The work of Weelkes[1] is also of the very greatest interest, but his temperament seems to have been different from that of either Bennet or Bateson. His music is hardly ever perfectly free from a sort of quaint angularity and slight stiffness which, in his best compositions, seems somehow to add a very pleasant tinge of piquancy, but which, in his less happy moments, produces a certain hard and unsympathetic impression. He has a fondness for a kind of agreeably antique restraint of style; and, though harmonically fully as advanced as any of his fellows, he occasionally diverges into a method which comes closer than is natural with most of them to the rigid ecclesiastical tonality, as in the expressively strong and massive six-part elegy 'Cease now, delight',[2] or the fine five-part madrigal 'Your beauty it allureth'.[3] But these features do not in the least detract from the charm of his music, which is among the most strongly individual of the period, though perhaps he is inclined to be more unequal than most, and occasionally three or four works on end may show but little to interest. The best known of his larger madrigals is his six-part contribution to the *Triumphes of Oriana*, 'As Vesta was from Latmos' hill descending',[4] which is one of the very finest in the collection, and is full of massively elaborate counterpoint singularly powerful in effect; but many others of his five- and six-part madrigals are equally strong, and occasionally, as in 'Those spots upon my lady's face'[5] or the delicious 'Sweet heart arise',[6] he indulges in a delicate softness that is on the whole rather foreign to him. He is seen at his most individual in moods of tragic despair. Nothing could surpass the poignancy of the opening

[1] *English Madrigal School*, vols. ix–xiii.
[2] Ibid., vol. **x, p. 113.**
[3] Ibid., vol. ix, p. 62.
[4] Ibid., vol. xiii, p. 72.
[5] Ibid., vol. ix, p. 99.
[6] Ibid., vol. x, p. 22.

of 'O Care, thou wilt despatch me' or its wonderful sequel 'Hence, Care, thou art too cruel':[1]

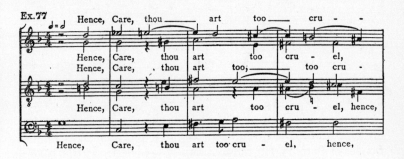

But there is more in him than pathos. The six-part 'Like two proud armies' and 'Mars in a fury'[2] are splendid examples of robust polyphony; and in 'Thule, the period of cosmography' and 'The Andalusian merchant' (from the same collection)[3] he most skilfully uses the medium to suggest the strange remoteness of far distant lands. Perhaps his instinct for massiveness is even more striking when he confines himself to a fewer number of parts—as, for example, in the powerful ending of 'Ay me! my wonted joys',[4] designed for four high voices, or still more in the three-part 'Cease sorrows now'[5] (perhaps the finest three-part madrigal in existence) of which we quote the splendid ending:

[1] Ibid., vol. xi, pp. 19 and 25.
[2] Ibid., vol. xii, pp. 1 and 38.
[3] Ibid., pp. 44 and 53.
[4] Ibid., vol. ix, p. 44.
[5] Ibid., p. 29.

Weelkes's balletts with *fa la* burdens differ from Morley's better-known examples of the style in being on the whole rather more formal and, so to speak, masculine; and in some of them, perhaps, the touch is a little too heavy. But the best—such for example, as 'To shorten winter's sadness', 'Hark, all ye lovely saints above', 'Lady, your eye my love enforced', and perhaps most of all, 'On the plains fairly trains'[1]—are flawless little gems, slightly less modern in tone[2] than Morley's, especially in rhythm, but perhaps somewhat more artistically solid; they should be sung, there can be no doubt, quite quickly, with any amount of delicate light and shade and accent, and real laughter in the voices. His three-part *Ayeres or Phantasticke Spirites*[3] are, however, on the whole much inferior, though they are interesting as a rare example of Elizabethan musical humour. The words are very odd and often quite unintelligible —'The gods have heard my vows' (No. 8) is a paraphrase of Horace's unpleasantly bitter ode to Lyce,[4] with a *fa la* refrain; and though there is much very ingenious, if rather heavy, counterpoint, and quaint wit, such as the illustration of Messalina going 'up and down the house a-crying, for her monkey lies a-dying' (No. 12), yet the twenty-five little pieces are of only slight artistic importance, in spite of their frequent spirit and point—the best are those with rather more reasonable words, such as 'The nightingale' (No. 25) or the very charming 'Upon a hill the bonny boy' (No. 5). The book ends very inappropriately with a very serious but on the whole rather dull elegy entitled 'A remembrance of my friend M. Thomas Morley', beginning 'Death hath deprived me' (No. 26).

The secular vocal music of Byrd is a curious instance of the limitations of a great man. Thirty out of the forty-seven *Songs of Sundrie Natures*[5] are secular, and yet it is hard to discover any particular genius of any kind in any of them, while in the remaining seventeen there is, as we have previously noticed, really noble work. Indeed, in an age that was, on the whole, so decidedly non-ecclesiastical in its art, the disposition of Byrd is noteworthy; he seems to become a new man when he touches religious words. It

[1] *English Madrigal School*, vol. x, pp. 5, 32, 71, 17.
[2] 'Welcome sweet pleasure' (ibid., p. 68), however, is as purely a squarely harmonized tune as any nineteenth-century part-song; but it is one of the least interesting of the balletts.
[3] Ibid., vol. xiii.
[4] *Odes*, iv, 13.
[5] *English Madrigal School*, vol. xv.

is true that, as we shall shortly see, he could write secular instrumental music equal to the very best of his time; but somehow, consciously or unconsciously, he inclined to the view that vocal music
should be primarily religious. A few exceptions there no doubt are;
two of the *Psalmes, Songs, and Sonnets*[1]—'This sweet and merry
month of May' (No. 9), and especially 'Come jolly swains' (No. 13),
with its delightful half-realistic setting of the refrain 'We smiling
laugh, while others sigh repenting', are full of gay charm of a subtle
kind. But when we have mentioned two or three other less remarkable specimens of his secular choral works—the graceful 'Though
Amaryllis dance in green' (*Psalmes, Sonets, and Songs of Sadnes
and Pietie*, No. 12),[2] and the dignified 'Wounded I am' and the
rather charming though quaint and stiff dialogue between two
shepherds, 'Who made thee, Hob, forsake the plough' (*Songs of
Sundrie Natures*, Nos. 17 and 41)—we are left with a very considerable residue that is merely heavy and dull. We have only to look
at his painfully ponderous setting of the playful poetry of 'When
I was otherwise than now I am' (ibid., No. 30) to realize how un-
willingly this great genius sported with Amaryllis in the shade;
and his contemporaries knew it well enough. It is perhaps significant that he did not contribute to the *Oriana* collection, in spite
of the fact that he was at the height of his fame when it was issued.
Peacham, in his *Compleat Gentleman*,[3] speaks of him as 'naturally
disposed to Gravity and Piety', rather than to 'light Madrigals or
Canzonets'; though he softens the partial depreciation by compar-
ing some of the secular works very favourably with Italian models,
which indeed they resemble on the whole more than they do contemporary English compositions.

The other supreme religious composer of the time, Orlando
Gibbons, seems to have taken the same general austere view of
vocal music; but his divergence into the secular field in his solitary
volume of *Madrigals and Mottets*[4] produced far more satisfactory
results. Though he calls these twenty pieces by this double title,
there is no line of demarcation to be drawn among them, and the
words of all are non-religious in character; but at the same time he
strikes out a special line for himself (possibly taking his cue from

[1] *English Madrigal School*, vol. xvi.
[2] Ibid., vol. xiv, p. 60. This, like other pieces in the same collection, was
originally written for soprano solo with strings.
[3] 2nd ed. (1634), p. 100.
[4] *English Madrigal School*, vol. v.

some particularly fine works by Wilbye produced fourteen years
earlier), and so we have a volume that is neither strictly secular nor
strictly religious, but rather, so to speak, 'ethical'. Without one
single exception, the words of all these pieces deal ultimately with
sadness or death, or preach some moral lesson; there is nothing
definitely religious anywhere, but the whole tone is distinctly an-
tagonistic to the general current of the time as shown in contemporary vocal music, and occasionally, as in the insistence on 'Lais,
now old' and her 'winter face' (No. 13), passes into sombre bitter-
ness. Gibbons does not, as Byrd did, force himself to uncongenial
work; but he sets himself to find words which satisfy his moods,
and discards all others. All these splendid madrigals, which must
indeed rank with the very greatest music of the age, are massive
and, so to speak, reserved in style; but the composer's seriousness
does not lead him towards an older harmonic language—on the
contrary he deals freely in augmented chords (which, indeed, are
occasionally found in the works of White as well as in those of Byrd
and most Elizabethans) and shows practically, in these works, no
traces of definite modal influences. 'The silver swan' (No. 1), exquisite though it is, is one of the slightest in the book, though none
could be more polished in expression; perhaps the finest are the
subtle and strong 'Now each flowery bank' (No. 12), the lengthy,
solemnly impressive 'What is our life' (No. 14), and 'How art thou
thrall'd', with a second part, 'Farewell all joys' (Nos. 7 and 8), the
last pages of which are truly magnificent. Perhaps we may quote
the beautiful close of 'Dainty fine bird that art encaged' (No. 9), to
show how Gibbons treats words that come as close as any used by
him ever to do the typical madrigalian sentiments:

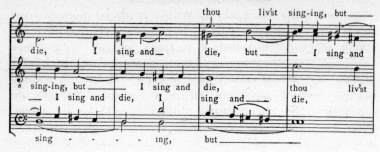

Apart from this one volume, Gibbons is not known to have written any secular vocal music, except a setting for voices and viols of 'The Cries of London'[1]—a quaint experiment of a realistic and humorous kind; two similar works by Dering, and two or three more by other composers, are in existence. They find their closest parallels in earlier French productions, like those of Jannequin; but in English music they are purely isolated apparitions of no artistic importance, except in so far as they may be considered to show the beginnings of a feeling for dramatic musical expression of a popular kind.

Morley is a very interesting figure, 'one of the most sympathetic in the history of English music'.[2] We have already noted his achievements as ecclesiastical composer and as theorist, and later on mention will also be made of his instrumental work; here we are concerned with him as madrigalist. His madrigals,[3] canzonets,[4] and balletts[5] are (even though showing, as they occasionally do, considerable modal influences) undoubtedly the most modern in tone of all the vocal music of the period; he has great command over

---

[1] Edited by J. F. Bridge (Novello).
[2] W. Nagel, *Geschichte der Musik in England* (1894–7), vol. ii, p. 125.
[3] *English Madrigal School*, vol. ii.
[4] Ibid., vols. i and iii.   [5] Ibid., vol. iv.

varied and piquant rhythm of a distinctively secular character, and
he has a frank delight in tune for its own sake. Hardly anything,
indeed, could well be more charmingly fresh and graceful than
such well-known little gems as 'Now is the month of maying'
(*Balletts*, No. 3), or 'My bonny lass she smileth' (ibid., No. 7);
and though the book of balletts which contains these is much his
most familiar work, the canzonets and madrigals show even more
attractive features. The balletts, taking them as a whole, are pure
dance-measures, non-contrapuntal in character, and as a rule slight
in texture, however polished; they lack on the one hand the tender
lyrical vein that we find in the best work of Dowland, and on the
other the intellectual solidity of the madrigals of Wilbye or Bennet.
The music is similar in style to Gastoldi's five-part *balletti* (1591);
some of the resemblances are too close to be fortuitous. Morley himself, in his *Plaine and Easie Introduction*,[1] says of the ballett: 'A
slight kind of musick it is, & as I take it devised to be daunced to
voices'; and very possibly he did not attach any special importance
to his work in this line. Anyhow, there seems to be no evidence of
any such plagiarism either in connexion with any of the rest of his
work, or with any of the compositions of any of his famous contemporaries; and the apparent inference is that Morley did not think it
worth while to lay claims to the customary complete proprietorship.
The two best-known of the balletts are certainly, on the whole, the
most modern in quality; though 'Lady, those cherries plenty' (No.
16) is also very delightful, and 'Singing alone' (No. 5) and 'I saw my
lovely Phillis' (No. 8) show rather more elaboration of texture, as
also does 'Leave alas this tormenting' (No. 19), which is designed
on lines rather more spacious than usual. The opening of 'What
saith my dainty darling?' (No. 9) may perhaps be quoted as a typical example of Morley's ordinary ballett-style:

Ex.80

[1] p. 180.

But, if we wish to see Morley's secular vocal music at its best, we should turn to the madrigals and the canzonets, the latter being really indistinguishable from the former, except that they are, as a rule, somewhat slighter in scope. Some of the two-part canzonets (notably, 'Go ye, my canzonets'[1]) are singularly ingenious and charming specimens of their very difficult form, and in all Morley makes full use of the resources of counterpoint, while at the same time preserving unimpaired his singular modernity of style; sometimes, as in the three-part canzonet, 'Do you not know how love lost first his seeing?',[2] he adopts a sort of cross between the methods of the ballett and the madrigal, starting with a purely rhythmical tune, and ending with a dominant pedal-point, but also employing contrapuntal detail considerably more fully than in the works of the harmonic type. As a rule, however, anything like part-song methods is not to be seen in the canzonets and madrigals, the deliciously smooth and rich interweaving of parts in the two- and three-part canzonets is of altogether exceptional quality, and in matter of

---

[1] *English Madrigal School*, vol. i, p. 1.
[2] Ibid., p. 84.

technique the madrigals can hold their own with any. But yet when we take up Morley's madrigals directly after a course of Wilbye, Weelkes, or Gibbons, or even Bennet or Bateson, we seem to miss something; in a sense Morley speaks our own language more fluently than they do—his dainty laughter is as fresh and entrancing now as it ever was, his rhythmical schemes might have been devised yesterday, and his tunes haunt us as they did his contemporaries—but the instrument he plays has only one string. We know well enough, from the Burial Music and other religious work, that his nature was very far from lacking in emotional depth; but he seems to have felt throughout that anything of the kind was out of place in the secular field. The madrigals of his great contemporaries, even if, like Bateson, they are essentially light-hearted composers, yet show sooner or later something below the surface of the words; there is some largeness of style, some reflection of the choral traditions that had been built up by ecclesiastical music. But Morley is from first to last sensuous and nothing more, as pure and delightful as a composer can be, but that is all; in the exquisitely beautiful three-part canzonet, 'Deep lamenting, grief bewraying'[1] there is neither grief nor lamenting, and in the equally delightful madrigals, 'Lady, why grieve you still me?' and 'O sweet alas!'[2] (one of Morley's most perfect masterpieces), the utmost emotionalism he can secure is a sort of playful delicate tenderness. Words that to Wilbye would suggest touches, however passing, of real feeling suggest to Morley nothing but charming *insouciance*; he has 'but fed on the roses and lain on the lilies of life'. But still, to criticize Morley's madrigals harshly is like breaking a butterfly on the wheel; it is only in comparison with some of the work of his fellows that we feel his own limitations, and when we remember that the ultimate criterion of a work of art is its handling of the given material, it is impossible to deny Morley a place among the few quite flawless craftsmen in the history of English music. Gems like 'Good morrow, fair ladies', 'What ails my darling' (*Canzonets to three voyces*, Nos. 6 and 18), 'April is in my mistress' face', 'The fields abroad with spangled flowers', 'Come lovers follow me', 'Besides a fountain' (*Madrigals*, Nos. 1, 10, 11, and 14), and many more, will keep his name green as long as musicians know the value of charm of sound; and his two editorial contributions to the *Oriana* collection—'Arise, awake' and

---

[1] Ibid., p. 44.
[2] Ibid., vol. ii, pp. 24 and 73.

'Hard by a crystal fountain'[1] placed before the rest an ideal of sunny melody and brightness that none of them equalled, far less surpassed.

We may now briefly consider the music of the other contributors to the great collection.[2] All the madrigals reach a high standard, and there is nothing that can be called unworthy work; though the productions of some of the men who are to us little if anything more than names—Norcome, Ellis Gibbons, Holmes, Hunt, Lisley, Edward Johnson—are, by the side of the best, relatively more or less uninteresting. But others who are also only stars of inferior magnitude are represented by very charming work; Nicolson's 'Sing shepherds all', Marson's 'The nymphs and shepherds danced Lavoltos' (with its delightful tripping runs on dotted rhythms), Cavendish's slight but very sunny 'Come gentle swains', the elder Hilton's 'Fair Oriana, beauty's queen' (with its very pretty bell-like refrain), Cobbold's dainty 'With wreaths of rose and laurel' (which Burney, very hastily, ranked the highest of the whole set), Milton's 'Fair Orian in the morn', and especially Carlton's 'Calm was the air', of which we may quote the exquisitely fresh and placidly antique opening, which secures the atmosphere of the words as perfectly as does any madrigal of the period:

Ex.81

¹ *English Madrigal School*, vol. iii, pp. 123 and 131 (also in vol. xxxii).
² Ibid., vol. xxxii.

all these are well worthy to hand down to posterity the names of men who (apart from the remarkably talented and far too neglected Carlton) are otherwise little known. Tomkins's 'The fauns and satyrs tripping' is imaginative and original, if not somehow quite mature. His other madrigals, however, published in 1622,[1] are much more remarkable, and rank but little below the best; usually they are joyous and fairly light in style, but show plenty of solid technical ability. Besides the general dedication of the set, in the usual fulsome manner, to the Earl of Pembroke, these madrigals are individually inscribed—a very rare custom. No. 1 is headed 'To my deare Father, Mr. *Thomas Tomkins*', No. 28 (the last) 'To my sonne, *Nathanael Tomkins*', while others bear the names of various relatives, 'Doctor *Douland*', 'my ancient & much reverenced Master, *William Byrd*' (a particularly sportive *fa la*), 'Mr. *Orlando Gibbons*' (also very amatory), and so on. The dedication of two of the very lightest numbers to the two most serious composers of the day is odd; but perhaps Tomkins was gifted with a special sense of humour.

---

[1] Ibid., vol. xviii.

Jones's 'Fair Oriana, seeming to wink at folly' is only an average work of one who also chiefly devoted himself to ayres; and John Mundy's 'Lightly she whipped o'er the dales' is a bright, but not particularly remarkable, example of a composer who was rather hardly treated by Burney and Nagel but nevertheless wrote some very polished things, notably, 'Of all the birds that I have heard' (No. 10 of the mixed sacred and secular *Songs and Psalmes* of 1594):[1]

with a delightfully unexpected ending. East, whose 'Hence stars! too dim of light' heads the *Oriana* collection, wrote several volumes of madrigals of, on the whole, no very special merit, though the breezy three-part 'How merrily we live'[2] keeps his memory green. The last of the second set (1606) has the curious title 'O metaphysical Tobacco'; the third set (1610) includes 'Pastorals, Anthemes, Neopolitanes, Fancies, and Madrigales'. The fine end of Farmer's 'Fair nymph, I heard one telling' rather overshadows the earlier portions, and his style is not as a rule quite up to the great level, though he could occasionally write very delightful things like 'You pretty flowers', or 'O stay, sweet love' (both in the 1599

---

[1] *English Madrigal School*, vol. xxxv (pt. 2), p. 1.   [2] Ibid., vol. xxx, p. 13.

collection),[1] and massive bits of contrapuntal work like the eight-part 'You blessed bowers' from the same set. The one contributor to *Oriana* who yet remains unnoticed is Kirbye, who published a book of madrigals in 1597; his *Oriana* work shows him as an interesting composer, a little stiffer in style than most, and with a sort of manly quaintness that is individual and attractive, though he lacks the gaiety of feeling and the easy technique of nearly all his colleagues. When he is at his best, as in 'Sleep now, my Muse' (from the set of 1597),[2] he can write music of a singular kind of grave tender charm, instinct with a quiet solemn beauty. There are two versions of this madrigal, one in four parts and one in six, the latter slightly expanded; the comparison between the two is deeply interesting, and the technical alterations show curious forecasts of Bach's methods under similar circumstances. 'Up then, Melpomene' (with its second part 'Why wail we thus?')[3] shows really very considerable power of a sombre kind, and more variety than usual with him. As a rule, however, he seems to have a partiality for what might be called the rather stiffly lugubrious style; he is very fond of amorously melancholy words, and his madrigals are on the whole inclined to be depressing in effect—not that they are 'serious' in the sense applicable to many by Wilbye and especially Gibbons, but Kirbye writes as if he were nearly always gloomily lovesick. Yet he can occasionally rise to deal with moods of a loftier character, and does so very successfully, as at the place in 'Why wail we thus?' where all the voices climb to the top of their registers at the words 'And is enstalled now in heaven's height'; and anyhow his massive solid workmanship, free from the least vestige of mere prettiness, commands cordial respect. In several ways he seems to have had much in common with Byrd; we shall notice later (in Chap. XIV) certain curious traits of harmony which, though often met with elsewhere, are perhaps most frequent in the works of these two composers.

A number of madrigal composers of the period were not included in *The Triumphes of Oriana*, for one reason or another. Bateson's 'When Oriana walked to take the air'[4] was intended for that collection but arrived too late and instead was inserted by the publisher at the beginning of his first book of madrigals. Pilkington's setting of the same words[5] may also have been intended as a contribution;

---

[1] Ibid., vol. viii, pp. 1 and 23.
[2] Ibid., vol. xxiv, pp. 25 and 152.
[3] Ibid., p. 133.
[4] Ibid., vol. xxi, p. 1.
[5] Ibid., vol. xxv, p. 133.

in the form in which it was published in his first set of madrigals
(1614) the last line appears as 'In heaven lives Oriana'—a clumsy
alteration of the original text which may have been suggested by
Bateson's 'Hark, hear you not?'[1] but is certainly out of place in its
context. His madrigals in general show a pleasant fancy, though
they are not strikingly individual and are apt to be rather square in
rhythm. It is difficult to see why Farnaby was not represented in the
Oriana collection; his four-part canzonets[2] had been published in
1598. Probably Ward (whose madrigals issued in 1613 contain fine
massive work, notably the fairly well-known 'Die not, fond man'),[3]
Gibbons, Ford, and Vautor were too young to be included; Gibbons
certainly was only eighteen. Ford, though now wellnigh solely
known by the accompanied songs that will shortly be noticed,
wrote some very charming three-part madrigals of a comparatively
slight kind,[4] including a setting of 'Sigh no more, ladies';[5] one of
them, 'My love is like a garden full of flowers,' is notable for the very
modern use of the pause-mark for emotional effect. Vautor, who was
in the service of Sir George Villiers (d. 1606), is one of the most
original of the madrigalists. His *Songs of divers Ayres and Natures*
(1619)[6] include the vivacious 'Mother, I will have a husband' (in
the style of the French *chanson*), the expressive and imaginative
setting of Sidney's 'Lock up, fair lids', the vivid Oriana madrigal,
'Shepherds and nymphs', and the charmingly picturesque and justly
popular 'Sweet Suffolk owl'.

The elder Ferrabosco (though his madrigals were included in
Arkwright's *Old English Edition*, vols. xi and xii) hardly seems to
demand notice in the present work, inasmuch as, great as was his
reputation in England, he resided largely in his native Italy, where
indeed all his music was originally published, except one madrigal
contributed to a collection issued at Antwerp. His work, though not
at times devoid of a certain quaint gracefulness, is as a rule rather
stiff and dull, showing powerful ecclesiastical influences in its
tonality, and very little rhythmical freedom; the one trait which he
may have acquired from his residence in England is a fondness for

[1] *English Madrigal School*, vol. xxi, p. 131.
[2] Ibid., vol. xx.
[3] Ibid., vol. xix, p. 180.
[4] Oxford, Christ Church, 736–8.
[5] Edited by P. Warlock, *Four English Songs of the early 17th Century*,
No. 4 (Oxford University Press).
[6] *English Madrigal School*, vol. xxxiv.

certain harmonic curiosities common in the works of his great
friend Byrd and other Englishmen (see Chap. XIV).

Of the solo songs with string accompaniment some are virtually
indistinguishable from madrigals, with voice and viols associating
on equal terms. Others present melodies obviously influenced by
the metrical psalm tunes, round which the instruments weave
a contrapuntal fabric. Others again, by avoiding independent
rhythms, subordinate the accompaniment to the singer. Byrd's
lullaby 'My little sweet darling',[1] perhaps the best known and
certainly one of the most beautiful of the solo songs, seems to
owe its inspiration to folk-song, while the anonymous 'This merry
pleasant spring'[2]—a very gay and spirited composition—throws
the voice-part into strong relief by its bird imitations and *fioriture*.
In *Pyramus and Thisbe* Shakespeare caricatured the verbal repetitions often found in the songs in the choirboy plays. Such repetition, however, is not necessarily ludicrous: there is a simple pathos
in the recurrent appeal for pity in Parsons's 'Pandolpho',[3] the end
of which may be quoted:

Ex.83

Pan-dol-pho. Pan-dol-pho, some

pi - ty, Pan - dol - pho, some pi - ty, Pan - dol - pho.

---

[1] Warlock, *The First Book of Elizabethan Songs* (Oxford University Press),
p. 14.

[2] Ibid., p. 5.

[3] Idem., *The Second Book of Elizabethan Songs*, p. 16.

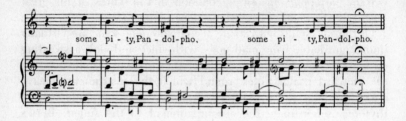

some pi - ty, Pan - dol - pho,   some pi - ty, Pan - dol - pho.

The subordination of an accompaniment to a melodic line is even more marked in the lutenists' ayres.[1] It is true that there are examples in them of contrapuntal treatment, but these are rarely continuous: a song like Danyel's 'Can doleful notes', where the lute accompaniment suggests the texture of a string quartet, is unusual. Nevertheless, the accompaniments are, in their slight impressionistic sort of style, extraordinarily well designed as a rule; and it is very much to be regretted that some modern versions sacrifice this delicate artistic economy for something much more 'complete', but heavy and lifeless. The net result, however, was that, as the ayres became more and more popular, and the influence of the Italian *nuova musica* spread in England, the old contrapuntal traditions of vocal music gradually lost their force. Not indeed that the purely English composers of ayres were attracted by the declamatory innovations of Monteverdi and his school; apart from Dowland's later work the Anglo-Italian Ferrabosco the younger is practically the only one who shows such influences, and in his case they are somewhat marked. In general the aim of the lutenist composers was to be lyrical; they set the words in plain strophic form, and avoided all musical elaboration or anything which would distract attention from the poetry. But the means varied; and it was realized that lyrical directness was not at all inconsistent with considerable rhythmical flexibility. The very square-cut manner shown in such rather stilted, though pure, songs as Dowland's 'Now, O now, I needs must part' (I, 6), or yet more his 'Away with these self-loving lads' (I, 21), is not at all common, and Dowland himself shows it but rarely after his first book; and even there the great bulk of the songs are more of the type of the exquisite 'Awake, sweet love' (I,

---

[1] Modern editions by E. H. Fellowes in the *English School of Lutenist Song Writers*, 1st and 2nd series.

19), from which we may quote the first bars of the version for solo voice and lute:

tinted, so to speak, in shades of delicate grey, and full of a quiet beauty and tender charm that raise their composer to a very high place among English artists. Sometimes his rhythm is clearly modelled on French practice, with its imitation of classical scansion; the opening of 'Come away, sweet love' (I, 11) will serve as an example:

Such a faithful adherence to the rhythm of the words demands the co-operation of the poet if the music is to fit all the stanzas equally well. There are, in fact, many examples where the author of the words has been at pains to provide an exact correspondence; but there are others where there is a conflict between words and music which can only be resolved by some modification in performance. The setting of the first verse of 'Come, heavy Sleep' (I, 20) is admirable:

But as it stands it cannot be said to be a perfect match for the second verse:

> Come, shadow of my end, and shape of rest,
> Allied to Death, child to the black-faced Night.

In his later songs Dowland shows plainly the influence of the new declamatory style. The opening of 'Welcome, black night' (IV, 20) is pure recitative:

It would be a mistake to pretend that Dowland is a composer with only one mood. That he was capable of gaiety is evident from pieces like the delightful 'Daphne was not so chaste' (III, 4), which recalls the rhythms of Morley's balletts. At the same time there was in him undoubtedly a very strong inclination to pathos. We see it in the well-known 'Flow, my tears' (II, 2), familiar as 'Dowland's Lachrymae', and many others of the same kind, or again, very impressively, in the two songs with additional parts for treble and bass viol—'Go, nightly cares' and 'From silent night' (IV, 9 and 10). One of his most moving songs, 'In darkness let me dwell',[1] was published in his son's anthology *A Musicall Banquet* (1610)—a piece remarkable for its sombre colouring and particularly for the way in which the setting of the opening words recurs at the end as an expression of passionate regret.

If we turn to the work of the lutenists in general we shall no doubt find a certain amount of monotony: a good many of the composers are never capable of really distinctive work that grips and retains the attention. But it is unfair to compare the songs, as some have done, to scentless flowers; the motto which a contemporary hand has written in the British Museum copy of Jones's *Musicall Dreame* —'musica medicina doloris'—comes nearer the mark. Campian's 'Divine and Morall Songs' (the description of his first book of ayres) may occasionally wear a gravely austere face, as in the beautiful 'Most sweet and pleasing are thy ways, O Lord', but it is an austerity that overflows with tranquil happiness; and in the same collection the song 'Never weather-beaten sail' has a refrain 'O come quickly, sweetest Lord, and take my soul to rest', which is quite trippingly lilting, almost to a dance-measure, in its innocent joyousness. As a

---

[1] Printed with *A Pilgrimes Solace (Fourth Book of Airs)*, ed. Fellowes, pt. ii, p. 116.

short but complete example of the ayres, we may quote the following from the Campian-Rosseter book of 1601—this particular song is by Rosseter, and there are five verses in all (the tablature of the accompaniment has already been given on p. 86):

Ex.88

And would you see my mis - tress' face? It is a flow-ery gar - den place, Where knots of beau - ties have such grace That all is work and no - where space, Where no - where space.

Rosseter is, however, not by any means the most distinguished of the company of ayre-writers; but this particular example has been chosen as in several respects very typical. Danyel and Pilkington—a distinctly attractive composer, whose style is considerably the most madrigalian of all the lutenists, and whose 'Rest, sweet nymphs', 'Now peep, bo-peep', 'With fragrant flowers', and a good many more, are beautifully graceful and polished—could do work of a considerably more solid kind; and Campian, as in the charming song (IV, 7) which begins as follows:

Ex.89

There is a gar-den in her face, Where ro-ses and white li - lies grow;

could very often produce melodies more flowing and more distinctive in outline, as could also Morley, and, though less frequently, Ford (whose 'Since first I saw your face' is one of the most familiar of all Elizabethan pieces), Corkine, and Robert Johnson. But 'And would you see my mistress' face?' is very typical of the great bulk of the ayres in its dainty stiffness, its deliberate rhythm, its half-sequential melody, its exquisitely finished 'impressionistic' harmony; practically every composer shows the type. It will be observed that the lute accompaniment follows the general outline of the tune; this is the general rule, but there are exceptions, as in the vigorous twanging C major chords on the accented beats at the beginning of No. 15 of Jones's second book, with its delightful opening phrase:

Ex.90

Dain - ty, dain - ty, dain - ty dar - ling.

Jones is one of the liveliest of the lutenists. Songs like 'My father fain would have me take' (V, 15), 'My complaining is but feigning' (IV, 6) and 'Think'st thou, Kate, to put me down' (III, 12) have the simplicity and the natural charm of folk-song. It is not surprising that 'Sweet Kate' (IV, 2) should have become one of the most popular of the lutenists' ayres, though it is unfortunate that so few singers appear to realize that it was written as a duet. Jones's simplicity, however, is not naïvety; its apparent artlessness is the product of a neat and skilful craftsmanship. An admirable example of his sense of proportion is the song 'Go to bed, sweet muse' (III, 3), which is short enough to be quoted complete:

135

Ex.91

Go to bed, sweet muse, take thy rest. Let not thy soul be so op-press'd.

Though she de-ny thee, she doth but try thee Wheth-er thy mind will

ev-er prove un-kind. O love is but a bit-ter sweet jest.

A different temperament is revealed in Danyel's songs. His book
includes a number of lighter pieces, but his supreme excellence is
to be found in his serious songs, of which we may mention particularly the exquisite 'If I could shut the gate against my thoughts'
and the two elaborate song-sequences—'Mrs. M. E., her funerall
teares for the death of her husband' and 'Can doleful notes'. The
opening of the 'Funeral tears' will give some idea of Danyel's eloquence in grief:

Ex.92

Grief, grief, grief, grief,

keep with-in and scorn to show but tears,

Since joy can weep as well as thou. Dis - dain to

sigh, for so can slen - der cares, Which but from i - dle caus - es grow.

The text of 'Can doleful notes' begins:

> Can doleful notes to measur'd accents set
> Express unmeasur'd griefs which time forget?
> No, let chromatic tunes, harsh without ground,
> Be sullen music for a tuneless heart.

The composer has interpreted this freely by using chromatic progressions of a kind familiar in the works of Weelkes, Farnaby, and
Dowland, and inherited by English writers from the Italian madrigalists. The whole sequence has a poignant intensity not easily
matched in the work of Danyel's contemporaries. In both sequences
the lute part is very fully worked out, with a consistent polyphonic
texture. This, as we have seen, is unusual in the work of the lutenists, who are generally content to provide a fairly straightforward
accompaniment. One or two examples of a more elaborate kind,
however, are to be found in Dowland, including 'In darkness let
me dwell'; and there is also the anonymous and extremely pathetic
and beautiful song, 'O death, rock me asleep',[1] of an unusually

---

[1] Brit. Mus. Add. 15117, fol. 3ᵛ. A modernized text is printed in Wooldridge's

extended and organized type, where the lute accompaniment is designed on a sort of ground bass.

We have already, in the previous chapter, mentioned the two or three pieces in the collections of keyboard music of this period which are the work of composers of the earlier generation; for the rest—though we cannot always feel quite certain of the date of the items to which no name is attached—they are by the contemporaries of the transcribers, and fall within the period we are now considering. Those by Sweelinck and other foreign composers lie of course outside our inquiry; but their inclusion is interesting as showing the range of sympathies of English music-lovers. These pieces are of all sorts and kinds—dance tunes, preludes, contrapuntal fantasias, variations on popular tunes of the day, variations on plainsong melodies, arrangements of madrigals, descriptive programme music, and so on; in the Forster and Cosyn collections in the Royal Music Library several vocal pieces are also included. The *Parthenia* collection (1611),[1] being the only music of this kind that was thought worthy of print at the time, represents, on the whole, the style at its highest level; the others are specially interesting as showing the music that was in general vogue—several numbers of presumably more than ordinary popularity are met with in two or three of them as well (in some cases) as in isolated manuscript copies. But it can hardly be gainsaid that, as a rule, the instrumental performers of Elizabethan times were apparently satisfied far more easily than the singers; it is only very rarely that, in reading through this music for the virginals, we see anything even approximately like the maturity of style and technical mastery that are so splendidly obvious in the great choral music. The composers, even the greatest, seem—with but few and passing exceptions—to have regarded instrumental music, as, so to speak, a trifling thing; they dallied with it for amusement, but, reserved their serious energies for other work. No doubt, at the time, the actual novelty of sound cast a glamour over the essential inferiority of material; but to us, for whom there is no such novelty, the main impression left by the great mass is, compared with that left by most of the choral music, one of somewhat monotonous dullness.

Not indeed that there is any lack of variety as regards the osten-

---

Old English Popular Music (1893), vol. i, p. 111—though why it should be included in that work is difficult to see.

[1] Facsimile edition with commentary by O. E. Deutsch (1942).

sible plans of the pieces; they vary in length from a few bars to several pages, and in difficulty from simple chords to rapid virtuosity that very distinctly tests even a modern pianist's fingers. But there is a strong family likeness about them all: and, apart from a handful of examples at either end of the scale of merit, they differ on the whole very little in quality. We see the frank enjoyment of instrumental expression as such, quite apart from the value of the thing expressed; apart from the variations, and the tentative experiments in the direction of fugues, there is practically never anything of the nature of a thematic subject, and very little in the way of organized structure. As a matter of fact, vocal music had had a long start, and it is only reasonable that it should show much more certainty of style than a branch of art that had not existed in England more than fifty or sixty years when the earliest of the works we are now considering was written. Musicians took some time to acquire a real sense of organic instrumental composition, which indeed was not perfectly developed till long after vocal music had reached its full maturity. The harmonic texture of the virginal music of Byrd and Morley and Gibbons is exactly the same as that of their choral work, whether ecclesiastical or secular; it is sober and restrained, essentially diatonic in character, and to a very large extent confined to the chords and progressions used in strict counterpoint. But combined with this we see pages and pages of the merest 'passage-work', which are obviously inspired by nothing else than the attractiveness of playing notes, no matter how artistically meaningless, at a quicker pace than voices could sing them. In a few cases—chiefly in the works of Bull—these passages take the form of arpeggios, broken octaves, or repeated notes; but as a rule they are built on scale-formulas. Scale-playing, as such, had a fascination for these early instrumental composers that we find hard to realize; the mere succession of notes in fixed and persistent alphabetical order was a novelty to men whose ideas of music had been almost entirely gained from choral compositions, and when these successions were heard in extensions beyond the range of voices, and also at a brilliant speed, the fascination was complete, irrespective of the artistic interest which listeners would have demanded when singing was in question. No doubt the greatest men represented in these collections rose often above this level, and even the lesser often confined themselves to decorative ornamentation of a sporadic rather than continuous kind; but still it is impossible to

avoid noticing the curious parallel between these early virtuosos
and their descendants in these latter days, shown in the similar
delight in pure finger-work as such.

It is in the dance tunes that passages of this kind are seen least
(though when the dance tune is taken as the basis of variations
the treatment is exactly the same as with variations on themes of
other types). Pavanes, galliards, courantes, and allemandes—spelt,
according to the vague fashions of those times, in many different
ways—are the most common. As a specimen of this sort of music at
its finest we may quote the beginning of Byrd's beautiful and stately
'Pavana, the Earle of Salisbury' from *Parthenia* (No. 6); indeed,
there is probably nothing more balanced and artistically complete
in all the literature of virginal music:[1]

Gibbons's 'The Lord of Salisbury, his Pavin', from the same collection (No. 18), is also a very fine piece, larger and perhaps in certain
respects of somewhat subtler expressive character, but the dance-
measure has here altogether vanished, and with it has vanished
some of the structural mastery; another by him in the 'Fitzwilliam
Virginal Book' (No. 292) is of a transitional type, but also noteworthy music. Of the dance movements current at this time the
allemandes or almans retain perhaps the most of the original swing,
and three by Robert Johnson and a 'Meridian Alman' set by Giles
Farnaby ('Fitzwilliam Virginal Book', Nos. 145–7, and 291), for
example, have a briskness of movement that is very pleasant; but
as a rule these pieces, though solid in general style, and harmonically very pure, are neither specially enlivening nor artistically of

[1] The original ornament ⪦ is here replaced by what appear to be its two
eighteenth-century equivalents.

much importance, though occasionally there are instances of the same material being used in different numbers of a dance-suite which are interesting as early experiments in unification. All that can be said for most of them is that they are free from the flimsy passage-work that marks a great deal of the other music in these collections.

The preludes ('Praeludium' is the usual title) are indeed almost invariably nothing but mere casual running up and down the keyboard or equally casual strings of chords; they are, however, always very short. The fantasias vary much in character; sometimes, as in the case of Gibbons's fine 'Fantazia of foure parts' in *Parthenia* (No. 17), or in certain examples in the Fitzwilliam book by Philips and others, which show something like definite fugal texture of an elementary type, the workmanship is essentially choral in character and grave and dignified in tone, sometimes—as in an example by Morley (Fitzwilliam book, No. 124)—the music contains nothing but essentially instrumental figures and somewhat vague florid passages. As a rule, however, the fantasias strike a sort of mean between these extremes; the numerous examples by Giles Farnaby are (like those just mentioned) practically the heralds of instrumental fugues, inasmuch as they start in the 'subject and answer' manner which later customs made orthodox, but at the same time they show their divergence from choral methods in occasional introduction of rapid ornamentation. Some pieces by Philips are specially clear and well designed, but the counterpoint of most of these fantasias is, as a rule, of a somewhat uncertain character; the subjects rarely recur in any recognizable form, and the pieces, considered as wholes, are very loose in texture. Indeed, even in the massive fantasia by Gibbons to which reference has just been made, though there is no sort of definitely instrumental effect from first to last, we nevertheless see the technical relaxation of style in several passages which, like many places in Mendelssohn's pianoforte fugues, cannot by any ingenuity be scored in separate parts.

A special kind of this contrapuntal fantasia is shown in the pieces by Bull, Byrd, and others on the favourite 'Ut re mi fa sol la' formula —the first six notes of the scale repeated in various positions;[1] in

---

[1] A curious modern survival may be noted in the opening bars of one of the best-known of Hungarian folk-melodies, occurring in Liszt's fourteenth rhapsody and in Francis Korbay's *Hungarian Melodies* (1891) to the words 'Far and high the cranes give cry' (vol. i, no. 3).

these we see the nearest approach to persistence of subject that the music of these collections shows, as the formula runs like a connecting thread throughout the whole, though its shortness and lack of thematic distinctiveness militate against the effect. An example by Bull in the Fitzwilliam book (No. 51) is of special interest by reason of the extreme ingenuity with which the formula is made to appear in many different keys, the method involving rapid modulations, the notation of which is at times complicatedly enharmonic; this piece is indeed remarkable on many grounds, showing that (unless Elizabethan ears were extraordinarily insensitive) some kind of approach to equal temperament must have been known, and also containing a section of extremely complex cross-rhythms that is a belated survival of the 'proportional system' common in the church music of the earlier centuries.[1] On the whole, this fantasia is more curious than artistic, in spite of Bull's distinct feeling for structural balance shown in the emphasizing of the main key after all the modulations; Byrd's two pieces on the same six notes (Fitzwilliam book, Nos. 101 and 102) show considerably more musical feeling and some rather subtle development of the theme, and in Byrd's fantasia called 'The Bells' (Fitzwilliam book, No. 69) we can also see how he could make something out of unpromising materials—in this case merely strings of notes of different lengths contrapuntally combined in such manner as to suggest, very effectively in its way, a peal of bells of different sizes, rung unequally. The virginal books show a few other examples of this sort of early programme music; but this bright if over-long piece is certainly the best. The third to the fifth numbers of 'My Ladye Nevell's Booke' consist of a sort of little suite known as 'Mr. Byrd's Battle', including sections respectively entitled 'The Marche before the Battell', 'The Souldiers Sommons: the Marche of Footemen', 'The Marche of Horsemen', 'The Trumpetts', 'The Irishe Marche', 'The Bagpipe and the Drone', 'The Flute and the Droome', 'The Marche to the Fighte', 'The Retreat', 'The Galliarde for the Victorie';[2] but this innocently playful production is of no more than historical interest. Another equally futile work, from the artistic point of view, is a fantasia in the Fitzwilliam book (No. 3) by John Mundy describing 'Faire Wether', 'Lightning', 'Thunder', 'Calme Wether', in vaguely alter-

[1] See W. Apel, *The Notation of Polyphonic Music* (1942), pp. 145–95, for an account of these rhythmical methods.

[2] Later versions of the suite include three further pieces: see Hilda Andrews, *My Ladye Nevell's Booke*, pp. 38–9.

nating little sections of a totally formless character, ending with five bars to depict 'A Cleare Day'.

We may briefly pass over the versions of madrigals of Marenzio, Lassus, and other composers, most of which are by Philips: they are as a rule mere transcriptions of the voice-parts, except that the long notes are ornamented with turns and trills and the larger intervals are often filled up with semiquavers. This indefinite kind of work had in it no germ of anything artistically worthy; but the variations, which are on the whole the most interesting branch of all the virginal music, demand more notice. It was natural that composers should turn to the variation form when desiring to write pieces as far as possible on purely instrumental lines and also of some length; the contrapuntal fantasias, however non-vocal in ornamental detail, were nevertheless based on choral tradition, and the little dance tunes and fancy pieces were not sufficiently important always to satisfy composer and listener. So there grew up a form of instrumental music consisting of variations, frequently very many in number, on some well-known melody by a contemporary composer, some extract from ecclesiastical plainsong, or, more frequently, one of the delightful secular popular songs of the time, such as 'The carman's whistle', 'Bonny sweet Robin', 'Walsingham', 'All in a garden green', and very many more (see Chap. XIII). Variations on dance tunes and on 'grounds' are also occasionally met with. It has been suggested that the variations on Church melodies were written for the organ, not the virginals, and this is no doubt true as regards the composer's primary intention; but nevertheless, except for the fact that the subject itself is not ornamented, there is really not the least essential difference in style between, for example, Bull's treatment of 'Salvator mundi' (Fitzwilliam book, No. 45) and 'The king's hunt' (ibid., No. 135). In both we see great ingenuity in devising brilliant instrumental passages which, within the limits necessitated by the harmonic language of the time, are effectively varied and contrasted, and anyhow show a curiously speculative and daring mind; but the themes are never developed except from the point of view of the purely technical virtuoso.

No doubt composers differed in their reliance on mere fingerwork; a good many of Bull's variations have practically no other interest, and some (such as those in the Fitzwilliam book on 'Walsingham', No. 1, and on 'Ut re mi fa sol la', No. 215[1]) seem to have

---

[1] This is not the same as the fantasia previously mentioned; it is a string

been designed for no other purpose than to show to what dazzling heights performers could rise—the very difficult and brilliant fireworks of the latter are really curiously modern in many ways. But others, especially Byrd, while not rivalling Bull in his precocious instinct for keyboard effectiveness, managed, while devising their variations on the general principle of more or less rapid successions of notes in different forms, to give occasional glimpses of a subtler idea of transmutation of the character of the theme; these attempts are not at all common, and when they do show themselves are usually very transient, but still they are evidence that some composers had notions of variations that should not be merely more or less mechanically technical in character. Not, indeed, that we should judge Bull or his followers too hardly; the frank delight in the merely, so to speak, physical capabilities of an instrument is historically a necessary precursor to the understanding of its less superficial possibilities, and, after all, Bull's passages never sink to the level of later things like the Alberti bass and similar lazy makeshifts which sinned against a known ideal. Perhaps a bar or two of one of Bull's typical variations (No. 22 of those on 'Walsingham') may be quoted as an example of his style:

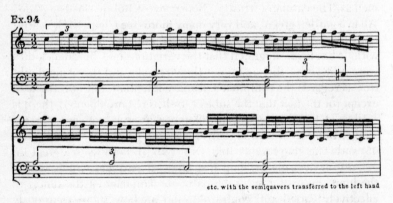

etc. with the semiquavers transferred to the left hand

The four men who figure most prominently in all this music are Bull, Byrd, Gibbons, and Giles Farnaby—Bull, the daring virtuoso, with extraordinary insight into the future, but with only a scanty endowment of real musicianship—Byrd, the rather austere and angular genius, occasionally unbending very delightfully, but

of technical variations on the phrase of six notes ascending and descending so as to form a sort of little tune that never changes.

as a rule showing here, as in his secular madrigals, that his heart was really elsewhere, and probably rather despising the public that welcomed him chiefly as a brilliant performer—Gibbons, massive and dignified, with a vein of tenderness appearing from time to time, but on the whole a little too solid for the material and the instrument at his command—and Farnaby, less capable in a way than the other three, but gifted with a sort of quaint romanticism of style that is now and then curiously modern in outlook, causing indeed the little pieces called his 'Dreame' (Fitzwilliam book, No. 194):

Ex.95

his 'Reste' (ibid., No. 195), and his 'Humour' (ibid., No. 196) to sound like a forecast, in lace ruffles, of Schumann's *Kinderscenen* (the way in which the 'Ut, re, mi' formula creeps into the third is quite in the style of the later composer's jests). No one can fail to admire much in the work of these men, especially the three latter; but still, however much we appreciate the delicate charm of some of these pieces, we cannot help recognizing the enormous gap in distinctiveness of material and maturity of handling between them and the great choral work of the same period. At the present day we sing the music of Byrd and Gibbons because it was written for all time; we play their music because it recalls to us, as nothing else can, the transient fashions of a day that is past.

In addition to the solo music for keyboard instruments and lute we have also a mass of music for instrumental ensembles, principally for consorts of viols. Dance tunes figure here, as in the solo instrumental music; sometimes they are set simply, in homophonic style, sometimes they are treated in a more stylized fashion, with contrapuntal elaboration. But the chief field for the exercise of instrumental polyphony was the 'In nomine' and the fantasia (or fancy). The origin of the 'In nomine' and its long vogue have already been mentioned in the previous chapter. It is obvious that there is a link with vocal music in the use of the traditional plainsong, though the treatment may be purely instrumental. The fancy, on the other hand, though it began as an imitation of the motet, was a purely original form of composition. Morley considered it to be the most important type of instrumental music, and described it admirably as 'when a musician taketh a point [i.e. a subject] at his pleasure, and wresteth and turneth it as he list, making either much or little of it according as shall seeme best in his own conceit'.[1] The mood might change as in the motet or madrigal, but the composer was not subject to the demands of a text; he had merely to exercise his fancy. The opening of a four-part fancy by Coprario[2] will illustrate a style of writing, fluid and expressive, which became, so to speak, standardized by constant repetition:

Ex.96

The whole of this example, with the exception of the last two bars, is concerned with the 'wresting and turning' of the first 'point'; the second 'point' is introduced by the second violin in the last bar but one and is then developed in its turn, and followed by others. The

[1] *A Plaine and Easie Introduction* (1597), p. 181.
[2] Edited by A. Mangeot (Augener).

eloquent and tranquil ending deserves quotation:

Ex.97

There is nothing in this piece beyond the capacity for voices; yet from the first bar to the last one has the impression that it has been conceived wholly in terms of instruments. In many of the fancies the instrumental character of the music is, indeed, strongly marked. This was not a late development; on the contrary, such unmistakable signs as a succession of repeated notes occur already in Tye's 'In nomines'.[1] Another characteristically instrumental detail is the use of very short melodic fragments, which are passed from one instrument to another in close imitation. A good many of the fancies are, like the example from Coprario, grave and even austere in character, but this is by no means universal. Many show considerable vivacity,[2] while others alternate liveliness and solemnity. Coprario's fancy is all of a piece, without any clearly defined sections; but it is very common to find a marked differentiation between

---

[1] E. H. Meyer, *English Chamber Music* (1946), p. 88.
[2] See, for example, a four-part fancy by Ward, ed. Mangeot (Augener).

the various parts of the composition. In such cases homophony, as in the madrigal, may be used as a contrast to the prevailing polyphony; and the sections into which the piece falls will bear a strong resemblance, in miniature, to the movements of the later sonata. The following section, taken from the middle of a three-part fancy by Lupo,[1] is an example not only of a more homophonic form of treatment but also of a popular, dance-like character often found in contrast to the motet style of the polyphonic sections:

Ex.98

* ♩ ♩ *in MS.* † 𝄴 *in MS.*

Dance rhythms also influenced the subjects that were used for fugal treatment; there are several instances in Gibbons's three-part fancies,[2] which show a very lively invention and real dignity and solidity of style. The influence of dance rhythms is one obvious point of contact with the keyboard music of the time. Another is the use of the 'Ut re mi fa sol la' formula as a *canto fermo*; in a four-part fancy by the younger Ferrabosco,[3] the hexachord appears successively in C, D♭, D, E♭, E, F, F♯, and G, ending on the third of the chord of C major. The manipulation of this arbitrary material results in some curiously kaleidoscopic changes of tonality.

[1] Printed in Meyer, op. cit., pp. 144–7.
[2] Edited by E. H. Fellowes (Stainer & Bell).
[3] Printed by E. Walker, 'An Oxford Book of Fancies', in *The Musical Antiquary*, Jan. 1912, pp. 70–3.

The fancy, like the madrigal, was intended not merely to delight performers but also to give pleasure to listeners. The complexity of the writing, however, must often have proved a stumbling-block to people who had not specially musical ears. Christopher Simpson, writing after the Restoration, says that the fancy had by that time become 'much neglected, by reason of the scarcity of auditors that understand it'.[1] We may guess that instrumental music was less practised by amateurs than singing, and this would explain why so little of it was printed. The only music for viols to be printed, apart from examples included in vocal collections such as those of Byrd and Morley, were the nine three-part fantasias of Gibbons (1609) and Michael East's collection entitled *The Seventh Set of Bookes* (1638). The publications of compositions for a mixed ensemble or for alternative resources were more numerous, but the total is still considerably less than the issue of madrigals and ayres. The mass of manuscript material for viols, however, testifies to a widespread cultivation of the purest form of chamber music, much of which is worthy to take its place beside the vocal music of the period. To the modern ear it is likely to sound 'abstract'; but there is plenty of evidence to show that contemporary musicians, who indulged so freely in emotion in the madrigal and ayre, were conscious of instrumental music as something equally expressive. This is true both of the fancies and of dance movements. East's fancies bear such significant titles as 'Desperavi, Peccavi, Vidi, Poenitet, Credidi, Vixi, Triumphavi'. Dowland's *Lachrimae* (1605),[2] founded on the song 'Flow, my tears', appeared with the sub-title 'Seaven Teares figured in seaven passionate Pavans' and the motto 'Aut furit, aut lachrimat, quem non fortuna beavit' (Either he rages or weeps, whom fortune has not blessed). Anthony Holborne's *Pavans, Galliards, Almains and other short Aeirs* (1599) have titles such as 'The Tears of the Muses' and 'The Image of Melancholy'. The use of pathetic chromaticism by composers like Ravenscroft and Tomkins[3]—an obvious analogy to its employment in madrigals and ayres—is a pointer in the same direction. The individualism of the age and the emphasis on subjective emotion in poetry and song encouraged a form of instrumental composition which was intimate both in its resources and its expression.

[1] *A Compendium of Practical Musick* (1667), p. 142.
[2] Edited by P. Warlock (Oxford University Press).
[3] An example by Tomkins is edited by E. H. Fellowes (Stainer & Bell).

V

MUSIC UNDER CHARLES I AND THE COMMONWEALTH

THE chief composers to be mentioned during this period are the two brothers Henry and William Lawes, Charles Colman, John Wilson, John Jenkins, John Hilton the younger, Martin Peerson, Nicholas Laniere, William Child, Benjamin Rogers, Christopher Gibbons, and Matthew Locke.

Henry Lawes, the elder of the two brothers, was born in 1596 and died in 1662. He became a gentleman of the Chapel Royal in 1626, but devoted himself chiefly to secular vocal music. He was held in the highest esteem by his contemporaries: Milton (for whose *Comus* he wrote the original music) and Herrick (many of whose songs he set) wrote poems praising him both as composer and performer. William Lawes was born in 1602. He was a pupil of Coprario and became one of the king's musicians after the accession of Charles I in 1625. At the outbreak of the Civil War he joined the Royalist army, and was killed at the siege of Chester in 1645. His music consists principally of instrumental pieces and secular songs; but he also wrote a few anthems and psalms.

Many other composers of this time applied themselves principally to the writing of music for masques and other purposes of secular entertainment. Charles Colman (who died probably in 1664), chamber musician to Charles I and composer to Charles II, is entirely known by such work, as also is Nicholas Laniere (1588–1666), master of the king's music to Charles I and Charles II—a versatile person, who was also a singer and a painter and spent some years in Italy buying pictures for the Royal collection as the agent of Charles I. John Wilson (1595–1674) was one of the court musicians to Charles I, Professor of Music at Oxford from 1656 to 1661, and afterwards gentleman of the Chapel Royal, in succession to Henry Lawes. He was also chiefly a composer of songs, but occasionally diverged into religious music, as in his *Psalterium Carolinum* (1657),[1] settings for three voices, with organ or theorbo

---

[1] The sub-title is 'The Devotions of His Sacred Majestie in his Solitudes and Sufferings'.

accompaniment, of metrical adaptations of the Psalms by Thomas Stanley.

Of Martin Peerson (d. 1650) hardly anything is known, except that he was master of the choristers at St. Paul's Cathedral. His *Mottects or Grave Chamber Musique*, published in 1630, have an organ accompaniment and represent the transition from the madrigals to the later style; he had previously published *Private Musicke, or the Firste Booke of Ayres and Dialogues* (1620), and was one of the contributors to Leighton's *Teares or Lamentacions*, of which mention has been made in the last chapter. John Hilton the younger (1599–1657), parish clerk and organist of St. Margaret's, Westminster, wrote a small quantity of church and instrumental music, but is chiefly known by his *Ayres or Fa La's for three voyces* (1627), and his collection of *Catches, Rounds, and Canons* (1652), by himself and other contemporary composers. Christopher Gibbons (1615–76), the second son of the great Orlando, was organist of Winchester Cathedral from 1638 until the Civil War, and after the Restoration held similar posts at the Chapel Royal and Westminster Abbey. He wrote a considerable quantity of ecclesiastical and instrumental music, most of which still remains in manuscript; in 1653 he joined with Matthew Locke, fifteen years his junior, in the composition of the *Masque of Cupid and Death*.

John Jenkins (1592–1678) spent most of his life as a member of the households of aristocratic patrons, chiefly in Norfolk; he was a famous performer and wrote a very large quantity of instrumental music, in addition to some songs and anthems. Benjamin Rogers (1614–98), William Child (1606–97), and Matthew Locke (*c.* 1630–77) form links between this period and the next. Rogers, like Jenkins, was in his day famous chiefly as an instrumental composer, but he is now best known by his ecclesiastical music, of which he wrote a large amount: he was at different times chorister and lay-clerk at St. George's Chapel, Windsor, organist of Christ Church Cathedral, Dublin, and organist of Magdalen College, Oxford. Most of his church music seems to have been written after the Restoration; most of his instrumental music before. William Child (a pupil of Bevin at Bristol) was organist of St. George's Chapel, Windsor, and after the Restoration also became one of the organists of the Chapel Royal; he was primarily a church composer and wrote numerous services and anthems, as well as motets and psalms, but some secular songs and instrumental pieces are also in existence. Matthew

Locke may almost be counted as a composer of the Restoration period, during which most of his work was written, but for certain traits which, as we shall see, connect him rather more closely with his older than with his younger contemporaries. He started his musical life as a chorister of Exeter Cathedral, under Edward Gibbons (uncle of Christopher), and at the Restoration became composer in ordinary to Charles II. His compositions were very numerous and varied, including anthems and other church music, songs and incidental music for plays, and suites and other instrumental works; he was also a fluent and acrimonious pamphleteer.

The 'new music' inaugurated in Italy at the close of the sixteenth century by Caccini and Monteverdi and their school soon showed its results in England, though the English composers were less radical than the Italians; like the makers of the English Reformation they compromised. The Italian ideal of emotionally exact expression of intense dramatic feeling did not make the same appeal to English musicians of the early seventeenth century; no one thought of setting tragic extracts from *King Lear* or *Macbeth* as Galilei set the story of Ugolino from Dante's *Inferno,* and no one here argued, as Count Bardi's coterie in Florence did, about the nature of the stage music of the Greeks. But the principles of declamatory recitative were known and applied, and as early as 1617 Ben Jonson's masque *Lovers made Men* 'was sung (after the Italian manner) *Stylo recitativo,* by Master *Nicholas Lanier*; who ordered and made both the Scene, and the Musicke'.[1]

In the previous chapter we have seen, and remarked on, various signs of the coming change; but it was not till the end of the first quarter of the seventeenth century that the new order of things took even moderately clear form. The madrigals died hard; but once an organ accompaniment, even if optional, was admitted—as in the publications of Peerson (1630)[2] and Porter (1632)—the old form was extinct. Church music, it is true, drifted gradually into the new paths, but it was but little practised; solo vocal secular music was the chief, virtually the only, line on which the transition could

[1] Works, ed. C. H. Herford, P. and E. Simpson, vol. vii (1941), p. 454.
[2] The title-page of Peerson's *Mottects or Grave Chamber Musique* says that they are 'fit for Voyces and Vials, with an Organ Part; which, for want of Organs, may be performed on Virginals, Base-Lute, Bandora, or Irish Harpe.' Some slightly earlier works of Philips (published abroad) seem to show the earliest examples of the use of figured bass by an Englishman.

firmly be based. The music-lovers of the generation before the Civil War found their chief enjoyment in the masques, the origin of which has already been noticed. Popular as they had been in the reign of James I, they became more and more so under the auspices of his son; indeed, Charles I seems himself to have possessed considerable taste for the fine arts. Nearly every year saw the production of a new masque, and in some years as many as four or five were brought to performance; occasionally they were simply excrescences on plays, after the model of the masque in *The Tempest*, but more frequently they were independent and self-contained works. The one best known to us (though by no means a typical example) is Milton's *Comus*, produced, with music by Henry Lawes, at Ludlow Castle in 1634; but Shirley and the other lingering upholders of the Elizabethan drama brought out many works in which the traditions of Ben Jonson, Beaumont and Fletcher, Middleton, and the rest were faithfully carried on and combined with music by the brothers Lawes, Laniere, and other composers of the time. These masques (to the actual music of which we shall return later) were in no sense a new departure, as Italian opera was. Dramatically, the form was a natural development, and musically it was intimately connected with the great mass of songs with lute accompaniment. Neither at this nor at any other time does English music show anything like an artificial, theoretical creation of a new method.

The Civil War, and the consequent supremacy of Puritanism, altered the artistic aspect of England very deeply. The services in churches and cathedrals were suppressed, the choirs disbanded, and, at any rate in some cases, the organs and the libraries were destroyed by the soldiers of the Parliament; the blow to ecclesiastical music was very heavy, and there was no alleviation till the accession of Charles II. Nevertheless the Puritans have often been gravely maligned. In some cases, as at St. Paul's, York, and Lincoln Cathedrals, and certain colleges at Oxford and Cambridge, the organs (though they were forced to remain silent) were not even removed from the buildings, and no order to burn choir-books was ever authoritatively given. It is true that some extremists condemned music of every kind indiscriminately, and doubted the propriety even of unison psalm-singing in public worship; but Cromwell himself and many of his chief supporters were ardent music-lovers, and the vast body of Puritans never for a moment questioned the lawfulness of the ordinary practice of

153

the art, confining their prohibitions to profane music on the Sabbath, organs and choirs in churches, and stage plays.[1] Many, indeed —such as Prynne, the famous author of the virulent *Histriomastix* (1633)—while inveighing against what they considered the misuse of music, go out of their way to express their sense of the praiseworthiness of the art itself;[2] and there is abundant evidence that, though some of the extremists looked askance at it, ordinary secular music, both vocal and instrumental, flourished greatly during this period. Probably it flourished all the more in consequence of the suppression of other branches of the art; composers, unable to write anthems or services, turned necessarily to songs and instrumental pieces. There had been very little actual publication of music under Charles I (the energy of the publishers of the madrigalian era was extinct), but in the ten years from 1650 to 1660 a great number of works issued from the press; and, indeed, we may fitly date the never-ceasing stream of English music publications from the Commonwealth. Numerous, however, as these works are and valuable as is the evidence they afford of the widely spread practice of music under the Puritan régime, artistically they come to very little; the taste of English composers had sadly degenerated in fifty years.

John Playford, who afterwards became clerk of the Temple Church, was the first regular music-publisher in England. In 1651 he brought out a collection of folk-tunes, entitled *The English Dancing Master*, edition after edition of which continued to appear far into the eighteenth century; at first it contained 104 dance tunes, but later editions (which include some tunes that seem to be of foreign origin) were much enlarged. This was his first publication, and the great success of it and *A Musicall Banquet*—a miscellaneous collection of rounds and catches and pieces for viols, issued in 1651—encouraged him to proceed in his venture; in 1655 he brought out the first edition of *An Introduction to the Skill of Musick*, which remained a standard work for two or three generations, and, in addition to his new issues, he reprinted various older works, such as *Parthenia* and Michael East's fantasias for viols, besides selling 'remainders' of Elizabethan madrigals. The new publications included several volumes of *Ayres and Dialogues* by

[1] The evidence has been fully presented by Percy Scholes, *The Puritans and Music* (1934).

[2] 'That Musicke of itselfe is lawfull, usefull, and commendable, no man, no Christian dares denie, since the Scriptures, Fathers, and generally all Christian, all Pagan authors extant, do with one consent averre it' (*Histriomastix*, p. 274).

Henry Lawes and others (some being the work of several different composers), collections of rounds and canons, and of instrumental pieces, with some theoretical treatises.

The evasion of the law prohibiting stage plays is one of the most striking features of this musical activity. The Civil War had put an end to the court masques; but masques of a similar kind continued to be written for amateurs. One of the most important of these was Shirley's *Cupid and Death* (1653), with music by Locke and Gibbons. Further, in May, 1656, a sort of miscellaneous performance was given at Rutland House in London, with music by Henry Lawes, Colman, Cooke, and Hudson; this seems to have been an experiment to discover whether operas would be permitted, and, no objection being raised, the opera of *The Siege of Rhodes*, to a libretto by Davenant, and with music by Locke in addition to the four others just named, was produced in the following autumn. There were twelve singers and six instrumentalists, and the address to the reader claimed that they and the five composers were 'the most transcendent of *England* in that art, and perhaps not unequal to the best Masters abroad'. Another opera, *The Cruelty of the Spaniards in Peru*, was performed at the Cockpit, in Drury Lane, every afternoon for some time in 1658, and this was followed by *The History of Sir Francis Drake* in 1659. *The Siege of Rhodes* was revived in a modified form after the Restoration, but the popularity of the spoken drama prevented the immediate development of English opera.

Small as was the quantity of ecclesiastical music produced during this period, Barnard's *Selected Church Music*, published in 1641, is nevertheless one of the most important collections that we possess. The compiler was a minor canon of St. Paul's Cathedral and an ardent admirer of the great style that was rapidly passing away; his selection includes services (nearly all complete) by Tallis, Strogers, Bevin, Byrd, Ward, William Mundy, Parsons, Morley, Gyles, Orlando Gibbons, and Woodson—several of these being represented by more than one work—forty-two full anthems by Tallis, Tye, Byrd, Hooper, Farrant, Shepherd, W. Mundy, O. Gibbons, Batten, White, Gyles, Parsons, and Weelkes, and twelve verse anthems by Byrd, Ward, W. Mundy, Morley, O. Gibbons, Batten, and Bull. Barnard issued his work in ten part-books; no cathedral or library now possesses a complete set, but the British Museum has a manuscript score (Add. 30087) made from a collation of part-books from different libraries, aided by an organ-book of Batten (Tenbury 791). He had the intention of supplementing this compilation with another devoted to living composers; but the Civil War put a stop to his researches, and, indeed, the volumes we have were brought out only just in time. Apart from Barnard's work, these thirty-five years show very few issues of sacred music; there are a few volumes of psalms for private use by Child and the brothers Lawes, and one or two other things, besides several psalters with tunes.

Though the composers who were in the prime of life during this period, and are therefore included in this chapter, produced the majority of their church music after the Restoration, it yet seems on the whole most convenient to mention it here. And, indeed, though both Child and Rogers lived to be over eighty years of age and consequently outlived Purcell himself, who was under a year old when the Commonwealth came to an end, yet we can see in their work, and especially in that of Child, traces of the transitional period that are not visible in the anthems of the true Restoration composers like Purcell, Blow, Wise, or Humfrey.

Of the Anglican service music produced during Charles I's reign, which was very small in extent, the best example remaining is William Lawes's anthem 'The Lord is my light,' which was included in Boyce's collection. Here the massive ecclesiasticism of Gibbons has altogether disappeared; the work is simple and melodious and has strong echoes of the secular style of the time. But it is, nevertheless, clean and dignified; there are no forecasts of the methods which were popular a generation later, and the anthem is, in its rather slight way, distinctly attractive. Locke was another composer of rather later date, who, while devoting himself chiefly to secular work, also produced a few anthems. 'Lord, let me know mine end',[1] 'How doth the city sit solitary', or 'O give thanks unto the Lord'[2] are all earnest work, showing attempts at emotional expression, which, if somewhat aimless and meandering, are yet not at all without interest. They sound like sincere endeavours to do something outside their composer's natural methods. 'O give thanks' is, perhaps, the best, and, indeed, the florid recitatives *in tempo* for the bass voice, followed each time by the refrain 'for his mercy endureth for ever' for the upper voices, are quite good and effective, as

---

[1] Edited by E. J. Dent and C. B. Rootham (Year Book Press).
[2] Edited by J. E. West (Novello).

is also the way in which all the voices join at the end. But still, compared with even the less important anthems of the previous period, Locke's work comes to very little; the old order had gone and the men to lead the new had not yet arrived. Christopher Gibbons is another of these transitional figures; he has suffered the usual neglect which attaches to the son of an incalculably greater father, and very few of his compositions seem to have been published. But he is worthy of being better known than he is; in some ways, indeed, his anthems are more transitional than those of either William Lawes or Locke, inasmuch as, confining himself mainly to religious music, he has not, as they have, a fairly strong secular method on which to fall back. He wanders rather ineffectually between reminiscences of his father's style and echoes of the new church music that the younger men were writing for Charles II's court; but though the result of this vacillation is that hardly any work of his is really satisfactory all through, yet he often strikes forcible and expressive, if isolated, notes of his own. Occasionally, as at the opening of 'Above the stars my Saviour dwells':

Ex.99

A - bove the stars my Sa-viour dwells

he drops into a phrase which shows real power, and, we might almost say, grandeur; but then he will diverge into vagueness, and write roulades on the word 'and' in the middle of an otherwise quite sedate passage and perpetrate other things which show his curiously mixed state of mind. But he does not by any means deserve his present total neglect.

Child's earliest sacred publication was *The First Set of Psalmes* for three solo voices, with organ or theorbo accompaniment, issued in 1639. They may be considered as in some respects forming a bridge between the verse anthems of the madrigalian era and those of the Restoration; but in essentials they are far closer to the latter. The attempts at direct expressiveness forecast those of Humfrey thirty years afterwards, and the curious and rather crude realism of the florid setting of words like 'O thou most *high*,' or 'That she should *fly* as a bird' has also many parallels in the work of the next generation. The music is essentially declamatory, as that of the older composers never was; but at the same time there is dignity and restraint, and nothing too obviously secular. But in the better-known works of Child's later years we see, on the whole, a declension of ideal; in earlier days he could never have penned a work like the anthem 'Praise the Lord, O my soul', scrappy and altogether undistinguished, with an unpleasant sort of air of conscious modernity about it, and a poor 'gabbling Hallelujah'[1] at the end.

Child was indeed too advanced in years when the new style was introduced to assimilate it thoroughly; his psalms had broken with the old traditions, but his attempts to write 'cheerful music' of the new fashionable kind are usually somewhat forced. Occasionally, as in the eight-part anthem 'Sing we merrily unto God',[2] or in the E minor service, he makes a heroic endeavour to fuse the best elements of the old and new in one; and, in spite of lapses here and there, he manages it very successfully, though anyhow, in comparison with the work of men like Orlando Gibbons, the result is distinctly weak. As a rule Child's Restoration work shows him trying to fit himself to his times without a very clear idea of how to set about the process; he tries to paint individual words without any of the musical interest that mere vocalization may sometimes give to florid realism, as in this extract from the Creed of the Service in D:

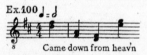

Ex.100

Came down from heav'n

or introduces fashionable dissonance, as in the Magnificat from the Service in E minor:[3]

Ex.101

the hun-gry with—— good things

He— hath fil - led— the hun - gry with good things

---

[1] This expressive phrase is quoted from Parry, *Oxford History of Music*, vol. iii (2nd ed., 1938), p. 272; he does not, however, mention this peculiarly typical instance.   [2] Edited by H. G. Ley (Novello).
[3] This is the reading of Oxford, Christ Church, 525, 1002, and 1246. Other manuscripts avoid the dissonance on the fourth beat of the second complete bar.

Indeed, musicianly as he can be when the necessity of being up to date is not before his eyes, Child must be counted as a distinctly second-rate composer. An exception is the Latin motet 'O bone Jesu',[1] of which we may quote the beautiful end:

This is full, from first to last, of real, solemn feeling expressed in modern but perfectly congruous terms.

The anthems and services of Rogers afford no problems. Though an almost exact contemporary of Child, and, therefore, also a great deal older than the leading Restoration composers, Rogers is more resolutely an adherent of the new order (he seems to have confined himself almost entirely to instrumental music in his earlier life) and his work shows none of Child's vacillation; he is a much more equable composer, and though never attaining anything like the height of Child's motets, never sinks quite so low. Still, we notice in some works, such as his Service in D, or his anthem 'Teach me, O Lord', a certain sort of dignified if somewhat dull solidity that shows that he was after all a son of the age of Gibbons; the old

[1] Edited by H. G. Ley (Novello). Fellowes (*English Cathedral Music*, p. 124) doubts the authenticity of this motet. On the other hand, it is ascribed to 'Dr. Childe' both in Brit. Mus. Add. 33235 and in Oxford, Christ Church, 14.

traditions died hard, and even in the work of a thoroughly un-imaginative composer like Rogers they still faintly linger. As we shall shortly see, the great geniuses of the new time, men like Purcell and Blow, could, when they pleased, write massive contra-puntal work of the highest kind, but with them it was a spontaneous effort; when Child and Rogers abandon their attempts to be melo-diously attractive, and endeavour to copy the 'grand style', the results almost always sound like rather unwilling reminiscences of the dominating traditions of their boyhood.

We might have imagined that the new methods of secular art, the external forms of which have already been described, would have resulted in something which, by its melodic and rhythmical attractiveness, would compensate, more or less adequately, for the loss of the older type; but when we examine the musical output of this time, in the secular as well as in the ecclesiastical field, our main feeling is one of great disappointment. We read Milton's son-net 'To Mr. H. Lawes on the Publishing his Airs':

> *Harry*, whose tunefull and well measur'd song
> First taught our English Music how to span
> Words with just note and accent, not to scan
> With *Midas* eares, committing short and long,

but, on looking into the ayres for ourselves, find it very hard to see anything to justify such enthusiasm. It is grossly untrue to say that Lawes was the first English composer to accentuate his words rightly; all the great madrigal writers (if we criticize their music, as we needs must, without allowing ourselves to be disturbed by any fettering idea of bar-lines) had a keen sense of 'just note and accent'. All that Lawes and his contemporaries attempted was to follow as closely as they could the rhythmical outlines of non-musical speech; they listened to their poet friends reading their own verses, and then tried to produce artificially exact imitations in musical notes. From the artistic point of view such proceedings are of course hopeless at the outset; they attempt to combine in-commensurable things. And indeed Lawes, like all his followers, is not consistent; sometimes he pulls up at the end of each line, after the fashion of the elementary reciter (compare Blow's well-known setting of these words):[1]

---

[1] *Ayres and Dialogues*, book i (1653), p. 22.

Ex.103 It is not that I love you lesse   Then when before your feet I lay,

But to pre-vent the sad en-crease   Of hopeless love I keep a-way.

sometimes he rambles on with absolute vagueness, following
another equally elementary model (the last bar of the quotation
is an echo):[1]

Ex.104 Im - bre la-chry-ma-rum lar - go, Ge-nas spar-go, qua-vis au-ro-ra;

De - us ci-to tu ve-ni-to, nunc nunc si-ne mo - ra, O-ra:

sometimes, as in the *Comus* songs, he copies reading of a cultured
kind, and sometimes (indeed quite frequently) he gives up his unnecessary problem altogether, and writes music which, whether
declamatory or lyrical, has no conscious concern with merely
literary considerations. In this last vein Lawes is at his best and
often writes music which, slender as it is, possesses a charming
fragrance of style, as, for example, this song, 'To his Mistress,
upon his going to travell':[2]

---

[1] Ibid., p. 36.
[2] Ibid., p. 20. The words are from Beaumont and Fletcher's *The Spanish
Curate* (1647).

Ex. 105

Dear - est, do not now de - lay me, Since thou know'st I must be___ gone; Wind and tide 'tis___ thought doth stay me, But 'tis___ wind that must be blown From thy___ breath whose___ na - tive smell In - dian___ o - dours___ doth___ ex - cell.

Historically, no doubt, these songs of Lawes are the direct precursors of the solo vocal work of the end of the century; but Purcell's declamatory rhapsodies show a largeness and mastery of handling to which these earlier composers never even approximately aspired.

Henry Lawes was much the most famous composer of his day, but it is very hard for us to see any qualities in his work which differentiate it in any noteworthy manner from that of his brother William or Laniere or Colman or Wilson, or indeed several others; in all there is the same attempt at refined expressiveness, the same slightness of technique, the same occasional charm and more frequent dullness. All, in addition to the songs (whether independent or forming part of masques), also wrote numerous monologues and dialogues, which resemble more closely than any other English music does the Italian *nuova musica* at the beginning of the century, insomuch as they strive to portray, for purely domestic use, histrionic or semi-histrionic situations of a classical, allegorical, or pastoral character; in the collections of the period we frequently find such items as a Lament of Venus over the body of Adonis, or of Ariadne when deserted by Theseus in Naxos, or dialogues between Charon and Philomel, between Time and a Pilgrim, between Cleon and Caelia or Sylvia and Thyrsis. Sometimes these innocent attempts at a sort of dramatic *vraisemblance* become almost comic, as, for example, in a pastoral dialogue, 'Did not you once, Lucinda,' by Colman,[1] where the bass voice explosively interjects the one word 'No!' at regular intervals; but, in the main, there are no differences between the styles of these pieces and of the songs, except that the purely lyrical view is very rarely, if ever, perceptible, even momentarily.

In the masque of *Cupid and Death*,[2] the joint work of Locke and Christopher Gibbons, and in Locke's opera *Psyche*, which, though produced during the reign of Charles II, belongs in musical essentials to the earlier period, we see this transitional style in its most ambitious shape. The former is, perhaps, the most elaborate of all extant masques, and contains, in addition to a large number of dances and other short instrumental pieces, some of which are very quaint and interesting, vocal music of all kinds—songs, both lyrical and florid, more or less declamatory recitative-like movements, and choruses, which are usually combined with solo work. The music to *Cupid and Death* does not seem ever to have been printed; but Locke's music for Shadwell's *Psyche* was published in 1675, along with some instrumental incidental music to *The Tempest*,[3] in which occurs a somewhat remarkable 'Curtain Tune', designed on an extended basis of a long *crescendo* and *accelerando* followed by a long *diminuendo* and *rallentando*, obviously dramatic in intention, and by no means unsuccessful. The title of the combined publication is *The English Opera*. In a long preface the composer, who had obviously an excellent conceit of himself, expounds the meaning which he attaches to the term—an amusing piece of vainglorious writing. *Psyche* itself is in fact an imitation of the *comédie-ballet* with the same title by Molière and Lully,[4] and the first of a series of 'operas' in which music was employed as a substantial supplement to spoken drama. The music recalls the pre-Restoration masques; occasionally there are tunes which forecast to some extent the melodic style of Purcell, as, for example, the fine swinging 'Song

---

[1] *Select Musicall Ayres and Dialogues* (1652), pt. ii, p. 12.
[2] Complete text in *Musica Britannica*, vol. ii.
[3] Edited by W. G. Whittaker (Oxford University Press).
[4] See E. J. Dent, *Foundations of English Opera* (1928), chap. vi.

at the Treat of Cupid and Psyche' in Act III, 'All joy to fair Psyche,' and the choruses are generally more or less simple and straightforward in manner, but, as a rule, Locke rambles along exactly in the general style of Lawes, and the fact that the work is designed for public stage presentation and not, like the old masques, for a private occasion, does not make the least difference. Sometimes, however, there are attempts at complex work of a type to which the amateurish talent of Lawes never aspired; a little chorus of devils in Act V is in six parts, and in the scene in the 'Rocky Desart' the 'Two despairing Men' and the 'Two despairing Women,' after alternating phrases in the ordinary style, join in a sort of canon '4 in 1'—but the result (as also in the case of a canon '4 in 2' in the *Tempest* music) is rather uncomfortable, and certainly suggests that Locke was not at home in counterpoint.

The sole work by any composer belonging to this period that attaches itself entirely to the madrigalian style is the collection of *Ayres or Fa La's* for three voices published by the younger Hilton[1] —'these unripe First-fruits of my Labours,' he calls them—in the year 1627, just at the close of the great time. These twenty-six pieces are full of dainty charm, and deserve to be much better known than they are; the variety of the *fa la* refrains (found in all except No. 17, 'When Flora frowns'), with their diverse rhythms and complicated cross-accents, is remarkable, and the best numbers, such as 'Fly, Philomel' (No. 25), 'Leave off, sad Philomel' (No. 11), or 'Now is the summer springing' (No. 19):

Ex.106

[1] *Musical Antiquarian Society*, vol. xiii.

are quite worthy of a place beside Morley's balletts, to which they bear, in general mood, a very strong resemblance. They are the last pure specimens of the style; Peerson's collection of 1630 has an organ part, which introduces a different tone, and Walter Porter's so-called *Madrigales and Ayres* of 1632 were furnished with 'Toccatos, Sinfonias and Rittornellos *to them*, after the manner of Consort *Musique*', and consequently represent a final break with the past.[1]

Hilton's name is now most familiar as the editor and part-composer of a collection of catches, rounds, and canons published in 1652 under the title of *Catch that catch can*. His delightful canon 'Come, follow me. Whither shall I follow?' is one of the most justly popular of all rounds. Many of these pieces were reprinted from three collections issued by Thomas Ravenscroft in 1609–11 with the fanciful names of *Pammelia*, *Deuteromelia*, and *Melismata*.[2] This purely secular development of the old ecclesiastical partiality for canonic writing had started at an early period in musical history; even if we omit 'Sumer is icumen in' from our consideration, yet it is plain enough that such highly elaborate and rhythmically complex early work as one of the four-part rounds on the 'Ut, re, mi, fa, sol, la' formula,[3] or the five-part 'Come follow me merrily, my mates'[4] must have had many predecessors, even though nothing of the kind

---

[1] For examples of Porter's work see G. E. P. Arkwright, 'An English Pupil of Monteverdi', in *The Musical Antiquary*, July 1913, pp. 236–57.

[2] All the rounds in Ravenscroft's collections have been edited by Peter Warlock (Oxford University Press).

[3] Ibid., p. 8.

[4] Ibid., p. 20.

was published before *Pammelia*. The Elizabethan dramas are full of allusions to the prevalence of catch-singing; very often no doubt this was of the merest elementary kind, as shown in the trivial production 'Hold thy peace, thou knave',[1] mentioned in *Twelfth Night* (ii. 3), which must have been very well within the powers of Sir Toby Belch and Sir Andrew Aguecheek, even in their most convivial moods. But the Ravenscroft collections contain many things of real artistic value, and *Catch that catch can* gave the initial impulse to a popular movement which for a hundred years or more flooded England with miniature works in this form—many, no doubt, mere bacchanalian effusions remarkable for nothing except the ingenious impropriety of the words, but many others (such as, in the present period, William Lawes's stately and beautiful 'She weepeth sore'[2]—perhaps the finest bit of work its composer ever produced), marked by musicianly feeling as well as technical skill, and, by the very nature of the medium, free from the rhythmical vagaries so often shown in the airs and dialogues.

The chief feature of the instrumental music during this period was the continued popularity of the fancy and the 'In nomine'. The most important composers of this form of concerted music were William Lawes and the versatile and long-lived Jenkins, described by Anthony Wood as 'the mirrour and wonder of his age for musick'.[3] Lawes was a finished artist with a very original turn of mind and a strongly developed feeling for the medium. The opening of one of his six-part fancies[4] will show clearly enough how far instrumental music had forgotten its vocal origin:

Ex.107

---

[1] Warlock's edition, p. 29.

[2] *Catch that catch can* (1652), p. 107.

[3] *Life and Times of Anthony à Wood*, ed. A. Clark (1891–1900), vol. i, p. 209.

[4] Printed in E. H. Meyer, *English Chamber Music*, pp. 265–70. The original is in Oxford, Bodleian, Mus. Sch. b. 2.

This is perhaps even more evident in the second section which begins:

Ex.108

* G in the original

The end of the piece is beautifully contrived, with the touching simplicity of the three-part writing rudely interrupted by the passionate outburst of the last three bars:

Ex.109

There is none of Lawes's extravagance in Jenkins; and if we were to take extravagance as the mark of originality, we should have to say that he was less original. His melodic invention, however, is genial and engaging, and he shows not only a subtle mastery of contrapuntal writing but also a very real sense of continuity. Only the reproduction of a complete composition would fully represent these qualities; but the opening of one of his four-part fancies[1] may give some idea of them:

Ex. 110

Jenkins also composed a large number of suites of dance tunes, as did Rogers, Colman, William Lawes, Locke, and others. Such music

[1] Edited by A. Mangeot (Augener).

was less ambitious than the fancy, but in its melodious courtliness it is often very attractive. Locke's compositions include a 'concert of 4 parts' which is in effect a set of suites,[1] each consisting of a fantasia followed by two dance movements and an 'ayre', and so combining the elements of the fancy and the dance-suite. The fantasias in these suites, often very expressive and closely knit, have many points of resemblance to Purcell's (see p. 211); it would indeed not be surprising if Purcell had used Locke as a model. The grave beauty of this extract from the fantasia in No. 5 would not seem out of place in a work by the younger composer:

Ex. 111

We also see occasionally the influence of the new style of the Italian trio sonata, for example in the opening of the fantasia in No. 2, which has very much the air of a canzona for two violins and continuo:

Ex. 112

[1] Edited by P. Warlock and A. Mangeot (Chester).

The violin, as we have seen, was accepted only with some hesitation as a serious instrument in its own right. Hence it is not surprising that the earliest English sonatas for two or more violins, bass viol, and continuo were the work of a composer who at the time was in foreign employment. William Young's sonatas (together with a set of dance movements) were published at Innsbruck in 1653, with a dedication to the Archduke of Austria;[1] only one copy is known, in the University Library at Upsala. The general plan of the Italian sonata is faithfully observed. Each sonata has several contrasted movements, including as a rule a fugal canzona and a slow movement in sarabande rhythm. The music on the whole is rather monotonous in style, and if it were not for the historical priority of the publication would hardly call for comment. One movement is unusual—the 'Resposte' in the eleventh sonata, where four violins and the bass viol have florid solo passages in concerto style above a simple supporting bass for the keyboard instrument. In England the violin had already been used in association with other instruments in a set of fantasias by William Lawes,[2] who died in 1645; these works are particularly interesting in having a fully written out part for organ or harp. It was not, however, until after the Restoration that the combination of two or more violins and bass viol, with or without *basso continuo*, came to be regarded as normal. Jenkins in his old age wrote a number of fantasias for two violins and bass viol which show an appreciation of the new medium remarkable in one of his years.[3] Here already are the clear outlines and pointed rhythms with which we are familiar in the continental music of the late seventeenth century. There is also some demand on virtuosity —the result, no doubt in part, of the brilliant execution of Thomas Baltzar (see p. 178). Indications of advanced technical accomplishment are also to be found in Christopher Simpson's fantasias entitled *Monthes and Seasons* for violin, two bass viols, and continuo.[4] The writing of elaborate parts for the bass viol was not peculiar to Simpson; Jenkins wrote a number of works in which considerable demands are made on the players.[5] The cultivation of the bass viol as a solo instrument at this period is in fact characteristic of English

---

[1] Edited by W. G. Whittaker (Oxford University Press).
[2] An example for two violins, bass viol, and organ or harp is printed in Meyer, op. cit., pp. 271–7. The original is in Oxford, Bodleian, Mus. Sch. d. 229, 238–40.
[3] For an example see Meyer, op. cit., pp. 288–93.
[4] Ibid., p. 226.   [5] Ibid., p. 222.

instrumental music and goes back to the early years of the century.[1] Alfonso Ferrabosco the younger, for instance, had published in 1609 a set of 'lessons' for one, two, and three bass viols. A particular result of this cultivation was the improvisation and composition of 'divisions on a ground', or florid variations on a bass. In the works of Simpson, their chief exponent, whose treatise *The Division-Violist* (1659) is authoritative, they were not only technically effective but designed with considerable taste and skill.

[1] See C. W. Hughes, 'The Music for Unaccompanied Bass Viol', in *Music and Letters*, July 1944, pp. 149–63.

VI

PURCELL AND HIS CONTEMPORARIES

THE short life of Henry Purcell (1659–95) has, from the biographical point of view, but little interest or variety. He was the son of Thomas Purcell, who became a gentleman of the Chapel Royal, a member of the King's private music and a composer for the violins, and died in 1682.[1] His younger brother Daniel, who died in 1717, was also a musician of some note, and the family talent descended to Edward, Henry's youngest son, and in a flickering manner to the fourth generation. The Purcell whose fame has extinguished that of his relatives entered the Chapel Royal as a chorister and studied successively under Cooke, Humfrey, and Blow; in 1679 he obtained the appointment of organist of Westminster Abbey, which he held till his death sixteen years later. He was also a composer for the violins, like his father, and one of the organists of the Chapel Royal. His works are very numerous, and include masterpieces in every department of music practised in his time; he wrote twenty-four odes (nine 'welcome songs' to Charles II and James II, six odes on Queen Mary's birthday, four odes for St. Cecilia's Day, and five for other occasions), music for forty-nine stage plays (ranging from a few interpolated numbers to complete operas), a great mass of anthems, services, and miscellaneous vocal pieces with religious words, another mass of secular songs, duets, trios and catches, and instrumental music, including (besides the theatre overtures and airs) sonatas for strings and keyboard, fantasias in three, four, five, six and seven parts, organ pieces, and a number of works of all kinds for harpsichord. Of all these the only works published during the composer's lifetime were the *Sonnata's of III Parts* (1683), the earliest of the St. Cecilia odes, *Welcome to all the pleasures* (1684), the music to *Dioclesian* (1691), songs from some of the dramatic music, and a number of songs and harpsichord pieces contributed to various collections. His widow subsequently published *A Choice Collection of Lessons for the Harpsichord or Spinnet* (1696), *A Collection of Ayres, compos'd for the Theatre*—instrumental pieces from the music to thirteen of the plays (1697), *Ten Sonata's in Four Parts* (1697), *Te Deum and Jubilate* (1697),

[1] See J. A. Westrup, *Purcell* (3rd ed., 1947), App. E.

172

and a large selection of songs of various kinds issued under the title of *Orpheus Britannicus*, the first editions of the two books of which appeared in 1698 and 1702. Later editions of these brought forward still more songs, after which publication ceased for a long time. The composer was also a theorist of distinction, as is shown in his elaborate work in the 1694 edition of Playford's publication *An Introduction to the Skill of Music*.

Cooke, Humfrey, and Blow have been named as Purcell's teachers; Henry Cooke (usually styled 'Captain' in remembrance of his rank in the Royalist army during the Civil War), was master of the children of the Chapel Royal from 1660 till his death in 1672, and accordingly, though an indifferent composer himself, had the earliest training of all the greatest musicians of the time. Pelham Humfrey (1647–74) was one of Cooke's pupils and became his son-in-law; in 1664 he was sent to France and Italy (his expenses being defrayed by Charles II out of the Secret Service funds), and on his return in 1667 was appointed a gentleman of the Chapel Royal, succeeding on Cooke's death in 1672 to the post of master of the children. Though he died at the age of twenty-seven, he left behind him a large quantity of anthems and secular vocal music; while still a boy at the Chapel Royal, he had joined with his fellow choristers Blow and Turner in the joint production of what is generally known as the 'Club Anthem'. John Blow (1649–1708) was two years his junior, and joined the Chapel Royal as a chorister about the same time; in 1674 he succeeded Humfrey as master of the children at the Chapel Royal, with which in various capacities he was connected till his death. He was also organist of Westminster Abbey from 1668 to 1679, when he made room for his pupil Purcell, on whose death, in 1695, he resumed the post, and held it for the rest of his life. He was a very voluminous composer in every branch of music except the dramatic, for which he wrote but little; a great quantity of his work is still, however, unprinted. William Turner (1651–1740) the longest-lived of this group of composers, was a native of Oxford and a fellow chorister of Humfrey and Blow at the Chapel Royal, of which he subsequently was appointed a gentleman, holding singing appointments also at St. Paul's Cathedral and Westminster Abbey; his compositions consist chiefly of church music and songs. Michael Wise (*c.* 1648–87) was another of 'Captain Cooke's boys', as they were called, and subsequently organist of Salisbury Cathedral, a gentleman of the Chapel Royal,

and master of the choristers at St. Paul's Cathedral; his principal
productions were for church use. Thomas Tudway (d. 1726) was
yet another of this distinguished band of choristers; most of his later
life was spent at Cambridge, where he was organist of King's and
Pembroke Colleges, and (from 1705) university professor. He composed a considerable quantity of church music, but is now best known
by the six large manuscript volumes of cathedral music of various
composers which he selected and edited for the Earl of Oxford.

Jeremiah Clarke was a Chapel Royal chorister under Blow, and
was probably born about 1673 (he sang at James II's coronation in
1685); he held at various times the appointments of organist of
Winchester College, organist, master of the children, and vicar-
choral of St. Paul's Cathedral, and organist of the Chapel Royal,
composing numerous anthems, odes, and other vocal works,
besides incidental music for plays and pieces for harpsichord. In
1707 he committed suicide in a fit of despondency caused by a
love-disappointment. John Golding[1] (c. 1667–1719) was a pupil
of Child, whom he succeeded in his post at St. George's Chapel,
Windsor; his compositions are almost exclusively ecclesiastical.

Two amateur composers of the time deserve mention. Robert
Creyghton (c. 1639–1734) was the son of the Cambridge professor
of Greek and Bishop of Bath and Wells, and showed hereditary
tendencies, succeeding his father in the professorship and holding
a canonry at Wells for sixty years. He was exclusively a composer
of services and anthems, but Henry Aldrich (1647–1710), dean of
Christ Church, Oxford, was more versatile, producing in addition
to his labours in both scholarship and architecture, secular vocal
music as well as a quantity for church use, and acquiring a valuable
musical library which he bequeathed to the college.

John Eccles (c. 1660–1735) is, on the other hand, known almost
entirely by his music for dramatic pieces, though he occasionally
attempted other styles. He started writing for the theatre in 1681,
and wrote assiduously for many years: but in later life he abandoned all composition except of the official odes which his duties
as Master of the King's Band required of him. The music to
D'Urfey's *The Comical History of Don Quixote*, parts i and ii
(1694) was the joint work of himself and Purcell.

The restoration in 1660 of the temporarily interrupted monarchi-

---

[1] For the spelling of his name see E. H. Fellowes, *Organists and Masters of
the Choristers of St. George's Chapel in Windsor Castle* (1939), p. 53.

cal régime had an immediate bearing on the musical life of the country; the organs in the churches awoke from their long silence, and there was on all sides an eager activity to unearth the forgotten anthems and services and to train up a new generation of choristers. The recovery did not take long; the old choir-books, though neglected, do not seem at all generally to have been destroyed, and in 1663 James Clifford, a minor canon of St. Paul's Cathedral, published a collection of the words of the anthems used there, which reached a second edition in the following year and comprised several hundred specimens from the times of Tye and White down to Humfrey and Blow, then mere children. But still the interregnum had done its work; it was not now possible for a church composer to revive the secret of the old style. The Puritan suppression of ecclesiastical music had given a powerful impulse towards secular forms; and when the Restoration composers began to write anthems and services, they found themselves irresistibly led to do so on lines much more akin to the declamatory solo songs than to the old continuous contrapuntal work. We have already seen, in the last chapter, the beginnings of this change in ecclesiastical music; but it was enormously accelerated by the régime of the Commonwealth.

Charles II's personal tastes had, no doubt, some influence. In his residence abroad he had acquired a great liking for the new French music; and one of his earliest acts after the new Chapel Royal had become firmly established was to send its most promising pupil, Pelham Humfrey, to France and Italy. He was also particularly fond of the violin; his string orchestra of twenty-four players was formed in imitation of the *Vingt-quatre violons du roi* at Louis XIV's court, and means had to be found for permitting it to play in the Chapel Royal services as well as in secular surroundings. And so a sort of authoritative standard of church music was set up, to include declamatory expressiveness, skilful solo vocalization and instrumental interludes—indeed, these instrumental sections were often so long and so entirely unconnected with the rest of the work that the worshippers must have found some difficulty in realizing that they were listening to an anthem at all. *Ritornelli*, as such, were not an absolute novelty (we find examples, though of a quite sedate and congruous type, in a considerable number of anthems of the madrigalian period), but the tone of the violins—'better suiting a tavern or playhouse than a church', as Evelyn says in his diary[1]—

[1] 21 Dec. 1662.

offended many persons who were quite ready to welcome the other features of the new style; however, after the accession of William III they disappeared for good from the organ-loft, and even in Charles II's reign they do not seem (if a remark of Tudway's[1] is trustworthy) to have been very much in evidence when the king himself was not present. But the declamation and the general preference of solo to choral work were essential and sharply differentiating elements of the new order.

The reopening of the theatres did away with the necessity for the subterfuges to which, as we have seen, the earliest English operas were indebted for their appearance; and consequently the opera, in the proper sense of the word, gave place to the tragedy or comedy with incidental music. In addition to the songs there was, however, a good deal of playing, both before the performance began and between the acts; indeed, many persons, we hear, used to come specially early so as not to miss the instrumental introductions.[2] But, partial as contemporary taste was to declamation and quasi-dramatic dialogue in domestic vocal music, there seems to have been a feeling that ordinary conversational speech was unsuitable for musical setting on the stage; Dryden[3] suggests that it should only be so employed when supernatural beings or heroes are concerned. We cannot, however, draw any hard and fast line between such musically illustrated plays and operas in the proper sense; Purcell's music to *Dioclesian*, for example, is so extensive in amount and so large in scope that it virtually overbalances the rest of the play. Moreover, masques still continued in favour during this period, and indeed considerably longer, though not to anything like the same extent as in the earlier part of the seventeenth century; and here, as before, the music continued to be an altogether essential feature, though—apart from those imbedded in the plays set by Purcell—nothing of real artistic importance was produced in the form.

Besides all this stage music of various kinds to English words, we see at this time the first beginnings of foreign influence in the dramatic field. Performances of Italian opera were planned more than once in Charles II's reign; and though the project came to nothing, a French opera, *Ariane ou le Mariage de Bacchus*, with

---

[1] Brit. Mus. Harl. 7338, fol. 2v–3.
[2] L. Magalotti, *Travels of Cosmo the Third, Grand Duke of Tuscany* (1821), p. 191.　　　　　[3] Preface to *Albion and Albanius* (1685).

music by Louis Grabu (an inferior protégé of Charles II) was performed in London in 1674, and a French company gave Lully's *Cadmus et Hermione* there in 1686.[1] Indeed, quite apart from Charles II's own artistic circle, there was in his reign a rapid extension of the knowledge of both French and Italian music in England. Nicola Matteis, a distinguished Italian violinist did much to make English listeners familiar with Italian instrumental style; and there can be no doubt that Purcell and most of his contemporaries were strongly affected by these influences. At the same time Pietro Reggio, a fashionable singing-teacher, was making for his friends collections of Italian vocal music, through which the knowledge of men like Carissimi and Stradella became widely diffused; and there was also a more or less continuous stream of amateurs who travelled to Paris or Rome and brought back with them news of the latest productions of Lully or Corelli. English music was in fact becoming a cosmopolitan art; though as yet there was not the very least sacrifice of anything individual in the endowment of our great composers.

The public concert, as an institution, dates in England from the Restoration period; previously music, unless ecclesiastical or dramatic in character, had been essentially the art of a small circle. The largess of aristocratic patronage and the profits of publication were the composers' rewards. But with the middle of the seventeenth century there came a change; the world of fashion tended more and more to be centralized in the metropolis, and, with the abandonment of the country coteries and quasi-feudal households of the nobility, the musician (unless attached to some provincial cathedral) found himself more and more obliged to be a Londoner, while the rapid advance of technical attainments, both instrumental and vocal, simultaneously produced a more marked differentiation between the professional and the amateur. It is in the latter years of the Commonwealth that we see the first signs of the new order; Oliver Cromwell gave State concerts at Whitehall,[2] performances in London taverns seem, if we may judge from a passage near the beginning of Pepys's diary,[3] to have been familiar occurrences, and at Oxford, where Anthony Wood's memoirs[4] give us the picture of

[1] See J. A. Westrup, *Purcell* (3rd ed., 1947), pp. 108–10.
[2] See Percy Scholes, *The Puritans and Music* (1934), pp. 49 and 143.
[3] 18 Feb. 1660.
[4] *Life and Times of Anthony à Wood*, ed. A. Clark (1891–1900), vol. i, pp. 204–6, 273–5.

a vigorous musical life, weekly concerts were held in six of the colleges as well as in private houses. The remarkable playing of Thomas Baltzar, a violinist from Lübeck, who came to England in 1656 and was, after the Restoration, appointed a member of Charles II's private music, gave a great impulse towards virtuosity. Public concerts after the Restoration began modestly with meetings in a house near St. Paul's Cathedral, where people could drink and smoke and sing catches and listen to organ music. These were followed, in 1672, by a series of concerts given at Whitefriars by John Banister, formerly one of the King's violinists, and later continued in other buildings. Here music, both vocal and instrumental, was performed, according to the original advertisement, 'by excellent masters' at four o'clock every afternoon, and the charge for admission was one shilling. Six years later Thomas Britton, an itinerant coal-dealer with a keen love for music, started at his house in Clerkenwell weekly concerts (at first open, afterwards with an annual subscription of ten shillings), which lasted till 1714 and grew gradually into very considerable fame (Handel was, in their last years, a frequent performer); while about 1680 a room in Villiers Street was opened and became much in request for fashionable performances, and before the end of the century we hear of several more. These concerts came to a culmination in the celebrations of St. Cecilia's Day (22 November), of which we first hear in 1683, and subsequently every year (with two or three exceptions) till 1703. They were managed by a body called the Musical Society, which commissioned a distinguished poet to write an ode in praise of music, and a distinguished composer to set it. This was performed at a concert given, from 1684 onwards, at Stationers' Hall; and, in addition to this, there was also, during the last ten years of the celebrations, a special service, with music of particular importance, at St. Bride's Church, Fleet Street. Among the poets who lent themselves to these occasions were Dryden and Congreve, and among the composers Purcell, Blow, Turner, Clarke, Eccles, and Daniel Purcell; and there is no doubt that they filled a very noteworthy place in the musical life of London. The celebrations after 1703 were of a much less regular character; Pope's well-known ode was written in 1708, but not set till long afterwards. Handel reset, in 1736 and 1739, both of Dryden's odes, written for the 1697 and 1687 festivals.

We may now proceed to discuss in some detail the actual music of the period. Blow, whose life covered the whole of it, is undoubtedly far the greatest of the Restoration composers, after his great pupil; and much of his church music[1] is of really noble quality, though some of the best still remains unpublished. He is by no means free from the mannerisms and weaknesses common in greater or less degree to all his contemporaries, even Purcell himself; he is by no means an equal composer, and his harmonic and structural technique is not always that of the assured master. But the finest of his anthems show him as possessing notable power, expressiveness, and individuality of utterance: 'I beheld, and lo, a great multitude'[2] and 'I was in the spirit' (an adaptation of 'And I heard a great voice'),[2] which for some reason difficult to understand are his most generally familiar works, are, however, far from representing him at his best—clean and stately though they are, they lack the marked originality of many others. The Services in A, G,[3] and E minor (especially the first) and anthems like the eight-part 'God is our hope and strength',[4] 'O sing unto God', or the six-part 'Sing we merrily',[5] contain much that is Blow's own—massive vigour and direct expression, combined with a harmonic inventiveness that, in spite of an occasional lapse, is usually as successful as it is novel; we cannot, indeed, doubt that he gave Purcell the lead in many directions where the younger man specially distinguished himself. But, as a rule, we see Blow's church music at its finest in the anthems where the words afford opportunity for pathos and deep feeling. 'O Lord, I have sinned' (written for the funeral of General Monk in 1670), 'O God, wherefore art thou absent?',[6] or 'My God, my God, look upon me' (1697):[7]

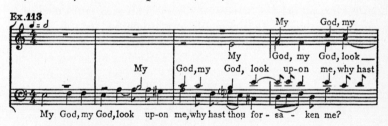

Ex.113

My God, my God, look up-on me, why hast thou for-sa-ken me?

---

[1] A list is printed in Grove's *Dictionary* (4th ed.), vol. i, pp. 396–8.
[2] Edited by V. Novello (Novello).
[3] The evening service edited by H. Watkins Shaw (Stainer & Bell).
[4] Edited by H. Statham (Oxford University Press).
[5] Edited by C. Macpherson (Novello).
[6] Edited by J. E. West (Novello).
[7] Edited by G. Bantock (Curwen). The composer's autograph is in Brit. Mus. Add. 30932, fol. 128.

contain a great deal of extremely touching music; the emotions are portrayed with tenderness and dignity, and the schemes are balanced and organic. Blow has, indeed, a singular gift for writing short phrases of quite exceptional expressiveness, as, for example, the opening of 'How doth the city sit solitary':

Ex.114

or this from 'Save me, O God':[1]

<hr>

[1] Edited by J. E. West (Novello).

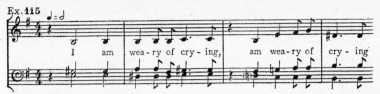

or other things in 'Turn ye to me', and, indeed, many other anthems. Some little-known Latin motets also show him in his best form: the five-part 'Salvator mundi'[1] is very powerful and massive, and four two-part motets on ground basses (a device particularly popular with English composers of this period) are most interesting: the first three are all on practically the same scale-subject, though in different keys and different rhythms, the fourth, 'Cantate Domino,'[2] is a specially fine brilliant work on a strong, swinging rhythm, beginning:

[1] Edited by R. R. Terry (Novello).   [2] Oxford, Christ Church, 14, fol. 109ᵛ.

Indeed, Blow's is really one of the outstanding names of English music; it is not difficult, it is true, to point to works where he has nothing very special to say for himself, and he is not altogether to be relied on for sustaining the interest of a lengthy piece from start to finish, but there are things in the best of his sacred compositions which can very well stand comparison with any contemporary music of any nationality.

Blow's two most famous fellow choristers, Humfrey and Wise, have left nothing behind them of such singular merit; but as Humfrey died at the age of twenty-seven, it may fairly be argued that he might have been one of the great men had he lived to fulfil his early promise. The anthems 'Have mercy upon me, O God', 'Hear, O heavens', or 'Like as the hart', may be taken as typical of his style, but, indeed, it varied hardly at all; in all his work we find a curious mixture of notable if not always perfectly convincing endeavours to be expressive and pathetic, combined with extreme scrappiness of structure and perfunctory instrumental interludes. Not infrequently he makes experiments in harmony, as in 'Thou art my King, O God', and 'By the waters of Babylon'. He might very well have steadied himself as he grew older; but, apart from certain pages here and there, where we see signs of something greater, his work leaves the impression of a highly talented but superficial youth, with whom desire for immediate popularity among the admirers of the new style was the strongest motive. Still, he was no doubt the pioneer of the declamatory and expressive church music, and he was a teacher of Purcell; and he might have done great things in opera, anyhow, had he lived. The opening of 'Like as the hart'[1] may be quoted as a typical example of his style at its best:

Ex. 117

[1] Oxford, Christ Church, 22, p. 80.

Wise's anthems are more mature and never give, as some of Humfrey's do, the impression that the popular effect is the one thing needful; he has more affinity with the older composers, and is much less affected by dance rhythms than Humfrey—while even when, as in the fresh, though very simple, 'Awake up my glory'[1]

[1] Edited by B. Luard Selby (Stainer & Bell).

he drops into them, he is somehow more of a solid musician. The anthem 'Thy beauty, O Israel'[1] shows him at his best—the expression is well-devised and sincere, and the section for bass solo, 'Ye mountains of Gilboa,' is a really fine piece of declamation:

Ex. 118

BASS SOLO

Ye moun - tains of Gil - bo - a, let there be no dew, no dew, nei-ther let there be rain up-on you nor fields of—— of-fer-ings

and there are some very beautiful things also in 'The ways of Zion do mourn'.[2] But Wise's art is, on the whole, of an indeterminate character; he never rises to any really steady loftiness of style, and has only elementary notions of structure. He deserves our cordial respect as an earnest and talented musician, but he was by no means a genius.

Much less so, still, were composers like Tudway and Turner, in whose anthems we see how decorously jejune the ecclesiastical music of the time could become in the hands of worthy but utterly commonplace men. Aldrich himself, widely cultured and versatile though he was, produced little that is worth rescuing from the great mass of his solidly dull pages, and Creyghton's 'I will arise',[3] though considerably more individual, does not come to very much. But it is notable how soon the specifically instrumental features of the Restoration anthem disappeared; it was only the popularity of solo music that proved lasting. Clarke and Golding come just at the end of the period, and in them we see already all the marks of the early eighteenth-century school, though they, like the rather younger and much greater Croft, show occasional traces of the methods of the men of a hundred years before. These are the more noticeable in the case of Golding, some of whose best works still remain unprinted:

[1] Edited by W. H. Harris (Novello).
[2] Edited by C. H. Kitson (Bayley & Ferguson).
[3] Edited by G. Bantock (Curwen).

we find in him, it is true, a good deal of the ordinary Restoration rhythmical and structural methods, but in anthems like the five-part 'Hear me, O God', or the six-part 'O Lord God of hosts', he gets back in the direction of the large contrapuntal designs, and becomes really fine. He has nothing like the genius of Blow (leaving Purcell altogether out of the question), but he seems to have been a close student of the work of both, and not only does he (as in anthems like those just mentioned) occasionally look back, as they sometimes do, to older ways of expression, but sometimes, as in the fine florid declamation at the beginning of 'O Lord my God!' or in the ground basses of the two-part verse anthem 'O Lord God of hosts' (an entirely different work from the six-part anthem with the same title), he copies Purcellian phraseology with singular exactitude. Golding is, indeed, an attractive sort of composer; he wrote, it is true, plenty of undistinguished music, but at his best he is worthy of more attention than he has usually received.

Clarke was a man of distinctly slighter calibre, though his facile melodiousness has kept several of his works alive. His 'Praise the Lord, O Jerusalem'[1] is very popular and superficial in tone, consisting of little tiny sections in different rhythms, loosely patched together, and technically very mild indeed; but 'I will love thee, O Lord',[1] and 'How long wilt thou forget me?',[2] the two others selected by Boyce for his collection, are considerably better. They show distinct immaturity of structural handling, and aim at nothing higher than a sort of agreeable charm; but they are clean and pleasing in their not very strong way and show some feeling for expressive setting of words. But Clarke is altogether a somewhat feeble talent; he possesses, with all his pleasant manners (which are quite adequate for some excellent hymn tunes), very little real artistic backbone, and somehow his music does not seem incongruous with his personal character as shown in his sentimental history. Perhaps Golding and Clarke might be considered to be more fitly coupled with the younger Croft at the head of the next period than at the close of this; but still they are in some ways closer to the main current of music during the lifetime of Purcell than to that of the succeeding generation, and it is by reference to the one supreme composer of the period that the places of the lesser men have to be judged.

[1] Edited by V. Novello (Novello).
[2] Edited by J. E. West (Novello).

Purcell touched, as no one else did, the music of his age at every point, and has left great works in every department; but it is eminently characteristic of the period that he was not, altogether, most at home in his church music. Not, indeed, that there is in any way the sort of discrepancy that we found between Byrd's sacred and secular work; Purcell produced the greatest religious music of his time, and it is only by comparison with his other work that we occasionally feel in it the pressure of certain conventions and a certain lack of spontaneity. Not even his genius could make a flawless artistic whole out of the typical Restoration anthem with its short disconnected movements, often varied by instrumental *ritornelli* (which many modern editors, with a scandalous lack of conscientiousness, reduce to minute fractions of the originals); and a considerable number of Purcell's anthems follow this artificial scheme, which is similar to that of the court odes. At the same time, in his earlier work he clearly modelled himself, with certain differences of idiom, on the pre-Commonwealth composers—for example, in the five-part 'Remember not, Lord, our offences', or in the six-part 'O God, thou hast cast us out'; and the eight-part fragment 'Hear my prayer, O Lord'[1] is a splendid piece of *a cappella* counterpoint, modern indeed in tonality but combining in the highest degree the strong massiveness of the older type with touching expression and flawlessly unified in design:

---

[1] Edited by J. E. West (Novello).

In some ways, indeed, this section of an incomplete work may fairly be taken as representing Purcell's anthems at their highest point; the average verse anthem, always open as it is to the temptation to write round the idiosyncrasies of individual voices, but rarely reaches the same austere grandeur. And even here he is not at all fairly represented by some of his best-known works; 'Rejoice in the Lord alway' (known as the 'Bell Anthem' on account of the descending scale which forms the ground bass of the introductory symphony)[1] or 'Behold, I bring you glad tidings' are little more than clean, naïve music, vigorous and pure, but without much that is really at all individual, and even anthems like the charmingly delicate 'Thy word is a lantern'[2] or the powerful and impressive

[1] *Purcell Society*, vol. xiv, p. 155.
[2] Edited by J. F. Bridge (Novello).

'They that go down to the sea in ships' hardly, taken as a whole, represent Purcell at his best. These last contain fine melody and noble declamation; but we miss in them the strong sweep that we see in other less popular works, like the above-mentioned 'Hear my prayer, O Lord', the superbly brilliant eight-part anthems 'My heart is inditing' (written for the coronation of James II)[1] and 'O praise God in his holiness'[2]—the former especially a very large work free from any trace of lively prettiness—or, in a totally different style, the grandly solemn and sombre funeral sentences—'Man that is born of a woman', 'In the midst of life',[3] with its wonderfully pathetic, half-realistic setting of 'the bitter pains of eternal death':

Ex.120

and 'Thou knowest, Lord, the secrets of our hearts' (the early setting),[4] with its vivid and expressive treatment of 'suffer us not at our last hour, for any pains of death, to fall away from thee.'

[1] *Purcell Society*, vol. xvii, p. 69. [2] Ibid., vol. xiv, p. 21.
[3] Ibid., vol. xiii*a*, p. 1. [4] Ibid., p. 6.

Purcell's anthems are indeed far more unequal than the sacred works of men like Byrd and Gibbons; he was torn two ways at once, as they never were. He was of an accommodating disposition, and does not seem to have had any rooted objection to producing what, after all, is artistically in some sense patchwork; not, indeed, that he ever, save in the very rarest instances, gives the impression of indulging in anything remotely like slovenliness, but he does not seem to concern himself, in many works, about more than the adequately musicianly treatment of details in each separate section as such. Indeed, of all great musicians, he takes, so to speak, the shortest views; but, nevertheless, as a rule, we feel this defect but very slightly in admiration of the loftiness and maturity of the expression and the earnestness of the handling of the materials in the portions where he really takes himself seriously. Apart from those that have been already mentioned, works like 'Blessed is he whose unrighteousness is forgiven',[1] 'O Lord God of hosts', 'Why do the heathen?',[2] 'Blessed are they that fear the Lord', 'Be merciful unto me, O Lord', 'O sing unto the Lord',[3] and others that might easily be named contain very noble music, rich sometimes in pathetic expression, sometimes in powerful solo declamation, sometimes in massive choral dignity. With all their imperfections, Purcell's anthems form a collection of splendid music, even if we feel that his true greatness is hardly, save for a handful of exceptions, represented in them to a really adequate extent.

Purcell seems to have been less attracted towards the Anglican service than most of his contemporaries, and all that he is known to have written for it is a Te Deum and Jubilate in D, an unusually complete Service in B♭, and an Evening Service (after the ordinary plan) in G minor;[4] but he is at a high level in them all. The real greatness of the first-named was very largely obscured till modern times owing to the fact that it was almost exclusively known merely through the strange edition of Boyce, who, in addition to unwarranted harmonic alterations, inserted many pages of what is purely his own work. The Jubilate is structurally the more shapely of the two pieces, the Te Deum showing a good deal of the scrappiness of design that we so often find in some of the Restoration composers' best music; but both alike contain much that is of a singularly massive brilliance, together with finely dignified expression and deep

[1] Ibid., p. 71.
[2] Ibid., vol. xvii, p. 1.
[3] Ibid., p. 119.
[4] Ibid., vol. xxiii.

restrained feeling. It is clear that Purcell, in spite of not infrequent lapses into structural fragmentariness and rather mechanical rhythmical formulas, recognized that the work was one that demanded some of his best efforts. And, indeed, in the great Service in B♭ we can see similar evidence that the old liturgical words made a strong appeal to him, seldom as (probably owing to the far greater scope for 'modern effects' available in anthems) he brought himself to set them; it was, perhaps, with a desire to associate his name with a uniquely monumental work in this field that he added to what was already a complete service (morning, evening, and communion) another, consisting of settings of the alternative canticles. Here again, though there are still occasional structural weaknesses unknown to men like Byrd and Gibbons, there are none of the court conventionalities of the 'popular' anthems; the music is both religious and human, and the fresh dignity of the whole exercises powerful fascination. Passing touches, in the cadences, of older tonal systems add a sort of flavour of delicate austerity; and yet the whole is essentially modern in sentiment, and there is none of that false antiquarianism into which many continental seventeenth-century composers so easily and so fatally lapsed. Purcell was always himself, however much he absorbed from his surroundings. The Evening Service in G minor also contains fine things, notably a long and really splendid Gloria to the Nunc Dimittis, but on the whole it is decidedly inferior to the B♭ service.

But to see Purcell's sacred music in what is perhaps its most striking aspect, we should turn from the anthems and services, magnificent as they often are, to the works written to religious words but intended apparently for private use. They are very numerous and of all kinds; we have dramatic scenes, 'hymns', sometimes for solo voices and sometimes for trio or quartet, and various untitled pieces, chiefly declamatory in character. Some of them may, perhaps, have been sung chorally, but they would seem to have been, at any rate originally, designed for single vocal parts throughout, and the writing is always unlike that shown in the full anthems. It is, indeed, as a rule more declamatory and, so to speak, rhapsodical than that shown in the solo portions of the average verse anthem, essentially flexible and unfettered by definite thematic material as the latter usually is; and in the few cases (such as 'We sing to him whose wisdom') where Purcell altogether abandons the style, the music is comparatively quite uninteresting.

Throughout all there are practically no connecting thematic links, save such as are afforded by the ground basses on which some of these pieces are built; we shall have further opportunities of seeing how markedly partial Purcell was to this particular structure, and these sacred vocal works show examples as fine as any of the better-known secular movements in the form. As a rule, the ground bass movements are for a solo voice, among which the exquisitely fresh and melodious 'Now that the sun' (an 'Evening Hymn'),[1] built up with astonishing ingenuity on a very straightforward figure:

is pre-eminent; but sometimes they are for voices in combination. The end of the four-part 'Beati omnes qui timent Dominum'—a very florid Hallelujah, with semiquaver scales, on an instrumental ground bass—is an interesting variant of the composer's ordinary methods, and the Hymn for two tenors and bass, 'Since God so tender a regard' is, though containing three movements, built throughout in simple but finely impressive style on the foundation of a ground bass, the middle movement being in $\frac{3}{2}$ time but keeping the same notes. Apart from cases like these, there is as little definite tunefulness in these hymns and scenes as in the anthems and services—Purcell seems to have considered regular flowing melody inappropriate to religious music as a rule; but there is one notable exception in the five-voice hymn 'Early, O Lord, my fainting soul', which is not remarkable save for a treble solo passage containing a splendidly swinging tune:

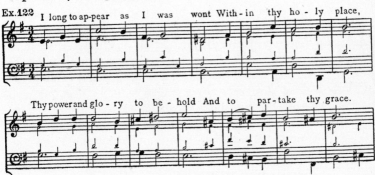

---

[1] Edited by W. G. Whittaker (Oxford University Press).

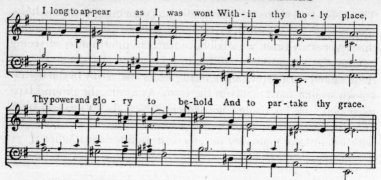

But undoubtedly the free declamatory style is the most typical. Works like the bass solo 'Awake, and with attention hear'—a sort of gorgeous rhapsody in a good many movements—the splendidly massive 'Awake, awake, ye dead' (a 'Hymn upon the last day' for two basses),[1] the fine sombre 'Thou wakeful shepherd' (a 'Morning Hymn' for soprano),[2] the powerful four-part 'O all ye people, clap your hands',[3] or the deeply pathetic and expressive 'O, I'm sick of life' for three voices and 'Ah! few and full of sorrow' for four:

Ex.123

[1] Edited by A. Moffat (Bayley & Ferguson).
[2] Edited by W. G. Whittaker (Oxford University Press).
[3] Edited by J. F. Bridge (Novello).

represent Purcell's genius in a form to which there is hardly any
parallel in the whole range of the art. There is no ostensible reason
anywhere why the music should continue in one way rather than in
another: and yet, somehow, the effect of the whole apparently in-
consequential work is thoroughly organic. The risks are enormous,
and no doubt in a very considerable number of cases we feel that
they have not been successfully met; but Purcell's best works of this
kind, whether to sacred or secular words, show very conclusively
to what heights pure rhapsody can attain in the hands of a great
master. It is strange that a work like 'Ah! few and full of sorrow',
with its extraordinary subtlety both of expression and of harmony,
is comparatively so little known; the dramatic scene 'Saul and the
Witch of Endor' ('In guilty night') is the most famous of these sacred
fantasias, but in spite of its simple dignity and its extremely impressive 'very slow' close, it is, as a whole, much stiffer than the others
already mentioned, and its superior reputation is only accidental.

One work indeed there is, and that one of Purcell's very greatest
masterpieces, that stands, so to speak, midway between the anthems
and the varied productions we have just been considering; this is
the psalm 'Jehova, quam multi sunt' for tenor and bass solos and
five-part chorus.[1] In this lengthy and most nobly imagined work—
the section 'Ego cubui et dormivi' is one of the most solemnly beautiful inspirations in all English music:

Ex.124

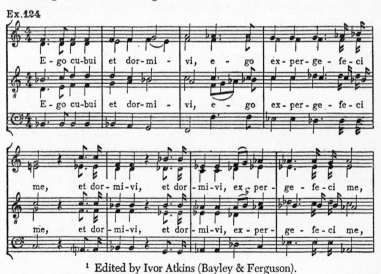

[1] Edited by Ivor Atkins (Bayley & Ferguson).

we see nothing of the conventionalities of many of the anthems, nothing of the ramblings of many of the hymns; the whole thing is firmly organized from start to finish, and there is not the least declension of ideal anywhere. If we were regrettably forced to pin our faith in Purcell as a religious composer on one work alone, it is to this psalm perhaps that most of those who are familiar with it would turn.

But to see Purcell in his most consistently individual mood we must turn from his religious compositions to those written for the stage. *Dido and Aeneas* (1689)[1] is the only dramatic production of his that can really be called an opera. All his others consist of more or less extensive incidental music to plays—the kind of work that no other great composer ever undertook except now and then. Though Beethoven's music to *Egmont* and Schumann's to *Manfred* show what they could do with congenial situations, a great deal of Purcell's activity in this line would have seemed to them hackwork below a serious composer's dignity; yet it was here that the flame of his genius burned brightest. The libretto of *Dido and Aeneas* is dramatically scrappy and often, indeed, ridiculous, but the music is full of varied characterization, from the great dying song of Dido

---

[1] Vocal score edited by Edward J. Dent (Oxford University Press). The full score published by the Purcell Society (vol. iii) is not wholly reliable.

(which has always, and very justly, been one of Purcell's most famous things), or the very tender and graceful last chorus 'With drooping wings ye Cupids come', to the swinging sailor tunes or the picturesque witches' scenes. The composer's favourite triple syncopated rhythm is noticeable at once in a tune like this:

Ex.125

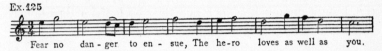

Fear no dan-ger to en-sue, The he-ro loves as well as you.

and, indeed, all through the opera Purcell is already the individual genius; but, mature though it certainly is, it does not show (apart from Dido's unsurpassable 'When I am laid in earth') his very greatest qualities. On the other hand, in the incidental music to *The Prophetess, or the History of Dioclesian* (1690), *King Arthur* (1691), and *The Fairy Queen* (1692), we see the composer at his best almost from their first pages to their last; and splendid as is much of the work for other plays, it is these that most of all deserve our close attention.

Dioclesian[1] (as the first of these is now usually known) is most familiar by the masque, which forms practically the whole of the music to the fifth act; but the earlier portions contain much that is equally fine. The overture is not, indeed, much of an exception to the rule that these movements are less interesting than other portions; but the second of its three sections, though as usual partially fugal in style, is remarkable as being built throughout on a continued ♫ ♫ ♫ ♫ rhythm, without the least disguise or cessation from start to finish. But the short 'act tunes' and other dance-measures scattered about the play are far finer and include some of Purcell's most charming work in this line, in which he was so especially at home; the chaconne at the beginning of the third act, written for two recorders in canon over a ground bass, is specially ingenious, and the 'Butterfly dance' in the following act shows him at his daintiest. It is true that the 'soft music' during the arrival of the 'dreadful monster', and the thunder and lightning dance of the Furies, seem very mild today; Purcell had very little capacity for the blood-curdling. But we readily pass over these comparative failures and turn rather to such things as 'Let the soldiers rejoice', or 'With dances and songs', or 'What shall I do to show how much I love her?'—all

[1] *Purcell Society*, vol. ix.

typically lyrical tunes, with finely organized phrases; and in the alto solo with trumpet obbligato 'Sound, Fame, thy brazen trumpet sound', we find a different style, consisting of massive florid writing (above a surging *moto perpetuo* bass) that leads in splendidly digni- fied manner to the large chorus 'Let all rehearse in lofty verse', which strikes a more powerful and, so to speak, epic note than the rest. But the masque is on the whole the most individual portion of *Dioclesian*; from Cupid's first wonderful phrase:

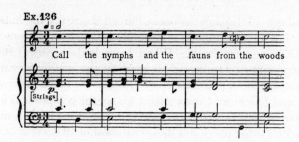

Ex.126

Call the nymphs and the fauns from the woods

[Strings]

to the stirring trio, 'Triumph, victorious Love' and the brilliant little chorus that follows, it is crowded with lovely dewy music, some of the most polished and fascinating that even Purcell ever wrote, and full of an open-air freshness that hardly any one else in the history of the art has succeeded in attaining so perfectly. And there is no lack of contrast; the rollicking Bacchanals and the amorous shep- herds are equally brilliantly portrayed, and swinging as the rhythms always are their varieties are endless.

The incidental music to *King Arthur*[1] is generally recognized as Purcell's masterpiece, and on the whole it deserves its reputation; though it would be easy to find equally fine numbers in many other works, yet perhaps none is so steadily large in style all through. The overture in the minor key, in two movements and for strings alone,[2] is, as in *Dioclesian* and elsewhere, much less interesting than the rest of the work; but on the other hand Purcell never wrote any- thing more finely organized than the spacious passacaglia in the fourth act, the structure of which is very remarkable. Like all pas- sacaglias, it is on a ground bass throughout, but it differs from

---

[1] *Purcell Society*, vol. xxvi.
[2] Another overture, also in two movements, but in D major and with the addition of trumpets to the score, is attached to the work in some copies. It is borrowed from the birthday ode for Queen Mary, *Arise, my Muse* (1690).

nearly all others in being a combination of numerous vocal and instrumental pieces. First there is a long instrumental introduction, which is followed by a beautiful song (of which there is no trace in the introduction), 'How happy the lover', set for soprano solo and repeated by chorus, still on the same bass; then we have another long instrumental ritornello, with the ground bass somewhat varied —sometimes more florid in various ways, sometimes inverted. Then there is a duet for soprano and bass soloists with the ground persisting still, but now in a simpler form; a new chorus on the ground in its original form follows and is succeeded by a trio for 'three nymphs' (with the ground inverted, and slightly altered after two repetitions) and that by a trio for 'three sylvans' (with a simplified form of the ground, not inverted). Then the nymphs sing again over the ground in its original form, and a chorus (with the ground first varied and finally as at the start) ends this astonishing piece; technically there is nothing finer in all the music of the period, but perhaps, apart from 'How happy the lover', the actual thematic interest is not at the level of the less definitely ingenious parts of the work. But in all the acts we have pages that make irresistible appeals to all music-lovers alike: the powerful sacrificial scene, the charming wayward fairy music of Philidel and Grimbald, the scene of Cupid and the Cold Genius, with its picturesquely realistic shivering vocal effects, are all, in their very different ways, unsurpassable examples of Purcell's grasp of situations as wholes. And then there are the immortal tunes—'How blest are shepherds' (notice the delicious way in which the 'drums and trumpets' are expressed):

Ex. 127

How blest are shepherds, how hap-py their las - ses, While drums and trumpets are sound-ing a - larms. O - ver our low - ly sheds all the storm pas - ses,

And when we die 'tis in each o-ther's arms, All the day on our herds and flocks em-ploy-ing, All the night on our flutes and in en-joy-ing.

and 'Fairest isle, all isles excelling', and other less-known melodies, like 'Love has a thousand ways to please', with its entrancing first phrase (from the dialogue 'You say 'tis love creates the pain'), or a delicate piece of quasi-declamation like the duet 'Two daughters of this aged stream are we'. We have indeed no specimens of that peculiar, almost gossamer-like daintiness that we find pre-eminently in *Dioclesian* and *The Fairy Queen*; but on the other hand we have qualities of perhaps a somewhat stronger kind which those works do not exhibit, at any rate to the same extent.

Yet it is conceivable that many Purcell-lovers, if they were by some painful necessity reduced to parting with all his works save one, would cling longest to *The Fairy Queen*,[1] the text of which is an adaptation of Shakespeare's *A Midsummer Night's Dream*. Until the beginning of this century only a few selections from the very large work had been previously published (and that only during Purcell's own lifetime) and the complete score had indeed been given up as lost till it was discovered in the library of the Royal Academy of Music. All this mass of incidental music shows, it is true, comparatively little variety of mood, for which the dramatic situations give no opportunity; there is little evidence of the serious side of Purcell's genius and comparatively little evidence of his technical brilliancy. Yet perhaps no long work of his is so absolutely crowded with melody; tunes as purely lyrical as any in existence meet us on wellnigh every page. The little instrumental pieces, the 'Dance of the Followers of Night' (a delightful double canon), the dances of 'The Green Men', 'The Haymakers', and so on—songs like

[1] *Purcell Society*, vol. xii.

'Sing while we trip it', 'See, even Night herself is here', 'If love's a sweet passion', 'Now the night is chas'd away', 'Here's the summer, sprightly gay'—all these, if indeed they strike no emotionally deep vein, are unsurpassable for sheer grace; and occasionally Purcell diverges into somewhat different channels, as in the extraordinarily clean and strong duet for two altos 'Let the fifes and the clarions', the vigorous florid soprano solo 'Hark! the ech'ing air', which has all the Handelian vocal brilliance without any of his not infrequent conventionality, Winter's remarkable song, 'Next Winter comes slowly', largely based on the chromatic scale, or impressive ground bass movements like 'O let me weep' (rather of the type of Dido's great song in *Dido and Aeneas*), and the alto song for a Chinese man, 'Thus, thus, the gloomy world'. The scene of the drunken poet and the fairies has throughout unusual characterization; it is full of real humour and fresh charm, and the fairy music is exquisite. Indeed, no one, save Mendelssohn, has equalled Purcell in that particular sort of lightness of style that such work demands, if it is to be really successful; and this music of the older composer's may worthily stand by the side of the best portions of the masterpiece, inspired by the same play of Shakespeare, that was written some century and a half later.

But, indeed, the wealth of music that Purcell scattered up and down these Restoration plays is wellnigh endless; literary considerations never seem to have affected him in the least (probably the atrocious manglings of Shakespeare left him totally unmoved), and he set anything to which he was asked to put his hand. It is really only a series of accidents that have preserved to our concert audiences gems like the Ariel songs from *The Tempest*,[1] or 'Nymphs and shepherds' and 'In these delightful pleasant groves' (both from *The Libertine*[2]), or 'I attempt from love's sickness to fly in vain' (from *The Indian Queen*[3]), more than others which are really quite as entrancing, or powerful declamatory *scenas* like 'Let the dreadful engines' (from *The Comical History of Don Quixote*, part i[4]), or 'Ye twice ten hundred deities' (from *The Indian Queen*[5]), more than others of equal dramatic splendour; while just occasionally, as in the case of 'Britons, strike home' (from *Bonduca*[6]), music which is a little more obvious than Purcell

[1] Ibid., vol. xix, pp. 132–45.   [2] Ibid., vol. xx, pp. 45 and 51.
[3] Ibid., vol. xix, p. 74.   [4] Ibid., vol. xvi, p. 143.
[5] Ibid., vol. xix, p. 49.   [6] Ibid., vol. xvi, p. 80.

usually is has acquired, probably owing to patriotic words, a fame that, in comparison with other work, it hardly deserves. Similarly, the so-called 'Golden' sonata has, purely by reason of its name, supplanted—for concert-goers—the whole of Purcell's other chamber music. The researcher among the original sources for this mass of music will find unexpected treasures everywhere; the ghost scene in *Oedipus*[1] is quite superb from start to finish, and the extended music to *The Indian Queen*, again, shows exceptional power, especially in the trio 'What flatt'ring noise is this, at which my snakes all hiss?',[2] where two of the three voices sing only the last word, with remarkable effect. Things there are no doubt which are more or less perfunctory and uncharacteristic, the sort of work that any capable contemporary composer could have turned out; but, on the whole, especially considering Purcell's extraordinary fertility, the average level is very high—higher, indeed, than that of the majority of the great composers. All these dusty plays, with their scanty blossoms of poetry among acres of bombast, owe wellnigh all of whatever vitality they possess to the fact that Purcell wrote music for them. The instrumental music forms, indeed, the best and most complete evidence we have of his system of harmony and part-writing in general, as such a large mass of his other work is set down merely with figured basses. The overtures themselves are nearly always rather ordinary in style; but the 'airs' and dances are of inexhaustible interest. Perhaps a bourrée from the music to Congreve's *The Old Bachelor*[3] may be quoted as typical of the ordinary style of the more lively specimens:

Ex.128

---

[1] *Purcell Society*, vol. xxi, pp. 1–18. [2] Ibid., vol. xix, p. 37.
[3] Ibid., vol. xxi, p. 29.

The spontaneous charm of these little pieces, harmonically polished in every detail, according to Purcell's own very individual methods, is really astonishing; and it says much for Restoration playgoers that they could appreciate work of this kind, even though it claimed merely to be a more or less unimportant adjunct to the drama, while the fact that it was published separately in *A Collection of Ayres, compos'd for the Theatre* would seem to show that it was familiar quite apart from the original contexts.

Apart from Purcell's works, the most notable dramatic production by a composer of this period is Blow's elaborate *Venus and Adonis* masque,[1] which clearly influenced *Dido and Aeneas*. Though Blow was decidedly most at home in sacred music, this is a very interesting work, and interesting not only in its merits but in its defects; on the one hand, we have charming and really distinctive music, like the 'Gavatt' of Graces, or especially the final scene for Venus and chorus, 'With solemn pomp let mourning Cupids bear' (which is in Blow's best style), and on the other we have a certain amount of crudity. The harmony is not always convincing; there are occasional moments when the scheme of tonality seems to fall to pieces, and the tunes, pleasant though they are usually, are inclined to meander along anyhow, without showing any particular trace of the sort of organized balance that Purcell exhibits as a rule, even in his freest declamation. But, nevertheless, the work is, as a whole, well worth attention; stiff and uncertain as parts of it are, there is yet much that is really fresh and individual; we may notice some curious quaintnesses, as this passage from the 'Cupids' lesson' scene in Act II:

[1] Edited by Anthony Lewis (Lyre-Bird Press).

201

Ex.129

or the laugh of Venus a little later, which is a typically modern vocal effect:

Ex.130

Although it is called a masque, *Venus and Adonis* is in effect a miniature opera, set to music throughout. It acknowledges a double debt—to French instrumental music and to the Italian chamber cantata.

The stage music of John Eccles also deserves a few words; overshadowed as he was by Purcell, with whom he sometimes collaborated, he yet possessed a fresh and not undistinguished talent, though somewhat unpolished and narrow in scope. His work for *The Comical History of Don Quixote*, parts i and ii, published together with Purcell's, has many points in it; his song for Sancho Panza, "'Twas early one morning,'[1] has a sort of jovial dashing vigour that is quite attractive, though the difference in maturity of touch between it and Purcell's emotionally very similar 'Song sung by a galley-slave' ('When the world first knew creation') is unmistakable. And, similarly, the song on a ground bass in Eccles's 'Dirge':

---

[1] Printed without a bass.

Ex.131

Couch'd___ in the dark and si-lent grave,

contrasts rather badly with Purcell's work of the kind; there is plenty of expressiveness, and the bass is excellent, but he cannot quite handle his material. Nevertheless, Eccles could write very pleasantly in his way—the song 'A soldier and a sailor'[1] from the music to Congreve's *Love for Love*, for example, has a first-rate swing about it; and, though he cannot compare with his great contemporaries, his popularity was by no means undeserved.

Purcell's odes form an important section of his compositions, and they contain some of his very finest work, however much we cannot avoid regretting that a great genius should have lent himself to the enhancing of these reams of loathsome flattery of whatever sovereign happened to be on the throne, and other royalties, down to the Duke of Gloucester, aged six, to whom an ode of specially sickening adulation is inscribed. Of the six birthday odes for Queen Mary[2] the third, 'Welcome, welcome glorious morn', dating from 1691, contains some very beautiful tunes, such as 'To lofty strains her tuneful lyre she strung' (written for a high bass, with numerous top G's) and 'I see the round years successively move', and is throughout strong music, more individual and more lyrical in its flow than the 1689 and 1690 odes, clean and vigorous though they are. Its successor, 'Love's goddess sure was blind this day', has an intimate, even elegiac, character which is in marked contrast to the pompous magnificence of the odes for 1693 and 1694. The latter of these, 'Come, ye sons of art away', is a splendid work, unfortunately known to most music-lovers only by the infectiously buoyant duet for two altos, 'Sound the trumpet'. The concluding section, 'See, Nature rejoicing has shown us the way', for soloists and chorus, is a remarkable example of Purcell's genius for creating significant melodies out of the simplest material. The music seems to bubble

---

[1] Printed (without the words) by Hawkins, *A General History*, &c. (1875 ed.), p. 786.

[2] *Purcell Society*, vols. xi and xxiv.

over with happiness. The 'welcome songs' for Charles II and James II[1] also show plenty of fine work, though, in general, less mature in style than the Queen Mary odes. There is everywhere evidence of technical assurance and of an instinct for contrast. The music is not a mere counterpart of formal compliments; it has a vivacity and picturesqueness that rise above the empty conceits of the text. Particularly remarkable are the frequent orchestral ritornellos, often very subtly organized, which show a consistent mastery of instrumental style. The alternation of strings and recorders in the welcome song for the Duke of York, 'What, what shall be done in behalf of the man?' (1682), is very happily contrived:

Ex.132

A word is also due to the Duke of Gloucester's birthday ode 'Who can from joy refrain?',[2] written in 1695 and so one of its composer's very latest productions; the alto solo 'A prince of glorious race descended', founded on a ground bass and succeeded by a long

---

[1] *Purcell Society*, vols. xv and xviii.   [2] Ibid., vol. iv.

instrumental section on the same subject, is notably fine stately music, and the whole ode (though it contains no tunes of outstanding merit) shows Purcell in a brilliant vein.

In addition to these royal *pièces d'occasion* there are the well-known 'Yorkshire Feast Song' ('Of old when heroes'),[1] and the series of odes written for the festivities of St. Cecilia's Day. D'Urfey, the author of the words of the Yorkshire Ode, has recorded his opinion that it is one of the finest compositions that Purcell ever made,[2] and the view has found general acceptance. It is a breezily joyous work from start to finish, and is memorable for tunes like the strenuous, swinging alto song 'Sound, trumpets, sound', or the lovely tenor air on a ground bass 'So when the glitt'ring queen of night'. For the St. Cecilia's Day celebrations Purcell wrote altogether five works—the already-mentioned Te Deum and Jubilate in D (1694), a Latin hymn 'Laudate Ceciliam' (1683),[3] and three odes, 'Welcome to all the pleasures', 'Raise the voice', and 'Hail, great Cecilia';[4] of these three the first was written for the inaugural festival in 1683, the second is undated,[5] and the third was produced in 1692. The Latin hymn is a work of an unusual type that seems to be based on specific Italian models, and it is partly written in notes of the old shapes, probably to give a sort of ecclesiastical look to the page. The form is curious, and is as follows:

1. Symphony.

    (*a*) A sort of Maestoso; common time, in the usual dotted rhythm.

    (*b*) A $\frac{3}{2}$ movement, no doubt faster.

2. (?) Chorus (three parts) in the same rhythm as No. 1 *b*, and really a continuation of it.

3. A sort of Largo; florid writing for three solo voices.

4. A bass solo, leading to a repetition of No. 2.

5. Repetition of No. 1 in its entirety.

6. A movement for three solo voices, less florid and with more ensemble work than No. 3.

7. Repetition of No. 2 in its entirety.

This is a very interesting attempt at elaborate structural unity, and is hardly paralleled elsewhere in the English music of the period,

[1] Ibid., vol. i.   [2] *Songs Compleat*, vol. i, p. 114.
[3] *Purcell Society*, vol. x.   [4] Ibid., vols. viii and x.
[5] Two manuscripts of subsequent date mention 1683 as the year of production; but this seems highly unlikely in view of the indubitable fact that 'Welcome to all the pleasures' was written for that occasion.

whether by Purcell himself or by any other composer; and apart from this fact the work contains, with all its markedly Italian influences, a great deal of really individual and highly attractive material. It is, indeed, considerably finer, on the whole, than the two earlier of the English odes, bright and effective though they are; in 'Welcome to all the pleasures' we may specially notice the charming short final chorus, and in 'Raise the voice' the section 'Mark, mark how readily each pliant string'—first a soprano solo, then a three-part chorus, and then a 'symphony', the whole being built up, with great ingenuity, on an elaborate ground bass. But the great 1692 ode is of altogether different quality; it was apparently recognized at the time as one of its composer's masterpieces, and it has always remained one of his most famous works, even if we feel that some of his others show him in more subtle mood than was possible in a composition of a decorative and ceremonial character. It is far larger in style and scope than the others; its fine florid recitatives are equal to any Purcell ever wrote, and the whole work is marked by a sort of spacious brilliance of an exceptional kind. The details are frequently elaborate and always highly effective, and every part is finely organized in a straightforward way; not, indeed, that the words receive, or really admit of, any special subtlety of treatment, but there is no smallness of style anywhere and the whole bears the unmistakable impress of distinction. The score displays some interesting orchestral features; the instrumental prelude is unusually extended and complex, consisting of no fewer than six movements; (1) a sort of pompous fanfare, (2) a 'Canzona'—here a double fugato, (3) a section entitled 'Adagio' in the dominant minor key—a sort of sarabande, (4) a busy allegro movement, (5) a short 'Grave' in the tonic minor, (6) No. 4 *da capo*. Altogether Purcell seems in this ode to have set himself consciously to plan on large lines; there are very few of his works which show so much deliberate desire to impress, even if we, for whom there is no longer the attraction of technical novelty, may feel that, in spite of all its beauties, it must yield in individuality of appeal to other works of which possibly Purcell's contemporaries thought less enthusiastically.

Blow, like Purcell, wrote a number of odes for the court and for the celebrations of St. Cecilia's Day, but seems to have been less able to adapt himself to circumstances: the music, on the whole, does not reach a very high level. Earlier than any one of these is the setting of Cowley's 'Awake, awake, my lyre',[1] written for Oxford in 1678 and performed there in the following year. Like much of Blow's work, it does not reveal a very strong personality; its mildly elegiac flavour is hardly a match for Cowley's fervent verse. But its simplicity and gravity are a welcome change from the pomposity of much of the ceremonial music of the time. A number of the separate movements from Blow's odes were published in the collection of his songs entitled *Amphion Anglicus* (1700), which seems to be arranged on a definite plan, in so far as it opens with a rambling 'Prologue'[2] and ends with an 'Epilogue', 'Sing ye muses', for four voices and two violins. No doubt the volume cannot compare with Purcell's *Orpheus Britannicus* in general interest; Blow's touch is much less sure and his inspiration less steady. But still the average music-lover of today, who knows the volume merely by the beautiful minuet song to Waller's words, 'The self-banished',[3] does Blow a great injustice; stilted though a good many pages are, there are many others that show really individual melody and fine, solid workmanship. Among the best may be mentioned 'Shepherds, deck your crooks'[4]—a beautifully dewy and fresh piece for solo and chorus, very well designed, and throughout strikingly light in touch, with a delightful *moto perpetuo* bass—or 'Rise, mighty monarch',[5] a fine, massive declamatory bass song (from the New Year's ode of 1684, 'My trembling song awake')—or the breezy, pastoral two-part song 'Bring, shepherds, bring the kids and lambs' (from a wedding ode)—or the vigorous setting of the familiar satirical poem, 'Of all the torments'—or the buoyant 'Song upon the Duke of Gloucester', son of Princess Anne, built on a good

[1] Edited by H. Watkins Shaw (Hinrichsen).
[2] The words are quaint:
> Welcome, welcome, ev'ry Guest:
> Welcome to the Muses' Feast:
> Musick is your only cheer,
> Musick entertains the Ear:
> The sacred Nine observe the Mode,
> And bring you dainties from abroad:
> The delicious *Thracian* Lute,
> And *Dodona's* mellow Flute,
> With *Cremona's* racy Fruit,
> At home you have the freshest Air;
> Vocal, Instrumental Fare.
> Our English Trumpet nothing has surpast.
[3] *Old English Edition*, vol. xxiii, p. 16.
[4] Ibid., p. 26.
[5] Ibid. p. 12.

nautical sort of ground bass—or the bass song, 'Arms, arms, arms, he delights in', with a really splendid opening, which has all Purcell's power of declamation, and yet is individual—or 'The fair lover and his black mistress',[1] from which we may quote a few bars in illustration of its finely flowing and organized tune, full of vigorous life and spirit:

It is true that Blow cannot somehow, save in a handful of exceptional cases (such as the last of these), sustain himself at his best level throughout a song; phrases which a superior genius would have turned to first-rate account are left in, so to speak, a straggling condition, and many of the tunes seem somehow just a little less good than they might have been. Blow's real greatness was shown in other fields: in the long dedication to Princess Anne of Denmark prefixed to *Amphion Anglicus* he says of his '*Church Services*, and *Divine Compositions*': 'To those, in truth, I have ever more especially consecrated the Thoughts of my whole Life. All the rest I consider but as the Blossoms, or rather the Leaves; those I only esteem as the Fruits of all my Labours in this kind.' Yet he had

---

[1] *Old English Edition*, vol. xxiii, p. 1.

plenty of ideas, and sometimes, indeed, is curiously advanced in technique; the song 'Musick's the cordial of a troubled breast', accompanied by two violins and bass (from the 1684 ode for St. Cecilia's Day, 'Begin the song') has a real look of Bach, with its interweaving part-writing, and its solo bass voice sometimes doubling the instrumental bass, sometimes curling round it, and sometimes quite independent, making pure four-part harmony quite after Bach's model.

The collections of the time, such as *The Banquet of Musick*, *Deliciae Musicae*, and the rest, are full of solo songs, but they are nearly all little more than weak reflections of those of Purcell and Blow, and require hardly any notice. Occasionally, as in Humfrey's 'I pass all my hours in a shady old grove',[1] or, at the other end of the period, several songs of Clarke, we strike a vein of melody which, if not very strong, is, nevertheless, individual; and here and there, even among the works of quite inferior men, we come across something good, as, for example, the really notably beautiful, as well as very clever, 'Be gentle, Phyllis, since I'm yours'[2] by Berenclow, finely organized on an exceedingly simple ground bass. But to wade through these volumes is, on the whole, a monotonous task; Purcell did everything so much better than any one else.

The number of Purcell's songs and duets which never, so far as we can definitely judge, were intended for insertion in a play or other extended production is over 130;[3] but apart from 'Bess of Bedlam' ('From silent shades') very few are familiar even by name save to professed Purcellian students. It is a pity that singers have not the enterprise to explore this treasury. Things like the two-part 'When Myra sings', with its exquisite end, the glowing 'Anacreon's defeat', the powerful 'Fly swift, ye hours', the very impressive 'O solitude, my sweetest choice', on a ground bass, and plenty of others, contain most beautiful music; and a self-contained section of a lengthy 'Elegy on the death of Mr. John Playford' ('Gentle shepherds, you that know') may be quoted in full as one of its composer's most tender and pathetic pages—the skill with which the accentuation of the ground bass is varied is typical of Purcell's methods:

[1] *Choice Songs and Ayres*, book i (1673). Edited by L. Bridgewater (Boosey & Hawkes).
[2] *The Banquet of Musick*, book vi (1692).
[3] *Purcell Society*, vols. xxii and xxv.

Ex 134

There are numerous catches and rounds, usually of a more or less definitely bacchanalian character, by Purcell[1] and his contemporaries scattered up and down Playford's various collections; but it is only occasionally that the coarseness of the bulk of the words is redeemed by any special point or humour in the music, which, as a rule, lacks both the *finesse* of the earlier type and the pleasant cheerfulness of the best examples of the later. Sometimes, it is true, we meet with really astonishingly brilliant little things, but, on the whole, these pothouse effusions add nothing worth mentioning to the artistic reputation of either Purcell or any of the others. The preface to the *Pleasant Musical Companion* can complacently remark that the pieces contained in it 'will neither give Offence to the nicest Judgments, or be ingrateful to the most delicate and distinguishing Ears';[2] but, except for the sake of completeness, we might, indeed, have left the whole of these trifling compositions unmentioned.

In the instrumental music of the period Purcell is again by far the greatest figure. The fantasias for viols, written when he was twenty-one, are perhaps his most remarkable achievement. There are three in three parts, nine in four parts (all carefully dated), one in five parts,[3] and two 'In nomines' in six and seven parts respectively. In writing works of this kind Purcell was following an old tradition, of which he was in fact the last practitioner. But though the general plan of the pieces is traditional, the idiom is often surprisingly up to date. In these fantasias he brought to a dying art a burning sincerity and a vivid imagination rarely found in works of this kind. The opening of the fifth four-part fantasia will serve to illustrate the sinewy polyphony which Purcell made the vehicle of his ideas and which he wielded with such skill and assurance:

Ex. 135

---

[1] *Purcell Society*, vol. xxii.
[2] Quoted from the fifth edition (1707).
[3] The fantasias in three, four, and five parts are edited by P. Warlock and A. Mangeot (Curwen).

A passage from the first four-part fantasia, more homophonic in style, is characteristic of his sense of colour and the range of his harmonic vocabulary:

Ex. 136

* The E♯'s in this bar are written as F♮ in the original.

There is a marked difference of style in the twenty-two trio sonatas, written in the new Italian manner of which Purcell himself was so ardent an advocate. Though twelve of them are described as being in three parts and the remaining ten in four, there is really no such difference as this would suggest, as all are alike written for two violins and bass viol or violoncello, with organ or harpsichord doubling the bass and also supplying harmonies on the lines of the indicated figures. The *Sonatas of III Parts*[1] are on the whole distinctly slighter and less interesting works than the others, though their structure is on the same general lines. No. 6 in C major, with the ingenious twofold augmented canon in its opening movement, is, perhaps, the finest, though there are plenty of other striking movements, such as the charming Canzona of No. 3 in D minor and the impressive Largo of No. 9 in C minor. But the *Sonatas of IV Parts*[2] are of altogether more important calibre; though we see, in general outline, the plan of four alternating slow and quick movements (beginning with a slow one) which, later on, became the classical sonata form in Bach and Handel, yet Purcell often enlarges and alters. No. 6 in G minor consists, indeed, solely of a very long and remarkably fine Passacaglia on a five-bar ground bass theme, the irregular rhythm of which secures all the needed variety, even though it is never even once transposed or altered, as is very often the case with the composer's ground bass pieces; and of the other nine all but one are in five movements (even if we may not count Nos. 3, 5, and 7 as being in six, short as the extra sections are), while Nos. 7 and 9 begin with a quick measure and so display still more flexibility of design. While it is true that Purcell does not in these works show his full individuality as we can see it elsewhere, yet in a sense they are his most serious efforts; there is not the faintest trace of any desire to please any one but himself, and no scrappiness of structure. He was working on Italian models rather than giving free play to his own ideas, and consequently the typical Purcellian note is hardly sounded fully in these sonatas; but there are splendid things everywhere, and Purcell can by no means altogether succeed in hiding himself behind his serious counterpoint. Fugal subjects like these from Nos. 4 and 7 respectively of the second set:

Ex.137

Ex.138

are full of a sort of breezy directness that reminds us of many things in the theatre music, and, indeed, all over these sonatas we find pages of massive joyousness expressed with singularly clear-cut workmanship, varied by charmingly delicate sections like the last two of No. 2, or the final Vivace of No. 8—a piquant outburst on a *moto perpetuo* bass, which is a delightful contrast to the fine long Largo that precedes it; but on the other hand there are not a few pages which are relatively characterless and, so to speak, vaguely cosmopolitan. Extremely fine as are the best things in these sonatas, and polished as they all are right through, Purcell required something else than abstract Italian models to arouse his most individual powers.

But we must not depreciate his harpsichord music,[1] which, like the sonatas, contains very beautiful things—as a rule slighter and daintier than the works we have just been examining and less influenced by 'serious' models. In these little suites and dance-like pieces we come much nearer Purcell's typical methods, though nearly all are designed on a tiny scale; the *Choice Collection of Lessons*, in particular, is bright with a sort of dewy freshness of singularly attractive quality, and some of the 'Grounds' rise to higher flights, while at the same time retaining the individuality of utterance more definitely than most of the sonatas do. Indeed, we could not find any solo instrumental music of the seventeenth century, whether in England or on the Continent, showing finer qualities, both of design and expression, than this Ground in C minor:[2]

Ex.139

where the refrain alternates with subtly expressive variations, and there are not a few others, such as the delightful 'Ground in

---

[1] *Purcell Society*, vol. vi.   [2] Ibid., p. 51.

Gamut',[1] that fall very little, if at all, short of this. Indeed, this solo work is, for distinctive qualities, comparable with nothing in the same medium in English music, save a small handful of the best work of the madrigalian era, to which, indeed, it is much superior; by the very nature of the instruments for which it was written, it could not aim at anything like grandeur, but it caught what it did aim at with both its hands and held it fast.

Certainly no other composer of Purcell's time came even approximately near rivalling him in this respect; Blow's genius seems to have collapsed entirely when he dealt with instrumental forms. The next best harpsichord composer of the men born under the Commonwealth or Charles II was Clarke,[2] whose work is indeed more vital, slight though it is, than the more ambitious productions of the older men like Rogers. A collection of suites published in 1707 is not without considerable expressiveness of a somewhat mild kind; and the *Choice Collection of Ayres for the Harpsichord or Spinett* (1700), the joint work of Clarke, Blow, Croft (see p. 243), and two quite unimportant composers named Francis Piggot and John Barrett, contains a few tiny things of Clarke like the 'Trumpett Minnuett', 'The Serenade', and two or three marches (one, 'The Prince of Denmark's March', is entitled 'Round O', viz. Rondo), which are really, in their evanescent style, extremely fresh and spirited, and much brighter than anything else in the collection, which is, as a whole, decidedly dull and both melodically and harmonically lacking in notable quality. It is of interest, however, to note that the music is prefaced by some 'Directions to the Learner', from which we gather that the contemporary way of fingering the scale of C major was to use the thumb only once in two octaves (in either hand), two of the middle fingers being continually passed one over the other; this was also, we know, the fingering adopted by Purcell. The thumb was only just coming into use in England; the figures employed were 1, 2, 3, 4, 5, the first indicating the thumb of the right hand, but the little finger of the left.

The main feature of the whole of the music of the Restoration period is the emergence of the art into the full atmosphere of secularity and publicity; the old church chains were definitely snapped,

[1] Ibid., p. 33.
[2] Modern editions in J. A. Fuller Maitland, *The Contemporaries of Purcell*, vol. v (Chester), and *At the Court of Queen Anne* (Chester).

and with them also went (purely accidental as was the connexion) the old intimate appeal to the few. Now the appeal was gradually becoming more indiscriminate; gradually there becomes visible the pressure on a composer to write to satisfy an audience, to underline his effects, to do something or another to secure success among his inferiors in artistic knowledge. The great men fought on the whole manfully for the rights that are the indefeasible heritage of every creative worker who preserves his self-respect; but they could not altogether stem the current, and sometimes indeed they were swept away by it. It is not believable that a supreme genius like Purcell could have been personally satisfied with the scrappiness of some of his work: it is obvious enough that it was written, in as musicianly a style as he could, to satisfy the rather elementary tastes of people who could not bring their minds to grasp organisms of any sort of largeness. No doubt, as a general rule, the music of Purcell's time preserves a certain dignity of manner and at its highest rises, as we have seen, to sheer splendour; but still there is an element of uncertainty about it. Virile and subtle as it is, it is not always immaculate in taste; it is of extraordinary interest, but it leads virtually nowhere. What might have been the course of English music, but for Handel's influence, it is idle to speculate; certainly Purcell's genius had no immediate successor, but his music was widely reverenced, and might have borne great fruit, had it been allowed free scope. As it is, English music of the last quarter of the seventeenth century is an artistic cul-de-sac.

VII

HANDEL IN ENGLAND

I⊤ is a singular fact that the composer who has left the deepest impress on English music should have been a German who came to this country as an upholder of a purely Italian art; and yet, even if his influence had been evanescent, it would be difficult for a historian of anything less than the whole of music to rank him as other than an English musician. George Frideric Handel lived in or near London for over forty-five years; and he was a naturalized Englishman. Few music-lovers know, and fewer ever hear, a note of the music that he wrote either in Germany or in Italy; it was exclusively for English audiences that he wrote every work in virtue of which he is one of the great composers, and of all these few seem to have been performed abroad during his lifetime, high as was the honour in which his name was always held. After the nine arias to religious poems by Barthold Heinrich Brockes,[1] which probably date from 1729, Handel never set a line in his native language; from that time forward he was, so far as his countrymen by birth were concerned, artistically dead.

It was as a writer of Italian opera that Handel came to England; but this fashionable exotic was then of very recent growth. Purcell's influence had apparently died with him; *Dido and Aeneas* had opened the way to a land of promise, but no one seemed sufficiently interested in the prospect to proceed any farther. And so, with that curious partiality for the musical traditions of any nation but its own that the English public has so often shown, the music-purveyors of the time turned to Italy for something fresh. It was not indeed the first time that Italy had influenced English vocal art. The madrigals of Marenzio and Croce and Gastoldi and other Italians of the period were, as we have already seen, well known in this country and had much bearing on the secular music of the Elizabethans; and Purcell himself declared, in the preface to his *Sonatas of III Parts* (1683), that he had 'faithfully endeavour'd a just imitation of the most fam'd Italian Masters'. But the English madrigal, though the original idea was foreign, was the natural expression of the

---

[1] Edited by Herman Roth (Breitkopf & Härtel). For the date see Max Seiffert, 'Händels deutsche Gesänge', in *Liliencron-Festschrift* (1910), pp. 297–314.

genius of some of our greatest men, and Purcell's music was far more than a mere copy of the Italian style; Italian opera in England, on the other hand, remained to the end of its days an 'exotick and irrational entertainment'.[1] It was exotic, not so much because the majority of the listeners did not understand the language—the music was the chief thing to which to listen, and they could easily learn what the words were about—but because it was strangely believed that no other language was admissible for artistic opera; and it was irrational, because the composer's own designs were fettered at every turn by the necessity of conciliating the singers. The musical world has never seen a race of men and women whose outlook was so entirely bounded by the horizon of their own little vanities as the great vocal stars of the early eighteenth century; solo singers have indeed been as a rule, up to a time that is within living memory, artistically the lowest class of musicians, but the full-blown, tyrannously selfish conceit of the *prima donna* and *primo uomo* of Handel's day was something quite unique. On pain of a displeasure which would have wrecked the whole concern, the composer had continually to be writing his music round the particular voices of Cuzzoni or Faustina, Caffarelli or Farinelli, affording suitably frequent and varied opportunities for personal display, minimizing mutual jealousies, and consequently letting the organic features of his work take care of themselves; opportunities for anything like dramatic characterization were few and far between, and the net result was a collection of stereotyped airs strung together by the slenderest threads. The audiences cared nothing for the story of the opera, even if they could have understood the formal recitatives in which the actors carried on the narrative (which were indeed practically invariably omitted on publication); the entertainment was simply a concert with scenery and costume, in which singers competed strenuously with each other for the favour of the arbiters of taste and fashion.

Had Italian opera in England not been supported by the genius of Handel, it is quite possible that it would have perished in its earliest infancy; before Handel's arrival in 1710 its validity was very precarious. Italian musicians had been attached to the courts of Charles II and James II, but the invasion of the concert world seems to have begun in 1693, when the *London Gazette* announced

[1] Samuel Johnson, *Lives of the English Poets*, ed. G. B. Hill (1905), vol. ii, p. 160.

that 'the Italian Lady, that is lately come over, who is so famous for her singing' would sing at York Buildings every Tuesday, and at Freeman's Yard, Cornhill, every Thursday, throughout the season; Signor Tosi, the celebrated author of a treatise on singing, gave a 'Consort of Musick' in Charles Street, Covent Garden, in April of the same year, and was emboldened by its success to do the same weekly, at York Buildings, throughout the ensuing winter.[1] In the subsequent years we hear of occasional similar concerts by Italian singers; at the beginning of the eighteenth century they became increasingly frequent, and in 1703 Signora Francesca Margarita de l'Épine gave a series of 'positively last' appearances throughout the summer season,[2] but nevertheless remained in England for many years, and was one of the chief stars in Handel's earlier operas. At one of her appearances at Drury Lane Theatre on 5 February 1704, a servant of Mrs. Tofts, a rival singer, hissed and threw oranges at her, and was thereupon taken into custody by the police; Mrs. Tofts wrote to the *Daily Courant* indignantly denying all complicity,[3] but no one seems to have believed her. This is probably the earliest instance of operatic jealousy in England; later on it was usually expressed more adroitly. In 1703 and 1704 there were a few attempts to return to the old type of English opera; an act of Purcell's *Fairy Queen* was performed, Locke's *Psyche* was revived, and *Circe* was given with the addition of 'Bacchanalian Musick'.[4] A 'new Entertainment of Vocal and Instrumental Musick (after the manner of an Opera)', called *Britain's Happiness*, was also produced at the Drury Lane and Lincoln's Inn Fields theatres in two versions, the former the joint work of Weldon and Dieupart, the latter solely by Leveridge.[5] But the run of these works was very short, and on 16 January 1705, *Arsinoe*, a regular opera 'after the Italian manner: All Sung', was produced at Drury Lane; the music seems to have been adapted from various Italian songs by Thomas Clayton, who had been a member of the Royal band in the previous reign. The words were taken from an Italian libretto some thirty years old, but the whole performance was in English, except for some Italian songs before and after the opera by Signora de l'Épine; indeed, the English public does not seem to have had the least wish for the Italian language

[1] *London Gazette*, 9 and 23 Jan., 3 Apr., 26 Oct. 1693.
[2] *Daily Courant*, 29 May, 8 June 1703, &c.
[3] Ibid., 8 Feb. 1704.
[4] Ibid., 29 Jan. 1703, 8 June, 13 July 1704.
[5] Ibid., 22 Feb., 7 Mar. 1704.

in itself, and it was only the superior merit of the Italian-speaking singers who visited England in increasing numbers that ultimately banished from the opera-houses the language of their frequenters. The first opera to be sung in Italian, Jakob Greber's *Gli Amori d'Ergasto*, was produced at the opening of the new theatre in the Haymarket on 9 April 1705,[1] but it was nearly five years before it had a successor. The transition was gradual: when *Camilla*, written by Marc' Antonio Bononcini (a younger brother of the more famous Giovanni Battista), one of the most celebrated of contemporary Italian operas, was first performed in England on 30 March 1706, with much success, it was sung in English; on 6 December 1707, however, a bilingual performance was given, three of the vocalists (including Valentini, one of the earliest of the *castrati*) singing in Italian and the rest in English. Similar performances were frequently given for the next year or two, Alessandro Scarlatti's *Pirro e Demetrio* (in which Nicolini, a famous *castrato*, first appeared in England) sharing with *Camilla* and a pasticcio entitled *Thomyris* the chief popular honours. The nationalists tried to hold their own with a handful of productions, including an extremely poor setting of Addison's *Rosamund* by Clayton (1707). But the fashion set by the wonderful voices of the singers who knew no language but Italian grew rapidly too strong to be resisted; in January 1710 *Almahide*, sung wholly in Italian apart from English intermezzi, was produced, and was quickly followed by Francesco Mancini's *L'Idaspe fedele* and a year later by a pasticcio called *Etearco*.[2] With the production of Handel's *Rinaldo* on 24 February 1711, English opera, though never becoming altogether extinct, meekly tendered its submission.

Though Handel, who was born at Halle in 1685, was only twenty-five at the time of his first appearance in England, he was already a musician of great and wide reputation, both as composer and as executant. While resident in Hamburg between 1704 and 1706 he had produced numerous works of importance with much success; and during his subsequent stay of from three to four years in Italy, where he visited all the principal cities, his pen had been busy with operas, oratorios, serenatas, psalms, motets, and a mass of smaller

---

[1] See A. Loewenberg, *Annals of Opera* (1943), p. 58.

[2] The composer of *Almahide* is unknown, but Burney (op. cit., vol. iv, p. 211) is inclined to attribute it to Bononcini. No. 13 of *The Spectator* may be consulted for an amusing account of Mancini's work; 'the lion in *Hydaspes*' was a famous butt for a long time.

things, both vocal and instrumental. Of all these the opera *Agrippina*, brought out at Venice in 1709, was the most brilliantly successful; and the enthusiastic approbation of Prince Ernest Augustus of Hanover and of several English noblemen who happened to be in Venice at the time had no doubt much to do, firstly with Handel's appointment as Kapellmeister to the Elector of Hanover six months later, and secondly, with the warm welcome he received when, having obtained leave of absence from his duties, he came to England in the autumn of 1710.

Rinaldo (in which music from earlier operas was incorporated) met with a success that altogether dwarfed that achieved by any previous opera in England; but Handel only stayed in London seven or eight months, and then returned to Germany. The duties of Kapellmeister at a quiet court, however, were not to his taste; the applause of a large public was throughout his whole career the breath of life to him, and the autumn of 1712 saw him back again in London. *Teseo* rivalled *Rinaldo* in popularity, and Handel forgot altogether about his duties on the other side of the Channel; he wrote a patriotic *Te Deum* for the celebration of the Peace of Utrecht, received a life pension from Queen Anne, and settled down comfortably to a pleasant existence, enjoying the favour of the court and aristocracy and the friendship of all congenial spirits in the society of London. When his neglected master ascended the English throne as George I, there was naturally a withdrawal of royal support; but ultimately the truant was forgiven and his pension augmented.

For more than half of all the years that Handel spent in England he was *par excellence* a writer of operas. Fortune varied; sometimes he lived in the full sunshine of popular success, sometimes the expenditure considerably overbalanced the receipts—indeed to the extent of the virtual bankruptcy of the composer, who added to his musical activities those of the impresario. From 1717 to 1720, when no Italian operas were given in London, he lived at the country seat of the Duke of Chandos near Edgware, occupying himself mainly with *Acis and Galatea*, the *Chandos Anthems*, and the masque of *Esther*, which later became his first oratorio; but till he was over fifty years of age opera was his main pursuit. Indeed, he only ultimately turned his attention elsewhere in consequence of the disastrous effects due to a combination of rivalries—a competing opera house under the musical direction of Giovanni Battista

ini, supported by an influential section of the nobility, and
cratic success in the shape of *The Beggar's Opera* (1728),
a piece made up of popular melodies gathered from all sources,
which drew crowds to the theatre in Lincoln's Inn Fields. Against
his ill fortune he struggled for some time; but in 1732 a revival of
Esther (in concert form) had met with great favour, and had turned
his thoughts into other channels. By 1735 he had not explored the
new vein farther than *Deborah* and *Athaliah*, both of which were
produced in 1733; but he continued to perform these oratorios on
Wednesdays and Fridays in Lent and other occasions as alternatives
to the operas. *Saul* and *Israel in Egypt* were brought out in 1739.
Finally, after 1741, when it became quite certain that opera would
no longer pay, he turned altogether in the new direction; obviously
the preliminary expenses, at any rate, were less heavy, and the oratorios had the attraction of a certain novelty. They were not meant
to be devotional, but were practically as much 'polite and elegant
entertainments' as anything else given in the theatres, though
treated in a different style and with different accessories—indeed,
Israel in Egypt and *Messiah* are the only ones in which the outlook
is in any way sharply differentiated from that of the secular works.

The first performance of *Messiah* took place at Dublin on 13
April 1742; Handel spent the best part of a year in Ireland, and it is
curious that, considering the exceptionally warm welcome with
which he met, he never revisited it. Indeed, it was not for some
time further that his position in London was fully secure; though
Bononcini had left England in 1733, his aristocratic partisans still
did their best to stand in Handel's way, giving specially brilliant
parties on the nights when the oratorio performers sang and made
'brave hallelujahs',[1] and generally making themselves as objection-
able as they could, while the royal favour which Handel continued
to enjoy was not much more practically valuable than such things
usually are. The result was that after, between 1743 and 1745, producing *Samson, Semele, Joseph and his Brethren, Hercules,* and
Belshazzar, Handel suffered heavy financial losses; but though he
was seriously ill in 1745 neither his power of composition nor his
enterprise suffered any permanent check. The foundations of success were established by *Judas Maccabaeus,* written in 1746 to com-
memorate the suppression of the 1745 rebellion. It appealed to the

[1] *The Letters of Horace Walpole*, ed. Mrs. Paget Toynbee, vol. i (1903),
p. 328 (24 Feb. 1743).

imagination of the public, and its subject-matter attracted the Jewish community. His later oratorios, *Alexander Balus* (1747), *Joshua* (1747), *Solomon* (1748), *Susanna* (1748), *Theodora* (1749), and *Jephtha* (1751), met with varying degrees of appreciation, but his old age was on the whole serene and comfortable; opposition gradually died away, and he was at length left in undisturbed enjoyment of the position to which his genius entitled him. But the affliction of blindness, though borne with a patience very exceptional in so naturally impatient a man, darkened the end; and after the completion of *Jephtha* he composed hardly anything but a few additional numbers to earlier works, the most important being those written for a largely revised English version, under the title of *The Triumph of Time and Truth* (1757), of an early oratorio of 1708, already revised, but still in Italian, in 1737. He died on 14 April 1759, and was buried in Westminster Abbey six days later.

We are not here concerned with the works that Handel wrote for performance outside England; and indeed, apart from a few things here and there in *Rodrigo* (1707) or *La Resurrezione* (1708), in the chamber cantatas, or in the Passion music to Brockes's poem *Der für die Sünden der Welt gemarterte und sterbende Jesus* (1716), they are of merely historical interest, while much of the material was utilized in improved form in the composer's later productions. As we have already said, it is by the music written for English audiences that his name lives; and it would consequently seem impossible, German though he was by blood, to omit consideration of them in a history of English music. To the historian London is Handel's artistic home fully as much as Vienna is that of non-Austrians like Beethoven or Brahms.

The thirty-six Italian operas that Handel wrote in England[1] are, save for a small handful of selected songs, little more than a name to the great majority of present-day music-lovers; they have been totally overshadowed by the oratorios, and the particular kind of audience to which, in their entirety, they appealed has been extinct for many a long year. Earlier in this chapter we have seen of what the ideal opera of Handel's aristocratic patrons consisted; and remembrance of all this, combined with the realization of the virtual impossibility of staging nowadays an entire Handelian opera in its original shape, has prevented most musicians from undertaking anything like an adequate examination of the huge

---

[1] *German Handel Society*, vols. lviii–xciv.

mass of operatic work that Handel left behind him. It has consequently become traditional to speak of it as greatly inferior to
that of the oratorios, yet very many, after carefully reading through
the operas, will be inclined to feel that serious injustice has been
done to them; unequal in merit though they are, these neglected
volumes contain some of their composer's most beautiful music.

   No doubt we find in all of them a great deal of more or less
perfunctory work: there are many pages of mere conventional vocal
display, and the current of melodic inspiration sometimes runs very
thin. Anything like dramatic individualization is of but rare occurrence; as a general rule all the characters, however virtuous or
vicious, and of whatever age or race, sing the same sort of music.
But, as we shall shortly see, Handel's operas have no monopoly of
dullness; and indeed, if we compare the average solo numbers of
the oratorios and the operas, it may fairly be argued that the opera
level is on the whole the higher. We must, indeed, remove the oratorio choruses out of the sphere of comparison; apart from the regular concluding ensembles of soloists and occasional short fragments
of choral work—*Giustino* (1737) shows several examples, but they
are not common—the operas have no choruses. But if the operas
never reach the massive dignity of the finest choral parts of the
oratorios, there are very few of the oratorio airs which can rival the
melodic breadth and the distinctive, subtle polish that we find not
infrequently among the operas. Take for example the really superb
'Vieni, torna' from *Teseo* (1713), from which we may quote the concluding symphony as typical of the sonorous part-writing and grand
swing of the whole:

Ex.140 *Andante, ma non troppo allegro*

[STRINGS & BASSOONS]

scored with massive richness, and full of a strong emotional exaltation for the like of which we might search in vain through oratorio after oratorio; or again there is the hardly inferior contralto air from the same opera, 'Le luci del mio bene,' a great spacious melody that is astonishingly little known, full of warmth and vocally most effective. Massive tunes of this kind are most rare in the strictly religious oratorios (the half-secular cantatas show more of them), but, though indeed very few reach the level of 'Vieni, torna', they occur fairly often in the operas; the phrases are finely balanced, and the whole melody is firmly conceived as an organic unity—not too usual a feature in Handelian melodies, unfortunately. More frequent, and in their way no less beautiful, are the airs in which the melody takes shorter flights. 'Rendi 'l sereno al ciglio' from *Sosarme* (1732) is one of the most perfect examples of an air of this kind in the deeply tranquil, pathetic, vein; 'Voglio dire al mio tesoro' from *Partenope* (1730), 'Voi dolci aurette al cor' from *Tolomeo* (1728), or 'Con rauco mormorio' from *Rodelinda* (1725), are fine specimens in other moods. And the florid arias, more or less mere vocalism though a good many of them are, rise not infrequently, as in 'Confusa si miri' from *Rodelinda*, or 'Del minacciar del vento' from *Ottone* (1723), to a sort of distinctiveness of utterance that we very rarely see in similar numbers from the oratorios. Dramatic characterization is, as has been said, not common, and in many operas the various personages all sing music that for all practical purposes is dramatically interchangeable; but there are exceptions, and, indeed, not altogether so few as is sometimes thought. As a rule, it must be remembered, the libretto affords no glimmer of assistance towards the attainment of such an end; but when it displays some sort of dramatic possibility, Handel usually rises to the occasion—not, indeed, as a revolutionary like Gluck would have done (Handel was a pure conservative in such things), but still far more definitely and successfully than any of his contemporaries. Certain striking situations, such as the madness of the hero in *Orlando* (1733), Handel can depict with what, considering the heavy trammels of the operatic conventions, is very real power; the sirens' song in *Rinaldo* (1711), with its hauntingly persistent cadence rhythm, produces a curiously soporific effect; and one of the greatest things in the operas, the contralto air 'Stille amare' from *Tolomeo*, with its wonderfully expressive introductory 'accompanied recitative', paints with singularly touching pathos the dying utterances of the hero—the end indeed is an example, and a very beautiful one too, of sheer realism:

Ex. 141 *Larghetto*

Stil-le a-ma - re, già vi sen - to tut-te in se - no, la

mor - te a chia-mar, vi sen - to

(cade spirante sopra il sasso)

tut - te in se-no, la mor-te a ...

Though, it is true, they will have to wade through many dull pages and often undergo the disappointment of meeting arias with beautiful opening phrases that come to very little afterwards, yet singers of an enterprising turn of mind have in these volumes of Handel's operas a rich and almost unworked mine; the best-known songs, such as 'Lascia ch' io pianga' from *Rinaldo*, 'Verdi prati' from *Alcina* (1735), or 'Ombra mai fù' from *Serse* (1738), fine as they are, only represent one sort of operatic air, and that not the greatest.[1]

Before we turn to a consideration of the choral works, something must be said of Handel's instrumental music. The mass of such work is considerable, including, besides seventeen suites and a great

[1] A representative selection of Handel's operatic arias has been edited by W. G. Whittaker, with English versions by A. G. Latham (Oxford University Press).

quantity of smaller pieces for harpsichord, numerous concertos for organ and for orchestra, and chamber sonatas. Much of this is conventional, in the sense that familiar procedures recur again and again. But we have only to compare Handel with his contemporaries to see that there is much more in him than the casual assembling of stock formulas. This is particularly so in cases where he has borrowed material from other composers. The second movement of the organ concerto in D minor (Op. 7, No. 4), for example, is adapted from an air for oboe, trumpet, and orchestra in Telemann's *Tafelmusik*;[1] but in its tautness and controlled energy it is unmistakably superior to the original. Most of Handel's mature instrumental music was specifically written for public performance or to attract subscribers. Its appeal is direct, its lines are clearly drawn, it pays respect to the eighteenth-century conceptions of good taste; but in doing so it constantly reveals the mind of a superior craftsman. The dignity of the violin sonata in A major (Op. 1, No. 3), the lazy grace of the recorder sonata in C major (Op. 1, No. 7), the pompous assertiveness of the first B♭ organ concerto (Op. 4, No. 2) are typical examples of the way in which Handel's vivid imagination illuminates the conventions of this time. Perhaps he is seen at his best in the twelve *concerti grossi* for strings (Op. 6). The variety of mood and treatment is very striking. The end of the first movement of No. 1 in G major is a notable example of his harmonic subtlety:

Ex. 142
Solo Violins
Solo Cello
Strings and Continuo

---

[1] *Denkmäler deutscher Tonkunst*, years lxi–lxii, p. 94.

Equally characteristic is the fugue in No. 6 in G minor, forthright in manner and full of nervous energy:

Ex. 143

Throughout the instrumental works there are constant associations with the vocal music. Not only is there frequently identity of material; there is also a similarity of mood. As in early eighteenth-century music in general we are made aware of the extent to which opera dominated the minds of composers, even though the influence was so often unconscious.

Handel and his public more or less habitually included, under the general name of oratorios, various choral works to which more modern custom generally denies the title; but it is on the whole most convenient to consider in one large group the strictly religious oratorios, the works which nowadays would probably be called cantatas, and such extended service music as the Chandos and other anthems. Roughly speaking, the same qualities are shown in them all alike; and to separate them with any rigid lines of de-marcation is to give false impressions. As we have seen, the oratorio was in Handel's day an 'entertainment' just as much as was the opera; and there was little place in the Anglican service of the time for the expression of the spirit that breathes through the church cantatas of Bach. Handel's German Passions show how much he could, in a different environment, adapt himself to the tastes of his countrymen by birth: the absolute difference between their style and that of the oratorios is most startling. But to the average member of his London audiences any artistic expression of pietism of the North German type would have seemed both dull and impertinent; and the composer was consequently thrown back on a style which remains in essentials virtually the same whether the words are of a religious character or not.

The history of art can hardly show a parallel to the enormous influence which Handel exercised over English music for wellnigh a century after his death; even yet the composer's name is a sort of national fetish with thousands of people who could not for their lives see any difference of quality between the best and the worst things in *Messiah* or *Israel in Egypt*. *Messiah* is, indeed, still a part of the average Englishman's religion, and he criticizes its music no more than he criticizes its words; and though it is true that now almost all Handel's other large works are, as wholes, but seldom performed, many extracts from them still display their popular halo almost untarnished by lapse of time and changes of fashion. Yet, passionate as has been the English worship of Handel, we have treated our idol very badly; no other composer who ever lived has had to suffer a tithe of the indignities that we have heaped, and still heap, on his head. The score of *Messiah* is full of careful directions that at least ninety-nine per cent. of our performances complacently and totally ignore, and only a handful of organists have any notion of even the proper chords of the Dead March in *Saul*; singers with famous names distort his rhythm out of all recognition, and insert top notes that would have driven him wild, and comparatively few people seem to think that it matters in the very least degree whatever. There is no doubt that he expected his singers to ornament the text of their arias, in accordance with the taste of his time;[1] the fault of our ordinary modern alterations is that they are grossly unhistorical. Until quite recent times hardly any pianoforte arrangement of Handel's music was in existence which did not blandly neglect most of the details of his part-writing, and indeed insert chords the like of which neither he nor his contemporaries ever wrote; and the most vilely ignorant 'traditions' of all kinds have sprung up round wellnigh every page of his works. Mozart's 'additional accompaniments'—the earliest of an entirely unnecessary company—were first heard in England in 1805, and were severely

[1] See Max Seiffert, 'Die Verzierung der Sologesänge in Händel's *Messias*', in *S.I.M.G.*, 1906–7, pp. 581–615.

and judiciously criticized. Bartleman, the great bass singer of the time, declined to take part in a performance where they were to be used, and carried his point. Of late years a very considerable cleansing process has been set on foot, and performances of *Messiah* with the original orchestration are less uncommon than they used to be; but there is still a vast amount more to be done.

Of course Handel's faults lie on the surface plainly enough. We have only to compare the carelessly conventional twirlings of airs like that of Septimius in *Theodora*:[1]

with the decorative vocal writing of Purcell or Bach, or contrast with the methods of other great men such things as (in *Joshua*) the orchestral elucidation of Achsah's words:

> Or who will not on Jordan smile
> Releas'd from bondage on the Nile?[2]

Indeed no other composer can even attempt to rival Handel in his power of intensely irritating those who have the strongest and sanest admiration for his genius. He was at once too careless and too practical; he lacked the steady self-criticism which rejects inadequate material and, when the material is adequate, looks to its polished presentation, and at the same time he kept an unnecessarily steady finger on the pulse of his visible public, and, so far as

[1] *German Handel Society*, vol. viii, p. 79.
[2] Ibid., vol. xvii, p. 22.

a man of genius could, wrote for the taste of the moment in the spirit of the mere impresario. Though it is true that in the process he never sacrificed personal self-respect, he took up oratorio, as indeed he took up everything else, because he thought it would pay. His sadly unenterprising contemporary at Leipzig—a mere 'musical director in a commercial city', as Burney[1] describes him— had to wait for something like a century and a half before his supremacy was generally realized; but now the judgements are reversed, and the old idol has been displaced. It would be a thousand pities, however, if *Messiah* were to disappear into the limbo of those artistic works for which the relatively unmusical public retains a superstitious reverence long after the musicians themselves have come to a final, and on the whole—at any rate in comparison—an adverse, judgement.

After all, a great man is to be judged by his greatness; and the student of Handel's oratorios lives in a state of continual exultant surprise. He may for example be examining the recitatives, and deploring the almost entire absence of the living spirit that breathes through those of Purcell and Bach, when suddenly he comes across wonderful pages like 'Deeper and deeper still' (which has nothing to do with 'Waft her, angels,' before which it is usually sung) in *Jephtha*,[2] or 'Thy rebuke hath broken his heart' in *Messiah*;[3] he may be wading through the instrumental movements—the overtures, the battle symphonies and the rest—and his attention is suddenly caught by a miraculously impressive thing like the Dead March in *Saul*, or one or two other numbers in *Judas Maccabaeus* or *Samson*. In gratitude for the gift of magnificent music like 'The people shall hear'[4]—full of the thrill that only the immortal things possess—we may well be content to forget the dullness of the surrounding pages of *Israel in Egypt*; and the great movements of *Messiah* more than cover a multitude of sins.

It is very interesting to note how, on the whole (leaving *Messiah*, which in many respects stands by itself, out of the question) the fire of inspiration burnt more steadily in the non-religious choral works than in those to which we would now, at any rate in England, restrict the name of oratorio. *Acis and Galatea*[5] and

---

[1] *A General History of Music* (1776–89), vol. iv, p. 595.
[2] *German Handel Society*, vol. xliv, p. 170.
[3] Ibid., vol. xlv, p. 162.
[4] Ibid., vol. xvi, p. 226.
[5] Ibid., vol. iii.

Semele[1] are perhaps the most equal compositions Handel ever wrote; they possess a sort of freshness and flow of inspiration, and a polished delicacy of workmanship, that, except sporadically, are hardly to be seen in most of the oratorios. It is no doubt difficult for any but convinced devotees to see in *Acis and Galatea* the deep psychological power with which it has been credited, and the overture would fit any other oratorio or opera or cantata practically as well; but there is about the work, taken as a whole, a singular charm and fragrance, the touch is unusually light, and the level of invention, melodic and the rest, unusually high. A chorus like 'Wretched lovers' or an air like 'Love in her eyes sits playing' will show Handel in his most vitalized mood; there are hardly any traces of heaviness or conventionality, and, delicate as is the touch, the grand style is, in all but a comparatively small handful of pages, plainly evident. And there is considerably more characterization than usual, though it is true that there is not much subtlety; the fact that Polyphemus nearly invariably sings in unison with the instrumental bass gives a special gruff quality to his music, and the trio 'The flocks shall leave the mountains', with the delightful pastoral melody for Acis and Galatea, and the giant's undercurrent of rage, finally bursting out *solo* as he rolls the rocks on the lovers, is in its way a really dramatic conception.

Though rather more unequal in quality, *Semele* shows the same fine distinction of utterance; we find, it is true, a few airs like Semele's 'Myself I shall adore' or 'No, no, I'll take no less' or Athamas's 'Despair no more shall wound me', which contain otiose *fioriture* that are practically invisible in *Acis*, but these are of no importance in view of the splendid quality of the great work. The airs 'Awake, Saturnia' (one of Handel's very finest inspirations), 'Oh sleep, why dost thou leave me?', 'Where'er you walk' (marked *Largo e pianissimo per tutto*—a curiously definite indication, which is not always, unfortunately, observed in performance), the choruses 'Now Love, that everlasting boy', 'Bless the glad earth with heavenly lays', the scenes of the waking of Somnus (his drowsy music is of special and uncommon beauty), of Jupiter's oath (followed by three bars for timpani *soli*) and his remorse, of Semele's death—all in their various ways show Handel in some of his most notably original moods; the fire of inspiration burns brightly, and the workmanship never falters. And here again, as in *Acis*, we see that the composer,

---

[1] Ibid., vol. vii.

when he took trouble over his work, could give his characters really individual music to sing; perhaps the most striking example is Juno's spiteful little air 'Above measure is the pleasure which my revenge supplies', which fits the words with a quite exceptional fidelity.

The rest of Handel's secular choral works, of which *Hercules*[1] and the three odes—*St. Cecilia's Day, Alexander's Feast,* and *L'Allegro*[2]—are the chief, are considerably less fine, though all have some arresting features. *Hercules,* which is designed on the scale of a large oratorio, is for the most part a dull grey sort of work, relieved, however, by a few striking pages, such as the scene of Hercules's agony:

Ex. 146

Was it for this un-num-ber'd toils I bore?

[STRINGS]

Oh Ju-no and Eu-rys-the-us, I absolve ye! Your keenest mal-ice

yields to De-jan-i-ra's; Mis-ta-ken, cru-el,

---

[1] *German Handel Society,* vol. iv.
[2] Ibid., vols. xxiii, xii, vi.

Dejanira's splendidly powerful and passionate recitative and air
'Where shall I fly?', Iole's tender and expressive 'My father', and a
small handful of other airs and choruses; the orchestral portrayal
of Hercules's madness in the *sinfonia* to the third act, with its spasmodic alternations of *Largo* and *Furioso,* is an interesting essay in
realism. The odes are more distinctive, and the short one for St.
Cecilia's Day is one of Handel's most attractive works on a small
scale; 'The trumpet's loud clangour'—a tenor solo followed by a
chorus—is a brilliantly stirring piece, with a sort of Purcellian
directness of style, and the final chorus has singular strength and
dignity. *L'Allegro* and *Alexander's Feast,* in spite of a considerable
amount that is merely perfunctory, also contain some of Handel's
notable work. The former is the slighter of the two, and many of its
numbers—including some of the most delicate and picturesque,
such as the *siciliano* 'Let me wander not unseen', and 'Oft on a plat
of rising ground'—are very short; 'There let the pealing organ blow'
contains altogether only seventeen bars of very bare music written
out; the rest consists of the indications for three separate organ
interludes (the last marked 'very soft'), which are left entirely to the
mercy of the performer—who would usually, of course, have been
Handel himself. But there is plenty of pleasant music, and the

differentiation of the characters[1] is on the whole decidedly well
carried out. *Alexander's Feast* is stronger, and the words are set
with real appreciation of their varied moods; the chorus 'Behold,
Darius great and good' is very touching in its way, but the finest
part is the connected string of numbers at the beginning of Part II
—from 'Now strike the golden lyre' to the famous 'Revenge, Timotheus cries'—which are throughout full of brilliantly stirring music
in their composer's most vitalized and individual manner. None of
these works, taken as complete wholes, equal *Acis and Galatea* or
Semele; but still, purely conventional as many pages in them are,
we do not somehow see in them (except perhaps in *Hercules*) the
specially bald type of conventionality that the oratorios, at their
worst, can display.

Again, the lengthy *The Triumph of Time and Truth*[2]—a sort of
semi-oratorio, a moral allegory containing a few religious 'applica-
tions' and ending with a Hallelujah chorus—is in most respects
quite different in style from the strict oratorios, except as regards
the numbers which are adapted from other works. This is one of
Handel's most irretrievably neglected productions, and yet it contains some of his most fresh and charming music. The hunting
chorus 'Oh, how great the glory', and the tenor solo 'Dryads, sylvans' with chorus 'Lo, we all attend on Flora' (both not to be found
in the earlier versions of the work), are singularly piquant and
graceful, and many of the airs of the various characters (Beauty,
Pleasure, Deceit, Time) are in different ways of strikingly individual quality—for example, Time's air 'Loathsome urns, disclose
your treasure':

Ex. 147

---

[1] *L'Allegro* and *Il Penseroso* are mixed up, chiefly in alternate numbers,
throughout Parts I and II; *Il Moderato*—Jennens's misplaced addition to
Milton—has Part III to itself.
[2] *German Handel Society*, vol xx.

The whole work is indeed somewhat slight in texture, and at its best it hardly does more than charm; but, apart from the numbers actually borrowed more or less closely from various religious choral works and organ concertos, there is an unusual freshness about its pages.

Indeed, we may carry this train of investigation a little farther and examine in the strictly religious oratorios themselves the passages—not, it is true, very many—where there is some close and definite opposition between secular and religious elements; where such contrast is necessarily required by the libretto, it is as a rule hard to deny that Handel's individuality shows itself considerably more on the non-religious side. Compare, for example, in *Saul*[1] the powerfully picturesque trio that describes Goliath, 'Along the

[1] Ibid., vol. xiii.

monster atheist strode', with the tame respectability of the immediately succeeding 'The youth inspired by thee, O Lord'; in *Samson*
and *Belshazzar*[1] the pagan choruses are as a general rule (there are
a few exceptions) distinctly the more interesting; and though the
choruses of Christians in *Theodora*[2] include such fine strong work
as 'He saw the lovely youth' and 'O love divine' (an impressive final
chorus, with a sombre, pathetic dignity) and others, yet there is
something about 'Queen of summer, queen of love' and 'Venus,
laughing from the skies', trifles as they are, that strikes a rarer and
a subtler note.

But it would be gravely unfair to press this line of argument too
far. Almost all this secularly tinged work, exquisitely fresh and
charming though it is, yet, when everything has been said, is of
slender character; in sheer beauty Handel never surpassed and
rarely equalled it, but it never touches any even moderately deep
springs of feeling. To see Handel at his greatest we must look elsewhere. The non-secular oratorios (with which we may group choral
works like the Chandos and other extended anthems, the Te Deums,
and the funeral anthem on the death of Queen Caroline) are of
various characters—sometimes, as *Messiah*, exclusively religious—
sometimes, as *Saul* or *Belshazzar*, vivid drama—sometimes, as
Joshua or *Joseph* or *Jephtha*, a blend of Biblical history with interpolated 'love interest'—sometimes, as *Solomon* or *Israel in Egypt*,
a sort of pageantry of imposing choruses. But in wellnigh every one
of the whole lengthy series we shall find, if we look carefully, something of great distinction; *Messiah* is, no doubt, on the whole the
most equal of the set, but others, such as *Saul* and, to a somewhat
less degree, *Susanna* or *Samson* or *Solomon*, run it very close, and
some of the more uneven works, such as *Israel in Egypt*, contain
inspirations that rank with anything Handel ever wrote. It is a pity,
for Handel's own sake, that the uncertain chances of things have
caused some of his finest pages to be far less known than others
of inferior quality; for every one person who knows the colossal
'Tremble, guilt' (from the chorus 'Righteous heaven') in *Susanna*,[3]
there are at least a thousand who admire the perfunctory 'Honour
and arms', and when we think of an oratorio duet, it is not of 'Joys
in gentle trains appearing' in *Athaliah*,[4] with its delicious Purcel-

---

[1] *German Handel Society*, vols. x and xix.   [2] Ibid., vol. viii.
[3] Ibid., vol. i.
[4] Ibid., vol. v.

lian melody,[1] but of the conventional 'The Lord is a man of war'.

But when we have ferreted out for ourselves the really great pages in the oratorios, not even the most modern-minded revolutionary can fail to be impressed with the sort of elemental grandeur that inspires them. The stern majesty of such pieces as 'Envy, eldest born of hell' in *Saul*, or 'By slow degrees the wrath of God' in *Belshazzar*, or 'How dark, O Lord, are thy decrees' in *Jephtha*, or 'He comes to end our woes' in *Esther*,[2] or the two mighty choruses in *Israel in Egypt* and *Susanna* that have already been named is, in its own way, unique in music; the touch is that of a hammering Titan. There is no compromise, no rounding of the sharp edges; the primevally massive music is simply hurled in our faces, to take or to leave. And though no doubt Handel is seen at his greatest in choruses like these and others—*Messiah* has several—which depend for their enormous impressiveness on sheer strength, wielded in the simplest and most direct manner, yet—within some definite limits—he has remarkable versatility; rapturous brilliance and deep pathos are both well within his reach, and occasionally, as in 'May no rash intruder' in *Solomon*,[3] the lion 'will roar you an 't were any nightingale'. The method of massive simplicity is no doubt a risky one to be adopted even by a great genius, when he is in the habit (as Handel was) of writing in a terrible hurry; both the composer and his audience are very liable to be misled by the undeniable sort of effect that can be produced by a sufficiently dignified and serious reiteration of anything whatever—witness 'Immortal Lord of earth and skies' in *Deborah*,[4] and many more. Handel is the only great composer who has placed a virtually blind reliance on the method; very often it plays him false, but when his trust in it is justified, then we must needs bow the head. In solo work the percentage of successes is no doubt smaller than in choral, as the

---

[1] The influence of Purcell upon Handel's style is not really very often noticeable to any degree worth mentioning, but when it is plainly visible, it is curiously thorough, affecting sometimes not only melody, but harmony, rhythm, part-writing, and everything. The Utrecht Te Deum shows it most markedly in the religious music; but perhaps the most remarkable instance of all is the secular chorus 'Queen of summer' in *Theodora*, every note of which bears the unmistakable sign-manual of the older composer. *The Triumph of Time and Truth* shows several other nearly equally striking examples, and *Acis and Galatea* has not a little of the Purcellian spirit.

[2] *German Handel Society*, vols. xl and xli.

[3] Ibid., vol. xxvi.

[4] Ibid., vol. xxix.

medium (at any rate as clothed in the eighteenth-century phrase-ology) offers fewer chances; but still, when we remember miraculous things like 'He shall feed his flock' (*Messiah*) or 'Total eclipse' (*Samson*), we do not feel inclined to complain. It is true that Handel was content to turn out masses of merely ordinary work, in a sort of patient certainty that sooner or later the inspiration would come. But when it did come, then we have the real Handel—the man on whose grave Beethoven said he would kneel bareheaded.[1]

Handel's technique presents many points of interest; most of it, no doubt, is derived from Italian sources, but he vastly improved on his masters. He had an extraordinary command over all the minutiae of smoothly balanced choral writing; it all looks so simple, but no one else has ever done it in just the same way. His counter-point runs on velvet; and he can produce effects of dazzling brilliance by magnificently unacademical methods, as in this cadence from the chorus in *L'Allegro*[2] 'These delights if thou canst give':

Ex.148 *Allegro*

Mirth, with thee we mean to live

which is full of wonderful technical points—the sudden drop into consecutive octaves for soprano and tenor on their most telling notes (with the alto out of the way), and the crashing full chords at the end—reached by consecutive fifths, but what does that matter? And so far as the orchestration of his day would allow, he has the sense of colour as no one had before; *Saul* is full of it, and so is one of his most sincerely felt works, the very fine funeral anthem on the death of Queen Caroline (1737),[3] while all over the operas we see experimental devices, always interesting, and often highly success-ful. We may mention in particular the use of the cello as a solo instrument, the writing of *obbligato* parts for bassoons, the intro-duction of instruments like the harp and mandoline for the sake of exotic colour, and the brilliantly effective employment of two, or even four, horns. The voluptuous aria 'V'adoro, pupille', sung by

[1] *Beethoven: Impressions of Contemporaries* (1927), p. 152.
[2] *German Handel Society*, vol. vi.   [3] Ibid., vol. xi.

Cleopatra in *Giulio Cesare*, derives not a little of its charm from the use of a chamber ensemble on the stage.

A paragraph may be added on the question of Handel's well-known plagiarisms.[1] During the last hundred years or so evidence has been accumulating to show that, besides borrowing very largely from himself, he appropriated from many other contemporary or earlier composers, both small and great, laying them under contributions of all kinds, ranging from mere single phrases up to virtually complete long movements. Famous composers like Carissimi, Lotti, Graun, Keiser, and Telemann[2] were so utilized, as well as a number of others of less fame, such as Clari, Muffat, Habermann, and Kerl. In *Israel in Egypt*, for example, the chorus 'Egypt was glad when they departed' is copied wellnigh note for note from an organ canzona by Kerl;[3] and several passages in *Jephtha* are taken from Masses by Habermann which were published four years earlier. We are faced with the task of accounting for what looks suspiciously like flagrant dishonesty. It has been the general custom to return a verdict of guilty without extenuating circumstances; but that is really going rather too far. Very many composers—Palestrina, Bach, Haydn, Beethoven, Brahms, and numbers of others of less fame—have frequently taken fragments of alien material as 'texts' for their own discourses, or as, so to speak, interesting quotations; they very rarely, it is true, specify them as borrowed—a highly reprehensible habit which has caused immense confusion—but in most cases their first hearers probably recognized them easily enough (just as Virgil and Tennyson no doubt assumed that their readers would recognize the word-for-word translations from Theocritus and Homer), and, anyhow, they are only mere fragments and nothing more.

Handel adopted the same method, but with two vital differences. Often he borrows, not mere themes, but great slices of a movement, and sometimes the whole of one; perhaps he will change here and

[1] Most of the material evidence is presented by Sedley Taylor, *The indebtedness of Handel to works by other composers* (1906), with complete examples in musical notation. See also P. Robinson, *Handel and his orbit* (1908), and 'Handel, or Urio, Stradella and Erba' in *Music and Letters*, Oct. 1935, pp. 269–77.

[2] For Telemann see M. Seiffert, *Beihefte zu den Denkmälern deutscher Tonkunst*, vol. ii (1927).

[3] Oddly enough, Hawkins (*A General History*, &c., 1875 ed., p. 597) published this canzona (originally printed in 1686) as an example of Kerl's style without ever recognizing its Handelian interest.

there in various ways, perhaps not at all. And further, what he does borrow has little of the salience and point which alone can justify the proceeding; nearly everything that he lays under contribution is as dull stuff as can be, and, unless they had a sense of style keen enough to detect the differences of technique, which to us now are sometimes quite plain, his audiences probably never suspected anything. He certainly was in the habit of working in a terrible hurry, and yet his borrowings cannot have been altogether due to laziness; his manuscript books in the Fitzwilliam Museum at Cambridge show that he took great pains to lay up a sort of store of things from which to copy, and, when he does alter and improve, he goes about the business in the spirit of a very careful and conscientious teacher of composition. And there is not the least reason whatever to suppose that he saw anything to be ashamed of in the proceeding; we must not forget the extraordinary prevalence in his day of pasticcios of every conceivable kind, made up out of the works sometimes of a single composer, sometimes of several (whose names were frequently unspecified) all mixed up together—it was considered interesting and important to advertise works as 'new and original', and no one troubled very much, if at all, about such a thing as artistic homogeneity. The case of Bononcini's forced retirement from England, though continually quoted, is not really parallel. He was charged with formally claiming as his own composition a madrigal presented (through the medium of Greene) to the Academy of Ancient Music, which was really the work of Lotti; this was obviously deliberate deceit, which no one would have thought of justifying by talking about pasticcios. But it is most doubtful if he was guilty; apart from the evidence in his favour mentioned by the unsympathetic Hawkins,[1] it seems impossible that a man of his great talents and his high position could have been such a short-sighted fool. He never opened his lips in his defence; but that fact is capable of two interpretations, and Lotti himself was of the opinion that the letter on which the Academy relied was a forgery. Handel displayed, we must regretfully confess, a greediness of an altogether unique and most deplorable character, and psychologically his proceedings are very puzzling, even if we attribute them to ill health;[2] but both his friends and his enemies have made rather too much of a moral question of the matter.

[1] Op. cit., p. 862.   [2] See E. J. Dent, *Handel* (1934), pp. 106–7.

VIII

HANDEL'S CONTEMPORARIES

CROFT, Greene, Boyce, and Arne—the first a little older, the other three a little younger than Handel—are the four most prominent composers to be dealt with in this chapter; but there are several others besides, to whose biographies a few words are due.

William Croft—or Crofts, as his name was also written—was born in 1678; he was a chorister at the Chapel Royal under Blow, whom in 1708 he succeeded in the posts of organist of Westminster Abbey and master of the children and composer to the Chapel Royal, of which he had previously been appointed organist—at first jointly with Clarke, and after his death in sole charge. He published many songs, besides instrumental music, overtures and entr'actes for stage plays, and odes for occasions of public rejoicing; but his fame is derived almost entirely from his music for the services of the church. Most of his finest works are contained in a collection he issued in 1724 under the title of *Musica Sacra*—the earliest example of ecclesiastical music engraved in score on plates; three years after its publication he died at Bath, and was buried in Westminster Abbey. The preface to *Musica Sacra* shows a very attractive character; it is a modest and thoughtful expression of his ideas on church music, and the quiet heartfelt homage to Purcell shows a self-effacing generosity of spirit not too common with musicians of Croft's age—indeed, contrasted with the ordinary preface of either the seventeenth or eighteenth centuries, it reads, to an extent almost unique, like the work of an artist and a gentleman.

Maurice Greene, the other great anthem-writer of the period, was seventeen years Croft's junior, being born in 1695. In his boyhood a chorister of St. Paul's Cathedral, he was at the age of twenty-three elected its organist; and he subsequently combined this position, after the pluralist fashion of the times, with those of organist and composer to the Chapel Royal (in succession to Croft), professor of music at Cambridge, and master of the King's music. In 1750 he inherited from a cousin a country estate in Essex, and, though still holding all his former offices, spent, it would appear, most of his time in collecting material for the publication in score of a representative selection of English church music—a project that was interrupted by his death in 1755, but was subsequently carried out by his pupil Boyce, to whom the task was bequeathed. In the earlier part of his life he was an intimate friend of Handel, who used frequently to play the organ at St. Paul's; but he declined to take sides in the operatic rivalry between Handel and Bononcini until the irascibility of the former threw him, apparently against his will, into the ranks of the latter's vehement partisans. Greene's chief publication was issued in 1743, and was entitled *Forty Select Anthems*; but he also brought out various other works, both vocal and instrumental. Very much of his music remains, however, still in manuscript; it includes numerous odes for various festal occasions, an oratorio on the subject of Jephtha, and dramatic compositions.

William Boyce was born in 1710; and like Greene, whose pupil he was, began his musical career as a chorister at St. Paul's. For many years he held the post of composer to the Chapel Royal, for some time simultaneously with Greene, whom he succeeded in 1755 in the mastership of the King's music; he was also conductor of the Three Choirs Festivals at Gloucester, Worcester, and Hereford, and held various organ appointments at London churches, though owing to the increase of the deafness from which he suffered for the greater part of his life he gave up most of his work some time before his death in 1779. He wrote a large quantity of vocal and instrumental music, both secular and ecclesiastical; but his name is best known by his fine collection of cathedral music of the sixteenth and seventeenth centuries, the original idea of which was, as we have seen, due to Greene. Though it is to be regretted that he did not make more exhaustive researches among the earlier composers, and indeed did not always select the finest examples of those of later date, yet the three large folio volumes remain a very worthy monument, and undoubtedly did very much to spread the fame of the masterpieces of Gibbons and Purcell and many more. Boyce was, however, not an ideal editor, and he has given considerable trouble to subsequent researchers; but his sins in these matters probably disturbed no one in his own time or for long afterwards.

The name of Thomas Augustine Arne is at present by far the best known among the English-born composers of the time, of whom, indeed, he was the most popular among his contemporaries. He was born in 1710, and was at first designed for the legal profession; unlike Croft, Greene, and Boyce, he seems to have written nothing for the Anglican Church, though he produced two oratorios entitled

The Death of Abel and *Judith*. At a performance of the latter work in 1773 (it was originally produced in 1761) female voices were for the first time in England introduced into oratorio choruses, the upper parts of which had always previously been sung by boys. He confined himself almost entirely to music connected with the stage or with popular places of entertainment like Vauxhall and Ranelagh, and composed an immense mass of work of this kind; his incidental music to adaptations of Milton's *Comus* (1738), Shakespeare's *As You Like it* (1740), and *The Tempest* (1746) contains some of his most familiar songs, while the elaborate opera *Artaxerxes* (1762) shows him in his most ambitious mood. Arne, who died in 1778, seems to have had his musical character a good deal spoilt by the success which he achieved directly his talents were allowed full scope; his correspondence generally shows him in the light of the 'jealous and self-seeking tradesman'[1] rather than the artist, and when desirous of obtaining a commission to write fresh music for a revival of Dryden's *King Arthur* in 1770, he can, in a letter to Garrick, refer to Purcell's original settings of the songs as 'infamously bad—so very bad that they are privately the objects of sneer and ridicule to the Musicians'. 'I wish you wou'd only give me leave to *Doctor* this performance—I would certainly make it pleasing to the Public', he adds;[2] and sentiments like these came with unpleasant frequency from his pushing pen.

A few short biographical notes may now be given concerning the other more or less noteworthy composers of the time. The date of John Weldon's birth is 1676; he was apparently a pupil of Purcell and held organ appointments at New College, Oxford, and from 1708 (on Blow's death) at the Chapel Royal, of which he was afterwards—from 1715 till his death in 1736—one of the court composers. His music is mainly ecclesiastical in character. Charles Stroud, a pupil of Croft, and organist of Whitehall, who died very young in 1726; Charles King (1687–1748), a pupil of Blow and Clarke and vicar-choral of St. Paul's; Thomas Kempton, organist of Ely Cathedral from 1729 to 1762; James Kent (1700–76), chorister at the Chapel Royal under Croft, and afterwards organist, from 1731 to 1737, of Trinity College, Cambridge, and from 1737 till

[1] G. E. P. A[rkwright], 'Dr. Arne and His Songs', in *The Musical Gazette*, Dec. 1902, p. 157.

[2] W. H. Cummings, 'Dr. Arne and Rule Britannia' (1912), p. 69. A facsimile of this letter was issued as an extra supplement of *The Musical Times*, Jan. 1896.

1774 of Winchester Cathedral and College; Thomas Kelway (d. 1749), organist of Chichester Cathedral; William Hayes (1706–77), organist for over forty years of Magdalen College, Oxford, and professor of music in the university; John Travers (d. 1758), a pupil of Greene and organist of the Chapel Royal; James Nares (1715–83), organist of York Minster and from 1756 onwards Greene's successor at the Chapel Royal—all these may be taken in various ways and degrees as typical exponents of the church music of the time below the high level of Croft, Greene, and Boyce. Nares and Travers showed some good work in other departments; but most of the rest —except Hayes, who was more versatile and set Collins's *Ode to the Passions* and a *Masque of Circe*—confined themselves chiefly to producing material for their church duties.

Among the primarily instrumental composers the names of William Babell (d. 1723), Thomas Roseingrave (1690–1766), Charles John Stanley (1713–86), and Joseph Gibbs (1699–1788) may be mentioned as typical; but some of the better-known men, especially Boyce and Arne, wrote a good deal for harpsichord and for strings. John Christopher Pepusch (1667–1752), though a Prussian by birth, resided in England for the last fifty years of his life; he preceded Handel as organist to the Duke of Chandos, and was subsequently music director at Lincoln's Inn Fields Theatre, and organist of the Charterhouse. He wrote a large quantity of instrumental music, besides odes, masques, and motets, and some elaborate theoretical treatises; but his best-known work was the selection and adaptation of the tunes for *The Beggar's Opera*—the brightest and most popular example of the ballad opera in England.

Mention has been made in the previous chapter of the blow dealt to Handel's operatic schemes by the success of this work, first performed in January 1728 and enormously popular in the twentieth century in Frederic Austin's version; the music consisted merely of popular melodies of the time ('wild, rude, and often vulgar', the fashionable Burney calls them[1]), adapted to Gay's words and harmonized by Pepusch, who also supplied an overture based on one of the tunes. Other 'ballad operas', as they were called, soon sprang up to emulate its enormous success. *The Beggar's Opera* does its best to justify its form by the dramatic fiction that it was originally intended for the wedding ceremonies of a beggar and a ballad-singer; but later on no one troubled to express any sort of apology.

---

[1] *A General History of Music*, vol. iv, p. 635.

Four more works of this type appeared in 1728, and eleven in 1729. The hey-day of ballad operas lasted barely a decade; but as we shall subsequently see, they left their influence on later English opera, which for a long time combined the composer's own work with selections from the temporarily favourite songs of both native and foreign birth. The Italian opera, however, though discarded by Handel himself, continued to exist simultaneously with more or less success; and some of the chief contemporary English composers, such as Boyce and Arne, brought out operas in which the dialogue was set to music and not spoken, as was, and remained for a long time after, the general practice of English opera, which in that respect conformed to the French and German methods. It is easy to see the reason for the popularity of the ballad operas in the contrast they presented to the stilted and artificial proceedings of the Italian stage, which even the genius of Handel could not succeed in making tolerable, except to a fashionable coterie; and besides their democratic appeal to the ordinary man, the individual tunes themselves are often of very great artistic merit, and anyhow were free from the irritating roulades and posturings which were the breath of life to the singers of the opposition form of entertainment.[1] The patrons of *The Beggar's Opera*, for example, heard in addition to admirable folk-tunes, native and foreign, some of Purcell's most beautiful songs (though it is true that 'Britons, strike home' is reduced to only six bars) and extracts from Handel himself; and it is not surprising that the ordinary unaristocratic music-lover preferred such an entertainment to the rival stage performances—even though it was liable to the censure of stern moralists like Burke, who could not endure to hear any praise of a production so subversive in social tendency,[2] or Johnson, who declared: 'There is in it such a *labefactation* of all principles as may be injurious to morality.'[3]

The first half of the eighteenth century saw the foundation of several still existing musical institutions of different kinds. The Three Choirs Festival of Gloucester, Worcester, and Hereford was started at Gloucester in 1724, and has been held at each city triennially ever since, except during the war years 1914–18 and 1939–

---

[1] Later on, however, it seems that singers frequently ornamented the simple tunes with their own 'airs and graces': sometimes these were definitely printed —there is a typical elaborate example in Shield's *Rosina*.

[2] J. Morley, *Burke* (1879), p. 111.

[3] *Boswell's Life of Johnson*, ed. G. B. Hill (1887), vol. ii, p. 367.

45; it was some forty years before Birmingham copied the example, and there (and at other places subsequently) the festivals were of less regular occurrence than they have always been in the western cathedral cities. The Royal Society of Musicians was founded in 1738 and was warmly supported by Handel, Arne, Boyce, and others; it still survives as a charitable institution for aged and indigent musicians and their families. Three years later the now somewhat unobtrusive Madrigal Society was inaugurated by John Immyns, secretary to Pepusch; Hawkins gives a very charming account of the meetings, which were originally attended mainly by working men, united in their appreciation of the older style of music and 'not less distinguished by their love of vocal harmony, than the harmless simplicity of their tempers, and their friendly disposition towards each other'.[1]

Another institution, which became extinct at the close of the century but had great influence while it lasted, was the Academy of Ancient Music, which was founded in 1710; numbers of motets and madrigals of nearly all the great sixteenth-century masters, both English and foreign, were in the regular repertory, which also included works by later and contemporary composers. Almost all the prominent musicians resident in England were members; and the concerts must have been of great value in keeping alive the taste for a style so unlike that generally practised at the time. Reference has been made in the previous chapter to the connexion of the Academy with Bononcini's retirement from England—the one fact in its history which has kept its name familiar to the general reader.

We cannot help noticing, all through this period, a great extension of the artistic evils, the beginning of which we have already seen in Purcell's day. Composers were all too rapidly adopting the idea that they were the servants of a public that had to be pleased on the spot; it was Burney's opinion that if 'Sebastian Bach and his admirable son Emanuel . . . had been fortunately employed to compose for the stage and public of great capitals . . . they would doubtless have simplified their style more to the level of their judges' and 'by writing in a style more popular, and generally intelligible and pleasing, would have extended their fame',[2] and this exactly voices the attitude of the English public towards music, which demanded

---

[1] *A General History of the Science and Practice of Music* (1875 ed.), p. 887.
[2] *A General History of Music*, vol. iv, p. 595.

at all costs that it should not be bored. To this were due all the pasticcios of favourite tunes, all the interpolations of organ or vocal solos between the parts of oratorios, all the ornamental alterations with which one singer tried to secure more applause than his or her rivals; sometimes the matter was put very frankly indeed, as in a delightful announcement in a Dublin paper of 1742 that

'Mr. Arne . . . intends, between the Acts of his Serenatas, Operas, and other Musical Performances, to intermix Comic Interludes . . . intended to give Relief to that grave Attention, necessary to be kept up in Serious Performances.'[1]

Mattheson remarks that in Vauxhall Gardens in London 'many concerts are given for money';[2] when things like those quoted above resulted from the decline of private patronage, it was difficult for thinking men not to regret modern democratic customs. Some there were in England, no doubt, who felt that there was something wrong; Hawkins's memoir prefixed to the second edition of Boyce's 'Cathedral Music' (1788) expresses his views with considerable incisiveness and eloquence, and though he wrote outside the period we are now considering his remarks apply with full force to the earlier time. His description of J. C. Bach and Abel, who 'like most of that profession who are to live by the favour of the public . . . had two styles of composition, the one for their own private delight, the other for the gratification of the many', is singularly pointed.

A considerable number of books on musical subjects were published during this period. Essays on aesthetics, in particular, were numerous; perhaps the most interesting is the *Essay on Musical Expression* (1752) by Charles Avison (*c.* 1710–70), which is full of good sense, set out in pleasant style; it was controverted, somewhat ponderously, by William Hayes. Notice should also be made of the valuable *Art of Playing on the Violin* (*c.* 1740, the first treatise ever printed on the subject), the work of Francesco Geminiani (1667–1762), a distinguished violinist who was settled in London or Dublin nearly all his later life.

We have now to consider the musical output of the English-born composers of this period; and turning, as before, first to ecclesiastical music (to which, indeed, most of them devoted their primary

[1] W. H. Grattan Flood, 'Dr. Arne's Visits to Dublin', in *The Musical Antiquary*, July 1910, p. 217.

[2] *Grundlage einer Ehren-Pforte* (1740), p. 101: 'Es werden in diesen Gärten, dahin jedermann gehen und sich erlustigen kann, viele Concerte für Geld gehalten.'

energies), we find that among the oldest, and perhaps also, on the whole, the most noteworthy of all, is Croft. We have already seen something of the man's attractive character in his preface to his *Musica Sacra*; and this attitude of modest dignity is reflected in his work. He is best known now by his fine hymn tunes, 'St. Anne', 'St. Matthew', and 'Hanover'. The first and last have been attributed to others, but probably without justification. It is true that versions of 'St. Anne' exist which are ascribed to one Denby, otherwise unknown; but Croft's contemporaries, Hart and Church, distinctly acknowledged his authorship, and probably Denby was merely an arranger.[1] 'Hanover' has been ascribed to Handel, but on no trustworthy evidence. These tunes are noteworthy as among the earliest purely English products entirely untouched by Genevan or other outside influences; indeed, the great massive swing of the triple measure of 'Hanover' was possibly quite a novelty at the time for such music, and it certainly possesses a distinct character of its own. But these, admirable in all ways as they are, represent only one, and that the less important side of Croft's church music; while it is true that some of his anthems fall short of them in qualities of solidity and masterly directness of style, yet his best works show features which demand for their portrayal much more space than a hymn tune can afford. Like some of the younger anthem-writers of his time, he not infrequently hovers visibly between his allegiance to the older and stronger ideals and his desire to meet the insistent contemporary demands for elegance and grace; occasionally he spoils what would otherwise be very fine works by unfortunate reminiscences of the perfunctory concluding Hallelujahs of the earlier generation, as in 'Praise the Lord, O my soul' (*Musica Sacra*, I), or by bald strings of consecutive thirds and sixths, as in 'God is gone up with a merry noise'[2] or 'Give the King thy judgements'. On the whole, he seems least at home when attempting what we might call 'brilliant' anthems. In 'The heavens declare the glory of God' (*Musica Sacra*, II), for example, in spite of the broad and dignified character of one of its 'Hallelujah' sections, there is a great deal of purely conventional bustling around; and his orchestrally accompanied anthems, especially those written for festive occasions, such as 'Rejoice in the Lord' (ibid., I) or 'O give thanks' (ibid., II), are usually, in spite of their largeness of outline,

---

[1] See Grove's *Dictionary* (4th ed.), vol. iv, p. 499.
[2] Edited by V. Novello (Novello).

disfigured by a quantity of what are nothing but massively reiterated 'tags'. But at his best—and in most of his works he is, even if
not continuously, in his really good vein somewhere—he is a very
attractive composer, with a real sense for lofty dignity of phrase,
and a distinct individuality of his own. The music of his Burial
Service cannot rank with that of either Morley or Purcell; but it
is sincere and impressive, and its sentiment, if not altogether great,
is thoroughly manly. Sometimes, as in 'O Lord, rebuke me not'
(ibid., I):[1]

'O Lord God of my salvation' (ibid., I), or 'Hear my prayer, O Lord' (ibid., I)[1] which begins in four parts and gradually increases to eight, the music is finely austere and solid, sometimes approaching really noble sombreness; and again, in a work like 'O Lord, thou hast searched me out' (ibid., I),[1] he can strike a vein of really beautiful and original melody—or, as in 'Be merciful unto me' or 'Put me not to rebuke',[2] can show a manly expressiveness that very worthily fits the words. His emotions are always well under control, as befits the eighteenth-century scholar and gentleman, and he never moves us very much; but in the roll of English church musicians there are very few who are more deserving of our sincere and cordial respect. He was probably the last who felt, more or less habitually, the influence of his great predecessors in that field; and in sober dignity and quietly sincere musicianship he is, when at his best, a true successor to the fine traditions.

Weldon was two years Croft's senior in age, but he outlived him by nine years; and his music certainly owes less to the older models. In many ways he forecasts the rather sentimental attitude of later English composers of religious music, notably, *mutatis mutandis*, Sterndale Bennett; the older notion of the essential value of restraint and dignity has almost if not quite disappeared, and in their place we have a style which is melodious enough in a somewhat weak manner and marked by rather elementary elegance, but is clean and in its way expressive. 'O God, thou hast cast us out', 'Who can tell how oft he offendeth?' (supposed to be in seven parts, but the full passages are of microscopically small duration), 'In thee, O Lord,

---

[1] Edited by C. Hylton Stewart (Oxford University Press).
[2] Edited by G. Bantock (Curwen).

have I put my trust',[1] 'Hear my crying',[2] and others like them, are on the whole of rather flimsy texture; they are the work of a man with a good deal of capacity for agreeable sentiment but little command over solid technique. Perhaps his best work, though it seems wellnigh forgotten now, is a long sort of *scena* in several movements, entitled 'The Dissolution' (Happy the man), which was published in the second edition of Playford's *Harmonia Sacra*, book I (1703); this is much more Purcellian than Weldon's ordinary anthems, and shows a good deal of rather powerful declamation and some finely swinging rhythms. But most of his work is, compared with that of his best contemporaries, merely second-rate; it is the beginning of a style that has in later days done its best to wreck English church music, though Weldon himself always, as has been said, retained a certain cleanness and refinement.

Greene was some twenty years younger than Croft and Weldon and belonged entirely to the Handelian period; we find in him occasional traces of the great earlier style, but they are less common than with Croft, though, when the old influence does make itself felt, the results are finer, perhaps, than anything Croft could achieve. Greene undoubtedly was a genius, though the fire of inspiration burnt fitfully; works like 'Sing unto the Lord a new song', 'Arise, shine', 'O clap your hands', 'I will sing of thy power', the five-part 'Let my complaint come before thee', 'The Lord, even the most mighty God, hath spoken', 'God is our hope and strength', or the eight-part 'How long wilt thou forget me, O Lord' (all in *Forty Select Anthems*) are really fine music, broad and massive in style, and instinct with individual dignity, in spite—in some of them—of the presence of a certain amount of what may be called Handelian generalities. The Anniversary Commemoration anthem, 'Hearken unto me, ye holy children',[3] written in 1728 for King's College, Cambridge, is a large work with full orchestral accompaniments, full of musicianly vigour from start to finish; in this field Greene was quite at home, and frequently produced really brilliant effects. But he could also be subtle, and, indeed, two anthems—'Lord, let me know mine end'[4] and 'Lord, how long wilt thou be angry?' (both in *Forty Select Anthems*), the latter beginning:

---

[1] Edited by J. E. West (Bayley & Ferguson).
[2] Edited by H. G. Ley (Oxford University Press).
[3] Oxford, Bodleian, Mus. d. 36, fol. 64^v.
[4] Edited by E. Bullock (Oxford University Press).

may without much hesitation be ranked as the finest masterpieces produced by a native-born Englishman in the whole period we are considering, and indeed as quite worthy to stand side by side with the great anthems of earlier times; both are full, from the first bar to the last, of nobly expressive solemnity—the sombre, never-ceasing, funeral march rhythm of 'Lord, let me know mine end' is superbly conceived—and the workmanship of both is of a very high type, even if we, perhaps, feel a certain lack of balance about the structure of 'Lord, how long wilt thou be angry?' But he was a composer of very unequal powers; and any one who sets himself, in admiration of these special anthems, to read through Greene's complete sacred compositions will find very few others that attain anything like this level. His best anthems are nearly all full; of these, six five-part works which survive in manuscript[1] are in their way specially interesting as expressive, if at the same time artificial, revivals of the old ecclesiastical tonalities, each of which is faithfully represented: deliberate archaism like this is almost unknown in English eighteenth-century music. But he more usually wrote verse anthems, which in the majority of cases are marked by a sort of mechanically monotonous style that retains enough musicianship to avoid (as a rule, but not invariably[2]) conventional triviality but not enough to produce anything of living interest. Our impression of Greene is indeed that of a man who, somehow, neglected and more or less frittered away a very splendid talent; for natural genius, his name certainly ranks among the foremost few in the list of English musicians of the last two centuries.

Boyce was, as we have seen, selected by Greene as his musical legatee; but as a composer he is a much smaller man.[3] The five-part anthem 'O where shall wisdom be found?' (the authenticity of which has been questioned[4]) and the four-part 'By the waters of Babylon' represent his church music at its best: they are solid, dignified work, thoroughly sincere and clean, but not very specially worthy of remembrance. His large eight-part 'O give thanks' (in B♭, not to be confused with a four-part anthem in the key of C with the same title) is also in some respects not at all unattractive, and the fashionable consecutive thirds and sixths are here managed considerably more satisfactorily than usual; 'Give the King thy judgements', the five-part 'Turn thee unto me', 'Save me, O God', and others, have plenty of solid merit in their way, and the end of 'If we believe that Jesus died' is fine and tender. There is much that we can temperately admire; but the expression is, as a rule, somewhat formal and stilted, and altogether a course of Boyce's church music leaves us with the confused and somewhat somnolent recollection of many very conscientious but rather dull pages. His workmanship is, as

[1] See E. Walker, 'The Bodleian Manuscripts of Maurice Greene', in *The Musical Antiquary*, Apr.–July 1910, pp. 149–65, 203–14.

[2] For example, the miserably perfunctory accompaniment-figures in 'O praise the Lord of heaven', or the empty twirlings of 'Behold, I bring you glad tidings'.

[3] His anthems were published by Vincent Novello in four volumes.

[4] See E. H. Fellowes, *English Cathedral Music* (1941), pp. 184–5.

a rule, within its narrow limits, very accurate and adequate; but occasionally it breaks down altogether. One of the most curious of all anthems is Boyce's eight-part 'Blessing and glory', forty-eight bars altogether, arranged in four little sections, (*a*) twelve bars of what is called eight-part work, but is never anything like it, (*b*) twelve bars of a four-part Hallelujah[1] on a jumping dotted rhythm, (*c*) twelve bars of a four-part 'Verse', and (*b*) repeated to finish: it is true, however, that Boyce very rarely drops to elementary emptiness of this kind—on the whole he is an eminently respectable composer, whose solid, good-natured face, looking out at us underneath the carefully arranged wig, is exactly typical of his music.

The rest of the church music of the period does not come to much. The least negligible of the remaining men is no doubt William Hayes, most of whose services and anthems—'Praise the Lord, O Jerusalem' is probably the best—are the work of a solid if as a rule rather uninspired and uninspiring musician, free from meretriciousness and, when allowance is made for the elegant posturings which his patrons demanded, not unattractive; we can hear his music with a certain satisfaction, and with him the conscious graces of the time rarely degenerate into flimsiness. It is true that he shows a partiality for one of the most unfortunate features of the anthems of the Restoration period—the incongruous bustling 'Hallelujah' finales: perhaps the worst case is in 'O give thanks', where each voice repeats the word some twenty times on end without pausing to take breath. But as a rule Hayes's music is very tolerable, if we do not have too much of it at once. His lesser contemporaries, though their music still to some extent survives, come to little or nothing; Stroud's 'Hear my prayer' has some agreeably melodious pages, and is clean and nice enough in its rather ordinary way. Kempton is a distinctly worthy if unimaginative composer, and Travers's 'Ascribe unto the Lord', in spite of the conscious elegance of its opening tenor solo and a good deal of rather meaningless floridity, is on the whole vigorous, pleasant music, but Kelway and King and Nares and Kent have extremely little to say to justify their existence. We can, however, no doubt distinguish to some extent between them; Kelway and King, in spite of their extreme dullness, are as a rule, free from

---

[1] Boyce has not so many perfunctory 'Hallelujah sections' as most of his contemporaries; but, on the other hand, he sometimes (as in 'Lord, what is man') interjects the word explosively at intervals—which is no artistic improvement.

the flimsiness which marks very much of the sacred work of Nares and still more that of the formerly much overrated Kent—one of the poorest, though one of the most popular, composers of the time.

Indeed, Hawkins's epigrammatic judgement on King's works— 'no one cares to censure or commend them, and they leave the mind just as they found it'[1]—applies to very much of the church music of this period. Apart from the best works of Croft and Greene these stacks of services and anthems contain hardly any music that would be worth remembering for a quarter of an hour were there not such a dearth of anything better. Boyce and Weldon and Hayes have their points, like any second-rate man who has capacity enough to make some use of good training; and Boyce once or twice showed something of his own. But nearly all this music has retained whatever vitality it still possesses solely through the associations of the daily routine of churches and cathedrals. Croft and Greene are the only composers who can really stand upright and look the world of art in the face: and fine as are their best things, the bulk of even their work will not bear comparison with that of Blow in the earlier generation, not to mention Purcell.

But besides religious music for the church we have also to consider that intended for the concert room; most of it, in default of the artificial support just mentioned, has now vanished into obscurity, but it is certainly not in any way of different merit. However, in the period we are now regarding, oratorios were not so very common; the fashion started by Handel took some little time to spread, and it is not till the next generation that we find the fever in full career. A fair number, indeed, of works of the kind were produced by Handel's contemporaries; but, with one exception, they do not seem to demand detailed notice from the artistic standpoint. The influences from the great men of the past which inspired Greene to such works as 'Lord, how long wilt thou be angry?' did not operate with respect to a perfectly new art-form, which from its origin was a theatrical entertainment: the men who had always associated religious words with the organ loft moved at first uneasily and tentatively when required to transport their sentiments to the concert room. Handel's oratorios no doubt succeeded all the more from the fact that he approached them from the opera-house and not from the cathedral: and similarly the best oratorio music of the period by

[1] *A General History of the Science and Practice of Music* (1875 ed.), p. 798.

a native-born Englishman was the work of one who wrote nothing for the Anglican Church.

The earlier of Arne's two oratorios, *The Death of Abel* (1744), which was produced in the same year as Handel's *Belshazzar*, survives only in the charmingly melodious 'Morning Hymn of Eve'; his second, *Judith* (1761), is more important, even though we can hardly echo Dibdin's opinion that it is 'one of the most noble compositions that ever stampt fame on a musician'.[1] The printed score contains only arias and duets besides the overture; the recitatives and choruses survive in manuscript (Brit. Mus. Add. 11515-7). None of the music is in the faintest degree large in style, and the duet for two sopranos 'Oh thou on whom the weak depend' is hopelessly feeble and conventional: but still there is a great deal of very melodious tunefulness of a very pleasant kind, such as 'Adorn'd with ev'ry matchless grace' or 'Vain is beauty's gaudy flow'r', or several other airs. Once, in 'Sleep, gentle cherub',[2] Arne manages to produce a little piece of somewhat remarkable delicacy and beauty; and he can also write vigorously effective music like the bass airs 'Hail, immortal Bacchus' and 'Conquest is not to bestow', in the latter of which the voice is almost always in unison with the whole string band, the upper harmony being supplied by two oboes and two horns. The whole work is, in spite of a fair amount of the ordinary decorous nothings of the age, very agreeable in its light style: and 'Sleep, gentle cherub' should be far better known than it is.

The secular vocal work of Arne is at the present time (at any rate in selections) much the most familiar music of the period, apart from that of Handel himself; and, indeed, there is much reason for its survival. We need not, perhaps, dwell on 'Rule Britannia', an extract from *Alfred* (1740);[3] it is only patriotism that has gathered this comparatively undistinguished strain out of its forgotten context—though it is true that the version generally current today is garbled in notes, in words, and in the way the two are fitted together. But, unequal composer though he was, Arne at his best possessed an individual vein of melody which, if not for a moment comparable with that of Purcell, is, nevertheless, genuine and pure; it is true that its range is not wide, and its emotion not deep, but

---

[1] *The Professional Life of Mr. Dibdin* (1803), vol. i, p. 75.
[2] *Old English Edition*, vol. ii, p. 47.
[3] Edited by Adam Carse (Augener).

still it lives and breathes, even after two hundred years have elapsed. Some of his Shakespearean songs, such as 'Where the bee sucks', 'Under the greenwood tree', or 'Blow, blow, thou winter wind', show, slender though they are, real marked freshness of style; and some less-known songs are perhaps still better. We have already remarked the grace of the best songs in the oratorios; and in the same style (Arne's methods hardly ever vary, whether he is dealing with oratorio or the stage or neither one nor the other) we may notice 'Not on beds of fading flow'rs' from *Comus*[1] or 'Arise, sweet messenger of morn' from *Alfred*[2]—both of a singularly charming delicacy—or 'O come, O come, my dearest' from *The Fall of Phaeton* (1736)[3]—a sparkling, polished little gem in its way:

As a rule, Arne's talent shows itself at its best in dainty tunefulness; he could very rarely rise to anything more powerful, but there are occasional, though very few, exceptions, such as the song from *Alfred*, 'Vengeance, O come inspire me'[4]—a brilliantly vigorous Prestissimo that really stirs the blood. But after all, Arne, it must

---

[1] *Old English Edition*, vol. ii, p. 23. The complete work is printed in *Musica Britannica*, vol. iii.

[2] Ibid., p. 44. [3] Ibid., p. 49.

[4] Ibid., p. 32.

be confessed, cannot long remain at such a level as he reached in work such as has just been named; he very easily dropped to an average sort of style, melodious enough in its way, but complacently undistinguished, and quite easily forgettable. *Artaxerxes*, the opera which was supposed by contemporary criticism to be his master-piece, is, to the reader who approaches it with a decided, if tem-pered, enthusiasm for Arne's talents, a very great disappointment. The great bulk of it is ordinary decorously stilted work (such as is seen, indeed, from start to finish in two other popular productions of his, the music to *Elfrida* and to *The Fairy Prince*); on the whole, he seems to have aimed at a certain impressiveness, and in the result to have produced a mass of conventional formulas. Occasionally, no doubt, we come across things of worth; the *siciliana* movement in the tenor scena, 'O much lov'd son', has a good deal of expressive-ness, and the soprano air, 'Let not rage, thy bosom firing', and the familiar 'Water parted from the sea' display Arne's pleasant melo-diousness very agreeably. But both here and elsewhere Arne prac-tically failed altogether when attempting anything on a large scale; when he tries to be floridly grand he almost invariably falls into purely second-rate and empty Handelianism (the ambitious but very poor song, 'The soldier tir'd of war's alarms', is a typical in-stance). Arne, indeed, is a somewhat small man possessed of one special talent, by which alone he lives. But this one gift of pleasant, fresh tunefulness has certainly never been at all too common; and though he cannot rank with the really great English composers, yet he occupies a very worthy niche of his own in our temple of art.

Greene's secular vocal music is far less familiar than Arne's; but much of it is of quite excellent quality. Songs like 'Go, rose'—dainty and elegant, if a shade stilted—he wrote in quantities; but we see this side of him to most advantage in such works as his setting of Pope's *Ode on St. Cecilia's Day* (1730) and (especially) in the dramatic pastoral entitled *Phoebe* (1748).[1] The former shows but a slight amount of the conventionality so usual in festival odes of the period; its final chorus 'Thus song could prevail' is very breezy and pointed, and the *siciliana* duet 'By the streams that ever flow' is full of delicate grace. *Phoebe* is a charming work that well deserves the attention of a tardy publisher; some pages, indeed (such as the last

[1] The manuscripts are in the Bodleian Library (Mus. d. 36, fol. 11 and d. 53), with many others by Greene.

chorus), do not amount to much, but the *allegro e piano* chorus 'From piercing steel or whelming wave', with its striking setting of 'and melt thy anger with her tears', is of a distinctly uncommon kind, and the solo numbers are full of most pleasant music. Tunes like 'Phoebe fears each bird that flies' or 'Ah, could we love like him' or the duet 'As round thine arm this chain I tie' show eighteenth-century melody in its most agreeable forms; and the vigorous bass air 'Like the young god of wine' displays some real characterization. It is true that Greene's secular work is, like his ecclesiastical, unequal; but at its best it shows, as much as the finest of the anthems do, talent of a quite exceptional kind.

A few words may be given to some other contemporary secular works. Croft's *Musicus apparatus academicus*—consisting of two odes on the Peace of Utrecht, one in Latin and one in English, written for his doctor's degree at Oxford in 1713—is a good specimen of his straightforward talent; it is not so individual as many of his anthems, but the English ode, 'With noise of cannon and of rattling drums', is not without a good deal of Purcellian spirit and directness, and has plenty of solid merit. Again, his song 'My time, O ye Muses, was happily spent' is very charming, almost worthy of Purcell himself; in lyrical work Croft's touch is, indeed, not infrequently unusually light, and he has plenty of distinction of utterance. Some of Boyce's music to stage plays has vigour and tunefulness, and his 'Heart of oak', from *Harlequin's Invasion* (1759), is a fine melody, which well deserves its continued fame; in this field he was extremely prolific, and shoals of songs, often excellent of their kind, but lacking, as a rule, the finish of the best of Arne or Greene or Croft, are to be met with in the collections of the time.

The instrumental music of Handel's contemporaries is very considerable in bulk. Much of it sounds like a faithful imitation of his style, but without the driving force of his invention; the same turns of phrase, the same harmonic progressions recur over and over again. Yet it is all, or nearly all, very worthy work; only very rarely do we see any of that sort of careless vulgarity which was creeping into the inferior class of instrumental music on the Continent, and the vast majority of all these sonatas and concertos and harpsichord pieces are marked by dignified solidness and sober geniality. But even excellent qualities like these do not serve to dispel the dullness that is caused by the absence of living inspiration. Still, there are exceptions to this generalization. The eight symphonies by Boyce[1] have an individuality which few of his contemporaries achieved in this field. The style appears on the surface to be Italian; but there is also a ripe English quality which makes itself felt from time to time —a happy example is the gigue at the end of the first symphony, bluff and unmistakably nautical:

The music is everywhere alive and shows plainly enough the hand of the practical musician. Two of the symphonies (Nos. 3 and 4) are in fact overtures to dramatic entertainments, while a third (No. 6) is the overture to the serenata *Solomon* (1743); a thorough search would probably reveal a similar origin for the remaining five. The dramatic overtures are a reminder of Boyce's practical association with the theatre, and further evidence of the close connexion between opera and instrumental forms which has been mentioned already. The strange thing is that a composer who could show such vigour and spontaneity in his instrumental music should have produced so many dull anthems. There is also excellent work in his trio sonatas, which Burney tells us 'were longer and more generally purchased, performed, and admired, than any productions of the kind in this kingdom, except those of Corelli'.[2] Here the style is less up to date than in the symphonies; there are echoes of an older tradition, and a certain affinity with Purcell's works for the same medium. As an instrumental composer Arne was on the whole inferior to Boyce. But there is much that is agreeable in his orchestral

---

[1] Edited by C. Lambert (Oxford University Press).
[2] *A General History of Music*, vol. iii, p. 620.

works—the gigue in the overture to *The Judgment of Paris*[1] is not an unworthy companion of the one in Boyce's first symphony; and his trio sonatas, though slight, sometimes achieve a genuine eloquence—for example, in the third movement of No. 2 in G major.[2] Occasionally, lesser-known composers, like William Babell and Joseph Gibbs, produced pieces of considerable grace and spirit; there is a charming violin sonata in B♭ by the former,[3] and a 'Corno' from a sonata in E♭ by the latter[4] is unusually pointed and individual.

Among the many keyboard pieces which faithfully observe the conventions of the period mention must be made of a really charming harpsichord sonata by Nares[5] (whose anthems, as we have seen, are by no means among the best), which is marked by unusual freshness of both style and matter and a facility of expression surprising in so ordinarily second-rate a composer. Particularly interesting at this period is the enthusiasm shown by several English musicians for the works of Domenico Scarlatti, largely as a result of the advocacy of Thomas Roseingrave, who had met him in Italy as a young man and published a collection of his sonatas in two volumes.[6] The subscribers to this edition included Avison, Arne, Boyce, Greene, Pepusch, and Stanley. Avison showed his admiration for Scarlatti in a peculiar way, by arranging forty-eight of his sonatas for orchestra to form twelve *concerti grossi* (1744). Among the other enthusiasts were John Worgan (1724–90), who published a further selection of Scarlatti's pieces, and Joseph Kelway (younger brother of Thomas), described by Burney as 'at the head of the Scarlatti sect' in England.[7] Kelway had a reputation as a performer of Scarlatti's sonatas, but was less successful in imitating that composer's idiosyncrasies in his own compositions for the harpsichord. Roseingrave himself published, among other works, a set of *Fifteen Voluntarys and Fugues* for organ or harpsichord,[8] which show an original, though rather wayward, talent. His fondness for chromaticism and dissonance earned the disapproval of Burney, who speaks

[1] Edited by A. Carse (Augener).
[2] Edited by H. Murrill (Hinrichsen).
[3] Edited by A. E. Moffat (Novello).
[4] Edited by O. Peiniger (Lucas).
[5] Edited by H. G. Ley (Year Book Press).
[6] See R. Newton, 'The English Cult of Domenico Scarlatti', in *Music and Letters*, Apr. 1939, pp. 138–56.
[7] *A General History of Music*, vol. iv, p. 665.
[8] Edited by A. V. Butcher (Hinrichsen).

of his harmony as 'intolerably harsh and ungrateful' and his modulation as 'licentious and extravagant'.[1] These mannerisms are not the mark of greatness; but it is at least refreshing to find an English composer of this period who was prepared to resist the influence of Handel and make some attempt at finding a style of his own.

[1] Op. cit., vol. iv, p. 266.

MUSIC UNDER THE LATER GEORGES

ONE of the oldest composers whose works will come under review in the present chapter is Benjamin Cooke (1734–93); he was for many years organist of Westminster Abbey, and composed a large quantity of music of all kinds, of which the glees are considerably the most noteworthy. Slightly junior was Jonathan Battishill (1738–1801); in his earlier life he devoted himself chiefly to theatre music and songs, but afterwards turned more in the direction of anthems and other works intended for church use. When a youth he had acted as Boyce's deputy in the organist's duties at the Chapel Royal, and his admiration for the older composer lasted throughout his life, and inspired his dying wish to be buried close at hand in St. Paul's Cathedral; he composed very little during the last twenty-five years of his life, when he seems to have spent much of his time in book-collecting, and at no period was he nearly so prolific as the majority of his contemporaries. Samuel Arnold (1740–1802), for example, produced forty-nine dramatic works, five oratorios—the most famous being *The Prodigal Son* (1773)—and very many anthems and services, and instrumental pieces both for orchestra and for harpsichord, besides collecting a large quantity of English eccle-siastical music of the seventeenth and eighteenth centuries, which was issued as a sort of continuation of Boyce's *Cathedral Music*, and performing multifarious duties as editor and conductor and organist of the Chapel Royal and subsequently of Westminster Abbey. Arnold was indeed, however superficially, one of the most versatile and indefatigable musicians of the time; and most of the rather younger composers who concerned themselves at all with ecclesiastical music devoted themselves to it more exclusively, with the exception of Thomas Attwood (1765–1838), who, like Battishill, wrote primarily in early life for the stage, and later on for the church, while producing songs and glees and instrumental pieces more or less continually all through his career. Originally a chorister at the Chapel Royal, he subsequently studied at Naples and then at Vienna under Mozart, who expressed high opinions of him;[1] he was organist of St. Paul's Cathedral for more than forty years, and held also various court appointments. In his last years he was an intimate

---

[1] *Reminiscences of Michael Kelly* (1826), vol. i, p. 228.

friend of Mendelssohn, whose genius he was one of the first Englishmen to recognize; he was also one of the founders of the Philharmonic Society, and one of the first professors of the Royal Academy of Music.

Two composers of the period, chiefly known by their ecclesiastical music, are John Clarke-Whitfield (1770–1836) and William Crotch (1775–1847). The former was successively organist of Armagh Cathedral, Trinity and St. John's Colleges, Cambridge, and Hereford Cathedral, besides being from 1821 onwards professor at Cambridge; the latter was chiefly connected with Oxford, where he was for fifty years professor, besides holding organ appointments at Christ Church and St. John's College. Crotch was perhaps the most juvenile infant prodigy ever known, as he was an organ-player at the age of two, was the subject of philosophical papers at the Royal Society at three, and at four gave a course of daily public recitals in London. His chief works were the oratorios *The Captivity of Judah* (1789) and *Palestine* (1812) and a considerable number of anthems; he also published his professorial lectures and various other theoretical writings.

Samuel Wesley (1766–1837) is, however, the most important figure of the time; he was the son of the famous hymn-writer and nephew of the founder of Methodism, and the younger brother of a capable organist who never fulfilled his promise as an infant prodigy. He himself was also unusually precocious, being at the age of ten a skilled performer on organ, harpsichord, and violin, and also a prolific composer; but a severe accident with which he met when he was twenty-one (he fell into a building excavation on a dark evening and injured his skull) rendered him throughout the rest of his life subject to attacks of something like insanity, frequently prolonged for a considerable period, which unfitted him for the holding of any regular appointment. His works include Masses and many shorter works for the services of the Roman Church, several Anglican anthems and services, other choral works, and a quantity of glees and songs, besides numerous instrumental compositions of all kinds, symphonies, concertos, chamber music, and solos. He was acknowledged as the leading organist of his day; and he was the first Englishman to appreciate to the full the genius of Johann Sebastian Bach, whose cause he propagated with the utmost enthusiasm.[1]

[1] See *Letters of Samuel Wesley to Mr. Jacobs*, ed. E. Wesley (1875).

Wesley never attempted to write for the stage; but, besides the composers already named, several others of this period wrote for hardly anything else. Michael Arne (1741–86), a son of his better-known namesake, wrote a large mass of incidental music for plays in the intervals of fantastic chemical experiments in search of the philosopher's stone; and Thomas Linley (1733–95)—first a fashionable singing-teacher at Bath, and afterwards director both of oratorio and stage music at Drury Lane Theatre—produced many very successful works of the same kind.[1] The kind of ballad opera which is chiefly represented by the names of Charles Dibdin (1745–1814), William Shield (1748–1829), and Stephen Storace (1763–96) is, however, the most typical dramatic product of the time. The first-named was a chorister in Winchester Cathedral, where he received the desultory musical education which was all he ever acquired save by his own efforts. He devoted himself entirely to stage pieces and songs, being in most cases the author of the words as well. He was also a novelist, and the author of a voluminous *History of the Stage* (1795), as well as of a nearly equally voluminous autobiography (1803). The theatrical world was his home throughout his life, and his 'table entertainments', in which he appeared at once as author, composer, singer, and accompanist, carried his songs all over England. William Shield was a musician in the stricter sense of the word, though his early education was hardly more adequate—he was in his youth apprenticed to a boat-builder; he wrote some instrumental music and some theoretical works, and was the leading viola-player in London, but his chief fame is derived from the songs in his dramatic compositions—operas, farces, and pantomimes—of which he wrote a very large number, *Rosina* (1782) being one of the best and most successful. Stephen Storace, son of an Italian double-bass player settled in London, and brother of Nancy Storace, who was the original Susanna in Mozart's *Le Nozze di Figaro*, studied in Italy, and after some travels on the Continent returned to England, and in the eight years from 1788 to his early death in 1796 produced a considerable quantity of stage music of various kinds, of which *The Haunted Tower* (1789), *No Song, no Supper* (1790), *The Pirates* (1792), and *The Cherokee* (1794) seem to have been the

[1] Three sons and three daughters of his were all musicians of more or less fame; Thomas Linley the younger (1756–78), who was a friend of Mozart and was drowned at the age of twenty-two, and Elizabeth Ann (1754–92), who became the wife of Sheridan, were the most gifted.

most noteworthy. Other composers of music of similar kind, whose names may be mentioned in passing, were James Hook (1746–1827), who, in addition to numerous dramatic works and songs, composed some choral music on an extended scale, as well as concertos and sonatas; John Davy (1763–1824), composer of 'The Bay of Biscay' among a mass of other things; and William Reeve (1757–1815); but a good many others were nearly as prominent. John Braham (1777–1856) was a tenor singer of exceptional ability, who for very many years held a unique position; he composed all the music of his own part in the majority of the operas in which he sang —his well-known 'The Death of Nelson' occurs in *The Americans* (1811).

Henry Rowley Bishop (1786–1855) was for a long time perhaps the most prominent composer in England. He was connected chiefly with the stage, holding appointments at the chief London theatres and at Vauxhall for many years, during which he produced in all (including some adaptations of operas by Arne, Auber, Boieldieu, Mozart, Meyerbeer, and Rossini) more than one hundred and thirty dramatic works of various kinds; he also wrote several choral concert works, including a sacred cantata entitled *The Seventh Day* (1833), and numerous smaller compositions. He also held university professorships at Edinburgh (from 1841 to 1843) and Oxford (from 1848 till his death) and numerous conducting appointments. A knighthood was conferred on him by Queen Victoria in 1842; this is the earliest instance of such a thing being given by the sovereign to a musician.[1] Charles Edward Horn, Bishop's exact contemporary in birth (1786–1849), was the son of Karl Friedrich Horn, who in 1810 published, in conjunction with Wesley, an English edition of Bach's *Wohltemperirtes Clavier*. Like Bishop, he concerned himself chiefly with stage music, of which he produced a very large quantity, in much of which he sang himself, but also wrote some oratorios and numerous songs and glees. He was the first prominent English composer to visit America, where he lived from 1833 to 1843, and from 1847 (with a brief interval) till his death.

As we have seen, many of the composers already mentioned wrote glees; but several others made a virtual speciality of unaccompanied vocal music. Of these perhaps the most important

[1] Three earlier knighthoods were conferred by Lords Lieutenant of Ireland. See *Hinrichsen's Musical Year Book, 1945–6*, p. 39.

was Samuel Webbe (1740–1816), the father of a similarly named son who was also a composer, though of less note; for many years he held the principal offices at the Catch Club and the Glee Club—the chief societies for the encouragement of such forms of composition—and carried off a very large proportion of the prizes offered. John Stafford Smith (1750–1836), son of a cathedral organist, was from 1784 onwards one of the musical officials of the Chapel Royal; his compositions consist, however, almost exclusively of glees and similar works, but he also devoted much time to musical antiquarianism, producing *A Collection of English Songs* (1779) and *Musica Antiqua* (1812), and acquiring a very valuable library of printed and manuscript music, much of which was carelessly dispersed at his death and seems to have entirely disappeared. Richard John Samuel Stevens (1757–1837) was also an organist—at the Temple Church and the Charterhouse—who devoted himself as a composer mainly to glee-writing; Stephen Paxton (1735–87), his brother William Paxton (1737–81), and the Earl of Mornington (1735–81), father of the Duke of Wellington and professor of music at Dublin, were also distinguished in the same field. John Wall Callcott (1766–1821), though an organist and theorist, also wrote little music besides his very numerous glees, catches, and canons; in later life (from 1808 onwards) he produced nothing at all, as his mind gave way under overwork of lecturing and teaching. His son-in-law William Horsley (1774–1858) was also an organist and theorist (he edited, though with very little understanding, the reprint of the first book of Byrd's *Cantiones Sacrae* for the Musical Antiquarian Society) who was chiefly famous as a composer of glees; but Reginald Spofforth (1770–1827) and William Beale (1784–1854), the last of the composers of this kind who need be noticed, seem to have devoted themselves entirely to such work without venturing, even in passing, into other departments.

John Field (1782–1837) may claim a paragraph to himself as virtually a denationalized native of these islands; he was an Irishman by birth and belonged to a musical family that had long been settled in Dublin, but he spent most of his life abroad. He was in early life an apprentice to Clementi, who gave him pianoforte lessons and whom he served as salesman to the firm of Clementi and Co. in London; afterwards he travelled through France, Germany, and Russia, still on the firm's business, and showing off their pianos in the different centres. His remarkably fine playing attracted general attention, and in 1804 he abandoned his post and settled in Russia, where he remained till 1832, being held in the highest esteem alike as performer, composer, and teacher. The next few years he spent in travelling, playing in London and Paris and afterwards in Italy, where, however, his concerts failed to attract and he sank into great poverty; he was rescued from a hospital in Naples, where he had lain for many months, by a Russian family, with whom he travelled back to Moscow, playing with the greatest success at Vienna on the way, but his health never returned, and he died soon after his arrival in Russia. His compositions include seven piano concertos, and many works of smaller dimensions; he is, however, now almost exclusively known by his Nocturnes, which, as will be seen later, are of unusual historical importance.

As a sort of counterbalance to this continentalized Englishman, two composers may be mentioned who, though foreigners by blood, made this country their home throughout virtually the whole of their musical lives. Muzio Clementi (1752–1832), a Roman by birth, was sent to England as a boy, and apart from three or four continental concert-tours remained here till his death; a pianist of extraordinary attainments, he may, through his influence as player and teacher, be counted the originator of piano technique, and he also displayed his versatile talents as the head of a very successful publishing and manufacturing business. He wrote a large number of compositions, chiefly for his own instrument; among these the well-known studies entitled *Gradus ad Parnassum* (1817) are noteworthy. His pupil, John Baptist Cramer (1771–1858, his life thus exactly spanning the gap between Tartini and *Tristan*), the son of a Mannheim violinist who for nearly thirty years held a distinguished position in England, was, like Clementi, virtually an Englishman, though he often travelled abroad and lived in Germany and France from 1835 to 1845; he followed in the steps of his master, not only as a virtuoso and composer but also as music-publisher. His famous piano studies are now his sole remembered works; but he had great influence in his day, and was the only contemporary pianist of whose powers Beethoven had any opinion.[1]

In spite of a few persistent questioners like Wesley (who was continually disparaging Handel in comparison with J. S. Bach), the most salient feature of English music during the whole of this

[1] F. G. Wegeler and F. Ries, *Biographische Notizen über Ludwig van Beethoven*, ed. A. C. Kalischer (2nd ed., 1906), p. 119.

period was, after all, the worship of the great Anglo-German and the oratorio form which he had popularized. The blind adoration of Handelian methods in almost every branch of the art laid a dead weight on English music which crushed out of ninety-nine of every hundred composers any vital originality that they might otherwise have displayed; and the public's insatiable appetite for oratorios forced into this channel all who wished to produce serious work on a certain scale. Religious music, in any conceivable sense of the word, these tons of oratorios are not, any more than they are artistic music; the whole thing is mere glazed conventionality. The poetasters of the day evolved, with apparently absolute indiscrimination, librettos from wellnigh every page of the Bible (sometimes to the original words, sometimes to bald versifications); and when the composers were not making oratorios of their own, they were still compiling them out of the mangled remains of other men's music. Turning over these dusty tomes, we meet, over and over again, with music of Handel himself or of Haydn or Mozart or many more in the most astonishingly perverted guises. One of the most unconsciously humorous of all is Arnold's anthem version[1] of the remarkably secular overture to Arne's *Artaxerxes*. The shibboleth of 'sacred music' satisfactorily quieted any uneasy artistic conscience. Nothing has been a greater hindrance to English music than this phrase, which, as used by far too many persons from Handel's day to our own, has no sort of warrant from religion or art or common sense or anything beyond a fetish-like conventional superstition.

The term oratorio was used indeed very vaguely. Handel himself, as we have seen, used it to include practically any choral work performed in a concert room or a theatre; towards the end of the century it was also used to denote any performance, even of the type of a variety entertainment, given during Lent, the general season for oratorios in the strict religious sense. These miscellaneous 'oratorio concerts', usually given at the two chief theatres, continued to be in vogue for a long time; but their artistic influences were of the slenderest importance.

Heavy as was the weight of foreign influence on most English music during the eighteenth century, the period nevertheless saw the birth of two specifically native forms of art. In the previous chapter we have described the rise of the ballad operas: and some half-century later an equally English product, the glee, rose with

[1] 'O be joyful unto the Lord.'

great rapidity to a pre-eminent popularity, which it retained till the beginning of the Victorian era. We have already seen how Pepusch and Immyns fostered, in the Madrigal Society, the old taste for unaccompanied singing even among Italianized surroundings; and the glee clubs that came into existence towards the end of the century were similarly designed to combine social and artistic pleasures in ways other than were afforded by catches like those of Restoration times—though these still continued to enjoy a great vogue as relaxations from more serious music-making. The glee[1] indeed was a compromise; it was more definitely melodious and rhythmical than the madrigal, and more especially laid out for solo male voices, while at the same time it preserved the artistic interests of more or less continuous rather than strophic design and a certain amount of contrapuntal elaboration, as well as the homogeneity of tone resulting from the absence of accompaniment. Accompanied choruses have been sometimes styled glees; but that is, strictly, a misuse of the name. The Glee Club *par excellence* was founded in 1787 and had a life of seventy years; the rather earlier, but still existing, Noblemen's and Gentlemen's Catch Club, founded in 1761 (which for many years offered annual prizes for the best glees, catches, and canons), and the later Concentores Sodales (1798–1847), both displayed similarly great activity in encouraging this form of art. The still existing Hibernian Catch Club (probably the oldest musical society in Europe today) had been founded in Dublin as early as 1680. Popularity, however, gradually brought with it a certain declension of taste: glees consisting of mere bald successions of plain chords became too frequent, and the homogeneity of manner which the masters of the form show, even when the words demand brief and sharply contrasted sections, gave place, in the inferior specimens, to a fragmentary and inorganic style.

At the same time there was considerable interest shown in the older English composers, especially those for the church; Boyce's collection of cathedral music found continuations in the large publications edited by Arnold (1790) and by John Page (1800), a cathedral singer himself. And at about the same time the first two histories of music written by Englishmen appeared—Sir John Haw-

---

[1] From the Anglo-Saxon *gliw* or *gléo* = entertainment, music. Charles Colman's 'To Bacchus, we to Bacchus sing', described as 'a Glee, with *Chorus* for three voyces' (in Playford's *Select Musicall Ayres and Dialogues*, 1652, p. 42), seems to be the earliest use of the term in printed music.

kins's in 1776 and Charles Burney's at intervals from 1776 to 1789. Both are of great value still, though more recent research has altered many things in them and neither author possessed any very exceptional qualities. Hawkins was not himself a practical musician, and his main strength lay in his antiquarian researches; Burney, though technically skilled (his books on the contemporary state of music in continental countries are full of interest), had a curious prejudice against the earlier secular music, especially madrigals,[1] and an equally (to us) curious belief in the permanent importance of every third-rate Italian opera produced in London in his own time. Stafford Smith's *Musica Antiqua* (1812)—a collection of nearly two hundred pieces, mainly English—is, though unorganized and virtually unedited, of very great interest, and forms a valuable supplement to the numerous musical extracts printed by Hawkins and Burney; already in 1779 he had published *A Collection of English Songs*, chiefly from the so-called 'Fayrfax Book'.[2] Both Burney and Smith, like practically all their contemporaries, express unbounded complacency with the position of English music in their time; but they seem on the whole to have referred more to the standard of performance than to the quality of the native productions, though they certainly rated the latter considerably higher than posterity has been inclined to do.

It is true, indeed, that about the end of the eighteenth century English music-lovers could hear a great deal of admirable vocal and instrumental performance; the days of singers like Caffarelli and Farinelli might be over, but on the other hand music was far more widely cultivated, and the general average of technical attainment was far higher. The Ancient Concerts (1776–1848) set a worthy standard and did much to keep alive the knowledge of Purcell and of the madrigalian composers, even though the reigning Handelworship led the directors to devote an altogether disproportionate share of wellnigh every programme to Handelian extracts. The meaning of the title was that no compositions written during a floating period of twenty years previously were included in the programmes. The Vocal Concerts (1792–1822) also largely advanced musical knowledge, especially between the years 1800 and 1815. Another enterprise, known as the Professional Concerts, did much

---

[1] 'There is doubtless more nerve, more science, and fire, in the worst of Handel's choruses, than in the greatest efforts of these old madrigalists' (vol. iii, p. 131).   [2] Brit. Mus. Add. 5465.

to popularize the works of Haydn; and it was owing to the secession from these concerts of a German violinist named Johann Peter Salomon (1745–1815), who started rival performances of his own, that the composer himself was induced to visit this country in 1791–2 and 1794–5. Haydn seems to have recognized that he learned much by his visits, especially through the opportunities, wider than any obtainable abroad, of hearing choral singing, both accompanied and unaccompanied; he was present in 1791 at the last Handel Commemoration held in Westminster Abbey, when more than a thousand performers took part—the first of these festivals was held in 1784 and there were several others in the intermediate years. In the purveying of instrumental music foreigners took the lead; Karl Abel (1725–87) a distinguished German *viola da gamba* player, and John Christian Bach (1735–82), a son of the great Sebastian and himself a composer of considerable facility but little artistic steadiness, were the joint conductors of a series of fashionable concerts from 1765 to 1782, and their successes as aristocratic teachers and performers attracted many other continental musicians to England. Some of these, like Clementi, made this country their permanent home—Cramer was, as we have seen, the son of such an immigrant and virtually an Englishman all his life— while others, like Dussek and Moscheles, returned to the Continent after some (in the latter case, twenty) years of exile; but to all foreign musicians we offered, as indeed we have done ever since, generous inducements to settle in our midst, and the methods they set were followed, sometimes rather too slavishly, by our own professors. However, the foundation of the Philharmonic Society in 1813 and the Royal Academy of Music in 1823 did much to keep the balance fair; and the numerous recurrent provincial festivals of which we hear during this period, in addition to the older events at Gloucester, Worcester, and Hereford, spread taste through districts usually untouched to any great extent by the foreign-loving fashions of the metropolis.

Over the music of this period one artistic figure towers, that of Samuel Wesley. It is true, indeed, as we shall see later, that he wrote a considerable mass of purely commonplace work; but after all a composer must be judged at his best, and it is in virtue of the finest of his religious productions that he takes place, beyond all possible question, among the great English musicians. He is differentiated from many of his contemporaries by the fact that he wrote no ora-

torios after the age of eleven; but *Ruth*,[1] the airs in which are said
to have been written at the age of six, and *The Death of Abel*[2] are
quite as good as the grown-up work of most other composers of the
time. 'Hail liberty' and 'Go, my Ruth, the pattern fairest' are, in
their graceful flow and solid harmonic foundation, astounding productions for an infant of six or seven; and a contemporary book of
mixed vocal and instrumental music contains some things of quite
Mozartian promise, for example, 'And now another day is gone'[3]—
a tune of real point, well organized and furnished with an excellent
bass:

Ex. 153

His other ecclesiastical works in large forms consist of several
masses and a long and elaborate 'Confitebor'[4] on an oratorio scale.

[1] Brit. Mus. Add. 34997.
[3] Ibid. 34998, fol. 44.
[2] Ibid. 34999, fol. 1–80[v].
[4] Ibid. 35002.

The Mass in C, *Missa de Spiritu Sancto*,[1] written at the age of eighteen, is a really good work in a rather obvious style—very strong and clean, but not specially individual; the 'Confitebor' is, however, much more mature, and was apparently (though with more than doubtful justice) considered by its composer as his masterpiece. In it we see strong traces of Italian influence, chiefly of the Leo and Pergolesi type—though the fine unaccompanied chorus 'Mandavit in aeternum', with its noble closing pages, looks back to the golden age of Italian art—and there is a good deal of florid writing of a sometimes rather perfunctory character, brilliant bravura for soprano solo, and so on; but the chorus just mentioned, and, in different styles, the Mozartian duet 'Redemptorem misit populo' and the last chorus 'Sicut erat' strike notes that are not very easily forgotten. Prefixed to the score is a very high commendation by Burney, and it is no doubt just what one whose eclecticism ran in the fashionable channels liked; but still it is on the whole a distinctly fine work, and if we object to the otiose instrumental *ritornelli*, it may be counted as a sign of grace to the composer, that he (or some one presumably under his directions) has subsequently struck a pencil through many of them. But Wesley was at his greatest where he had nothing (or next to nothing) to think of but choral voices; the few works that he wrote for the Anglican church service—such as the massive anthem 'Thou, O God, art praised in Sion' and some others—are far above the ordinary type, but still to see him at the climax of his powers we must turn to the motets or antiphons that were, there can be no doubt, written for the Roman ritual. The gorgeously powerful and impressive eight-part 'In exitu Israel' is a masterpiece that places its composer on a very lofty pedestal; and the also more or less familiar 'Exultate Deo' and 'Dixit Dominus' fall only a little below in grand dignity of manner.

Three other men—Battishill, Attwood, and Crotch—did something to keep church music alive in those dead days; and of these Battishill must certainly be ranked first, in virtue of such things as his anthems 'Call to remembrance'[2] and 'O Lord, look down from heaven'.[3] The former has secured the wider fame, and it no doubt represents the standard eighteenth-century manner at its very best; it is gracefully melodious and also almost always quite strong, and

---

[1] Brit. Mus. Add. 35000.
[2] Modern edition published by Oxford University Press.
[3] Edited by G. C. Martin (Novello).

its expressive climaxes are built up in really fine, vigorous style. It is sincere, and does its best to live up to its ideals; there are a few touches of the empty conventions of the time, but they are only very few, and the earlier portion (which is considerably the greater) shows many traces of the influence of the Elizabethans in its dignity and its massive technique. But the austerer 'O Lord, look down from heaven' is really Battishill's masterpiece, and represents the high-water mark of English church music between Greene and the younger Wesley; instead of the mosaic of little pieces that we so often find, it is one continuous movement throughout, of altogether first-rate quality from start to finish, and full of variety and artistic life:

There is not perhaps the individuality of the best work of his predecessors Croft or Greene; but there is none of the slight flavour of sentimentality which rather spoils the second part of 'Call to remembrance', and there are no conventional loose ends about the workmanship. It is a matter for much regret that Battishill never again rose to the height of this remarkably fine anthem, with which English church music, even in its worst days, need not be ashamed to speak with its enemies in the gate.

The talent of Attwood was of a slenderer kind, and he never rose anywhere near the height of 'O Lord, look down from heaven'. He was, as we have seen, a pupil of Mozart; and his general manner is rather like a dim reflection of his master's less inspired moments. Of Handelian traits there is hardly a vestige; the new influence has practically ousted the old altogether. The anthem 'Let the words of my mouth',[1] for example, is marked by an agreeable, if not particularly dignified, sort of sparkle of a singularly Mozartian type:

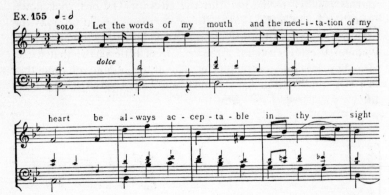

and the graceful turns of harmony in the Epiphany anthem 'O God, who by the leading of a star' show a vein not previously struck in English church music. But there is no real individuality of utterance; Attwood nearly always seems to be repeating a well-learned lesson. Often no doubt he repeats it really admirably; the little hymn 'Come, holy Ghost' is in its way charming, and, in a larger style, the extended anthems 'Teach me thy way, O Lord', and 'They that go down to the sea in ships' are (like many more) pleasing and refined, with good melody and well-devised harmony, and altogether the work of a musician and a gentleman. It is all quite enjoyable in its mild way, but it all comes to very little; and a course of Attwood leaves really a more unsatisfactory total impression than a course of men who may write much worse music than ever he did but at the same time occasionally blunder into something that grips attention.

Ten years younger than Attwood, and nearly forty younger than Battishill, Crotch represents yet another style. He has little or none of the graceful if ineffectual purity of Attwood, still less of the massive power to which Battishill could rise; he is dominated by the Handelian traditions, and owes, unlike Battishill, nothing to any influence of earlier date. On the whole, his anthems are not much

---

[1] *Attwood's Cathedral Music*, ed. T. A. Walmisley, p. 220.

more than decorous Georgian work, clean and dull, with somewhat stilted expression and much formal padding; occasionally he tries, without much success, to be realistically modern, as at the passage 'though the earth be moved' in the anthem 'God is our hope and strength', or the rather elementary trumpet fanfare in 'The Lord, even the most mighty God, hath spoken'. But he rises above the majority of his fellows, inasmuch as he can, not infrequently, display a sort of polished if old-fashioned melodiousness that is even now not at all unattractive, as in the well-known 'How dear are thy counsels' and others; and once, in 'My God, my God, look upon me', he very largely drops his conventions, and writes really pathetic, sincere music—not particularly deep, but in its way of distinct tender beauty:

279

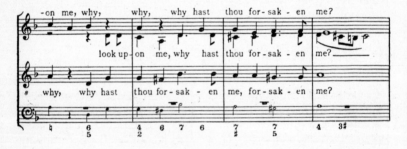

This, however, is indeed a solitary example of Crotch's best work; but his large oratorio *Palestine*[1] may be accepted as a satisfactory compendium of whatever other excellences he possessed. And, as a matter of fact, it is impossible to deny that *Palestine* is the one and only even moderately outstanding English oratorio in the century between Arne's *Judith* and Bennett's *The Woman of Samaria*, countless as were the works of that kind produced during those years; a good deal of it is no doubt a somewhat unappetizing mixture of

---

[1] Edited by B. Tours (Novello).

Handelian odds and ends with the consciously polite elegancies of 1812, but the criticism of it as 'stucco made to look like stone' is perhaps a little unfair. The dramatic chorus 'Let Sinai tell' is in its way not at all unimpressive, and the still frequently heard quartet 'Lo, star-led chiefs' is very agreeable music; Crotch does not try to do more than he can adequately manage, he occasionally has quite happy ideas, and his workmanship is thoroughly solid and dignified. But 'the best in this kind are but shadows'; and Crotch, like Attwood, has to suffer the penalties which sooner or later are the lot of composers who have no minds to call their own.

But still the other church music of the time shows traces of hardly even any one else's mind. Arnold was a person of great fame in his day, but he is now very nearly unreadable, though the vapidly respectable 'Who is this that cometh?' is still heard in our cathedrals; Clarke-Whitfield—an amiably unobjectionable composer, who occasionally had rather happy ideas which his technique was not strong enough to develop—also still survives to some extent. After all, only a very few of the church composers of these dark days dropped to the painful insipidity of such things as 'Jackson in F';[1] as a rule they knew and loved their Handel well enough to keep them free from anything like *ad captandum* cheapness of effect. Most of them had no capacity worth mentioning for anything beyond accurate counterpoint; but their music is nothing worse than intolerably dull. It was reserved for a later generation of English church musicians to discover that dullness could be blended with other more harmful qualities.

There is a strong family likeness about all the catches and canons and glees of this period; however much they may differ in musical quality—and at the worst they are very dull and undistinguished—they almost all show the same sense of vocal effect, the same flowing ease of style, the same decorous cheerfulness which, in the best specimens, result in the production of works which, though for the most part artistically very slight, are very agreeable and thoroughly fulfil a worthy end. Sometimes—rather illegitimately, but there is perhaps no other handy word available—the term glee is used to include works in the ordinary glee style, but provided with independent instrumental accompaniment; but these cases are comparatively rare, and the great bulk of this secular vocal literature whether, as with some glees, of considerable dimensions, or, as

[1] Attributed to William Jackson (1730–1803), organist of Exeter Cathedral.

with the catches and canons, merely a few bars long, reverts to the older ideals of unaccompanied singing, which had been wellnigh forgotten by composers for a century and a half. We have, indeed, noticed earlier the catches of the Purcellian epoch; but there was then nothing like the same wide artistic interest shown in this form of composition. Occasionally, as in parts of Webbe's fine 'Discord, dire sister' and especially Beale's 'Awake, sweet Muse', Morning-ton's 'As it fell upon a day', and Samuel Wesley's singularly beauti-ful 'O sing unto my roundelaie', we hear a sort of echo of the great madrigalists of the older time; and there is often plenty of solid workmanship shown, even when the methods are entirely un-affected by Elizabethan influences.

As a rule, the composers of the best glees did little noteworthy work in other fields. Battishill's charming, though very slender, 'Amidst the myrtles' is one of the best of the few specimens of good secular work by the anthem-writers of the time, who as a general rule—Attwood's 'Hark, the curfew's solemn sound' is a well-known instance—were by no means at their best outside their organ-lofts. Samuel Wesley himself, apart from the charming piece just men-tioned and the expressive 'Here shall the morn' (the words adapted from four lines in Pope's *Elegy to the Memory of an Unfortunate Lady*),[1] produced little of any special merit in this field; when he attempts great poetry, as in the settings of 'The glories of our birth and state'[2] and 'Roses, their sharp spines being gone',[3] he drops into mere stiff, stilted commonplace, and his ordinary social glees, whether purely convivial or more decorous in tone, do not equal the best specimens of those who found their primary medium of expres-sion in such work.

Narrow as the range of the typical glee-composers is, we can without much difficulty distinguish their individual characteristics, though it is true that very many of their works are in a sort of nega-tive style that was common to all. Webbe's 'When winds breathe soft' or 'Discord, dire sister', the closing section of which[4] may be quoted:

---

[1] Brit. Mus. Add. 35005, fol. 59ᵛ.
[2] Edited by E. G. Monk (Novello).
[3] Brit. Mus. Add. 14343, fol. 53.
[4] *Catches, Canons and Glees*, ed. Thomas Warren, vol. xi, p. 21.

Grazioso

Ex.157 But love - ly Peace in an - gel's form, de - scend - ing

quells the ris - ing storm: Soft ease and sweet con - tent____ shall

reign, and Dis - cord nev - er rise____ a - gain.

may be taken as representatives of the best glees of the ordinary mould—solid, tuneful music, excellent in workmanship and admirably effective; or we may select Cooke's well-designed 'As now the shades of eve' or some of the glees of Mornington, a musicianly composer with (at his best) a sort of aristocratic distinction of style that places him rather apart from the others. The melodious glees of Stevens and Spofforth—the former's 'Ye spotted snakes' or 'The cloud-capt towers' or 'Sigh no more, ladies', or the latter's 'My dear mistress' or 'Hail, smiling morn'—though slighter than some others, are clean, pleasant music; and Stephen Paxton's 'How sweet, how fresh', or his brother William's 'Breathe soft ye winds', while somewhat artificially pastoral in style, and rather more consciously polite than most, are, nevertheless, quite dainty and agreeable. With Callcott and Horsley we see rather more divergence of manner; the latter's admirable 'By Celia's arbour' or 'See the chariot at hand' or the eight-part ode 'Daughter of faith, awake' hardly seem to be from the same pen as the very poor and stilted 'When shall we three meet again?' (the words of which are not by Shakespeare), and

Callcott shows the same inequalities. Among his works we see the exceedingly dull 'Forgive, blest shade' and the very elementary setting of the 'Erlking' side by side with the breezy, spirited 'You gentlemen of England' (often known as 'Ye mariners of England') and pleasantly solid and musicianly pages like 'In the lonely vale of streams' or 'With sighs, sweet rose' or 'Who comes so dark?' or 'Father of heroes'; Callcott, indeed, though he never equalled the best work of Webbe and one or two others, is perhaps the most prominent figure of the time in this field, and certainly one of the most prolific.

A feature which markedly separates the English glee from the male-voice music of other countries is the prominent part assigned to the high counter-tenor or alto voice—a particular development of falsetto singing which has persisted in our cathedral choirs from the time of Charles II to the present day, but has never been known abroad. The quotation from 'Discord, dire sister' given above exemplifies very well the kind of writing that is specially suited to this type of voice.

Apart from the glees, which stand by themselves in a separate group, the whole of the secular vocal music of the time is coloured through and through by the influences springing from the ballad operas; nearly all the work is of virtually the same general type, and it never makes any difference whether it was primarily intended for theatrical surroundings or not. It is to Arne and the traditional folk music of earlier date that ultimately the parentage of all these numerous songs must be ascribed; but in the sixty years that this period covers we see a gradual decline, from the earlier generation represented by Shield and Hook and Dibdin and Storace to the later represented by Horn and Bishop. Shield was perhaps the most naturally gifted of all; a song like 'The wolf' is, indeed, poor stuff, but on the other hand some of the tunes in *Rosina*—which seems to have been generally considered his best opera—are of singular grace and purity. *Rosina* was published as 'composed and selected' by Shield; it is very often, throughout these ballad operas, quite impossible to be certain of the authorship of particular songs. Probably, however, the songs otherwise unspecified may be taken as Shield's own work; but it is certainly nothing more than a probability, which is always liable to exceptions. Shield's music is, as a rule, free from the conventional floridities that disfigure much contemporary work, though he descends to them occasionally, and then falls completely to pieces. A really very charming little work like 'O happy fair' stands out prominently among its weaker fellows; and rather more conventional music like the also well-known 'The thorn' is yet in its way quite pure and pleasant.[1] Hook's style is a little more consciously elegant; he has a special partiality for a sort of feminine daintiness, and undoubtedly, in his own line, he is a composer of a real, though slender, distinction. 'O listen to the voice of love', 'The blackbird', 'The lass of Richmond hill', and others are, if less artistically strong than the best work of Shield, very graceful little songs, and 'pretty' in the worthy sense of that often abused word.

Storace again, though less capable than Shield or Hook, often produced tunes that are worth the remembrance of posterity; like Shield he falls to pieces when he attempts to be advanced and floridly elaborate, but ballad operas like *No Song, no Supper* or *The Cherokee* contain melodies which to the lovers of the contemporary type may appeal as among the best of their kind, and *No Song, no Supper* shows, in a very graceful little quintet (a harmonized ballad-like tune), an exception to the rule of the almost universal inferiority of the concerted to the solo numbers. Dibdin has survived for us almost exclusively as a composer of songs connected with the sea; but his ballad operas are, as a rule, much like those of the rest. Admirable tune though 'Tom Bowling' is, he but rarely reached that level; and he is certainly a much less polished composer than Shield or Hook, or indeed than Storace. His amiable, inoffensive songs are all of one general type, and do not amount to very much, clean and healthy though the music is; occasionally he can turn a phrase quite happily, but, as a rule, he confines himself to such a setting of his words, whether they be sentimental or jovial, as shall be just sufficiently interesting to carry them along, and not so much so as to be capable of remembrance on its own merits. Others, too, there were, like the elder Linley—a graceful composer with a style in many respects much resembling Shield's—or his rather less capable son (the composer of 'O bid your faithful Ariel fly'), or John Percy (1749–97), with his charming if rather characterless 'Wapping old stairs', who at this time produced work which, slender though it is, is at its best, like that of the four more prominent composers first mentioned, a genuine and welcome legacy to the

---

[1] The familiar 'The Arethusa' is not by Shield. It is an adaptation of the country dance tune 'The Princess Royal', first published in 1730.

store of English music. It is notable, however, that nearly all the vitalized songs written at the latter end of the eighteenth century were the work of composers who are virtually unknown in other fields. The elder Linley and Shield produced, it is true, excellent concerted vocal music; but almost all the solo songs of the best-known glee-writers are singularly perfunctory, and those of the church musicians are no better. Arnold's still fairly familiar 'Flow, thou regal purple stream' comes to much less than the best bacchanalian songs of the pure secularists; Attwood's lyrics are singularly feeble, and the shoals of songs by Samuel Wesley in the British Museum manuscript volumes, in spite of the variety afforded by the frequent use of foreign languages such as French and Greek and the occasional emergence of some moderately good tune of the folk-song type, are on the whole a mere mass of dullness. The times had certainly changed since a primarily ecclesiastical musician like Boyce could write 'Heart of oak'.

At its worst the music of Shield and his followers was indeed thin and dull, but it always retained a certain freedom and naturalness of utterance. But later on the type of song which the ballad operas had popularized declined in spontaneity and became stiff and pompous. Horn could sometimes turn out clean and fairly solid work of an agreeable, if rather starchy, type; but most of his music is a sort of quasi-professional attempt at an imitation of the older essentially democratic style. He is, indeed, a capable workman, and is never guilty of the theatrical emptiness of things like his contemporary Braham's 'Death of Nelson'; but nearly all the early fresh charm has withered, and 'The deep, deep sea' is a very miserable successor to the older sailor songs. 'Cherry ripe' and some other similar melodies show traces of Shield's grace and easy tunefulness; but even here the touch is considerably heavier. Bishop also represents an undeniable decline, but in a somewhat different direction. He could, indeed, from time to time show himself the possessor of a certain vein of pleasing, if slender, melody, and things like 'Tell me, my heart' or 'Should he upbraid' are in their rather stilted way agreeable enough; very trifling though they are from a strictly artistic standpoint, there is a certain air of courtly, old-fashioned politeness about their easy-going strains which has not yet lost its attraction. But Bishop's average work fell much below this level; his general style is one of rather feeble sentimentality, lacking the sort of solidity of Horn's and also the distinctiveness of the older composers. A paltry tune like 'Home, sweet home', first associated with these words in the opera *Clari, or the Maid of Milan* (1823), represents fairly well the sort of music to which he was capable of rising in his ordinary moods; in its way it is not altogether inexpressive, but the whole is conceived on, artistically, a thoroughly low plane. Bishop was indeed a distinctly capable sort of musician, and his operas show considerably more power over the technique of choral writing than had been evident in the native stage music for many years previously; but there is no real sincerity in his careless, popularity-hunting work, and, apart from a small handful, his songs have virtually nothing to say to the musician. His best things show, indeed, that he possessed talents that, combined with more steadiness of aim, might have produced something really vital; but all that he did was to squander his endowment.

During all this period native instrumental music was at a very low ebb. Vocal music could stand out fairly well against the cult of the imported foreigner; he took no interest in anthem or glee, and if alien oratorios were sometimes produced, at any rate they had to be translated, and, moreover, English composers wrote many more. But instrumental music had neither the refuge of ecclesiasticism nor that of conviviality to which to retreat, nor could it call on the support of the national language; the consequence was that it fell instantly before the onslaught of the foreigner, and we may safely say that no instrumental work of even second-rate merit was produced by any resident English-born composer during the whole period. A few placidly ineffectual organ pieces, a few tentative attempts to do something with the new pianoforte, a few childish imitations of the new foreign orchestral works—these are all we have. When we examine the volumes of Wesley's instrumental compositions, we are at once struck by the astonishing difference in quality between them and his vocal masterpieces; the latter speak with a living voice, the former are virtually, one and all, mere vague routine work. Dim visions there are now and then of something vital; there is a symphony in $B\flat$[1] with an Andante less square in rhythm than most, and a finale unusually flexible and nicely freakish in a Haydnesque style—at a very considerable distance. Some of the organ concertos[2] show curious features: the finale of No. 3 in C is based on 'Rule Britannia', and No. 1 in D contains an exact transcription (duly acknowledged) of the D major fugue from the

[1] Brit. Mus. Add. 35011, fol. 91.   [2] Ibid. 35009.

first book of Bach's *Das wohltemperirte Clavier*, given straight through twice over, first as an organ solo, and then scored for full orchestra—when the brass, unable, in the days before valves, to play more than the natural notes, confines itself to incongruously military fanfares edged in here and there whenever the harmony allows. A movement like this, sandwiched in between Wesley's own decorous platitudes, must have sounded very strange; at any rate he seems to have been determined to force his beloved Bach down his auditors' throats somehow. But hardly any of Wesley's own instrumental work (or indeed, for that matter, little of his choral either) shows the remotest trace of Johann Sebastian's influence; all these symphonies and the rest are steeped in the facile mellifluousness of John Christian Bach, to whose temporary influence on English music we have already referred. And where Samuel Wesley failed, it was out of the question for lesser men to succeed; even the inferior Handelianism that marked so much of the instrumental work of the mid-eighteenth century was far preferable to this bastard sort of style, which borrowed the skeleton outlines of the new forms being built up by Haydn and Mozart while absolutely failing to fathom their meaning, and at the same time, though retaining odds and ends of Handel's phraseology, lost the grasp of his methods also. Indeed, this state of things lasted till the advent of Sterndale Bennett; it is extraordinary how microscopically little influence Haydn and Mozart, popular as they were, had on English instrumental composers of the time, except as regards the merest externals. English music threw itself back on the vocal medium, and in the instrumental field hardly tried even to copy the great men, much less to compete with them.

Practically the sole noteworthy instrumental music of the time from an English pen was not written in England. Field wrote, as we have seen, a very large quantity of music, most of which is today in an irretrievably dusty condition; but the little volume of his Nocturnes still possesses much more than historical interest. The name, since so often degraded, seems to be his own invention (though its Italian equivalent, *notturno*, was in use in the late eighteenth century in the sense of 'serenade'); these slender piano pieces are indeed curiously original for their date. It is easy to see their deep influence on Chopin's nocturnes, as regards the types of melody and also, especially, the methods of writing for the instrument; and we can also see how in both one and the other the expressiveness sometimes, in their less happy moments, comes rather perilously near sentimentality. It is by a handful of the nocturnes that Field really lives; a piece like that beginning as follows (a most beautiful thing, and its composer's masterpiece):

Ex.158 *Poco adagio*

or the nocturnes in A♭ and C minor, or some few others, are full of singularly refined and limpid music which has a very real distinction of manner—distinction indeed of a kind that very many little piano pieces by composers far greater on the whole than Field fail to display. Field's instrument has only one string—his notions of structure are as a rule somewhat elementary, and outside the nocturnes his music is not significant; but the best of these exquisitely polished little miniatures, with their delicate melodies and their shy fugitive gracefulness, will long serve to keep his name fragrant.

Clementi wrote nothing so individual as his pupil's nocturnes. Yet the wide range of his invention and his infallible mastery of the keyboard explain fully why he was one of the most influential composers of his time, admired by his contemporaries and by many of his successors. For him counterpoint was a natural means of expression, equally at home in study and sonata; and at the same time he knew, like Haydn and Beethoven, how to make harmony the vehicle of intense emotion. The sombre minor opening of his D major sonata, Op. 40, No. 3,[1] is in the truest sense pathetic music, deeply felt and firmly controlled:

[1] No. 14 in the selection edited by Franklin Taylor (Augener).

Ex. 159 *Adagio molto*

He belongs, indeed, as a composer to two worlds—to the *galant* traditions of the eighteenth century, in which he was brought up, and to the new urgency of romanticism. His long life embraced profound changes in musical composition, many of which are reflected in his work. He was four years older than Mozart, and when he died Schumann was already launched on his career as a composer. Perhaps his most remarkable achievement was the *Gradus ad Parnassum*, unique in the literature of pedagogy for its combination of the most thorough technical discipline with a charming fancy and a versatile imagination.

X

EARLY VICTORIAN MUSIC

WE may perhaps take some thirteen composers, arranged in order of birth, as typical of English music during this period—Pearsall, Goss, John Barnett, Balfe, Hatton, Sebastian Wesley, Loder, George Macfarren, Henry Smart, Walmisley, Pierson, Bennett, and Ouseley.

Robert Lucas Pearsall (1795–1856) was a wealthy amateur of an old Worcestershire family: he was born at Clifton, but the greater part of his life was spent in Germany, at Mainz, Carlsruhe, and finally at Wartensee, on the Lake of Constance. He was always keenly interested in literary and archaeological subjects as well as music, and in addition to his compositions produced several theoretical and antiquarian works. His numerous specimens of ecclesiastical music still remain almost entirely in manuscript; his published works consist nearly exclusively of choral songs and madrigals.

John Barnett, who was born in 1802, and died, after many years' retirement, in 1890, was a second cousin of Meyerbeer, his father's name being similarly Beer before his settlement in England; he was of mixed Prussian and Hungarian blood, but always counted himself an Englishman. He sang in opera as a boy with much success; and except for numerous songs and some larger works that were never published, devoted himself entirely to dramatic music, until, in middle life, he established himself as a singing teacher at Cheltenham, when he practically abandoned composition except on a small scale. *The Mountain Sylph*, produced in 1834, is his most famous opera.

John Goss (1800–80) was a chorister of the Chapel Royal and a pupil of Attwood, whom he succeeded as organist of St. Paul's Cathedral; apart from some glees, his noteworthy compositions consist entirely of ecclesiastical music. A similar concentration is shown in the work of Samuel Sebastian Wesley (1810–76), a son of Samuel Wesley; like Goss, he started his musical life at the Chapel Royal, and was subsequently organist of Hereford Cathedral, Leeds Parish Church, and Winchester and Gloucester Cathedrals. Thomas Attwood Walmisley (1814–56) was another composer of the same school; he was the son of Thomas Forbes Walmisley, a composer of agreeable glees, and was a pupil of his godfather Attwood. His adult life was spent at Cambridge, where he was professor of music and organist simultaneously of three colleges, as well as of St. Mary's Church; his chief works are contained in the volume of *Cathedral Music* published after his death by his father, but he also wrote a good many specimens of secular vocal music.

Michael William Balfe (1808–70), was, on the other hand, an almost exclusively operatic composer. Born in Dublin, he removed to England when a boy, but for several years led a roving life on the Continent, studying in more or less desultory fashion at Rome and Milan, and afterwards appearing as an opera singer in many other Italian cities as well as in Paris. Throughout his life, indeed, Balfe had a strong predilection for the Continent, and produced works in Germany, Austria, and Russia, as well as in France and Italy; but after 1833 he resided chiefly in London, and, abandoning public singing after a few years, devoted himself almost entirely to operatic composition. His most successful works were *The Siege of Rochelle* (1835), *The Bohemian Girl* (1843), *The Rose of Castille* (1857), and *Satanella* (1858).

Edward James Loder (1813–65) was similarly chiefly an operatic composer; he was the son of a music-publisher at Bath, and studied under Ferdinand Ries at Frankfort. Of his dramatic works *The Night Dancers*, produced in 1846, is the most remarkable; he also wrote numerous songs, a set including some of the best of them being issued by subscription after his enforced retirement, owing to cerebral disease, in 1856. John Liptrot Hatton (1809–86) spent, like Loder, much of his life in performing the duties of a theatrical conductor; but his stage, as well as his ecclesiastical, music has been forgotten in the popularity of his songs for one or more voices, of which he wrote a very large number.

George Alexander Macfarren (1813–87) was one of the most industrious musicians of his time, in spite of the blindness from which he suffered for the greater part of his life; he succeeded Bennett, his junior in age, both as professor of music at Cambridge and as principal of the Royal Academy of Music, of which he had been for many years one of the chief teachers. Oratorios, operas, cantatas, symphonies, and other orchestral works, and very numerous smaller instrumental and vocal compositions, poured in profusion from his pen; and, in addition to his teaching work, he was also busy as editor, critic, and lecturer, besides producing several theoretical treatises. His contemporary, Henry Smart (1813–79), was the nephew of Sir George Smart, a well-known organist and conductor, and the son of another musician. He held various organ appointments in London, and composed much solo music for his instrument, as well as anthems and services; he also wrote numerous songs for one or more voices, an opera, and several cantatas, including *The Bride of Dunkerron* (1864), his best-known work on a large scale.

Henry Hugo Pierson[1] (1815–73), the son of an Oxford clergyman who afterwards became Dean of Salisbury, was educated at Harrow and Cambridge, and originally intended for the medical profession. He studied music chiefly in Germany, where he became acquainted with Mendelssohn and the other leading composers of his time, including Schumann, who reviewed his songs in the *Neue Zeitschrift für Musik* with quite exceptional insight and great friendliness. In 1844 he was appointed to the Reid professorship at Edinburgh, but he soon resigned the post, and for the rest of his life resided principally in Germany, where his talents were far more appreciated than in his native country. He wrote, indeed, a couple of oratorios, *Jerusalem* and *Hezekiah* (the latter was never quite completed), which were performed at the Norwich Festivals of 1852 and 1869; but his other chief works, such as the elaborate music to the second part of Goethe's *Faust* (1854) and his numerous orchestral compositions, were intended primarily for German audiences. In addition to these he wrote operas (two, *Leila* and *Contarini*, were produced at Hamburg in 1848 and 1872 respectively), and a large quantity of songs. His death passed almost unnoticed in England, but called forth noteworthy tributes of admiration from the German press.

Frederick Arthur Gore Ouseley (1825–89), the son of a distinguished orientalist and Ambassador to Persia and Russia, was a musician of an altogether different type. He was an infant prodigy both as performer and as composer, and throughout his life retained remarkable technical facility in various directions; he succeeded Bishop in 1855 as professor of music at Oxford (holding the post till his death) and shortly afterwards founded St. Michael's College at Tenbury in Herefordshire for the education of boys, with special reference to music. His compositions are almost entirely ecclesias-

[1] Originally Pearson, but he changed the spelling on taking up his residence in Germany.

tical in character, consisting chiefly of anthems; he also edited the complete sacred music of Gibbons and other collections, and published several theoretical works.

The most prominent early Victorian composer, William Sterndale Bennett (1816–75), has still to be mentioned. He was the son and grandson of musicians, and began his musical career as a chorister in King's College Chapel at Cambridge; he then studied at the Royal Academy of Music, and in 1836, having even then produced numerous important works that had created a remarkable impression, proceeded to Leipzig, where he became intimately acquainted with both Mendelssohn and Schumann, both of whom expressed the most enthusiastic prophecies of his future. In 1856 he was appointed professor of music at Cambridge, and in 1866 principal of the Royal Academy of Music, holding both appointments till his death; he was also well known both as pianist and as conductor, and did very much to promote in England the proper appreciation of Bach and other great foreign composers. He wrote nothing for the stage, except incidental music to Sophocles' *Ajax* (dramatic music very unlike that ordinarily known by that name at the time), but left behind him specimens of all other kinds of composition—a symphony, several concert overtures, several concertos and a large quantity of solo music for piano, an oratorio, *The Woman of Samaria* (1867), a 'Pastoral', *The May Queen* (1858), odes for festival occasions, concerted chamber music, and numerous anthems and songs.

By the beginning of the Victorian period the Handelian domination had lost a little of its formerly overpowering weight—the programmes of the Sacred Harmonic Society (founded in 1832) are in this respect much more reasonable than those of the Ancient Concerts; but it nevertheless survived for many more years with very slightly diminished vigour. Perhaps its most marked effect was the establishment in 1859 (after a preliminary experiment in 1857) of triennial Handel Festivals at the Crystal Palace, consisting of four days' music performed by a monster chorus and orchestra of several thousand persons; these events were very popular with the public, but from the musician's point of view they did great harm in encouraging the glorification of mere size and perpetuating radically false notions of Handel's artistic methods. Down to 1880 they were conducted by Michael Costa (1808–84), an Italian of Spanish extraction who came to England in 1829, when quite a youth; for very many years he was the leading conductor in this country, and both at the opera and in the concert-room produced, in spite of his complete insensibility to deeper artistic considerations, notable results in the shape of performances of a disciplined skill quite unknown before. It was not, however, till the advent of Hans Richter (1843–1916) in 1877 that English audiences knew what really great conducting meant—as a fine art in addition to all-round musicianship.

The main cause of the weakening of the sheer monopoly of Handelian influence was the enormous popularity of Mendelssohn. He visited this country on several occasions, and the fascination of his personal character won him hosts of friends; the first performance of *Elijah* at Birmingham in 1846 was the crowning event of his career, and at his death a year later the English musical world talked as if the sun had fallen from the sky. For a generation more, after which a steady decline began, Mendelssohnianism remained astonishingly powerful; though it was not long before it became confined—though not to so extreme a degree as in the case of Handelianism—to a comparatively small number of works. To these two dominations all English musicians of serious aims had more or less whole-heartedly to bow the knee, so long as they did not, like Pierson, prefer a voluntary exile; even if here and there individuality declined to be crushed altogether, yet it was by the canons of Handel and Mendelssohn that the English public (even while extending a personal welcome to revolutionary foreigners like Berlioz) inevitably judged all native work, except such as frankly appealed to lower tastes, or, like Pearsall's, presented virtually no points of contact.

Opera was, however, a side issue. The English Georgian opera was a mere medley of tunes strung together on the very slenderest dramatic thread; but the early Victorian period saw the production of several works which, slight as they were, were nevertheless designed with some attention to continuity of interest and propriety of stage effect. Barnett's *The Mountain Sylph* and Loder's *Nourjahad*, both of which came out in 1834, and other quickly succeeding works of Balfe, Macfarren, Vincent Wallace (1812–65), and Julius Benedict (1804–85)—a German who settled in England when a young man, and was prominent in fashionable circles for many years—are all, in their different ways, far more worthy of the name of opera than any works of Bishop and his contemporaries; they have some sort of theatrical *raison d'être*, insignificant as nearly all of them are musically. But in spite of these signs of a more promising future, and occasional performances in English translations of German masterpieces (sometimes also, indeed, given in the original), the status of opera in the native language still remained inferior; popular as individual works of the kind often were, the prestige that is the outcome of fine performance and fashionable support attached almost solely[1] to the exotic Italian opera, which enjoyed its palmiest days in early Victorian times. Though works by English composers, translated into Italian (Balfe's *Il Talismano*, for example), were very occasionally included in the repertory, and among the crowd of great foreign singers one or two English names may be observed, on English music as such it had hardly any bearing whatever. Still more than is the case nowadays, the vast majority of the audiences went to hear individual singers, without much concern about the music that they sang; the system was a hothouse for vocal stars and all the evils that they bring with them, and on anything like native effort of an individual character it was as purely a dead-weight as the influence of Handel or Mendelssohn was in other branches of the art. And it had a very long life; from the beginning of the eighteenth century for about a hundred and eighty years onwards Italian was the one and only language of aristocratic opera in England; and then, partly through managerial competition and partly through a growing sense of the absurdity of the whole business, the system, which had for some time been moribund, finally expired. The subsequent revival of foreign opera in a reasonable guise, through the business talents of Augustus Harris, belongs to the following chapter.

We have seen how the figure of Samuel Wesley dominated ecclesiastical music at the beginning of the nineteenth century; and similarly his son Sebastian stands at the head of English church musicians of early Victorian times. Indeed, he is the Anglican composer *par excellence*; unlike his father, he wrote nothing for any other ritual, nor even an oratorio, and his works for any other medium than a church choir with organ accompaniment are almost all artistically quite negligible. But in his own field he was undeniably a very remarkable man; we miss in his own compositions the grandeur of style visible in the church music of the great past days, clear echoes of which still sounded in the best work of his father, but, on the other hand, we find in Sebastian Wesley's finest anthems

---

[1] Malibran and others of the renowned cosmopolitan singers of the day sometimes, however, sang in English versions of foreign operas.

a style which is his own and which has plenty to say for itself. It is unfortunate that a very early work like 'The wilderness' should have somehow come to be generally accepted as typical; in spite of its noteworthy picturesqueness and melodic flow it has a certain vein of rather weak elegance that Wesley afterwards altogether discarded. 'Blessed be the God and Father' is another anthem a good deal below its composer's best level, the popularity of which has perhaps rather hampered the appreciation of his more subtle things; and even the Service in E, though strong, fresh, sincere work, possessing plenty of individuality, also hardly reaches the summit of Wesley's achievement. The long, elaborate 'O Lord, thou art my God' and the pathetic 'Wash me throughly' are better examples of what their composer could do; but, though tastes may to some extent differ, many would be inclined to name as the highest the exquisite 'Thou wilt keep him in perfect peace' and perhaps especially 'Cast me not away'—a short masterpiece of flawless dignity and deep feeling, with a touchingly beautiful close:[1]

[1] This is the text of the first edition. Wesley's revised edition (in current use) has some minor readjustments of the parts and in bar 9 substitutes a semibreve A for the minims B A in the bass.

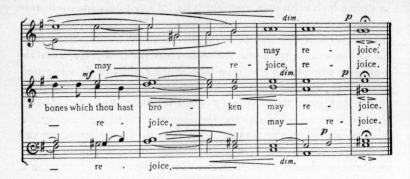

Sebastian Wesley's best work has indeed an attractiveness all its own. His genius was not capable of taking wide views, and his style is always—using the term in no derogatory sense—somewhat feminine in character; temperate, cultured, and devotional, it lives and moves and has its being in the cathedral chancel. But while we are bound to recognize that his music, even at its best, lacks the full measure of that indefinable universal appeal beyond the bounds of race and creed that we find in the work of the great men, and in the handful of his father's best things, yet there is not the least doubt that he is one of the very foremost names in English artistic history in the nineteenth century. Like most composers, he wrote poor music occasionally; but through all the work that is worthy of remembrance we see many fine features—a notable instinct for beautifully polished part-writing, a dignified melodiousness of style, a sense of organic proportion which shows itself in the absense of any triviality of detail, and, above all, a certain innate distinction which, by some turn of phrase or harmony, keeps him on the straight path even when he seems temporarily to be diverging from it. No doubt his music does not appeal to all alike, and it is perhaps with a somewhat conscious effort that some, not in personal sympathy with its composer's temperament, have to realize that it is worth taking on its own terms; but though, as has been said, it is not universal music, it is none the less music that is artistically individual, and the work of a man who in his narrow sphere was a real genius. But the sphere was narrow, and it is singular how even the organ is, so to speak, extraneous to it; wherever the accompaniment does more than double the voices it is (except in a mere handful of instances) commonplace in texture. For example, at the passage 'For the Lord hath spoken it' in the anthem 'O Lord, thou art my God' the organ, for no ostensible reason, suddenly dashes into eight bars of singularly poor semiquaver scales up and down, which quite ruin an otherwise very fine page; Wesley's feeling for close texture in vocal writing was very remarkable, but, like almost all organ-loft composers between Purcell's day and his own, he had no sort of similar instinct for instrumental writing as such—it was, to him and to all of his school, a mere Cinderella.

Goss, like Wesley, was to all intents and purposes a church musician pure and simple; but he has nothing like the other's individuality of manner. His work is, as a rule, little more than 'organist's music', but it is that on the very highest plane; and through nearly all of it there runs a very agreeable vein of sedately graceful expressiveness joined to solid technical skill. 'The wilderness', 'If we believe that Jesus died', 'Praise the Lord, O my soul', 'Lift up thine eyes', 'Come and let us return', and a good many more are thoroughly musicianly work; their well-ordered paths are not disturbed by any special fire of inspiration, but they deserve and command our sincere respect. Goss did indeed occasionally give way to a somewhat saccharine type of emotionalism, as in 'O Saviour of the world', but the taste is perfectly clean, and the expression is always refined; and if we can point to a good many pages in his works that are merely stiff and commonplace, yet we can, on the other hand, point to some others which attain the level of the permanently remembered things. Perhaps Goss shows himself at his highest in some short anthems comparatively little known; 'Lord, let me know mine end',[1] the close of which may be quoted:

Ex.161 *Lento*

[1] Adapted from the first movement of 'Brother, thou art gone before us'.

299

is indeed rather surprising to those who are familiar merely with his ordinary style. But as a rule he is the worthy, conscientious workman, not the imaginative artist.

T. A. Walmisley was a composer of much the same general type, though he never rose to Goss's highest level. His Service in D minor and his anthem 'If the Lord himself had not been on our side' are not marked by very much original distinctiveness, but they are, especially the former, finely massive, dignified work, with a high ideal to which the composer does his best to attain. No doubt he suffers from occasional lapses; the anthem just mentioned—on the whole both his largest and his best—falls into some rather weak melodiousness in the middle portion, and the well-known short 'Not unto us, O Lord' is a little inclined to sentimentality. But still Walmisley is one of the company of church composers who sought after high things; he never reached greatness, but we cannot but commend his earnest talent. The Evening Service in A by Stephen Elvey (1805–60), the brother of a better-known and more prolific but less meritorious composer, shows very similar qualities.

Before we pass on to criticize the religious work of the composer who is the most prominent all-round musician of the period, a few words may be given to two men of very different types, who each, in different ways, exercised considerable influence. The anthems of Henry Smart, like his numerous organ works, achieved a great popularity in a wide circle; they can never artistically be ranked higher than pleasing Sunday-school music, usually quite inoffensive and nicely put together, but they are historically interesting as among the earliest of successful attempts to write down to the intelligence of the average church-goer—considerably more worthy, it is true, than some later attempts of similar aim. Ouseley never trod that path, and always wrote with a lofty ideal; his inspiration, or anything approaching it, visited him very rarely. His work is massive and sincere, but it is usually very dull; however, he deserves a word or two of commendation, not only for his excellent technical workmanship, sometimes of a brilliantly elaborate kind, but also for one or two emergences into a really vitalized atmosphere—such as the anthem 'Is it nothing to you?', which is notably strong, solemn, and beautiful music and should keep Ouseley's name in fragrant remembrance when most of his pages are forgotten.

The religious music of Sterndale Bennett consists of eight anthems, a few sacred duets and hymn tunes, and the oratorio *The Woman of Samaria*. Some of the anthems, such as 'O that I knew where I might find him', are melodiously expressive, without, however, possessing the distinguishing features of the best church compositions of Goss or Sebastian Wesley; but by common consent the oratorio is Bennett's most typical work in the ecclesiastical field. We shall shortly have an opportunity of considering his other music; and we shall find that—as with the work of his master, Mendelssohn, who had an overwhelming influence on him—his best religious pages never rise to anything like the artistic height of his best secular work. We shall see later ample evidence of Bennett's talents; but *The Woman of Samaria* gives us little assistance in our search. Apart from a few things, such as the last chorus 'And blessed be the Lord God of Israel', the work is decorously dead; the libretto is totally lacking in any artistic vitality, and nearly all the music is similarly steeped in conventionalism. It is refined in its feeble way, but, curiously enough, even Bennett's technique fails him more or less; the elementary dull devices of the opening chorale-chorus are as unlike Bach's methods (with which they have sometimes, astoundingly, been compared) as anything can be, and, indeed, the

301

whole work is a sad legacy from the mature pen of the young genius who had written the *Naiads* overture more than thirty years before. Bennett is the outstanding instance in music of a man who might have reached real greatness being slowly but very effectually killed by his environment.

Macfarren's oratorios are of slightly later date, but they still belong essentially to the early Victorian period; in them the Handelian influence, which is almost invisible with Bennett, again makes itself felt, though Mendelssohn is still the primary force. His *St. John the Baptist*, which was enthusiastically welcomed as a great masterpiece when produced at the Bristol Festival of 1873, may fitly be taken as a type; the anthems and the other oratorios show the same qualities with hardly an exception. We see an obvious desire to be dramatic and up to date; the overture, we are told, is intended 'to suggest the state of expectancy that preceded the Advent', and the 'Shofar' or trumpet-call at the beginning of the overture, followed by what serves for the chief subject—a very elementary quaver-phrase in C minor—comes again, with a few bars of the quavers in the major key, just at the end of the last chorus, at the words 'until the day should dawn, and the day-star should arise'. Indeed, the oratorio sometimes shows a sort of childlike dramatic characterization that would hardly have been possible to a composer possessing any sense of humour; and throughout Macfarren's tentative modernities are pathetically ineffectual. He can do what, in its way, is quite admirable academic work, such as the clever fugue on the old 'Hanover' tune; but otherwise the oratorio is a mere tissue of innocent, respectable commonplaces. And yet, as we shall shortly see, some of Macfarren's secular music shows that he had real blood in his veins; somehow it seems to have been a sort of point of honour with him (as with many others) to set religious words to dull platitudes.

Pierson's oratorios represent, however, a cross-current, though they are in no sort of way so revolutionary as other works by him, to which we shall come later. *Jerusalem* and *Hezekiah* owe next to nothing to either Handel or Mendelssohn; there are a few occasional traces of Spohr, as in the quintet 'Blessed are the dead' in *Jerusalem*, but, as a rule, Pierson shows all the independence of the bold but somewhat ignorant amateur. He has plenty of ideas, but no sort of technical mastery; his command over vocal part-writing is, on the whole, very poor compared with the average academic contem-

porary work, fine phrases come to untimely and entirely unnecessary ends, and the whole style is a singular mixture of earnest
idealism and uneducated unorthodoxy. He has an exceptional fondness for instrumental writing as such—witness, in *Jerusalem*, the
long overture, or the long instrumental symphony 'representing the
march of the Romans against Jerusalem' (a very angular march
indeed), or the long curious 'recitando con affetto' for unaccompanied violoncellos at the words 'this is the second death'; and
altogether his figure is very much out of place in early Victorian
England. The oratorios contain, in spite of their crudity as wholes,
some striking work; the chorus 'Holy, holy, holy' in *Jerusalem* has
a fine, austere atmosphere about it, and other things also are notable.
But Pierson can hardly ever get through a complete movement
without a lapse of expression or technique somewhere. Had he
known what to do with his ideas, he would have been one of the
really remarkable English composers; as it is, he remains an isolated
figure of ineffectual revolt.

All through this period English opera was artistically very much
on the down grade, even if dramatically, as we have seen, there was
a certain improvement on the traditions hallowed by the successes
of men like Bishop, in virtue of which opera had been a sort of third-
rate theatrical medley, totally devoid alike of art and of sense. True,
a work like Loder's *The Night Dancers* has glimpses of something
better; in the middle of much that is altogether commonplace there
is occasionally something that has a certain stylishness and character of its own, something that, altogether elementary though it be,
has yet a touch of individuality of a kind. But mid-Victorian opera
is mainly represented by the work of Balfe, a fragment of which
lingers still; *The Bohemian Girl* has even now not quite lost all its
popular attraction for certain tastes, and it may be confessed that
perhaps on the whole one might do worse. Artistically it is not worth
a moment's consideration—the tunes are empty beyond expression,
and there is not a particle of any workmanship to carry them off; yet
there is nothing worse than emptiness, and the rubbish is quite un-
pretentious and decent. Highly coloured vulgarity is a later development to which Balfe gives no countenance; we go to sleep over his
middle-class, tawdry melodies, but we are not actively irritated by
them. No doubt in his day Balfe was thought a great man; he strove
to rival the favourite Italian operas, and wrote in the fashionable
bravura style for the prima donnas—Elvira's part in *The Rose of*

Castille is technically as difficult as any soprano music in existence. But it is all artistically dead beyond the very faintest hope of resurrection; and we need not feel any cause for lament. Balfe, however, was the best of his particular type; Wallace's *Lurline* and *Maritana* which (especially the latter) long rivalled *The Bohemian Girl* in popularity, are considerably poorer, and indeed advance a good many steps on the road to sheer vulgarity, though of a good-natured and unpretending order. Barnett's *The Mountain Sylph*, the general influence of which seems visible also in Macfarren's stage works, was no doubt artistically more ambitious, and tried to strike out a less superficially attractive line; but the whole, in spite of a good deal of well-wrought and pleasant music (much of that sung by the Sylphs, and also of that sung by the malignant supernaturals, has a considerable amount of point and invention), was far too mild and ineffectual to create any real permanent life for English opera.

Pierson's lengthy incidental music to *Faust* is marked by altogether different methods, and it is plain that his ideal was artistically far higher than that of most of his contemporary countrymen. The scene of Ariel and the Fairy Chorus, with its delightful opening tune:

Ex.162 *Allegretto*

Wann der Blü - then Früh - lings - Re - gen
ü - ber al - les schwe - bend sinkt

the very delicate and graceful scene of Euphorion, the vigorous song of Lynceus, and plenty of things in the final chain of choruses —all these are well worthy of close attention; though it must be confessed that the frequent pages of sheer amateurish incoherence are decidedly irritating and would prevent any enterprising lover of Pierson's talent from attempting to revive the work as a whole.

The cantata was an art-form increasingly popular throughout mid-Victorian times, though virtually unknown before; due in its origin to the rapid growth of small choral societies, it became a favourite medium for the expression of a sort of mild romanticism— a flavour of the stage tempered by the respectability of the concert-room. With later composers the idea was developed in different and more promising forms; in its early emasculate guise, the cantata offered little or no scope for really living artistic work. Bennett's *The May Queen,* to a singularly ridiculous 'drawing-room' libretto by H. F. Chorley, is the most familiar and indeed probably the best example of the type; but it is very innocent and obvious all through. Robin Hood's bass solo "'Tis jolly to hunt' does indeed bring into this atmosphere of a boarding-school prize-giving a whiff of fresh air from the woods: but the relief is only temporary. Not that there is not a good deal of delicate if commonplace refinement about *The May Queen,* but the whole thing is respectably lifeless; and such a very watery romanticism is perhaps worse than none at all. Mac-farren's *Songs in a Cornfield* (1868)—a cantata for female voices— is a work of more or less the same kind, though less pretentious; it has been acclaimed as his best production, but its refined melodious futilities have gone down into the dust already. Music without some sort of life-blood in it has singularly little chance of passing beyond the circle of friendly sympathizers to which it makes its first appeal; *The May Queen* is inclined to outstay her welcome, but it is after all only the music of the disreputable character that enables the work occasionally to be heard. And almost all the rest of the cantatas of the time are now unknown even by name; while no one who has turned over their dusty pages wishes to revive them.

On the other hand, the unaccompanied secular vocal music of the time contains, among much that is ordinary, some really fine work. Pearsall—certainly the best English writer of such music since the madrigalian period—left behind him some notable gems, mixed up, unfortunately, with much of an inferior kind. In the vein of the pure part-song as distinguished from the madrigal, Pearsall is virtually negligible: clean as they are, things like 'The hardy Norseman'[1] or

[1] The composer says the tune of this is an 'ancient popular song'—con-siderably modernized, in all probability.

'O who will o'er the downs' come to little or nothing. But when he gives free play to his love for the Elizabethans, the result is altogether different; it is true that sometimes (the six-part 'Light of my soul' is a specially good instance) we see that the giant's robe does not quite fit, and anyhow there remains something indefinable about the great madrigalists of the past which eludes the imitation even of a brilliantly clever disciple like Pearsall. But still, all allowances made, Pearsall's best madrigals are exceedingly musicianly and vitalized work, with a very real air of distinction about them. 'Sing we and chaunt it'[1] and 'No, no, Nigella' have an almost Morleyan brightness and swing: and 'Take heed, ye shepherd swains', 'Down in a garden fair', 'Let us all go maying', 'Why do the roses?', and a good many others, are most agreeable in their polished solid technique and their frank individual melody. Occasionally, indeed, Pearsall can become really massive, as in 'Lay a garland' (a most beautiful stately thing), 'Great God of love', or 'O ye roses', the beginning of which may be quoted:

---

[1] Published both in an eight-part and in a four-part form; the former is far the more effective.

307

It is true that, as has been said, we perhaps feel just a faint touch of conscious antiquarianism about such work as this; but still it is singularly living and imaginative, and incalculably more musical than anything the average English composer of the time could produce—fully as musical indeed as anything since Purcell. Not that good work is altogether absent from the mass of glees and part-songs of the period; the slight but pleasant talent of Hatton, for example, is seen to advantage in such things as 'April showers', 'Summer eve', 'Spring, ye flowrets', and others of the same type—agreeably tuneful, effectively written, and harmonically clean, if occasionally a little sugary. Walmisley's charming 'Sweete floweres, ye were too faire', various things of Goss, and especially some very interesting Shakespearean part-songs of Macfarren—work that possesses undoubted vitality—are also worthy of mention as honourable survivors of an undistinguished crowd; but even they would not, in a period of greater really artistic fecundity, take an outstanding position. Pearsall's best works, however, are very well worthy to be remembered on their own merits, as but little early- or mid-Victorian music is.

In solo vocal music the period can boast of hardly anything worthy of even a distant comparison with the finest works of Pearsall. Reams of the kind of music that is very fairly represented by such things as Balfe's once famous 'The arrow and the song' were more or less conscientiously turned out; but it is virtually all mere waste-paper. A few things, however, rise above the average level, and may deserve brief notice: Hatton's 'To Anthea', for example, is (though it has been greatly overrated) quite pleasant, cleanly written work. The songs of Loder present a somewhat curious problem; many of them are very distinctly commonplace or worse, but occasionally he could attain something much higher. 'Robin Hood is lying dead' has a good sort of folk-tune swing about it, as well as considerable pathos; and 'The brooklet'[1] (a setting of a translation of Müller's 'Wohin' from *Die schöne Müllerin*) is a solitary, but very real, masterpiece—exquisitely polished in detail and full of melodic distinction:

Ex. 164

I heard ___ a brook-let gush-ing ___
From its rock-y foun-tains near ___
Down in-to the val-ley rush-ing ___
So fresh and won-drous clear,

[1] No. 7 of *Twelve Songs, Sacred and Secular* (n.d.). Reprinted (transposed) in J. Goss, *An Anthology of Song* (1929), p. 101.

so won - drous clear.

But this, which might not be in the very least ashamed of comparison with the standard classical songs of the same type, is merely a single (and indeed, compared with Loder's average work, an almost unbelievable) effort; and to judge its composer by it would be to do him an honour of which he is very far from worthy. Yet Bennett, a musician of far finer general calibre than Loder, produced no song that is anything like its equal; 'May Dew' (Op. 23, No. 2) and others of the same graceful, easy style are pleasant enough, but their somewhat diluted Mendelssohnianism does not come to very much. And Bennett's songs show a dreary quantity of mere respectable sentiment; the sugariness is clean, but it very soon palls on the taste, and there is hardly any sign of the distinction that marks some of the instrumental work. Heine seen through English mid-Victorian spectacles, as in Bennett's setting of 'Mädchen mit dem rothen Mündchen', is by no means a specially attractive vision.

Pierson wrote a large number of songs to both English and German words, but here again we meet with disappointment: his setting of Tennyson's 'Claribel'—undoubtedly his best song—has some extremely beautiful and delicate bits of melody, but as a whole it lacks shape. The lyrical gift was indeed denied to Pierson; and his attempts to deal with concentrated emotion such as inspires the words of 'Take, O take those lips away', or 'O wert thou in the cauld, cauld blast', or 'My love's like the red, red rose', are overdone and theatrical. His dramatic ballads, again, in spite of plenty of real musical feeling, are always exaggerated and inclined to degenerate into rhapsodical dullness; as in his instrumental work, he never, with all his original talent, produces anything really 'foursquare without blame'. But still he shows sparks of the real fire of inspiration; and somewhat dim though they may be, they are brilliant compared with the microscopic glimmer which is all of which wellnigh every other mid-Victorian song-writer, when at his highest level, can boast.

There was a great dearth of instrumental music at this period; indeed, apart from Bennett's and the historically interesting work of Pierson, none demands even passing notice, though occasional symphonies and overtures came from the pens of composers who were much more at home in their organ lofts or their lecture rooms, and every now and then, as in a remarkable organ prelude in F♯ minor by Ouseley, we find really imaginative work in the middle of a dreary waste. Bennett, however, showed his talents at their best in instrumental music, though all his finest pieces are early in date. The third pianoforte concerto in C minor (1834), with its earnestness and structural finish, the polished and thoughtful *Parisina* overture (1835), and, most noteworthy of all, the remarkably beautiful overture entitled *The Naiads* (1836):

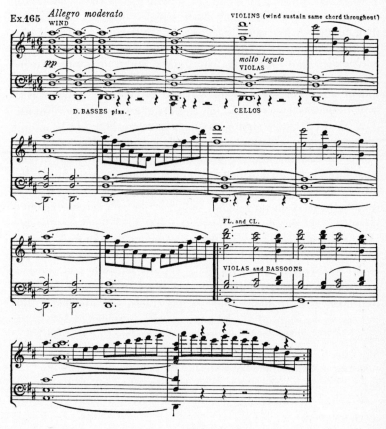

were all written before he was twenty-one; the *Wood-nymphs* over-ture (1838)—a companion to *The Naiads,* and though hardly equal in fascination still a work of unusual promise—the fourth piano-forte concerto in F minor (1836), with its charming Barcarolle, and the very graceful water-colour sketches for pianoforte known as *The Lake, The Millstream,* and *The Fountain* (1835) are also quite youthful works; and it is no cause for wonder that both Mendels-sohn and Schumann warmly heralded the coming of a new genius out of the dark West. The former overflowed with affectionate admiration,[1] and the latter, besides pouring out sincere praise in the *Neue Zeitschrift für Musik,*[2] dedicated his *Études Sympho-niques* to the young Englishman, and in the finale utilized, in a playfully delicate manner all his own, an air from Marschner's opera *Der Templer und die Jüdin* (1829), where England is bidden to rejoice in the prowess of her knights; but the composer whose career began with such brilliant auspices soon lost his early freshness of genius. Even in his first review Schumann noted the great strength of Mendelssohn's influence; later on he regretfully confessed that Bennett could only do one particular kind of thing, and that his talent was becoming mere mannerism. And even in his one special vein he never recovered his early fertility of invention; the 'Fantasie-Overture' on Moore's *Paradise and the Peri* (1862)[3] has charming passages, but it is certainly not as a whole equal to *The Naiads,* and the G minor symphony (1864–7), though starting with a movement that has a good deal of polished grace, greatly declines in interest afterwards. Again, the pianoforte pieces practically never show again the stylishness, slight though it be, of the early *Three Musical Sketches,* to which reference has already been made; the Toccata (1854) and the 'Rondeau à la Polonaise' (1855) have their points, but they are mere reflections of a vanishing talent.

It is indeed easy to overrate the promise of the early works; though the Mendelssohnian influence is not so strong as altogether to overburden the delicate, rather shy refinement which was Ben-

[1] See, for example, the testimonial he sent when Bennett was competing for the Edinburgh professorship in 1843 (*Musical Times,* Nov. 1943, p. 351), and the letter he sent to Bennett on the same occasion (J. R. Sterndale Bennett, *The Life of William Sterndale Bennett,* 1907, p. 153).

[2] Translated in R. Schumann, *Music and Musicians,* 1st series, pp. 140, 210, 222, and 284, 2nd series, pp. 114, 119, and 540.

[3] See the authorized analysis in the programme-book of the Jubilee Phil-harmonic concert in July 1862, for which this overture was expressly written.

nett's own endowment, yet we can see that something more robust was necessary to secure the really outstanding artistic position in European music which his friends prophesied for him. The pages are rather too much tinged with rose-water; but still the beautiful finish of the phrasing, the fastidious avoidance of anything even remotely coarse or heavy, the highbred grace and charm—all these were sufficiently different from the general run of English music of the time to give rise to very great hopes. And though the restricted outlook was obvious even at the start, yet this was a negligible fault in the work of one who was little more than a boy; the foundation was ready, but nothing worth mentioning was ever built upon it— the polished charm degenerated into gentlemanly commonplace, the limpid technique into stereotyped dryness. Like Mendelssohn, Bennett had derived his pianoforte writing from the Clementi-Hummel school, and ultimately from harpsichord music like that of Domenico Scarlatti, though adding elements of his own; the rapid surface glitter of his finger passages, for which a sort of immaculately neat, emotionless precision is the main requisite, is somewhat trying for the ordinary modern pianist, who thinks mainly of such things as tone-colour or richness of sound; and in his later works he subsists, as a rule, almost entirely on such subdued brilliance of effect, and moves uneasily in slower tempi, where there is more time for his attenuated inventiveness to make itself felt. But a certain sort of musicianly pride which Bennett retained, even in his weaker moods, prevented him from ever yielding to mere display, and consequently almost all his pianoforte music has fallen, as it were, between two stools; there is not enough intellectual or emotional content for the pianist who is not specially interested in technique as such, and the average pianist who is so interested prefers music that, while being less difficult, sounds more so.

Bennett was a classicist in his failings as well as in his virtues, and he carried his classicism even into his excursions into the field of programme music; both the pianoforte sonata *The Maid of Orleans* (1869–73) and the greatly superior orchestral overture *Paradise and the Peri* are plentifully labelled with quotations calculated to impress the special poetic content on the listener, but the composer does his very best to retain the orthodox structural schemes, which sometimes conflict oddly with the necessities of the narrative. The early overtures are merely 'mood music' after the pattern of Mendelssohn's, and not, in the strict sense, pro-

313

gramme music at all; *Paradise and the Peri*, however, eminently restrained though it is in style, is in essence—with its ticketed themes and its triangle-bell—an adventuress, of unwontedly shy and refined mien, into the domain of Berlioz and Liszt.

It is interesting to compare this delicately timid modernity with the orchestral work of Bennett's contemporary Pierson, whose vocal compositions we have already described; his concert overture *Romeo and Juliet*, his symphonic poem *Macbeth*, and all the rest seem now indeed as unknown in their composer's adopted country as in that of his birth, but historically they are somewhat notable. In speaking of Pierson's other works we have remarked his defiant rejection of the Handelian and Mendelssohnian traditions of the England of his day, and his incorrigible amateurishness of technique; but the music to *Faust*, violently opposed to the orthodox classical traditions though it is, is yet hardly so revolutionary as *Macbeth*, which to the typical English composer of the period must have seemed like a nightmare. Pierson's model seems to be Berlioz, but he has even less steadiness of method than that wayward genius, and far less technical ability. These curious works are designed (if one can use the word design at all in connexion with them) in a style that is throughout incoherently formless; there is no thematic invention to speak of, and the sections jostle each other with no sort of intelligible sequence of idea. *Macbeth* is full of quotations from Shakespeare (in German) written over various passages. We have the witches represented by a sort of dialogue between a trombone (labelled 'first witch'), a clarinet ('second witch'), and a cornet ('third witch'), with accompaniment for double basses *tremolando* in three parts—a purely Berliozian effect; we have marches for the Scottish and English armies (singularly alike in general character), a witches' dance, banqueting music, and many other things all mixed up anyhow and poetically labelled right and left—all the last pages have quotations from the play every few bars.

But there is no actuality about it all; it tries to be dramatically blood-curdling but only succeeds in being, as a rule, respectably dull. There is a great deal of elaborate emotional indication, such as 'con espansione, calando sempre più dolcissimo ed appassionato', and so on, and many ingenious colour effects quite after Berlioz's models (cymbals *soli*, &c.), the scoring being unusually complicated, and not at all unimpressive; indeed, Pierson is in very many ways a sort of early Richard Strauss, using unrevolutionary harmony but otherwise altogether 'emancipated' from classical leading-strings—far more so indeed than Strauss, as Pierson seems to have a sovereign contempt for structural technique of any kind. And yet this queer stuff has many signs of a dim but notable talent that might have blossomed into something really great had Pierson received from his countrymen a little sympathy and kindly discipline, instead of blank stares combined with objurgation. The sombrely expressive end of *Romeo and Juliet*, for example, shows, in its vague, uncertain way, glimmerings of something much deeper than Bennett, with his facile acceptance of things, ever reached; though there can be no doubt that Pierson's muddled amateurishness contrasts extremely badly with the other's polished skill. Nearly every one would much rather listen to Bennett's orchestral writings than to Pierson's; but to the student of artistic psychology the latter is on the whole the most interesting figure of mid-Victorian music.

A word or two may perhaps be given to a composer not hitherto mentioned, Francis Edward Bache (1833–58), a pupil of Bennett; in his brief life of ill-health he succeeded in creating on his friends an altogether exceptional impression. It is hard, however, to see in his published works more than a very mild and undistinguished talent; but there is no doubt that his technical musicianship was decidedly above the average of his time, and he might, had he lived, have done something to justify what to us seems an altogether too partial laudation due to the influence of his enthusiastic personality.

THE ENGLISH RENAISSANCE

IN this chapter biographical details will naturally divide into two classes, of composers whose work lies wholly in the nineteenth century and of those whose activity belongs equally to the twentieth. Among the former the most prominent name is that of Arthur Seymour Sullivan (1842–1900). The son of a military bandmaster, he began his musical career as a chorister of the Chapel Royal, which he quitted for the Royal Academy of Music and still later for the Leipzig Conservatorium; after returning to England in 1862 he held occasional organ and conducting appointments and was principal of the National Training School of Music (forerunner of the Royal College of Music) from 1876 to 1881, but devoted himself chiefly to composition, producing a large number of works, including examples of every department except chamber music. The numerous light operas which he wrote in conjunction with W. S. Gilbert met one and all with exceptional success, not only in England but also in America and Australia: and it is by these and a certain number of detached songs that his name is most widely familiar. His junior, Arthur Goring Thomas (1850–92), began the study of music somewhat late in life, working at Paris and afterwards at the Royal Academy of Music in London: his operas *Esmeralda* (1883) and *Nadeshda* (1885) are his most important works, but he also produced many non-dramatic pieces, including several cantatas and a large number of songs, chiefly to French words. Among other late Victorian composers the names may be mentioned of John Stainer (1840–1901), organist of Magdalen College, Oxford, and St. Paul's Cathedral and professor at Oxford, and Joseph Barnby (1838–96), precentor of Eton College and principal of the Guildhall School of Music, who, with the older John Bacchus Dykes (1823–76), precentor of Durham Cathedral, were the leaders of an influential school of anthem- and hymn-writers.

The second group of composers includes Alexander Campbell Mackenzie (1847–1935), Charles Hubert Hastings Parry (1848–1918), Frederic Hymen Cowen (1852–1935), Charles Villiers Stanford (1852–1924), and Edward Elgar (1857–1934).[1] Mackenzie, the

[1] Composers born after 1857 will be found on pp. 340–3.

eldest of this quintet, was a native of Edinburgh and studied at the Royal Academy of Music in London; for some years he followed the calling of a violinist in a German orchestra and subsequently resided for some time at Florence. In 1888 he was elected principal of the Royal Academy of Music, and he also for several years conducted the Philharmonic and other important concerts. In the latter part of his life he did not show himself so prolific a composer as in his younger days, and even then his output was not very large; but he produced a considerable quantity of music in several of the most important branches. Among his chief vocal works are the oratorio *The Rose of Sharon* (1884, revised 1910), the operas *Colomba* (1883, revised 1912), *The Troubadour* (1886), and *The Cricket on the Hearth* (1901), and the cantatas *The Story of Sayid* (1886) and *The Dream of Jubal* (1889); his numerous orchestral compositions do not, however, include any work on a symphonic scale (apart from concertos for violin and piano), and, except for a handful of early works, he neglected concerted chamber music.

Parry did not adopt the musical profession until after some time spent in other pursuits, and he was never attached as a student to any musical institution; but he was a fertile composer ever since his Eton days. Till rather past his thirtieth year he devoted himself chiefly to concerted chamber music; but though a few similar works of later date saw the light and he also produced some symphonies and other important orchestral compositions, his mature activities were directed mainly towards choral forms. *Prometheus Unbound* (a setting of portions of Shelley's poem), written for the Gloucester Festival of 1880, was the earliest work in which his real *métier* was displayed: settings of Shirley's *The Glories of our Blood and State* (revised 1914) and of Milton's *Blest Pair of Sirens* followed in 1883 and 1887 respectively, and these were followed in turn by a practically continuous stream of choral works either definitely sacred or what might perhaps be called 'ethical' in character— among the principal of which may be mentioned the oratorios *Judith* (1888), *Job* (1892), and *King Saul* (1894), settings of Pope's *Ode on St. Cecilia's Day* (1889), Milton's *L'Allegro ed Il Pensieroso* (1890), the choric song from Tennyson's *The Lotos-Eaters* (1892), Bridges's *A Song of Darkness and Light* (1898), A. C. Benson's *Ode to Music* (1901), *War and Peace* (1903), *Voces Clamantium* (1903), *The Love that casteth out Fear* (1904), and *A Vision of Life* (1907, revised 1914). Besides his very numerous compositions, both in these large, and also in smaller, shapes such as songs, Parry found time for various literary works of very high value—the chief of which are *The Evolution of the Art of Music* (1896), *The Music of the Seventeenth Century* (volume III of the *Oxford History of Music,* 1902),[1] *Johann Sebastian Bach* (1909), and *Style in Musical Art* (1911); he was also director of the Royal College of Music from 1894 until his death, and from 1900 to 1908 professor of music at Oxford.

Cowen was born in Jamaica but received his musical education at Leipzig. His 'Scandinavian' symphony (1880) was the first work to give him a prominent position, though he had been known both as composer and as pianist for a considerable time previously; his powers were later shown in several other symphonies as well as in numerous other orchestral works, three operas—*Thorgrim* (1890), *Signa* (1893), and *Harold* (1895), numerous oratorios and cantatas, of which a setting of Collins's *Ode to the Passions* (1898) is perhaps the chief, and a very large quantity of solo songs, while he was also for many years one of the prominent conductors of England.

Stanford was born in Dublin but in 1870 removed to Cambridge, which from that time became a chief centre of his influence, first as organist of Trinity College (from 1873 to 1892) and afterwards as professor of music, a post that he held from 1887 until his death; he also taught composition at the Royal College of Music and held various important conductorships. Of all the composers of the English renaissance he was the most versatile, as well as perhaps the most prolific. Besides very numerous instrumental compositions, both chamber and orchestral, including several symphonies, he produced a considerable quantity of music for the stage, his operas, *Shamus O'Brien* (a *Singspiel* after the older model, with spoken dialogue, 1896) and *Much Ado about Nothing* (1901) being the most important; his choral works include two oratorios, *The Three Holy Children* (1885) and *Eden* (1891), a Requiem (1897), a Te Deum (1898), and a Stabat Mater (1907) and many secular pieces, such as, among others, Tennyson's *The Revenge* (1886) and *The Voyage of Maeldune* (1889), and Henley's *The Last Post* (1900), besides a large quantity of church music, part-songs, and solo songs.

Edward Elgar, a native of Worcester, is a unique example of a composer who was, virtually, altogether self-taught. Till about his fortieth year he was little known; he preferred to live outside the

---

[1] A second edition, revised by E. J. Dent, appeared in 1938.

whirl of the recognized musical circles, and never held any official position of any importance except the professorship at Birmingham from 1905 to 1908, and the mastership of the King's music from 1924 until his death. His principal works are the oratorios *The Dream of Gerontius* (1900), *The Apostles* (1903), and its sequel *The Kingdom* (1906), the choral ode *The Music-Makers* (1912), two symphonies (1908 and 1911), concertos for violin (1910) and 'cello (1919), the 'Enigma' variations (1899), the Introduction and Allegro for strings (1905), the symphonic study *Falstaff* (1913), and a small group of chamber works.

It was only during the last twenty-five years of the nineteenth century that the renaissance of English composition gradually grew in strength; but in other departments of music signs of the new order were visible at an earlier date. In 1855 August Manns (1825–1907) started at the Crystal Palace a lifetime's work that had a great and most beneficial influence; not only did he first introduce to English audiences the orchestral compositions of Schubert and Schumann and many more, but it was to him, foreigner though he was by blood, that nearly all the composers of this period owed their first public encouragement. Manns's labours were ably seconded by George Grove (1820–1900), for many years secretary to the Crystal Palace Company, and subsequently the first director of the Royal College of Music (who was also the real inventor of the analytical programme and the editor of the first complete musical dictionary in the English language); and in the field of chamber music the St. James's Hall Popular Concerts (1859–98) did a great work in familiarizing the English public with the finest renderings of all the classical masterpieces (though it was no part of their manager's scheme to make experiments or to do anything for native composers), and from 1848 onwards Charles Hallé (1819–95) did valiant service in a similar direction in London and the north of England, where the orchestra known by his name was formed in 1857. Even more remarkable as an educative force was the series of orchestral 'Promenade' concerts inaugurated by Robert Newman at Queen's Hall in 1895, with Henry Wood (1869–1944) as conductor. The success of these concerts has been such that they now attract a very much larger audience to the Albert Hall, which became their home when Queen's Hall was destroyed in the 1939–45 war. Undoubtedly the popularity of orchestral concerts has increased so much that it distinctly threatens to silence the quieter appeal of chamber music; but in spite of this very regrettable fact, nothing shows better the enormous advance in musical appreciation than a comparison of the programmes of a 'Promenade' concert to-day and of its parallel sixty years ago, when the Crystal Palace had a virtual monopoly of symphonic music in or near London. In vocal music, however, the revival came somewhat later. The older generation of solo singers did not feel to any appreciable extent the same pressure towards the universal choice of high-class music which has become every year more and more weighty; it was only the younger singers who felt obliged to render at least an outward homage to the ideal which had long ruled in the instrumental field. In choral music, again, it was some time before we recognized that something more than mere military drilling is necessary in modern technique; and the new era of opera is virtually a product of the present century. But in every department, plentiful as are the opportunities for deeper culture that still remain, the advance that coincided with the renaissance of composition has been very remarkable; an English-born and home-staying musician has now a position of perfect artistic equality with his continental colleague.

Again, we can see in the teaching world how the old Royal Academy of Music was awakened to a new existence by the establishment of the Royal College of Music in 1882, and how they, with other institutions and individual teachers, moved with the times in raising the average quality of the music taught to young people. And we cannot pass by the Tonic Sol-fa movement (the Association was founded in 1853, the College in 1863), which had enormous influence in diffusing elementary musical knowledge among certain classes of the community; it was indeed often greatly hampered by a quite unnecessary connexion with musicianship of the very poorest kind, but freed from these shackles and taken for what it was worth—merely an easy means to the end which all musicians have in common, and not a sort of panacea that can afford to dispense with the one universal language of the staff notation—it proved that it could do a lasting work in English music. The People's Concert Society (founded in 1878) and others of similar aims did finely artistic work in the poorer quarters of London, and the competition festivals (beginning in the eighties) greatly fostered good music in provincial districts; indeed, though the wide diffusion of music among relatively uneducated persons often had the great drawback of extinguishing the memory for traditional folk-songs, yet it proved—what ought to have been known before—that artistic appreciation is quite independent of social distinctions and that there is no sort of foundation for the pernicious doctrine that it is ever necessary for a musician to sing or play down to the supposed level of any audience in existence. And simultaneously the musician himself became far less narrowly professional, far more interested in the whole wide world of intellect and art.

Opera ramified in several directions. At Covent Garden 'grand opera' of the cosmopolitan type, with foreign conductors and chiefly foreign singers, to obtain whom Europe and America were scoured year by year, survived until 1939; to it we owed the maintenance of what as a rule was a distinctly high level of performance, though the excessive prices often charged were prohibitive to very many of the music-lovers who would have been the best appreciators. This régime may be said to have taken its rise from the productions of German operas in 1882 and 1884, though it was not till 1887 that it was firmly established; it had the drawback of reviving the old type of fashionably ill-mannered audience that during the decay of operatic fortunes was very little in evidence, but nevertheless, in spite of the vagaries of its arbiters, it did a great deal (especially by the popularization of the later works of Wagner) to broaden taste and to help on the general movement of the renaissance. For English composers, however, Covent Garden did very little; a few works were performed once or twice, and then pusillanimously dropped out of the repertory for good and all. But as early as 1875 the Carl Rosa Company (the venture of a German violinist who had married a brilliant singer), after some years in America, started to give operas in London, performing all the works in English and getting together the best native talent that could be procured; a considerable number of operas by English composers were commissioned and brought to a first hearing under its auspices, but after the death of its founder in 1889 it became overshadowed by the revival of cosmopolitan opera, and turned its attention from London to the provinces. As for the English Opera House in London, specially built and opened with a flourish of trumpets in 1891, it merely performed Sullivan's *Ivanhoe* till the public was tired, then diverged to André Messager's *La Basoche*, and directly afterwards acknowledged its failure and became a music-hall (now the Palace Theatre).

But it is in a department of stage music untouched by the directors of either the cosmopolitan or the purely English opera that the greatest success was won. Since the days of Shield and his contemporaries English light opera had gradually drifted downhill till all relics of even the faintest musical culture vanished; but the great vogue of Offenbach's Parisian operettas in the fifties and sixties suggested to a theatre conductor of the name of German Reed (1817–88) the foundation of stage entertainments with music that should appeal to a different class of audience. These prospered for many years, and it was to them that Sullivan (whose *Cox and Box*, written and produced in 1867, was revived under Reed's auspices) owed the beginnings of his popular success; Frederic Clay (1838–89), some of whose work (more especially that of earlier date) is of quite pleasant quality in its kind, was also brought to light through this channel. Throughout the seventies and eighties Sullivan, with the admirable assistance of W. S. Gilbert as his librettist, poured forth a continuous stream of light operas, nearly all of which were received with unbounded applause; and though those subsequently produced with other collaborators did not attain the same popular success, the general musical type remained unchanged. But in this field, and in this alone, English music proceeded to go backwards instead of forwards. These works, and contemporary imitations from the less able pens of Alfred Cellier (1844–91) and Edward Solomon (1853–95), really created a new sort of audience, able to pronounce a financially very weighty verdict but possessing very little artistic discrimination; and their legitimate if, as a rule (especially in the matter of libretti), decidedly inferior descendants appeared in the flood of musical comedies which swamped London theatres and enthroned on a very solid cash basis ideals of verbal and musical vulgarity which, in spite of occasional works of better quality, have not yet been overthrown.

We may now turn to consider the actual musical output of this period. Sullivan was, beyond all question, the most widely popular English composer of the nineteenth century; and the impress that he left on one department of English music was undoubtedly very deep. The comic operas written to the libretti of W. S. Gilbert made his reputation and form indeed his chief title to fame. Though we cannot forget that a considerable share of the success they achieved was due to the brilliantly sparkling wit of his collaborator, it has become increasingly evident that they survive by virtue of the music. Gilbert's humour now seems old-fashioned and his libretti have the air of period pieces, but the music is as fresh as ever. Sullivan was not only a master of the *buffo* style; he also had a genius for parody. A generation to whom nineteenth-century 'grand opera' is virtually a closed book may not realise how mercilessly witty are imitations like the waltz song in *The Pirates of Penzance* (1880) or the chorus of conspirators in *H.M.S. Pinafore* (1878). We even have a parody of Italian *opera buffa* in the opening scene of *The Gondoliers* (1889)—a parody so faithful that we seem almost to be listening to Rossini. All this is done with a technical expertness which conceals the craftsman's hand. Sometimes indeed the composer aims higher: 'The ghosts' high noon' in *Ruddigore* (1887) is not unworthy of a place in serious opera. But for the most part he is content to amuse and to charm, and he errs only when the text tempts him to sentimentality, or when he tries to stretch his invention beyond the limits of a lyrical style. Two details call for particular comment—an almost Schubertian flair for modulation, of which 'Three little maids from school' in *The Mikado* (1885) provides a good example, and a happy knack of choosing contrasted keys for his soloists in an ensemble ('A regular royal queen' in *The Gondoliers* is a case in point). The orchestration, unobtrusive, neat, and pointed, enhances the vivacity of the music: the scores are full of happy touches like this from *The Mikado*:

In his serious music he is less consistent. He had imbibed all the orthodox Mendelssohnian traditions of his student days and was also attracted by the frank *bonhomie* of the lighter works of Schubert, whose music he did much to make known; and the results are visible, when he is at his best, in admirably clear and economically effective orchestration, dexterous, smooth workmanship and an easy and continual flow of natural and, in its slight way, thoroughly individual tunefulness. In a few works—the *Di Ballo* overture (1870), much of the incidental music to *The Tempest* (1862), the song 'Orpheus with his lute' (1878), and a handful of other things—Sullivan shows the finish and fluent melodiousness of the comic operas under more independent conditions; they are essentially light music, but the melodies have point and charm of their own and are not mere background. He might, indeed, with his fresh and distinctive gifts, have gone far, had he been endowed also with anything like steadiness of ideal; his best pages are nearly all comparatively early, but even then he turned out a great deal of very inferior music and in later years the success of the operas seems to have blunted his capacity for really vitalized work on independent lines. We can never recollect without shame that the composer who stood for contemporary English music in the eyes of the world could put his name to disgraceful rubbish like 'The lost chord' or 'The sailor's grave' (1872) or, in what purported to be serious artistic work, sink to the abysmally cheap sentimentality of the opening tune of the *In Memoriam* overture (1866) or the 'O pure in heart' chorus in *The Golden Legend* (1886); and indeed there is a pitiful amount of this kind of thing. The sacred cantata *The Martyr of Antioch* (1880), apart from a certain amount of a sort of mildly pleasant picturesqueness, alternates between dullness and vulgarity, and sometimes attains both at once; while the more ambitious oratorio *The Light of the World* (1873) has hardly enough vitality even to be vulgar. The later orchestral pieces, such as the *Macbeth* overture (1888), come to singularly little, and *Ivanhoe* (1891), the one serious opera, is a purely elementary work all through, with a few fairly dramatic pages, but as a rule mere commonplace, the one really living thing being the bass air of Friar Tuck, which comes more or less close to the Savoy style; all the exciting situations are treated as mere theatrical business with not a trace of workmanship worth mentioning, and the deadly dullness of nearly all of the opera passes belief. In *The Golden Legend* Sullivan no doubt pulled himself together to some extent; the Prologue (apart from the conventional chromatics), the end of Scene I, parts of the 'Journey to Salerno', of the love-duet, of the Epilogue—these show traces of the early talent, less satisfactory because more pretentious, but in their rather superficial way romantically pleasant enough. And indeed, apart from the painful lapses in the already mentioned 'O pure in heart' and at the end of 'O gladsome light', the rest of the work is hardly ever anything worse than dull drawing-room music; but for the best-known English composer in the very prime of life, and putting forth his full powers, *The Golden Legend* is, as a whole, a melancholy production. After all, Sullivan is merely the idle singer of an empty evening; with all his gift for tunefulness he never could raise it to the height of a real strong melody, of the kind that appeals to cultured and relatively uncultured alike as a good folk-song does—often and often, on the other hand (but chiefly outside the operas), it sank to mere vulgar catchiness. He laid the original foundations of his success on work that, as a matter of fact, he did extremely well, and it would have been incalculably better for the permanence of his reputation if he had realized this and set himself, with sincerity and self-criticism, to the task of becoming—as he might easily have become—a really great composer of musicianly light and humorous music. But anything like steadiness of artistic purpose was never one of his endowments; and without that, a composer, whatever his technical ability may be, is easily liable to degenerate into a mere popularity-hunting trifler.

Goring Thomas's artistic nature was far more steadfast, though just occasionally, as in the popular song 'A summer night' and some other things, he turned out definitely low-class work; he never, on the other hand, attained the distinctiveness of utterance which marks Sullivan's style at its very best, though his general average is much higher. He is certainly the most Parisianized of nineteenth-century composers; his training shows itself in nearly every page of his music, and his most characteristic and picturesque songs—'Le jeune pâtre,' for example—have all the polished delicacy and slightly sentimental charm that are such salient features in modern French work. Thomas is an interesting instance of a composer possessing plenty of style but at the same time little individuality; his music at its best is full of point, but exactly the same points have also been made by others. His refined technique, his dainty turns of phrase, can be matched over and over again in contemporary French music; not that he is anything like a plagiarist, but this way of doing things seems somehow to be in the air of the boulevards, and the reverse of the same picture is seen in the permanent deficiency to write music possessing real emotional grip. Light music of the aristocratic type is his *métier*; and, like his models, he pursues his aim with, as a rule, undeniable skill and success. It is in the operas that his work is seen on the largest scale; and though, there as else-where, the current of inspiration sometimes runs distinctly thin, there is much of very real interest. *Esmeralda* (1883) in particular—perhaps his best composition—is a distinctly attractive work which deserves reviving; the more serious portions are, it is true, the less successful, but there is a great deal of delicate sparkle and charm (as in Esmeralda's 'Swallow song', for example) not at all unworthy of Bizet himself, and the rollicking but thoroughly refined opening chorus should appeal to lovers of stage 'Kermesse Music' who are justly tired of some other popular specimens. *Nadeshda* (1885) is a little more theatrical and a little less spontaneous; there are plenty of good pages in the opera, but the handling is rather more heavy. But in nearly all Thomas's work, whether for the stage or the concert-room, we see signs of an undeniable talent that might, but for his early death, have resulted in something worthy of a more permanent remembrance than his actual output is likely to attain.

Cowen's talent is also of the lighter type, but it differs from Goring Thomas's in being at the same time much more varied and also, in a way, considerably less thorough. There is also no trace worth mentioning of French influence; the style is in many respects a sort of combination of Sterndale Bennett and Sullivan, with the addition of elements of Cowen's own. We can see the resemblance to Sullivan in the very regrettable capacity for per-petrating inferior shop-ballads, and also, in a worthier manner, in the talent for cleverly dainty and effective orchestration; while the influence of Bennett can be traced in the graceful ease of the workmanship at its best and in the fondness for what may perhaps be called drawing-room pictorialism, though the colouring is in-clined, as a rule, to lack the purity of Bennett's. But the pages where he treats subjects of a more or less fairylike character show him in his most individual mood; the best parts of *The Sleeping Beauty* (1885) or *The Water-Lily* (1893) are very polished and delicate works—not more, it is true, than ballet music, but touched with an exceptionally light hand and in that slender way sometimes very charming. It is, so to speak, water-colour work like Bennett's, but is far more piquant than serenely classical (as is that of the older composer); nor is it exactly French or Mendelssohnian—it is, in its slight, evanescent style, something that may fairly be called Cowen's own. Though, indeed, it is not so very often that he is really at his best; he is unfortunately capable of writing a good deal of music where the daintiness of touch degenerates into mere refined com-monplace or still lower into mere triviality—for example, the well-known 'Elegance and grace' gavotte from the first *The Language of Flowers* suite (1880) does most of the rest of the work scant justice. And as a general rule he is less happy in his more serious moods; *Ruth* (1887) and *Thorgrim* (1890), which may fairly be taken as typical of his oratorios and his operas, are rather obvious works, containing a good deal of suave picturesqueness of a kind, but (es-pecially the former) singularly little that is at all solidly satisfying. And the same may be said of his symphonies and other non-fairylike instrumental music; there is plenty of cleverness and, more espe-cially in the Adagio of the 'Idyllic' symphony (1897) and the first movement of the 'Scandinavian' (1880), with its happily designed opening, there is interesting material, but somehow there is a lack of vitality about the works as wholes. In the 'Welsh' symphony (1884) in particular, we see how his style is inclined to become uncertain when he feels he must not indulge his desire to be frankly pretty; that really is his *métier*, and at his best he can exercise it with a graceful adroitness that compels the admiration even of those who may feel that it is but a small thing on which to found a reputation. It is true that there are occasional glimpses of something more: the setting of Collins's *Ode to the Passions* (1898)—probably Cowen's best work—shows plenty of vitalized utterance of a considerably more solid kind than usual, and not a few pages in it combine their composer's usual melodiousness with definite emotional strength. But to this level, we must confess, he rises but seldom.

Mackenzie, Cowen's senior by five years, was a composer of undeniable talent and serious aims, whose development seems, for some reason or other (probably pressure of non-creative work), to have come more or less to a standstill in early middle life. A sort of quiet but nevertheless warm picturesqueness is the quality chiefly shown in his best compositions, such as the beautiful orchestral ballad to Keats's poem *La Belle Dame sans merci* (1883), the dirge in *The Dream of Jubal* (1889), the finest portions of *Colomba* (1883, revised 1912) and *The Troubadour* (1886), *The Rose of Sharon* (1884, revised 1910), and *The Story of Sayid* (1886); he also showed with success a partiality for works based on the general lines of his native folk-melodies, such as the three Scottish rhapsodies for orchestra (1880, 1881, 1911), the 'Pibroch' suite for violin (1889), and others. His first opera, *Colomba*, contains many pages of very real living grace and charm; it is strongly influenced no doubt by the methods of Bizet's *Carmen*, but not to such an extent as to cause any sacrifice of individuality. *The Troubadour*, though its peculiarly blood-curdling libretto hindered its success, also contains some of its composer's most romantic work and shows plenty of delicate characterization; indeed, Mackenzie always seemed to find a special attraction in the stage, small in amount as was his output in that field. The libretto of the oratorio *The Rose of Sharon*, his most important choral work, is based on the *Song of Solomon*, with the rather incongruous additions of a prologue and epilogue (both of which were omitted in the revised edition), and the emotional fervour of the Eastern love-poem affords chances of which some admirable use has been made; the 'Sleep' scene in the third part is one of Mackenzie's most remarkable and imaginative pages, and some of the choruses, though redolent of what might be called highly modernized Mendelssohnianism, are in their way decidedly impressive. But the oratorio unfortunately declines in interest towards the end: and indeed its composer's talent was of a somewhat uncertain order. He had plenty of versatility, and never wrote below his own musicianly standards—the fun of the *Britannia* nautical overture (1894), for example, though rather obvious, is very workmanlike—but a considerable quantity of his music does not show any particular distinctive qualities of any kind. Mackenzie, indeed, is the salient representative of the purely transitional school; with some contemporaries whose work runs in very similar channels, he seems to have recognized the unworthiness of anything short of the highest ideal, without, save sporadically, being able to make any notable personal contribution towards its attainment.

The great bulk of the music that later Victorian composers wrote for the services of the Anglican church is something altogether *sui generis*; and the deepest impress upon it is not that of any Englishman but of a foreigner attached to another creed. To Dykes, Barnby, and Stainer, Gounod, whether they fully recognized the fact or not, was an influence incomparably greater than Sebastian Wesley or Goss, though the latter, in his inferior moods, shows signs of the change of ideal; the methods of the *Messe solennelle* and 'Nazareth' are visible everywhere, but nevertheless the work is definitely, so to speak, non-mystical—it is Gounod's ideal in terms of Protestantism. Sullivan's church music represents, it is true, something of a divergence from the main stream; as a rule, it is more straightforward and old-fashioned in type, and things like 'Onward! Christian soldiers', or such parts of the elaborate 'Festival Te Deum' (1872) as the 'We therefore pray thee' section or the military band march at the end, show a sort of good-natured, frank, more or less healthy vulgarity that is not visible in the work of the others. Indeed, Sullivan's church music shows traces of many influences; some pages are diluted, but not, in its way, at all unpleasant Mendelssohnianism, others suggest Gounod's *Roméo et Juliette*, others the Savoy operas. But in the hymns and services and anthems of Dykes, Barnby, and Stainer there is not this conflict of styles; their work is all of a piece. No doubt Stainer, very much the most gifted of the three, could occasionally produce music of a different order, as, for instance, the picturesque and powerful opening section of the eight-part anthem 'I saw the Lord'; but (as indeed the rest of this anthem exemplifies somewhat markedly) the effort was never long-sustained. The general work of these three and their numerous followers is, as a matter of fact, remarkably homogeneous. The musical historians of centuries hence will be able to date things like the 'Sevenfold Amen' or the tune of 'Lead, kindly light' within a decade or two as infallibly as a skilled paleographist dates a medieval manuscript; there has been no music like it before, and it is highly improbable that there will ever be music like it again. Fortunately, Stainer's reputation depends not on his music but on his services to scholarship. Musicians today have no use for *The Crucifixion* (1887), but *Dufay and his Contemporaries* (1898) and the volumes of *Early Bodleian Music* (1901) are still known and valued by historians. Stainer was also instrumental in founding the Musical Association in 1874. Barnby in turn deserves to be remembered for the services he rendered by performing Bach's Passions at a time when they were still little known. If the music of this period was often negligible, the activity shown in reviving and studying the music of the past was not. The Purcell Society was founded in 1876 with the object of publishing an edition, still unfortunately incomplete, of that composer's works. The Plainsong and Medieval Music Society followed in 1888. Byrd's Masses were revived at the Brompton Oratory by Thomas Wingham (1846–93), and the enthusiasm of Lionel Benson brought to light many of the works of the English madrigalists. The first volume of Grove's *Dictionary of Music and Musicians* appeared in 1879, while in 1901 the *Oxford History of Music* was launched with Wooldridge's pioneer work on the music of the early Middle Ages. The scholarship that promoted these studies was earnest and sincere; and it is no depreciation to say that much of it has since been superseded.

We now come to the trio of composers who were the really significant leaders of the English renaissance; of these the eldest was Parry, and indeed his work shows the most affinity to the methods of the older classics. In some of his earlier instrumental compositions—for example, the duo for two pianofortes in E minor (1876) or the partita for violin and pianoforte in D minor (1886)—we find indeed sections which produce a somewhat anachronistic effect by their frank adoption of eighteenth-century formulas, and on the whole, in spite of the many admirable pages in such works as the 'Cambridge' symphony (1883, revised 1887), especially the slow movement, one of Parry's very finest inspirations, or the symphonic variations for orchestra (1897) or the B minor trio for piano and strings (1884), and others besides, he is not at his best in instrumental writing; massive and earnest as the musicianship invariably is, the thematic invention is not, as a rule, of very special individuality, and the touch is inclined to be heavy. With certain notable exceptions, like the fine part-song 'There rolls the deep' (No. 4 of *Six Modern Lyrics*, 1897), the same may, to a greater or less extent, be said of the smaller vocal compositions; it is when using the spacious medium of chorus and orchestra combined that Parry's true *métier* is displayed

Bach and Brahms, and to a considerably less degree, Handel and Mendelssohn, were the sources out of which Parry developed his own thoroughly characteristic style as exemplified in his mature choral works; and it is curious that his earliest writing for that medium is to a very large extent unaffected by any of them. *Prometheus Unbound* (1880), his first really important production, has never yet come to its own; but both it and the slightly later setting of the ode from Shirley's *The Contention of Ajax and Ulysses*, 'The glories of our blood and state' (1883), show features that the later work lacks. It is easy to see that in certain respects the technical handling is less mature than it afterwards became; but nearly every page of Shirley's ode, and in *Prometheus* such things (among several others) as the 'Light of life' chorus and the splendid closing scene, are instinct with a sort of youthful and yet deep emotional thrill that the more restrained later work very rarely shows in anything like the same form. If we seek for a definite birthday for modern English music, 7 September 1880, when *Prometheus* saw the light at Gloucester and met with a distinctly mixed reception', has undoubtedly the best claim; and it is difficult to avoid a certain feeling of regret that in his later years Parry left this particular vein wellnigh untouched. But in the later style, seen at its best in such works as *Blest Pair of Sirens* (1887), *Job* (1892), *L'Allegro ed il Pensieroso* (1890), *De Profundis* (1891), *Invocation to Music* (1895), *Ode to Music* (1901), *The Lotos-Eaters* (1892), the Te Deum in F major (1900), and, though perhaps in a more unequal degree, in many others besides, there are plenty of compensations. There is real nobility of manner about the finest specimens of his broad choral writing with its powerful dignified climaxes—nobility of a kind that is the reverse of common in modern English or any other compositions; he has the Handelian love of straightforward piling up of great masses of sound and he manages such effects with consummate skill, though it must be confessed that at times he shows another and less attractive type of neo-Handelianism in allowing his instruments to bustle around in a rather vaguely genial fashion to fill up the gaps when the current of inspiration temporarily fails —an interlude in the finale of the *St. Cecilia's Day* ode (1889) is perhaps the most striking lengthy example of this trait. But his general outlook is distinctly more akin to that of Bach; there is something of the same large-hearted disregard of relatively unimportant matters, something of the same love of massive intellectualism. Not of course that Parry (any more than Bach, or any one else worth mentioning) is, in the abusive sense of a much misunderstood word, an 'academic' composer; he is quite at home in plenty of things besides counterpoint. It is true that he never again caught the lyrical rapture of the best parts of *Prometheus Unbound*; but the fresh spring-like grace and the happy gravity or grave happiness of the best numbers of *L'Allegro* (in many respects indeed Parry has a singular affinity with Milton), the solemn impressiveness of such pages as the dirges in the *Invocation to Music* and *War and Peace* (1903), from the latter of which a section may be quoted:[1]

Ex. 167 *Andante*

Dark earth un-der them, skies a - bove, This is the rest that

---

[1] Vocal score, p. 50. By permission of Novello and Co., Ltd.

the finest parts of *The Love that casteth out Fear* (1904), or the two
great sections in *Job*, the delicate pathos of the Eurydice music in
St. Cecilia's Day or the 'Tears' chorus in the *Song of Darkness and
Light* (1898), the picturesque expression of the sea-pictures in the
Invocation or the honeyed languor of *The Lotos-Eaters*, the jovial
humour of *The Pied Piper of Hamelin* (1905) or the Aristophanic
plays—all these show real versatility of style, though it is easy to see
in them all the same hand at work, and the same strong feeling for
the spacious things. In his later years Parry attempted some new
fields, such as organ music, in which he was particularly successful,
and unison choral songs, including among other fine things 'England' (1918), one of the noblest of our patriotic tunes. His chief
new works, however—perhaps the masterpieces of his whole career,
at the very end of which they were written—were the series of extended motets for unaccompanied chorus, called by the general
name of *Songs of Farewell* (1916–18): the best of them, such as 'At

the round earth's imagined corners', 'There is an old belief', or 'Lord, let me know mine end', reach heights of tranquil and massive spiritual dignity to which few British composers have attained.

It is true that Parry is far from being an equal composer; composition was indeed only one of the elements in an extraordinarily busy life, but still he produced a very large mass of music. Occasionally he may write pages of mere bluff breeziness without any adequate impulse behind them, and the firm touch occasionally becomes ponderous; but hardly any composers in the history of the art give a more vivid impression of unswerving sincerity of aim, and when the flame of his genius burns brightest, it stirs our blood with a real living heat. It is, however, very curious that the oratorio *Judith* (1888)—the one composition in which (in spite of fine things here and there, such as, especially, Meshullemeth's ballad 'Long since in Egypt's plenteous land') Parry rather approaches the commonplace—should have been for a time one of his most successful productions; both libretto and music hark back very largely to traditions which had fully served their time, and it is a remarkable illustration of their firm clutch on the hearts of Victorian choral societies and their patrons that so reactionary a work should have had such a vogue.

Like Parry, Stanford never from the first wrote anything to tarnish the purity of his ideal; but his temperament led him into somewhat different paths. His Irish blood showed itself not only in his frequent researches into the rich store of his native folk music but also in his versatile susceptibility to many and various influences; individual as his utterance is, it is, so to speak, a very composite blend. Quite apart from the Irish folk-songs that he edited, and many movements coloured more or less by such influences, he produced in the opera *Shamus O'Brien* (1896) and the choral ballad *Phaudrig Crohoore* (1896) something that is virtually Irish folk music itself; *Shamus O'Brien* in particular—one of the most deliciously open-air works in all British music—is crammed full of tunes which, without any suspicion of plagiarism, seem to suggest that their composer had lived in the wilds of Ireland all his life. We see French influence, especially that of Bizet, in considerable tracts of *The Three Holy Children* (1885) and *The Veiled Prophet of Khorassan* (1881), signs of the later Verdi in the Requiem (1897) and the Te Deum (1898), of Sebastian Wesley in the Anglican anthems and services, of Brahms in the chamber music and of a variety of composers in *The Travel-*

ling Companion (1919[1]); and yet all this roving results in something really characteristic, something that is unmistakably Stanford himself. Though it cannot, save occasionally, be said of his music that it suggests the incommensurable things in art (for which we have indeed still, in the main, to look to foreign work), it always shows a singular deftness of handling and a sort of brilliant, sensitive adaptability of mood that we do not see elsewhere in English music in at all the same forms; the style at its best is full of vitality, and the musicianship, even when the themes are not specially striking, is invariably impeccable.

In certain respects, perhaps, Stanford displays his most distinguished manner when working on a small canvas. The subtle imaginativeness of songs like 'The Fairy Lough' or 'Homeward bound' is extraordinary; and, in a brighter mood, the choral settings of Elizabethan pastorals are marked by an exquisitely polished delicacy that perhaps no other modern English musician has equalled. Again, movements like the beautiful slow section of the 'Irish' symphony in F minor (1887) are altogether his own; and so is wonderfully picturesque sea music like *The Revenge* (1886) or *The Voyage of Maeldune* (1889), the latter of which, especially, contains some of his very best work. Speaking generally, he seems (apart from the 'Irish' symphony and rhapsodies, and similarly quasi-native music like the 'Irish Fantasies' for violin) to be less at home in instrumental compositions than in those where the addition of words gives a special stimulus; and in vocal music he seems most inspired by words that afford, so to speak, a certain amount of concrete imagery. His large ecclesiastical works, such as the Mass in G, the Requiem, the Te Deum, and the Stabat Mater (1907) exemplify this in different ways. The first-named is perhaps the least interesting of his mature compositions and the second and third, in spite of admirable sections—most of all the very fine Introit and Kyrie of the Requiem—do not, as wholes, fairly represent him; the colouring is often strikingly rich, almost voluptuous—as is especially shown in the feathery Sanctus of the Requiem or the grandiose last pages of the Te Deum—but the general effect is somehow not altogether successful. On the other hand the Stabat Mater, a very vivid and expressive setting, is undoubtedly the masterpiece of all his larger choral works; and in *Eden* (1891), curiously unequal though the long oratorio is, several numbers of the 'Heaven' section, the first

[1] First performed, 1925.

chorus of devils, parts of the 'Vision of Good', and most of all the very solemn and tender 'Vision of Christ' and final pages, are in their different ways very arresting music, and the last-named portion shows the composer in his loftiest vein. Loftiness is again the distinguishing feature of the early setting of Whitman's great *Ode to Death* (1884), the varying moods of which are very successfully caught. There is nobility, too, in Beatrice's dirge at the end of *Much Ado about Nothing* (1901), of which the instrumental introduction may be quoted:[1]

Ex. 168

and, at the opposite extreme, we see Stanford's strong sense of humour, quite apart from Irish influences, in the delightful Dogberry music in the same opera. Generally speaking, however, he seems most attracted by two things—Irish national music and a sort of broadly Tennysonian romanticism. He avowedly uses a considerable number of his native folk-tunes as material in several of his works, and, apart from these, he very frequently writes original music that breathes an exactly similar spirit; and, when in this mood, he almost invariably produces results of a really vital attractiveness and charm. His Tennysonian spirit shows itself in his great partiality for words dealing with nature, especially with the sea, or expressing the romantic side of patriotism; in these and similar veins he is again completely at home, and possesses a singular power of subtle pictorialism that is entirely devoid of the faintest exaggeration and yet is very direct and vivid. Stanford was a prolific writer, and in some of his very numerous compositions he may fail

[1] Vocal score, p. 194. By permission of Boosey and Hawkes, Ltd.

to be more than the skilful craftsman; but it is quite certain that his best work will, in virtue of the living imaginativeness that inspires it, survive among the permanently notable achievements of English art.

Few things in the history of modern music are more remarkable than Elgar's sudden leap into something like world-wide fame; indeed, no composer has had an artistic career like his. Like Berlioz, he was a free lance, self-taught, and influenced very slightly by the current traditions of his time; but unlike Berlioz, whose work is all of a piece from the very start, Elgar began on lines almost entirely alien to his later methods. All composers, even the greatest, have of course written relatively inferior (often very inferior) work at some period or other; and some have only for the first time found themselves artistically in middle life, like Wagner, or in old age, like Verdi. But Elgar, till he was considerably over thirty years of age, was known chiefly by, so to speak, smart society music—the kind of production that seeks and finds its reward in the West End drawing-room, clever and shallow and artistically quite unpromising; and even in the days of his high fame he had (at any rate for a long time) the heavy millstone of aristocratic fashionableness hanging round his neck and may over and over again well have prayed to be delivered from his friends. Indeed, there was no particular reason for any one to prophesy any special future for him: in the best work of the transition period there were no doubt points of interest of various kinds—the pleasant picturesqueness of *The Black Knight* (1893) and the Serenade for strings (1892), several parts of *King Olaf* (1896), especially the powerful 'Challenge of Thor', and the very fine sombre 'Lament' in *Caractacus* (1898)—but still these were so much overbalanced by things like the conscientious sentimentality of the great bulk (though not indeed all) of the *The Light of Life* (1896), the rather blatant hardness of the last section of *The Banner of St. George* (1897) and the 'Imperial March' (1897), and the superficial appeal of the salon music, that it seemed decidedly doubtful whether the obvious talent would ever result in anything really vital. It was not until 1899 that Elgar found his fully individual method of expression in some fine *Sea Pictures* for contralto and orchestra, and in the astonishingly subtle and imaginative 'Enigma' variations for orchestra. *The Dream of Gerontius* (1900), in which the new style was first shown on an extended scale, had to wait some time for its second performance, and three years before it was heard in London, but after its great success in Germany its composer's popularity swelled rapidly to enormous proportions. It was fairly obvious from the start that the movement which began in London with the performance of *The Dream of Gerontius* at Westminster Cathedral in 1903 was to some extent of a merely evanescent character; and the comparatively cool reception accorded to *The Kingdom* (1906), which is certainly by no means inferior to Elgar's other mature works, seemed to show that it had already nearly spent itself, as was bound sooner or later to be the case. But though pessimistic voices were heard prophesying that Elgar would find his level by the side of people like the composers of *The Redemption* or *The Resurrection of Lazarus*, yet the reality proved to be far otherwise. The oratorios found their natural home at the Three Choirs Festivals, and *Gerontius* became a classic in the composer's lifetime.

Apart from a certain number of small works, either several years old or written in imitation of earlier models, Elgar published nothing after 1899 which does not bear his own characteristic sign-manual; and in slender productions like the Greek Anthology lyrics for male voices (1903) or other similarly most remarkable part-songs like 'Weary wind of the west' (1903) or 'Evening scene' (1906) the individual vitality of utterance is quite as conspicuous as in the large choral works or orchestral compositions such as the *In the South* overture (1904). In feeling for colour—colour of every conceivable kind—Elgar is surpassed by no composer of his time, and he shows, like his contemporary and admirer, Richard Strauss, a singular power of reaching the essence of the words he chooses to set—especially when they give opportunity for the expression of emotional drama or religious feeling in the terms of mystical but modern Catholicism. The sort of entrancing, unearthly charm of such music as the songs of the Angel in *Gerontius* or the setting of the Beatitudes in *The Apostles* (1903) is without parallel in English work; it is wonderfully subtle and intimate, and yet the appeal which it makes is very direct. He threads the mazes of the most elaborate polyphony with easy assurance; vividness, courage, modernity inspire every page of the works by which he bids fair to live.

In his oratorios, however, we cannot help noticing here and there a lack of sustained thematic inventiveness, a deficiency in the power of broadly organic construction; even when, in a way, quite original, the material sometimes consists of scraps of music, neither individually nor collectively of any particular interest beyond mere colour, joined together by methods not altogether convincing. Occasionally also there seems an undue reliance on a rather hot-house type of emotionalism, which every now and then comes near degenerating into a somewhat forced pseudo-impressiveness; the melodramatic bars that depict the suicide of Judas in *The Apostles* set on edge the teeth of listeners who have felt to the full the drama-tic power of the pages that precede them, and there are parts of Gerontius's confession of faith which, though sincere, nevertheless suggest an atmosphere of artificial flowers. Sometimes the splen-dour of the frame tends to hide the picture; and in the picture itself, when we do see it, the gorgeous colour tends to hide the drawing. This opulence is less a drawback in the large-scale orchestral works —the two symphonies (1908 and 1911), the violin concerto (1910), and the symphonic study *Falstaff* (1913)—which show in many ways an increased breadth of outlook with, occasionally, a touch of austerity seldom felt before. Some of them are, no doubt, open to the charge of over-luxuriance in length, though to shorten them in performance, as is sometimes done, plays havoc with their structure. The chamber music, however, is considerably terser. Among this the fine piano quintet (1918) certainly ranks first: but both the string quartet (1918) and the violin sonata (1918) have many characteristic beauties, even though showing, as they do, that their necessarily narrow range of colour-schemes is rather uncongenial to Elgar's normal methods. All three works have that curiously nostalgic flavour which is particularly evident in the works of his maturity —it is found in the violin concerto, in the choral ode *The Music Makers* (1912), and, most noticeably, in the 'cello concerto (1919), the most intimate of all his orchestral works and the most restrained in orchestration. Like all romantic artists he identifies himself with his work. This is explicit in *The Music Makers*, where he quotes from his own compositions to illustrate the text; but it is also true of the second symphony, which, contrary to currently accepted opinion, has nothing whatever to do with Edward VII (beyond the dedica-tion)—it represents rather the passionate pilgrimage of the soul, as Elgar himself admitted.[1] The result is an intensely personal form of self-expression, which may arouse the warmest sympathy but may also repel. There is no doubt that *Falstaff* is his greatest orchestral work. It combines a mastery of symphonic structure with a quite

---

[1] See W. H. Temple Gairdner, *W. H. T. G. to his Friends* (1930), p. 157.

remarkable gift for character-drawing, which might well have made him a successful opera-composer in any country but his own. Elgar himself provided a commentary on the work; but no programme is needed to appreciate its logic, its wit, and its alternation of exuberance and pathos.

Among Elgar's contemporaries mention must be made first of Ethel Smyth (1858–1944): her works include several operas, a Mass and other choral pieces, chamber music, organ pieces, and songs (often with orchestral accompaniment). She also published a series of autobiographical volumes, which show exceptional literary gifts. One of the chief features of her very individual manner is the breadth of her line-drawing, so to speak: even if the material happens at times to be relatively uninteresting, her music is always very remarkably spacious in outlook and has caught not a little of the 'grand style' of the older classics. Virility is a strongly marked characteristic of her genius: there is some very powerful music in the opera *The Wreckers* (1906), and such things as the 'Anacreontic Ode' and, in particular, the choral setting of the Elizabethan *Hey nonny no* are of a biting grimness uncommon in English music. But she was also thoroughly at home in quieter veins—the song 'Chrysilla', the organ prelude and fugue on 'O Traurigkeit, O Herzeleid', the slow movement of the string quartet, and the beautiful Incarnatus and Sanctus of the unequal but very striking Mass (1893) are salient instances: and the delightful comic opera *The Boatswain's Mate* (1916) is full of rollicking humour and the freshest light-heartedness expressed with easily masterful technique. She was, however, a composer of moods, liable to rather disturbing outbursts of a sort of freakishness, which is particularly noticeable in the curious cantata *The Prison* (1931): and even when her work is all of a piece, temperament not infrequently outruns invention.

A brief reference is also due to Arthur Somervell (1863–1937). Much of his life was spent in valuable work in the field of musical education; but he found time to compose several large-scale works, including the *Normandy* variations for piano and orchestra (1912), the symphony *Thalassa* (1912), and a violin concerto (1932). His oratorios for parish choirs, *The Passion of Christ* (1914) and *Christmas* (1926), are also notable for a taste and artistry not often found in modest productions of this kind. But his reputation as a composer virtually rests on a single work—the cycle of songs from Tennyson's

Maud (1898).[1] In his larger works his ready acceptance of tradition argues a certain lack of self-criticism. But in *Maud* a familiar idiom becomes the servant of imagination: the music convinces by its sincerity and by the perfection with which it matches the mood and the expression of the poem. Here, as though by accident, the words have struck fire from the composer, and the result is a minor masterpiece.

Frederick Delius (1863–1934) was the son of a Bradford wool merchant, and from 1889 till his death lived in France. His works include several operas, choral pieces of considerable dimensions, many orchestral pieces more or less of the 'programme' type, concertos, some chamber music, and a comparatively slender output of music in the smaller forms. Delius was a curiously isolated figure among composers, and his music is personal in a special sense, both in conception and in technique: it often sounds, it is hardly paradoxical to say, like the work more of an amateur of great genius than of a professional musician. His style is full of subtly imaginative, broodingly thoughtful sensitiveness, most at home with the half-lights, and aristocratic to the finger-tips: quite casual touches, such as the haunting refrain of the song 'Irmelin' or the strangely beautiful harmonies of the last page of *Brigg Fair* (1907), can arrest us in a way difficult to define. He can also be grimly powerful or massively plain-speaking on occasion, as in the orchestral *Lebenstanz* (1911) or, in particular, the setting of Nietzsche's 'Tiefe Ewigkeit' poem that forms the finale of the long *Mass of Life* (1905): but such pages are excrescences on his normal style, the general outlook of which is very uniform. In intensity, it is true, his music is very often curiously unequal—for example, the elaborate *Songs of Sunset* (1907) for soli, chorus, and orchestra, and, indeed, many other pages, do little more than drift along: once or twice, as in the piano concerto (1906), the individual touch seems to fail him altogether, and he seems to have little sense of drama or of humour. But when he is at his best—as in the profoundly expressive setting of Whitman's *Seadrift* (1903), in the wordless choral songs *To be sung of a summer night on the water* (1917), in the lyrical portions of his chief opera *A Village Romeo and Juliet* (1901), in such orchestral poems as *Brigg Fair* and *In a summer garden* (1908), in the unaccountably neglected violin concerto (1916)—he is one of the great modern composers, saying, and saying very beautifully,

[1] Reissued in 1907 with an additional song: 'Maud has a garden of roses.'

vital things that no one has said before. Perhaps we may feel that, fully alive as the music is, it is alive in a world of its own, and rather a limited and aloof world: but anyhow we must needs be grateful for the high privilege of entrance.

Granville Bantock (1868–1946), was, on the other hand, a composer who, though attempting a more limited range of art-forms, gave himself freely to many diverse influences. His works include hardly any specimens of abstract instrumental music, nor did he publish any opera (in the strict sense of the word): apart from a large number of pieces of small dimensions, mainly vocal, he devoted himself mainly to extended works for chorus and orchestra, or for orchestra alone on definite subjects, generally literary. Orientalism, Liszt, Wagner, Debussy, the Elizabethans, Mendelssohn (in some early work and in the first movement of the violin sonata), Irish (in the rest of the same sonata) and other folk music—all at one time or another contributed to the making of his own very amalgamated personality: but all through his career his vivid and adventurous musical imagination functioned most readily under a non-musical spur. His odd experiments in religious music, *Christ in the wilderness* (1907) and *Gethsemane* (1910), are failures—mysticism was not part of his endowment—nor do the grandiose, though textually simple enough, unaccompanied choral symphonies, *Atalanta in Calydon* (1912) and *Vanity of Vanities* (1914), really fulfil their aims: the concrete, the pictorial, attracted him most powerfully. Among the orchestral pieces we see him at his best in the finely polished, delicate imaginativeness of the tone-poems on Shelley's *Witch of Atlas* (1902) and Ernest Dowson's *Pierrot of the Minute* (1908) or, most of all, in the singularly vivid and picturesque 'Hebridean' symphony (1916)—the section that is based on the superb 'Seagull of the land under waves' tune is one of the most impressive things in our music: or, among the vocal works, in the thrilling end of Part II and considerable sections of Part III of *Omar Khayyám* (1906–9) or many pages (especially towards the end) of the choral ballet *Pan in Arcady* (1914), a work that, though unequal, is on the whole of specially characteristic interest. But, sincerely impulsive and technically brilliant as Bantock's work is, it has the defects of its qualities. Almost always, his music is short-breathed: it fastens ardently on whatever comes to hand at the moment, but organic unity, in the big sense of the word, it rarely seems either to attain or indeed to attempt. He has often large and powerful conceptions, but—the tone-poem on Browning's *Fifine at the Fair* (1912) is a salient instance—he prefers their external, paintable features to those that may lie deeper: and he seems at times more interested in the details and colour of expression than in the actual value of the thematic material that has to be so expressed. His fiery eagerness was a great asset to English music: but perhaps at the end we shall come back most often to some things where he has taken his art more purely and himself more quietly, such as 'On Himalay' (1908), a part-song that is a polished masterpiece of deep tranquil beauty, or the 'Atthis' section of the *Sappho* song-cycle (1906), with its great sweeping lines of melody and harmony and its sombrely restrained passion.

Henry Walford Davies (1869–1941) was active in other directions. He published only a small quantity of purely instrumental music, and that of relative unimportance: the great bulk of his music was vocal, and whether writing in large or small forms, he was often attracted by words of a more or less religious type. Among his larger compositions, he is seen at his best in the *Song of St. Francis* (1912): an extremely attractive work, full of delicately thoughtful expressiveness and sober charm, quiet-voiced but with ample breadth and manly dignity in its refinement. The setting of the medieval morality play *Everyman* (1904), by which he first won wide fame, is less equal and mature but has many masterly pages: and part-songs like 'These sweeter far than lilies are' (1913), 'Magdalen at Michael's gate' (1914), or 'Love is a torment' (1914)—very varied in style but all built on finely spacious lines—or the weirdly powerful solo song 'This ae nighte' (1905) or the daintily humorous unbendings, from the *Peter Pan* string quartet (1909) to the concerted nursery rhymes, show how successfully versatile he can be. No doubt in the course of his prolific production he wrote a good deal in which the palpable sincerity and musicianship do not rise to anything urgent: the refinement becomes over-cool and we miss the note of passion, whether austere or the reverse. But his *via media* always aimed high: and in his position as professor of music in the University of Wales and in his numerous broadcasts, both to schools and to adults, he had further opportunities of notably valuable work, extended much beyond the normal academic field.

XII

MUSIC IN THE TWENTIETH CENTURY

IN England, as elsewhere, the present century has seen many changes, both in the musical life of the country and in styles of composition. Orchestral music has become increasingly popular, though there has been no corresponding development in public taste. Opera, as in the past, has had many vicissitudes. The excellent work done by Sir Thomas Beecham (b. 1879) and by the British National Opera Company could not disguise the fact that a national opera is not possible without the support of the State. The popularity of opera among the public at large undoubtedly owes much to the modest performances given at the Royal Victoria Hall (the 'Old Vic') by Miss Lilian Baylis (1874–1937), and to the rather more ambitious productions which were possible after the re-opening of Sadler's Wells Theatre in 1931. The lasting enthusiasm for ballet which was aroused by the visit of Diaghilev's company after the 1914–18 War made possible the creation of a ballet company, as well as an opera company, at Sadler's Wells, and subsequently at Covent Garden. Interest in old music has deepened considerably. The practical enthusiasm for Bach shown by men like W. G. Whittaker (1876–1944) at Newcastle and Sir Hugh Allen (1869–1946) at Oxford has borne fruit everywhere. The publication on an extensive scale of English music of the sixteenth and seventeenth centuries has made familiar much that was previously unknown even to serious students of the subject. At Haslemere Arnold Dolmetsch (1858–1940) showed not only that old music could be performed on the instruments for which it was designed but also that they were in fact indispensable for its proper interpretation. But perhaps the most far-reaching influence of our time has been the growth of broadcasting. It is undeniable that its influence has sometimes been bad, and that mistakes have often been made. But against this must be set the creation of a new standard of orchestral playing with the formation of the B.B.C. Orchestra in 1930 and the dissemination of a vast amount of music, old and new, which would otherwise have remained a closed book to musicians in general.

The enrichment of our musical experience has not been without its effect on composers. The influence, for example, of the revival

344

of sixteenth-century music, of the rediscovery of English folk-song by Cecil Sharp, and of the music of the Russian ballet has in some cases been very marked. There has, however, been little inclination to accept without question the latest trends in European music. There was a short period after the 1914–18 War when younger composers showed a curious irresponsibility in imitating foreign fashions. But on the whole English musicians have been conservative, as in the past; atonality, for instance, has had no solid or permanent adherents. Conservatism, however, has not meant the acceptance of outworn idioms; on the contrary, there have been several composers who have created an individual language of their own—a language which is none the worse for being intelligible. The English renaissance of which we spoke in the last chapter has proved to be no mere ephemeral resurgence; its influence is with us still.

In many ways the impression made by the work of Ralph Vaughan Williams (b. 1872) has been among the most powerful forces in English music in the present century. His compositions consist mainly of vocal music in both the larger and the smaller forms, orchestral works, and chamber music: he has also written for the stage and in the smaller instrumental forms. His genius did not develop early, and practically all his music dates from after his thirtieth year: but since then there have been several periods, fairly definitely distinguishable from one another, though the same strong individuality is palpably spreading itself through all. The first period consists mainly of solo songs, and reaches its climax in the justly familiar settings of Stevenson's *Songs of Travel* (1905–7); the poetry of Whitman furnishes the great choral landmarks of the second in *Toward the Unknown Region* (1907, revised 1918) and the *Sea Symphony* (1910, revised 1918); the third is more varied with the song-cycle settings of Herbert's *Five Mystical Songs* (1911), the choral fantasia on Christmas carols (1912), and the orchestral *London Symphony* (1914, revised 1920); in the fourth we have the *Pastoral Symphony* (1922), the fourth, fifth, and sixth symphonies (1935, 1943, and 1948), the operas *Sir John in Love* (1929) and *The Pilgrim's Progress* (1951), the ballet *Job* (1930), and various choral works.

Vaughan Williams has touched contemporary music at many points; but English folk music (of which he has made many remarkably personal arrangements) has influenced him most of all, sometimes on the surface of his work, but more often in subtler matters of phrase and rhythm and tonality. His melodic speech is singularly flexible and varied, and so are his harmonic methods and his colour-schemes: and his best works stand very high among the great things of today in their large human outlook, their probing of the essential and disregard of all else, their subtle insight into deep and spacious moods. There are marked contrasts in his work, which though it has its mannerisms is nowhere bound to a single idiom. The violence and fierce tension of the fourth symphony are as different from the tranquil musing of the *Pastoral Symphony* as they are from the mellow philosophy of the fifth symphony. The finale of the sixth symphony, again, breathes a reticence which is far removed from the urgency and the expansiveness of the opening movement. There are striking contrasts too in *Job* and in *Flos Campi* for solo viola, wordless chorus, and small orchestra (1925), where the music sounds a note of ecstasy rare in the work of English composers. The same qualities of mystical absorption appear in the early *Fantasia on a Theme of Tallis* for string orchestra (1910) and in the unjustly neglected oratorio *Sancta Civitas* (1926), while the racy humour of *Five Tudor Portraits* (1936) is a vivid reminder of the composer's versatility. Of his operas *Hugh the Drover* (1914[1]) is the most successful. *Sir John in Love,* which uses the text of *The Merry Wives of Windsor,* suffers from an incomplete realization of the demands of the stage; *The Poisoned Kiss* (1928[2]), an operetta with dialogue, is full of charming music which deserves a less naïve libretto. *The Pilgrim's Progress* (1951) is more a meditation on familiar idioms than an opera, and the action is too static for the dramatic implications of the story. The most original of his stage works is the setting of Synge's *Riders to the Sea* (1927[3]) in a sort of continuous recitative which acknowledges the ascendancy of the words and at the same time translates them into music.

Different as the two individualities palpably are, it is a natural step from the work of Vaughan Williams to that of Gustav Holst (1874–1935): their names can be mentally coupled as can no other pair of names among twentieth-century composers. Holst's output includes operas, a considerable quantity of choral and some solo vocal music, together with orchestral suites: other forms of instrumental music

---

[1] First performed, 1924.
[2] First performed, 1936.
[3] First performed, 1937.

do not seem to have attracted him. He is another instance of slowly ripening genius, and it was only towards the latter part of his career that his real power was displayed. On the whole, he was less versatile than his contemporaries—such things as the orchestral *Beni-Mora* suite (1910), an astonishingly brilliant and invigorating piece of first-class ballet-music, were by-products; his powerful individuality, as a rule, held firmly to one straight path. Like Vaughan Williams, he aimed at the essentials and disregarded everything else: but his speech is more starkly direct and his texture, equally masterly in its technique, is considerably simpler. Often, as in the *Hymn of Jesus,* a setting of a Gnostic ritual (1917), or the *Neptune* section of the spacious orchestral suite *The Planets* (1917), he strains normal harmonic language very severely: but the strain comes, not from any complexity of inside detail, but simply from the meeting of massive forces none of which will give way. The note of austerity is very strong in Holst's music, evident particularly in later works, such as the *Choral Symphony* (1924), the orchestral *Egdon Heath* (1927), and the settings of poems by Humbert Wolfe (1929): the different sections of *The Planets* strike very different moods and not with equal convincingness, but all through there is an almost defiant refusal of any compromise, any shading of the outlines of the thoughts. He was greatly attracted by Indian mysticism, and set many translations from Sanskrit literature: in the best of the *Rig Veda Hymns*—such as the choral 'Funeral hymn' (1910) or the solo 'Sky' and 'Creation' (1907–8)—we have pages of a nakedly stern impressiveness that is altogether unique. But it is in the splendid setting of Whitman's *Ode to Death* (1919), one of the chief landmarks of modern English music, that we see Holst's massive powers at their fullest: his straight path has widened without losing any of its straightness. Elsewhere we may often feel that his moods are inclined to renounce overmuch: no doubt they are always palpably and intensely sincere, but their appeal does not always last—except for listeners endowed with a particular temperament unconnected with the power of artistic appreciation. When the first freshness of the curious beauty of such things as the four religious songs for voice and violin (1917) has passed off, some of us may perhaps feel as if we had been shut up in a small room and asked to part with a large share of our musical birthright: it is true that the music fits the words like a glove, but the frequent recourse to medievalist conceptions is in itself significant, and with Holst, as with

Vaughan Williams, the retrogressive idiom may at times pass into mannerism.

Two contemporaries of Vaughan Williams and Holst—Coleridge-Taylor and Hurlstone—died before the 1914–18 War. Samuel Coleridge-Taylor (1875–1912) was of mixed West African and English blood. He was a prolific writer throughout the whole of his life: his instrumental music was, as a rule, of comparatively small size, but his very numerous vocal compositions ranged from songs up to large-scale choral works. He made his great early fame with the short cantata *Hiawatha's Wedding-Feast* (1898), a work full of fresh naïve beauty expressed in charmingly childlike fashion and with ample technique: slightly earlier was the orchestral Ballade in A minor (1898), larger in scale and scope and full of exceptional musical promise—but it remains his masterpiece. His great talent failed to develop: the first of the *Hiawatha* sequels, *The Death of Minnehaha* (1899), has equal sincerity and attempts to be more spacious, but the spontaneity was already fading, and in his largest work, the oratorio *The Atonement* (1903), inspiration had given out. All through his life, however, he retained the power of freshness of utterance when writing in the dance-like rhythms, slow and fast, that especially appealed to him: and it would seem that his best work, slight as it is and small in extent compared with his total output, is likely to live on as the expression of a personality individual and very attractive, in spite of its narrowness and immaturity.

William Yeates Hurlstone (1876–1906) was, except for a few songs and part-songs, an exclusively instrumental composer. His largest orchestral work, and perhaps his masterpiece, is a sensitive and finely wrought set of Variations on a Swedish air (1904): but he was chiefly known as the leading pioneer of the younger school of chamber-music writers. In this field he was prolific: most typical, perhaps, is the very attractive Phantasy string quartet in A minor, which won the first of the prizes founded by W. W. Cobbett (1847–1937). Hurlstone had hardly, at the time of his early death, reached fully individual expression: but his quietly thoughtful and firmly based musicianship had great influence on his contemporaries.

Rutland Boughton (b. 1878) has confined himself almost entirely to vocal music in different forms—stage pieces, music for chorus and orchestra, songs, and part-songs. His best-known work is the noteworthy opera *The Immortal Hour* (1914), which has enjoyed the honour, unprecedented for any English work of its calibre, of a lengthy series of daily performances: though unequal in inspiration, at its best it is distinguished by a very individual feeling for a kind of beauty that, though very subtle, is expressible in simple texture and by a singularly fascinating glamour very well suited to its Celtic subject. He has been much attracted by the rugged prose-poetry of Edward Carpenter, and in the fine extended choral ode *Midnight* (1907), as also, on a much smaller scale, in the song 'The dead Christ', he shows qualities not displayed in his more familiar work—a rather grim kind of powerfulness and a very sensitive reaction to the artistic aspects of subjects that most composers would pass by: the imaginative 'Early dawn' part-song shows very well what he can do with delicately picturesque colour, and there is ample humour in his choral Variations on folk-songs (1905). But his work is often unbalanced and aims at more than it is able to secure: and it is perhaps at times open also to the charge of attitudinizing, though the attitudes are always quite sincere.

Joseph Holbrooke (b. 1878) has been a very prolific composer in many departments, in all of which he has consistently pursued a steady path of his own: he has written several extended music-dramas, many works of the symphonic-poem type, choral or purely orchestral, and a great quantity of chamber music as well as of smaller pieces, vocal and instrumental. He puts into all he attempts the full weight of his clever, forcible seriousness: though the seriousness does not indeed by any means exclude outbursts of humour—as in the brilliant *Pickwick* string quartet (1911), one of his best-rounded and most attractive works. He is, generally speaking, most at home with subjects that give scope for vividness and strongly marked contrasts, as in the picturesque setting of Poe's *The Bells* (1906) or in the symphonic poem *Byron* (1906), though he can also deal effectively—as, for example, in parts of the dramatic symphony *Apollo and the Seaman* (1908) or the 'Absence' slow movement of the string quartet in D minor—with quieter moods. But his ardour often in its haste disregards the subtler and finer issues, and it is usually in front of his power of invention: many pages of the bulky operas *The Children of Don* (1911) and *Dylan* (1914) surge along in massive style without saying anything distinctive, and he is very liable—the scena *Marino Faliero* (1905) is a typical example—to drop into mere sharp-cornered turgidity. No English composer has worked with more consistent ideals: but his music is often apt to strive and cry aloud unnecessarily, and much of its appeal has been consequently, in the long run, weakened.

Frank Bridge (1879–1941) was a leading example of what, in the best sense of the word, we may call the professional composer: finely equipped by nature and training, with his feet firmly on solid ground, and never attempting anything of which he was not perfectly sure. A highly skilled string-player himself, he is seen at his best in his chamber music, of which he wrote large quantities: such works as the string sextet in E♭ (1912) or the string quartet in G minor (1915) or the piano-quartet phantasy in F♯ minor (1910) are among the very best specimens we can show, always full of artistic vitality and dignity and effectiveness and often, in versatile fashion, notably beautiful as well. He also wrote choral and orchestral works —the picturesque suite *The Sea* (1910), with its specially fine 'Moonlight' slow movement, should be mentioned—and many smaller instrumental and vocal things, grave and gay, and quite at home in either mood. Sometimes he may seem to have written ahead without much impulse or his great technical mastery may have allowed him to throw off what are not much more than skilful exercises in the styles of other men: but musicianship so fine must always be very attractive, even if there were not (as there is) plenty behind the technique. This is true also of his later works, such as the third or fourth string quartets (1926 and 1937), where his adoption of a new and rather forbidding idiom is entirely free from any suggestion of experiment.

John Ireland (b. 1879) has, apart from songs and the choral setting of J. A. Symonds's *These things shall be* (1937), restricted himself almost entirely to instrumental music, the great bulk of which is non-orchestral. His songs, the best of which are among the finest of today, present a very uncommon problem: they differ no doubt very much in musical interest, but they also differ to an extraordinary degree in actual style. He seems to steep himself so much in the various kinds of poetry he sets that, apart from an irreducible common measure of technique, he becomes, for each kind of poetry, a virtually new composer: there is hardly any common musical ground between, for example, his setting of Arthur Symons's 'The adoration' (where he comes perhaps nearest his normal instrumental idioms) and equally beautiful songs with other poetical outlooks. Vocal music apart, Ireland's work is very unified in manner, however diverse in range of expression: the orchestral prelude *The*

Forgotten Rite (1913), the second violin sonata in A minor (1917), such piano solos as the *Rhapsody* (1915), *The Island Spell* (1913), the sonata (1920), and the suite *Sarnia* (1941), and the splendid piano concerto (1930) may perhaps be taken as landmarks. We see a very strongly marked individuality, contemptuous of all mere airs and graces, and inclining more to the bitter than to the sweet: the music can when required be mystical or massively tender or, after a fashion, playful and brilliant, but anyhow it is reticent and never gives itself away. No modern English music is more finely personal: but however much its, at times, somewhat difficult moods may clarify on intimate acquaintance, we cannot help frequently feeling a sense, so to speak, of conflict. It is a genuinely big force, but the struggle is not quite over: an ardently alive imagination is always at work in many directions, but it has not always, perhaps, succeeded in fully clearing the path before it.

The great bulk of the work of Cyril Scott (b. 1879) consists of songs and piano music; but he has also written a good deal of other instrumental music, chamber and orchestral, three operas, and some large-scale vocal music. We may disregard the many things— 'Asphodel' and the setting of Ernest Dowson's 'The valley of silence' are typical examples—which are not at all more than deft drawing-room music (the drawing-room is often, also, rather over-heated), and there are also a good many other pages which, though their delicate charm is undeniable, are quite slight: Scott's real powers are shown only when he is writing on somewhat larger scales. The larger scale is indeed in essence rather one of style than of dimensions—the five piano *Poems* (1912), certainly among his very best works, are all comparatively short: but size is usually an element in it, and one of his longer published works, the setting for soli, chorus, and orchestra of Crashaw's *Nativity Hymn* (1914), is on the whole his finest. In it, as in the *Poems*, there is a temperament that has things of its own to say and its own way of saying them: there is a quick, sensitive mind functioning, readily open to all sorts of subtle impressions, and translating them into a very warm, lusciously flexible musical language, the appeal of which, though limited, is very fascinating. On the other hand, the restlessly rich harmonic and rhythmic idioms often (as, notably, in the piano sonata) end in a nervous monotony of effect, and a suspicion of something like artificiality and preciousness is often lurking just under the surface: all mainly sensuous art has anyhow to pay an inevitable price, though we may perhaps feel, at any rate in certain moods, that the price is quite possibly worth while.

Arnold Bax (b. 1883) was for some while best known by music more or less correlated with the contemporary 'Celtic Twilight' school of literature: but his work has broadened considerably. He has produced seven symphonies, several symphonic poems and other orchestral works, extended specimens of chamber music, choral works of varied types, and many songs and piano pieces. He is seen at his best in such things as the vividly picturesque orchestral poem *November Woods* (1917) or the very subtle and sensitive 'Phantasy' for viola and orchestra (1920) or, most of all, in the elaborate eight-voice motet 'Mater, ora filium' (1921), a cleanly masterful piece that takes the highest rank in our choral music for its finely individual imagination and its powerful blend of classical dignity with latter-day thematic material. However, the notably spacious manner of this motet is rather alien to Bax's normal methods: his line is normally, if the analogy is permissible, that of the painter rather than of the sculptor. The impressionist painter, also: solid as is his technique, and firmly based as is his innate subtle sense of beauty, he generally prefers to suggest rather than to say, and to suggest something rather remote, perhaps at times a little exotic. Not that he lacks virility—the sonata No. 2 in G major (1919) is one of the most virile of modern piano works, the *Overture to a Picaresque Comedy* (1930) is full of rumbustious energy, and some of the songs ('A rann of exile', for example) have great strength: but whether in his passionate or his contemplative moods, he is normally somewhat of a visionary: and, when he is not at his best, his visions are apt to relax and wander. Bax's contemporary Lord Berners (1883–1950) was a composer of a very different cast. Though a romantic at heart he made his name largely by music of a satirical character, which employs romantic idioms only to make fun of them. Among his successful essays in parody are the orchestral *Fantaisie espagnole* (1920), which is a repertory of Spanish and pseudo-Spanish idioms, and *Valses bourgeoises* for piano duet (1919). He found his true *métier*, however, in ballet. In *Luna Park* (1930), *The Triumph of Neptune* (1926), and *A Wedding Bouquet* (1937)—the last with chorus—he shows a technical dexterity and a lively humour which are admirably adapted to the fantasies represented on the stage.

Of the composers born between 1885 and 1900 George Kaye

Butterworth (1885–1916) was, like Hurlstone, a premature loss to English music, though he was much less influenced by the older classical models and developed much more quickly. His output, however, was very slender, consisting only of a small handful of comparatively short orchestral works and a dozen or so songs: but he had already perfect technical mastery and a distinctive style that promised great things. He was largely influenced by folk music —the bulk of his orchestral work, indeed, is partially based on folk-material, the idyll *The Banks of Green Willow* (1913) being specially noteworthy—and he was most at home with moods at once simple and intense: when he tried to deal with more sophisticated ideas (as in his setting of Wilde's 'Requiescat') his touch was much less sure. His masterpiece is the orchestral rhapsody *A Shropshire Lad* (1913), based on a theme from his two song-cycles to Housman's words, a work full of extraordinarily delicate and emotionally moving imaginativeness. Benjamin Dale (1885–1943) made his reputation while still a student with a remarkable piano sonata in D minor (1902), and this was followed by a delicately imaginative suite for viola and piano (1907) and a sensitive setting of Christina Rossetti's *Before the Paling of the Stars* (1912); but a rigorous self-criticism seems to have prevented him from developing his undoubted talent.

Arthur Bliss (b. 1891) has been much more productive and also less consistent in style. He first became known as a composer after the 1914–18 War with some vivacious works which typified the current revolt against romanticism—among them the impudent but very stimulating *Rout* for wordless voice and ten instruments (1919). This phase did not last. Before long he showed that he was, like Berners, a romantic at heart, though fully alive to the influence of modern idioms. The charming pastoral *Lie Strewn the White Flocks* for chorus and small orchestra (1928) still retains much of the vivacity of Bliss's earlier work, but is is matched with a warmth of imagination which skilfully recreates the drowsy summer heat of Greece and Sicily. Romanticism, too, is the impulse behind the sincere and often moving *Morning Heroes* (1930), a tribute to the men who fell in the 1914–18 War. The piano concerto (1939), though designed on a big scale, is on the whole less successful; it makes expansive gestures, but they are apt to be self-conscious, and the keyboard writing, though difficult, does not make the best use of the solo instrument. In ballet—particularly in the forceful and very dramatic

Checkmate (1937)—Bliss is thoroughly at home. In his opera *The Olympians* (1949), on a libretto by J. B. Priestley, he has adopted what may be called a traditional operatic idiom, strongly influenced by nineteenth-century romanticism; the music is full-blooded and warm-hearted, though there is a certain lack of continuity and not always a clear realization of the demands of the stage. Perhaps he is seen at his best in his chamber music—particularly in the mellow clarinet quintet (1938) and the more astringent string quartet No. 1 (1941). He is certainly one of the most resourceful of modern English composers, and for that reason has been successful in writing music for the cinema. Sometimes one has the impression that there is in his work a conflict between the heart and the head—a conflict which is generally resolved most happily when the heart takes command. He has been impervious to the influence of folk-song; his spiritual affinity with Elgar is unmistakable.

Of the other composers of this generation Herbert Howells (b. 1892) has preferred to work mainly in the smaller forms, where his fastidious craftsmanship and disciplined imagination have found a natural outlet. He has shown, however, in his *Hymnus Paradisi* for soloists, chorus, and orchestra (1950) that he not only has the capacity for large-scale work but is also master of an eloquence that can rise to the heights of a noble theme. E. J. Moeran (1894–1951), like Vaughan Williams, uses the idioms of folk-song without self-consciousness. He is primarily a lyrical composer, and for that reason his symphony (1937), which lacks coherence, is less convincing than his violin concerto (1943), which successfully employs a rhapsodic style. His settings of Elizabethan songs for unaccompanied chorus combine the manner of the madrigalists with the harmonic language of Delius—a combination that is effective except where the discrepancy is emphasized. The influence of Delius is equally apparent in the work of Peter Warlock (1894–1930), the pen-name of Philip Heseltine, who was also active in transcribing and publishing English music of the sixteenth and seventeenth centuries. His reputation rests almost entirely on his songs, of which he wrote nearly a hundred. He was, by his own choice, a miniaturist, with a finely developed literary taste and an instinctive sense of style. In the long history of English songs his work holds an honourable place. There is a considerable range of mood—from the roistering good-humour of 'Captain Stratton's Fancy' to the moving intimacy of 'Sleep'. His song-cycle *The Curlew* (1923), a setting of poems by Yeats, with accompaniment for flute, cor anglais, and string quartet, matches beautifully the nostalgic melancholy of the text.

We turn now to the composers born in the present century. The oldest of these is Edmund Rubbra (b. 1901), a pupil of Holst, to whom he has devoted a short but illuminating monograph (1947). His assured mastery and his wholly individual style are the product of a slow but continuous process of development. The foundation of his style is a contrapuntal habit of mind, which derives ultimately from sixteenth-century polyphony but is developed in his own way. One might have expected such an influence to produce its most powerful effect in vocal music; but in fact Rubbra has been less successful here than in instrumental music. His madrigals and motets show a sensitive awareness of their texts, but the sometimes excessive demands made on the voices and a certain stiffness in the treatment seem to cramp, to some extent, the spontaneity and the freedom of the music. His symphonies are free from these limitations. In the first (1937), and to a lesser degree in the second (1937), the exuberance of the ideas resulted in too strenuous and complex a texture. In the third symphony (1940) there is a new simplicity and a firmer discipline. Here, as in the fourth symphony (1942), the polyphony seems to expand without effort. The music grows by a steady process of accumulation, each idea generating without effort its successors. Rubbra pays no regard to current fashions; he is content to remain himself. Dissonance of a purely modern kind may be found side by side with traditional harmony, though tradition is often illuminated by a new and refreshing approach. Instrumental colour is less important than the melodic lines. Hence the reproach that has sometimes been made that the scoring is insensitive. This reproach has far less justification in the fifth symphony (1948), which is no less closely knit than its predecessors but shows a more acute feeling for orchestral sonority. It is significant that the emphasis on polyphony does not exclude lyricism; it has its place in the symphonies, as well as in smaller works such as the second violin sonata (1932), the 'cello sonata (1947), the piano trio (1950), and the settings of Spenser's *Amoretti* for voice and string quartet (1936). Melody is the vital impulse that runs through all Rubbra's work. We are conscious everywhere of a purposeful determination, and of a passionate absorption in the very stuff of music.

William Walton (b. 1902), like Bliss, has absorbed the influence of Elgar without making any attempt to imitate his style. At first he seemed uncertain of his direction. It is hardly surprising that the early piano quartet (1918–19), though a remarkable work for a boy, should afford comparatively little evidence of the personality that was to emerge later; and the *Façade* music (1922), originally written for a chamber ensemble and designed to accompany the recitation of poems by Edith Sitwell, was primarily a fashionable entertainment—wonderfully clever in its sophisticated way and full of wit expressed with complete technical assurance, but with little in it to suggest the serious artist. The brilliant overture *Portsmouth Point* (1925) marks a new departure; here we have the rhythmical subtlety and the compelling nervous energy that were to appear in later works such as the *Sinfonia concertante* for piano and orchestra (1927), the oratorio *Belshazzar's Feast* (1931), and the symphony (1935), and a command of the material that suggests a vigorous creative intelligence. *Belshazzar's Feast* challenged the traditional conception of oratorio as decisively as Elgar's *Dream of Gerontius* had thirty years before. In retrospect it may seem extravagantly assertive; but there is no denying the intensity of imagination that has gone into it. Some of that assertiveness appears also in the finale of the symphony, which has the air of attempting to storm the battlements of an impregnable city; it is spectacular music, but it does not completely match the nimble *diablerie* of the scherzo or the restrained melancholy of the slow movement. The viola concerto (1929), which remains unsurpassed by Walton's later works, is in a different category. Predominantly elegiac in character, it touches the springs of emotion without violence, and leaves printed on the mind a curiously disturbing impression of regret. In his later works Walton has never quite recaptured the same freedom of imagination. The violin concerto (1939), the string quartet (1947), and the violin sonata (1950), though they contain much that is effective, seem to suffer from a certain inhibition; the effort of creation, instead of finding its natural consummation in the finished work, has left its mark on the music, and the nostalgia which was so movingly expressed in the viola concerto has become almost a mannerism.

Composition was only one of the activities of Constant Lambert (1905–51). He was an excellent conductor, particularly of ballet, and a shrewd critic; his *Music Ho!* (1934), though tinged with pessimism, is a penetrating and quick-witted analysis of the music of our time. His setting of Sacheverell Sitwell's *The Rio Grande* for chorus, solo pianoforte, and orchestra (1929) deserves its popularity. The unusual medium, which excludes wood-wind, is handled with remarkable assurance. The piano part is made up of keyboard formulas, but is none the less brilliant in effect. Jazz idioms are used, not in any spirit of parody but with complete sincerity; and the sentimental ending, very moving in its simplicity, forms an admirable contrast to the brassy glitter of the more exuberant pages. Lambert wrote nothing else which captured the public imagination, perhaps because he never discovered a wholly consistent style. There is considerable charm, however, in his ballet *Horoscope* (1938), and his most elaborate composition, *Summer's Last Will and Testament* for chorus and orchestra (1936), reveals a serious purpose and an intensity of imagination not always found in his work. His contemporary Alan Rawsthorne (b. 1905) has been more successful in developing a style of his own. He can be resourceful in lighter work—for instance, the lively and amusing *Street Corner* overture (1944), but his gifts find their fullest expression in music of a more serious character, such as the *Symphonic Studies* for orchestra (1938), the first piano concerto (1942), and the violin concerto (1948). His musical language is highly concentrated, and he expresses himself with a terseness which suggests the working of a keenly analytical mind —the chaconne in the piano concerto is a very impressive study in the cumulative development of comparatively simple material. The violin concerto, undoubtedly his best work, shows an understanding of the genius of the instrument which is anything but common at the present day; and in its willingness to declare emotion it proves that the spirit of romanticism, however different the language, is not dead. Michael Tippett (b. 1905), like Rubbra, thinks in terms of polyphony, but with less ease and confidence; the complex texture of his second symphony (1945) seems at times to defeat its own object. There is no doubt that an intensely musical mind is at work here; but the impulses do not appear to be wholly co-ordinated and we miss the joyous freedom in creation which is the sign of the complete artist. His oratorio *A Child of our Time* (1941) has a tragic insistence which needs more contrast than is provided by the introduction of negro spirituals.

Benjamin Britten (b. 1913) is the most prolific, and certainly one of the most imaginative, composers of our time. He acquired at an early age a technical facility which not only made the solution of problems comparatively easy but also encouraged him to create his own. He has on occasion used polyphony as a means of expression —for instance, in the early *A Boy was born* for unaccompanied chorus (1934) and in the first string quartet (1941)—but there is nothing to show that it has at any time been the natural channel for his invention. He is rather an impressionist—not in the same sense as Debussy or Ravel, of whose influence there is no trace in his work, but in his delight in sonority for its own sake. His work is full of experiments in sound which are wonderfully successful but leave one wondering whether they serve any end beyond themselves. Britten always appears to be intensely interested in the means by which music is produced, but not always so interested in the invention of significant material. In a sense he has no recognizable style of his own; the influence of widely different composers—for example, Verdi and Busoni—can be detected. But these influences are often disguised by his extraordinary flair for saying the right thing at the right moment.

Undoubtedly his most considerable achievement is the opera *Peter Grimes* (1945). Here his gift for creating atmosphere finds the fullest scope. The background of the drab and sordid life of a Suffolk seaside village is brought vividly before our eyes. The bustling activity of the court-room scene, the fishermen working at their nets in the bright morning light, the homely solemnity of the Sabbath day, the horrors of storm at sea, and the air of tension that hangs over a fog-bound coast—all these find their expression in music which often achieves its effects by the simplest means. The hero of the opera, in fact, is not so much the sadistic fisherman from whom it takes its name as the village which passes judgement on him. In *The Rape of Lucretia* (1946), founded on a play by André Obey, no such background was possible, and the opera resolves itself into a series of episodes, memorable largely for the imaginative scoring for a small chamber ensemble. Britten used the same resources for the comic opera *Albert Herring* (1947), an amusing extravaganza which suffers a little from a certain immaturity in the composer's wit. His touch, indeed, is surer than his taste; his version of *The Beggar's Opera* (1948) shows a quite extraordinary insensitiveness to the period flavour of the original melodies.

Though he has written works in the larger forms Britten's talent is primarily lyrical. His *Spring Symphony* for soloists, chorus, and orchestra (1949) is in effect a suite, in which the several texts provide the foundation for a picturesque interpretation. *Les Illuminations* (1939), a setting of poems by Arthur Rimbaud for voice and string orchestra, is a relatively early example of his skill in matching the imagery of poetry with an equally imaginative texture in sound. This is even more evident in the *Seven Sonnets of Michelangelo* (1942) and the *Serenade* for tenor, solo horn, and strings (1943). The latter work assembles texts from a number of poets—among them Tennyson, Blake, Ben Jonson, and Keats; for each of them Britten has provided music which is at once simple and suggestive. Here, as elsewhere, it is the originality of the conception that is most striking; the audacious setting of Jonson's 'Queen and huntress, chaste and fair', based on a hunting jig for the horn, ignores convention as though it had never existed and does so with complete success. In such small-scale work Britten is completely at home; we find the same certainty in the charming *Ceremony of Carols* for boys' voices and harp (1942) or the unaccompanied *Hymn to St. Cecilia* (1942). In all these later works the perkiness which sometimes marred his earlier compositions has given way to a severer self-discipline. If he were less prodigal of his gifts and could spare the time for self-examination we might well find that his achievement would equal his capacity.

It is not possible in a short survey to do more than mention some of the other composers who have been active during this half-century: Gordon Jacob (b. 1895), whose flair for orchestration is stronger than his invention, genial and attractive though that often is; Gerald Finzi (b. 1901), a disciple of Vaughan Williams, whose gifts have found their chief expression in a number of very sensitive songs—in particular, settings of poems by Thomas Hardy; Lennox Berkeley (b. 1903), trained in Paris, whose instinct for precision and economy is most happily employed in smaller works such as the delightful sonatina for recorder and harpsichord (1940); and Howard Ferguson (b. 1908), whose relatively small output includes an effective piano sonata in a neo-Brahmsian idiom (1940). There are also not a few younger men and women of promise, whose achievement is not yet substantial enough for discussion. The opportunities open to them are considerable. Broadcasting offers more chances of performance than the public concert hall and enables their work to reach a wider audience. Film music is not only a source of income but also provides valuable practice in the exercise of craftsmanship; its one serious danger is that it may encourage a style of writing appropriate as illustration but not sufficiently coherent or individual to deserve recognition in its own right. There is every sign that our composers are alive to their opportunities and aware of their responsibilities. It will be for the historian of the future to determine what in their work is merely talented and what can be accounted evidence of genius.

XIII

FOLK MUSIC

FOLK music is a term of curiously, but perhaps, inevitably, loose signification. Some would include under it all tunes, whether by known composers or not, and from the earliest times down to the music-hall ditty or hymn-tune of today, which have for some reason or other become, if as a rule only temporarily, part of what may be called the artistic life of a considerable number of people, just as proverbs or fragments of literature of various kinds become part of common speech. Others would agree with this except in so far as they exclude all music of the last century which is not anonymous; others, again, would omit from the older work all signed compositions of any date except the national, patriotic tunes; while still others prefer to define folk music as 'evolved music', and exclude everything except tunes having their original birth among the un-learned classes of society, by whom they have been handed down by a purely oral tradition. Perhaps it may be most convenient for our present purpose if we here define folk music as (1), in the strict sense, including all tunes that, whether originally designed mono-phonically or not, have come at one period or another to be very generally so regarded, and (2), in the narrower sense to which we shall here confine ourselves (the rest of the field having been covered in previous chapters), including such tunes as were, in the minds of their technically unskilled makers, independent (so far as we can discover) of any necessary harmonic support. We have to remember that folk music does not 'spring from the hearts of the people' in the sense that it is the work of nobody in particular; some individual brain is ultimately responsible for every note of it, even if, as may usually be the case, it may be the brain of some one lacking the power to place his thoughts on paper. We may meet with the same tune in dozens of slightly varying forms (even on the lips of the same singer), and we may even be able to trace the gradual melting of one tune into another totally different; but at every stage there must necessarily be some one more or less consciously at work who, however technically unlearned, is in essentials as much a musical composer as any holder of that title. Folk music is indeed, like all things dependent on oral tradition, in a fluid state, and the researcher practically never finds really firm ground under his feet; but nevertheless we certainly cannot draw any hard and fast line between it and what is called 'composed music'. The Essex singer who remarked to an inquirer that 'if you can get the words, the Almighty will send you the tune' is continually quoted by the enthusiasts; but unfortunately the particular tune in question,[1] though very beautiful, is clearly an imperfect reminiscence of something else, and anyhow the hundreds of cases of the same tune being traditionally fitted to many different sets of words, and vice versa, play havoc with the theory of divine inspiration.

With the words which are more or less closely connected with most folk music we have not here to deal; but there is no denying the merits of the great bulk of the tunes. Even when least distinctive in quality—and many have certainly little enough to boast of in this respect—they have still the touch of natural sincerity which goes far to cover a multitude of those negative sins which are all that can be laid to their charge; and when at their best, they give us melody that the greatest composers would have been proud to sign. To suit tastes more sophisticated than those of their own makers and original hearers, the tunes have been harmonized and 'arranged' in countless fashions—sometimes extremely well, sometimes extremely badly; but, unless we are prepared to accept the theory that the concert-room is the only place for hearing music, it is a fairly arguable question whether the work, even when in first-rate hands, wants doing at all. In the field of British folk music we have the wonderfully pointed and polished settings of Byrd, Morley, and other Elizabethans, and in later times the finely musicianly versions of men like Vaughan Williams and R. O. Morris, to make us forget the too frequent miserable productions of arrangers without either taste or knowledge; but still it is not altogether a paradox to say that the better the work is done, the more does the essential *naïveté* of the folk-tune tend to disappear, and the more does it become merged in the general mass of musicians' music. There is of course no denying that, save in the rarest instances, the only ground we have for calling a tune originally monophonic is that no original harmonization of it is known: and these are obviously shifting sands on which to build theories. To the musical historian with a strong desire for strictly logical classification, folk music is the most irritatingly elusive of all the matters with which he has to deal; but after all we need not allow that to interfere with our enjoyment.

[1] 'Bushes and briars' (*Journal of the Folk-Song Society*, vol. ii, p. 143).

And the student of British folk music has not only to contend with the difficulty that any day it may be discovered that the tune with which he is concerned is not, in the restricted definition of the word, folk music at all. Though the popular tunes of England, Wales, Scotland, and Ireland have their own broadly racial characteristics, yet there are some which, while obviously unlike foreign folk music, are, so to speak, cosmopolitanly British, or at any rate share in the typical features of the tunes of at least two of the four nations. Favourite melodies become disseminated in widely separate localities, and the Cheviot Hills and the Irish Channel themselves are far from being insurmountable barriers. Sometimes we can say with considerable confidence that a tune found in both Scotland and Ireland is really English in origin; sometimes again the reverse is the case, as with such well-known tunes as 'The girl I left behind me' and 'The Arethusa', which, long supposed to be pure English, are most probably pure Irish. But though the finest melodies of each race bear upon them unmistakable signs of their origin, there remain a very great many of less distinctive quality, about which the researcher can really not make any dogmatic assertions; folk-tunes are so continually subject to slight modifications that even certain typically racial characteristics are no infallible guide to the ultimate source. And further, some of the older historians of folk music, chiefly those of Scottish blood, were by no means averse to a certain amount of enthusiastic but deliberate stealing, in the interests of patriotism.

One point connected with the whole of British folk music is now, after long misunderstanding, perfectly clear. Until a comparatively recent period the belief was firmly held—apparently on purely *a priori* grounds—that the 'ecclesiastical modes' were confined to the service of the church, and that we owe the modern scale-system to the natural instinct of the makers of folk-tunes. As a matter of fact, the major and minor scales are by no means uncommon in ancient church compositions, and in folk music modal tonality is extremely frequent down to the present day. A vast amount of havoc has been worked in the past by arrangers careless or ignorant of this; sharpened leading-notes and all sorts of things have been illegitimately inserted right and left in order to make the tunes 'sound proper', and many well-known melodies ('The last rose of summer' is an instance) have in consequence become traditional in a hopelessly vulgarized form. No doubt we have to discard from the category of normal modal tunes those frequent circular melodies which, whatever may be their scale, are designed so as to lead straight on from one verse to the next, the last notes being altered at the conclusion of the whole; we have also to remember the difficulty that at times is found in taking down an unusual type of tune from the lips of uncultivated singers possessing no special capacity for exact intonation or exact rhythm. But, after every allowance has been made, there still survives a very large and quite indubitable mass of modal music that has entirely outlasted the fashions of modern composition; and in consequence folk-tunes are, so far as tonality is concerned, the most varied of all. In British folk music the Dorian, Mixolydian, and Aeolian are the modes normally found; the Phrygian is distinctly rare,[1] and the Lydian is almost unknown. Sometimes, however, the tonalities become confused (a Mixolydian scale with an occasionally flattened third is fairly often noticeable) or the same melody is found in different modes, as well as, perhaps, in the ordinary major scale also; the minor scale is by no means common.[2]

Quite apart from folk-tunes in the usual sense of compositions of some shape and structure (whether they are associated with secular words or take the form of carols makes no musical difference), the researcher may diverge into some by no means uninteresting by-paths: nursery ditties, sailors' 'shanties', street cries, and similar half unconscious artistic utterances are often curious and attractive, and very possibly of considerable antiquity. Lavender-sellers, in particular, seem to be prone to what are virtually hereditary musical formulas, handed down from parent to child—sometimes, indeed, antiphonal in character, the two halves of the formula being alternately sung by two persons on either side of a street.

It is only with regard to the folk music of England itself that we can make any chronological division of our material. Quite apart from the oral traditions of what we may call the relatively uncultured classes of society, we have a large mass of documentary evidence of folk music ranging over a space of about two hundred and fifty years, from 1500 to 1750, with a certain amount of still earlier

---

[1] Sometimes (the fine English tune 'The trees they grow so high', in the form in which it is quoted in the *Journal of the Folk-Song Society*, vol. ii, p. 95, is an instance) a melody has been claimed as Phrygian on the strength of an unimportant final note to a short syllable, whereas really it is pure Aeolian in every essential that counts.

[2] See further C. J. Sharp, *English Folk-Song: Some Conclusions* (1907), pp. 54–72.

work of which, in the first and second chapters of this book, we have already spoken. Clearly we cannot draw a hard and fast line between the traditional melodies and those derived from written sources; there are no tangible differences of style, and as soon as any collector of today places on paper the songs he hears from the peasantry, he is creating documentary evidence which, in essentials, is, so far as we can tell, identical with that on which we depend for most 'non-traditional' folk music. The sharp distinction made in Wooldridge's *Old English Popular Music* is misleading. The written folk-melodies may be divided into two great classes, dating from before and from after the middle of the seventeenth century; minor subdivisions can be traced, but they are unimportant. In the sixteenth century our sources consist, to start with, of miscellaneous 'commonplace books' and vocal arrangements, and afterwards of lute books and virginal books containing settings of the popular tunes of the time, sometimes with elaborate variations on them— these, dating from round about 1600, are the most valuable sources we possess; early in the seventeenth century these are supplemented by Ravenscroft's *Pammelia*, *Deuteromelia*, and *Melismata*, and subsequent collections of catches and similar settings of familiar melodies, published both in England and in the Netherlands. Authorities of this latter kind are very numerous after the Restoration, and, in addition, we have the numerous editions of *The English Dancing Master*,[1] and, in the eighteenth century, the ballad operas; while, in both the earlier and later periods, we often find folk-tunes imbedded in works of which the greater part is the composition of perfectly well-known men. In some cases we first meet in the latter half of the seventeenth century with tunes the style of which is obviously earlier—the Mixolydian 'The merry milkmaids' is a familiar and excellent instance: and some specially popular melodies, such as 'Greensleeves', 'Sellenger's Round', 'Packington's Pound', 'Trenchmore', 'John come kiss me now', 'The hunt is up', 'Walsingham', 'The woods so wild', 'Row well ye mariners', 'Hanskin',[2] and so on, are found, often with different words, under different titles, and in different forms, both in early authorities and in those of post-Restoration times, though the eighteenth-century ballad operas confined themselves practically entirely to tunes of the more modern type. Not only in English, but in all folk music, the numer-

---

[1] Modern edition by Leslie Bridgewater and Hugh Mellor (1933).
[2] All printed in H. E. Wooldridge, *Old English Popular Music* (1893), vol. i.

ous diversities of melodies (which sometimes, by cumulative small changes, become almost unrecognizable) give the student considerable trouble to discover the earliest shape. 'The British Grenadiers', for example, seems to be an eighteenth-century derivative of a sixteenth-century tune.[1] One of the most curious modifications in effect is that of the jovial Elizabethan dance melody called at first 'Quodling's delight',[2] which appeared in the seventeenth century as 'Goddesses':[3]

Ex.169

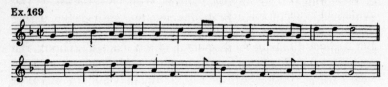

and was later transformed into the pathetic eighteenth-century tune so well known as 'The oak and the ash'.[4] Mere changes of pace, apart from anything else, can produce startling transformations; 'Admiral Benbow',[5] one of the most delightfully rollicking of eighteenth-century tunes:

Ex.170

was used for the Christmas carol 'The virgin unspotted',[6] 'The land o' the leal' is simply 'Scots wha hae' sung slowly, and indeed no sort of fixed emotional character ever seems to have attached to these melodies, which were, from every point of view, common property.

The triple division into lyrical songs, narrative ballads, and tunes mainly connected with dancing (though possibly vocal in origin), meets us in the folk music of every nation; but there are no rigid

---

[1] Wooldridge, op. cit., vol. i, p. 262. The original tune is called 'Nancie' in Morley's version in the 'Fitzwilliam Virginal Book' (No. 12). It also occurs in Valentin Haussmann's *Rest von polnischen und andern Täntzen* (1603), reprinted in *Denkmäler deutscher Tonkunst*, year xvi, p. 134.

[2] A version by Giles Farnaby is in the 'Fitzwilliam Virginal Book' (No. 114).

[3] *The English Dancing Master* (1650), p. 52.

[4] Wooldridge, op. cit., vol. i, p. 276.

[5] Ibid., vol. ii, p. 92.

[6] Cecil J. Sharp, *English Folk-Carols* (1911), No. 15.

lines of demarcation between the three. In English music, ancient as was the custom of ballad-singing by harper and minstrel, ballad tunes (in the strict sense of the word) are later than the other two kinds; whatever early specimens may have existed have been lost, and the ballads so popular in the sixteenth century were chiefly sung to tunes originally intended for lyrics or dances. More than one historian has referred to the possibility that the melodies of 'Sumer is icumen in' and the Agincourt song may, in virtue of the melodic and rhythmical directness of style they exhibit, be examples of ancient folk-tunes; and the thirteenth-century dance tunes discussed on p. 15 bear equally the marks of popular origin. But it is not till about the beginning of the sixteenth century that we have something like a regular literature of folk music; no doubt such existed continuously in earlier times, but there was little chance of its preservation in permanent form till the trained composers began to apply themselves to secular as well as to ecclesiastical work, and to vie with one another in exercising their skill in the embellishment of favourite popular melodies.

The gap was bridged by the carols, which meet us continually in fifteenth-century manuscripts, and to which reference has already been made;[1] they differ in no essentials from contemporary secular pieces, but they were set, it would appear, far more frequently. Towards the year 1500 the phrases become more and more balanced and organized, as we see in such tunes as 'Nowell, nowell, this is the salutacyon'[2] (familiar today in what as a rule is a somewhat modernized shape) or 'As y lay upon a nyȝt',[3] the burden of which runs:

Ex. 171

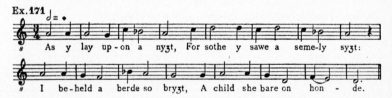

As y lay up-on a nyȝt, For sothe y sawe a seme-ly syȝt:

I be-held a berde so bryȝt, A child she bare on hon - de.

and simultaneously we find for the first time (at least in any profusion) melodies to secular words which bear the impress of folk

---

[1] Sometimes the tunes may have been the composition of the arrangers, sometimes not; we have no evidence either way.

[2] J. Stainer, *Early Bodleian Music*, vol. ii, p. 183; Wooldridge, op. cit., vol. i, p. 30.

[3] Stainer, op. cit., vol. ii, p. 130.

music. The earliest of these, such as 'A, the syghes that come froe my herte', 'Westron wynde', 'Blow thy horne, hunter', 'I have bene a foster',[1] 'The lytell prety nygtyngale',[2] diverse as they are in style, nevertheless show many qualities in common. All (except 'Blow thy horne, hunter', and that has a sort of little supplementary codetta of a different kind) end with a decorative cadence, the last word of the poetry being extended beyond the normal rhythmical limit. Here we may suspect the hand of the arranger. It is true that a good many of these early tunes are rather vague and colourless; but the best of them (and not a few are of really high quality) show somewhat remarkable appreciation of the sentiment of the words—'A, the syghes', in particular, is singularly pathetic in expression. The manuscripts present these tunes sometimes unaccompanied, sometimes set in plain vocal harmony with the melody in the tenor, sometimes in the form of what is known as 'broken plainsong', the melody being expanded in rhythm and occasionally interspersed with rests, the whole forming a more or less elaborate concerted vocal composition:[3] the instrumental settings came into vogue rather later.

The Elizabethan age was as prolific in folk-tunes as in everything else; music seems to have been greatly in vogue among the lower as well as the upper classes, and the dramatists are constantly alluding to popular melodies by name. Shakespeare, for example, mentions 'Sick, sick',[4] 'Fortune my foe',[5] 'Light o' love',[6] 'Calen o custure me',[7] 'Whoop, do me no harm, good man',[8] 'Heart's ease',[9] 'Come o'er the bourne, Bessy',[10] 'Peg-a-Ramsey',[11] and others, including the rollicking tune of which Mrs. Ford says: 'They [i.e. Falstaff's words and deeds] do no more adhere and keep place together than the Hundredth Psalm to the tune of Greensleeves':[12]

[1] = forester. The foregoing are all printed in Wooldridge, op. cit., vol. i.
[2] *Songs and Madrigals by English Composers of the Close of the Fifteenth Century* (1891), pt. i, p. 8.
[3] Reference has been made in chapter iii (p. 50) to the Masses by Tye, Shepherd, and Taverner on the 'Western Wynde'. Note that there are two tunes with this title. The one used by Tye, Shepherd, and Taverner is different from the one in Brit. Mus. Royal App. 58 (Wooldridge, op. cit., vol. i, pp. 37–8).
[4] *Much Ado about Nothing*, iii. 4.   [5] *The Merry Wives of Windsor*, iii. 3.
[6] *The Two Gentlemen of Verona*, i. 2; *Much Ado about Nothing*, iii. 4.
[7] *Henry V*, iv. 4.   [8] *The Winter's Tale*, iv. 3.
[9] *Romeo and Juliet*, iv. 5.   [10] *King Lear*, iii. 6.
[11] *Twelfth Night*, ii. 3. For the tunes see Wooldridge, op. cit., vol. i.
[12] *The Merry Wives of Windsor*, ii. 1. Cf. v. 5. The version of the tune quoted here is derived from the lute setting in Trinity College, Dublin, MS.

Ex.172

and such fragments of popular poetry as those in *Hamlet* or *The Winter's Tale* were no doubt sung by Ophelia or Autolycus to their proper tunes, some of which are still in existence.[1] Very many tunes of extremely fine quality, including some still well known like 'There were three ravens' or 'The hunt is up',[2] date from this time; we find indeed all kinds, some beautifully expressive and rhythmically flexible like 'Now the spring is come' or 'Bonny sweet Robin':[3]

Ex.173

some buoyantly vigorous like 'Lord Willoughby'[4] or perhaps the most contemporaneously popular of all tunes, 'Sellenger's Round'[5] (a singularly perfect example of a Mixolydian superficially resembling a major-scale melody):

Ex.174

412, p. 104. Another contemporary version, from William Cobbold's 'New fashions' (Brit. Mus. Add. 18936–9), is quoted by J. F. Bridge, *Shakespearean Music in the Plays and Early Operas* (1923), p. 79.

[1] E. W. Naylor, *Shakespeare and Music* (2nd ed., 1931), pp. 184–5, 189–91.
[2] Wooldridge, op. cit., vol. i, pp. 75 and 86.
[3] Ibid., pp. 194 and 153.   [4] Ibid., p. 152.   [5] Ibid., p. 256.

But, whatever the style, nearly all later sixteenth-century folk-tunes show a singular vitality of utterance; and for the first half of the next century the bulk of such music still has more or less the same qualities. Very many tunes are still purely modal, and some, such as 'The woods so wild' or 'Come o'er the bourne, Bessy'[1] are very probably of earlier date than their first occurrence in Elizabethan collections.[2]

The folk-melodies for which our earliest documentary evidence dates between 1650 and 1800 are, as a rule, of a different character; we find them in great profusion in numerous collections of contemporary popular songs and dances (the most voluminous being Playford's *The English Dancing Master*, which was first brought out in 1650 and was reprinted as *The Dancing Master* in enlarged forms seventeen times down to 1728), in the ballad operas, and in the common broadsides. Many older melodies were, however, continually being reprinted, usually in more or less different and inferior shapes; and we are, in fact, largely driven back on internal evidence in estimating the date of any particular example. It is easy, nevertheless, to see a gradual weakening of the type; the increasing neglect of the modal tonalities means a loss of variety, and there is a decline in melodic and rhythmic inspiration. But, less notable though the general average is, we still find a large number of very fine tunes with a vital character all their own, such as, to take a casual handful, 'Come, lasses and lads', or 'Here's a health unto his majesty', or 'Down among the dead men', or 'Pretty Polly Oliver'[3]—a model of graceful melodic curve:

Ex. 175

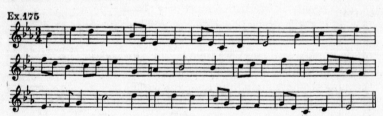

or two, in their very different ways, equally splendid tunes from later editions of *The Dancing Master*, both of which, in the absence of any known accompanying words, seem to have dropped into oblivion—'Portsmouth':[4]

---

[1] Wooldridge, op. cit., vol. i, pp. 119 and 121. [2] See p. 46.
[3] All in Wooldridge, op. cit., vol. ii. [4] Ibid., p. 88.

Ex. 176

and 'Pall Mall':[1]

Ex. 177

What many people call 'typical English tunes'—sturdy, swinging, healthy, but rather insensitive melodies like 'The Vicar of Bray' (a corruption of the Morris dance 'Country Gardens'[2])—occur by shoals during the eighteenth century; as also do others of the softer and (using the word in a good sense) more sentimental kind, which are now best known through their offspring in the works of Arne.

Traditional English melodies for which we have nothing but nineteenth-century (or, it may be, twentieth-century) evidence are of all sorts and shapes. Reference has already been made to the general features which they bear in common with other British folk music; but the caution against dogmatic judgements of date and origin applies to them more than to any of the rest. Though some of our oldest folk-tunes are in the plain major scale, yet, probably, the more strongly modal the tune, the earlier it is likely to be; and where definitely modal tonality is found together with melodic *fioriture* common in sixteenth-century folk music but not later, there is at any rate a presumption that the tune is of considerable antiquity.[3] But all such speculations must necessarily be more or

---

[1] *The Dancing Master* (11th ed., 1701), p. 125. The imperfect key-signature of this edition is rectified in later editions.

[2] Cecil J. Sharp, *English Folk-Song: Some Conclusions* (1907), p. 112.

[3] See, for example, the picturesque Dorian 'Bristol Town' (*Journal of the Folk-Song Society*, vol. i, p. 148).

371

less conjectural, in the absence of any datable evidence; it is quite possible that, in remoter parts of the country, lovers of the older style may have retained the older types longer.

But historical doubts need not hinder us from enjoying the music that has been collected in such abundance from all parts of England, as well as from the southern Appalachian Mountains of North America.[1] Much of it has not, save in the eyes of enthusiasts beyond the reach of argument, any particular artistic merit, except that of clean unaffectedness; but we find all shades of gradation from the kind of tune that any capable and healthily minded musician could produce at the rate of a dozen an hour up to a mass of really splendid melodies like 'The ship in distress' (Dorian), the Irish-like 'Farewell, Nancy' (Aeolian),[2] 'Salisbury Plain' (Aeolian), 'Brigg fair' (Dorian), 'As I walked out one May morning' (Aeolian), 'Covent Garden' (Aeolian),[3] or indeed many more, with, at a rather lower melodic level, a large number of charmingly piquant and pointed things like 'The wraggle-taggle gipsies',[4] 'My Johnny was a shoemaker',[5] or 'The bobtailed mare'.[6] The folk-tunes of the counties at either of the extreme ends of England show certain features of their own. There is a historically close connexion between the Cornish and Irish races; and the best known of Cornish folk-songs—the very charming 'Where be going?'[7]—has, though it retains a definite individuality of style, a distinctively Celtic lilt that is also noticeable in greater or less degree in other tunes from the same district. In Northumbria, on the other hand, we find, as is natural, a close approximation to the Lowland Scottish type; 'John Peel (an old border tune originally known as 'Where will bonnie Annie lie?') is no doubt English enough, but on the other hand 'The Keel Row' is equally Scottish, and the great majority of the tunes in Bruce and Stokoe's collection *Northumbrian Minstrelsy* (1882) show

[1] See Cecil J. Sharp, *English Folk Songs from the Southern Appalachians*, 2 vols. (1932).

[2] Cecil J. Sharp and Charles L. Marson, *Folk Songs from Somerset*, 3rd ser. (1906), pp. 64 and 58.

[3] *Journal of the Folk-Song Society*, vol. i, p. 150; vol. ii, pp. 80 and 195; vol. iii, p. 113.

[4] Sharp and Marson, op. cit., 1st ser. (1904), p. 18.

[5] Lucy E. Broadwood and J. A. Fuller Maitland, *English County Songs* (1893), p. 181.

[6] *Journal of the Folk-Song Society*, vol. i, p. 219.

[7] Harold Boulton and Arthur Somervell, *Songs of the Four Nations* (1892), p. 58.

(when they possess distinctive qualities at all, as very many of them entirely fail to do) strong affinities for their still more northern neighbours. Beautiful melodies like 'Bonny at morn' or 'Sair fyel'd, hinny'[1] are, both in sentiment and in technical features,[2] inseparable from a tune like that quoted later from the other side of the Cheviots, 'I'll bid my heart be still'.

The Island of Man is a little world of its own in language, and its folk music, though much mixed with outside influences, has certain individual characteristics. It is, as a rule, somewhat melancholy in mood and has a special partiality for the Dorian scale; the structure which repeats the same two strains for the first and fourth, and for the second and third, lines is very frequent. There is much in collections of Manx music that fails to create any marked impression, and there are many approximations to Irish methods; but still, tunes like the familiar passionate and majestic 'Mylecharane' and the less-known beautiful Dorian 'The sheep under the snow':[3]

Ex. 178

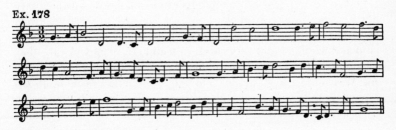

have a tinge of expression not exactly paralleled elsewhere in the British Islands.

Considerably the least artistically interesting of the four large departments of British folk music is that contributed by the Welsh people. As we have seen in Chapter I, music was cultivated in Wales to a relatively advanced degree in quite early times; and the old quasi-official status of the art in the national life is still preserved, in what to the non-Welshman seems a curiously quaint and artificial fashion, in the ceremonies of the 'Eisteddfod'. But we have, until comparatively recent times, practically nothing but mere legend on

---

[1] *Northumbrian Minstrelsy*, pp. 88 and 92.

[2] Both are pure Aeolian, apart from an improbable sharp seventh on the penultimate note of the middle section of the latter; cf. W. G. Whittaker, *Collected Essays* (1930), p. 63.

[3] W. H. Gill, *Manx National Songs* (1896), pp. 34 and 1. The editor's version of the latter has sharps in the cadences: these have been omitted in the example.

which to rely for any definite facts about Welsh music; and there is no sort of reason for yielding to the blandishments of enthusiastic natives, who would claim an eighth-century date for the tune of 'Morva Rhuddlan' and the status of 'the most ancient specimen of music in existence' for some tablature for the Welsh harp, first noted in a manuscript of the time of Charles I (Brit. Mus. Add. 14905).[1] Welsh folk music stands in an unusual position in showing a relatively small number of modal melodies (the fine Dorian 'Britain's Lament'[2] and the expressive 'Breuddwyd y Bardd'[3] are examples); the majority are in the ordinary major or minor keys. This fact does not by any means necessarily imply that they are more modern than other folk-tunes; but it is hard to deny the presence of a more or less sophisticated tone about all but the really finest specimens. Tunes of the very frequently recurring type of 'Jenny Jones' or 'The Ash Grove' ('Llwyn onn'),[4] with their politely complacent rhythm and their rather colourless arpeggio-like phrases, are not really, in spite of their fresh cleanness, of any artistic importance; these and many others show a certain lack of sensitiveness of style that we do not find nearly so often in the folk-melodies of England and Scotland and very rarely indeed in those of Ireland—they are much more akin to those of the western continental nations. But still Welsh music is individual enough, even in its artistic faults; its typical melodies are easily differentiated from those of other races. Characteristic features are a fondness for triple time, an avoidance of rhythmical organization save of the very simplest nature, an emotional expressiveness of a direct and slightly heavy kind, a certain monotony of invention; yet Wales has produced plenty of fine tunes, though of a somewhat limited range. The slow, steady, majestic swing of the melody known as 'The red piper's'[5] is an inspiration of really great power:

Ex. 179

---

[1] Facsimile edition by H. Lewis (1936). Cf. G. Reese, *Music in the Middle Ages* (1940), p. 391.

[2] Alfred Moffat, *The Minstrelsy of Wales* (1906), p. 13.

[3] J. Lloyd Williams and Arthur Somervell, *Sixteen Welsh Melodies*, pt. ii (1909), p. 56.

[4] Moffat, op. cit., pp. 2 and 88.

[5] Ibid., p. 170.

and, similarly, melodies such as 'Morva Rhuddlan'[1] or 'David of the white rock'[2] or 'Ton-y-Botel'[3] (a very noble specimen of a traditional hymn-tune) are marked by artistic strength of a high order. And again, in the tenderer vein, we have the beautiful 'Gwenith Gwyn':[4]

Ex. 180

and others of the same general type, such as 'All through the night',[5] or 'The blackbird'[6]—a charmingly graceful tune in five-bar rhythm; and many more might be mentioned. But still, taken as a whole, Welsh music lacks subtlety; and we cannot avoid drawing unfavourable deductions from the fact that it has admitted into its national song-literature a miserably feeble effusion like Brinley Richards's 'God bless the Prince of Wales' and the hardly less commonplace modern patriotic anthem 'Land of my fathers'.

Scottish folk music consists of two parts, that of the Lowlands and that of the Highlands; being the products of different races, they show different characteristics, though as in all British folk music, one style slides into the other by infinitesimal gradations. Beyond

[1] Ibid., p. 45.   [2] Ibid., p. 37.
[3] *The English Hymnal* (2nd ed., 1933), No. 108.
[4] Moffat, op. cit., p. 171.   [5] Ibid., p. 4.
[6] Ibid., p. 106.

the borders of Scotland the Lowland tunes bear the greatest affinity to the English, the Highland to the Irish.

Lowland folk-tunes are very largely modal, the favourite scale being the Aeolian, though two fine specimens, 'The Brume o' the Cowdenknowes' and 'Wae's me for Prince Charlie',[1] are respectively Dorian and Mixolydian:

Ex. 181

Ex. 182

This latter is an early eighteenth-century version of a rather less organized tune, 'Lady Cassilis' Lilt', that is found in the Skene manuscript[2] of some hundred years earlier date—a collection of songs and dances (written in lute tablature) which is the oldest extant trustworthy authority for Scottish national music, though it contains English tunes as well. Of the Aeolian melodies there may perhaps be quoted the wonderfully organized 'Katherine Ogie':[3]

Ex. 183

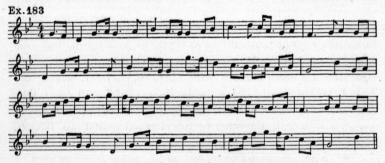

[1] Moffat, *The Minstrelsy of Scotland* (2nd ed., 1896), pp. 69 and 4.
[2] Edited by W. Dauney, *Ancient Scotish Melodies, from a manuscript of the reign of King James VI* (1838), p. 228.   [3] Moffat, op. cit., p. 278.

the subtly picturesque 'Ca' the yowes': [1]

Ex. 184

and a very expressive Border tune known to the words 'I'll bid my
heart be still' (and to many others also): [2]

Ex. 185

and the pure major scale, which is not very common, is found in one
of the most ancient and most beautiful of all, the familiar 'Ay
waking, O!', [3] as well as in 'The twa sisters o' Binnorie', [4] a noble
specimen of a rare type of half-declamatory, half-lyrical tune of
extended compass. Pentatonic tunes, based on a scale containing
only five notes, are not of very frequent occurrence in the Lowlands.
The very beautiful original form of 'Gala Water' [5] is a specially
good example, and another is found in the ancient air 'The bridegroom grat': [6]

Ex. 186

This last example may serve to introduce a brief digression on the
curious vicissitudes which the conception of Scottish music has
undergone, quite apart from the natural fusion of one country's
style with another's that we are always finding in our examination
of British folk-tunes. This particular tune was fitted by Lady Anne
Lindsay to the words of her 'Auld Robin Gray', but it has now been

[1] Ibid., p. 36.   [2] Ibid., p. 73.
[3] Ibid., p. 22.
[4] W. Christie, *Traditional Ballad Airs* (1876), vol. i, p. 40; cf. G. Greig and
A. Keith, *Last Leaves of Traditional Ballads and Ballad Airs* (1925), pp. 9–13.
[5] See Grove's *Dictionary* (4th ed.), vol. iv, p. 697.
[6] Ibid.

completely supplanted by a nineteenth-century English production
of vastly inferior quality; indeed, during the previous century the
deliberate manufacture of Scottish tunes was a favourite industry
with London composers. There was at the time a great fashion for
them; but they were, as a rule, hopelessly mangled by the whole-
sale addition of the so-called 'Scottish snap'—the ♫. rhythm—
which is of very rare occurrence in the old genuine versions,[1] and
Hook and many others turned out shoals of so-called 'Scottish
songs', which were really entirely their own work. The same thing
has indeed been done on the farther side of the Cheviots; according
to Burns the neatly pentatonic 'Ye banks and braes of bonnie Doon'
was the joint concoction of a couple of gentlemen in Edinburgh,[2]
and the much more trivial 'Annie Laurie', which figures on most
programmes as an old traditional tune, is the long-unavowed composition of Lady John Scott, who died as late as 1900.

The genuine Lowland music is, however, as a rule, of very fascinating artistic quality. It is on the whole much the most at home in
slow tunes, which are very often marked by a kind of severe but,
nevertheless, tender beauty of an altogether exceptional order, that
sets their unknown composers high among the lastingly remembered melodists; they are almost always, so to speak, tinted in
shades of grey, but the colour is of the purest. Quick melodies of
the type of 'Jenny Nettles'[3] or 'The Piper of Dundee'[4] again, are
marked by a sort of fine delicately sparkling gaiety that is not visible
elsewhere; but real notable distinctiveness is not perhaps so common as among the slower tunes. Certain qualities, such as the broad,
calm happiness of some of the English melodies, or the fiery majesty
of some of the Irish, we do not see; when the Lowland folk music
tends towards the straightforwardly placid, as, for example, in
'Afton Water'[5] and others of a similar character, the inspiration
burns rather fitfully and the tools seem blunted, and the intensely
vivid Irish imagination, which blazes in such outbursts as the
melody of 'Avenging and bright fall the swift sword of Erin', finds
only a dim reflection in the Jacobite songs.

[1] What is perhaps the best-known tune exemplifying this feature, 'Robin
Adair', is a bastard 'Scottish' version of a pure Irish song, 'Eileen aroon'.
[2] The Letters of Robert Burns, ed. J. de L. Ferguson (1931), vol. ii, p. 274.
See further J. Glen, Early Scottish Melodies (1900), pp. 55–7.
[3] Moffat, op. cit., p. 80.
[4] J. Hogg, The Jacobite Relics of Scotland, 2nd ser. (2nd ed., 1874), p. 43.
[5] Moffat, op. cit., p. 56.

The Highland Gaelic folk music is certainly more versatile in mood, though it does not equal the special excellences of the Lowland; it is on the whole more primitive in expression, and has, combined with a certain spirituality of its own, something of the Irish power of direct utterance of nearly all the great simple emotions, though it is less sensuously beautiful in melodic outline. Sometimes the tunes are curiously rugged in form, wandering on in more or less vague rhythm from one phrase to the next, as, for example, in this fine half-barbaric North Highland tune 'Och o ro u':[1]

Ex.187

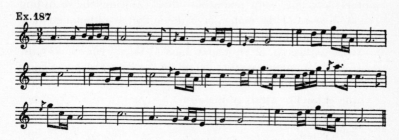

and even when the rhythmical structure is more balanced, there will often be a good deal of irregularity of detail. Tunes like these, which are formally quite unlike any others found in the British islands, give the impression of considerable antiquity, though we have little or no direct evidence on which to lean; but on the other hand we equally often find pure Gaelic tunes which are artistically balanced as finely as the best Irish specimens, as, for example, the beautiful melody now best known to the modern words 'Mo chailin dileas donn':[2]

Ex.188

or the massively picturesque pentatonic 'A chuachag nan craobh' ('O cuckoo of the grove'):[3]

[1] K. N. Macdonald, *The Gesto Collection of Highland Music* (1895), p. 4.
[2] Moffat, op. cit., p. 94; cf. L. Macbean, *The Songs and Hymns of the Gael* (1900), p. 16.
[3] See p. ix.

Ex. 189

Another very fine, stern pentatonic tune (omitting the third and seventh degrees of the scale, not, as here, the second and sixth) is the melody from the island of St. Kilda 'Cumha h'Irteach', quoted in the 'Gesto' collection of Highland music;[1] this is rather unlike the tunes of the mainland and the Hebrides, and the Orkney islands, again, have folk-melodies of a rather distinctive character, as, for example, 'Elorelo',[2] a special favourite of Scott:

Ex. 190

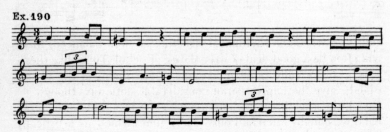

It will be seen that this last is a hexatonic tune, omitting one degree of the scale entirely; this is a particularly common characteristic in Highland music, and some very striking instances can be seen in the superb 'Laoidh Molaidh' ('Hymn of Praise'), 'Fear a Bhàta', and the Hebridean 'Soraidh' ('Farewell').[3] Researches into Gaelic music have been a good deal too much left in the hands of enthusiastic but unscientific amateurs, and our knowledge of it is as yet not based on any very firm foundations; but there is no doubt that it is of very rich artistic value, and in many ways approximates more closely than any other extant folk music to primitive conditions.

The real traditional Highland instrument is a kind of jews'

[1] Macdonald, op. cit., p. 22.
[2] D. Balfour, *Ancient Orkney Melodies* (1888), No. 1.
[3] Moffat, op. cit., pp. 74, 162, 194.

harp; the bagpipes were introduced later, and it was only in the eighteenth century that Scottish dance music was rendered on the violin by Niel Gow (1727–1807) and his school, many of whom were also composers. Old laments, reels, and strathspeys exist in profusion: many of the finest, especially the frequently very passionate and beautiful laments, were very probably originally vocal, but the many quick dance tunes, both Scottish and Irish, that are virtually exclusively based on the notes of an alternating couple of triads (the lower one invariably major) separated by the interval of a tone, were no doubt designed from the start for the special scale of the pipes—though the style was obviously adaptable to other instruments and is indeed occasionally found in the dance music of England, as in the 'Cobbler's hornpipe'.[1]

The Irish temperament is peculiarly prone to patriotism of a kind that is too enthusiastic to trouble itself overmuch about such mundane concerns as facts; and in this amiable weakness native writers on Irish music have their share. Thus 'Sumer is icumen in' has, it would appear, been stolen from the Irish melody 'The summer is coming' (joined by Moore to the words 'Rich and rare were the gems she wore')[2]—though only the first four notes are in the least degree similar, and we first hear of it five hundred and fifty years after the time of the Reading *rota*. Power, again, who is alleged to be an Anglo-Irishman, has to be claimed, without the slightest evidence, as the earliest and most distinguished member of the first British school—apparently because it is *a priori* intolerable that he should have to be ousted by a mere Englishman like Dunstable; and we are given to understand that 'The Coolin' (adapted by Moore to the words 'Though the last glimpse of Erin'),[3] a beautiful tune the first documentary evidence of which occurs in the late eighteenth century, probably dates from the year 1296 or 1297 'inasmuch as it must have been composed not long after the passing of the Statute 24th of Edward I, in 1295, which forbade "the degenerate English in Ireland" to imitate the native Irish "by allowing their hair to grow in coolins"'.[4] But we need not rely on arguments of this very doubt-

[1] H. E. Wooldridge, *Old English Popular Music*, vol. ii, p. 80.
[2] *The Irish Melodies of Thomas Moore*, ed. C. V. Stanford (1895), p. 18; cf. *The Bunting Collection of Irish Folk Music and Songs*, ed. D. J. O'Sullivan, pt. i (1927), p. 21.
[3] Ibid., p. 11.
[4] W. H. Grattan Flood, *A History of Irish Music* (4th ed., 1927), pp. 66, 87, 94–7.

ful type to show that Ireland has had a musically distinguished history. In the first chapter of this book we have noted evidence of the early artistic proficiency of the Irish race; and there seems no doubt that for some hundreds of years Irish minstrelsy was considerably more cultured and advanced and at the same time more honoured and appreciated than similar developments on the other side of St. George's Channel. We know nothing, however, about the harmony (if any) employed by the medieval harpers, nor have we any definite evidence that the tunes we know now existed in the same forms prior to their earliest documentary appearances—not, at any rate, so much as to carry any melody farther back than the ancient English tunes of 1500 or thereabouts. We have a few passing references; an extract from the Talbot Papers of 1602[1] tells us of the great popularity at Elizabeth's court of Irish tunes (several of which are indeed referred to by Shakespeare),[2] and Spenser refers to minstrels and bards in terms which suggest the influence of his own experience of native music in Ireland.[3] But we are thrown back virtually entirely on the folk music itself, of much of which the actual composers are definitely discernible—among them O'Carolan, a famous itinerant harper (1670–1738), who wrote many of the best-known Irish melodies.

Few musicians have been found to question the assertion that Irish folk music is, on the whole, the finest that exists; it ranges with wonderful ease over the whole gamut of human emotion from the cradle to the battlefield, and is unsurpassed in poetical and artistic charm. If musical composition meant nothing more than tunes sixteen bars long, Ireland could claim some of the very greatest composers that have ever lived; for in their miniature form the best Irish folk-tunes are gems of absolutely flawless lustre, and though of course some of them are relatively undistinctive, it is very rare to meet with one entirely lacking in character. The publication of numerous collections of arrangements by Stanford and others, and of the huge mass of melodies transcribed in the middle of the last century by George Petrie (1789–1866), has attracted special attention to this field; and there is no branch of folk music which has been investigated with more artistic thoroughness. Nearly

[1] Edmund Lodge, *Illustrations of British History, Biography, and Manners* (2nd ed., 1838), vol. ii, p. 578.
[2] Grattan Flood (op. cit., pp. 169–77) cites eleven; but for some of these the evidence seems insufficient.
[3] *The Faerie Queene*, III. xii. 5.

all Irish tunes show a singular sensitiveness of feeling; it is true that
frequently they do not seem emotionally to fit the words with
which they were in their earliest days connected (Moore, on the
other hand, had a wonderful genius for writing round the essential elements in an older tune), but as mere successions of notes
without words of any kind they are full of a subtle vitality which
can give delicate and distinctive sparkle to more or less humorous
dance-measures of no particular melodic loftiness, and also rise to
such strains as 'It is not the tear' (originally 'The sixpence')[1]—a
wonderful example of what can be crowded into a restricted structural scheme:

Ex. 191

or 'If the sea were ink'[2]—a magnificently majestic and solemn
march to which Moore's 'Lay his sword by his side' is exactly suited:

Ex. 192

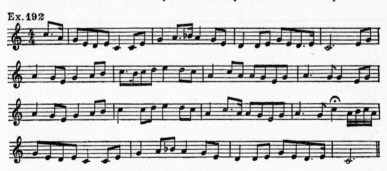

or the tune generally known as 'The Londonderry Air',[3] with an
emotionally organized design of quite exceptional power:

[1] *The Irish Melodies of Thomas Moore*, p. 70.
[2] Ibid., p. 238; cf. George Petrie, *The Complete Collection of Irish Music*,
ed. C. V. Stanford (1902–5), No. 770.
[3] Petrie, *The Ancient Music of Ireland* (1855), p. 57 (with a B♮ in bar 6).
Anne Gilchrist (*Journal of the English Folk Dance and Song Society*, Dec.
1934, pp. 115–21) argues that the original tune must have been in $\frac{3}{4}$ time.

Ex. 193

In form, as well as in melody, the best Irish folk music is exceptionally polished. We very rarely[1] find the somewhat luxuriant flexibility of metre that is far from infrequent in Highland melodies and not at all unknown in English; even balanced structures such as those of the exquisite 'The Dove' in three-bar rhythm,[2] or 'One Sunday after Mass',[3] in which there is a two-bar refrain after each half of the tune, or 'Draherin O Machree'[4] or 'Have you been at Carrick?'[5] which consists of four sections of five bars each, or 'At the mid hour of night',[6] which has five-bar phrases, are exceptional, and nearly all Irish melodies are built on an ordinary sixteen-bar framework subdivided into fours. But the phrases have a quite exceptional freedom from anything like either vagueness or stiffness of line; the melodies never tie themselves into knots, and the rhythmical basis is always firm and coherent. Sometimes, as in the beautiful tune known as 'The flight of the earls' or 'The boys of Wexford':[7]

Ex. 194

[1] No. 125 in the complete Petrie collection is an instance.
[2] Petrie, *The Complete Collection of Irish Music*, No. 614.
[3] Ibid., No. 633; cf. Moffat, *The Minstrelsy of Ireland* (1897), p. 212.
[4] P. W. Joyce, *Ancient Irish Music* (1873), p. 40; Moffat, op. cit., p. 90.
[5] Joyce. *Irish Music and Song* (1888), p. 10; Moffat, op. cit., p. 70.
[6] *The Irish Melodies of Thomas Moore*, p. 96.
[7] C. V. Stanford, *Songs of Old Ireland* (1882), p. 26.

we have a sort of miniature epitome of sonata-form; indeed this structure may quite possibly have occurred for the first time in Irish folk music, though in the default of exact dating we can never dogmatize. A distinctive feature that occurs in very many tunes is the reiteration of the key-note at the end of a phrase—a reiteration that is strictly melodic, and not, as in some Scottish tunes like 'There was a lad was born in Kyle', mainly due to the rhythmical exigencies of a dance-measure. Sometimes, as in the very graceful and tender tune familiar to the words 'My love's an arbutus',[1] this reiterated note would seem to be the dominant of the key; but as a matter of fact the melodies which seem to show this exception are really Mixolydian, though (it may be) harmonized on Hypoionian lines in the major key a fourth higher. The feature shows itself not only in the ordinary major or Ionian mode (in which, however, it seems most frequently to occur) but in the three other modes common in Irish music; a specially powerful example is seen in the well-known magnificent Aeolian tune 'Remember the glories of Brien the brave' or 'Molly McAlpin'.[2]

[1] Ibid., p. 62. The melody is known as 'Coola Shore' (Petrie, op. cit., No. 507).

[2] *The Irish Melodies of Thomas Moore*, p. 3; cf. *The Bunting Collection*, pt. ii (1930), p. 24.

XIV

GENERAL CHARACTERISTICS

WE have seen, in the first two chapters of this book, how English composers in the Middle Ages developed a characteristically smooth art of harmonic progression which had a considerable influence on the Continent. By the sixteenth century such smoothness had become an integral part of polyphonic writing everywhere, but the enervating effect of continuous euphony was avoided by the use of dissonant suspensions and passing notes. In Palestrina dissonance is a practice governed by almost rigorous conventions;[1] and though other Continental composers show some variety of treatment, there is sufficient unanimity to suggest a common practice. English composers of this period, however, are much less bound by convention. They show, for example, more variety in the treatment of suspensions and in their ornamental resolution, and a richer and more varied use of passing dissonance.[2] In particular they show a curious attachment to a form of dissonance which arises neither from suspensions nor from the use of passing notes. An attempt at a short systematic treatment of this most interesting question is (even though it strikes a more technical note than the rest of this book) the more necessary in that it has frequently been obscured in the past by editorial vagaries, which have resulted in the alteration —sometimes silent, sometimes with an airy reference to 'obvious misprints'—of passages which, strange as they may sound, are quite certainly intentional.

The ultimate origin of it all is what is known as *musica ficta*. This extempore insertion of accidentals not indicated in the music was definitely sanctioned by the theorists of the earliest times for such purposes as avoiding progressions of augmented intervals, or securing sharpened leading-notes in cadences. By the fourteenth century it became quite common to write these accidentals in the music; but the practice was not systematized, and indeed the later fifteenth-century Flemish composers seem on the whole to have reverted to the older custom of leaving the accidentals to the singers. It is not

---

[1] See K. Jeppesen, *The Style of Palestrina and the Dissonance* (2nd ed., 1946).
[2] See R. O. Morris, *Contrapuntal Technique in the Sixteenth Century* (1922).

surprising to find a lack of method in sixteenth-century music; sometimes the accidentals were inserted, sometimes not, and the only thing for us to do is, by the collation of a large number of instances, to try to form some general rules for our guidance in a kind of chaos rendered worse by the occasional occurrence of what are undoubtedly slips of the pen and misprints.

It is in what are called 'false relations' that the crux lies. In the music of the Elizabethan age we find all possible kinds, from the ordinary:

Ex. 195

ev - er more and more to - wards us

in Batten's anthem 'O praise the Lord',[1] to this rather more striking example from Byrd's 'Sed tu, Domine, qui non derelinquis' (*Cantiones Sacrae*, I, No. 7),[2] which, in one form or another, is of constant occurrence as a cadence figure in English music down to Purcell and Blow:

Ex. 196

and, further, to this abrupt instance from one of Byrd's *Songs of Sundrie Natures* (No. 27)—'Penelope that longed for the sight':[3]

[1] *Tudor Church Music*, 8vo ed., No. 56.
[2] *Collected Vocal Works* (ed. Fellowes), vol. ii, p. 52.
[3] *English Madrigal School*, vol. xv, p. 176.

But the specially English feature (though by no means unknown on the Continent) is the very frequent simultaneous employment of 'false relations' so that the major and minor thirds of the same root are sounded together; sometimes, as at the end of Weelkes's 'Cease sorrows now' (see Ex. 78, p. 116), the effect is very pathetic and beautiful, sometimes it is very expressive, as at the end of Tallis's 'Absterge, Domine'[1]—an obvious extension of the cadence figure just mentioned:

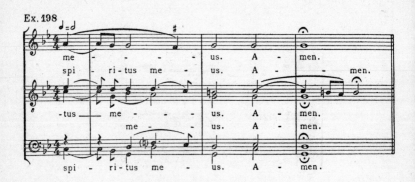

or in this extract from Gibbons's fine anthem 'If ye be risen again with Christ':[2]

---

[1] *Tudor Church Music*, vol. vi, p. 186 (the key signature is accidentally omitted on this page, and the clef on the second line is wrong).
[2] Ibid., vol. iv, p. 217.

Ex. 199

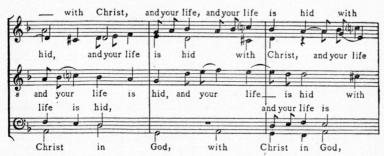

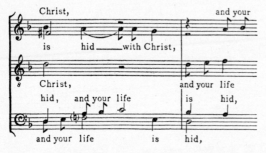

Ouseley quaintly remarks: 'The Composer has fallen into the error
of attempting to represent the antagonism of the ideas of Life and
Death by the use of discords utterly intolerable to modern ears.'[1]
Perhaps, however, the F♯ in the penultimate bar (which occurs
in only two manuscripts) was not held long enough to clash with the
F♮ in the bass—at the end of a phrase, as here (and the same kind
of passage occurs very often), the duration of the note may be
merely conventional. Sometimes the clash is harsher in effect, as in

[1] *A Collection of the Sacred Compositions of Orlando Gibbons* (1873),
p. 85, n.

389

this example from the madrigal 'Ah, cruel hateful fortune' by Kirbye,[1] who, like Byrd, shows a great partiality for this kind of thing:

Ex.200

It is, of course, against all evidence to credit such passages to personal initiative, but it is curious how very many English composers seem to have been totally unaffected by this tendency. Tye is the earliest of the great men concerned, Croft the last. The clash may also occur in instrumental music, for example, the 'Voluntary' by Alwood in the Mulliner book[2] and many instances in the Fitzwilliam book. Of the later composers, Child, Purcell, Wise, and Blow are the most partial to the style, and there are one or two final echoes of it in Croft's works—in the Te Deum of the Service in E♭, for example, or in the anthem 'O Lord, rebuke me not' (see Ex. 149, p. 251). Child and Blow show numerous examples—the latter, indeed, is as partial to it as Byrd and Kirbye themselves—and in Purcell we find a considerable number of specimens, like this from the five-part anthem 'Lord, how long wilt thou be angry?':[3]

Ex.201

[1] *English Madrigal School*, vol. xxiv, p. 113.
[2] *Musica Britannica*, vol. i, p. 13.   [3] Edited by J. A Westrup (Novello).

or a very similar one in the eight-part anthem 'O praise God in his holiness':[1]

Ex.202

Praise him on the well tun-ed cym-bals

Things like these are quite different in kind from the consecutive sevenths of the Restoration composers and other little harmonic mannerisms with which the musical historian meets more or less frequently; and it does not help matters much to argue that with a system of unequal temperament they would sound a fraction less curious, nor to throw out despairing suggestions that perhaps we do not quite understand the notation. Nor can we, in a gallant radicalism, alter everything so as to make it sound well from a nineteenth-century point of view; sometimes, it is true, only a very slight alteration is needed, and in those cases it is quite possible that such may have been made by performers, but very many other cases, exactly similar in essentials, refuse to be altered except by a process of upsetting the music right and left. Nor, again, can we, in a gallant purism, consistently decline to supply any accidentals whatever to a manuscript; the frequent result is that the music seems right from no point of view at all. No doubt, when the passage is got over at a good speed, the effect is only transient, and anyhow it is less noticeable on voices than on instruments; still, when all has been said, some explanation is necessary. And, indeed, after a sufficiently extensive acquaintance, we begin to see that there is really at the bottom of it all a definite system; and the very minute handful of passages which cannot be included under it can be left to be examined each on its own merits, and relegated, if we think fit, to the category of slips of the pen or misprints, the existence of which nobody denies. This principle is very simple, being nothing more than the adherence of each part to its own independent scale-scheme. A good illustration is this passage from Milton's 'If that a sinner's sighs':[2]

[1] *Purcell Society*, vol. xiv, p. 32.
[2] *Old English Edition*, vol. xxii, p. 26.

Ex.203

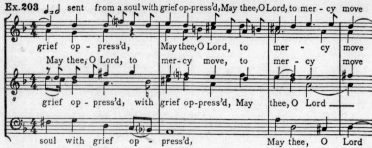

where a B♮ in the tenor, though not in the original, is logical.
Authentic examples of the melodic interval of an augmented second
are not unknown in the madrigalian period but they are very rare.[1]
The principle of independent movement is a simple and natural
extension of the doctrine of horizontalism that is the foundation of
polyphonic music. Sometimes, indeed, we almost seem to see the
composer adopting it consciously, as in this extract from the second
section of the overture to Blow's *Venus and Adonis*:[2]

Ex.204

where the clash in the second bar is explained by the fact that there,
and in that bar alone, the scale-schemes of the second violin and
viola are necessarily in conflict. A passage in Purcell's anthem 'Out
of the deep', where the ascending and descending melodic minor
scales slowly grind against one another, is equally salient:

Ex.205

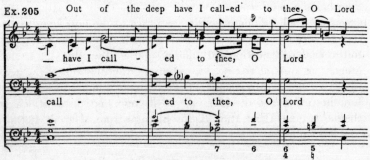

[1] See E. H. Fellowes, *The English Madrigal Composers* (1921), p. 118.
[2] Edited by Anthony Lewis (Lyre-Bird Press), p. 3.

As for the two and a half closely printed pages of 'Dr Blow's crudities' which the usually amiable Burney indignantly sets forth,[1] they may be divided into three fairly equal classes—things explicable on the above lines, other kinds of things, not altogether successful, but about which it is pedantic to trouble overmuch, and things that show really brilliant harmonic originality, rising at times to something like genius.

No doubt it is not always easy to see the true application of the principle; there are various doubtful places. Once or twice, indeed, the principle itself may seem to betray us, as in the well-known extract from Byrd's 'Civitas sancti tui' (*Cantiones Sacrae*, I, No. 21),[2] familiar in its English version 'Bow thine ear':

which stands thus in the printed part-books of 1589 and also in Barnard's collection; Boyce, in the reprint in his *Cathedral Music*, omitted the sharp, and has consequently drawn down on his head a storm of scholarly abuse, which (though he has plenty of genuine editorial sins to answer for) he hardly seems to deserve. It is quite arguable that it may be an error due to a mistaken impression that the phrase was a full close. On the other hand this is not the only example of an augmented sixth in Byrd's *Cantiones Sacrae*;[3] and though the introduction of such a chord may seem out of place to the modern ear, its occurrence is quite conceivable, under certain circumstances, on the basis of the principle mentioned—which, indeed, is not by any means intended to exclude the possibility of hesitation about borderland cases of this and a few other kinds. All that is claimed is that it affords a working hypothesis for the artistic

---

[1] *A General History of Music* (1776–89), vol. iii, pp. 449–51.
[2] *Collected Vocal Works*, vol. ii, p. 159.
[3] See E. H. Fellowes, *William Byrd* (2nd ed., 1948), p. 70, and cf. his *The English Madrigal Composers* (1921), p. 114.

explanation of certain features characteristic of English music, which in the older reprints were too often suppressed.

These characteristics, as will have been noticed, occur only at certain periods; and, indeed, the lack of steady continuity is one of the most striking features of English musical history. In all other countries the art has run a course which has undergone normal developments and has been unaffected by spasmodic rises and falls; in England, on the other hand, it has oscillated violently between extremes, or what may virtually be considered such. English music was in the very forefront of artistic endeavour in the first half of the fifteenth century; then came a period of partial relapse until it awoke to some seventy or eighty years of splendid activity (*c.* 1540–1620), during the whole of which time it poured forth works that could rank with the very greatest of any contemporary foreign composers. Again there was a relative darkness till the Purcellian period, the brilliance of which owed its origin primarily to French and Italian methods; but this brief efflorescence of some twenty years, during which English music again at least equalled any written abroad, was followed by a long dark stretch till, this time under German influence, a new birth came in the later Victorian days. Not that foreign impulses denationalized English music; they merely gave the stimulus, and our own composers worked out their own native styles for themselves. But, since the time of Dunstable, we have never reciprocated; unless we may be allowed to trace the influence of the nocturnes of Field (who, after all, spent most of his life abroad) on those of Chopin, no compositions by even the greatest men of English blood since the fifteenth century seem to have had any germinating force outside their own country. The influence of early English instrumental music abroad was chiefly one of performance, not of composition, and the stimulus given to the *Singspiel* by *The Beggar's Opera* cannot be regarded as due to the impulse of any specifically national style. The greatest of the foreigners whom we have adopted sacrificed, when he set foot on English soil, all chance of guiding the course of continental music; we have taken freely from other nations, but we have not given back.

This sort of isolation, due partly to insularity of position and partly to a certain insularity of temperament, has resulted in a curious ignorance among foreign musicians of even the finest English music. It is true that in the sixteenth and seventeenth centuries compositions by Englishmen living in their native country were occasionally reprinted abroad. East printed Morley's balletts in Italian, for exportation, in 1595, the year of their first appearance in their original form; the same volume was also published, with German words, at Nuremberg in 1609, and German editions of the *Canzonets or little short songs to three voyces* (1593) were published at Cassel and Rostock in 1612 and 1624 respectively. Reference has been previously made to the numerous foreign issues of music by Englishmen temporarily or more or less permanently residing abroad. We have also, of course, in fairness to recollect that until fairly recently much of our most noteworthy work remained in manuscript or in part-books practically unprocurable outside English libraries. But still, the complacent scorn with which the country of Byrd and Purcell has been almost universally treated up to very recent times is totally unpardonable. 'An English composer—no composer' was the remark made by a friend of Schumann's when Bennett was announced to play his third piano concerto in Leipzig;[1] and some thirty years later, Ambros, though not himself agreeing with the opinion that England has been 'from the very beginning down to the present day a completely unmusical country', quotes it as practically universally held in Germany.[2] Indeed, Naumann, in his voluminously elaborate *Illustrierte Musikgeschichte* (1880–5), gives exactly four astonishingly perfunctory pages (out of some 1,200) to the whole of English music, passing over, without the slightest mention, all Elizabethan church and madrigal composers and 'Sumer is icumen in' itself, and even a scholar like Nagel was apparently under the impression that our artistic life came to a total and permanent stop about the year 1700. It is only quite lately that this prejudiced ignorance has begun to disappear as foreign musicians have become better acquainted with the works of English composers, both ancient and modern.

One of the favourite taunts of continental criticism has been to assert that every English composer was merely an organist; and, while we might retort that the same could be said of Bach, it is no doubt true that ecclesiastical influences have played here a part that is altogether exceptional. We have never had any fixed and

---

[1] R. Schumann, *Music and Musicians*, trans. by Fanny Ritter, 1st series, p. 212.
[2] *Geschichte der Musik*, vol. iii (3rd ed., 1893), p. 452. The first edition of this volume was published in 1868.

powerful secular tradition, either in opera or in the instrumental field; our religious music has always been something of our own, and fine as is the work we have produced in other departments, we have turned to them only spasmodically. It is true that at the present time the ecclesiastical hold is weakening very rapidly, and the younger school writes very little church music; but still an exceptional proportion of English musicians hold or have held, as conditions of livelihood, posts to which not all of them would have aspired had other channels, open to their foreign fellow artists, been open to them also. The inferior composer of the quasi-clerical order has for more than two hundred years been a peculiarly Anglo-Saxon product; other nations have known bad religious music, but they have not, like us, been deluged with it. Nor have they suffered, to anything like the same extent, from the application to artistic matters of totally non-artistic canons of judgement; it is only in England that musicianship has been really seriously hampered by the unmusical seekers after edification.

England, again, is the only country that can show a perfectly continuous output of hymn-tunes; magnificent tunes have been written elsewhere at various times, but the current has never, except here, run at all steadily. While on the one hand the English Reformation did a great disservice to art in causing the noble plainsong melodies to be one and all forgotten for over three hundred years by the whole community, except the small number of adherents of the older traditions, yet, on the other, it gave rise to a musical literature that was far from an unworthy substitute. The superb Lutheran chorales, though introduced to England as early as 1539 in Coverdale's *Goostly Psalmes*, never took root here, and have only, like the plainsong melodies, been revived during the last hundred years; but the psalm-tunes owing their birth to western European, especially Genevan, Protestantism (not a few of which are very possibly adaptations of secular folk-melodies, as are some Lutheran chorales) were quickly assimilated into the national life, and some of the greatest musicians of both the mid-sixteenth century and the madrigalian period arranged them in parts for congregational use (the melody being, as a rule, placed in the tenor), and also imitated their style, more or less closely, in original compositions. We possess some splendid little masterpieces of this kind from the avowed pens of Tallis and Gibbons; but in most cases it is impossible for us to determine the real authorship of the tunes in the very numerous psalters between the 1556 edition of Sternhold (in which the so-called 'church tunes' first appear, in an unharmonized shape) and Playford's in 1677, the last of its kind—the arranger of a tune not previously met with may be also the composer, or he may not. All these melodies, many of which, such as the 'Old Hundredth', 'St. Mary', 'Winchester Old', 'London New', 'St. Michael', 'French Tune (or Dundee)', 'Windsor', 'St. Flavian', 'Old 137th', and plenty of others are still happily very familiar, attain a very lofty standard of merit; and many also, like the superb Dorian 'Martyrs', which we first find in the Scottish Psalter of 1635:[1]

Ex. 207

and others showing equally grand sternness, have been more or less forgotten in the competition with hymn-tunes of a less uncompromising type. The different psalters display varying methods of harmonization; that published in 1599 by Richard Allison (and indeed entirely his own work) shows the Elizabethan style at its purest, but in the mixed collections known under the names of Day, East, and Ravenscroft, and others as well, there is a steadily maintained artistic level, though some of the musicians who contributed were more at home in such tasks than were others. And until about the middle of the nineteenth century we still retained the power of producing distinguished music in this restricted field; the old 'church tunes' of doubtful authorship once left behind, we pass to the admirable work of Clarke and Croft, and on to that large literature of later eighteenth- and early nineteenth-century hymn-tunes of which, on the stronger side, Howard's 'St. Bride', and on the softer, Miller's 'Rockingham' (an adaptation of an eighteenth-century melody) are typical examples, where in spite of a distinct declension of grandeur and at times a certain partiality for over-decoration the sentiment is still as a rule pure and dignified and the musicianship sound and clean. No doubt this later manner has but little of the melodic inventiveness and emotional force that were the glories of the older; but yet (even when we remember how some of the inferior eighteenth-century hymn-composers ran riot with 'polite' experiments in very doubtful taste) the rapid declension of

---

[1] *The Scottish Psalter of 1635*, ed. by R. R. Terry (1935), pt. ii, p. iv.

hymn-writing after 1860 presents an astonishing contrast. We have already referred to the main features of later Victorian church music; and it is enough to say that the composers of hymn-tunes led the way in the fall to the easy popularity of inferior sentimentalism. But in this, as in other branches of ecclesiastical art, a wholesome reaction is now in full swing. Heroic and not altogether unsuccessful efforts have been made to oust the bad familiar tunes and replace them by others more worthy of congregational affection; and composers like Parry, Stanford, and Vaughan Williams have enriched English hymnody with tunes not unworthy of a place with the masterpieces of the past. So far as hymns are concerned, the process of purification has been chiefly due in the first instance to the High Church section of the Anglican communion; see, for example, the admirable collection *Songs of Syon*, edited by G. R. Woodward (4th ed. 1923). Very little incentive has been afforded by other religious bodies; but some of the larger collections of a general type, such as the 1904 edition of *Hymns Ancient and Modern*, the *English Hymnal* (2nd ed. 1933), and *Songs of Praise* (2nd ed. 1931), have given considerable impulse to the movement of reform.

We must nevertheless remember that this purification consists to a large extent in the revival or introduction of fine old hymn-tunes of non-English origin—a cosmopolitanism possible in our less rigid rituals but unfamiliar abroad. Indeed, there is no other country that has so cordially, throughout its whole artistic history, welcomed foreign music and musicians of all kinds—sometimes to our advantage, sometimes to the reverse. On the credit side of the resulting account we can point to our freedom from the curse of a narrow, jealous patriotism, our ready openness to impressions from outside, our cordiality towards alien singers and instrumentalists; on the other side, however, there has been the often strongly marked tendency, that no other country's artistic history has shown, to neglect and depreciate native work in comparison with foreign, even when the latter is only equally good or even worse. This trait was visible at an early stage of our musical career; Morley, for example, inveighs strongly against the current practice of extolling Italian music to the disadvantage of equally good or better productions by Englishmen.[1] Again, in the Restoration period, there is ample evidence that, at any rate in fashionable circles, foreign performers and foreign compositions had a vogue in many cases quite incom-

[1] *A Plaine and Easie Introduction to Practicall Musicke* (1597), p. 179.

mensurate with their merits; but the eighteenth century, and the first half (or rather more) of the nineteenth, show this characteristic in its fullest force. The main cause was no doubt the domination of the aristocratic Italian opera; its regular *habitués* felt and expressed a sort of lordly contempt for home products, and a very large number of British performers—chiefly during the last century—considered themselves in honour bound to sink their nationality under Italianized disguises of various kinds. And quite apart from all this our religious music for about a hundred and fifty years was almost entirely subservient to the successive influences of three composers of foreign birth. Even if we claim the first of these as to all intents and purposes an Englishman, and the influence exercised by the Handelian oratorio as virtually altogether native, nevertheless the fact remains that it was consciously imposed upon us from outside, and was not in any sense a natural development of any previous existing English art; and the later reigns of Mendelssohn and Gounod (especially the third, happily short though it was) were definitely foreign in character. All three dominations were gravely detrimental in so far as they dictatorially imposed certain methods on all British composers who had any desire for recognition in the field of religious music; we may admire non-British work as much as we like and can, but it should be as learners, not as slaves.

The reaction from all this has resulted in a movement of considerable strength in the direction of what is somewhat vaguely described as nationalism; but this too has its dangers. We certainly do not want anything like protection in the field of art; if a non-British is better than a British work, every one worthy to be called the possessor of a musical taste must needs prefer the former. We have, it is true, a definite right to ask that native work shall have fair chances and that it shall not be ousted by inferior competition from outside; there is still room for very considerable improvement of this kind, but to ask more is to abnegate any artistic standpoint worth the name. It is ridiculous and worse to ask English singers to sing home-made productions to the exclusion of Schubert, Brahms, or Fauré; nor should we desire England as a whole to adopt the sort of narrowly parochial attitude which has in Wales and Ireland, for example, gravely injured any sustained artistic production by resident natives. However much a composer's race may be shown in his music, his ideals must be cosmopolitan; all great music speaks a world language, not a dialect—and this holds good with the really great folk-melodies as much as with any other branch of the art. The ideal of a national school of composers may very easily mean a wilful narrowing of our artistic heritage, a feebly patriotic blunting of the edge of our judgement; and, after all, the musician who (save occasionally when seeking alien texts for his own individual discourses) borrows his material from his native folk-tunes shows himself, just as much as if he borrowed from any other quarter, a common plagiarist who is not strong enough to invent material of his own.

What really do we mean by calling any composer 'English' in tone? We have seen in the last chapter that there are certain broadly general characteristics marking the folk-tunes of the various portions of the British islands; and in the light of these several features we can, if we like, say that Vaughan Williams is more English than Elgar, or Stanford more Irish than either, or, among past centuries, Purcell more English than Byrd, or Arne than Wilbye. But judgements like these connote neither praise nor blame; no composer writes in a chamber hermetically sealed from all external influences, and all that we mean is that some composers have been attracted, more than others have, by the general types of phrase or the general emotional moods exemplified in their native folk music. A skilled ethnologist might be able to discover the common denominator of, let us say, Tallis and Sullivan, but the attempt is hardly worth making; folk music, as the production of the more or less 'natural' man, gives the general main characteristics, but in art, as in everything else, nationality is broad enough to include nearly all imaginable varieties. So far as the individual composer is concerned, it is not a matter for either credit or discredit if his temperament leads him to keep close to the norm of his race; the only vital consideration is the value, in the general terms of all races, of his artistic output.

There are no doubt certain subsidiary aspects in which the English musical world of today, looked at from other than the composer's point of view, shows features of a unique character. Musical degrees, for example, are virtually unknown on the Continent; they are first heard of at Oxford and Cambridge towards the end of the fifteenth century, but had little or no bearing on the musical life of the country till past the middle of the nineteenth. Their early history is very obscure;[1] they probably originated out of the cus-

---

[1] See C. F. Abdy Williams, *Degrees in Music* (1893). I may, perhaps, also be allowed to refer to my own article on the subject in Grove's *Dictionary* (4th

tom of granting degrees in the single arts of the medieval *trivium* and *quadrivium*, and may in some respects have been similar to the long extinct degrees in grammar. Until the middle of the nineteenth century their acquisition involved no formal examination of any kind, nothing more indeed than the presentation of an 'exercise' under very vague conditions, and the graduates held, as compared with other members of the universities, a position of the most anomalous description. Most of the younger universities also confer these degrees, and the regulations for their attainment differ widely; in one or two cases a test of performance is required, but as a rule the examinations are concerned purely with composition and the history and theory of music. Honorary degrees are also not infrequently granted; and the Archbishop of Canterbury, as the inheritor of the ancient rights of the occupants of the see as legates of the Pope, possesses and occasionally exercises the eccentric privilege of conferring them on the advice of expert musicians. Musical degrees have no doubt been of service in setting certain standards of scholastic proficiency; though, on the other hand, the curious passion for ornamental letters that consumes a large section of the British public sometimes leads to foolish misunderstandings of their strictly artistic value.

This love of tangible results in the shape of titles and certificates is indeed, in the field of music, a specially British characteristic: and during the last sixty or seventy years we have increasingly suffered from a tyranny of examinations that at the present day is rampant in every direction. For the higher professional standards such things are no doubt necessary; but it is the special eccentricity of English musicians to travel up and down the country passing and 'plucking' children all day long. In their anxiety for the magic pieces of paper the parents forget that any teacher worth the name knows infinitely more about his pupils than any peripatetic examiner, however patient and fair-minded, can possibly do; and even if we charitably concede to examinations a share of the credit for the great advance in the quality of the music taught in schools during the last generation, nevertheless no impartial observer can do otherwise than keenly regret the stereotyped methods of teaching which most of their syllabuses almost inevitably tend to engender. Inspection is all very well, but musical examinations, as too often carried on today,

ed.), vol. ii, pp. 32–8 (see also supplementary vol., pp.153–5) for fuller details than are possible here.

are neither educational nor artistic; and a pitiful amount of time and energy is wasted on them.

In certain respects, indeed, we in England have perhaps been rather specially prone to take an inartistic view of music; a good-humoured, indiscriminating tolerance of irreconcilable contrasts is a peculiarly common attribute, and in art as in other things we have a singular gift for keeping our minds in watertight compartments. The folk-tune and the shop-ballad are alike 'simple music', the greatest performer is he or she who commands the highest fees, and we innocently imagine that the sales of a work of art have some sort of an inherent ratio to its permanent value. Of course we are very far from having a monopoly of vulgar music, but in no other country, perhaps, have prominent composers written such with their eyes open, purely for the sake of money, nor has this kind of thing elsewhere hampered the real progress of the art to anything like so considerable an extent.

Still, there is no sort of reason to be pessimistic about English music. Our leading performers, institutions, and critics can on the whole fully bear comparison with those abroad; and the Londoner has quite exceptional opportunities for hearing every kind of music interpreted by the finest artists of every nationality. And the impartial historian who looks back on our long line of composers, and compares it with what other nations can show, will perhaps—more than either we or they are generally inclined to admit—think it not unworthy of our pride. We have indeed to confess that in instrumental music and opera we have done comparatively little, and even in song and choral music, where our strength has lain, we have never produced a man for whom the term genius seems too small—none of the few supreme kings of the art has been English. At the same time we can look back on five centuries of continuous creative work, from Dunstable to the present day; and though we have had periods of mere respectability, the same is true of every other race. And we have had at any rate one period during which the average level of English work was at least as high as the average level of any other music has been at any period whatsoever. No doubt we have slept the sleep of the dull too often and too long; but now we are awake again. The present is hopeful, the future bright.

BIBLIOGRAPHY

THE bibliography, which does not pretend to be exhaustive, includes mainly books and articles in periodicals. References are given to collections of music published in series or in substantial volumes with introductions, but not to reprints of individual works, many of which are cited in footnotes to the text. Where reprints form part of a general series, such as *Tudor Church Music*, they are listed under the title of the series; where they are the work of individual editors, under the editors' names.

GENERAL

COLLES, H. C.: *Voice and Verse: a Study in English Song* (London, 1928).

DAVEY, HENRY: *History of English Music* (2nd ed., London, 1921).

FARMER, HENRY GEORGE: *A History of Music in Scotland* (London, 1947).

FELLOWES, EDMUND H.: *English Cathedral Music* (2nd ed., London, 1943).

—— *Organists and Masters of the Choristers of St. George's Chapel in Windsor Castle* (London, 1939).

FLOOD, W. H. GRATTAN: *A History of Irish Music* (4th ed., Dublin, 1927).

GALPIN, FRANCIS W.: *Old English Instruments of Music* (3rd ed., London, 1932).

KIDSON, FRANK: *British Music Publishers, Printers and Engravers* (London, 1900).

LAFONTAINE, H. CART DE: *The King's Musick* (London, 1909).

LOEWENBERG, ALFRED: *Annals of Opera, 1597–1940* (Cambridge, 1943).

PULVER, JEFFREY: *A Biographical Dictionary of Old English Music* (London, 1927).

—— *A Dictionary of Old English Music and Musical Instruments* (London, 1923).

RIMBAULT, EDWARD F.: *The Old Cheque-Book, or Book of Remembrance, of the Chapel Royal* (London, 1872).

SCHOLES, PERCY A.: *The Mirror of Music, 1844–1944.* 2 vols. (London, 1947).

WEST, JOHN E.: *Cathedral Organists, Past and Present* (2nd ed., London, 1921).

WHITE, ERIC WALTER: *The Rise of English Opera* (London, 1951).

CHAPTER I

The Beginnings of English Music

APEL, WILLI: *The Notation of Polyphonic Music* (Cambridge, Mass., 1942).

BUKOFZER, MANFRED F.: 'The First Motet with English Words'. *Music and Letters*, July 1936, pp. 225–33.

BIBLIOGRAPHY

BUKOFZER, MANFRED F.: 'Gymel, the Earliest Form of English Poly-
phony'. *Music and Letters*, Apr. 1935, pp. 77–84.
—— *Geschichte des englischen Diskants und des Fauxbourdons nach
den theoretischen Quellen* (Strasbourg, 1936).
—— *Studies in Medieval and Renaissance Music* (New York, 1950).
—— '"Sumer is icumen in": a Revision'. *University of California Pub-
lications in Music*, vol. ii, No. 2 (1944), pp. 79–114.
COUSSEMAKER, C. E. H. DE: *Scriptorum de musica medii aevi nova series.*
4 vols. (Paris, 1864–76).
ELLINWOOD, LEONARD: 'John Cotton or John of Affligem'. *Notes*, Sept.
1951, pp. 650–9.
FRERE, W. H.: *The Winchester Troper.* Henry Bradshaw Society, vol. viii
(London, 1894).
HANDSCHIN, JACQUES: 'The Summer Canon and its Background'. *Musica
Disciplina*, vol. iii (1949), pp. 55–94.
—— 'Über Estampie und Sequenz'. *Zeitschrift für Musikwissenschaft*,
vol. xii (1929–30), pp. 14–18.
HUGHES, DOM ANSELM: *Worcester Mediaeval Harmony* (Burnham,
1928).
LEVY, KENNETH JAY: 'New Material on the Early Motet in England'.
Journal of the American Musicological Society, vol. iv, No. 3 (1951),
pp. 220–39.
PIRROTTA, NINO: 'On the Problem of "Sumer is icumen in"'. *Musica
Disciplina*, vol. ii (1948), pp. 205–16.
REESE, GUSTAVE: *Music in the Middle Ages* (New York, 1940).
SCHOFIELD, BERTRAM: 'The Provenance and Date of "Sumer is icumen
in"'. *The Music Review*, May 1948, pp. 81–6.
STAINER, JOHN: *Early Bodleian Music.* 3 vols. (London, 1901).
TREND, J. B.: 'The First English Songs'. *Music and Letters*, Apr. 1928,
pp. 111–28.
WAESBERGHE, J. SMITS VAN: *Johannis Affligemensis De Musica cum
Tonario* (Rome, 1950).
WOLF, JOHANNES: 'Die Tänze des Mittelalters'. *Archiv für Musikwissen-
schaft*, vol. i (1918–19), pp. 10–42.
WOOLDRIDGE, H. E.: *Early English Harmony* (London, 1897).

CHAPTER II

Music in the Fifteenth and Early Sixteenth Centuries

BUKOFZER, MANFRED F.: 'Fauxbourdon revisited'. *The Musical Quarterly*,
Jan. 1952, pp. 22–47.
—— 'The First English Chanson on the Continent'. *Music and Letters*,
Apr. 1938, pp. 119–31.
—— *Geschichte des englischen Diskants und des Fauxbourdons nach
den theoretischen Quellen* (Strasbourg, 1936).
—— 'John Dunstable and the Music of his Time'. *Proceedings of the
Musical Association*, vol. lxv (1938–9), pp. 19–43.

BUKOFZER, MANFRED F.: 'A Newly Discovered Fifteenth-Century Manuscript of the English Chapel Royal—Part II'. *The Musical Quarterly*,
Jan. 1947, pp. 38–51.

—— *Studies in Medieval and Renaissance Music* (New York, 1950).

—— 'Über Leben und Werke von Dunstable'. *Acta Musicologica*, vol.
viii (1936), pp. 102–18.

COLLINS, H. B.: 'John Taverner's Masses'. *Music and Letters*, Oct. 1924,
pp. 322–34.

—— 'John Taverner—Part II'. *Music and Letters*, Oct. 1925, pp. 314–
29.

—— *Missa 'O quam suavis'* (Burnham, 1927).

COUSSEMAKER, C. E. H. DE: *Scriptorum de musica medii aevi nova series.*
4 vols. (Paris, 1864–76).

Denkmäler der Tonkunst in Österreich, years vii, xi (1), xix (1), xxvii (1),
xxxi, xl (Vienna, 1900–33).

FULLER MAITLAND, J. A., and ROCKSTRO, W. S.: *English Carols of the
Fifteenth Century* (London, n.d.).

HUGHES, DOM ANSELM: 'The Works of Robert Fairfax'. *Music and
Letters*, Apr. 1949, pp. 118–20.

Madrigals by English Composers of the Close of the Fifteenth Century
(London, 1893).

Musica Britannica, vol. iv: *Mediaeval Carols*. Edited by John Stevens
(London, 1952).

M[YERS], L. S.: *Music, Cantelenas, Songs, &c. from an Early Fifteenth
Century Manuscript* (London, 1906).

RAMSBOTHAM, A., COLLINS, H. B., and HUGHES, DOM ANSELM: *The Old
Hall Manuscript*. 3 vols. (Burnham, 1933–8).

REESE, GUSTAVE: *Music in the Middle Ages* (New York, 1940).

SCHOFIELD, BERTRAM: 'A Newly Discovered Fifteenth-Century Manuscript of the English Chapel Royal—Part I'. *The Musical Quarterly*,
Oct. 1946, pp. 509–36.

*Songs and Madrigals by English Composers of the Close of the Fifteenth
Century* (London, 1891).

STAINER, CECIE: 'Dunstable and the Various Settings of O Rosa Bella'.
Sammelbände der internationalen Musikgesellschaft, vol. ii
(1900–1), pp. 1–13.

STAINER, JOHN: *Early Bodleian Music*. 3 vols. (London, 1901).

STEVENS, JOHN E.: 'Rounds and Canons from an Early Tudor Song-
Book'. *Music and Letters*, Jan. 1951, pp. 29–37.

TREFUSIS, LADY MARY: *Songs, Ballads and Instrumental Pieces composed by King Henry the Eighth* (Oxford, 1912).

Tudor Church Music (London, 1923–9), vols. i, iii, x.

VAN, GUILLAUME DE: 'A Recently Discovered Source of Early Fifteenth-
Century Polyphonic Music, the Aosta Manuscript'. *Musica Disciplina*, vol. ii (1948), pp. 5–74.

WOOLDRIDGE, H. E.: *Early English Harmony* (London, 1897).

—— *The Polyphonic Period, Part II* (1st ed., Oxford, 1905; 2nd ed.,
London, 1932).

CHAPTER III

Music of the Mid-Sixteenth Century

ARKWRIGHT, G. E. P.: *The Old English Edition* (London and Oxford, 1889–1902), vol. x.

BOYD, MORRISON COMEGYS: *Elizabethan Music and Musical Criticism* (Philadelphia, 1940).

COLLINS, H. B.: 'Thomas Tallis'. *Music and Letters*, Apr. 1929, pp. 152–66.

DONINGTON, ROBERT, and DART, THURSTON: 'The Origin of the In Nomine'. *Music and Letters*, Apr. 1949, pp. 101–5.

ELLINWOOD, LEONARD: 'Tallis' Tunes and Tudor Psalmody'. *Musica Disciplina*, vol. ii (1948), pp. 189–203.

HUNT, J. ERIC: *Cranmer's First Litany, 1544, and Merbecke's Book of Common Prayer Noted, 1550* (London, 1939).

MILLER, HUGH M.: 'Sixteenth-Century English Faburden Compositions for Keyboard'. *The Musical Quarterly*, Jan. 1940, pp. 50–64.

Musica Britannica, vol. i: *The Mulliner Book*. Edited by Denis Stevens (London, 1951).

PFATTEICHER, CARL: *John Redford, Organist and Almoner of St. Paul's Cathedral* (Cassel, 1934).

REESE, GUSTAVE: 'The Origin of the English *In Nomine*'. *Journal of the American Musicological Society*, vol. ii, No. 1 (1949), pp. 7–22.

STEVENSON, ROBERT: 'John Marbeck's "Noted Booke" of 1550'. *The Musical Quarterly*, Apr. 1951, pp. 220–33.

Tudor Church Music (London, 1923–9), vols. v, vi, x.

WOOLDRIDGE, H. E.: 'The English Metrical Psalter'. Grove's *Dictionary of Music and Musicians* (4th ed., London, 1940), vol. iv, pp. 267–81.

CHAPTER IV

The Madrigalian Era

ANDREWS, HILDA: *My Ladye Nevells Booke* (London, 1926).

ARKWRIGHT, G. E. P.: 'Early Elizabethan Stage Music'. *The Musical Antiquary*, vol. i (1909–10), pp. 30–40, vol. iv (1912–13), pp. 112–17.

—— *The Old English Edition* (London and Oxford, 1889–1902), vols. i, xi–xii, xxi–xxii.

BORREN, CHARLES VAN DEN: *The Sources of Keyboard Music in England* (London, 1913).

BOYD, MORRISON COMEGYS: *Elizabethan Music and Musical Criticism* (Philadelphia, 1940).

BRENNECKE, ERNEST: *John Milton the Elder and his Music* (New York, 1938).

CAMPIAN, THOMAS: *Works*. Edited by Percival Vivian (Oxford, 1909).

COLE, ELIZABETH: 'In Search of Tregian'. *Music and Letters*, Jan. 1952, pp. 28–32.

DART, R. THURSTON: 'The Cittern and its English Music'. *The Galpin Society Journal*, No. 1 (1948), pp. 46–63.

—— 'Morley's Consort Lessons of 1599'. *Proceedings of the Royal Musical Association*, vol. lxxiv (1947–8), pp. 1–9.

EINSTEIN, ALFRED: 'The Elizabethan Madrigal and "Musica Transalpina"'. *Music and Letters*, Apr. 1944, pp. 66–77.

ENGELKE, BERNHARD: *Musik und Musiker am Gottorfer Hofe*, vol. i (Breslau, 1930).

FELLOWES, EDMUND H.: *The Complete Works of William Byrd*. 20 vols. (London, 1937–50).

—— *The English Madrigal Composers* (Oxford, 1921).

—— *The English Madrigal School*. 36 vols. (London, 1913–24).

—— *English Madrigal Verse, 1588–1632* (Oxford, 1920).

—— *The English School of Lutenist Song-Writers*. 31 vols. (London, 1920–32).

—— *Orlando Gibbons and his Family* (2nd ed., London, 1951).

—— *William Byrd* (2nd ed., London, 1948).

FULLER MAITLAND, J. A., and SQUIRE, W. BARCLAY: *The Fitzwilliam Virginal Book*. 2 vols. (London and Leipzig, 1899).

GLYN, MARGARET H.: *About Elizabethan Virginal Music and its Composers* (London, 1924).

—— *Orlando Gibbons: Complete Keyboard Works*. 5 vols. (London, 1924–5).

HAYES, GERALD R.: *The Viols, and Other Bowed Instruments* (London, 1930).

HEURICH, HUGO: *John Wilbye in seinen Madrigalen* (Prague, 1931).

KASTENDIECK, M. M.: *England's Musical Poet: Thomas Campion* (New York, 1938).

LAWRENCE, W. J.: 'Notes on a Collection of Masque Music'. *Music and Letters*, Jan. 1922, pp. 49–58.

MANIFOLD, JOHN: 'Theatre Music in the Sixteenth and Seventeenth Centuries'. *Music and Letters*, Oct. 1948, pp. 366–97.

MEYER, ERNST H.: *Die mehrstimmige Spielmusik des 17. Jahrhunderts in Nord- und Mitteleuropa* (Cassel, 1934).

—— *English Chamber Music* (London, 1946).

MILLER, HUGH M.: 'The Earliest Keyboard Duets'. *The Musical Quarterly*, Oct. 1943, pp. 438–57.

—— 'John Bull's Organ Works'. *Music and Letters*, Jan. 1947, pp. 25–35.

MORLEY, THOMAS: *A Plaine and Easie Introduction to Practicall Musicke*. Shakespeare Association Facsimiles, No. 14 (London, 1937).

NAYLOR, EDWARD W.: *An Elizabethan Virginal Book* (London, 1905).

NEWTON, RICHARD: 'English Lute Music of the Golden Age'. *Proceedings of the Musical Association*, vol. lxv (1938–9), pp. 63–90.

OBERTELLO, ALFREDO: *Madrigali italiani in Inghilterra* (Milan, 1949).

Parthenia or the Maydenhead of the first musicke that ever was printed for the Virginals. Facsimile edition (Cambridge, 1942).

PATTISON, BRUCE: *Music and Poetry of the English Renaissance* (London, 1948).

PLATT, PETER: 'Dering's Life and Training'. *Music and Letters*, Jan. 1952, pp. 41–9.

SCHOFIELD, BERTRAM, and DART, THURSTON: 'Tregian's Anthology'. *Music and Letters*, July 1951, pp. 205–16.

SQUIRE, W. BARCLAY: 'Collections of Virginal Music'. Grove's *Dictionary of Music and Musicians* (4th ed., London, 1940), vol. v, pp. 545–52.

Tudor Church Music (London, 1923–9), vols. ii, iv, vii–ix.

WALKER, ERNEST: 'An Oxford Book of Fancies'. *The Musical Antiquary*, vol. iii (1911–12), pp. 65–73.

WARLOCK, PETER: *The English Ayre* (London, 1926).

—— *Thomas Whythorne: an unknown Elizabethan composer* (London, 1927).

WELCH, CHRISTOPHER: *Six Lectures on the Recorder* (London, 1911).

WESTRUP, J. A.: 'Domestic Music under the Stuarts'. *Proceedings of the Musical Association*, vol. lxviii (1941–2), pp. 19–53.

—— 'Foreign Musicians in Stuart England'. *The Musical Quarterly*, Jan. 1941, pp. 70–89.

CHAPTER V

Music under Charles I and the Commonwealth

ARKWRIGHT, G. E. P.: 'An English Pupil of Monteverdi'. *The Musical Antiquary*, vol. iv (1912–13), pp. 236–57.

DENT, EDWARD, J.: *Foundations of English Opera* (Cambridge, 1928).

HART, ERIC FORD: 'Introduction to Henry Lawes'. *Music and Letters*, July 1951, pp. 217–25; Oct. 1951, pp. 328–44.

HUGHES, CHARLES W.: 'John Gamble's Commonplace Book'. *Music and Letters*, Oct. 1945, pp. 215–29.

—— 'The Music for Unaccompanied Bass Viol'. *Music and Letters*, July 1944, pp. 149–63.

—— 'Porter, Pupil of Monteverdi'. *The Musical Quarterly*, July 1934, pp. 278–88.

LEWIS, ANTHONY: 'Matthew Locke: a Dynamic Figure in English Music'. *Proceedings of the Royal Musical Association*, lxxiv (1947–8), pp. 57–71.

MEYER, ERNST H.: *English Chamber Music* (London, 1946).

Musica Britannica, vol. ii: *Cupid and Death* (Locke and Gibbons). Edited by Edward J. Dent. (London, 1951).

NORTH, ROGER: *Memoirs of Musick*. Edited by Edward F. Rimbault. (London, 1846).

—— *The Musicall Gramarian*. Edited by Hilda Andrews (London, 1925).

PARRY, C. HUBERT H.: *The Music of the Seventeenth Century* (2nd ed., London, 1938).

SCHOLES, PERCY A.: *The Puritans and Music in England and New England* (London, 1934).

WESTRUP, J. A.: 'Foreign Musicians in Stuart England'. *The Musical Quarterly*, Jan. 1941, pp. 70–89.

WOOD, ANTHONY: *Life and Times of Anthony à Wood.* Edited by Andrew Clark. 5 vols. (Oxford, 1891–1900).

CHAPTER VI

Purcell and his Contemporaries

ARKWRIGHT, G. E. P.: *The Old English Edition* (London and Oxford, 1889–1902), vols. xxiii—xxv.

DAY, CYRUS LAWRENCE, and MURRIE, ELEANOR BOSWELL: *English Song-Books, 1651–1702* (London, 1940).

DENT, EDWARD J.: *Foundations of English Opera* (Cambridge, 1928).

HOLLAND, A. K.: *Henry Purcell: the English Musical Tradition* (London, 1932).

HUSK, WILLIAM H.: *An Account of the Musical Celebrations on St. Cecilia's Day* (London, 1857).

LAWRENCE, W. J.: *The Elizabethan Playhouse and other Studies.* 2 vols. (Stratford-upon-Avon, 1912–13).

—— 'The English Theatre Orchestra: its Rise and Early Characteristics'. *The Musical Quarterly*, Jan. 1917, pp. 9–27.

NICOLL, ALLARDYCE: *A History of Restoration Drama, 1660–1700* (2nd ed., Cambridge, 1928).

NORTH, ROGER: *Memoirs of Musick.* Edited by Edward F. Rimbault. (London, 1846).

—— *The Musicall Gramarian.* Edited by Hilda Andrews (London, 1925).

PARRY, C. HUBERT H.: *The Music of the Seventeenth Century* (2nd ed., London, 1938).

Purcell Society. 26 vols. (London, 1878–1928).

QUERVAIN, FRITZ DE: *Der Chorstil Henry Purcell's* (Berne, 1935).

SCOTT, HUGH ARTHUR: 'London's Earliest Public Concerts'. *The Musical Quarterly*, Oct. 1936, pp. 446–57.

SHAW, H. WATKINS: 'Blow's Use of the Ground Bass'. *The Musical Quarterly*, Jan. 1938, pp. 31–8.

—— 'John Blow, Doctor of Music'. *The Musical Times*, Oct.–Dec. 1937, pp. 865–7, 946–9, 1025–8.

—— 'John Blow's Anthems'. *Music and Letters*, Oct. 1938, pp. 429–42.

—— 'The Secular Music of John Blow'. *Proceedings of the Musical Association*, vol. lxiii (1936–7), pp. 1–19.

—— 'Tradition and Convention in John Blow's Harmony'. *Music and Letters*, Apr. 1949, pp. 136–45.

SQUIRE, W. BARCLAY: 'The Music of Shadwell's "Tempest"'. *The Musical Quarterly*, Oct. 1921, pp. 565–78.

WESTRUP, J. A.: 'Domestic Music under the Stuarts'. *Proceedings of the Musical Association*, vol. lxviii (1941–2), pp. 19–53.

—— 'Foreign Musicians in Stuart England'. *The Musical Quarterly*, Jan. 1941, pp. 70–89.

—— *Purcell* (3rd ed., London, 1947).

CHAPTER VII

Handel in England

DENT, EDWARD J.: *Handel* (London, 1934).

—— *Händel in England.* Hallische Universitätsreden 68 (Halle, 1936).

—— 'Italian Opera in London'. *Proceedings of the Royal Musical Association*, vol. lxxi (1944–5), pp. 19–42.

German Handel Society. 96 vols. (Leipzig, 1859–1902).

MÜLLER, ERICH H.: *The Letters and Writings of George Frideric Handel* (London, 1935).

NICOLL, ALLARDYCE: *A History of Early Eighteenth-Century Drama* (Cambridge, 1925).

ROBINSON, PERCY: *Handel and his Orbit* (London, 1908).

—— 'Handel, or Urio, Stradella and Erba'. *Music and Letters*, Oct. 1935, pp. 269–77.

—— 'Handel up to 1720: a new chronology'. *Music and Letters*, Jan. 1939, pp. 55–63.

SCOTT, HUGH ARTHUR: 'London Concerts from 1700 to 1750'. *The Musical Quarterly*, Apr. 1938, pp. 194–209.

—— 'London's First Concert Room'. *Music and Letters*, Oct. 1937, pp. 379–90.

SMITH, WILLIAM C.: *Concerning Handel* (London, 1948).

STREATFEILD, R. A.: *Handel* (2nd ed., London, 1910).

TAUT, KURT: *Verzeichnis des Schrifttums über Georg Friedrich Händel.* Händel-Jahrbuch, vol. vi (Leipzig, 1933).

TAYLOR, SEDLEY: *The Indebtedness of Handel to Works by Other Composers* (Cambridge, 1906).

YOUNG, PERCY M.: *The Oratorios of Handel* (London, 1949).

CHAPTER VIII

Handel's Contemporaries

ARKWRIGHT, G. E. P.: *The Old English Edition* (London and Oxford, 1889–1902), vol. ii.

AVISON, CHARLES: *An Essay on Musical Expression* (2nd ed., London, 1753).

BERGER, ARTHUR V.: 'The Beggar's Opera, the Burlesque, and Italian Opera'. *Music and Letters*, Apr. 1936, pp. 93–105.

CUMMINGS, WILLIAM H.: *Dr. Arne and Rule Britannia* (London, 1912).

FLOOD, W. H. GRATTAN: 'Dr. Arne's Visits to Dublin'. *The Musical Antiquary*, vol. i (1909–10), pp. 215–33.

HUGHES, CHARLES W.: 'John Christopher Pepusch'. *The Musical Quarterly*, Jan. 1945, pp. 54–70.

KIDSON, FRANK: *The Beggar's Opera; its Predecessors and Successors* (Cambridge, 1922).

LAMBERT, CONSTANT: 'Thomas Roseingrave'. *Proceedings of the Musical Association*, vol. lviii (1931–2), pp. 67–83.

BIBLIOGRAPHY

LANGLEY, HUBERT: *Doctor Arne* (Cambridge, 1938).

LAWRENCE, W. J.: 'Early Irish Ballad Opera and Comic Opera'. *The Musical Quarterly*, July 1922, pp. 397–412.

LYSONS, DANIEL: *History of the Origin and Progress of the Meetings of the Three Choirs of Gloucester, Worcester and Hereford* (Gloucester, 1812).

Musica Britannica, vol. iii: *Comus* (Arne). Edited by Julian Herbage. (London, 1951).

NEWTON, RICHARD: 'The English Cult of Domenico Scarlatti'. *Music and Letters*, Apr. 1939, pp. 138–56.

NICOLL, ALLARDYCE: *A History of Early Eighteenth-Century Drama* (Cambridge, 1925).

SCHULTZ, W. E.: *Gay's 'Beggar's Opera': its Content, History and Influence* (New Haven, 1923).

TUFTS, GEORGE: 'Ballad Operas: a List and Some Notes'. *The Musical Antiquary*, vol. iv (1912–13), pp. 61–86.

WALKER, ERNEST: 'The Bodleian Manuscripts of Maurice Greene'. *The Musical Antiquary*, vol. i (1909–10), pp. 149–65, 203–14.

CHAPTER IX

Music under the Later Georges

BARRETT, WILLIAM A.: *English Glees and Part-Songs* (London, 1886).

BARRINGTON, DAINES: *Miscellanies* (London, 1781).

BURNEY, CHARLES: 'Account of the Infant Musician Crotch'. *Philosophical Transactions of the Royal Society*, vol. lxix, part 1 (1779).

—— *An Account of the Musical Performances in Westminster Abbey and the Pantheon in Commemoration of Handel* (London, 1785).

CARSE, ADAM: *The Orchestra from Beethoven to Berlioz* (Cambridge, 1948).

CORDER, F.: 'The Works of Sir Henry Bishop'. *The Musical Quarterly*, Jan. 1918, pp. 78–97.

COX, H. B., and C. L. E.: *Leaves from the Journals of Sir George Smart* (London, 1907).

DALE, KATHLEEN: 'Hours with Muzio Clementi'. *Music and Letters*, July 1943, pp. 144–54.

DIBDIN, CHARLES: *The Musical Tour of Mr. Dibdin* (Sheffield, 1788).

—— *The Professional Life of Mr. Dibdin.* 4 vols. (London, 1803).

FARMER, H. G.: 'A Forgotten Composer of Anthems: William Savage (1720–89)'. *Music and Letters*, July 1936, pp. 188–99.

FOSTER, MYLES B.: *History of the Philharmonic Society* (London, 1913).

KELLY, MICHAEL: *Reminiscences of Michael Kelly.* 2 vols. (London, 1826).

LIGHTWOOD, JAMES T.: *Samuel Wesley, Musician* (London, 1937).

NORTHCOTT, RICHARD: *The Life of Sir Henry Bishop* (London, 1920).

OLDMAN, C. B.: 'Two Minuets by Attwood, with corrections by Mozart'. *The Music Review*, Nov. 1946, pp. 166–9.

PARKE, W. T.: *Musical Memoirs*. 2 vols. (London, 1830).

SAINT-FOIX, GEORGES DE: 'Muzio Clementi'. *The Musical Quarterly*, July 1923, pp. 350–82.

SCHOLES, PERCY A.: *The Great Dr. Burney*. 2 vols. (London, 1948).

—— *The Life and Activities of Sir John Hawkins* (London, 1952).

SQUIRE, W. BARCLAY: 'Some Novello Correspondence'. *The Musical Quarterly*, Apr. 1917, pp. 206–42.

TERRY, CHARLES SANFORD: *John Christian Bach* (London, 1929).

TREND, J. B.: 'Jonathan Battishill'. *Music and Letters*, July 1932, pp. 264–71.

WESLEY, ELIZA: *Letters of Samuel Wesley to Mr. Jacobs* (London, 1875).

CHAPTER X

Early Victorian Music

BACHE, CONSTANCE: *Brother Musicians: Reminiscences of Edward and Walter Bache* (London, 1901).

BANISTER, H. C.: *George Alexander Macfarren* (London, 1891).

BARRETT, WILLIAM A.: *Balfe: his Life and Work* (London, 1862).

BENNETT, J. R. STERNDALE: *The Life of William Sterndale Bennett* (Cambridge, 1907).

CARSE, ADAM: *The Orchestra from Beethoven to Berlioz* (Cambridge, 1948).

FULLER MAITLAND, J. A.: *English Music in the Nineteenth Century* (London, 1902).

GOTCH, ROSAMUND BRUNEL: *Mendelssohn and his Friends in Kensington* (London, 1934).

HUEFFER, FRANCIS: *Half a Century of Music in England, 1837–87* (London, 1889).

JOYCE, F. W.: *The Life of Sir F. A. G. Ouseley, Bart.* (London, 1896).

LEGGE, ROBIN H., and HANSELL, W. E.: *Annals of the Norfolk and Norwich Triennial Musical Festivals, MDCCCXXIV: MDCCCXCIII* (London, 1896).

SPARK, FREDERICK R., and BENNETT, J.: *History of the Leeds Musical Festivals, 1858–89* (Leeds, 1892).

SQUIRE, W. BARCLAY: 'Letters of Robert Lucas Pearsall'. *The Musical Quarterly*, Apr. 1919, pp. 264–97.

CHAPTER XI

The English Renaissance

ANDERTON, H. ORSMOND: *Granville Bantock* (London, 1915).

BEECHAM, THOMAS: *A Mingled Chime* (London, 1944).

COLLES, H. C.: *Symphony and Drama, 1850–1900* (London, 1934).

—— *Walford Davies* (London, 1942).

DUNHILL, THOMAS: *Sir Edward Elgar* (London, 1938).

—— *Sullivan's Comic Operas* (London, 1928).

412

FENBY, ERIC: *Delius as I knew him* (London, 1936).

FULLER, MAITLAND, J. A.: *English Music in the Nineteenth Century* (London, 1902).

—— *The Music of Parry and Stanford* (Cambridge, 1934).

GRAVES, CHARLES L.: *The Life and Letters of Sir George Grove* (London, 1903).

—— *Hubert Parry: his Life and Work*. 2 vols. (London, 1926).

GREENE, HARRY PLUNKET: *Charles Villiers Stanford* (London, 1935).

HALLÉ, CHARLES: *Life and Letters of Sir Charles Hallé* (London, 1896).

HESELTINE, PHILIP: *Frederick Delius* (London, 1923).

JACKSON, BARRY: 'Elgar's "Spanish Lady"'. *Music and Letters*, Jan. 1943, pp. 1–15.

MACKENZIE, ALEXANDER C.: *A Musician's Narrative* (London, 1927).

NETTEL, R.: *Music in the Five Towns, 1840–1914* (London, 1944).

REED, WILLIAM H.: *Elgar as I knew him* (London, 1936).

SHAW, BERNARD: *London Music in 1888–9* (London, 1938).

—— *Music in London, 1890–4*. 3 vols. (London, 1931).

SMYTH, ETHEL: *Impressions that remained*. 2 vols. (London, 1919).

—— *Streaks of Life* (London, 1921).

—— *A Final Burning of Boats* (London, 1928).

—— *As Time went on* (London, 1936).

STANFORD, CHARLES VILLIERS: *Pages from an Unwritten Diary* (London, 1914).

WOOD, HENRY J. *My Life of Music* (London, 1938).

CHAPTER XII

Music in the Twentieth Century

British Music of our Time. Edited by A. L. Bacharach (2nd ed., London, 1951).

DENT, EDWARD J.: *A Theatre for Everybody: the Story of the Old Vic and Sadler's Wells* (London 1945).

DICKINSON A. E. F.: *An Introduction to the Music of R. Vaughan Williams* (London, 1928).

ELKIN, ROBERT H.: *Royal Philharmonic* (London, 1947).

FOSS, HUBERT: *Ralph Vaughan Williams* (London, 1950).

GRAY, CECIL: *Peter Warlock* (London, 1934).

Hinrichsen's Musical Year Book, 1944, 1945–6, 1947–8, 1949–50.

HOLST, IMOGEN: *Gustav Holst* (London, 1938).

—— *The Music of Gustav Holst* (London, 1951).

HOWES, FRANK: *The Dramatic Works of Ralph Vaughan Williams* (London, 1937).

—— *The Later Works of R. Vaughan Williams* (London, 1937).

—— *The Music of William Walton*. 2 vols. (London, 1943).

LOWE, GEORGE: *Josef Holbrooke and his Work* (London, 1920).

Musical Britain 1951. Compiled by the Music Critic of *The Times*. (London, 1951).

RUBBRA, EDMUND: *Gustav Holst* (Monaco, 1947).

RUBBRA, EDMUND: 'The Later Vaughan Williams'. *Music and Letters*, Jan. 1937, pp. 1–8.
—— 'Symphony No. 5 in B♭, Op. 63; an Analysis'. *The Music Review*, Feb. 1949, pp. 27–35.
SAYERS, W. C. BERWICK: *Samuel Coleridge-Taylor: his Life and Letters* (London, 1915).
WHITE, ERIC WALTER: *Benjamin Britten: a Sketch of his Life and Works* (London, 1948).

CHAPTER XIII

Folk Music

(For collections of folk-tunes see the footnotes to the text, and the bibliographies of English, Irish, Scottish, and Welsh folk-song in Grove's *Dictionary of Music and Musicians*).

BRIDGE, J. FREDERICK: *Shakespearean Music in the Plays and Early Operas* (London, 1923).
DAUNEY, WILLIAM: *Ancient Scotish Melodies, from a manuscript of the reign of King James VI* (Edinburgh, 1838).
FITZGIBBON, H. MACAULAY: 'The Lute Books of Ballet and Dallis'. *Music and Letters*, Jan. 1930, pp. 71–7.
Journal of the English Folk Dance and Song Society. 1932– .
Journal of the Folk-Song Society. 8 vols. 1899–1931.
Journal of the Irish Folk Song Society. 1904– .
KIDSON, FRANK, and NEAL, MARY: *English Folk Song and Dance* (Cambridge, 1915).
NAYLOR, EDWARD W.: *Shakespeare and Music* (2nd ed., London, 1931).
O'NEILL, FRANCIS: *Irish Folk Music* (Chicago, 1910).
SHARP, CECIL J.: *English Folk-Song: Some Conclusions* (London, 1907).
—— *English Folk Songs from the Southern Appalachians*. 2 vols. (London, 1932).
TRAVIS, JAMES: 'Irish National Music'. *The Musical Quarterly*, Oct. 1938, pp. 451–80.
WHITTAKER, W. G.: *Collected Essays* (London, 1930).
WILLIAMS, IOLO A.: *English Folk-Song and Dance* (London, 1935).
WOOLDRIDGE, H. E.: *Old English Popular Music*. 2 vols. (London, 1893).

INDEX TO MUSICAL EXAMPLES

Agincourt song (15th cent.), Exs. 18–19 (p. 23).
'Angelus ad virginem' (14th cent.), Ex. 15 (p. 14).
Anon. (*see also* Folk-tunes):
  Agincourt song (15th cent.), Exs. 18–19 (p. 23).
  Angelus ad virginem (14th cent.), Ex. 15 (p. 14).
  As y lay upon a nyȝt (15th cent.), Ex. 171 (p. 367).
  Dance tunes (13th cent.), Exs. 16–17 (pp. 15–16).
  Deo gracias (Agincourt song, 15th cent.), Exs. 18–19 (p. 23).
  Edi beo thu hevene quene (13th cent.), Ex. 9 (p. 10).
  English descant (13th–14th cent.), Exs. 10–11 (pp. 11–12).
  Martyrs (hymn-tune), Ex. 207 (p. 397).
  Now wel may we merthis make (15th cent.), Ex. 20 (p. 24).
  O quam suavis Mass (16th cent.), Ex. 37 (p. 39).
  Passion according to St. Luke, The (15th cent.), Ex. 24 (p. 27).
  Puellare gremium (14th cent.), Exs. 13–14 (p. 13).
  Rejoice in the Lord always (16th cent.), Ex. 49 (p. 62).
  Rosa fragrans (13th cent.), Ex. 6 (p. 9).
  Salve virgo virginum (13th cent.), Exs. 7–8 (pp. 9–10).
  Sanctus et aeternus Deus (14th cent.), Ex. 12 (p. 12).
  Sumer is icumen in (13th cent.), Exs. 3–5 (pp. 7–8).
  Te Deum (13th cent.), Ex. 10 (p. 11).
  Ut tuo propitiatus (12th cent.), Ex. 1 (p. 5).
  Worldes blis ne last no throwe (13th cent.), Ex. 2 (p. 6).
Anthems:
  Above the stars my Saviour dwells (C. Gibbons), Ex. 99 (p. 157).
  Ah! few and full of sorrow (Purcell), Ex. 123 (p. 192).
  Bow thine ear (Byrd), Ex. 206 (p. 393).
  Cast me not away (S. S. Wesley), Ex. 160 (p. 297).
  Early, O Lord, my fainting soul (Purcell), Ex. 122 (p. 191).
  Glorious and powerful God (O. Gibbons), Ex. 66 (p. 98).
  Hear my prayer, O Lord (Purcell), Ex. 119 (p. 186).
  Hide not thou thy face (Farrant), Ex. 50 (p. 62).
  Hosanna to the Son of David (O. Gibbons), Ex. 64 (p. 96).
  How doth the city sit solitary (Blow), Ex. 114 (p. 180).
  If that a sinner's sighs (Milton), Ex. 203 (p. 392).
  If ye be risen again with Christ (O. Gibbons), Ex. 199 (p. 389).
  In the midst of life (Purcell), Ex. 120 (p. 188).
  Let the words of my mouth (Attwood), Ex. 155 (p. 278).
  Like as the hart (Humfrey), Ex. 117 (p. 182).
  Lord, how long wilt thou be angry? (Greene), Ex. 150 (p. 254).
  Lord, how long wilt thou be angry? (Purcell), Ex. 201 (p. 390).
  Lord, let me know mine end (Goss), Ex. 161 (p. 299).
  My God, my God, look upon me (Blow), Ex. 113 (p. 179).
  My God, my God, look upon me (Crotch), Ex. 156 (p. 279).
  O God, the rock of my whole strength (Wilbye), Ex. 68 (p. 101).
  O Lord, arise into thy resting place (Weelkes), Ex. 67 (p. 99).
  O Lord, I bow the knees (W. Mundy), Ex. 52 (p. 63).
  O Lord, in thy wrath rebuke me not (O. Gibbons), Ex. 65 (p. 97).
  O Lord, look down from heaven (Battishill), Ex. 154 (p. 277).
  O Lord, rebuke me not (Croft), Ex. 149 (p. 251).

Anthems (*cont.*):
  O Lord, the world's saviour (W. Mundy), Ex. 51 (p. 63).
  O praise God in his holiness (Purcell), Ex. 202 (p. 391).
  O praise the Lord (Batten), Ex. 195 (p. 387).
  Out of the deep (Purcell), Ex. 205 (p. 392).
  Rejoice in the Lord always (16th cent.), Ex. 49 (p. 62).
  Save me, O God (Blow), Ex. 115 (p. 181).
  Thy beauty, O Israel (Wise), Ex. 118 (p. 184).
Arne, Thomas Augustine:
  O come, O come, my dearest (*The Fall of Phaeton*), Ex. 151 (p. 259).
Aston, Hugh:
  Te Deum Mass, Ex. 38 (p. 40).
'As y lay upon a nyȝt' (15th cent.), Ex. 171 (p. 367).
Attwood, Thomas:
  Let the words of my mouth, Ex. 155 (p. 278).

Balletts, *see* Madrigals and balletts.
Bateson, Thomas:
  Hark, hear you not? (Oriana's farewell), Ex. 76 (p. 113).
Batten, Adrian:
  O praise the Lord, Ex. 195 (p. 387).
Battishill, Jonathan:
  O Lord, look down from heaven, Ex. 154 (p. 277).
Bennet, John:
  O grief, where shall poor grief? Ex. 75 (p. 111).
Bennett, William Sterndale:
  The Naiads, Ex. 165 (p. 311).
Blitheman, William:
  Te Deum, Ex. 55 (p. 67).
Blow, John:
  Cantate Domino, Ex. 116 (p. 181).
  How doth the city sit solitary, Ex. 114 (p. 180).
  My God, my God, look upon me, Ex. 113 (p. 179).
  O Nigrocella (The fair lover and his black mistress), Ex. 133 (p. 208).
  Save me, O God, Ex. 115 (p. 181).
  Venus and Adonis, Exs. 129–30 (p. 202), Ex. 204 (p. 392).
Boyce, William:
  Symphony No. 1 in B♭ major, Ex. 152 (p. 262).
Browne, John:
  Salve regina, Ex. 30 (p. 33).
  Stabat mater, Ex. 31 (p. 34).
Bull, John:
  Variations on 'Walsingham', Ex. 94 (p. 144).
Byrd, William:
  Bow thine ear, Ex. 206 (p. 393).
  Civitas sancti tui, Ex. 206 (p. 393).
  Domine, tu iurasti, Ex. 60 (p. 91).
  Haec dies, Ex. 62 (p. 94).
  Mass for three voices, Ex. 58 (p. 88).
  O lux, beata Trinitas, Ex. 63 (p. 94).
  O quam suavis est, Ex. 61 (p. 93).
  Pavana, the Earle of Salisbury, Ex. 93 (p. 140).
  Penelope that longed for the sight, Ex. 197 (p. 388).

Sed tu, Domine, qui non derelinquis, Ex. 196 (p. 387).
Vigilate, nescitis enim, Ex. 59 (p. 90).

Campian, Thomas:
  There is a garden in her face, Ex. 89 (p. 135).
Cantatas, Choral, *see* Oratorios.
Carlton, Richard:
  Calm was the air, Ex. 81 (p. 124).
Carols:
  As y lay upon a nyȝt (15th cent.), Ex. 171 (p. 367).
  Deo gracias (Agincourt song, 15th cent.), Exs. 18–19 (p. 23).
  Now wel may we merthis make (15th cent.), Ex. 20 (p. 24).
Child, William:
  O bone Jesu, Ex. 102 (p. 159).
  Service in D major, Ex. 100 (p. 158).
  Service in E minor, Ex. 101 (p. 158).
Clementi, Muzio:
  Sonata in D major, Op. 40, No. 3, Ex. 159 (p. 290).
Concertos, *see* Orchestral works.
Coprario, John:
  Fantasia in four parts, Exs. 96–7 (pp. 146–7).
Cornyshe, William:
  Salve regina, Exs. 32–3 (p. 35).
Croft, William:
  O Lord, rebuke me not, Ex. 149 (p. 251).
Crotch, William:
  My God, my God, look upon me, Ex. 156 (p. 279).

Damett, Thomas:
  Gloria, Ex. 21 (p. 24).
Dances (*see also* Folk-tunes):
  Anon. (13th cent.), Exs. 16–17 (pp. 15–16).
  Bourrée (Purcell), Ex. 128 (p. 200).
  Pavana, the Earle of Salisbury (Byrd), Ex. 93 (p. 140).
Danyel, John:
  Grief, keep within (Funeral tears), Ex. 92 (p. 136).
Davy, Richard:
  Passion according to St. Matthew, The, Ex. 34 (p. 36).
'Deo gracias' (Agincourt song, 15th cent.), Exs. 18–19 (p. 23).
Dering, Richard:
  O vos omnes, Ex. 72 (p. 106).
Dowland, John:
  Awake, sweet love, Ex. 84 (p. 131).
  Come away, sweet love, Ex. 85 (p. 131).
  Come, heavy Sleep, Ex. 86 (p. 132).
  Welcome, black night, Ex. 87 (p. 132).
Dunstable, John:
  Ascendit Christus, Ex. 29 (p. 32).
  Crux fidelis, Ex. 26 (p. 29).
  Kyrie eleison, Ex. 27 (p. 30).
  Praeco praeeminentiae, Ex. 28 (p. 31).
  Quam pulcra es, Ex. 25 (p. 29).

Eccles, John:
  Don Quixote, The Comical History of, Ex. 131 (p. 203).
'Edi beo thu hevene quene' (13th cent.), Ex. 9 (p. 10).
English descant (13th–14th cent.), Exs. 10–11 (pp. 11–12).

Fantasias for viols:
  Coprario, Exs. 96–7 (pp. 146–7).
  Jenkins, Ex. 110 (p. 168).
  Lawes (W.), Exs. 107–9 (pp. 166–7).
  Locke, Exs. 111–12 (p. 169).
  Lupo, Ex. 98 (p. 148).
  Purcell, Exs. 135–6 (pp. 211–12).
Farnaby, Giles:
  Giles Farnaby's Dreame, Ex. 95 (p. 145).
Farrant, Richard:
  Hide not thou thy face, Ex. 50 (p. 62).
Fayrfax, Robert:
  Albanus Mass, Ex. 36 (p. 38).
  Regali Mass, Ex. 35 (p. 37).
Field, John:
  Nocturne in A major, Ex. 158 (p. 289).
Folk-tunes (*see also* Carols):
  A chuachag nan craobh, Ex. 189 (p. 380).
  Admiral Benbow, Ex. 170 (p. 366).
  Bonny sweet robin, Ex. 173 (p. 369).
  Ca' the yowes, Ex. 184 (p. 377).
  Elorelo, Ex. 190 (p. 380).
  Goddesses, Ex. 169 (p. 366).
  Greensleeves, Ex. 172 (p. 369).
  Gwenith Gwyn, Ex. 180 (p. 375).
  If the sea were ink, Ex. 192 (p. 383).
  I'll bid my heart be still, Ex. 185 (p. 377).
  It is not the tear, Ex. 191 (p. 383).
  Katherine Ogie, Ex. 183 (p. 376).
  Lay his sword by his side, Ex. 192 (p. 383).
  Londonderry Air, Ex. 193 (p. 384).
  Mo chailin dileas donn, Ex. 188 (p. 379).
  Och o ro u, Ex. 187 (p. 379).
  O cuckoo of the grove, Ex. 189 (p. 380).
  Pall Mall, Ex. 177 (p. 371).
  Portsmouth, Ex. 176 (p. 371).
  Pretty Polly Oliver, Ex. 175 (p. 370).
  Quodling's delight, Ex. 169 (p. 366).
  Sellenger's Round, Ex. 174 (p. 369).
  The boys of Wexford, Ex. 194 (p. 384).
  The bridegroom grat, Ex. 186 (p. 377).
  The Brume o' the Cowdenknowes, Ex. 181 (p. 376).
  The flight of the earls, Ex. 194 (p. 384).
  The red piper's melody, Ex. 179 (p. 374).
  The sheep under the snow, Ex. 178 (p. 373).
  The sixpence, Ex. 191 (p. 383).

Gibbons, Christopher:
  Above the stars my Saviour dwells, Ex. 99 (p. 157).

Gibbons, Orlando:
Dainty fine bird that art encaged, Ex. 79 (p. 119).
Glorious and powerful God, Ex. 66 (p. 98).
Hosanna to the Son of David, Ex. 64 (p. 96).
If ye be risen again with Christ, Ex. 199 (p. 389).
O Lord, in thy wrath rebuke me not, Ex. 65 (p. 97).
Goss, John:
Lord, let me know mine end, Ex. 161 (p. 299).
Greene, Maurice:
Lord, how long wilt thou be angry? Ex. 150 (p. 254).

Handel, George Frideric:
Concerti grossi, Op. 6, No. 1, Ex. 142 (p. 227).
— No. 6, Ex. 143 (p. 228).
Hercules, Ex. 146 (p. 234).
Joshua, Ex. 145 (p. 231).
L'Allegro, Ex. 148 (p. 240).
Teseo, Ex. 140 (p. 224).
Theodora, Ex. 144 (p. 231).
Tolomeo, Ex. 141 (p. 226).
Triumph of Time and Truth, The, Ex. 147 (p. 236).
Hilton, John (the younger):
Now is the summer springing, Ex. 106 (p. 164).
Humfrey, Pelham:
Like as the hart, Ex. 117 (p. 182).

Jenkins, John:
Fantasia in four parts, Ex. 110 (p. 168).
Jones, Robert:
Dainty, dainty, dainty darling, Ex. 90 (p. 135).
Go to bed, sweet muse, Ex. 91 (p. 136).

Keyboard works:
Eterne rex altissime (Redford), Ex. 56 (p. 69).
Giles Farnaby's Dreame (Farnaby), Ex. 95 (p. 145).
Ground in C minor (Purcell), Ex. 139 (p. 214).
Nocturne in A major (Field), Ex. 158 (p. 289).
Pavana, the Earle of Salisbury (Byrd), Ex. 93 (p. 140).
Rejoice in the Lord always (16 cent.), Ex. 49 (p. 62).
Sonata in D major, Op. 40, No. 3 (Clementi), Ex. 159 (p. 290).
Te Deum (Blitheman), Ex. 55 (p. 67).
Variations on 'Walsingham' (Bull), Ex. 94 (p. 144).
Kirbye, George:
Ah, cruel hateful fortune, Ex. 200 (p. 390).

Lamentations:
Parsley, Ex. 54 (p. 66).
Tallis, Ex. 48 (p. 59).
White, Ex. 47 (p. 57).
Lawes, Henry:
Dearest, do not now delay me, Ex. 105 (p. 162).
Imbre lachrymarum largo, Ex. 104 (p. 161).
It is not that I love you less, Ex. 103 (p. 161).
Lawes, William:
Fantasia in six parts, Exs. 107–9 (pp. 166–7).

Locke, Matthew:
    Suite No. 2 for viols, Ex. 112 (p. 169).
    Suite No. 5 for viols, Ex. 111 (p. 169).
Loder, Edward James:
    The brooklet, Ex. 164 (p. 309).
Lupo, Thomas:
    Fantasia in three parts, Ex. 98 (p. 148).
Lute songs, *see* Solo songs.

Madrigals and balletts:
    Ah, cruel hateful fortune (Kirbye), Ex. 200 (p. 390).
    All pleasure is of this condition (Wilbye), Ex. 73 (p. 109).
    Calm was the air (Carlton), Ex. 81 (p. 124).
    Cease sorrows now (Weelkes), Ex. 78 (p. 116).
    Dainty fine bird that art encaged (O. Gibbons), Ex. 79 (p. 119).
    Happy, Oh! happy he (Wilbye), Ex. 74 (p. 110).
    Hark, hear you not? (Bateson), Ex. 76 (p. 113).
    Hence, Care, thou art too cruel (Weelkes), Ex. 77 (p. 115).
    Now is the summer springing (Hilton), Ex. 106 (p. 164).
    Of all the birds that I have heard (J. Mundy), Ex. 82 (p. 126).
    O grief, where shall poor grief? (Bennet), Ex. 75 (p. 111).
    O ye roses (Pearsall), Ex. 163 (p. 306).
    Penelope that longed for the sight (Byrd), Ex. 197 (p. 388).
    What saith my dainty darling? (Morley), Ex. 80 (p. 121).
'Martyrs' (hymn-tune), Ex. 207 (p. 397).
Masques, *see* Operas and stage music.
Masses:
    Albanus (Fayrfax), Ex. 36 (p. 38).
    Corona Spinea (Taverner), Exs. 40–1, 43 (pp. 42–4).
    Euge bone (Tye), Ex. 57 (p. 70).
    'French' (Shepherd), Ex. 53 (p. 65).
    O quam suavis (16th cent.), Ex. 37 (p. 39).
    Regali (Fayrfax), Ex. 35 (p. 37).
    Te Deum (Aston), Ex. 38 (p. 40).
    Three-part (Byrd), Ex. 58 (p. 88).
    Western Wynde, The (Taverner), Ex. 42 (p. 43).
    — (Tye), Ex. 44 (p. 53).
Mass movements (15th cent.):
    Credo (Power), Ex. 23 (p. 27).
    Gloria (Damett), Ex. 21 (p. 24).
    Gloria (Pycard), Ex. 22 (p. 25).
    Kyrie eleison (Dunstable), Ex. 27 (p. 30).
Milton, John:
    If that a sinner's sighs, Ex. 203 (p. 392).
Morley, Thomas:
    Agnus Dei, Ex. 69 (p. 102).
    What saith my dainty darling? Ex. 80 (p. 121).
Motets:
    Absterge, Domine (Tallis), Ex. 198 (p. 388).
    Agnus Dei (Morley), Ex. 69 (p. 102).
    Ascendit Christus (Dunstable), Ex. 29 (p. 32).
    Cantate Domino (Blow), Ex. 116 (p. 181).
    Civitas sancti tui (Byrd), Ex. 206 (p. 393).
    Crux fidelis (Dunstable), Ex. 26 (p. 29).

Domine, tu iurasti (Byrd), Ex. 60 (p. 91).
Haec dies (Byrd), Ex. 62 (p. 94).
Iste est Joannes (Philips), Ex. 70 (p. 103).
Jehova, quam multi sunt (Purcell), Ex. 124 (p. 193).
Miserere mei, Deus (Tye), Ex. 45 (p. 54).
O bone Jesu (Child), Ex. 102 (p. 159).
O lux, beata Trinitas (Byrd), Ex. 63 (p. 94).
Omnes gentes plaudite manibus (Tye), Ex. 46 (p. 55).
O quam suavis est (Byrd), Ex. 61 (p. 93).
O virum admirabilem (Philips), Ex. 71 (p. 104).
O vos omnes (Dering), Ex. 72 (p. 106).
Praeco praeeminentiae (Dunstable), Ex. 28 (p. 31).
Puellare gremium (14th cent.), Exs. 13–14 (p. 13).
Quam pulcra es (Dunstable), Ex. 25 (p. 29).
Quemadmodum (Taverner), Ex. 39 (p. 41).
Salve regina (Browne), Ex. 30 (p. 33).
Salve regina (Cornyshe), Exs. 32–3 (p. 35).
Sed tu, Domine, qui non derelinquis (Byrd), Ex. 196 (p. 387).
Stabat mater (Browne), Ex. 31 (p. 34).
Vigilate, nescitis enim (Byrd), Ex. 59 (p. 90).
Mundy, John:
Of all the birds that I have heard, Ex. 82 (p. 126).
Mundy, William:
O Lord, I bow the knees, Ex. 52 (p. 63).
O Lord, the world's saviour, Ex. 51 (p. 63).

'Now wel may we merthis make' (15th cent.), Ex. 20 (p. 24).

Operas and stage music:
Dido and Aeneas (Purcell), Ex. 125 (p. 195).
Dioclesian (Purcell), Ex. 126 (p. 196).
Don Quixote, The Comical History of (Eccles), Ex. 131 (p. 203).
Fall of Phaeton, The (Arne), Ex. 151 (p. 259).
Faust (Pierson), Ex. 162 (p. 304).
King Arthur (Purcell), Ex. 127 (p. 197).
Mikado, The (Sullivan), Ex. 166 (p. 323).
Much Ado about Nothing (Stanford), Ex. 168 (p. 336).
Old Bachelor, The (Purcell), Ex. 128 (p. 200).
Teseo (Handel), Ex. 140 (p. 224).
Tolomeo (Handel), Ex. 141 (p. 226).
Venus and Adonis (Blow), Exs. 129–30 (p. 202), Ex. 204 (p. 392).
Oratorios and choral cantatas:
Hercules (Handel), Ex. 146 (p. 234).
Joshua (Handel), Ex. 145 (p. 231).
L'Allegro (Handel), Ex. 148 (p. 240).
Theodora (Handel), Ex. 144 (p. 231).
Triumph of Time and Truth, The (Handel), Ex. 147 (p. 236).
War and Peace (Parry), Ex. 167 (p. 332).
Orchestral works:
Concerti grossi, Op. 6 (Handel), Exs. 142–3 (pp. 227–8).
Naiads, The (Bennett), Ex. 165 (p. 311).
Symphony No. 1 in B♭ major (Boyce), Ex. 152 (p. 262).
Organ solos, see Keyboard works.

Parry, Charles Hubert Hastings:
  War and Peace, Ex. 167 (p. 332).
Parsley, Osbert:
  Lamentations, Ex. 54 (p. 66).
Parsons, Robert:
  Pandolpho, Ex. 83 (p. 129).
Passion music:
  St. Luke (15th cent.), Ex. 24 (p. 27).
  St. Matthew (Davy), Ex. 34 (p. 36).
Pearsall, Robert Lucas:
  O ye roses, Ex. 163 (p. 306).
Philips, Peter:
  Iste est Joannes, Ex. 70 (p. 103).
  O virum admirabilem, Ex. 71 (p. 104).
Piano solos, *see* Keyboard music.
Pierson, Henry Hugo:
  Faust, Ex. 162 (p. 304).
Power, Leonel:
  Credo, Ex. 23 (p. 27).
'Puellare gremium' (14th cent.), Exs. 13–14 (p. 13).
Purcell, Henry:
  Ah! few and full of sorrow, Ex. 123 (p. 192).
  Dido and Aeneas, Ex. 125 (p. 195).
  Dioclesian, Ex. 126 (p. 196).
  Early, O Lord, my fainting soul, Ex. 122 (p. 191).
  Elegy on the death of Mr. John Playford, Ex. 134 (p. 210).
  Evening Hymn, Ex. 121 (p. 191).
  Fantasias in four parts, No. 1, Ex. 136 (p. 212).
  — No. 5, Ex. 135 (p. 211).
  Gentle shepherds, you that know, Ex. 134 (p. 210).
  Ground in C minor, Ex. 139 (p. 214).
  Hear my prayer, O Lord, Ex. 119 (p. 186).
  In the midst of life, Ex. 120 (p. 188).
  Jehova, quam multi sunt, Ex. 124 (p. 193).
  King Arthur, Ex. 127 (p. 197).
  Lord, how long wilt thou be angry? Ex. 201 (p. 390).
  Now that the sun, Ex. 121 (p. 191).
  Old Bachelor, The, Ex. 128 (p. 200).
  O praise God in his holiness, Ex. 202 (p. 391).
  Out of the deep, Ex. 205 (p. 392).
  Sonatas of IV Parts, No. 4, Ex. 137 (p. 213).
  — No. 7, Ex. 138 (p. 213).
  What, what shall be done in behalf of the man? Ex. 132 (p. 204).
Pycard:
  Gloria, Ex. 22 (p. 25).

Redford, John:
  Eterne rex altissime, Ex. 56 (p. 69).
'Rejoice in the Lord always' (16th cent.), Ex. 49 (p. 62).
'Rosa fragrans' (13th cent.), Ex. 6 (p. 9).
Rosseter, Philip:
  And would you see my mistress' face? Ex. 88 (p. 134).

'Salve virgo virginum' (13th cent.), Exs. 7–8 (pp. 9–10).

'Sanctus et aeternus Deus' (14th cent.), Ex. 12 (p. 12).
Services:
    Child in D major, Ex. 100 (p. 158).
    Child in E minor, Ex. 101 (p. 158).
Shepherd, John:
    'French Mass', Ex. 53 (p. 65).
Solo songs and arias (*see also* Folk-tunes):
    And now another day is gone (S. Wesley), Ex. 153 (p. 275).
    And would you see my mistress' face? (Rosseter), Ex. 88 (p. 134).
    Awake, sweet love (Dowland), Ex. 84 (p. 131).
    Come away, sweet love (Dowland), Ex. 85 (p. 131).
    Come, heavy Sleep (Dowland), Ex. 86 (p. 132).
    Couch'd in the dark and silent grave (Eccles), Ex. 131 (p. 203).
    Dainty, dainty, dainty darling (Jones), Ex. 90 (p. 135).
    Dearest, do not now delay me (H. Lawes), Ex. 105 (p. 162).
    Gentle shepherds, you that know (Purcell), Ex. 134 (p. 210).
    Go to bed, sweet muse (Jones), Ex. 91 (p. 136).
    Grief, keep within (Danyel), Ex. 92 (p. 136).
    I heard a brooklet gushing (Loder), Ex. 164 (p. 309).
    Imbre lachrymarum largo (H. Lawes), Ex. 104 (p. 161).
    It is not that I love you less (H. Lawes), Ex. 103 (p. 161).
    Loathsome urns, disclose your treasure (Handel), Ex. 147 (p. 236).
    Now that the sun (Purcell), Ex. 121 (p. 191).
    O come, O come, my dearest (Arne), Ex. 151 (p. 259).
    O Nigrocella (Blow), Ex. 133 (p. 208).
    Pandolpho (Parsons), Ex. 83 (p. 129).
    Stille amare (Handel), Ex. 141 (p. 226).
    The brooklet (Loder), Ex. 164 (p. 309).
    There is a garden in her face (Campian), Ex. 89 (p. 135).
    Welcome, black night (Dowland), Ex. 87 (p. 132).
    Worldes blis ne last no throwe (13th cent.), Ex. 2 (p. 6).
Stage music, *see* Operas.
Stanford, Charles Villiers:
    Much Ado about Nothing, Ex. 168 (p. 336).
Sullivan, Arthur Seymour:
    The Mikado, Ex. 166 (p. 323).
'Sumer is icumen in' (13th cent.), Exs. 3–5 (pp. 7–8).
Symphonies, *see* Orchestral works.

Tallis, Thomas:
    Absterge, Domine, Ex. 198 (p. 388).
    Lamentations, Ex. 48 (p. 59).
Taverner, John:
    Corona Spinea Mass, Exs. 40–1, 43 (pp. 42–4).
    Quemadmodum, Ex. 39 (p. 41).
    Western Wynde Mass, *The*, Ex. 42 (p. 43).
Te Deum (13th cent.), Ex. 10 (p. 11).
Tye, Christopher:
    Euge bone Mass, Ex. 57 (p. 70).
    Miserere mei, Domine, Ex. 45 (p. 54).
    Omnes gentes plaudite manibus, Ex. 46 (p. 55).
    Western Wynde Mass, *The*, Ex. 44 (p. 53).

'Ut tuo propitiatus' (12th cent.), Ex. 1 (p. 5).

Webbe, Samuel:
  Discord, dire sister, Ex. 157 (p. 283).
Weelkes, Thomas:
  Cease sorrows now, Ex. 78 (p. 116).
  Hence, Care, thou art too cruel, Ex. 77 (p. 115).
  O Lord, arise into thy resting place, Ex. 67 (p. 99).
Wesley, Samuel:
  And now another day is gone, Ex. 153 (p. 275).
Wesley, Samuel Sebastian:
  Cast me not away, Ex. 160 (p. 297).
White, Robert:
  Lamentations, Ex. 47 (p. 57).
Wilbye, John:
  All pleasure is of this condition, Ex. 73 (p. 109).
  Happy, Oh! happy he, Ex. 74 (p. 110).
  O God, the rock of my whole strength, Ex. 68 (p. 101).
Wise, Michael:
  Thy beauty, O Israel, Ex. 118 (p. 184).
Worldes blis ne last no throwe (13th cent.), Ex. 2 (p. 6).

GENERAL INDEX

Abel, Karl Friedrich, 249, 274.

'Abyde y hope hit be the beste' (15th cent.), 46.

Academy of Ancient Music, 242, 248.

Adler, Guido, 2 n.4.

Aelred, Abbot of Rievaulx, 3.

Agincourt song (15th cent.), 23–4, 367.

Alanus, Johannes, 20.

'Alas, departynge is ground of woo' (15th cent.), 22.

Aldrich, Henry, 174, 184.

Aleyn, 20.

Allen, Hugh Percy, viii, 344.

Allison, Richard, 397.

Alwood, Richard, 68, 390.

Ambros, August Wilhelm, 395.

'A, my dere son' (16th cent.), 41.

Ancient Concerts, 273, 294.

Andrews, Hilda, 84 n.5, 142 n.2.

'Angelus ad virginem' (14th cent.), 14.

Anne, Queen, 207–8, 221.

Anonymus of the British Museum (Anonymus IV), 4–5, 11–12.

Anthems:

  Mid-16th cent., 45, 51, 56–8, 61–5.

  Late 16th and early 17th cent., 81–2, 89–90, 96–102, 106–7.

  Mid-17th cent., 156–60.

  Late 17th cent., 175–6, 178–90.

  Early 18th cent., 238, 240, 250–7.

  Late 18th cent., 276–81.

  Early 19th cent., 296–301.

  Late 19th cent., 329–30.

Above the stars my Saviour dwells (C. Gibbons), 157.

Ah, helpless wretch (W. Mundy), 64.

Ah, helpless wretch (Ravenscroft), 106.

Almighty God, who by the leading of a star (Bull), 107.

And I heard a great voice (Blow), 179.

Arise, shine (Greene), 253.

Ascribe unto the Lord (Travers), 256.

Awake and stand up (East), 107.

Awake up my glory (Wise), 183.

Behold, I bring you glad tidings (Greene), 255 n.2.

Behold, I bring you glad tidings (Purcell), 187.

Behold, thou hast made my days as it were a span long (O. Gibbons), 96.

Be merciful unto me (Croft), 252.

Anthems (cont.):

  Be merciful unto me, O Lord (Purcell), 189.

  Blessed are they that fear the Lord (Purcell), 189.

  Blessed be the God and Father (S. S. Wesley), 297.

  Blessed is he whose unrighteousness is forgiven (Purcell), 189.

  Blessing and glory (Boyce), 256.

  Bow thine ear (Byrd), 90, 393.

  Brother, thou art gone before us (Goss), 299 n.1.

  By the waters of Babylon (Boyce), 255.

  By the waters of Babylon (Humfrey), 182.

  Call to remembrance (Battishill), 276–7.

  Cast me not away (S. S. Wesley), 297–8.

  Come and let us return (Goss), 299.

  Come, holy Ghost (Attwood), 278.

  Deliver me from my enemies, O God (Parsons), 65.

  From depth of sin (Byrd), 90.

  From Virgin pure this day did spring (Byrd), 95.

  Give the King thy judgements (Boyce), 255.

  Give the King thy judgements (Croft), 250.

  Glorious and powerful God (O. Gibbons), 97–8.

  God is gone up with a merry noise (Croft), 250.

  God is our hope and strength (Blow), 179.

  God is our hope and strength (Crotch), 279.

  God is our hope and strength (Greene), 253.

  Have mercy upon me, O God (Humfrey), 182.

  Hearken unto me, ye holy children (Greene), 253.

  Hear me, O God (Golding), 185.

  Hear my crying (Weldon), 253.

  Hear my prayer, O God (Batten), 107.

  Hear my prayer, O God (Stroud), 256.

  Hear my prayer, O Lord (Croft), 252.

  Hear my prayer, O Lord (Purcell), 186, 188.

  Hear, O heavens (Humfrey), 182.

Anthems (*cont.*):
Hide not thou thy face (Farrant), 62.
Holy, Lord God Almighty (Bateson), 101.
Hosanna to the Son of David (Gibbons), 96.
Hosanna to the Son of David (Weelkes), 99.
How dear are thy counsels (Crotch), 279.
How doth the city sit solitary (Blow), 180.
How doth the city sit solitary (Locke), 156.
How long wilt thou forget me? (Clarke), 185.
How long wilt thou forget me, O Lord? (Greene), 253.
I beheld and lo, a great multitude (Blow), 179.
I call and cry (Tallis), 60, 82.
If that a sinner's sighs (Milton), 391–2.
If the Lord himself had not been on our side (Walmisley), 300.
If we believe that Jesus died (Boyce), 255.
If we believe that Jesus died (Goss), 299.
If ye be risen again with Christ (O. Gibbons), 388–9.
In the midst of life (Purcell), 188.
In thee, O Lord, have I put my trust (Weldon), 252–3.
I saw the Lord (Stainer), 330.
Is it nothing to you? (Ouseley), 301.
I was in the spirit (Blow), 179.
I will arise (Creyghton), 184.
I will exalt thee (Tye), 57.
I will love thee, O Lord (Clarke), 185.
I will sing of thy power (Greene), 253.
Let God arise (Ford), 107.
Let God arise (Ward), 106.
Let my complaint come before thee (Greene), 253.
Let the words of my mouth (Attwood), 278.
Lift up thine eyes (Goss), 299.
Lift up your heads (O. Gibbons), 96–7.
Like as the hart (Humfrey), 182–3.
Lord, for thy tender mercies' sake (? Tye), 62.
Lord, how long wilt thou be angry? (Greene), 253–4.
Lord, how long wilt thou be angry? (Purcell), 390.

Anthems (*cont.*):
Lord, let me know mine end (Goss), 299–300.
Lord, let me know mine end (Greene), 253–4, 257.
Lord, let me know mine end (Locke), 156.
Lord, what is man (Boyce), 256 *n.* 1.
Lullaby, my sweet little baby (Byrd), 95.
Man that is born of a woman (Purcell), 188.
My God, my God, look upon me (Blow), 179–80.
My God, my God, look upon me (Crotch), 279–80.
My griefs are full (Ford), 107.
My heart is inditing (Purcell), 188.
Not unto us, O Lord (Walmisley), 300.
O be joyful unto the Lord (Arnold), 271.
O clap your hands (O. Gibbons), 96–7.
O clap your hands (Greene), 253.
O give thanks (Boyce), 255.
O give thanks (Croft), 250.
O give thanks (Hayes), 256.
O give thanks unto the Lord (Locke), 156.
O God, for thy name's sake (Franctynge), 65.
O God, the rock of my whole strength (Wilbye), 101.
O God, thou hast cast us out (Purcell), 186.
O God, thou hast cast us out (Weldon), 252.
O God, wherefore art thou absent? (Blow), 179.
O God, who by the leading of a star (Attwood), 278.
O God, wonderful art thou (Tomkins), 100.
O had I wings (Milton), 107.
O how glorious art thou (White), 58.
O Jesu, look (Kirbye), 107.
O Jesu meek (Ravenscroft), 106.
O Lord, arise into thy resting place (Weelkes), 99.
O Lord, give thy holy spirit (Tallis), 60.
O Lord God of hosts (Golding), 185.
O Lord God of hosts (Purcell), 189.
O Lord God of my salvation (Croft), 252.
O Lord, I bow the knees (W. Mundy), 63.

Anthems (cont.):
O Lord, I have sinned (Blow), 179.
O Lord, in thy wrath rebuke me not (O. Gibbons), 97.
O Lord, look down from heaven (Battishill), 277.
O Lord my God! (Golding), 185.
O Lord, rebuke me not (Croft), 251, 390.
O Lord, the maker of all thing (? Henry VIII), 45.
O Lord, the maker of all thing (W. Mundy), 45, 63.
O Lord, the world's saviour (W. Mundy), 63.
O Lord, thou art my God (S. S. Wesley), 297–9.
O Lord, thou hast searched me out (Croft), 252.
O Lord, turn thy wrath (Byrd), 90.
O praise God in his holiness (Purcell), 188, 391.
O praise God in his holiness (White), 58.
O praise the Lord (Batten), 387.
O praise the Lord, all ye heathen (Tomkins), 100.
O praise the Lord of heaven (Greene), 255 n. 2.
O Saviour of the world (Goss), 299.
O sing unto God (Blow), 179.
O sing unto the Lord (Purcell), 189.
O that I knew where I might find him (Bennett), 301.
O thou God almighty (Hooper), 107.
Out of the deep (Morley), 82, 102.
Out of the deep (Purcell), 392.
O where shall wisdom be found? (Boyce), 255.
Praise the Lord, O Jerusalem (Clarke), 185.
Praise the Lord, O Jerusalem (Hayes), 256.
Praise the Lord, O my soul (Child), 158.
Praise the Lord, O my soul (Croft), 250.
Praise the Lord, O my soul (Goss), 299.
Praise the Lord, ye children (Tye), 57.
Put me not to rebuke (Croft), 252.
Rejoice in the Lord (Croft), 250.
Rejoice in the Lord alway (Purcell), 187.
Rejoice in the Lord always (16th cent.), 61, 67.
Remember not, Lord, our offences (Purcell), 186.

Anthems (cont.):
Save me, O God (Blow), 180–1.
Save me, O God (Boyce), 255.
See, see, the Word is incarnate (O. Gibbons), 98.
Sing joyfully unto God (Byrd), 89.
Sing unto the Lord a new song (Greene), 253.
Sing we merrily (Blow), 179.
Sing we merrily unto God (Child), 158.
Sing we merrily unto God our strength (Byrd), 89.
Teach me, O Lord (Rogers), 159.
Teach me thy way, O Lord (Attwood), 278.
The almighty Trinity (Bennet), 101.
The heavens declare the glory of God (Croft), 250.
The Lord bless us (White), 58.
The Lord, even the most mighty God, hath spoken (Crotch), 279.
The Lord, even the most mighty God, hath spoken (Greene), 253.
The Lord is my light (W. Lawes), 156.
The ways of Zion do mourn (Wise), 184.
The wilderness (Goss), 299.
The wilderness (S. S. Wesley), 297.
They that go down to the sea in ships (Attwood), 278.
They that go down to the sea in ships (Purcell), 188.
Thou art my king, O God (Humfrey), 182.
Thou knowest, Lord, the secrets of our hearts (Purcell), 188.
Thou, O God, art praised in Zion (S. Wesley), 276.
Thou wilt keep him in perfect peace (S. S. Wesley), 297.
Through thee will we overthrow our enemies (Tomkins), 82.
Thy beauty, O Israel (Wise), 184.
Thy word is a lantern (Purcell), 187.
Turn thee unto me (Boyce), 255.
Turn ye to me (Blow), 181.
Unto the hills mine eyes I lift (Byrd), 91.
Wash me throughly (S. S. Wesley), 297.
Who can tell how oft he offendeth? (Weldon), 252.
Who is this that cometh? (Arnold), 281.
Why do the heathen? (Purcell), 189.
see also Motets.

Apel, Willi, 8 n.3, 15 n.3, 16 n.1, n.3, 17 n.1, 28 n.3, 47 n.1, 142 n.1.

Aristophanes, 333.

Arkwright, Godfrey Edward Pellew: on the authorship of 'Lord, for thy tender mercies' sake', 63 n.1; on Arne, 245 n.1; cited, 63 n.2, 79 n.2, 128, 165 n.1.

Arne, Michael, 267.

Arne, Thomas Augustine: life, 244–5; works, 258–60, 262–3; supported Royal Society of Musicians, 248; performances in Dublin, 249; subscribed to Roseingrave's edition of Scarlatti's sonatas, 263; operas adapted by Bishop, 268; overture to *Artaxerxes* arranged as an anthem by Arnold, 271; cited, 243, 246–7, 261, 371, 400.

ORATORIOS:
Death of Abel, The, 245, 258.
Judith, 245, 258, 280.

SONGS:
Adorn'd with ev'ry matchless grace, 258.
Arise, sweet messenger of morn, 259.
Blow, blow, thou winter wind, 259.
Conquest is not to bestow, 258.
Hail, immortal Bacchus, 258.
How cheerful along the gay mead (Morning hymn of Eve), 258.
Let not rage, thy bosom firing, 260.
Not on beds of fading flow'rs, 259.
O come, O come, my dearest, 259.
O much lov'd son, 260.
Rule Britannia, 258, 287.
Sleep, gentle cherub, 258.
The soldier tir'd of war's alarms, 260.
Under the greenwood tree, 259.
Vain is beauty's gaudy flow'r, 258.
Vengeance, O come inspire me, 259.
Water parted from the sea, 260.
Where the bee sucks, 259.

STAGE MUSIC:
Alfred, 258–9.
Artaxerxes, 245, 260, 271.
As You Like it, 245, 259.
Comus, 245, 259.
Elfrida, 260.
Fairy Prince, The, 260.
Fall of Phaeton, The, 259.
Judgment of Paris, The, 263.
Tempest, The, 245, 259.
Trio Sonatas, 263.

Arnold, Samuel: life, 265; arranged overture to Arne's *Artaxerxes* as an anthem, 271; edited cathedral music, 272.

ANTHEMS:
O be joyful unto the Lord, 271.
Who is this that cometh? 281.

ORATORIO:
Prodigal Son, The, 265.

SONG:
Flow, thou regal purple stream, 286.

Aston, Hugh: music student at Oxford, 21; 'Hornpipe' for keyboard, 47; Masses, 39–40.

'As y lay upon a nyʒt' (15th cent.), 367.

Atkins, Ivor, 107 n.4, 193 n.1.

Atonality, 345.

Attwood, Thomas: life, 265–6; works, 276–8, 282, 286; Goss and Walmisley his pupils, 291–2; cited, 281.

ANTHEMS:
Come, holy Ghost, 278.
Let the words of my mouth, 278.
O God, who by the leading of a star, 278.
Teach me thy way, O Lord, 278.
They that go down to the sea in ships, 278.

GLEE:
Hark the curfew's solemn sound, 282.

Auber, Daniel, 268.

Austin, Frederic, 246.

'Ave miles coelestis curiae' (14th cent.), 15.

Avison, Charles, 249, 263.

Ayres, *see* Lute-songs.

Babell, William, 246, 263.

Bach, Carl Philipp Emanuel, 248.

Bach, Johann Sebastian: church cantatas compared with English church music, 229; vocal writing compared with Handel's, 231–2; Burney's opinion of, 248; Samuel Wesley's enthusiasm for, 266, 270; English edition of his *Wohltemperirtes Clavier*, 268; Samuel Wesley's orchestral transcription of fugue from his *Wohltemperirtes Clavier*, book I, 287–8; Bennett compared with, 301; Passion music performed by Barnby, 330; influence on Parry, 331–2; music revived by Whittaker and Allen, 344; cited, 213, 241, 395.

Bach, John Christian, 249, 274, 288.

Bache, Francis Edward, 315.

Bagpipes, 381.

Balfe, Michael William: life, 292; works, 296, 303–4, 308; cited, 291, 295.

Balfe (*cont.*):
  OPERAS:
    Bohemian Girl, The, 292, 303–4.
    Rose of Castille, The, 292, 303–4.
    Satanella, 292.
    Siege of Rochelle, The, 292.
    Talismano, Il, 296.
Balfour, David, 380 n. 2.
Ballad operas, 246–7, 284–7, 365, 370.
Ballads, 366–7.
Ballet, 344–5, 352–4, 357.
  Checkmate (Bliss), 354.
  Horoscope (Lambert), 357.
  Job (Vaughan Williams), 345.
  Luna Park (Berners), 352.
  Triumph of Neptune, The (Berners), 352.
  Wedding Bouquet, A (Berners), 352.
Balletts, 77, 117, 121, 164–5.
  Fly, Philomel (Hilton), 164.
  Hark, all ye lovely saints above (Weelkes), 117.
  I saw my lovely Phillis (Morley), 121.
  Lady, those cherries plenty (Morley), 121.
  Lady, your eye my love enforced (Weelkes), 117.
  Leave alas this tormenting (Morley), 121.
  Leave off, sad Philomel (Hilton), 164.
  My bonny lass she smileth (Morley), 121.
  Now is the month of maying (Morley), 121.
  Now is the summer springing (Hilton), 164.
  On the plains fairy trains (Weelkes), 117.
  Singing alone (Morley), 121.
  To shorten winter's sadness (Weelkes), 117.
  What saith my dainty darling? (Morley), 121–2.
  When Flora frowns (Hilton), 164.
Baltzar, Thomas, 170, 178.
Banaster, Gilbert, 21.
Bandora, 79, 81, 84, 87.
Banister, John, 178.
Bantock, Granville: works, 342–3; as editor, 107 n. 1, 179 n. 7, 184 n. 3, 252 n. 2.
  CHORAL WORKS, UNACCOMPANIED:
    Atalanta in Calydon, 342.
    On Himalay, 343.
    Vanity of Vanities, 342.
  CHORAL WORKS WITH ORCHESTRA:
    Christ in the Wilderness, 342.

Bantock: Choral works with orchestra (*cont.*):
    Gethsemane, 342.
    Omar Khayyám, 342.
    Pan in Arcady, 342.
  ORCHESTRAL WORKS:
    Fifine at the Fair, 343.
    'Hebridean' symphony, 342.
    Pierrot of the Minute, The, 342.
    Witch of Atlas, The, 342.
  SONG-CYCLE:
    Sappho, 343.
Bardi, Giovanni, 152.
Bards, 1.
Barley, William, 80.
Barnard, John: *Selected Church Music,* 155–6; works printed in this collection, 60, 63, 65, 90, 106, 393.
Barnby, Joseph, 316, 329–30.
Barnett, John, 291, 295, 304.
Barrett, John, 215.
Bartleman, James, 231.
Bateson, Thomas: life, 73; works, 101, 111–14, 127–8; cited, 123.
  ANTHEM:
    Holy, Lord God Almighty, 101.
  MADRIGALS:
    And must I needs depart then, 112.
    Beauty is a lovely sweet, 112.
    Come follow me, fair nymphs, 113.
    Dame Venus hence to Paphos go, 113.
    Hark, hear you not? 112–14, 128.
    Live not, poor bloom, 113.
    Music some think no music is, 112.
    Sadness, sit down, 112.
    Strange were the life, 112.
    Sweet Gemma, 112.
    Sweet, those trammels of your hair, 112.
    The nightingale, 112.
    Thirsis, on his fair Phillis' breast reclining, 112.
    When Oriana walked to take the air, 112, 127.
Batten, Adrian: life, 74; anthems, 107, 155, 387; organ-book, 156.
Battishill, Jonathan: life, 265; anthems, 276–8; glee, 'Amidst the myrtles', 282.
Bax, Arnold, 352.
  A rann of exile (song), 352.
  Mater, ora filium (unaccompanied motet), 352.
  November Woods (orchestra), 352.
  Overture to a Picaresque Comedy (orchestra), 352.
  Phantasy for viola and orchestra, 352.

Bax (*cont.*):
  Piano sonata No. 2 in G major, 352.
  Symphonies, 352.
Baylis, Lilian, 344.
B.B.C. Orchestra, 344.
Beale, William, 269, 282.
Beaumont, Francis, 153, 161 *n.* 2.
Bede, The Venerable, 3.
Bedford, John of Lancaster, 1st Duke of, 19.
Bedingham, 20.
Beecham, Thomas, 344.
Beethoven, Ludwig van: music to *Egmont*, 194; his opinion of Handel, 240, of Cramer, 270; cited, 223, 241, 289.
Beggar's Opera, The: 222, 246–7; arranged by Pepusch, 246, by Austin, 246, by Britten, 358; influence abroad, 394.
Benedict Biscop, 3.
Benedict, Julius, 295.
Benet, John, 20.
Bennet, John: works, 101, 111–12; cited, 73, 114, 123.
  ANTHEM:
  The almighty Trinity, 101.
  MADRIGALS:
  All creatures now are merry-minded, 111.
  Come, shepherds, follow me, 112.
  Cruel, unkind, 112.
  O grief, where shall poor grief? 111.
  O sleep, fond fancy, 112.
  O sweet grief, 111.
  Rest now, Amphion, 112.
  The hunt is up, 111.
  Thirsis, sleepest thou? 112.
  Weep, O mine eyes, 111.
  Whenas I glance, 112.
Bennett, J. R. Sterndale, 312 *n.* 1.
Bennett, William Sterndale: life, 294; works, 301–2, 305, 310–15; influence on Cowen, 327; in Leipzig, 395; cited, 252, 288, 291–2.
  CHORAL WORKS:
  May Queen, The, 294, 305.
  Woman of Samaria, The, 280, 294, 301–2.
  ORCHESTRAL WORKS:
  Naiads, The, 302, 311–12.
  Paradise and the Peri, 312–14.
  Parisina, 311.
  Piano concerto No. 3 in C minor, 311, 395.
  —— No. 4 in F minor, 312.
  Symphony in G minor, 312.
  Wood-nymphs, The, 312.
  PIANO SOLOS:
  Fountain, The, 312.

Bennett, W. S.: Piano solos (*cont.*):
  Lake, The, 312.
  Maid of Orleans, The, 313.
  Millstream, The, 312.
  Rondeau à la Polonaise, 312.
  Toccata, 312.
  SONGS:
  Mädchen mit dem rothen Mündchen, 310.
  May Dew, 310.
Benson, Arthur Christopher, 317.
Benson, Lionel, 330.
Berenclow, Bernard Martin, 209.
Berkeley, Lennox, 359.
Berlioz, Hector, 295, 314, 337.
Berners, Gerald Hugh Tyrwhitt-Wilson, Lord, 352–3.
  Fantaisie espagnole (orchestra), 352.
  Luna Park (ballet), 352.
  Triumph of Neptune, The (ballet), 352.
  Valse bourgeoises (piano duet), 352.
  Wedding Bouquet, A (ballet), 352.
Bevin, Elway, 75, 151, 155.
Binchois, Gilles, 19.
Birmingham Festival, 248.
Bishop, Henry Rowley: life, 268; works, 286–7; cited, 293, 295, 303.
Bizet, Georges, 328.
Blake, William, 359.
Bliss, Arthur, 353–4.
  Checkmate (ballet), 354.
  Clarinet quintet, 354.
  Lie Strewn the White Flocks (chorus and orchestra), 353.
  Morning Heroes (chorus and orchestra), 353.
  Olympians, The (opera), 354.
  Piano concerto, 353.
  Rout, 353.
  String quartet No. 1, 354.
Blitheman, William, 49, 67–9, 84.
Blow, John: life, 173; works, 178–82, 201–2, 206–9; master of Purcell, 172, of Croft, 243, of King, 245; as an instrumental composer, 215; use of false relations, 390, 392; harmony criticized by Burney, 393; cited, 156, 160, 175, 185, 257, 387.
Amphion Anglicus, 207–8.
  ANTHEMS:
  And I heard a great voice, 179.
  God is our hope and strength, 179.
  How doth the city sit solitary, 180.
  I beheld and lo, a great multitude, 179.
  I was in the spirit, 179.
  My God, my God, look upon me, 179–80.

Blow: Anthems (*cont.*):
  O God, wherefore art thou absent? 179.
  O Lord, I have sinned, 179.
  O sing unto God, 179.
  Save me, O God, 180–1.
  Sing we merrily, 179.
  Turn ye to me, 181.
DUETS:
  Bring, shepherds, bring the kids and lambs, 207.
  Cantate Domino, 181.
MOTETS:
  Cantate Domino, 181.
  Salvator mundi, 181.
ODES:
  Awake, awake, my lyre, 207.
  Begin the song, 209.
  My trembling song awake, 207.
SERVICES, 179.
SONGS:
  A prince so young (Song on the Duke of Gloucester), 207–8.
  Arms, arms, arms he delights in, 208.
  It is not that I love you less (The self-banished), 207.
  Musick's the cordial of a troubled breast, 209.
  Of all the torments, 207.
  O Nigrocella (The fair lover and his black mistress), 208.
  Rise, mighty monarch, 207.
  Shepherds, deck your crooks, 207.
  Venus and Adonis, 201–2, 392.
Boccaccio, Giovanni, 76.
Boieldieu, François, 268.
Bononcini, Giovanni Battista: operatic rivalry with Handel, 221–2, 244; accusation of plagiarism, 242, 248; cited, 220.
Bononcini, Marc' Antonio, 220.
Boswell, James, 247 *n.*3.
Boughton, Rutland, 348–9.
  Choral variations on folk-songs, 349.
  Early dawn (part-song), 349.
  Immortal Hour, The (opera), 348–9.
  Midnight (choral ode), 349.
  The dead Christ (song), 349.
Boulton, Harold, 372 *n.*7.
Boyce, William: life, 244; works, 255–7, 261–3; *Cathedral Music*, 62, 156, 185, 189, 244, 249, 265, 272, 393; supported Royal Society of Musicians, 248; cited, 243, 246–7, 286.
ANTHEMS:
  Blessing and glory, 256.
  By the waters of Babylon, 255.

Boyce: Anthems (*cont.*):
  Give the King thy judgements, 255.
  If we believe that Jesus died, 255.
  Lord, what is man, 256 *n.*1.
  O give thanks (4 parts), 255.
  O give thanks (8 parts), 255.
  O where shall wisdom be found? 255.
  Save me, O God, 255.
  Turn thee unto me, 255.
  Harlequin's Invasion, 261.
  Heart of oak (song), 261, 286.
  Solomon, 262.
  Symphonies, 262–3.
  Trio sonatas, 262.
Brade, William, 85 *n.*2.
Braham, John, 268, 286.
Brahms, Johannes: influence on Parry, 331, on Stanford, 334; cited, vii, 223, 241, 399.
Bramston, Richard, 21.
Brewer, John Sherren, 2 *n.*1, *n.*3.
Bridge, Frank, 350.
Bridge, John Frederick, 105 *n.*4, 120 *n.*1, 187 *n.*2, 192 *n.*3, 368 *n.*12.
Bridges, Robert, 317.
Bridgewater, Leslie, 209 *n.*1.
Bristol Festival, 302.
British National Opera Company, 344.
Britten, Benjamin, 357–9.
CHAMBER MUSIC:
  String quartet No. 1, 358.
CHORAL WORKS:
  A Boy was born, 358.
  Ceremony of Carols, A, 359.
  Hymn to St. Cecilia, 359.
  Spring Symphony, 358–9.
OPERAS:
  Albert Herring, 358.
  Beggar's Opera, The, 358.
  Peter Grimes, 358.
  Rape of Lucretia, The, 358.
SONGS:
  Illuminations, Les, 359.
  Serenade, 359.
  Seven Sonnets of Michelangelo, 359.
Britton, Thomas, 178.
Broadcasting, 344, 359.
Broadwood, Lucy, 372 *n.*5.
Brockes, Barthold Heinrich, 217, 223.
Browne, John, 33–4, 41.
Browning, Robert, 343.
Bruce, John Collingwood, 372–3.
Bukofzer, Manfred F.: on the date of 'Sumer is icumen in', 8 *n.*2; on 'English descant', 11 *n.*1–3; cited, 15 *n.*1, 18 *n.*3, 19 *n.*4, 20 *n.*1, *n.*3,

Bukofzer (*cont.*):
25 *n.* 1, 27 *n.* 1, 28 *n.* 2, 30 *n.* 1, 52 *n.* 3.
Bull, John: life, 75; works, 107, 139, 141–4; pupil of Blitheman, 49; contributor to *Teares or Lamentacions of a Sorrowfull Soule*, 81; part author of *Parthenia*, 84; represented in the 'Fitzwilliam Virginal Book', 84, in Barnard's *Selected Church Music*, 155.
ANTHEMS:
Almighty God, who by the leading of a star, 107.
Deliver me, 107.
KEYBOARD WORKS:
Salvator mundi, 143.
The king's hunt, 143.
Ut re mi fa sol la (fantasia), 142.
Ut re mi fa sol la (variations), 143–4.
Walsingham, 143–4.
Bullock, Ernest, 253 *n.* 4.
Bunting Collection, The, 381 *n.* 2, 385 *n.* 2.
Burell, 20.
Burke, Edmund, 247.
Burney, Charles: *A General History of Music*, 272–3; on Cobbold's 'With wreaths of rose and laurel', 124; on John Mundy, 126; on J. S. Bach, 232, 248; on *The Beggar's Opera*, 246; on Boyce's trio sonatas, 262; on Joseph Kelway, 263; on Thomas Roseingrave, 263–4; comparison between Elizabethan madrigals and Handel's choruses, 273 *n.* 1; on Blow's 'crudities', 393; cited, 46, 64, 66.
Burns, Robert, 378.
Bury St. Edmunds Abbey, 4.
Busoni, Ferruccio, 358.
Butcher, A. Vernon, 263 *n.* 8.
Butterworth, George Kaye, 352–3.
Byrd, William: life, 72; works, 77–9, 87–98, 102, 117–19, 129, 139–42, 144–5; granted a monopoly of music-printing, with Tallis, 48, 73; contributor to *Teares or Lamentacions of a Sorrowfull Soule*, 81; Morley's *Plaine and Easie Introduction to Practicall Musicke* dedicated to him, 83; part author of *Parthenia*, 84; one of Tomkins's madrigals dedicated to him, 125; music for viols printed in his vocal collections, 149; represented in Barnard's *Selected Church Music*, 155; Masses revived at the Brompton Oratory, 330; use of false rela-

Byrd (*cont.*):
tions, 387–8, 390, of augmented intervals, 393; cited, 51–2, 60, 70, 103, 107–8, 127, 189–90, 362, 395, 400.
ANTHEMS:
Bow thine ear, 90, 393.
From depth of sin, 90.
From Virgin pure this day did spring, 95.
Lullaby, my sweet little baby, 95.
O Lord, turn thy wrath, 90.
Sing joyfully unto God, 89.
Sing we merrily unto God our strength, 89.
Unto the hills mine eyes I lift, 91.
Cantiones Sacrae (with Tallis), 48, 72, 94–5.
—— books I & II, 72, 79, 90–1, 93, 269, 387, 393.
DUET:
Who made thee, Hob, forsake the plough, 118.
Gradualia, 72, 89, 91–3.
Great Service, 92.
KEYBOARD WORKS:
Mr. Byrd's Battle, 142.
Pavana, the Earle of Salisbury, 140.
The Bells, 142.
Ut mi re, 142.
Ut re mi fa sol la, 142.
MADRIGALS:
Come jolly swains, 118.
Penelope that longed for the sight, 387–8.
This sweet and merry month of May, 118.
Though Amaryllis dance in green, 118.
When I was otherwise than now I am, 118.
Wounded I am, 118.
Masses, 72, 88–9, 330.
MOTETS:
Alleluia, ascendit Deus, 93.
Ave verum corpus, 93.
Civitas sancti tui, 90, 393.
Diliges Dominum Deum, 95.
Domine, tu iurasti, 91.
Effuderunt sanguinem, 90.
Haec dies, 93–4.
Laetentur coeli, 91.
Laudibus in sanctis, 93.
Ne irascaris, Domine, 90.
Non vos relinquam orphanos, 91.
O admirabile commercium, 93.
O lux, beata Trinitas, 94.
O quam gloriosum, 91.
O quam suavis est, 93.

Byrd: Motets (*cont.*):
Posuerunt morticinia, 90.
Sed tu, Domine, qui non derelin-
quis, 90, 387.
Sed veni, Domine, 90.
Tristitia et anxietas, 90.
Turbarum voces, 89.
Vide, Domine, afflictionem, 90.
Vigilate, nescitis enim, 90.
*Psalmes, Sonets, and Songs of Sad-
nes and Pietie*, 72, 77–9, 95, 118.
Psalmes, Songs, and Sonnets, 72, 78,
81, 89, 118.
SONG:
My little sweet darling, 129.
Songs of Sundrie Natures, 72, 90–1,
95, 117–18, 387.
Byttering, 20.

Caccini, Giulio, 152.
Caffarelli, Gaetano Majorano, detto,
218, 273.
Callcott, John Wall, 269, 283–4.
GLEES:
Erlking, 284.
Father of heroes, 284.
Forgive, blest shade, 284.
In the lonely vale of streams, 284.
Who comes so dark? 284.
With sighs, sweet rose, 284.
You gentlemen of England, 284.
Campian, Thomas: life, 74; works,
80–3, 133–5.
Divine and Morall Songs, 133.
*New Way of making fowre parts in
Counter-point, A*, 83.
SONGS:
Most sweet and pleasing are thy
ways, O Lord, 133.
Never weather-beaten sail, 133.
There is a garden in her face, 135.
Cantatas, Choral:
Banner of St. George, The (Elgar),
337.
Before the Paling of the Stars
(Dale), 353.
Bells, The (Holbrooke), 349.
Black Knight, The (Elgar), 337.
Blest Pair of Sirens (Parry), 317, 331.
Bride of Dunkerron, The (Smart),
293.
Caractacus (Elgar), 337.
Choral Hymns from the Rig Veda
(Holst), 347.
Choral Symphony (Holst), 347.
Christ in the Wilderness (Bantock),
342.
Crucifixion, The (Stainer), 330.
Death of Minnehaha, The (Cole-
ridge-Taylor), 348.

Cantatas, Choral (*cont.*):
De Profundis (Parry), 331.
Dream of Jubal, The (Mackenzie),
317, 328.
Everyman (Davies), 343.
Fantasia on Christmas Carols
(Vaughan Williams), 345.
Five Mystical Songs (Vaughan
Williams), 345.
Five Tudor Portraits (Vaughan
Williams), 346.
Flos Campi (Vaughan Williams),
346.
Gethsemane (Bantock), 342.
Glories of our Blood and State, The
(Parry), 317, 331.
Golden Legend, The (Sullivan),
325.
Hiawatha's Wedding Feast (Cole-
ridge-Taylor), 348.
Hymnus Paradisi (Howells), 354.
Hymn of Jesus (Holst), 347.
Invocation to Music (Parry), 331–3.
King Olaf (Elgar), 337.
L'Allegro ed Il Pensieroso (Parry),
317, 331–2.
Last Post, The (Stanford), 318.
Lie Strewn the White Flocks (Bliss),
353.
Lotos-Eaters, The (Parry), 317, 331,
333.
Love that casteth out Fear, The
(Parry), 317, 333.
Martyr of Antioch, The (Sullivan),
325.
Mass of Life, A (Delius), 341.
May Queen, The (Bennett), 294,
305.
Morning Heroes (Bliss), 353.
Nativity Hymn (Scott), 351.
Omar Khayyám (Bantock), 342.
Pan in Arcady (Bantock), 342.
Phaudrig Crohoore (Stanford), 334.
Pied Piper of Hamelin, The (Parry),
333.
Prison, The (Smyth), 340.
Prometheus Unbound (Parry), 317,
331–2.
Revenge, The (Stanford), 318, 335.
Rio Grande, The (Lambert), 357.
Seadrift (Delius), 341.
Sea Symphony, A (Vaughan Wil-
liams), 345.
Seventh Day, The (Bishop), 268.
Sleeping Beauty, The (Cowen), 327.
Song of Darkness and Light, A
(Parry), 317, 333.
Song of St. Francis (Davies), 343.
Songs in a Cornfield (Macfarren),
305.

Cantatas, Choral (*cont.*):
Songs of Sunset (Delius), 341.
Spring Symphony (Britten), 358–9.
Story of Sayid, The (Mackenzie), 317, 328.
Summer's Last Will and Testament (Lambert), 357.
These things shall be (Ireland), 350.
Toward the Unknown Region (Vaughan Williams), 345.
Vision of Life, A (Parry), 317.
Voces Clamantium (Parry), 317.
Voyage of Maeldune, The (Stanford), 318, 335.
War and Peace (Parry), 317, 332–3.
Water-Lily, The (Cowen), 327.
see also Odes, Oratorios.
Canzonets:
Deep lamenting, grief bewraying (Morley), 123.
Do you not know how love lost first his seeing? (Morley), 122.
Good morrow, fair ladies (Morley), 123.
Go ye, my canzonets (Morley), 122.
What ails my darling (Morley), 123.
Carissimi, Giacomo, 177, 241.
Carl Rosa Opera Company, 321.
Carlton, Richard, 73, 124–5.
Carols, 15th-cent., 22–4, 367.
Carpenter, Edward, 349.
Carse, Adam, 258 *n.*3, 263 *n.*1.
Carver, Robert, 52.
Catch Club, Hibernian, 272.
Catch Club, Noblemen's and Gentlemen's, 269, 272.
Catches:
Early 17th cent., 165–6.
Mid-17th cent., 151, 154–5, 165–6.
Late 17th cent., 211, 272, 282.
Late 18th cent., 272, 281–2.

Come follow me merrily, my mates, 165.
Come, follow me. Whither shall I follow? (Hilton), 165.
Hold thy peace, thou knave, 166.
She weepeth sore (W. Lawes), 166.
Ut re mi fa sol la, 165.
Causton, Thomas, 50, 61.
Cavendish, Michael, 78, 80, 124.
Cellier, Alfred, 322.
Chamber music:
Late 16th and early 17th cent., 81, 84–6, 145–9.
Mid-17th cent., 166–71.
Late 17th cent., 211–14.
18th cent., 227, 262–3.
19th cent., 330–1.

Chamber music (*cont.*):
20th cent., 339–40, 343, 348–51, 354–6, 358–9.
see also Fantasias, Sonatas, Trio sonatas.
Chandos, James Brydges, 1st Duke of, 221, 246.
Charles I, King: reception of his Queen, 73; household included Robert Johnson, 74, Alfonso Ferrabosco the younger, 76, William Lawes, 150, Charles Colman, 150, Nicholas Laniere, 150, John Wilson, 150; Wilson's *Psalterium Carolinum* composed in his memory, 150–1; his taste for fine arts, 153; publication of music in his reign, 154; church music during his reign, 156; tablature for the Welsh harp dating from his reign, 374; cited, 100.
Charles II, King: Nicholas Laniere master of his music, 150; Matthew Locke his composer in ordinary, 152; revival of church music at his accession, 153; church music by younger composers written for his court, 157; offices held by Purcell under him, 172; Purcell's 'welcome songs' for him, 172, 204; paid the expenses of Pelham Humfrey's visit to France and Italy, 173; taste in music, 175; instrumental music in the Chapel Royal in his reign, 175–6; plans for Italian opera in his reign, 176; Louis Grabu his protégé, 177; increase of knowledge of French and Italian music in his reign, 177; Thomas Baltzar a member of his private music, 178; Italian musicians at his court, 218; cited, 163, 215, 284.
Chaucer, Geoffrey, 14.
Child, William: life, 151; anthems, 156–60; use of false relations, 390.
ANTHEMS:
Praise the Lord, O my soul, 158.
Sing we merrily unto God, 158.
First Set of Psalmes, The, 157.
MOTET:
O bone Jesu, 159.
SERVICES:
D major, 158.
E minor, 158.
Chopin, Frédéric, 394.
Choral works, Unaccompanied, see Part-songs.
Choral works with orchestra, see Cantatas, Odes, Oratorios.

Chorley, Henry Fothergill, 305.
Christie, W., 377 n. 4.
Church, John, 250.
Church music: objections to elaboration in the Middle Ages, 3; effect of the Reformation, 49–52, of the Civil War and Puritanism, 153–4. *See also* Anthems, Hymn-tunes, Masses, Motets, Services.
Chybury, 20, 26.
Cittern, 81, 84, 87.
Clari, Giovanni Carlo Maria, 241.
Clark, Andrew, 166 n. 3, 177 n. 4.
Clarke, Jeremiah: life, 174; works, 184–5, 209, 215; composed music for St. Cecilia's day, 178; part author of *A Choice Collection of Ayres for the Harpsichord or Spinett*, 215; Charles King his pupil, 245; hymn-tunes, 397; cited, 243.
ANTHEMS:
  How long wilt thou forget me? 185.
  I will love thee, O Lord, 185.
  Praise the Lord, O Jerusalem, 185.
KEYBOARD WORKS:
  The Prince of Denmark's March, 215.
  The Serenade, 215.
  Trumpett Minnuett, 215.
Clarke-Whitfield, John, 266, 281.
Clay, Frederic, 322.
Clayton, Thomas, 219–20.
Clementi, Muzio: life, 270; *Gradus ad Parnassum*, 270, 290; piano sonatas, 289–90; relations with Field, 269; influence on Bennett, 313; cited, 274.
Clifford, James, 175.
Clovesho, Council of, 3.
Cobbett, Walter Willson, 348.
Cobbold, William, 124, 368 n. 12.
Cole, Charles Augustus, 19 n. 3.
Coleridge-Taylor, Samuel, 348.
Collins, Henry Bird, 18 n. 2, 24 n. 2, 25 n. 1, 26 n. 1–2, 38 n. 1, 50 n. 1, 55 n. 1, 65 n. 2–3, 104 n. 1.
Collins, William, 246, 318, 328.
Colman, Charles: life, 150; works, 162–3, 168, 272 n. 1; collaborated with Davenant, 155.
'Come follow me merrily, my mates' (17th cent.), 165.
Competition festivals, 320.
Concentores Sodales, 272.
Concerti grossi: Avison, 263; Handel, 227–9.
Concertos, Solo:
  Cello: Elgar, 339.

Concertos, Solo (*cont.*):
  Organ: Handel, 227; S. Wesley, 287–8.
  Piano: Bennett, 311–12; Bliss, 353; Delius, 341; Ireland, 351; Rawsthorne, 357; Walton (*Sinfonia concertante*), 356.
  Viola: Walton, 356.
  Violin: Delius, 341; Elgar, 339; Moeran, 354; Rawsthorne, 357; Somervell, 340; Walton, 356.
Concerts:
  17th cent., 177–8.
  18th cent., 248–9, 273–4.
  19th cent., 294–5, 319–20.
  see also Ancient Concerts, Crystal Palace Concerts, Professional Concerts, Promenade Concerts, St. James's Hall Popular Concerts, Vocal Concerts.
Congreve, William, 178, 200, 203.
Cooke (15th cent.), 20.
Cooke, Benjamin, 265, 283.
Cooke, Henry, 155, 172–3.
Cooper, John, *see* Coprario.
Cooper, Robert, 21.
Coprario, John: life, 74; instrumental music, 146–7; master of William Lawes, 74, 150; contributor to *Teares or Lamentacions of a Sorrowfull Soule*, 81; wrote music for masques, 83.
Corelli, Arcangelo, 177, 262.
Corkine, William, 74, 135.
Cornett, 87.
Cornyshe, William: master of the children of the Chapel Royal, 21; motets, 34–5; secular works, 40–1, 45.
Costa, Michael, 294–5.
Cosyn, Benjamin, 138.
Cotton, John, 4.
Coussemaker, Charles Edmond Henri de, 4 n. 2, n. 4, 5 n. 1–3, 9 n. 1, 19 n. 2, 20 n. 4–5.
Covent Garden Opera House, 321, 344.
Coverdale, Miles, 51, 396.
Cowen, Frederic Hymen: life, 318; works, 327–8; cited, 316.
CANTATAS:
  Ode to the Passions, 318, 328.
  Sleeping Beauty, The, 327.
  Water-Lily, The, 327.
OPERAS:
  Harold, 318.
  Signa, 318.
  Thorgrim, 318, 327.
ORATORIO:
  Ruth, 327.

Cowen (*cont.*):
ORCHESTRAL WORKS:
'Idyllic' symphony, 327.
Language of Flowers (I), *The*, 327.
'Scandinavian' symphony, 318, 327–8.
'Welsh' symphony, 328.
Cowley, Abraham, 207.
Cramer, John Baptist, 270, 274.
Cramer, Wilhelm, 270.
Crashaw, Richard, 351.
Creyghton, Robert, 174, 184.
Croce, Giovanni, 78, 217.
Croft, William: life, 243; works, 250–2, 261; part author of *Choice Collection of Ayres for the Harpsichord or Spinett*, 215; Stroud and Kent his pupils, 245; use of false relations, 390; cited, 184, 244, 246, 253, 257, 277, 397.
ANTHEMS:
Be merciful unto me, 252.
Give the King thy judgements, 250.
God is gone up with a merry noise, 250.
Hear my prayer, O Lord, 252.
O give thanks, 250.
O Lord God of my salvation, 252.
O Lord, rebuke me not, 251, 390.
O Lord, thou hast searched me out, 252.
Praise the Lord, O my soul, 250.
Put me not to rebuke, 252.
Rejoice in the Lord, 250.
The heavens declare the glory of God, 250.
Burial Service, 251.
Musica Sacra, 243, 250–2.
Musicus apparatus academicus, 261.
Service in E♭ major, 390.
Cromwell, Oliver, 105, 153, 177.
Crotch, William: life, 266; works, 278–81; cited, 276.
ANTHEMS:
God is our hope and strength, 279.
How dear are thy counsels, 279.
My God, my God, look upon me, 279–80.
The Lord, even the most mighty God, hath spoken, 279.
ORATORIOS:
Captivity of Judah, The, 266.
Palestine, 266, 280–1.
Crystal Palace Concerts, 319–20.
Cummings, William Hayman, 245 *n.* 2.
Cuzzoni, Francesca, 218.

Dale, Benjamin, 353.
Daman, William, 75, 107.

Damett, Thomas, 20, 24–5.
Dances:
13th cent., 15–16.
Early 16th cent., 47.
Late 16th and early 17th cent., 85, 140–1, 143, 145, 148.
Mid-17th cent., 168–9.
see also Folk dances, Playford.
Dante Alighieri, 152.
Danyel, John: lute-songs, 136–7; cited, 74, 134.
SONGS:
Can doleful notes, 130, 136–7.
Grief, keep within, 136–7.
If I could shut the gate against my thoughts, 136.
Dauney, William, 376 *n.* 2.
Davenant, William, 155.
Davey, Henry, viii, 61.
Davies, Henry Walford, 343.
CANTATAS:
Everyman, 343.
Song of St. Francis, 343.
CHAMBER MUSIC:
Peter Pan string quartet, 343.
PART-SONGS:
Love is a torment, 343.
Magdalen at Michael's gate, 343.
These sweeter far than lilies are, 343.
SONG:
This ae nighte, 343.
Davison, Archibald Thompson, 8 *n.* 3, 15 *n.* 3, 28 *n.* 3, 47 *n.* 1.
Davy, John, 268.
Davy, Richard, 21, 36.
Day, John: *Certaine notes set forthe in foure and three partes*, 50; psalters, 51, 61 *n.* 5, 397.
Debussy, Claude, 342, 358.
Degrees in music, 400–1.
Delius, Frederick: life and works, 341–2; influence on Moeran and Warlock, 354.
CHORAL WORKS:
Mass of Life, A, 341.
Seadrift, 341.
Songs of Sunset, 341.
To be sung of a summer night on the water, 341.
OPERA:
Village Romeo and Juliet, A, 341.
ORCHESTRAL WORKS:
Brigg Fair, 341.
In a summer garden, 341.
Lebenstanz, 341.
Piano concerto, 341.
Violin concerto, 341.
SONG:
Irmelin, 341.

Denby, 250.
Dent, Edward Joseph, 156 *n*. 1, 163 *n*. 4, 194 *n*. 1, 242 *n*. 2.
'Deo gracias' (Agincourt song), 23–4, 367.
Dering, Richard: works, 105–6; music published abroad, 75.
   Cantica Sacra, 105.
   Countrey Cryes, 120.
   Cryes of London, The, 120.
   MOTETS:
   Anima Christi, 105.
   Jesu, dulci memoria, 105.
   O vos omnes, 105–6.
Deutsch, Otto, 84 *n*. 2, 138 *n*. 1.
Diaghilev, Sergei, 344.
Dibdin, Charles: life, 267; works, 285; on Arne's *Judith*, 258.
Dieupart, Charles, 219.
Dimock, James Francis, 2 *n*. 1, *n*. 3.
Divisions on a ground, 171.
Dolmetsch, Arnold, 344.
Dowland, John: life, 74; works, 79–80, 130–3, 137; contributor to *Teares or Lamentacions of a Sorrowfull Soule*, 81; translated Ornithoparcus's *Micrologus*, 83; one of Tomkins's madrigals dedicated to him, 125; cited, 121.
   First Booke of Songes or Ayres, 79–80, 130–2.
   Lachrimae, 86, 149.
   Pilgrimes Solace, A, 132–3.
   Second Booke of Songs or Ayres, 133.
   SONGS:
   Awake, sweet love, 80, 130–1.
   Away with these self-loving lads, 130.
   Come away, sweet love, 131.
   Come, heavy Sleep, 132.
   Daphne was not so chaste, 133.
   Flow, my tears, 133.
   From silent night, 133.
   Go, nightly cares, 133.
   In darkness let me dwell, 133, 137.
   Now, O now, I needs must part, 130.
   Welcome, black night, 132.
   Third and Last Booke of Songs or Aires, 133.
Dowland, Robert, 133.
Dowson, Ernest, 342, 351.
Dryden, John, 176, 178, 245.
Duets, Vocal:
   As round thine arm this chain I tie (Greene), 261.
   Awake, awake, ye dead (Purcell), 192.

Duets, Vocal (*cont*.):
   Bring shepherds, bring the kids and lambs (Blow), 207.
   By the streams that ever flow (Greene), 260.
   Cantate Domino (Blow), 181.
   Did not you once, Lucinda (Colman), 163.
   Joys in gentle trains appearing (Handel), 238.
   Let the fifes and the clarions (Purcell), 199.
   Oh thou on whom the weak depend (Arne), 258.
   Sound the trumpet (Purcell), 203.
   Sweet Kate (Jones), 135.
   The Lord is a man of war (Handel), 239.
   Two daughters of this aged stream are we (Purcell), 198.
   When Myra sings (Purcell), 209.
   Who made thee, Hob, forsake the plough (Byrd), 118.
   You say 'tis love creates the pain (Purcell), 198.
Dufay, Guillaume, 19–20.
Duncan, J. M., viii.
Dunstable, John: life, 18–19; works, 28–33; the treatise *De quatuor principalibus* attributed to him by Ravenscroft, 5; Morley's criticism of his word-setting, 70; cited, 5, 20, 50, 381, 394, 402.
   Kyrie eleison, 30.
   MOTETS:
   Ascendit Christus, 31–2.
   Crux fidelis, 29–30.
   Praeco praeeminentiae, 30–1.
   Quam pulcra es, 28–9, 33.
   Regina coeli, 33.
   Veni, sancte spiritus, 30.
D'Urfey, Thomas, 174, 205.
Dussek, Jan Ladislav, 274.
Dygon, John, 21.
Dykes, John Bacchus, 316, 329.

East, Michael: organist of Lichfield Cathedral, 73; fantasias for viols, 81, 149; anthems, 107; madrigals, 126.
East, Thomas, 73, 395, 397.
Eccles, John: life, 174; music for St. Cecilia's day, 178; stage music, 202–3.
'Edi beo thu hevene quene' (13th cent.), 10.
Edward I, King, 381.
Edward VI, King, 48–51.
Edward VII, King, 339.
Edwards, Richard, 49, 66–7.

Einstein, Alfred, 6 n. 1.
Eleanor of Aquitaine, Queen of England, 6.
Elgar, Edward: life, 318–19; works, 337–40; influence on Bliss, 354, on Walton, 355–6; cited, 316, 400.
CANTATAS:
Banner of St. George, The, 337.
Black Knight, The, 337.
Caractacus, 337.
King Olaf, 337.
CHAMBER MUSIC:
Piano quintet, 339.
String quartet, 339.
Violin sonata, 339.
ODE:
Music-Makers, The, 319, 339.
ORATORIOS:
Apostles, The, 319, 338–9.
Dream of Gerontius, 319, 337–9, 356.
Kingdom, The, 319, 338.
Light of Life, The, 337.
ORCHESTRAL WORKS:
Cello concerto, 339.
'Enigma' variations, 337.
Falstaff, 339–40.
'Imperial March', 337.
In the South, 338.
Serenade for strings, 337.
Symphony No. 1 in A♭ major, 339.
Symphony No. 2 in E♭ major, 339.
Violin concerto, 339.
PART-SONGS:
Evening scene, 338.
5 Part-songs from the Greek Anthology, 338.
Weary wind of the west, 338.
SONG-CYCLE:
Sea Pictures, 337.
Elizabeth I, Queen: musicians in her service, 49, 75; The Triumphes of Oriana intended as a compliment to her, 78; popularity of Irish tunes at her court, 382; cited, 86, 100.
Ellinwood, Leonard, 4 n. 3.
Elvey, George Job, 300.
Elvey, Stephen, 300.
Engelke, Bernhard, 85 n. 2.
English descant, 11–14, 26.
English Hymnal, The, 375 n. 3, 398.
English Opera House, 321.
Épine, Margarita de l', 219.
Eton College manuscript, 33–6.
Evelyn, John, 175.
Examinations in music, 400–2.
Excetre, 20.

Fairfax, see Fayrfax.

Fa las, 77, 164; see also Balletts.
False relations, 387–94.
Fancies, see Fantasias for viols.
Fantasias for violins and other instruments, 170.
Fantasias for viols, 145–9, 166–9, 211–12; Byrd, 81, 149; Coprario, 146–7; East, 81, 149; Ferrabosco (the younger), 148; O. Gibbons, 84, 148–9; Jenkins, 166, 168; W. Lawes, 166–8; Locke, 169; Lupo, 148; Morley, 149; Purcell, 211–12; Ravenscroft, 149; Tomkins, 149; Ward, 147 n. 2.
Farinelli, Carlo Broschi, detto, 218, 273.
Farmer, John, 73, 126–7.
MADRIGALS:
Fair nymph, I heard one telling, 126.
O stay, sweet love, 126.
You blessed bowers, 127.
You pretty flowers, 126.
Farnaby, Giles: canzonets, 128; keyboard works, 140–1, 144–5; represented in the 'Fitzwilliam Virginal Book', 84; use of chromatic progressions, 137; cited, 75.
KEYBOARD WORKS:
His Dreame, 145.
His Humour, 145.
His Reste, 145.
Meridian alman, 140.
Quodling's delight, 366 n. 2.
Farnaby, Richard, 84.
Farrant, Richard: gentleman of the Chapel Royal, 49; church music, 62–4; secular works, 66; represented in Barnard's Selected Church Music, 155.
Fauré, Gabriel, 399.
Faustina Bordoni (Hasse), 218.
Fauxbourdon, 11, 22.
'Fayrfax Book', 273.
Fayrfax, Robert: life, 21; Masses, 36–8; cited, 41.
Fellowes, Edmund Horace: on Taverner's Mass Small Devotion, 44 n. 2; on the 'Wanley' manuscript, 45 n. 2; on English adaptations of Taverner's Masses, 51 n. 1; editor of Byrd's complete vocal and instrumental works, 72 n. 1; inventory of instruments at Hengrave Hall printed by him, 85 n. 5; on the date of Byrd's Masses, 88 n. 2; his reconstruction of services by Weelkes, 98; on the authenticity of Child's motet 'O bone Jesu', 159 n. 1; on

Fellowes (*cont.*):
  the spelling of Golding's name, 174 *n.* 1; on the authenticity of Boyce's anthem 'O where shall wisdom be found?', 255 *n.* 4; on augmented intervals in the madrigalian period, 392 *n.* 1, 393 *n.* 3; as editor, 90 *n.* 1, 93 *n.* 5, 130 *n.* 1, 133 *n.* 1, 148 *n.* 2, 149 *n.* 3, and references *passim* to the *English Madrigal School*; cited, 48 *n.* 1, 83 *n.* 1.
Ferdinand of Austria, Archduke, 85.
Ferguson, Howard, 359.
Ferguson, John de Lancey, 378 *n.* 2.
Ferrabosco, Alfonso (the elder): life, 75–6; madrigals, 128–9.
Ferrabosco, Alfonso (the younger): life, 75–6; lute-songs, 80; contributor to *Teares or Lamentacions of a Sorrowfull Soule*, 81; wrote music for masques, 83; influenced by the declamatory style, 130; music for viols, 148, 171.
Festivals: Birmingham, 248; Bristol, 302; Handel, 294; Three Choirs, 244, 247–8, 274.
Field, John: life, 269–70; nocturnes, 288–9; influence on Chopin, 394.
Film music, 354, 359–60.
Finzi, Gerald, 359.
Fitzgerald, J. F., 101 *n.* 2.
'Fitzwilliam Virginal Book': history and contents, 84; music in, 67–8, 140–5; false relations in, 390; cited, 72, 75, 366 *n.* 1–2.
Fletcher, John, 153, 161 *n.* 2.
Flood, William Henry Grattan, 249 *n.* 1, 381 *n.* 4, 382 *n.* 2.
Flute, 84, 87.
Folk-dances:
  Cobbler's hornpipe, 381.
  Country Gardens, 371.
  Goddesses, 366.
  Lady Cassilis' Lilt, 376.
  Pall Mall, 371.
  Portsmouth, 370–1.
  Quodling's delight, 366.
  The Princess Royal, 285 *n.* 1.
  see also Folk-songs, Playford.
Folk-songs, 361–85; used by Elizabethan and Jacobean virginal composers, 143; influence on Vaughan Williams, 345, on Butterworth, 353, on Moeran, 354.
  ENGLISH:
  Admiral Benbow, 366.
  All in a garden green, 143.
  As I walked out one May morning, 372.

Folk-songs: English (*cont.*):
  A, the syghes that come froe my herte, 368.
  Blow thy horne, hunter, 368.
  Bonny at morn, 373.
  Bonny sweet Robin, 143, 369.
  Brigg fair, 372.
  Bristol Town, 371 *n.* 3.
  Bushes and briars, 362 *n.* 1.
  Come, lasses and lads, 370.
  Come o'er the bourne, Bessy, 368, 370.
  Covent Garden, 372.
  Down among the dead men, 370.
  Farewell, Nancy, 372.
  Fortune my foe, 368.
  Greensleeves, 365, 368–9.
  Hanskin, 365.
  Heart's ease, 368.
  Here's a health unto his majesty, 370.
  I have bene a foster, 368.
  John come kiss me now, 365.
  John Peel, 372.
  Light o' love, 368.
  Lord Willoughby, 369.
  My Johnny was a shoemaker, 372.
  Nancy, 366 *n.* 1.
  Now the spring is come, 369.
  Packington's Pound, 365.
  Peg-a-Ramsey, 368.
  Pretty Polly Oliver, 370.
  Row well, ye mariners, 365.
  Sair fyel'd, hinny, 373.
  Salisbury Plain, 372.
  Sellenger's Round, 365, 369.
  Sick, sick, 368.
  The bobtailed mare, 372.
  The British Grenadiers, 366.
  The carman's whistle, 143.
  The hunt is up, 365, 369.
  The Keel Row, 372.
  The last rose of summer, 363.
  The lytell prety nygtyngale, 368.
  The merry milkmaids, 365.
  The oak and the ash, 366.
  There were three ravens, 369.
  The ship in distress, 372.
  The trees they grow so high, 364 *n.* 1.
  The Vicar of Bray, 371.
  The virgin unspotted, 366.
  The woods so wild, 365, 370.
  The wraggle-taggle gipsies, 372.
  Trenchmore, 365.
  Walsingham, 143–4, 365.
  Western wynde, 50, 368.
  Where be going? 372.
  Where will bonnie Annie lie? 372.

Folk-songs: English (*cont.*):
  Whoop, do me no harm, good man, 368.

IRISH:
  At the mid hour of night, 384.
  Avenging and bright fall the swift sword of Erin, 378.
  Caleno custure me, 368.
  Coola Shore, 385 *n*. 1.
  Draherin O Machree, 384.
  Eileen aroon, 378 *n*. 1.
  Have you been at Carrick? 384.
  If the sea were ink, 383.
  It is not the tear, 383.
  Lay his sword by his side, 383.
  Londonderry Air, 383–4.
  Molly McAlpin, 385.
  My love's an arbutus, 385.
  One Sunday after Mass, 384.
  Remember the glories of Brien the brave, 385.
  Rich and rare were the gems she wore, 381.
  The Arethusa, 285 *n*. 1, 363.
  The boys of Wexford, 384.
  The Coolin, 381.
  The Dove, 384.
  The flight of the earls, 384.
  The girl I left behind me, 363.
  The sixpence, 383.
  The summer is coming, 381.
  Though the last glimpse of Erin, 381.

MANX:
  Mylecharane, 373.
  The sheep under the snow, 373.

SCOTTISH HIGHLANDS:
  A chuachag nan craobh, 379–80.
  Cumha h'Irteach, 380.
  Elorelo, 380.
  Farewell, 380.
  Fear a Bhàta, 380.
  Hymn of Praise, 380.
  Laoidh Molaidh, 380.
  Mo chailin dileas donn, 379.
  Och o ro u, 379.
  O cuckoo of the grove, 379–80.
  Soraidh, 380.

SCOTTISH LOWLANDS:
  Afton Water, 378.
  Auld Robin Gray, 377.
  Ay waking, O! 377.
  Ca' the yowes, 377.
  Gala Water, 377.
  I'll bid my heart be still, 373, 377.
  Jenny Nettles, 378.
  Katherine Ogie, 376.
  Robin Adair, 378 *n*. 1.
  Scots wha hae, 366.
  The bridegroom grat, 377.

Folk-songs: Scottish Lowlands (*cont.*):
  The Brume o' the Cowdenknowes, 376.
  The land o' the leal, 366.
  The Piper of Dundee, 378.
  There was a lad was born in Kyle, 385.
  The twa' sisters o' Binnorie, 377.
  Wae's me for Prince Charlie, 376.

WELSH:
  All through the night, 375.
  Breuddwyd y Bardd, 374.
  David of the white rock, 375.
  Gwenith Gwyn, 375.
  Jenny Jones, 374.
  Llwyn onn, 374.
  Morva Rhuddlan, 374–5.
  The Ash Grove, 374.
  The blackbird, 375.
  The red piper's melody, 374–5.
  Ton-y-Botel, 375.

Fonteyns, 20.
Ford, Thomas: *Musicke of sundrie kindes*, 74; contributor to *Teares or Lamentacions of a Sorrowfull Soule*, 81; anthems, 107; three-part madrigals, 128; lute-songs, 135.
Foreign influences, 398–9.
Forest, 20, 28 *n*. 1.
Forster, William, 138.
Franctynge, John, 65.
Freemen's songs, 45.
Frere, Walter Howard, 5 *n*. 3.
Frottole, 77.
Fry, A. Ruth, viii.
Fuller Maitland, John Alexander, vii–viii, 22 *n*. 3, 52 *n*. 2, 68 *n*. 3, 84 *n*. 6, 215 *n*. 2, 372 *n*. 5.

Gairdner, William Henry Temple, 339 *n*. 1.
Galilei, Vincenzo, 152.
Galpin, Francis William, 87 *n*. 2.
Garlande, Jean de, 4–5.
Garrick, David, 245.
Gastoldi, Giovanni, 121, 217.
Gay, John, 246; see also *Beggar's Opera*.
Geminiani, Francesco, 249.
George I, King, 221.
Gibbons, Christopher: life, 151; collaborated with Locke in the music to Shirley's *Cupid and Death*, 151, 155, 163; anthems, 157; cited, 150.
Gibbons, Edward, 73, 152.
Gibbons, Ellis, 73, 124.
Gibbons, Orlando: life, 73; works, 95–8, 102, 118–20, 139–41, 144–5, 148; contributor to *Teares or Lamentacions of a Sorrowfull*

Gibbons, Orlando (*cont.*):
Soule, 81; part author of *Parthenia*, 84; represented in the 'Fitzwilliam Virginal Book', 84, in Barnard's *Selected Church Music*, 155, in Boyce's *Cathedral Music*, 244; one of Tomkins's madrigals dedicated to him, 125; use of false relations, 388–9; hymn-tunes, 396; cited, 51, 63, 99–100, 106–8, 112, 123, 127–8, 151, 156–9, 189–90.

ANTHEMS:
Behold, thou hast made my days as it were a span long, 96.
Glorious and powerful God, 97–8.
Hosanna to the Son of David, 96–7.
If ye be risen again with Christ, 388–9.
Lift up your heads, 96–7.
O clap your hands, 96–7.
O Lord, in thy wrath rebuke me not, 97.
See, see, the Word is incarnate, 98.
Cries of London, The, 120.
Fantasies for viols in three parts, 84, 148–9.

KEYBOARD WORKS:
Fantazia of foure parts, 141.
Pavana, 140.
The Lord of Salisbury, his Pavin, 140.
Madrigals and Mottets:
Dainty fine bird that art encaged, 119–20.
Farewell all joys, 119.
How art thou thrall'd, 119.
Lais, now old, 119.
Now each flowery bank, 119.
The silver swan, 119.
What is our life, 119.
Short Service in F major, 95.
Gibbs, Joseph, 246, 263.
Gilbert, William Schwenck, 316, 322.
Gilchrist, Anne, 383 *n*.3.
Giles, John Allen, 3 *n*.1.
Giles, Nathaniel, *see* Gyles.
Gill, W. H., 373 *n*.3.
Giraldus Cambrensis, 1–3.
Giustiniani, Leonardo, 28.
'Glad and blithe mote ꝫe be' (15th cent.), 23.
Glee Club, 269, 272.
Glees, 271–2, 281–4:
Amidst the myrtles (Battishill), 282.
As it fell upon a day (Mornington), 282.
As now the shades of eve (Cooke), 283.

Glees (*cont.*):
Awake, sweet Muse (Beale), 282.
Breathe soft, ye winds (W. Paxton), 283.
By Celia's arbour (Horsley), 283.
Daughter of faith, awake (Horsley), 283.
Discord, dire sister (Webbe), 282–4.
Erlking (Callcott), 284.
Father of heroes (Callcott), 284.
Forgive, blest shade (Callcott), 284.
Hail, smiling morn (Spofforth), 283.
Hark, the curfew's solemn sound (Attwood), 282.
Here shall the morn (S. Wesley), 282.
How sweet, how fresh (S. Paxton), 283.
In the lonely vale of streams (Callcott), 284.
My dear mistress (Spofforth), 283.
O sing unto my roundelaie (S. Wesley), 282.
Roses, their sharp spines being gone (S. Wesley), 282.
See the chariot at hand (Horsley), 283.
Sigh no more, ladies (Stevens), 283.
The cloud-capt towers (Stevens), 283.
The glories of our birth and state (S. Wesley), 282.
To Bacchus, we to Bacchus sing (Colman), 272 *n*.1.
When shall we three meet again? (Horsley), 283.
When winds breathe soft (Webbe), 282.
Who comes so dark? (Callcott), 284.
With sighs, sweet rose (Callcott), 284.
Ye spotted snakes (Stevens), 283.
You gentlemen of England (Callcott), 284.
Glen, John, 378 *n*.2.
Gloucester, William, Duke of, 203–4, 207–8.
Gluck, Christoph Willibald von, 225.
'Go hert hurt with adversite' (15th cent.), 22.
Golding, John, 174, 184–5.
Goldwin, *see* Golding.
Gordon, George Stuart, 84 *n*.1.
Goring Thomas, *see* Thomas.
Goss, John (1800–80): life, 291; works, 299–300, 308; cited, 329.

Goss (*cont.*):
ANTHEMS:
 Brother, thou art gone before us, 299 *n*. 1.
 Come and let us return, 299.
 If we believe that Jesus died, 299.
 Lift up thine eyes, 299.
 Lord, let me know mine end, 299–300.
 O Saviour of the world, 299.
 Praise the Lord, O my soul, 299.
 The wilderness, 299.
Goss, John (b. 1894), 309 *n*. 1.
Gounod, Charles, 329, 338, 399.
Gow, Niel, 381.
Grabu, Louis, 176–7.
Grattan Flood, *see* Flood.
Graun, Karl Heinrich, 241.
Greaves, Thomas, 74.
Greber, Jakob, 220.
Greene, Maurice: life, 243–4; works, 253–5, 260–1; association with Bononcini, 242, 244; subscribed to Roseingrave's edition of Scarlatti's sonatas, 263; cited, 246, 257, 277.
ANTHEMS:
 Arise, shine, 253.
 Behold, I bring you glad tidings, 255 *n*. 2.
 God is our hope and strength, 253.
 Hearken unto me, ye holy children, 253.
 How long wilt thou forget me, O Lord? 253.
 I will sing of thy power, 253.
 Let my complaint come before thee, 253.
 Lord, how long wilt thou be angry? 253–4, 257.
 Lord, let me know mine end, 253–4.
 O clap your hands, 253.
 O praise the Lord of heaven, 255 *n*. 2.
 Sing unto the Lord a new song, 253.
 The Lord, even the most mighty God, hath spoken, 253.
DUETS:
 As round thine arm this chain I tie, 261.
 By the streams that ever flow, 260.
Forty Select Anthems, 244, 253–5.
Ode on St. Cecilia's Day, 260.
Phoebe, 260–1.
SONGS:
 Ah, could we love like him, 261.
 Go, rose, 260.
 Like the young god of wine, 261.

Greene: Songs (*cont.*):
 Phoebe fears each bird that flies, 261.
Greig, Gavin, 377 *n*. 4.
Grounds: in music for virginals, 143; divisions for bass viol, 171; in Blow, 181, 208; in Purcell, 191, 195–7, 199, 204–5, 213–15.
Grove, George, 319, 330.
Gyles, Nathaniel, 81, 155.
Gymel, 10, 22.
Habermann, Franz Wenzel, 241.
Haddan, Arthur West, 3 *n*. 2.
Hadow, William Henry, viii.
Hallé, Charles, 319.
Handel, George Frideric: life and works, 217–42; operas, 223–6; oratorios, 229–41; instrumental works, 226–9; used the lute in *Esther*, 87; influence on English music, 216, 281, 288, 294–6, 331, 399; a friend of Maurice Greene, 244; music used in *The Beggar's Opera*, 247; supported Royal Society of Musicians, 248; hymn-tune 'Hanover' wrongly attributed to him, 250; Samuel Wesley's opinion of, 270; music borrowed for late 18th-cent. oratorios, 271; performed at Ancient Concerts, 273; commemorated at Westminster Abbey, 274; cited, 213, 243, 246–7, 258, 261, 302.
ARIAS, ENGLISH:
 Above measure is the pleasure, 234.
 Awake, Saturnia, 233.
 Despair no more shall wound me, 233.
 Dryads, sylvans, 236.
 He shall feed his flock, 240.
 Honour and arms, 238.
 Let me wander not unseen, 235.
 Loathsome urns, disclose your treasure, 236–7.
 Love in her eyes sits playing, 233.
 My father, 235.
 Myself I shall adore, 233.
 No, no, I'll take no less, 233.
 Oft on a plat of rising ground, 235.
 Oh sleep, why dost thou leave me? 233.
 Revenge, Timotheus cries, 236.
 Total eclipse, 240.
 Waft her, angels, 232.
 Where'er you walk, 233.
 Where shall I fly? 235.
ARIAS, ITALIAN:
 Confusa si miri, 225.
 Con rauco mormorio, 225.
 Del minacciar del vento, 225.

Handel: Arias, Italian (*cont.*):
  Lascia ch'io pianga, 226.
  Le luci del mio bene, 225.
  Ombra mai fù, 226.
  Rendi 'l sereno al ciglio, 225.
  Stille amare, 225–6.
  V'adoro, pupille, 240–1.
  Verdi prati, 226.
  Vieni, torna, 224–5.
  Voglio dire al mio tesoro, 225.
  Voi dolci aurette al cor, 225.
Chandos anthems, 221, 229, 238.
Der für die Sünden der Welt gemarterte und sterbende Jesus, 223.
Dettingen Te Deum, 238.
DUETS:
  Joys in gentle trains appearing, 238.
  The Lord is a man of war, 239.
Funeral anthem for Queen Caroline, 238, 240.
INSTRUMENTAL WORKS:
  Concerti grossi, 227–9.
  Organ concertos, 227.
  Recorder sonatas, 227.
  Violin sonatas, 227.
OPERAS:
  Agrippina, 221.
  Alcina, 226.
  Giulio Cesare, 240–1.
  Giustino, 224.
  Orlando, 225.
  Ottone, 225.
  Partenope, 225.
  Rinaldo, 220–1, 225–6.
  Rodelinda, 225.
  Rodrigo, 223.
  Serse, 226.
  Sosarme, 225.
  Teseo, 221, 224–5.
  Tolomeo, 225–6.
ORATORIOS, ODES, ETC.:
  Acis and Galatea, 221, 232–3, 236, 239 n. 1.
  Alexander Balus, 223.
  Alexander's Feast, 234–6.
  Athaliah, 222, 238–9.
  Belshazzar, 222, 238–9, 258.
  Deborah, 222, 239.
  Esther, 87, 221–2, 239.
  Hercules, 222, 234–6.
  Israel in Egypt, 222, 230, 232, 238–9.
  Jephtha, 223, 232, 238–9, 241.
  Joseph and his Brethren, 222, 238.
  Joshua, 223, 231, 238.
  Judas Maccabaeus, 222, 232.
  L'Allegro, 234–6, 240.
  Messiah, 222, 230–2, 238–40.
  Ode for St. Cecilia's Day, 234–5.
  Resurrezione, La, 223.

Handel: Oratorios, Odes, &c. (*cont.*):
  Samson, 222, 232, 238, 240.
  Saul, 222, 230, 232, 237–40.
  Semele, 222, 233–4, 236.
  Solomon, 223, 238–9.
  Susanna, 223, 238–9.
  Theodora, 223, 231, 238, 239 n. 1.
  Triumph of Time and Truth, The, 223, 236–7, 239 n. 1.
  Utrecht Te Deum, 221, 238, 239 n. 1.
Handel Festival, 294.
Handschin, Jacques, 16 n. 3.
Hanover, Elector of, *see* George I.
Hanover, Prince Ernest Augustus of, 221.
Hardy, Thomas, 359.
Harpers, 1, 367, 382.
Harris, Augustus, 296.
Harris, William Henry, 184 n. 1.
Hart, Philip, 250.
Harwood, Basil, viii.
Haslemere Festival, 344.
Hatton, John Liptrot, 291–2, 308.
Haussmann, Valentin, 366 n. 1.
Hawkins, John: *A General History of the Science and Practice of Music*, 272–3; attributed 'Rejoice in the Lord always' to Redford, 61; conjectured that the music of 'In going to my naked bed' was by Richard Edwards, 66–7; gave the name 'Queen Elizabeth's Virginal Book' to the 'Fitzwilliam Virginal Book', 84; failed to recognize Handel's 'Egypt was glad when they departed' as an adaptation of an organ canzona by Kerl, 241 n. 3; on Bononcini's alleged plagiarism, 242; on the Madrigal Society, 248; on the style of J. C. Bach and Abel, 249; on King's church music, 257; cited, 64, 203 n. 1.
Haydn, Franz Joseph: his music borrowed for late 18th-cent. oratorios, 271; attended the last Handel Commemoration in Westminster Abbey, 274; little influence on English instrumental music, 288; cited, 241, 289.
Hayes, Gerald, 85 n. 3.
Hayes, William: at Oxford, 246; attack on Avison, 249; church music, 256–7.
Heath, 50.
Heine, Heinrich, 310.
Hengrave Hall, 73, 85, 87.
Henley, William Ernest, 318.
Henrietta Maria, Queen, 73.
Henry II, King, 6.

Henry III, King, 5.
Henry V, King, 19–20.
Henry VII, King, 33.
Henry VIII, King: foreign musicians at his court, 21; as a composer, 21–2, 45; 'O Lord, the maker of all thing' wrongly attributed to him, 45, 63; cited, 41, 49, 51.
Herbert, George, 345.
Herford, Charles Harold, 152 n. 1.
Herrick, Robert, 113, 150.
Heseltine, Philip, see Warlock.
Hibernian Catch Club, see Catch Club.
Hill, George Birkbeck, 218 n. 1, 247 n. 3.
Hilton, John (the elder), 62, 73, 124.
Hilton, John (the younger), 80, 150–1, 164–5.
Histories of Music, see Ambros, Burney, Davey, Hawkins, Nagel, Naumann, Parry, Wooldridge.
Hogg, James, 378 n. 4.
Holborne, Anthony, 86, 149.
Holbrooke, Joseph, 349–50.
  CHAMBER MUSIC:
    Pickwick string quartet, 349.
    String quartet in D minor.
  CHORAL WORKS:
    Bells, The, 349.
    Byron, 349.
  OPERAS:
    Children of Don, The, 349.
    Dylan, 349.
  ORCHESTRAL WORK:
    Apollo and the Seaman, 349.
  SCENA FOR VOICE AND ORCHESTRA:
    Marino Faliero, 349.
'Hold thy peace, thou knave' (17th cent.), 166.
Holmes, John, 124.
Holst, Gustav: works, 346–8; Rubbra his pupil, 355.
  CHORAL WORKS:
    Choral Hymns from the Rig Veda, 347.
    Choral Symphony, 347.
    Hymn of Jesus, 347.
    Ode to Death, 347.
  ORCHESTRAL WORKS:
    Beni-Mora, 347.
    Egdon Heath, 347.
    Planets, The, 347.
  SONGS:
    Four songs for voice and violin, 347.
    Twelve songs by Humbert Wolfe, 347.
Homer, 241.

Hook, James, 268, 285, 378.
Hooper, Edmund: organist of Westminster Abbey, 74; contributor to Teares or Lamentacions of a Sorrowfull Soule, 81; represented in the 'Fitzwilliam Virginal Book', 84, in Barnard's Selected Church Music, 155; anthem by him, 107.
Horace, 117.
Horn, Charles Edward, 268, 286.
Horn, Karl Friedrich, 268.
Horsley, William, 269, 283.
Hothby, John, 20.
Housman, Alfred Edward, 353.
Howard, Samuel, 397.
Howells, Herbert, 354.
Hudson, George, 155.
Hughes, Anselm: on text-omissions in the Creed in 15th and 16th cent., 50 n. 1; as editor, 12 n. 1–4, 18 n. 2, 24 n. 2, 25 n. 1, 26 n. 1–2.
Hughes, Charles W., 171 n. 1.
Hughes-Hughes, Augustus, viii.
Hume, Tobias, 81.
Humfrey, Pelham: life, 173, 175; works, 182–3, 209; Purcell his pupil, 172; cited, 156–7.
  ANTHEMS:
    By the waters of Babylon, 182.
    Have mercy upon me, O God, 182.
    Hear, O heavens, 182.
    Like as the hart, 182–3.
    Thou art my king, O God, 182.
Hummel, Johann Nepomuk, 313.
Hunt, J. Eric, 49 n. 1.
Hunt, Thomas, 124.
Hurlstone, William Yeates, 348, 353.
Hylton Stewart, see Stewart.
Hymns Ancient and Modern, 398.
Hymn-tunes, 250, 396–8:
    Dundee, 397.
    French Tune, 397.
    Hanover (Croft), 250.
    London New, 397.
    Martyrs, 397.
    Old Hundredth, 397.
    Old 137th, 397.
    Rockingham (Miller), 397.
    St. Anne (Croft), 250.
    St. Bride (Howard), 397.
    St. Flavian, 397.
    St. Mary, 397.
    St. Matthew (Croft), 250.
    St. Michael, 397.
    Winchester Old, 397.
    Windsor, 397.
    see also Psalters.

Immyns, John, 248, 272.
Inglot, William, 84.

In nomines, 68, 145–7, 166, 211.
Instrumental music, *see* Chamber music, *Concerti grossi*, Concertos, Dances, Fantasias, In nomines, Keyboard music, Organ music, Overtures, Sonatas, Symphonic poems, Symphonies, Trio sonatas.
Ireland, John, 350–1.
  CHAMBER MUSIC:
  Violin sonata No. 2, 351.
  CHORAL WORK:
  These things shall be, 350.
  ORCHESTRAL WORKS:
  Forgotten Rite, The, 350–1.
  Piano concerto, 351.
  PIANO SOLO:
  Island Spell, The, 351.
  Piano sonata, 351.
  Rhapsody, 351.
  Sarnia, 351.
  SONG:
  The adoration, 350.
Irish music: instrumental playing in the 12th cent., 2; influence of folk music on Stanford, 334–6, on Bantock, 342; connexions with England and Scotland, 363; history and characteristics of, 381–5; parochial attitude to, 399; *see also* Folksongs, Irish.
Isorhythmic technique, 25, 30–1.

Jackson, William, 281 *n.* 1.
Jacob, Gordon, 359.
James I, King: musicians in his service, 74, 76; madrigal in his honour by Peacham, 83; violin in use at his court, 85; string ensemble music in his reign, 86; popularity of masques at his court, 153; cited, 100.
James II, King: Purcell's 'welcome songs' for, 172, 204; coronation of, 174, 188; Italian musicians at his court, 218.
Jannequin, Clément, 120.
Jekyll, F., ix.
Jenkins, John: life, 151; instrumental music, 168, 170; Anthony Wood's opinion of, 166; cited, 150.
Jennens, Charles, 286 *n.* 1.
Jeppesen, Knud, 386 *n.* 1.
Jervays, 20.
'Jesu Christes milde moder' (13th cent.), 10.
John of Salisbury, 1, 3.
Johnson, Edward, 84, 124.
Johnson, Robert (mid-16th cent.), 49, 64–6.
Johnson, Robert (early 17th cent.); court lutenist to James I and

Johnson, Robert (*cont.*):
  Charles I, 74; contributor to *Teares or Lamentacions of a Sorrowfull Soule*, 81; represented in the 'Fitzwilliam Virginal Book', 84; songs, 135; keyboard works, 140.
Johnson, Samuel: on Italian opera, 218; on *The Beggar's Opera*, 247.
Jones, Robert: lute-songs, 80–1, 135–6; madrigal in *The Triumphes of Oriana*, 126; cited, 74, 133.
  DUET:
  Sweet Kate, 135.
  First Booke of Songes and Ayres, 80–1.
  Musicall Dreame, A, 81, 133.
  Second Booke of Songs and Ayres, 80.
  SONGS:
  Dainty, dainty, dainty darling, 135.
  Go to bed, sweet muse, 135–6.
  My complaining is but feigning, 135.
  My father fain would have me take, 135.
  Think'st thou, Kate, to put me down, 135.
Jonson, Ben: friend of Alfonso Ferrabosco (the younger), 76; his masque *Lovers made Men* set by Laniere, 152; Britten's setting of 'Queen and huntress, chaste and fair', 359; cited, 82, 153.
Josquin des Près, 20.
Joyce, Patrick Weston, 384 *n.* 4–5.

Kalischer, Alfred Christlieb, 270 *n.* 1.
Keats, John, 328, 359.
Keiser, Reinhard, 241.
Keith, Alexander, 377 *n.* 4.
Kelly, Michael, 265 *n.* 1.
Kelway, Joseph, 263.
Kelway, Thomas, 246, 256, 263.
Kempton, Thomas, 245, 256.
Kent, James, 245, 256–7.
Kerl, Johann Caspar, 241.
Keyboard music:
  14th cent., 16–17.
  Early and mid-16th cent., 47, 67–9.
  Late 16th and early 17th cent., 138–45.
  Late 17th cent., 214–15.
  Early 18th cent., 226–7, 263–4.
  Late 18th cent., 288–90.
  Early 19th cent., 312–13.
  20th cent., 351–2, 359.
  see also Organ music, Sonatas.
Kindersley, Robert, 81.
King, Charles, 245, 256–7.

Kirbye, George: works, 107, 127; use of false relations, 390; cited, 73.
ANTHEM:
O Jesu, look, 107.
MADRIGALS:
Ah, cruel hateful fortune, 390.
Sleep now, my Muse, 127.
Up then, Melpomene, 127.
Why wail we thus? 127.
Kitson, Charles Herbert, 184 n. 2.
Knox, John, 52.
Korbay, Francis, 141 n. 1.

'Laetabundus' (sequence), 23.
Lafontaine, Henry Cart de, 85 n. 4.
Lambe, Walter, 20.
Lambert, Constant, 262 n. 1, 356–7.
Lamentations: Parsley, 66; Tallis, 59; White, 57–8.
Laniere, Nicholas, 150, 152–3.
Lassus, Orlandus, 58, 143.
Latham, Albert George, 226 n. 1.
Lawes, Henry: life, 150; songs, 160–2; wrote music for Milton's Comus, 153; collaborated with Davenant, 155; psalms, 156; cited, 164.
Lawes, William: life, 150; church music, 156–7; catches, 166; instrumental music, 166–8, 170.
Leighton, William: Teares or Lamentacions of a Sorrowfull Soule, 81; contributions by Wilbye, 101, Milton (the elder), 107, Peerson, 151.
Leo, Leonardo, 276.
Leveridge, Richard, 219.
Lewis, Anthony, 201 n. 1, 392 n. 2.
Lewis, Henry, 374 n. 1.
Ley, Henry George, 158 n. 2, 159 n. 1, 253 n. 2, 263 n. 5.
Lindsay, Lady Anne, 377.
Linley, Elizabeth Ann, 267 n. 1.
Linley, Thomas (the elder), 267, 285–6.
Linley, Thomas (the younger), 267 n. 1, 285.
Lisley, John, 124.
Liszt, Franz, 141 n. 1, 314, 342.
Locke, Matthew: life, 151–2; works, 156–7, 163–4, 168–9; collaborated with Christopher Gibbons in the music for Shirley's Cupid and Death, 151, 155, 163; collaborated with Davenant, 155; cited, 150.
ANTHEMS:
How doth the city sit solitary, 156.
Lord, let me know mine end, 156.
O give thanks unto the Lord, 156.
Concert of 4 parts, 169.

Locke (cont.):
Cupid and Death, 163.
Psyche, 163–4, 219.
Tempest, The, 163–4.
Loder, Edward James: life, 292; operas, 295, 303; songs, 308–10.
Lodge, Edmund, 382 n. 1.
Loewenberg, Alfred, 220 n. 1.
'Lord, for thy tender mercies' sake' (16th cent.), 62.
Lotti, Antonio, 241–2.
Louis XIV of France, King, 175.
Lovell, Thomas, 21.
Ludford, Nicholas, 21.
Lully, Jean-Baptiste, 163, 177.
Lupo, Theophilus, 81.
Lupo, Thomas, 81, 148.
Lute, 81, 86–7.
Lute-songs, 79–81, 130–8.
And would you see my mistress' face (Rosseter), 134–5.
Awake, sweet love (Dowland), 80, 130–1.
Away with these self-loving lads (Dowland), 130.
Can doleful notes (Danyel), 130, 136–7.
Come away, sweet love (Dowland), 131.
Come, heavy Sleep (Dowland), 132.
Dainty, dainty, dainty darling (Jones), 135.
Daphne was not so chaste (Dowland), 133.
Flow, my tears (Dowland), 133.
From silent night (Dowland), 133.
Go, nightly cares (Dowland), 133.
Go to bed, sweet muse (Jones), 135–6.
Grief, keep within (Danyel), 136–7.
If I could shut the gate against my thoughts (Danyel), 136.
In darkness let me dwell (Dowland), 133, 137.
Most sweet and pleasing are thy ways, O Lord (Campian), 133.
My complaining is but feigning (Jones), 135.
My father fain would have me take (Jones), 135.
Never weather-beaten sail (Campian), 133.
Now, O now, I needs must part (Dowland), 130.
Now peep, bo-peep (Pilkington), 134.
O death, rock me asleep (anon.), 137–8.
Rest, sweet nymphs (Pilkington), 134.

Lute-songs (*cont.*):
Since first I saw your face (Ford), 80, 135.
Sweet Kate (Jones), 135.
There is a garden in her face (Campian), 135.
Think'st thou, Kate, to put me down (Jones), 135.
Welcome, black night (Dowland), 132.
With fragrant flowers (Pilkington), 134.
Lyra viol, 81, 87.

Macbean, Lachlan, 379 *n*.2.
Macdonald, Keith Norman, 379 *n*.1, 380 *n*.1.
Mace, Thomas, 105 *n*.2.
Macfarren, George Alexander: life, 292–3; oratorios, 302; operas, 304; *Songs in a Cornfield*, 305; part-songs, 308; cited, 291, 295.
Mackenzie, Alexander Campbell: life, 316–17; works, 328–9.
CHORAL WORKS:
Dream of Jubal, The, 317, 328.
Rose of Sharon, The, 317, 328–9.
Story of Sayid, The, 317, 328.
OPERAS:
Colomba, 317, 328.
Cricket on the Hearth, The, 317.
Troubadour, The, 317, 328.
ORCHESTRAL WORKS:
Britannia, 329.
La Belle Dame sans merci, 328.
'Pibroch' suite, 328.
Macpherson, Charles, 179 *n*.5.
Madrigals, 46, 77–81, 107–29, 143, 148, 152, 217–18, 248, 273, 306–8.
Adieu, sweet Amarillis (Wilbye), 108.
Ah, cruel hateful fortune (Kirbye), 390.
Alas, what hope of speeding (Wilbye), 108.
All creatures now are merry-minded (Bennet), 111.
All pleasure is of this condition (Wilbye), 109.
And must I needs depart then (Bateson), 112.
April is in my mistress' face (Morley), 123.
Arise, awake (Morley), 123.
As fair as morn (Wilbye), 108.
As Vesta was from Latmos' hill descending (Weelkes), 114.
Ay me! my wonted joys (Weelkes), 115.

Madrigals (*cont.*):
Beauty is a lovely sweet (Bateson), 112.
Besides a fountain (Morley), 123.
Calm was the air (Carlton), 124.
Cease now, delight (Weelkes), 114.
Cease sorrows now (Weelkes), 115–16, 388.
Come follow me, fair nymphs (Bateson), 113.
Come gentle swains (Cavendish), 124.
Come jolly swains (Byrd), 118.
Come lovers follow me (Morley), 123.
Come, shepherds, follow me (Bennet), 112.
Come, shepherd swains (Wilbye), 108.
Cruel, unkind (Bennet), 112.
Dainty fine bird that art encaged (Gibbons), 119–20.
Dame Venus hence to Paphos go (Bateson), 113.
Die not, fond man (Ward), 128.
Down in a garden fair (Pearsall), 306.
Down in a valley (Wilbye), 108.
Fair nymph, I heard one telling (Farmer), 126.
Fair Oriana, beauty's queen (Hilton), 124.
Fair Oriana, seeming to wink at folly (Jones), 126.
Fair Orian in the morn (Milton), 124.
Farewell all joys (Gibbons), 119.
Flora gave me fairest flowers (Wilbye), 108.
Great God of love (Pearsall), 306.
Happy, O happy he (Wilbye), 109–10.
Happy streams whose trembling fall (Wilbye), 108.
Hard by a crystal fountain (Morley), 124.
Hark, hear you not? (Bateson), 112–14, 128.
Hence, Care, thou art too cruel (Weelkes), 115.
Hence stars! too dim of light (East), 126.
How art thou thrall'd (Gibbons), 119.
How merrily we live (East), 126.
I live and yet methinks I do not breathe (Wilbye), 108, 110.
In going to my naked bed (anon.), 66–7.
Lady, when I behold (Wilbye), 108.

Madrigals (*cont.*):

Lady, why grieve you still me? (Morley), 123.

Lais, now old (Gibbons), 119.

Lay a garland (Pearsall), 306.

Let us all go maying (Pearsall), 306.

Lightly she whipp'd o'er the dales (J. Mundy), 126.

Light of my soul (Pearsall), 306.

Like two proud armies (Weelkes), 115.

Live not, poor bloom (Bateson), 113.

Lock up, fair lids (Vautor), 128.

Long have I made these hills and valleys weary (Wilbye), 108, 110.

Mars in a fury (Weelkes), 115.

Mother, I will have a husband (Vautor), 128.

Music some think no music is (Bateson), 112.

My love is like a garden full of flowers (Ford), 128.

No, no, Nigella (Pearsall), 306.

Now each flowery bank (Gibbons), 119.

O Care, thou wilt despatch me (Weelkes), 115.

Of all the birds that I have heard (J. Mundy), 126.

Of joys and pleasing pain (Wilbye), 110.

Oft have I vowed how dearly I did love thee (Wilbye), 108.

O grief, where shall poor grief? (Bennet), 111.

Oh me, that I were young again! (Wilbye), 108.

O metaphysical tobacco (East), 126.

O sleep, fond fancy (Bennet), 112.

O stay, sweet love (Farmer), 126.

O sweet alas! (Morley), 123.

O sweet grief (Bennet), 111.

O ye roses (Pearsall), 306-8.

Penelope that longed for the sight (Byrd), 387-8.

Rest now, Amphion (Bennet), 12.

Sadness, sit down (Bateson), 112.

Shepherds and nymphs (Vautor), 128.

Sigh no more, ladies (Ford), 128.

Sing shepherds all (Nicolson), 124.

Sing we and chaunt it (Pearsall), 306.

Sleep now, my Muse (Kirbye), 127.

So light is love (Wilbye), 108.

Stay, Corydon, thou swain (Wilbye), 108.

Madrigals (*cont.*):

Strange were the life (Bateson), 112.

Sweet Gemma (Bateson), 112.

Sweet heart arise (Weelkes), 114.

Sweet honey-sucking bees (Wilbye), 108.

Sweet Suffolk owl (Vautor), 128.

Sweet, those trammels of your hair (Bateson), 112.

Take heed, ye shepherd swains (Pearsall), 306.

The Andalusian merchant (Weelkes), 115.

The fauns and satyrs tripping (Tomkins), 125.

The fields abroad with spangled flowers (Morley), 123.

The hunt is up (Bennet), 111.

The nightingale (Bateson), 112.

The nymphs and shepherds danced Lavoltos (Marson), 124.

The silver swan (Gibbons), 119.

Thirsis, on his fair Phillis' breast reclining (Bateson), 112.

Thirsis, sleepest thou? (Bennet), 112.

This sweet and merry month of May (Byrd), 118.

Those spots upon my lady's face (Weelkes), 114.

Thou art but young, thou sayest (Wilbye), 108.

Though Amaryllis dance in green (Byrd), 118.

Thule, the period of cosmography (Weelkes), 115.

Unkind, O stay thy flying (Wilbye), 110.

Up then, Melpomene (Kirbye), 127.

Weep, O mine eyes (Bennet), 111.

Weep, O mine eyes (Wilbye), 108.

What is our life (Gibbons), 119.

Whenas I glance (Bennet), 112.

When I was otherwise than now I am (Byrd), 118.

When Oriana walked to take the air (Bateson), 112, 127.

When Oriana walked to take the air (Pilkington), 127-8.

When shall my wretched life (Wilbye), 108.

Why do the roses? (Pearsall), 306.

Why wail we thus? (Kirbye), 127.

With wreaths of rose and laurel (Cobbold), 124.

Wounded I am (Byrd), 118.

Ye restless thoughts (Wilbye), 108.

You blessed bowers (Farmer), 127.

You pretty flowers (Farmer), 126.

Madrigals (*cont.*):
  Your beauty it allureth (Weelkes), 114.
  see also Balletts, Canzonets.
Madrigal Society, 248, 272.
Magalotti, Lorenzo, 176 *n*. 2.
Maitland, James Alexander, *see* Fuller Maitland.
Malibran, Maria Felicita, 296 *n*. 1.
Mancini, Francesco, 220.
Mangeot, André, 146 *n*. 2, 147 *n*. 2, 168 *n*. 1, 169 *n*. 1, 211 *n*. 3.
Manns, August, 319.
Mansi, Joannes Dominicus (Giovanni Domenico), 3 *n*. 2.
Manx music, 373.
Marbeck, John: life, 49; *Booke of Common Praier noted*, 49–50; cited, 73.
Marenzio, Luca, 78, 143, 217.
Markham, 20.
Marlowe, Christopher, 82.
Marschner, Heinrich, 312.
Marson, Charles Latimer, 372 *n*. 2, *n*. 4.
Marson, George, 124.
Martin le Franc, 19.
Mary I, Queen, 49.
Mary II, Queen: Purcell's birthday odes for, 172, 196 *n*. 2, 203–4.
Masques: Elizabethan, 87; Jacobean, 83, 153; Caroline, 153; in Shakespeare's *Tempest*, 153; Commonwealth, 155, 163–4; Restoration, 176, 201–2; in Purcell's *Dioclesian*, 195–6; 18th cent., 245–6, 258–9.
  Acis and Galatea (Handel), 221, 232–3, 236, 239 *n*. 1.
  Alfred (Arne), 258–9.
  Circe (Hayes), 246.
  Comus (H. Lawes), 153.
  —— (Arne), 245, 259.
  Cupid and Death (Locke and C. Gibbons), 155, 163.
  Venus and Adonis (Blow), 201–2, 392.
Masses:
  Albanus (Fayrfax), 37–8.
  Corona Spinea (Taverner), 41–5.
  De Spiritu Sancto (S. Wesley), 276.
  Euge bone (Tye), 52–3, 70.
  Four-part Mass (Byrd), 89.
  Five-part Mass (Byrd), 89.
  'French' (Shepherd), 65.
  Gloria tibi Trinitas (Taverner), 44, 68.
  L'homme armé (Carver), 52.
  Mass in D major (Smyth), 340.
  Mass in G major (Stanford), 335.

Masses (*cont.*):
  Mater Christi (Taverner), 44.
  O Michael (Taverner), 44.
  O quam suavis (early 16th cent.), 38–9.
  Regali (Fayrfax), 36–7.
  Small Devotion (Taverner), 44.
  Te Deum (Aston), 39–40.
  Three-part Mass (Byrd), 88.
  Western Wynde (Shepherd), 50, 368 *n*. 3.
  —— (Taverner), 43–4, 50, 368 *n*. 3.
  —— (Tye), 50, 53–4, 368 *n*. 3.
Mass movements (15th cent.), 24–7, 30.
Matteis, Nicola, 177.
Mattheson, Johann, 249.
Mayshuet, 20.
Mendelssohn-Bartholdy, Felix: contrapuntal writing compared with Gibbons, 141; fairy music compared with Purcell, 199; a friend of Attwood, 265–6; Pierson's acquaintance with, 293; admiration for Sterndale Bennett, 294; first performance of *Elijah* at Birmingham, 295; influence on Victorian music, 295–6, 399, on Sterndale Bennett, 301, 312, on Macfarren, 302, on Parry, 331, on Bantock, 342; cited, 313.
Merbecke, *see* Marbeck.
Messager, André, 321.
Meyer, Ernst Hermann, 147 *n*. 1, 148 *n*. 1, 166 *n*. 4, 170 *n*. 2–5.
Meyerbeer, Giacomo, 268, 291.
Michelangelo Buonarroti, 359.
Middleton, Thomas, 153.
Migne, Jacques Paul, 3 *n*. 3.
Miller, Edward, 397.
Milton, John (the elder): contributor to *The Triumphes of Oriana*, 74, 124, to *Teares or Lamentacions of a Sorrowfull Soule*, 81, 107; example of *musica ficta* from, 391–2.
Milton, John (the younger): *Comus* set by Henry Lawes, 150, 153, by Arne, 245, 259; sonnet to Lawes, 160; *L'Allegro* set by Handel, 236 *n*. 1, by Parry, 317.
Moeran, Ernest John, 354.
Moffat, Alfred, 192 *n*. 1, 263 *n*. 3, 374 *n*. 2, *n*. 4–5, 375 *n* 1–2, *n*. 4–6, 376 *n*. 1, *n*. 3, 377 *n*. 1–3, 378 *n*. 3, *n*. 5, 379 *n*. 2, 380 *n*. 3, 384 *n*. 3–5.
Molière, Jean-Baptiste Poquelin, dit, 163.
Monk, Edwin George, 282 *n*. 2.
Monk, George, 1st Duke of Albemarle, 179.

Monteverdi, Claudio, 130, 152.

Moore, Thomas, 381, 383.

Morley, John, Viscount, 247 n. 2.

Morley, Thomas: life, 72–3; works, 101–2, 120–4; on vocalizing, 46; on Dunstable's word-setting, 70; on singing as a social accomplishment, 76; edited *The Triumphes of Oriana*, 78; different versions of 'Out of the deep', 82; melodic style in lute-songs, 135; on the fancy, 146; instrumental music in his vocal publications, 149; represented in Barnard's *Selected Church Music*, 155; arrangements of folk-songs, 362, 366 n. 1; Italian and German editions of his vocal works, 395; on the fashion of preferring Italian music to English, 398; cited, 80, 83–4, 112, 117, 139, 165, 251.

BALLETTS:
I saw my lovely Phillis, 121.
Lady, those cherries plenty, 121.
Leave alas this tormenting, 121.
My bonny lass she smileth, 121.
Now is the month of maying, 121.
Singing alone, 121.
What saith my dainty darling? 121–2.

CANZONETS:
Deep lamenting, grief bewraying, 123.
Do you not know how love lost first his seeing? 122.
Good morrow, fair ladies, 123.
Go ye, my canzonets, 122.
What ails my darling, 123.
Canzonets or Little Short Aers to five and sixe Voyces, 80.
Canzonets or Little Short Songs to Three Voyces, 395.

CHURCH MUSIC:
Agnus Dei, 101–2.
Out of the deep, 82, 102.
Services, 101–2, 123, 251.
First Booke of Consort Lessons, The, 84.

KEYBOARD WORKS:
Fantasia, 141.
Nancie, 366 n. 1.

MADRIGALS:
April is in my mistress' face, 123.
Arise, awake, 123.
Besides a fountain, 123.
Come lovers follow me, 123.
Hard by a crystal fountain, 124.
Lady, why grieve you still me? 123.
O sweet alas! 123.

Morley, Thomas: Madrigals (*cont.*):
The fields abroad with spangled flowers, 123.
Plaine and Easie Introduction to Practicall Musicke, A, 46, 70, 72–3, 76, 83, 101, 121, 146, 398.
see also *Triumphes of Oriana, The*.

Mornington, Garrett Wellesley, 1st Earl of, 269, 282–3.

Morris, Reginald Owen, 362, 386 n. 2.

Morris, Richard, 10 n. 2.

Moscheles, Ignaz, 274.

Motets:
14th cent., 12–15.
15th cent., 28–33.
Early 16th cent., 33–5, 41, 45, 52.
Mid-16th cent., 54–61, 64–6.
Late 16th and early 17th cent., 181, 191, 193–4.
Late 17th cent., 181, 191, 193–4.
18th cent., 275–6.
20th cent., 333–4, 352, 355.

Absterge, Domine (Tallis), 60, 388.
Agnus Dei (Morley), 101–2.
Alleluia, ascendit Deus (Byrd), 93.
Anima Christi (Dering), 105.
Ascendit Christus (Dunstable), 31–2.
At the round earth's imagined corners (Parry), 333–4.
Ave, Dei patris filia (Johnson), 65.
Ave miles coelestis curiae (14th cent.), 15.
Ave verum corpus (Byrd), 93.
Beata Agnes (Philips), 103.
Beati omnes qui timent Dominum (Purcell), 191.
Cantantibus organis (Philips), 105.
Cantate Domino (Blow), 181.
Civitas sancti tui (Byrd), 90, 393.
Confitebor (S. Wesley), 275–6.
Crux fidelis (Dunstable), 29–30.
Derelinquat impius (Tallis), 60.
Diliges Dominum Deum (Byrd), 95.
Dixit Dominus (S. Wesley), 276.
Domine, tu iurasti (Byrd), 91.
Dum transisset Sabbatum (Johnson), 65.
Effuderunt sanguinem (Byrd), 90.
Exultate Deo (S. Wesley), 276.
Gaudent in coelis (Philips), 105.
Haec dies (Byrd), 93–4.
Hodie Beata Virgo Maria (Philips), 103.
Homo natus de muliere (Wilbye), 100.
In exitu Israel (S. Wesley), 276.
Iste est Joannes (Philips), 103.

Motets (*cont.*):
Jehova, quam multi sunt (Purcell), 193–4.
Jesu, dulci memoria (Dering), 105.
Laetentur coeli, (Byrd), 91.
Laudibus in sanctis (Byrd), 93.
Lord, let me know mine end (Parry), 334.
Mater, ora filium (Bax), 352.
Miserere mei (Tye), 54–5.
Miserere nostri (Daman), 107.
Miserere nostri (Tallis), 61.
Ne irascaris, Domine (Byrd), 90.
Ne reminiscaris, Domine (Wilbye), 100.
Non vos relinquam orphanos (Byrd), 91.
O admirabile commercium (Byrd), 93.
O bone Jesu (Carver), 52.
O bone Jesu (Child), 159.
O lux, beata Trinitas (Byrd), 94.
Omnes gentes plaudite manibus (Tye), 55–6.
O quam gloriosum (Byrd), 91.
O quam suavis est (Byrd), 93.
O sacrum convivium (Tallis), 60, 82.
O virum admirabilem (Philips), 104–5.
O vos omnes (Dering), 105–6.
Petrum Cephas ecclesiae (14th cent.), 15.
Posuerunt morticinia (Byrd), 90.
Praeco praeeminentiae (Dunstable), 30–1.
Puellare gremium (14th cent.), 12–13.
Quam pulcra es (Dunstable), 28–9, 33.
Quam pulcra es (Henry VIII), 45.
Quam pulcra es (Sampson), 41.
Quemadmodum (Taverner), 41.
Regina coeli (Dunstable), 33.
Salvator mundi (Blow), 181.
Salvator mundi (Tallis), 60.
Salve regina (Browne), 33.
Salve regina (Cornyshe), 34–5.
Sed tu, Domine, qui non derelinquis (Byrd), 90, 387.
Sed veni, Domine (Byrd), 90.
Spem in alium non habui (Tallis), 60–1.
Stabat mater (Browne), 34.
Stella coeli (Thorne), 64.
Sub Arturo plebs vallata (Alanus), 20.
There is an old belief (Parry), 334.
Tristitia et anxietas (Byrd), 90.
Turbarum voces (Byrd), 89.

Motets (*cont.*):
Veni, sancte spiritus (Dunstable), 30.
Vide, Domine, afflictionem (Byrd), 90.
Vigilate, nescitis enim (Byrd), 90.
Mozart, Wolfgang Amadeus: additional accompaniments to *Messiah*, 230–1; Attwood's teacher, 265, 277; Nancy Storace as Susanna in *Le Nozze di Figaro*, 267; adaptations of his operas by Bishop, 268; his music adapted for 18th-cent. oratorios, 271; influence on Attwood, 278; cited, 288, 290.
Muffat, Gottlieb, 241.
Müller, Wilhelm, 309.
Mulliner, Thomas, 67–9, 390.
Mundy, John: life, 73; represented in the 'Fitzwilliam Virginal Book', 84, 142–3; madrigal by him in *The Triumphes of Oriana*, 126.
Mundy, William: life, 49; anthems, 62–4; 'Rejoice in the Lord always' possibly by him, 62; father of John Mundy, 73; represented in Barnard's *Selected Church Music*, 155; cited, 57, 60.
ANTHEMS:
Ah, helpless wretch, 64.
O Lord, I bow the knees, 63.
O Lord, the maker of all thing, 45, 63.
O Lord, the world's saviour, 63.
Murrill, Herbert, 263 n.2.
Musica ficta, 386–7.
Musical Antiquarian Society, 269.
Musical Association, 330.
Musica Transalpina, 77–8.
'My Lady Carey's Dompe' (16th cent.), 47.
'My Ladye Nevell's Booke', 84, 142.

Nagel, Wilibald: on Morley, 120; on John Mundy, 126; limitations of his study of English music, 395; cited, viii, 76 n.2.
Nares, James: life, 246; anthems, 256–7; harpsichord sonata, 263.
Nash, Manfred J., viii.
Nationalism, 399–400.
Naumann, Emil, 395.
Naylor, Edward Woodall, 369 n.1.
'Nesciens mater virgo' (15th cent.), 22.
Newark, William, 21.
Newman, Robert, 319.
Newton, Richard, 79 n.3, 263 n.6.
Nicolini (Grimaldi), 220.
Nicolson, Richard, 124.
Nietzsche, Friedrich, 341.

Noblemen's and Gentlemen's Catch Club, *see* Catch Club.
Norcome, Daniel, 124.
Northumbrian music, 2–3, 372–3.
Novello, Vincent, 179 *n.* 2, 185 *n.* 1, 250 *n.* 2, 255 *n.* 3.
'Nowell, nowell, this is the salutacyon' (15th cent.), 367.
'Now wel may we merthis make' (15th cent.), 24.
'Now wolde I fayne sum merthis mak' (15th cent.), 46.

Obey, André, 358.
Obrecht, Jacob, 21.
O'Carolan, Turlogh, 382.
'O death, rock me asleep' (17th cent.), 137–8.
Odes:
    Alexander's Feast (Handel), 234–6.
    Arise, my Muse (Purcell), 196 *n.* 2, 203.
    Awake, awake, my lyre (Blow), 207.
    Begin the song (Blow), 209.
    Byron (Holbrooke), 349.
    Come, ye sons of art away (Purcell), 203.
    Hail, great Cecilia (Purcell), 205–6.
    Hymn to St. Cecilia (Britten), 359.
    Laudate Ceciliam (Purcell), 205–6.
    Love's goddess sure was blind this day (Purcell), 203.
    Midnight (Boughton), 349.
    Music-Makers, The (Elgar), 319, 339.
    Musicus apparatus academicus (Croft), 261.
    My trembling song awake (Blow), 207.
    Ode for St. Cecilia's Day (Handel), 234–5.
    Ode on St. Cecilia's Day (Greene), 260.
    —— (Parry), 317, 332–3.
    Ode to Death (Holst), 347.
    —— (Stanford), 336.
    Ode to Music (Parry), 317, 331.
    Ode to the Passions (Cowen), 318, 328.
    —— (Hayes), 246.
    Of old when heroes (Purcell), 205.
    Raise the voice (Purcell), 205–6.
    Welcome to all the pleasures (Purcell), 172, 205–6.
    Welcome, welcome, glorious morn (Purcell), 203.
    What, what shall be done in behalf of the man? (Purcell), 204.
    Who can from joy refrain? (Purcell), 204.

Odington, Walter, 4–5, 9.
Offenbach, Jacques, 322.
Okeghem, Johannes, 21.
Oldfield, Thomas, 84.
Old Hall manuscript, 18–20, 24–8, 30.
Old Vic, The, 344.
Oliver, 20.
Operas:
    17th cent., 155, 163–4, 176–7, 194–202.
    18th cent., 217–26, 245–7, 284–5.
    19th cent., 295–6, 303–4, 321–4, 326–8, 334–6.
    20th cent., 340–1, 345–6, 348–9, 354, 358.

    Agrippina (Handel), 221.
    Albert Herring (Britten), 358.
    Alcina (Handel), 226.
    Almahide, 220.
    Americans, The (Braham), 268.
    Ariane ou le Mariage de Bacchus (Grabu), 176–7.
    Arsinoe (Clayton), 219.
    Artaxerxes (Arne), 245, 260, 271.
    Beggar's Opera, The, 222, 246–7, 358, 394.
    Boatswain's Mate, The (Smyth), 340.
    Bohemian Girl, The (Balfe), 292, 303–4.
    Britain's Happiness (Leveridge), 219.
    —— (Weldon and Dieupart), 219.
    Camilla (M. A. Bononcini), 220.
    Children of Don, The (Holbrooke), 349.
    Clari, or the Maid of Milan (Bishop), 287.
    Colomba (Mackenzie), 317, 328.
    Contarini (Pierson), 293.
    Cox and Box (Sullivan), 322.
    Cricket on the Hearth, The (Mackenzie), 317.
    Cruelty of the Spaniards in Peru, The, 155.
    Dido and Aeneas (Purcell), 194–5, 199, 201, 217.
    Dioclesian (Purcell), 172, 176, 195–6.
    Dylan (Holbrooke), 349.
    Esmeralda (Thomas), 316, 326.
    Etearco, 220.
    Fairy Queen, The (Purcell), 195, 198–9, 219.
    Giulio Cesare (Handel), 240–1.
    Giustino (Handel), 224.
    Gli Amori d'Ergasto (Greber), 220.
    Gondoliers, The (Sullivan), 323.
    Harold (Cowen), 318.

Operas (*cont.*):
History of Sir Francis Drake, The, 155.
H.M.S. Pinafore (Sullivan), 323.
Hugh the Drover (Vaughan Williams), 346.
Immortal Hour, The (Boughton), 348–9.
Indian Queen, The (Purcell), 199–200.
Ivanhoe (Sullivan), 321, 325.
King Arthur (Purcell), 195–8, 245.
Leila (Pierson), 293.
L'Idaspe fedele (Mancini), 220.
Lurline (Wallace), 304.
Maritana (Wallace), 304.
Mikado, The (Sullivan), 323–4.
Mountain Sylph, The (Barnett), 291, 295, 304.
Much Ado about Nothing (Stanford), 318, 336.
Nadeshda (Thomas), 316, 326.
Night Dancers, The (Loder), 292, 303.
Nourjahad (Loder), 295.
Olympians, The (Bliss), 354.
Orlando (Handel), 225.
Ottone (Handel), 225.
Partenope (Handel), 225.
Peter Grimes (Britten), 358.
Pilgrim's Progress, The (Vaughan Williams), 345–6.
Pirates of Penzance, The (Sullivan), 323.
Pirro e Demetrio (Scarlatti), 220.
Poisoned Kiss, The (Vaughan Williams), 346.
Psyche (Locke), 163–4, 219.
Rape of Lucretia, The (Britten), 358.
Riders to the Sea (Vaughan Williams), 346.
Rinaldo (Handel), 220–1, 225–6.
Rodelinda (Handel), 225.
Rodrigo (Handel), 223.
Rosamund (Clayton), 220.
Rose of Castille, The (Balfe), 292, 303–4.
Rosina (Shield), 247 *n.* 1, 284.
Ruddigore (Sullivan), 323.
Satanella (Balfe), 292.
Serse (Handel), 226.
Shamus O'Brien (Stanford), 318, 334.
Siege of Rhodes, The, 155.
Siege of Rochelle, The (Balfe), 292.
Signa (Cowen), 318.
Sir John in Love (Vaughan Williams), 345–6.
Sosarme (Handel), 225.

Operas (*cont.*):
Talismano, Il (Balfe), 296.
Tempest, The (Purcell), 199.
Teseo (Handel), 221, 224–5.
Thomyris, 220.
Thorgrim (Cowen), 318, 327.
Tolomeo (Handel), 225–6.
Travelling Companion, The (Stanford), 334–5.
Troubadour, The (Mackenzie), 317, 328.
Veiled Prophet of Khorassan, The (Stanford), 334.
Venus and Adonis (Blow), 201–2, 392.
Village Romeo and Juliet, A (Delius), 341.
Wreckers, The (Smyth), 340.
see also Masques, Stage Music.
O quam suavis Mass (16th cent.), 38–9.
Oratorios:
18th cent., 221–3, 229–41, 244–5, 257–8, 266, 271, 280–1.
19th cent., 301–3, 325, 327–9, 331–7.
20th cent., 337–40, 346, 348, 356–7.

Alexander Balus (Handel), 223.
Apostles, The (Elgar), 319, 338–9.
Athaliah (Handel), 222, 238–9.
Atonement, The (Coleridge-Taylor), 348.
Belshazzar (Handel), 222, 238–9, 258.
Belshazzar's Feast (Walton), 356.
Captivity of Judah, The (Crotch), 266.
Child of our Time, A (Tippett), 357.
Christmas (Somervell), 340.
Death of Abel, The (Arne), 245, 258.
—— (S. Wesley), 275.
Deborah (Handel), 222, 239.
Dream of Gerontius, The (Elgar), 319, 337–9, 356.
Eden (Stanford), 318, 335–6.
Esther (Handel), 87, 221–2, 239.
Hercules (Handel), 222, 234–6.
Hezekiah (Pierson), 293, 302.
Israel in Egypt (Handel), 222, 230, 232, 238–9.
Jephtha (Handel), 223, 232, 238–9, 241.
Jerusalem (Pierson), 293, 302–3.
Job (Parry), 317, 331, 333.
Joseph and his Brethren (Handel), 222, 238.

Oratorios (*cont.*):
Joshua (Handel), 223, 231, 238.
Judas Maccabaeus (Handel), 222, 232.
Judith (Arne), 245, 258, 280.
— (Parry), 317, 334.
Kingdom, The (Elgar), 319, 338.
King Saul (Parry), 317.
L'Allegro (Handel), 234–6, 240.
Light of Life, The (Elgar), 337.
Light of the World, The (Sullivan), 325.
Messiah (Handel), 222, 230–2, 238–40.
Palestine (Crotch), 266, 280–1.
Passion of Christ, The (Somervell), 340.
Prodigal Son, The (Arnold), 265.
Resurrezione, La (Handel), 223.
Rose of Sharon, The (Mackenzie), 317, 328–9.
Ruth (Cowen), 327.
— (S. Wesley), 275.
St. John the Baptist (Macfarren), 302.
Samson (Handel), 222, 232, 238, 240.
Sancta Civitas (Vaughan Williams), 346.
Saul (Handel), 222, 230, 232, 237–40.
Semele (Handel), 222, 233–4, 236.
Solomon (Handel), 223, 238–9.
Susanna (Handel), 223, 238–9.
Theodora (Handel), 223, 231, 238, 239 *n.* 1.
Three Holy Children, The (Stanford), 318, 334.
Triumph of Time and Truth, The (Handel), 223, 236–7, 239 *n.* 1.
Woman of Samaria, The (Bennett), 280, 294, 301–2.
Orchestral music; *see Concerti grossi,* Concertos, Overtures, Symphonic poems, Symphonies.
Organ music: Alwood, 68; Blitheman, 67–9; Handel, 227; Ouseley, 311; Parry, 333; Redford, 68–9; Rosein-grave, 263–4; Shelby, 69; Smyth, 340; Tallis, 68; Taverner, 68; S. Wesley, 287–8.
Organum, 4–5.
Ornithoparcus, Andreas, 83.
'O rosa bella' (15th cent.), 28.
Orpheoreon, 87.
O'Sullivan, D. J., 381 *n.* 2.
Ouseley, Frederick Gore: life, 293–4; anthems, 301; organ prelude, 311; on Gibbons's use of false relations, 389; cited, 291.

Overtures, Concert:
Britannia (Mackenzie), 329.
Di Ballo (Sullivan), 324.
In Memoriam (Sullivan), 325.
In the South (Elgar), 338.
Macbeth (Sullivan), 325.
Naiads, The (Bennett), 302, 311–12.
Overture to a Picaresque Comedy (Bax), 352.
Paradise and the Peri (Bennett), 312–14.
Parisina (Bennett), 311.
Portsmouth Point (Walton), 356.
Romeo and Juliet (Pierson), 314–15.
Street Corner (Rawsthorne), 357.
Wood-nymphs, The (Bennett), 312.
Oxford, Robert Harley, 1st Earl of, 174.

Page, John, 272.
Palestrina, Giovanni Pierluigi da: contributor to *Il trionfo di Dori,* 78; compared with Byrd, 89; influence on Philips, 102; use of dissonance, 386; cited, 58, 241.
Pandora, *see* Bandora.
Parry, Charles Hubert Hastings: life, 317–18; works, 330–4; hymn-tunes, 398; on 'gabbling Halle-lujahs' in Restoration anthems, 158 *n.* 1; cited, viii, 316.
CHORAL CANTATAS:
Blest Pair of Sirens, 317, 331.
De Profundis, 331.
Glories of our Blood and State, The, 317, 331.
Invocation to Music, 331–3.
L'Allegro ed Il Pensieroso, 317, 331–2.
Lotos-Eaters, The, 317, 331, 333.
Love that casteth out Fear, The, 317, 333.
Pied Piper of Hamelin, The, 333.
Prometheus Unbound, 317, 331–2.
Song of Darkness and Light, A, 317, 333.
Vision of Life, A, 317.
Voces Clamantium, 317.
War and Peace, 317, 332–3.
INSTRUMENTAL MUSIC:
'Cambridge' symphony, 330–1.
Duo for two pianos in E minor, 330.
Organ works, 333.
Partita for violin and piano in D minor, 330.
Piano trio in B minor, 331.
Symphonic variations, 331.

Parry (*cont.*):
  ODES:
    Ode on St. Cecilia's Day, 317, 332–3.
    Ode to Music, 317, 331.
  ORATORIOS:
    Job, 317, 331, 333.
    Judith, 317, 334.
    King Saul, 317.
  PART-SONG:
    There rolls the deep, 331.
    Songs of Farewell, 333–4.
  STAGE MUSIC:
    Birds, The, 333.
    Clouds, The, 333.
    Frogs, The, 333.
  UNISON SONG:
    England, 333.
Parsley, Osbert, 49, 66.
Parsons, Robert: gentleman of the Chapel Royal, 49; church music, 64–5; secular vocal music, 66, 129–30; represented in the 'Fitzwilliam Virginal Book', 84, in Barnard's *Selected Church Music*, 155.
Parthenia, 84, 138, 140–1.
Part-songs and unaccompanied choral works:
    A Boy was born (Britten), 358.
    April showers (Hatton), 308.
    Atalanta in Calydon (Bantock), 342.
    Choral variations on folk-songs (Boughton), 349.
    Early dawn (Boughton), 349.
    Elizabethan Pastorals (Stanford), 335.
    Evening scene (Elgar), 338.
    Hey nonny no (Smyth), 340.
    Hymn to St. Cecilia (Britten), 359.
    Love is a torment (Davies), 343.
    Magdalen at Michael's gate (Davies), 343.
    On Himalay (Bantock), 343.
    O who will o'er the downs so free (Pearsall), 306.
    Part-Songs from the Greek Anthology (Elgar), 338.
    Phyllida and Corydon (Moeran), 354.
    Shakespeare Songs for four voices (Macfarren), 308.
    Songs of Springtime (Moeran), 354.
    Spring, ye flowrets (Hatton), 308.
    Summer eve (Hatton), 308.
    Sweete floweres, ye were too faire (Walmisley), 308.
    The hardy Norseman (Pearsall), 305.
    There rolls the deep (Parry), 331.
    These sweeter far than lilies are (Davies), 343.

Part-songs (*cont.*):
    To be sung of a summer night on the water (Delius), 341.
    Vanity of Vanities (Bantock), 342.
    Weary wind of the west (Elgar), 338.
    see also Balletts, Canzonets, Glees, Madrigals.
Pashe, William, 21.
Passion according to St. John, The (Byrd), 89.
Passion according to St. Luke, The (15th cent.), 27.
Passion according to St. Matthew, The (Davy), 36.
Patrick, Nathaniel, 74, 107.
Paxton, Stephen, 269, 283.
Paxton, William, 269, 283.
Peacham, Henry: on singing and playing as a social accomplishment, 76–7; madrigal in honour of James I, 83; on Philips, 103; on Byrd, 118; cited, 83–4.
Pearsall, Robert Lucas: life, 291; works, 305–8; cited, 295.
  MADRIGALS AND PART-SONGS:
    Down in a garden fair, 306.
    Great God of love, 306.
    Lay a garland, 306.
    Let us all go maying, 306.
    Light of my soul, 306.
    No, no, Nigella, 306.
    O who will o'er the downs so free, 306.
    O ye roses, 306–8.
    Sing we and chaunt it, 306.
    Take heed, ye shepherd swains, 306.
    The hardy Norseman, 305.
    Why do the roses? 306.
Pearson, Henry Hugo, *see* Pierson.
Pearson, Hugh Nicholas, 293.
Peerson, Martin: life, 151; contributor to *Teares or Lamentacions of a Sorrowfull Soule*, 81, 151; represented in the 'Fitzwilliam Virginal Book', 84; organ part in his *Mottects or Grave Chamber Musique*, 152, n. 2, 165; cited, 150.
Peiniger, Otto, 263 n. 4.
Pembroke, William Herbert, 3rd Earl of, 125.
Pennard, 20.
People's Concert Society, 320.
Pepusch, John Christopher: life, 246; arranged music for *The Beggar's Opera*, ibid.; association with the Madrigal Society, 248, 272; subscribed to Roseingrave's edition of Scarlatti's sonatas, 263.
Pepys, Samuel, 177.

Pergolesi, Giovanni Battista, 276.

Perosi, Lorenzo, 338.

Petrie, George, 382, 383 n. 2–3, 384 n. 1–3, 385 n. 1.

'Petrum Cephas ecclesiae' (14th cent.), 15.

Philharmonic Society, 266, 274.

Philips, Peter: life, 75; vocal music, 102–5; keyboard works, 141, 143; represented in the 'Fitz-william Virginal Book', 84; use of figured bass, 152 n. 2.

MOTETS:

Beata Agnes, 103.

Cantantibus organis, 105.

Gaudent in coelis, 105.

Hodie Beata Virgo Maria, 103.

Iste est Joannes, 103.

O virum admirabilem, 104–5.

Piano music, see Keyboard music, Sonatas.

Pierson, Henry Hugo: life, 293; works, 302–5, 310–11, 314–15; cited, 291, 295.

OPERAS:

Contarini, 293.

Leila, 293.

ORATORIOS:

Hezekiah, 293, 302.

Jerusalem, 293, 302–3.

ORCHESTRAL WORKS:

Macbeth, 314.

Romeo and Juliet, 314–15.

SONGS:

Claribel, 310.

My love's like the red, red rose, 310.

O wert thou in the cauld, cauld blast, 310.

Take, O take those lips away, 310.

STAGE MUSIC:

Faust, 293, 304–5, 314.

Piggot, Francis, 215.

Pilkington, Francis: madrigals, 74, 127–8; lute-songs, 74, 134; contributor to Teares or Lamentacions of a Sorrowfull Soule, 81.

Plainsong and Medieval Music Society, 330.

Playford, Henry, 253.

Playford, John: publications and reprints, 154–5; published Dering's three-part motets, 105 n. 3; catches published by him, 211.

Ayres and Dialogues, 154–5.

Cantica Sacra, 105 n. 3.

English Dancing Master, The, 154, 365, 366 n. 3, 370–1.

Introduction to the Skill of Musick, An, 154, 173.

Playford, John (cont.):

Musicall Banquet, A, 154.

Plummer, Charles, 3 n. 1.

Poe, Edgar Allan, 349.

Poole, Rachael, viii.

Pope, Alexander, 178, 260, 317.

Popular Concerts, St. James's Hall, 319.

Porter, Walter, 152, 165.

Power, Leonel, 19–20, 26–7, 381.

Priestley, John Boynton, 354.

Professional Concerts, 273–4.

Promenade Concerts, 319–20.

Prynne, William, 3 n. 3, 154.

Psalters, 51–2, 150–1, 156, 396–7; see also Hymn-tunes.

'Puellare gremium' (14th cent.), 12–13.

Purcell, Daniel, 172, 178.

Purcell, Edward, 172.

Purcell, Frances, 172.

Purcell, Henry: life, 172–3; works, 186–207, 209–15; declamatory style compared with Henry Lawes, 162; influence of Locke on, 163–4, 169; Italian influence on, 177, 212–13, 217–18; wrote music for St. Cecilia's day, 178; influence of Blow on, 179; a pupil of Humfrey, 182; influence on Golding, 185; florid vocal writing compared with Handel's, 231; recitative compared with Handel's, 232; influence on Handel, 239 n. 1; Croft's tribute to, 243; represented in Boyce's Cathedral Music, 244; Arne on his King Arthur, 245; music used in The Beggar's Opera, 247; music performed at the Ancient Concerts, 273; use of false relations, 390–2; cited, 111, 156, 160, 174, 176, 216, 248, 251, 257–8, 261–2, 299, 308, 387, 395, 400.

ANTHEMS:

Behold, I bring you glad tidings, 187.

Be merciful unto me, O Lord, 189.

Blessed are they that fear the Lord, 189.

Blessed is he whose unrighteousness is forgiven, 189.

Hear my prayer, O Lord, 186, 188.

In the midst of life, 188.

Lord, how long wilt thou be angry? 390.

Man that is born of a woman, 188.

My heart is inditing, 188.

O God, thou hast cast us out, 186.

Purcell, Henry: Anthems (*cont.*):
O Lord God of hosts, 189.
O praise God in his holiness, 188, 391.
O sing unto the Lord, 189.
Out of the deep, 392.
Rejoice in the Lord alway, 187.
Remember not, Lord, our offences, 186.
They that go down to the sea in ships, 188.
Thou knowest, Lord, the secrets of our hearts, 188.
Thy word is a lantern, 187.
Why do the heathen? 189.
Choice Collection of Lessons, A, 172, 214.
Collection of Ayres, compos'd for the Theatre, A, 172, 201.
DUETS:
Awake, awake, ye dead, 192.
Let the fifes and the clarions, 199.
Sound the trumpet, 203.
Two daughters of this aged stream are we, 198.
When Myra sings, 209.
You say 'tis love creates the pain, 198.
Fantasias for viols, 211–12.
HYMNS AND SACRED SONGS:
Ah! few and full of sorrow, 192.
Awake and with attention hear, 192.
Awake, awake, ye dead, 192.
Early, O Lord, my fainting soul, 191.
In guilty night, 193.
Now that the sun, 191.
O all ye people, clap your hands, 192.
O, I'm sick of life, 192.
Thou wakeful shepherd, 192.
We sing to him whose wisdom, 190.
In nomines, 211.
KEYBOARD WORKS:
Ground in C minor, 214.
Ground in Gamut, 214–15.
MOTETS:
Beati omnes qui timent Dominum, 191.
Jehova, quam multi sunt, 193–4.
ODES:
Arise, my Muse, 196 n.2, 203.
Come, ye sons of art away, 203.
Hail, great Cecilia, 205–6.
Laudate Ceciliam, 205–6.
Love's goddess sure was blind this day, 203.
Of old when heroes, 205.

Purcell, Henry: Odes (*cont.*):
Raise the voice, 205–6.
Welcome to all the pleasures, 172, 205–6.
Welcome, welcome, glorious morn, 203.
What, what shall be done in behalf of the man? 204.
Who can from joy refrain? 204.
OPERAS AND STAGE WORKS:
Bonduca, 199.
Dido and Aeneas, 194–5, 199, 201, 217.
Dioclesian, 172, 176, 195–6.
Don Quixote, The Comical History of, 199, 202.
Fairy Queen, The, 195, 198–9, 219.
Indian Queen, The, 199–200.
King Arthur, 195–8, 245.
Libertine, The, 199.
Oedipus, 200.
Old Bachelor, The, 200–1.
Tempest, The, 199.
Orpheus Britannicus, 173, 207.
Services, 172, 189–90, 205, 251.
Sonatas of III Parts, 172, 212–13, 217, 262.
Sonatas of IV Parts, 172, 200, 212–14, 262.
Songs, Sacred, *see* Hymns, *supra.*
SONGS, SECULAR:
A prince of glorious race descended, 204.
Britons, strike home, 199, 247.
Come unto these yellow sands, 199.
Dry those eyes, 199.
Fairest isle, all isles excelling, 198.
Fly swift, ye hours, 209.
From silent shades (Bess of Bedlam), 209.
Full fathom five, 199.
Gentle shepherds, you that know, 209–10.
Hark! the ech'ing air, 199.
Here's the summer, sprightly gay, 199.
How blest are shepherds, 197.
How happy the lover, 197.
I attempt from love's sickness to fly in vain, 199.
If love's a sweet passion, 199.
I see the round years successively move, 203.
Kind fortune smiles, 199.
Let the dreadful engines, 199.
Let the soldiers rejoice, 195.
Love has a thousand ways to please, 198.
Next Winter comes slowly, 199.
Now the night is chas'd away, 199.

Purcell, Henry: Songs, secular (cont.):
Nymphs and shepherds, 199.
O let me weep, 199.
O solitude, my sweetest choice, 209.
See, even Night herself is here, 199.
Sing while we trip it, 199.
Sound, Fame, thy brazen trumpet, 196.
Sound, trumpets, sound, 205.
So when the glitt'ring queen of night, 205.
This poet sings the Trojan wars (Anacreon's defeat), 209.
Thus, thus, the gloomy world, 199.
To lofty strains her tuneful lyre she strung, 203.
What shall I do to show how much I love her? 195.
When I am laid in earth, 195.
When the world first knew creation, 202.
With dances and songs, 195.
Ye twice ten hundred deities, 199.
Purcell, Thomas, 172.
Purcell Society, 330.
Puritanism, 153–4, 175.
Pycard, 20, 25–6.

Queldryk, 20.

Raleigh, Walter, 82.
Ramsbotham, Alexander, 18 n.2, 24 n.2, 25 n.1, 26 n.1–2.
Ravel, Maurice, 358.
Ravenscroft, Thomas: graduate of Cambridge, 75; anthems, 106; chromaticism in instrumental works, 149; publications, 83, 165–6, 365, 397; attributed the treatise De quatuor principalibus to Dunstable, 5; works by Bennet in A Briefe Discourse, 111.
ANTHEMS:
Ah, helpless wretch, 106.
O Jesu meek, 106.
Briefe Discourse of the true (but neglected) use of Charact'ring the Degrees . . . in Mensurable Music, A, 5, 83, 111.
Pammelia, Deuteromelia and Melismata, 165–6, 365.
Whole Booke of Psalmes, The, 397.
Rawsthorne, Alan, 357.
Reading Abbey, 8.
Recitative: in Lovers made Men (Laniere), 152; in Cupid and Death (Locke and C. Gibbons), 163; in Handel, 232–5.
Recorder, 87; see also Sonatas.
Redford, John, 49, 60–1, 68–9.

'Redit aetas aurea' (12th cent.), 6.
Reed, Arthur William, 61 n.3.
Reed, Thomas German, 322.
Reese, Gustave, 10 n.1, 374 n.1.
Reeve, William, 268.
Reggio, Pietro, 177.
'Rejoice in the Lord always' (16th cent.), 61, 67.
Richard I, King, 6.
Richard III, King, 21.
Richards, Brinley, 375.
Richardson, Ferdinando, 84.
Richter, Hans, 295.
Ries, Ferdinand, 270 n.1, 292.
Rimbaud, Arthur, 359.
Ritter, Fanny, 395 n.1.
Robertsbridge Abbey, 16.
Robertson, J., ix.
Robinson, Percy, 241 n.1.
Rockstro, William Smith, 22 n.3.
Rogers, Benjamin: life, 151; church music, 159–60; dance tunes, 168; keyboard works, 215; cited, 150, 156.
Rondel, 9.
Rootham, Cyril Bradley, 156 n.1.
Rosa, Carl, 321.
'Rosa fragrans' (13th cent.), 9.
Roseingrave, Thomas, 246, 263–4.
Rosseter, Philip, 74, 80, 82, 134–5.
Rossetti, Christina, 353.
Rossini, Gioacchino Antonio, 268.
Roth, Herman, 217 n.1.
Rowland, 20.
Royal Academy of Music, 266, 274, 320.
Royal College of Music, 320.
Royal Musical Association, see Musical Association.
Royal Philharmonic Society, see Philharmonic Society.
Royal Society, 266.
Royal Society of Musicians, 248.
Royal Victoria Hall, 344.
Rubbra, Edmund, 355, 357.
Amoretti, 355.
Cello sonata, 355.
Piano trio, 355.
Symphonies, 355.
Violin sonata No. 2, 355.
Rückert, Friedrich, vii.

Sackbut, see Trombone.
Sacred Harmonic Society, 294.
Sadler's Wells Theatre, 344.
St. Andrews psalter, 52.
St. Cecilia: commemoration of, 178; odes by Purcell, 205–6, Blow, 209, Greene, 260, Handel, 234–5, Parry, 332–3, Britten, 359.

St. Edmund, Hymn in honour of, 15.

St. Godric, 6.

St. James's Hall Popular Concerts, 319.

St. Magnus, Hymn in honour of, 2.

St. Stephen, Hymn to, 5.

Saintsbury, George, 6 n.2.

Salomon, Johann Peter, 274.

'Salve virgo virginum' (13th cent.), 9–10.

Sampson, Richard, 21, 41.

'Sanctus et aeternus Deus' (14th cent.), 12.

Savoy, Duke of, 76.

Scarlatti, Alessandro, 220.

Scarlatti, Domenico, 263, 313.

Schofield, Bertram, 8 n.2, 18 n.3.

Scholes, Percy Alfred, 3 n.3, 154 n.1, 177 n.2.

Schubert, Franz, 319, 324, 399.

Schumann, Robert: pieces by Giles Farnaby compared with his *Kinderscenen*, 145; music to *Manfred*, 194; on Pierson, 293; friendship with Bennett, 294; his *Études Symphoniques* dedicated to Bennett, 312; orchestral works introduced to England by Manns, 319; cited, 290, 395.

Scott, Cyril, 351–2.

Scott, Lady John, 378.

Scott, Walter, 380.

Scottish music: in the 12th cent., 2; 16th cent., 52; folk-song in Bantock's 'Hebridean' symphony, 342; connexions of folk music with England and Ireland, 363; Lowland folk music, 375–8; imitations of Lowland folk-songs in the 18th and 19th cent., 377–8; Highland folk music, 379–81; *see also* Folk-songs, Scottish Highlands and Scottish Lowlands.

Scottish snap, 378.

Seiffert, Max, 217 n.1, 230 n.1, 241 n.2.

Selby, Bertram Luard, 183 n.1.

Services: Bevin, 107; Blow, 179; Byrd, 92; Causton, 50; Child, 158; Croft, 251, 390; S. Elvey, 300; Farrant, 62; O. Gibbons, 95; Heath, 50; Jackson, 281; Morley, 101–2, 123, 251; Patrick, 107; Purcell, 189–90, 205, 251; Rogers, 159; Tallis, 51, 59–60, 62, 65; Tomkins, 100; Walmisley, 300; Weelkes, 98; S. S. Wesley, 297.

Shadwell, Thomas, 163.

Shakespeare, William: satire on choirboy plays in *Pyramus and Thisbe*,

Shakespeare (*cont.*):
79, 129; recorder scene in *Hamlet*, 87; *The Fairy Queen* an adaptation of *A Midsummer Night's Dream*, 198–9; Vaughan Williams's *Sir John in Love* a setting of *The Merry Wives of Windsor*, 346; references to popular songs in the plays, 368–9, 382; songs set by Robert Johnson, 74, Purcell, 199, Arne, 259, Macfarren, 308, Pierson, 310, Sullivan, 324; cited, 82, 245, 283, 314.

As You Like it, 245, 259.

Hamlet, 87, 369.

Henry V, 368.

King Lear, 368.

Macbeth, 314.

Merry Wives of Windsor, The, 346, 368.

Midsummer Night's Dream, A, 79, 129, 198–9.

Much Ado about Nothing, 368.

Romeo and Juliet, 368.

Tempest, The, 74, 153, 163, 199, 245, 259, 324.

Twelfth Night, 166, 368.

Two Gentlemen of Verona, The, 368.

Winter's Tale, The, 368–9.

Sharp, Cecil James: his rediscovery of English folk-song, 345; on the tonality of folk-songs, 364 n.2; on the origin of 'The Vicar of Bray', 371 n.2; as editor, 366 n.6, 372 n.1–2.

Shaw, Harold Watkins, 179 n.3, 207 n.1.

Shelby, William, 69.

Shelley, Percy Bysshe, 317, 342.

Shepherd, John: life, 49; Mass on 'Western wynde', 50, 368 n.3; other church music, 64–5; represented in Barnard's *Selected Church Music*, 155.

Sheridan, Richard Brinsley, 267 n.1.

Sheryngham, 46.

Shield, William: life, 267; works, 284–6; vocal ornaments in *Rosina*, 247 n.1; 'The Arethusa' not by him, 285 n.1; cited, 322.

Shirley, James, 153, 155, 317, 331.

Sichel, Gertrude, viii.

Sidney, Philip, 82, 128.

Simpson, Christopher, 149, 170–1.

Simpson, Evelyn, 152 n.1.

Simpson, Percy, 152 n.1.

Sims, W. R., viii.

Sitwell, Edith, 356.

Sitwell, Sacheverell, 357.
Skene manuscript, 376.
Smart, George, 293.
Smart, Henry, 291, 293, 301.
Smith, John Stafford, 269, 273.
Smyth, Ethel, 340.
  CHORAL WORKS:
  Hey nonny no, 340.
  Mass in D major, 340.
  Prison, The, 340.
  OPERAS:
  Boatswain's Mate, The, 340.
  Wreckers, The, 340.
Organ prelude and fugue on 'O
  Traurigkeit, O Herzeleid', 340.
  SONGS:
  Anacreontic Ode, 340.
  Chrysilla, 340.
  String quartet, 340.
Solomon, Edward, 322.
Solo songs:
  13th cent., 6.
  16th and early 17th cent., 79–83,
    129–38, 152–3.
  Mid-17th cent., 160–3.
  Late 17th cent., 190–2, 207–10.
  18th cent., 253, 258–61, 284–7.
  Early 19th cent., 308–10.
  Late 19th cent., 324–6.
  20th cent., 335, 337, 340–1, 343,
    345, 347, 349, 351–5, 359.
  Above measure is the pleasure
    (Handel), 234.
  Adorn'd with ev'ry matchless grace
    (Arne), 258.
  Ah, could we love like him (Greene),
    261.
  All joy to fair Psyche (Locke), 164.
  Amoretti (Rubbra), 355.
  Anacreontic Ode (Smyth), 340.
  And now another day is gone (S.
    Wesley), 275.
  And would you see my mistress'
    face (Rosseter), 134–5.
  Annie Laurie (Lady Scott), 378.
  A prince of glorious race descended
    (Purcell), 204.
  A prince so young (Blow), 207–8.
  A rann of exile (Bax), 352.
  Arise sweet messenger of morn
    (Arne), 259.
  Arms, arms, arms he delights in
    (Blow), 208.
  A soldier and a sailor (Eccles), 203.
  A summer night (Thomas), 326.
  Awake and with attention hear
    (Purcell), 192.
  Awake, Saturnia (Handel), 233.
  Awake, sweet love (Dowland), 80,
    130–1.

Solo songs (*cont.*):
  Away with these self-loving lads
    (Dowland), 130.
  Be gentle, Phyllis, since I'm yours
    (Berenclow), 209.
  Blow, blow, thou winter wind
    (Arne), 259.
  Britons, strike home (Purcell), 199,
    247.
  Buy new broom (Whythorne), 79.
  Can doleful notes (Danyel), 130,
    136–7.
  Captain Stratton's Fancy (War-
    lock), 354.
  Cherry ripe (Horn), 286.
  Chrysilla (Smyth), 340.
  Claribel (Pierson), 310.
  Come away, sweet love (Dowland),
    131.
  Come, heavy Sleep (Dowland), 132.
  Come unto these yellow sands
    (Purcell), 199.
  Confusa si miri (Handel), 225.
  Conquest is not to bestow (Arne),
    258.
  Con rauco mormorio (Handel),
    225.
  Couch'd in the dark and silent
    grave (Eccles), 203.
  Creation (Holst), 347.
  Curlew, The (Warlock), 354–5.
  Dainty, dainty, dainty darling
    (Jones), 135.
  Daphne was not so chaste (Dow-
    land), 133.
  Dearest, do not now delay me (H.
    Lawes), 162.
  Del minacciar del vento (Handel),
    225.
  Despair no more shall wound me
    (Handel), 233.
  Dryads, sylvans (Handel), 236.
  Dry those eyes (Purcell), 199.
  Fairest isle, all isles excelling (Pur-
    cell), 198.
  Five Mystical Songs (Vaughan Wil-
    liams), 345.
  Flow, my tears (Dowland), 133.
  Flow, thou regal purple stream
    (Arnold), 286.
  Fly swift, ye hours (Purcell), 209.
  Four songs for voice and violin
    (Holst), 347.
  From silent night (Dowland), 133.
  From silent shades (Purcell), 209.
  Full fathom five (Purcell), 199.
  Gentle shepherds, you that know
    (Purcell), 209–10.
  Go, nightly cares (Dowland), 133.
  Go, rose (Greene), 260.

Solo songs (*cont.*):

Go to bed, sweet muse (Jones), 135–6.

Grief, keep within (Danyel), 136–7.

Hail, immortal Bacchus (Arne), 258.

Happy the man (Weldon), 253.

Hark! the ech'ing air (Purcell), 199.

Heart of oak (Boyce), 261, 286.

Here's the summer, sprightly gay (Purcell), 199.

He shall feed his flock (Handel), 240.

Home, sweet home (Bishop), 287.

Homeward bound (Stanford), 335.

Honour and arms (Handel), 238.

How blest are shepherds (Purcell), 197.

How cheerful along the gay mead (Arne), 258.

How happy the lover (Purcell), 197.

I attempt from love's sickness to fly in vain (Purcell), 199.

If I could shut the gate against my thoughts (Danyel), 136.

If love's a sweet passion (Purcell), 199.

I heard a brooklet gushing (Loder), 309–10.

Illuminations, Les (Britten), 359.

Imbre lachrymarum largo (H. Lawes), 161.

In darkness let me dwell (Dowland), 133, 137.

I pass all my hours in a shady old grove (Humfrey), 209.

Irmelin (Delius), 341.

I see the round years successively move (Purcell), 203.

It is not that I love you less (Blow), 207.

It is not that I love you less (H. Lawes), 161.

Kind fortune smiles (Purcell), 199.

Lascia ch'io pianga (Handel), 226.

Le jeune pâtre (Thomas), 326.

Le luci del mio bene (Handel), 225.

Let me wander not unseen (Handel), 235.

Let not rage, thy bosom firing (Arne), 260.

Let the dreadful engines (Purcell), 199.

Let the soldiers rejoice (Purcell), 195.

Like the young god of wine (Greene), 261.

Loathsome urns, disclose your treasure (Handel), 236–7.

Love has a thousand ways to please (Purcell), 198.

Solo songs (*cont.*):

Love in her eyes sits playing (Handel), 233.

Mädchen mit dem rothen Mündchen (Bennett), 310.

Marino Faliero (Holbrooke), 349.

Maud (Somervell), 341.

May Dew (Bennett), 310.

Most sweet and pleasing are thy ways, O Lord (Campian), 133.

Musick's the cordial of a troubled breast (Blow), 209.

My complaining is but feigning (Jones), 135.

My father (Handel), 235.

My father fain would have me take (Jones), 135.

My little sweet darling (Byrd), 129.

My love's like the red, red rose (Pierson), 310.

Myself I shall adore (Handel), 233.

My time, O ye Muses, was happily spent (Croft), 261.

Never weather-beaten sail (Campian), 133.

Next Winter comes slowly (Purcell), 199.

No, no, I'll take no less (Handel), 233.

Not on beds of fading flow'rs (Arne), 259.

Now, O now, I needs must part (Dowlands), 130.

Now peep, bo-peep (Pilkington), 134.

Now that the sun (Purcell), 191.

Now the night is chas'd away (Purcell), 199.

Nymphs and shepherds (Purcell), 199.

O bid your faithful Ariel fly (Linley the younger), 285.

O come, O come, my dearest (Arne), 259.

O death, rock me asleep (early 17th cent.), 137–8.

Of all the torments (Blow), 207.

Oft on a plat of rising ground (Handel), 235.

O happy fair (Shield), 285.

Oh sleep, why dost thou leave me? (Handel), 233.

O let me weep (Purcell), 199.

O listen to the voice of love (Hook), 285.

Ombra mai fù (Handel), 226.

O much lov'd son (Arne), 260.

O Nigrocella (Blow), 208.

Orpheus with his lute (Sullivan), 324.

Solo songs (*cont.*):

O solitude my sweetest choice (Purcell), 209.

O wert thou in the cauld, cauld blast (Pierson), 310.

Pandolpho (Parsons), 129.

Phoebe fears each bird that flies (Greene), 261.

Queen and huntress (Britten), 359.

Rendi 'l sereno al ciglio (Handel), 225.

Requiescat (Butterworth), 353.

Rest, sweet nymphs (Pilkington), 134.

Revenge, Timotheus cries (Handel), 236.

Rise, mighty monarch (Blow), 207.

Robin Hood is lying dead (Loder), 309.

Rule Britannia (Arne), 258, 287.

Sappho (Bantock), 343.

Sea Pictures (Elgar), 337.

See, even Night herself is here (Purcell), 199.

Serenade (Britten), 359.

Seven Sonnets of Michelangelo (Britten), 359.

Shepherds, deck your crooks (Blow), 207.

Should he upbraid (Bishop), 286.

Since first I saw your face (Ford), 80, 135.

Sing while we trip it (Purcell), 199.

Sky (Holst), 347.

Sleep (Warlock), 354.

Sleep, gentle cherub (Arne), 258.

Songs of Travel (Vaughan Williams), 345.

Sound, Fame, thy brazen trumpet (Purcell), 196.

Sound, trumpets, sound (Purcell), 205.

So when the glitt'ring queen of night (Purcell), 205.

Stille amare (Handel), 225–6.

Swallow song (Thomas), 326.

Take, O take those lips away (Pierson), 310.

Tell me, my heart (Bishop), 286.

The arrow and the song (Balfe), 308.

The Bay of Biscay (Davy), 268.

The blackbird (Hook), 285.

The brooklet (Loder), 309–10.

The dead Christ (Boughton), 349.

The Death of Nelson (Braham), 286.

The deep, deep sea (Horn), 286.

The fairy lough (Stanford), 335.

The lass of Richmond Hill (Hook), 285.

Solo songs (*cont.*):

The lost chord (Sullivan), 325.

There is a garden in her face (Campian), 80, 135.

The sailor's grave (Sullivan), 325.

The soldier tir'd of war's alarms (Arne), 260.

The thorn (Shield), 285.

The valley of silence (Scott), 351.

Think'st thou, Kate, to put me down (Jones), 135.

This ae nighte (Davies), 343.

This merry pleasant spring (early 17th cent.), 129.

This poet sings the Trojan wars (Purcell), 209.

Thou wakeful shepherd (Purcell), 192.

Thus, thus, the gloomy world (Purcell), 199.

To Anthea (Hatton), 308.

To lofty strains her tuneful lyre she strung (Purcell), 203.

Tom Bowling (Dibdin), 285.

Total eclipse (Handel), 240.

'Twas early one morning (Eccles), 202.

Twelve songs by Humbert Wolfe (Holst), 347.

Under the greenwood tree (Arne), 259.

V'adoro, pupille (Handel), 240–1.

Vain is beauty's gaudy flow'r (Arne), 258.

Vengeance, O come inspire me (Arne), 259.

Verdi prati (Handel), 226.

Vieni, torna (Handel), 224–5.

Voglio dire al mio tesoro (Handel), 225.

Voi dolci aurette al cor (Handel), 225.

Waft her, angels (Handel), 232.

Wapping old stairs (Percy), 285.

Water parted from the sea (Arne), 260.

Welcome, black night (Dowland), 132.

We sing to him whose wisdom (Purcell), 190.

What shall I do to show how much I love her? (Purcell), 195.

When I am laid in earth (Purcell), 195.

When the world first knew creation (Purcell), 202.

Where'er you walk (Handel), 233.

Where shall I fly? (Handel), 235.

Where the bee sucks (Arne), 259.

Solo songs (*cont.*):
  With dances and songs (Purcell), 195.
  With fragrant flowers (Pilkington), 134.
  Worldes blis ne last no throwe (13th cent.), 6.
  Ye banks and braes of bonnie Doon (18th cent.), 378.
  Ye twice ten hundred deities (Purcell), 199.
  see also Folk-songs, Masques, Operas, Oratorios, Stage music.
Somervell, Arthur: works, 340–1; as editor, 372 *n.*7, 374 *n.*3.
  ORATORIOS:
  Christmas, 340.
  Passion of Christ, The, 340.
  ORCHESTRAL WORKS:
  Normandy variations, 340.
  Thalassa (symphony), 340.
  Violin concerto, 340.
  SONG-CYCLE:
  Maud, 340–1.
Sonatas:
  Cello: Rubbra, 355.
  Harpsichord: Nares, 263.
  Piano: Bax, 352; Bennett, 313; Clementi, 289–90; Dale, 353; Ferguson, 359; Ireland, 351; Scott, 351.
  Recorder: Berkeley, 359; Handel, 227.
  Violin: Babell, 263; Elgar, 339; Gibbs, 263; Handel, 227; Ireland, 351; Rubbra, 355; Walton, 356.
  see also Trio sonatas.
Songs, *see* Solo songs.
Songs of Praise, 398.
Songs of Syon, 398.
Sophocles, 294.
Spenser, Edmund, 82, 355, 382.
Spofforth, Reginald, 269, 283.
Spohr, Louis, 302.
Squire, William Barclay, viii, 68 *n.*3, 84 *n.*6.
Stage music:
  16th cent., 79, 83.
  17th cent., 163, 176, 194–203.
  18th cent., 219, 245–7, 258–61.
  19th cent., 304–5.

  Ajax (Bennett), 294.
  As You Like it (Arne), 245, 259.
  Birds, The (Parry), 333.
  Bonduca (Purcell), 199.
  Circe, 219.
  Clouds, The (Parry), 333.
  Don Quixote, The Comical History

Stage music (*cont.*):
  of (Purcell and Eccles), 199, 202–3.
  Elfrida (Arne), 260.
  Fairy Prince, The (Arne), 260.
  Fall of Phaeton, The (Arne), 259.
  Faust (Pierson), 293, 304–5, 314.
  Frogs, The (Parry), 333.
  Harlequins Invasion (Boyce), 261.
  Libertine, The (Purcell), 199.
  Love for Love (Eccles), 203.
  Oedipus (Purcell), 200.
  Old Bachelor, The (Purcell), 200–1.
  Tempest, The (Arne), 245, 259.
  —— (Sullivan), 324.
  see also Masques, Operas.
Stainer, Cecie, 28 *n.*2.
Stainer, John: life, 316; church music, 329–30; *Dufay and his Contemporaries*, 330; *Early Bodleian Music*, 15 *n.*2, 16 *n.*1, 18 *n.*1, 22 *n.*1–2, 23 *n.*2–3, 24 *n.*1, 46 *n.*1, 330, 367 *n.* 2–3; instrumental in founding Musical Association, 330.
Standley, 20.
Stanford, Charles Villiers: life, 318; works, 334–7; arrangements of Irish folk-songs, 382; hymntunes, 398; cited, 316, 381 *n.*2–3, 383 *n.*2, 384 *n.*7, 385 *n.*1, 400.
  CHORAL WORKS, SACRED:
  Mass in G major, 335.
  Requiem, 318, 334–5.
  Stabat Mater, 318, 335.
  Te Deum, 318, 334–5.
  CHORAL WORKS, SECULAR:
  Last Post, The, 318.
  Ode to Death, 336.
  Phaudrig Crohoore, 334.
  Revenge, The, 318, 335.
  Voyage of Maeldune, The, 318, 335.
  Elizabethan Pastorals, 335.
  Irish fantasies for violin and piano, 335.
  OPERAS:
  Much Ado about Nothing, 318, 336.
  Shamus O'Brien, 318, 334.
  Travelling Companion, The, 334–5.
  Veiled Prophet of Khorassan, The, 334.
  ORATORIOS:
  Eden, 318, 335–6.
  Three Holy Children, The, 318, 334.
  ORCHESTRAL WORKS:
  Irish rhapsodies, 335.
  'Irish' symphony, 335.

Stanford (cont.):
  SONGS:
    Homeward bound, 335.
    The fairy lough, 335.
Stanley, Charles John, 246, 263.
Stanley, Thomas, 151.
Statham, Heathcote, 179 n. 4.
Sterndale Bennett, see Bennett.
Stevens, Richard John Samuel, 269, 283.
Stevenson, Robert Louis, 345.
Stewart, Charles Hylton, 251 n. 1.
Stokoe, John, 372–3.
Storace, Nancy, 267.
Storace, Stephen, 267–8, 285.
  OPERAS:
    Cherokee, The, 267, 285.
    Haunted Tower, The, 267.
    No Song, no Supper, 267, 285.
    Pirates, The, 267.
Stove, 20.
Stradella, Alessandro, 177.
Strauss, Richard, 315, 338.
Strogers, Nicholas, 84, 155.
Strong, Thomas Banks, viii.
Stroud, Charles, 245, 256.
Stubbs, William, 3 n. 2.
Sturgeon, 20.
Sullivan, Arthur Seymour: life, 316; works, 321–7, 329; cited, 400.
  CANTATAS, CHORAL:
    Golden Legend, The, 325.
    Martyr of Antioch, The, 325.
  Festival Te Deum, 329.
  INCIDENTAL MUSIC:
    Tempest, The, 324.
  OPERAS:
    Cox and Box, 322.
    Gondoliers, The, 323.
    H.M.S. Pinafore, 323.
    Ivanhoe, 321, 325.
    Mikado, The, 323–4.
    Pirates of Penzance, The, 323.
    Ruddigore, 323.
  ORATORIO:
    Light of the World, The, 325.
  ORCHESTRAL WORKS:
    In Memoriam overture, 325.
    Overture di Ballo, 324.
    Macbeth overture, 325.
  SONGS:
    Orpheus with his lute, 324.
    The lost chord, 325.
    The sailor's grave, 325.
'Sumer is icumen in' (13th cent.), 7–8; assigned to the 14th cent. by Bukofzer, 8 n. 2; Schofield on date of, ibid.; compared with 'Sanctus et aeternus Deus', 12; alleged Irish origin of, 381; not mentioned by Naumann, 395; cited, 165, 367.

Sweelinck, Jan Pieterszoon, 84, 104, 138.
Swynford, 20.
Symonds, John Addington, 350.
Symons, Arthur, 350.
Symphonic poems:
  Apollo and the Seaman (Holbrooke), 349.
  Banks of Green Willow, The (Butterworth), 353.
  Brigg Fair (Delius), 341.
  Byron (Holbrooke), 349.
  Falstaff (Elgar), 339–40.
  Fifine at the Fair (Bantock), 343.
  Forgotten Rite, The (Ireland), 350–1.
  In a summer garden (Delius), 341.
  Lebenstanz (Delius), 341.
  Macbeth (Pierson), 314.
  November Woods (Bax), 352.
  Pierrot of the Minute, The (Bantock), 342.
  Shropshire Lad, A (Butterworth), 353.
  Witch of Atlas, The (Bantock), 342.
Symphonies: Bantock, 342; Bax, 352; Bennett, 312; Boyce, 262; Britten, 358–9; Cowen, 318, 327–8; Elgar, 339; Holst, 347; Moeran, 354; Parry, 330–1; Rubbra, 355; Somervell, 340; Stanford, 335; Tippett, 357; Vaughan Williams, 345–6; Walton, 356; S. Wesley, 287.
Synge, John Millington, 346.

Tablature: lute, 86; organ, 16–17.
Talbot Papers, 382.
Tallis, Thomas: life, 48; works, 58–61; owned the manuscript of a treatise by Leonel Power, 20; Bevin his pupil, 75; represented in the 'Fitzwilliam Virginal Book', 84, in Barnard's Selected Church Music, 155; use of false relations, 388; hymn-tunes, 396; cited, 51–2, 57–8, 62–6, 70, 72, 95, 107, 400.
  ANTHEMS:
    I call and cry, 60, 82.
    O Lord, give thy holy spirit, 60.
  Cantiones Sacrae (with Byrd), 48, 60–1.
  'Dorian' service, 51, 59–60, 62, 65.
  Keyboard works: Felix namque (two settings), 68.
  Lamentations, 59.
  MOTETS:
    Absterge, Domine, 60, 388.
    Derelinquat impius, 60.

Tallis: Motets (*cont.*):
 Miserere nostri, 61.
 O sacrum convivium, 60, 82.
 Salvator mundi, 60.
 Spem in alium non habui, 60–1.
'Tappster, drynker' (15th cent.), 22.
Tartini, Giuseppe, 270.
Taverner, John: master of the choristers at Christ Church, Oxford, 21; works, 41–5, 68; adaptations of his Masses to English words, 50–1; cited, 53, 368 *n*.3.
 MASSES:
 Corona Spinea, 41–5.
 Gloria tibi Trinitas, 44, 68.
 Mater Christi, 44.
 O Michael, 44.
 Small Devotion, 44.
 Western Wynde, 43–4, 50, 368 *n*.3.
 MOTET:
 Quemadmodum, 41.
Taylor, Franklin, 289 *n*.1.
Taylor, Sedley, 241 *n*.1.
Telemann, Georg Philipp, 227, 241.
Temperament, Equal, 142.
Tenbury, St. Michael's College, 293.
Tennyson, Alfred, Lord: settings of his poetry by Pierson, 310, Parry, 317, Stanford, 318, Somervell, 340–1, Britten, 359; cited, 241.
Terry, Richard Runciman, 101 *n*.3, 105 *n*.1, 181 *n*.1, 397 *n*.1.
Theocritus, 241.
Theorbo, 87.
'This merry pleasant spring' (16th cent.), 129.
Thomas, Arthur Goring, 316, 326–7.
 OPERAS:
 Esmeralda, 316, 326.
 Nadeshda, 316, 326.
 SONGS:
 A summer night, 326.
 Le jeune pâtre, 326.
 Swallow song, 326.
Thorne, John, 49, 64.
Three Choirs Festival, 244, 247–8, 274.
Tinctoris, Johannes de, 19–20.
Tippett, Michael, 357.
Tisdall, William, 84.
Tofts, Catherine, 219.
Tomkins, Nathaniel, 125.
Tomkins, Thomas: life, 74; works, 82, 100, 125; represented in the 'Fitzwilliam Virginal Book', 84; chromaticism in instrumental works, 149.
 ANTHEMS:
 O God, wonderful art thou, 100.

Tomkins, Thomas: Anthems (*cont.*):
 O praise the Lord, all ye heathen, 100.
 Through thee will we overthrow our enemies, 82.
 Madrigals, 125.
 Musica Deo sacra, 100.
 Services, 100.
Tonic Sol-fa Association, 320.
Tonic Sol-fa College, 320.
Tosi, Pier Francesco, 219.
'Tota pulchra es' (15th cent.), 22.
Tours, Berthold, 280 *n*.1.
Toynbee, Helen, 222 *n*.1.
Travers, John, 246, 256.
Trefusis, Lady Mary, 45 *n*.1.
Tregian family, 84.
Trend, John Brande, 6 *n*.2.
Trent codices, 18.
Trent, Council of, 51.
Trionfo di Dori, Il, 78.
Trio sonatas: Arne, 263; Boyce, 262; Purcell, 200, 212–14; Young, 170.
Triumphes of Oriana, The: described, 78; madrigals in, 107, 111, 114, 123–8; cited, 72–3, 107, 112, 118.
Trombone, 87.
Tudway, Thomas: life, 174; on instrumental accompaniment in the Chapel Royal, 176; anthems, 184.
Tunsted, Simon, 4–5.
Turner, William, 173, 178, 184.
Tye, Christopher: life, 48; works, 52–7; 'Lord, for thy tender mercies' sake' possibly by him, 62–3; clumsy part-writing in Euge bone Mass, 70; repeated notes in his 'In nomines', 147; represented in Barnard's Selected Church Music, 155; use of false relations, 390; cited, 50–1, 58, 60–1, 63–4, 66, 95, 175, 368 *n*.3.
Acts of the Apostles, 48, 51, 56.
 ANTHEMS:
 I will exalt thee, 57.
 Praise the Lord, ye children, 57.
 MASSES:
 Euge bone, 52–3, 70.
 Western Wynde, 50, 53–4, 368 *n*.3.
 MOTETS:
 Miserere mei, 54–5.
 Omnes gentes plaudite manibus, 55–6.
Tyes, 20.
Typp, 20.

University degrees in music, 400–1.
Unton, Henry, 87.
'Ut re mi fa sol la': keyboard fantasias by Bull, 141–2, by Byrd, 142; fan-

'Ut re mi fa sol la' (*cont.*):
tasia for viols by Alfonso Ferrabosco (the younger), 148; 17th cent. catch, 165.

'Ut tuo propitiatus' (12th cent.), 5.

Valentini (Valentino Urbani), 220.
Van, Guillaume de, 18 *n*.5, 28 *n*.2.
Variations:
Early 16th cent., 47.
Late 16th and early 17th cent., 143–4.
19th cent., 331, 337, 340, 348–9.

Anon: My Lady Carey's Dompe, 47.
Aston: Hornpipe, 47.
Boughton: Choral variations on folk-songs, 349.
Bull: Salvator mundi, 143; The king's hunt, 143; Ut re mi fa sol la, 143–4; Walsingham, 144.
Elgar: 'Enigma' variations, 337.
Hurlstone: Variations on a Swedish air, 348.
Parry: Symphonic variations, 331.
Somervell: *Normandy* variations, 340.
see also Grounds.
Vaughan Williams, Ralph: 345–6; compared with Holst, 347–8; with Moeran, 354; influence on Finzi, 359; folk-song settings, 362; hymn-tunes, 398; cited, 400.
CHORAL WORKS:
Fantasia on Christmas Carols, 345.
Five Mystical Songs, 345.
Five Tudor Portraits, 346.
Flos Campi, 346.
Sancta Civitas, 346.
Sea Symphony, A, 345.
Toward the Unknown Region, 345.
OPERAS:
Hugh the Drover, 346.
Pilgrim's Progress, The, 345–6.
Poisoned Kiss, The, 346.
Riders to the Sea, 346.
Sir John in Love, 345–6.
ORCHESTRAL WORKS:
Fantasia on a Theme of Tallis, 346.
Job, 345–6.
London Symphony, A, 345.
'Pastoral' symphony, 345–6.
Symphony No. 4, 345–6.
— No. 5, 345–6.
— No. 6, 345–6.
SONGS:
Songs of Travel, 345.
Vautor, Thomas, 128.

Vauxhall Gardens, 249.
Vecchi, Orazio, 83.
Verdi, Giuseppe, 337, 358.
Victoria, Queen, 268.
Villiers, George, 128.
Viol, 85–6, 170–1; *see also* Chamber music, Fantasias for viols.
Violin: at the court of James I, 85; chest of violins, 85–6; music for in the mid-17th cent., 170; 24 Violins, 175–6; Geminiani's treatise on, 249; *see also* Chamber music, Fantasias for violins and other instruments, Sonatas, Trio sonatas.
Virgil, 241.
Virginals, 85; *see also* Keyboard music.
Vivian, Percival, 83 *n*.2.
Vocal Concerts, 273.

Waesberghe, Jos. Smits van, 4 *n*.3.
Wagner, Richard, 270, 321, 337, 342.
Walford Davies, *see* Davies.
Walker, Ernest, 148 *n*.3, 255 *n*.1, 400 *n*.1.
Wallace, William Vincent, 295, 304.
Waller, Edmund, 161, 207.
Walmisley, Thomas Attwood: life, 291–2; works, 300, 308; editor of *Attwood's Cathedral Music*, 278 *n*.1.
Walmisley, Thomas Forbes, 291–2.
Walpole, Horace, 4th Earl of Orford, 222.
Waltham Holy Cross Monastery, 20.
Walton, William, 355–6.
CHAMBER MUSIC:
Piano quartet, 356.
String quartet, 356.
Violin sonata, 356.
Façade, 356.
ORCHESTRAL WORKS:
Portsmouth Point, 356.
Sinfonia concertante, 356.
Symphony, 356.
Viola concerto, 356.
Violin concerto, 356.
ORATORIO:
Belshazzar's Feast, 356.
Wanley manuscript, 45.
Ward, John: contributor to *Teares or Lamentacions of a Sorrowfull Soule*, 81; church music, 102, 106; madrigals, 128; fantasias for viols, 147 *n*.2; represented in Barnard's *Selected Church Music*, 155; cited, 73–4.
Warlock, Peter: songs, 354–5; as editor, 76 *n*.1, 79 *n*.1, 128 *n*.5, 129 *n*.1–3, 149 *n*.2, 165 *n*.2, 169 *n*.1, 211 *n*.3.

GENERAL INDEX

Warren, Thomas, 282 *n*. 4.

Warrock, Thomas, 84.

Webb, Clement Charles Julian, 4 *n*. 1.

Webbe, Samuel, 269, 282–4.

Weelkes, Thomas: organist of Winchester College and Chichester Cathedral, 73; works, 98–100, 114–17; contributor to *Teares or Lamentacions of a Sorrowfull Soule*, 81; chromaticism in, 115–16, 137; represented in Barnard's *Selected Church Music*, 155; use of false relations, 388; cited, 74, 80, 111, 123.

ANTHEMS:

Hosanna to the Son of David, 99.

O Lord, arise into thy resting place, 99.

Ayres or Phantasticke Spirites, 80, 117:

Ay me, alas, hey ho, 117.

Death hath deprived me, 117.

The gods have heard my vows, 117.

The nightingale, 117.

Upon a hill the bonny boy, 117.

BALLETTS:

Hark, all ye lovely saints above, 117.

Lady, your eye my love enforced, 117.

On the plains fairy trains, 117.

To shorten winter's sadness, 117.

MADRIGALS:

As Vesta was from Latmos' hill descending, 114.

Ay me! my wonted joys, 115.

Cease now, delight, 114.

Cease sorrows now, 115–16, 388.

Hence, Care, thou art too cruel, 115.

Like two proud armies, 115.

Mars in a fury, 115.

O Care, thou wilt despatch me, 115.

Sweet heart arise, 114.

The Andalusian merchant, 115.

Those spots upon my lady's face, 114.

Thule, the period of cosmography, 115.

Your beauty it allureth, 114.

SERVICES:

Evening Service for two trebles, 98 *n*. 2.

Short Morning and Evening Service for four voices, 98 *n*. 2.

Weever, John, 19.

Wegeler, Franz Gerhard, 270 *n*. 1.

Welch, Christopher, 87 *n*. 1.

Weldon, John: life, 245; church music, 252–3; stage music, 219; cited, 257.

Wellington, Arthur Wellesley, 1st Duke of, 269.

Welsh music, 2–3, 373–5, 399; *see also* Folk-songs, Welsh.

Wesley, Charles (the elder), 266.

Wesley, Charles (the younger), 266.

Wesley, Eliza, 266 *n*. 1.

Wesley, John, 266.

Wesley, Samuel: life, 266; works, 274–6, 282, 286–8; published, with Horn, an English edition of Bach's *Das wohltemperirte Clavier*, 268; enthusiasm for Bach, 270; cited, 267, 291, 296.

CHURCH MUSIC:

Confitebor, 275–6.

Dixit Dominus, 276.

Exultate Deo, 276.

In exitu Israel, 276.

Missa de Spiritu Sancto, 276.

Thou, O God, art praised in Zion, 276.

GLEES:

Here shall the morn, 282.

O sing unto my roundelaie, 282.

Roses, their sharp spines being gone, 282.

The glories of our birth and state, 282.

ORATORIOS:

Death of Abel, The, 275.

Ruth, 275.

ORCHESTRAL WORKS:

Organ concertos, 287–8.

Symphony in B♭ major, 287.

SONG:

And now another day is gone, 275.

Wesley, Samuel Sebastian: life, 291; works, 296–9; influence on Stanford, 334; cited, 277, 301, 329.

ANTHEMS:

Blessed be the God and Father, 297.

Cast me not away, 297–8.

O Lord, thou art my God, 297–9.

The wilderness, 297.

Thou wilt keep him in perfect peace, 297.

Wash me throughly, 297.

Service in E major, 297.

West, John Ebenezer, 107 *n*. 4, 156 *n*. 2, 179 *n*. 6, 180 *n*. 1, 185 *n*. 2, 186 *n*. 1, 253 *n*. 1.

Westrup, Jack Allan, 172 *n*. 1, 177 *n*. 1, 390 *n*. 3.

White, Robert: life, 48; works, 57–8; augmented chords in, 119;

White (*cont.*):
  represented in Barnard's *Selected Church Music*, 155; cited, 51–2, 60–1, 64, 66, 70, 95, 175.
ANTHEMS:
  O how glorious art thou, 58.
  O praise God in his holiness, 58.
  The Lord bless us, 58.
  Lamentations, 57–8.
Whitman, Walt, 336, 341, 345, 347.
Whittaker, William Gillies: revived Bach's works, 344; on the tonality of 'Sair fyel'd, hinny', 373 *n.*2; as editor, 163 *n.*3, 170 *n.*1, 191 *n.*1, 192 *n.*2, 226 *n.*1.
Whyte, *see* White.
Whythorne, Thomas, 76, 79.
Wilbye, John: at Hengrave Hall, 73, 85; works, 100–1, 107–11; contributor to *Teares or Lamentacions of a Sorrowfull Soule*, 81, 101; cited, 112, 119, 123, 127, 400.
ANTHEM:
  O God, the rock of my whole strength, 101.
MADRIGALS:
  Adieu, sweet Amarillis, 108.
  Alas, what hope of speeding, 108.
  All pleasure is of this condition, 109.
  As fair as morn, 108.
  Come, shepherd swains, 108.
  Down in a valley, 108.
  Flora gave me fairest flowers, 108.
  Happy, O happy he, 109–10.
  Happy streams whose trembling fall, 108.
  I live and yet methinks I do not breathe, 108, 110.
  Lady, when I behold, 108.
  Long have I made these hills and valleys weary, 108, 110.
  Of joys and pleasing pain, 110.
  Oft have I vowed how dearly I did love thee, 110.
  Oh me, that I were young again! 108.
  So light is love, 108.
  Stay, Corydon, thou swain, 108.
  Sweet honey-sucking bees, 108.
  Thou art but young, thou sayest, 108.

Wilbye: Madrigals (*cont.*):
  Unkind, O stay thy flying, 110.
  Weep, O mine eyes, 108.
  When shall my wretched life, 108.
  Ye restless thoughts, 108.
MOTETS:
  Homo natus de muliere, 100.
  Ne reminiscaris, Domine, 100.
Wilde, Oscar, 353.
William III, King, 176.
Williams, Charles Francis Abdy, 400 *n.*1.
Williams, John Lloyd, 374 *n.*3.
Williams, Vaughan, *see* Vaughan Williams.
Wilson, John, 150–1, 162.
Winchester Tropers, 5.
Windsor, St. George's Chapel, 19.
Wingham, Thomas, 330.
Wise, Michael: life, 173–4; anthems, 183–4; use of false relations, 390; cited, 156, 182.
Wode, Thomas, 52.
Wolf, Johannes, 47 *n.*2.
Wolfe, Humbert, 347.
Wood, Anthony: on Fayrfax, 21 *n.*1; on Jenkins, 166; on music-making in Oxford, 177.
Wood, Henry Joseph, 319.
Woodson, Leonard, 155.
Woodward, George Ratcliffe, 398.
Wooldridge, Harry Ellis, viii; *Early English Harmony*, 5 *n.*5, 6 *n.*3, 9 *n.*3, 10 *n.*1, 14 *n.*1, 15 *n.*3, 16 *n.*1, *n.*3; *Old English Popular Music*, 137 *n.*1, 365 *n.*2, 366 *n.*1, *n.*4–5, 367 *n.*2, 368 *n.*1, *n.*3, *n.*11, 369 *n.*2–5, 370 *n.*1, *n.*3–4, 381 *n.*1; *Oxford History of Music*, 41 *n.*2, 330; article on 'Psalter' in Grove's *Dictionary*, 51 *n.*2; misleading distinction between traditional and non-traditional folk-song, 365.
Worgan, John, 263.
'Worldes blis ne last no throwe' (13th cent.), 6.
Wynkyn de Worde, 45.

Yeats, William Butler, 355.
Yonge, Nicholas, 78.
York, James, Duke of, *see* James II.
Young, William, 85, 170.